THE
CAVE TEMPLES OF INDIA

THE
CAVE TEMPLES OF INDIA

BY

JAMES FERGUSSON,

D.C.L., F.R.S., V.P.R.A.S.

AND

JAMES BURGESS,

F.R.G.S., M.R.A.S.,

MEMBRE DE LA SOCIETE ASIATIQUE, ETC.;
ARCHAEOLOGICAL SURVEYOR AND REPORTER TO
GOVERNMENT, WESTERN INDIA.

PRINTED AND PUBLISHED BY ORDER OF HER MAJESTY'S
SECRETARY OF STATE, &c.

GYAN

Published by

Gyan Publishing House
5, Ansari Road
Daryaganj, New Delhi-110002
Phone: 011-47034999, 9811692060
E-mail: books@gyanbooks.com

Distribution Network
gyanbooks.com
India, USA, Canada, UK, Australia, France

ISBN : 978-81-212-2600-4 (HB)
First Published, 1880

2nd Impression 2021

Printed at: Gyan Press, Delhi.

The
Cave Temples of India
Author: James Fergusson; James Burgess

THE CAVE TEMPLES OF INDIA.

By JAMES FERGUSSON, D.C.L., F.R.S., V.P.R.A.S.,

AND

JAMES BURGESS, F.R.G.S., M.R.A.S.,

MEMBRE DE LA SOCIÉTÉ ASIATIQUE, ETC.; ARCHÆOLOGICAL SURVEYOR AND REPORTER TO GOVERNMENT, WESTERN INDIA.

Capital or Tee from a Rock-cut Dâgoba at Bhâjâ.

PRINTED AND PUBLISHED BY ORDER OF HER MAJESTY'S SECRETARY OF STATE, &c.

LONDON:

W. H. ALLEN & Co., WATERLOO PLACE; TRÜBNER & Co., LUDGATE HILL;
E. STANFORD, CHARING CROSS; AND W. GRIGGS, HANOVER STREET, PECKHAM.

1880.

FRONTISPIECE.

MANMODI CHAITYA CAVE, JUNNAR.
From a photograph.

CONTENTS.

PART I.—THE EASTERN CAVES.

By James Fergusson.

PART II.—CAVE TEMPLES OF WESTERN INDIA.

By James Burgess.

BOOK II.

BOOK III.—THE BRAHMANICAL CAVES.

BOOK IV.—THE JAINA CAVE-TEMPLES.

LIST OF PLATES.

Late Mahâyâna representation of Buddha on his Lotus Throne, with Attendants, from Cave No. XXXV. at Kanhêri.

LIST OF WOODCUTS.

PREFACE.

In the year 1843 I read a paper to the Royal Asiatic Society on the Rock-Cut Temples of India,[1] in which I embodied the results obtained during several journeys I had undertaken between the years 1836 and 1842 for the purpose of investigating their history and forms, together with those of the other architectural antiquities of India. It was the first attempt that had then been made to treat the subject as a whole. Many monographs of individual temples or of groups, had from time to time appeared, but no general description, pointing out the characteristic features of cave architecture had then been attempted, nor was it indeed possible to do so, before the completion of the first seven volumes of "Journal of the Asiatic Society of Bengal" in 1838. The marvellous ingenuity which their editor James Prinsep displayed, in these volumes, in deciphering the inscriptions of Aśoka and other hitherto unread documents, and the ability with which Turnour, Kittoe, and others who were inspired by his zeal, hastened to aid in his researches, revolutionised the whole character of Indian archæology. The history of Buddha and of early Buddhism, which before had been mythical and hazy in the extreme, now became clear and intelligible and based on recognized facts. The relation, too, of Brahmanism and the other Hindu religions to Buddhism and to each other were now for the first time settled, on a basis that was easily understood and admitted of a logical superstructure raised upon it.

When all this was done the remaining task was easy. It only required that some one should visit the various localities where the caves were situated, and apply, the knowledge so amassed, to their classification. For this purpose I visited the eastern caves at Katak and Mahâvallipur, as well as those of Ajaṇṭâ, Elurâ, Karlê, Kanheri,

[1] *Journal of the Royal Asiatic Society*, vol. viii., pp. 30 to 92, and afterwards republished with a folio volume of eighteen lithographic plates from my own sketches of the caves.

Elephanta, and others in the west, and found no difficulty in seeing at a glance, to what religion each was dedicated, and as little in ascertaining their relative ages among themselves. A great deal has been done since by new discoveries and further investigations to fill up the cartoon I then ventured to sketch in, but the correctness of its main outlines have never been challenged and remain undisturbed.

One of the first works to appear after mine was the "Historical Researches" of Dr. Bird, published in Bombay in 1847,"[1] but which from various causes—more especially the imperfection of the illustrations—was most disappointing. Though this has been almost the only other work going over the same ground, the interest excited on the subject, led to the formation of a Cave Commission in Bombay in 1848[2] for the purpose of investigating the history of the caves and taking measures for their preservation. One of the first fruits of their labour was the production, in August 1850, of a Memoir on the subject by the late Dr. Wilson, in the introductory paragraph to which he made the following statement, which briefly summarises what was then proposed to be done:—

"The Royal Asiatic Society of Great Britain and Ireland having, on the suggestion of James Fergusson, Esq., to whom we are so much indebted for the artistic and critical illustration of the architectural antiquities of India, represented to the Court of Directors of the East India Company the propriety of taking steps for the preservation, as far as possible, of the Cave Temples and other ancient religious memorials of this country, and for their full delineation and description, before the work of their decay and destruction

---

[1] Dr. Bird, in the preface to his *Historical Researches*, says:—

"The Court of Directors have at length responded to the Royal Asiatic Society's representation of the duty imposed on us, as a nation, to preserve the relics of ancient art, and have accordingly sent out orders to each presidency that measures be adopted to keep them from further decay. They are also about to institute an Archæological Commission for investigating the architectural character and age of the several monuments; an inquiry which, though long neglected, and left to other nations, less interested than ourselves in India, is likely to aid in dispelling the mist which for centuries has enveloped the historical age of these excavations and the object of their structure."

[2] The Bombay Cave-Temple Commsssion consisted of the Rev. Dr. J. Wilson, F.R.S., President; Rev. Dr. Stevenson, Vice President; C. J. Erskine, C.S.; Capt. Lynch, I. N.; Dr. J. Harkness; Venâyak Gangâdhar Shâstri; and Dr. H. J. Carter, Secretary, and was appointed in terms of a resolution (No. 2805) of 31st July 1848 of the Government of Bombay.

has made further progress, that honourable body has promptly responded to the call which has been addressed to it, and already taken certain steps for the accomplishment of the objects which are so much to be desired.[1] With reference to the latter of these objects, it has determined to appoint a general Commission of Orientalists to direct its accomplishment in the way which may best tend to the illustration of the history, literature, religion, and art of ancient India. Preparatory to the commencement of the labours of that Commission, and the issuing of instructions for its researches, another of a local character has, with the approbation of the Government of India, been formed by the Bombay Branch of the Royal Asiatic Society to make such preliminary inquiries about the situation and extent and general character of the antiquities, which are to be the subject of investigation, as may facilitate its judicious commencement and prosecution."[2]

This *first Memoir* was prepared by Dr. Wilson for the Bombay Cave Commission just referred to, in order to sketch the extent of the information then available on the subject, and to call forth additions from persons possessed of special local knowledge.

In September 1852 he read to the same Society his *Second Memoir*, containing short notices of the Aurangâbâd Caves and of a few others that had been brought to light during the preceding two years.

Previous to this, about July 1851, Lieutenant Brett had been employed to take facsimiles of the inscriptions from the caves,—a work strongly commended in the Court's despatch No. 13 of 4th May 1853. Reduced copies were made to accompany Dr. Stevenson's papers on the inscriptions,[3] but Lieutenant Brett's engagement was closed about the end of 1853, and his original copies were sent to England. In April 1856, Vishnu Shâstri Bâpat was engaged to continue Lieutenant Brett's work, and having some knowledge of the ancient characters and of Sanskrit, it was expected he would be serviceable in preparing translations also. Results were promised from time to time, but delayed till September 1860, when it was reported that the Pandit had translated 88 inscriptions into Marâthî; but he died next year, and no results of his work were ever pub-

---

[1] Despatches No. 15 of 29th May 1844, No. 1 of 27th January 1847, and No. 24 of 29th September 1847; also despatch of Lord Hardinge, No. 4 of 19th April 1847.

[2] *Jour. Bom. B. R. As. Soc.* vol. iii. pt. ii. p. 36.

[3] *Jour. Bom. B. R. As. Soc.*, vol. v.

lished; while the Commission itself ceased to exist early in 1861. It had, however, stirred up officers in different parts of the country to send in accounts of the antiquities in their districts, and among these the contributions of Sir Bartle Frere, Captain Meadows Taylor, Dr. E. Impey, Dr. Bradley, Sir W. Elliot, Mr. West, and others were valuable additions to our knowledge. At its instigation, also, the caves at Ajaṇṭâ, Aurangâbâd, and Elephanta were cleared of accumulations of earth and silt.

The fresco paintings in the Buddhist caves at Ajaṇṭâ being of very special interest, Captain Robert Gill was appointed by the Madras Government to make copies of them in oils. The work was one of considerable labour, but in the course of eight or ten years he sent home full-size copies of about thirty fresco paintings, many of them of very large size. The greater number of these paintings were exhibited in the Crystal Palace at Sydenham, where they were most unfortunately destroyed by fire in 1866. Five of them only escaped, having remained in the stores belonging to the India Office, and consequently were not exhibited.

From the time that Major Gill had been first appointed to copy them, till the destruction of his work, much of the fresco painting in the caves had fallen off or been destroyed. Still sufficient was left to make it desirable to secure fresh copies of what still remained, and in 1873 Mr. Griffiths, of the School of Art in Bombay, was engaged to make fresh copies. He has already spent three seasons at Ajaṇṭâ with some of his students, and has copied, with great fidelity, a considerable number of the fragments that still remain in a sufficiently perfect state, to make it worth while to reproduce them.[1]

Meanwhile the Secretary of State for India in Council in a despatch, dated in November 1870, proposed a survey of the architectural antiquities of Western India, and especially of the Cave-temples; but no progress was made till 1873, when the Hon. J. Gibbs, C.S., prepared a minute on the subject in which he sketched a scheme for the Archæological Survey, and to him chiefly belongs the credit of carrying into effect the objects of the despatch.

The drawings for this work have been collected during the

[1] These copies are now in this country, principally in the British Museum, and a small portion in the India Museum, South Kensington.

six seasons since the Archæological Survey of Western India was commenced, and some of them, with others not reproduced here, have appeared in the three volumes of reports already published. There is, however, a very large collection of careful drawings illustrative of many details of sculpture, especially at Ajaṇṭâ and Elurâ, which could not be reproduced in this work;[1] and it is hoped a further selection from them may form a prominent feature in, if it does not constitute, the next volume of the Survey Reports.[2] If presented on a sufficiently large scale, these drawings would be most interesting to all engaged in the practice of art, as well as to all amateurs. With the frescoes of Ajaṇṭâ and Bâgh, and perhaps a very few other additions, they would form a very complete illustration of Buddhist art in sculpture, architecture, and painting from the third before our era to the eighth century after it.

One of the objects proposed at the time this survey was sanctioned was, that I, conjointly with Mr. Burgess, should, when the proper time arrived, write a general history of Cave Architecture in India. A scheme for this work was submitted to the Duke of Argyll, then Secretary of State for India, and sanctioned by his Grace in 1871. In order to carry this into effect Mr. Burgess remained at home, in Edinburgh, during the season 1877–78 to write his part, which forms practically the second part of this book; but, owing to various causes it is not necessary to enumerate here, the whole of his part was not set up in type till just before his return to India in October last. The whole of my share, which forms practically the first part, was ready at the same time, and we were thus able to exchange parts and go over the whole together before his departure, and I was left to "make up" the whole and pass it through the press, which I have done during the past winter.

---

1 After this work had been almost wholly written Dr. Ed. W. West and his brother Mr. Arthur A. West placed in my hands a very large collection of notes and drawings from the Rock-Temples of the Bombay Presidency, collected and prepared by them whilst in India, with full permission to make any use I chose of them. I have used one of these plans and part of another, but I still hope to examine them more carefully and perhaps to make further use of so valuable a collection.—J.B.

2 Three volumes of *Reports* of the Survey and a collection of 286 Pâli Sanskrit and old Canarese inscriptions have already been published. The *Reports* contain accounts of the Cave Temples at Bâdâmi, in Kâthiâwâr, at Dhârsinva, Karusâ, Ambâ, and Aurangâbâd. Accounts of other groups had also appeared either separately or in the *Indian Antiquary*.

This arrangement, though inevitable under the circumstances, has, I fear, been in some respects unfavourable to the uniformity of the work. There is little doubt that if Mr. Burgess had been at home and in daily communication with me during the time the work was passing through the press, many points of detail might have been discussed and elaborated with more completeness than has been possible at a distance. There is, however, really nothing of importance on which we were not agreed before his departure. Had this not been the case, a better plan would probably have been to postpone indefinitely the appearance of the book. Had I been a younger man, I might possibly have recommended this course, especially if I had felt confident that the Indian Government would at any future period have sanctioned the necessary outlay. The abolition, however, of the establishment at Peckham, the dispersion of the India Museum, and other symptoms of economy in matters relating to literature and art, seem to render it expedient to proceed while there is the opportunity.

Supposing these personal difficulties had not existed, the work might certainly have been made more perfect if its publication had been delayed till the survey was complete, or at least more nearly so than it now is. At present our knowledge of the subject is rapidly progressive, and anything like completeness is consequently impossible. Since, for instance, Mr. Burgess' return to India in October last, two facts have been brought to light which have revolutionised our chronology of the old pre-Christian caves in the west, and gives our knowledge of them a precision that was not before attainable. One of these is the discovery of inscriptions in the Mauryan character (they have not yet been deciphered) in the caves at Pitalkhorâ. The other the discovery of the very old Vihâra at Bhâjâ, described in the Appendix. With two such discoveries in one season there is every probability that others of great if not of equal importance may be made, and give the history of the western caves a precision it cannot now pretend to possess.

One of the weak points in the chronology of the western caves arises from our inability to fix the dates of the Andhrabhṛitya kings, but in his last letter Mr. Burgess informs me that he has collected an immense number of inscriptions at Kârlê and elsewhere, which he is examining with the assistance of Mr. Fleet, Dr. Bühler, and the Pandits, and he hopes to make even this point quite clear.

In fact, if the survey is carried on for another couple of years, which I earnestly hope and trust it will be, and with the same success which has hitherto attended its operations, there will not be a single cave in Western India whose date and destination may not be ascertained with all the requisite certainty, nor any antiquities of importance in the Bombay presidency that will not have been investigated and described. Meanwhile, however, the present work may, at all events, serve to direct attention to the subject, and to some extent at least, supply a want which has long been felt by those interested in Indian archæology.

In order that readers may know exactly what part each of us took in the preparation of this book, it may be as well to explain that I wrote the whole of the first part (pp. 161), with the intention that it should serve as a general introduction to the whole, but at the same time Mr. Burgess contributed a certain number of pages, between 5 and 10 per cent. of the whole, even in this part.

In like manner the whole of the second part has been written by Mr. Burgess (pp. 162 to 512), but during its passage through the press I have interpolated even a greater proportion of pages on the various subjects of which it treats. Thus, as I have no reason to suppose there is any difference of opinion on any material point, the work may fairly be considered a combined production, for the whole of which we are jointly and severally responsible. I selected the whole of the woodcuts, and all the new ones were executed under my superintendence by Mr. Cooper. The whole of the plates, except the first, are reduced copies of a few from among the mass of drawings prepared by Mr. Burgess and his assistants during the progress of the survey, and were specially selected by him for this work to supply a want that had long been felt. At the present day photographs and sketches of almost all the caves can be had by anyone who will take the trouble to collect them, but correct plans and architectural details, drawn to scale, can only be procured by persons who have time at their disposal, and instruments and assistants which are only available for such a survey as that conducted by Mr. Burgess. The plates have been very carefully executed in photo-lithography by Mr. Griggs, under Mr. Burgess' superintendence, and serve to place our knowledge of the cave architecture of Western India on a scientific basis never before attainable.

The woodcuts of the Raths at Mahâvallipur are taken from a beautiful series of drawings of these curious monoliths prepared for me, at his own expense, by Mr. R. Chisholm, of the Public Works Department at Madras. I only regret that owing to various untoward delays they reached me so late that I was not able to avail myself of them to a greater extent than I have done.

JAMES FERGUSSON.

20, Langham Place,
March 1880.

NOTE.

A word should be said about the mode of spelling Indian names adopted in this work. The rules recently adopted by Government for spelling names of places, and for the transliteration of Sanskrit and other Indian words, have generally been adhered to, but well established names have not often been interfered with. Where, however, they have been spelt in a variety of ways,—and what Indian name has not?—as Iloura, Yeloora, Elura, Elora, Ellorah, Elloora, Veroola, &c., a compromise approximating to the local pronunciation has been used, as Elurâ, or the vernacular name has been adopted in Romanised form, with the broad or long sounds of vowel letters marked by a circumflex or caret, as Bhâjâ, Kârlê, Stûpa, &c. The cerebral letters *ṭ*, *ḍ*, *ṭh*, *ḍh*, *ṇ*, need not disturb though they hardly convey much meaning to the English readers. They are the hard sounds of these letters and in constant use in our own language; *ṛ* has been used freely for *ḍ*, as to many ears the sounds approximate closely, being formed with the tip of the tongue on the palate, and *ś* has a decidedly more delicate aspiration than *sh*.

Adjectivals are formed in the Indian language by lengthening the vowels, thus from *Śiva* is formed the word *Śaiva*, denoting anything relating to Śiva or a member of the sect devoted to him; so from *Vishṇu* is formed *Vaishṇava;* from *Buddha*—*Bauddha;* from *Jina*—*Jaina;* and from *Śakti*—*Śâkta*. "Buddhist" has, however, been generally used throughout this work instead of Bauddha, as it has from long use become so much more familiar to English ears than its more correct Indian synonym.—J.B.

THE CAVE TEMPLES OF INDIA.

PART I.

THE EASTERN CAVES.

INTRODUCTION.

From the earliest period at which the mention of India dawns upon us, among the records of the past, her name has been surrounded by a halo of poetic mystery, which even the research and familiarity of modern times, have as yet failed to entirely dispel. Of her own history she tells us but little, and it was only in comparatively modern times, when she came into contact with the more prosaic nations of the outer world, that we learned much regarding her former existence. So far as is at present known, no mention of India has yet been discovered among the records of Egypt or Assyria. No conquest of her country is recorded in the hieroglyphics that adorn the Temples of Thebes, nor been decyphered among the inscriptions on the walls of the palaces of Nineveh. It is even yet uncertain whether the Ophir or Tarshish to which the ships of Solomon traded and "brought back gold, and ivory, and algum "trees, and apes, and peacocks," can be considered as places in India, rather than some much nearer localities in Arabia or Africa. The earlier Greek writers had evidently no distinct ideas on the subject, and confounded India with Ethiopia in a manner that is very perplexing. It was not, in fact, till the time of the glorious raid of Alexander the Great, that the East and the West came practically into contact, and we obtain any distinct accounts, on which reliance can be placed, regarding that land which before his time was, to his countrymen, little more than a mythic dream. Fortunately, as we now know, the visit of the Greeks occurred at one of the most interesting periods of Indian history. It was just when the old Vedic period was passing away, to give place to the new Buddhist epoch; when that religion was rising to the surface, which for nearly 1,000 years continued to be the prevailing faith of northern India, at least. Though after that period it disappeared from the land where it originated, it still continues to influence all the forms of religious belief in the surrounding countries, to the present day.

The gleam of light which the visit of the Greeks shed on the internal state of India, though brilliant, was transitory. Before the great Mauryan dynasty which they found, or which they placed, on the throne of central India had passed away, her history relapsed, as before, into the same confused, undated, record of fainéant kings, which continued almost down to the Moslem conquest, a tangle and perplexity to all investigators. It is only in rare instances that the problems it presents admit of a certain solution, while the records of the past, as they existed at the time when the Greeks visited the country, were, as may well be supposed, even more shadowy than they became in subsequent ages.

It is so strange that a country so early and so extensively civilised as India was, should have no written chronicles, that the causes that led to this strange omission deserve more attention than has hitherto been bestowed on the subject by the learned in Europe. The fact is the more remarkable, as Egypt on the one hand and China on the other, were among the most careful of all nations in recording dates and chronicling the actions of their earlier kings, and they did this notwithstanding all the difficulties of their hieroglyphic or symbolic writing, while India seems to have possessed an alphabet from an early date, which ought to have rendered her records easy to keep and still more easy to preserve. There seems in fact to be no intelligible cause why the annals of ancient India should not be as complete and satisfactory as those of any other country in a similar state of civilisation, unless it lies in the poetic temperament of its inhabitants, and the strange though picturesque variety of the races who dwell within her boundaries, but whose manifold differences seem at all times to have been fatal to that unity which alone can produce greatness or stability among nations.

All this is the more strange, for, looked at on the map, India appears one of the most homogeneous and perfectly defined countries in the world. On the east, the ocean and impenetrable jungles shut her out from direct contact with the limitrophe nations on that side, while in the north the Himalayas forms a practically impassible barrier against the inhabitants of the Thibetan plains. On the west the ocean and the valley of the Indus equally mark the physical features which isolate the continent of India, and mark her out as a separate self-contained country. Within these boundaries there are no great barriers, no physical features, that divide the land into separate well defined provinces, in which we might expect different races to be segregated under different forms of government. There seems certainly no physical reason why India, like China, should not always have been one country, and governed, at least, at times, by one dynasty. Yet there is no record of any such event in her annals. Aśoka, in the third century B.C., may have united the whole of the north of India under his sway, but nothing of the sort seems again to have occurred till nearly 2,000 years afterwards, when the Moguls under Akbar and Aurangzib nearly accomplished what it has been left for us, to carry practically into effect. During the interval, India seems to have been divided into five great divisions, nearly corresponding to our five presidencies, existing as separate kingdoms and ruled by different kings, each supreme over a host of minor kinglets or chiefs, among whom the country was divided. At times, one of the sovereigns, of one of the five Indias, was acknowledged as lord paramount, nominally at least, but the country never was united as a whole, capable of taking a place among the great monarchies of the earth, and making its influence felt among surrounding nations. It never, indeed, was so organised as to be capable of resisting any of the invaders who from time to time forced the boundary of the Indus, and poured their hordes into her fertile and much-coveted plains. It is, indeed, to this great fact that we owe all that wonderful diversity of peoples we find in India, and, whether for good or for evil, render the population of that country as picturesquely various, as that of China is tamely uniform. It is this very variety, however, that renders it so difficult for even those who have long studied the question, on the spot, to master the problem in all its complexity of detail. It unfortunately, too, becomes, in consequence, almost impossible to convey to those who have not had these advantages, any clear ideas on the subject, which is nevertheless both interesting and instructive, though difficult and complex, and requiring more study than most persons are able or inclined to bestow upon it.

ETHNOGRAPHY.

The great difficulty of writing anything very clear or consecutive regarding Indian ethnography or art arises principally from the fact that India was never inhabited by one, but in all historical times, by at least three distinct and separate races of mankind. These occasionally existed and exist in their original native purity, but at others are mixed together and commingled in varying proportions to such an extent as almost to defy analysis, and to render it almost impossible at times to say what belongs to one race, what to another. Notwithstanding this, the main outlines of the case are tolerably clear, and can be easily grasped to an extent at least sufficient to explain the artistic development of the various styles of art, that existed in former times in various parts of the country.

When the Aryans, descending from the plateau of central Asia, first crossed the Indus to occupy the plains of the Panjâb, they found the country occupied by a race of men apparently in a very low state of civilisation. These they easily subdued, calling them *Dasyus*,[1] and treated as their name implies as a subject or slave population. In the more fertile parts of the country, where the Aryans established themselves, they probably in the course of time assimilated this native population with themselves, to a great degree at least. They still however exist in the hills between Silhet and Asam, and throughout the Central Provinces, as nearly in a state of nature[2] as they could have existed when the Aryans first intruded on their domains, and drove the remnants of them into the hills and jungle fastnesses, where they are still to be found. Whoever they were these Dasyus may be considered as the aboriginal population of India. At least we have no knowledge whence they came nor when. But all their affinities seem to be with the Himalayan and trans-Himalayan races, and they seem to have spread over the whole of what we now know as the province of Bengal, though how far they ever extended towards Cape Comorin we have now no means of knowing.

The second of these great races are the *Dravidians*, who now occupy the whole of the southern part of the peninsula, as far north at least as the Krishnâ river, and at times their existence can be traced in places almost up to the Nerbudda. It has been clearly made out by the researches of Bishop Caldwell[3] and others that they belong to the great *Turanian* family of mankind, and have affinities with the Finns and other races who inhabit the countries almost up to the shores of the North Sea. It is possible also that it may be

---

1 Confr. V. de St. Martin, *Geog. du Veda*, pp. 82, 99.

2 Gen. Dalton, *Descriptive Ethnography of Bengal* (Calcutta, 1872), is by far the best and most exhaustive work on the subject.

3 *Comparative Grammar of the Dravidian or South Indian Family of Languages* by Bishop Caldwell, 2nd edit., 1875.

found that they are allied to the Accadian races who formed the substratum of the population in Babylonia in very ancient times. It is not however known when they first entered India, nor by what road. Generally it is supposed that it was across the Lower Indus, because affinities have been traced between their language and that of the *Brahuis*, who occupy a province of Baluchistan. It may be, however, that the Brahuis are only an outlying portion of the ancient inhabitants of Mesopotamia, and may never have had any direct communication further east. Certain it is that neither they nor any of the Dravidian families have any tradition of their having entered India by this road, and they have left no traces of their passage in Sindh or in any of the countries to the north of the Nerbudda or Taptee. On the other hand, it seems so improbable that they could have come by sea from the Persian Gulf in sufficient numbers to have peopled the large tract that they now occupy, that we must hesitate before adopting such an hypothesis. When their country is first mentioned in the traditions on which the *Râmâyaṇa* is based, it seems to have been an uncultivated forest, and its inhabitants in a low state of civilisation.[1] In the time of Aśoka, however (B.C. 250), we learn from his inscriptions, confirmed by the testimony of classical authors, that the Dravidians had settled into that triarchy of kingdoms, the Chôla, Chêra, and Pândya, which endured till very recent times. From their architecture we know that these states afterwards developed into a comparatively high state of civilisation.

The third and by far the most illustrious and important of the three races were the *Aryans*, or Sanskrit speaking races, who may have entered India as long ago as 3,000 years[2] before the Christian era.[3] In the course of time—it may have taken them 2,000 years to effect it—they certainly occupied the whole of India north of the Vindhya mountains, as far as the shores of the Bay of Bengal, entirely

---

1 See *Indian Antiquary*, vol. viii. pp. 1–10.

2 Confr. V. de St. Martin, *Geog. du Veda*, p. 9.

3 I have always looked upon it as probable that the era 3101 years before Christ, which the Aryans adopt as the Era of the Kali Yug, may be a true date marking some important epoch in their history. But whether this was the passage of the Indus in their progress eastward, or some other important epoch in their earlier history, it seems impossible now to determine. It may, however, be only a factitious epoch arrived at by the astronomers, computing backwards to a general conjunction of the planets, which they seem to have believed took place at that time. Colebrooke's *Essays*, vol. i., p. 201; vol. ii., pp. 357, 475.

superseding the native Dasyus and driving the Dravidians, if they ever occupied any part of the northern country, into the southern portion, or what is now known as the Madras Presidency. There never was any attempt, so far as is known, on the part of the Aryans to exterminate the original inhabitants of the land. They seem on the contrary to have used them as herdsmen or cultivators of the soil, but they superseded their religion by their own higher and purer faith, and obliterated, by their superiority, all traces of any peculiar civilisation they may have possessed. At the same time, though they never seem to have attempted physically, to conquer or colonise the south, they did so intellectually. Colonies of Brahmans from the northern parts of India introduced the literature and religion of the Aryans into the country of the Dravidians, and thus produced a uniformity of culture, which at first sight looks like a mingling of race. Fortunately their architecture and their arts enable us to detect at a glance how essentially different they were, and have always remained. Notwithstanding this, the intellectual superiority of the Aryans made so marked an impression during long ages on their less highly organised Turanian neighbours in the south, that without some such material evidence to the contrary, it might be contended that the fusion was complete.

There are no doubt many instances where families and even tribes of each of these three races still remain in India, keeping apart from the rest, and retaining the purity of their blood to a wonderful extent. But as a rule they are so mixed in locality and so commingled in blood, that it is extremely difficult, at times, to define the limits of relationship that may exist between any one of the various peoples of India with those among whom they are residing. Their general relationships are felt by those who are familiar with the subject, but in the present state of our knowledge it is almost impossible to define and reduce them into anything like a scientific classification, and it certainly is not necessary to attempt anything of the sort in this place. The main features of Indian ethnography are distinct and easily comprehended, so that there is little difficulty in following them, and they are so distinctly marked in the architecture and religion of the people, that they mutually illustrate each other with sufficient clearness, for our present purposes at least. No one, for instance, at all familiar with the subject, can fail to recognise at a glance the many-storeyed pyramidal temples of the Dravidians, and to distinguish them from the curvilinear outlined towers universally employed by the northern people, speaking languages derived from the Sanskrit. Nor when he has recognised these can he hesitate in believing that, when any given temple was erected, the country was either inhabited, in the one case by Dravidians, or by an Aryan people, more or less, it may be, mixed up with the blood of the native Dasyus;[1] but in either case the architecture marks the greater or less segregation of the race, by the purity with which the distinctive features of the style are carried out in each particular instance.

HISTORY.

From the Greek historians we learn that at the time of Alexander the falsification of Indian history had only gone the length of duplication. If we assume the Kaliyug, 3101 B.C., to represent the first immigration of the Aryans, the time that elapsed between that epoch and the accession of Chandragupta is, as nearly as may be, one half of the period, 6,042 years[2], during which Aryan tells us 153 monarchs succeeded one another on the throne of India. As this is as nearly as may be the number of kings whose names are recorded in the Puranas, we may fairly assume that the lists we now possess are the same as those which were submitted to the Greeks, while as according to this theory the average of each king's reign was little more than 18 years, there is no inherent improbability in the statement. It is more difficult to understand the historian when he goes on to say, "During all this time the Indians had only the liberty of being governed by their own laws twice. First for about 300 years, and after that for 120."[3] If this means that at two different epochs during these 30 or rather 28 centuries the Dasyus had asserted their independence it would be intelligible enough. It may have been so. They had, however, no literature of their own, and could not consequently record the fact, and their Brahmanical masters were hardly likely to narrate this among the very few historical events they deign to record. If, however, it should turn out to be so, it is the one fact in Dasyu ancient history that has come down to our days.

---

[1] See *History of Indian Architecture*, p. 210 *et seq.*, 319 *et seq. in passim.*

[2] *Indica*, chap. ix.

[3] *Loc. cit.*

The ancient history of the Dravidian race is nearly as barren as that of the Dasyus. It is true we have long lists of names of Pâṇḍyan kings, but when they commence is extremely doubtful. There is no one king in any of the lists whose date can be fixed within a century, nor any event recorded connected with any of these fainéant kings which can be considered as certain. It is not indeed till inscriptions and buildings come to our aid after the 5th or 6th century of our era, that anything like history dawns upon us. Between that time and the 10th or 11th century we can grope our way with tolerable certainty, and by the aid of synchronisms with the other dynasties obtain a fair knowledge of what was passing in the south some 8 or 10 centuries ago.[1]

Though all this is most unsatisfactory from an historical point of view, it fortunately is of comparatively little consequence for the purposes of this work. It does not appear that the Dravidians ever adopted the Buddhist religion, to any extent at least, and never certainly were excavators of caves. The few examples that exist in their country, such as those at Undavalli and Mahâvallipur, are quite exceptional, and though extremely interesting from that very cause, would hardly be more so, if we knew more of the history of the great dynasties of the country in which they are situated. They are not the expression of any national impulse, but the works of some local dynasties impelled to erect them under some exceptional circumstances, we do not now know, and may never be quite able to understand.

We are thus for our history thrown back on the great Aryan Sanskrit-speaking race of northern India, and for our present purposes need not trouble ourselves to investigate the history of the long line of Solar kings. These from their first advent held sway in Ayodhya (the modern Oudh), till the time of the *Mahâ Bhârata* when, about 12 centuries before the Christian era, they were forced to make way to their younger but less pure cousins of the Lunar line. Even then we may confine our researches to the rise of the Sisunâga dynasty in the 7th century B.C., as it was under one of the earlier kings of this dynasty that Śâkya Muni was born about 560 B.C., and with this event our architectural history practically begins.

It is fortunate we may be spared this long investigation, for even the much lauded *Vedas*, though invaluable from a philological or

[1] Wilson, *Essay J. R. A. S.*, vol. iii. p. 199, *et seq.*

ethnographic point of view, are absolutely worthless in so far as chronology and history are concerned, while the Epics on which the bulk of our knowledge of the ancient history of India is based, present it in so poetic a garb that it is difficult to extract the small residuum of fact its passioned strophes may contain. For the rest of our ancient history we are forced to depend on the *Purâṇas*, which have avowedly been falsified in order to present the history subsequently to the *Mahâbhârata* or great wars of the Pandus as a prophecy delivered by the sage Vyâsa who lived contemporaneously with that event. In this case it happens that a prophecy written after the events it describes, is nearly as unreliable, as writings of the same class, that pretend to foresee what may happen in the future.

Had any fragments of contemporary Buddhist literature survived the great cataclysm that destroyed that religion in the 7th and 8th centuries of our era, we would probably know all that we now are searching for in vain. We know at all events that in the Buddhist island of Ceylon they kept records which when condensed into the history of the *Mahâwanso*[1] present a truthful and consecutive narrative of events. Meagre it may be, in its present form, but no doubt capable of almost infinite extension if the annals of the monasteries still exist, and were examined with care. In like manner we have in the half Buddhist country of Kashmir, in the *Râja Tarangini* the only work in any Indian language which, as the late Professor Wilson said, is entitled to be called a history.[2] If such works as these are to be found on the outskirts of the Buddhist kingdom, it can hardly be doubted that even fuller records existed in its centre. We have indeed indications in *Hiuen Thsang*[3] that in the great monastery of Nalandâ the annals of the central kingdom of Magadha were in his time preserved with all the care that could be desired. The Chinese pilgrims, however, who visited India between the 4th and 7th centuries were essentially priests. They came to visit the places sanctified by the presence and actions of the founder of their religion, and to gather together on the spot the traditions relating to him and his early disciples. Beyond this their great object was to collect the books containing the doctrines and discipline of the sect. Secular affairs and political events had no attraction for these pilgrims of

[1] Translated by the Hon. Geo. Turnour, 1 vol. 4to., Colombo, 1837.

[2] Translated by Wilson, *Asiatic Researches*, vol. xv. p. 1, *et seqq.*

[3] *Hiuen Thsang*, translated by Stanislas Julien, vol. iii. p. 41, *et seq.*

the faith, and they pass them over with the most supercilious indifference. It is true nevertheless that the great encyclopædia of Ma-twan-lin does contain a vast amount of information regarding the mediæval history of India, but as this has not yet been translated it is hardly available for our present purposes.[1]

Religions.

The religions of India are even more numerous than her races, and at least as difficult to describe and define, if not more so, as the two classes of phenomena are by no means conterminous, and often mix and overlap one another in a manner that is most perplexing. Yet the main outlines of the case are clear enough, and may be described in a very few words with sufficient clearness for our present purposes at all events.

First comes, of course, the religion of the great immigrant Aryan race, embodied in the hymns of the *Vedas*, and consequently called the *Vedic*. It seems to have been brought from the regions of Central Asia, and it and its modified forms were, to say the least of it, the dominant religion in India down to the middle of the third century before Christ. At that time Aśoka adopted the religion of Buddha and made it the religion of the State, in the same manner that Constantine made Christianity the religion of the Roman world, at about the same distance of time from the death of its founder.

For nearly 1,000 years Buddhism continued to be the State religion of the land, though latterly losing much of its purity and power, till the middle of the seventh century of our era, when it sunk, and shortly afterwards disappeared entirely, before the rising star of the modern Hindu form of faith. This last was a resuscitation of the old Vedic religion, or at least pretended to be founded on

[1] This was partially done by the late M. Pauthier, and his extracts republished, 1837, in the *Journal of the Asiatic Society of Bengal*, vol. vi. p. 61, *et seq.*, and *Journal Asiatique*, 1839; also partially by M. Stan. Julien in the *Journal Asiatique* and by M. Favre. These, however, are only meagre extracts, and not edited with the knowledge since acquired. There are scholars willing to undertake the task of translation, but the difficulty is to obtain a copy of the original work. There are several in the British Museum, but the rules of that establishment do not admit of their being lent outside their walls, and as the would-be translators live at a distance, we must wait till this obstacle is removed before we can benefit by the knowledge we might thus attain.

the *Vedas*, but so mixed up with local superstitions, and so overlaid with the worship of Śiva and Vishṇu, and all the 1001 gods of the Hindu Pantheon, that the old element is hardly recognisable in the present popular forms of belief. It is now the religion of upwards of 150,000,000 of the inhabitants of India.

Jainism is another form of faith which sprung up contemporaneously with Buddhism, and perhaps even a little earlier, for the date of nirvana of *Mahâvîra*, the last of the Tirthankars or prophets of the Jains, is 526 B.C., and consequently earlier than that of Buddha. It never rose, however, to be either a popular or a State religion till after the fall of its sister faith, when in many parts of India it superseded Buddhism, and now, in some districts, takes the place that was formerly occupied by its rival.

It would, of course, be vain to look for any written evidence of the religion of the Dasyus during the long period in which they have formed an important element in the population of Hindostan. They always were too illiterate to write anything themselves, and their masters despised them and their superstitions too thoroughly to record anything regarding them. What we do know is consequently only from fragments encrusted in the other and more advanced faiths, or from the practices of the people where they exist in tolerable purity in the remote districts of the country at the present day. From these we gather that they were Tree and Serpent worshippers, and their principal deity was an earth god, to whom they offered human sacrifices till within a very recent period. They seem too to have practised all kinds of fetish worship, as most men do, in their early and rude state of civilisation.[1]

The great interest to us, for the purposes of the present work, is, that if there had been no Dasyus in India, it is probable there would have been no Buddhist religion either there or elsewhere. Though Buddha himself was an Aryan of pure Solar race, and his

---

[1] In his *Hibbert Lectures* Professor Max Müller points out with perfect correctness, that the Aryans in India never were fetish worshippers, and argues, that as no fetishism is found in the *Vedas*, therefore it never existed, at least anywhere in India. From his narrow point of view his logic is unassailable, but he entirely overlooks the fact, that only a very small portion of the population of India ever was Aryan, or in their early stages knew anything of the *Vedas*. Nine-tenths of the population are of Turanian origin, and judging from the results, indulged in more degrading fetish worship than is to be found among the savages in Africa and America till partially cured of these practices by contact with the Aryans.

earliest disciples were Brahmans, still, like Christianity, Buddhism was never really adopted by those by whom and for whom, it first was promulgated. It was, however, eventually adopted by vast masses of the casteless tribes of India, and by mere weight of numbers they seem for a long time to have smothered and kept under the more intellectual races of the land. It always was, however, and now is, a religion of a Turanian people, and never was professed, to any marked extent, by any people of pure Aryan race.

As we do not know exactly what the form of the religion of the Dasyus really was, we cannot positively assert, though it seems most probable that it was the earliest existing in India; but at the same time, it is quite certain that the Vedic is the most ancient cultus of which we have any written or certain record in that country. It was based on the worship of the manifestations of a soul or spirit in nature. Their favourite gods were Indra, the god of the firmament, who gave rain and thundered; Varuna, the Uranos of the Greeks, the "all-enveloper," the king of gods, upholding and knowing all, and guardian of immortality; Agni, the god of fire and light; Ushas, the dawn; Vâyu and the Maruts or winds; the Sun, addressed as Savitri, Sûrya, Vishṇu; and other less distinctly defined personifications. The service of these gods was at first probably simple enough, consisting of prayers, praises, libations, and sacrifices. The priests, however, eventually elaborated the most complicated ritual probably ever invented, and of course, as in other rituals, they arrogated to themselves, through the proper performance of these rites, powers, not only superhuman, but even super-divine, compelling even the gods themselves to submit to their wills.

The system of caste—an essential feature of Brahmanism—had become hard and fast as early at least as the sixth century before Christ, and was felt, especially among the lower castes, to be an intolerable yoke of iron. Men of all castes—often of very low ones—in revolt against its tyranny, separated themselves from their kind, and lived lives of asceticism, despising caste as something beneath the consideration of a devotee who aspired to rise by the merits of his own works and penances to a position where he might claim future felicity as a right. The Tîrthakas and others of this class, perhaps as early as the seventh century B.C., threw aside all clothing, sat exposed to sun and rain on ant-hills or dung-heaps, or, clothed in bark or in an antelope hide, sought the recesses of forests and on mountain peaks, to spend their days apart from the world and its vanities, in order to win divine favour or attain to the power of gods.

The founder of Buddhism was one of these ascetics. Gautama "the Buddha" was the son of a king of Kapilavastu, a small state in the north of Oudh, born apparently in the sixth century B.C. At the age of 29 he forsook his palace with its luxuries, his wife and infant child, and became a devotee, sometimes associating with others of the class in their forest abodes in Behâr, and sometimes wandering alone, and, unsatisfied with the dreamy conjectures of his teachers, seeking the solution of the mystery of existence. After some six years of this life, while engaged in a long and strict fast under a pîpal tree near Gayâ, wearied by exhaustion like the North American Indian seers, he fell into a trance, during which, as he afterwards declared, he attained to Buddhi or "perfected knowledge," and issued forth as the Buddha or "enlightened," the great teacher of his age. He is called by his followers Śâkya Muni—the Muni or ascetic of the Śâkya race; the Jina, or "vanquisher" of sins; Śâkya Sinha, "the lion of the Śakyas;" Tathâgata, "who came in the same way" as the previous Buddhas, &c. He celebrated the attainment of the Buddahood in the stanzas—

> Through various transmigrations
> Have I passed (without discovering)
> The builder I seek of the abode (of the passions).
> Painful are repeated births!
> O house builder! I have seen (thee).
> No house shalt thou again build me;
> Thy rafters are broken,
> Thy ridge-pole is shattered,
> My mind is freed (from outward objects).
> I have attained the extinction of desires.[1]

With its dogma of metempsychosis, Vedantism and Brahmanism provided no final rest, no permanent peace; for to be born again, even in the highest heaven, was still to be under the empire of the law of change, and consequently of further suffering in some still future birth. Hence it had created and fostered the thirst for final death or annihilation as the only escape from this whirlpool of

[1] For Gogerly's version as well as Turnour's, see Spence Hardy's *Manual of Buddhism*, pp. 180, 181.

miseries. The mission Śâkya Muni, now at the age of 35, set before himself as the proper work of a Buddha, was to minister to this passion for extinction; to point out a new religious path for the deliverance of men from the endless series of transmigrations they had been taught it was their doom to pass through, and to be the liberator of humanity from the curse of the impermanency, sorrow, and unreality of existence. His royal extraction, his commanding dignity and persuasive eloquence, the gentleness of his manners, his ardour and self-denying austerities, the high morality and the spirit of universal kindness that pervaded his teaching, fascinated the crowds, and he soon attracted enthusiastic disciples who caught something of the fire of their master's enthusiasm, and who were sent forth to propagate his new doctrines.

Caste he set aside: "My Law," said Buddha, "is a law of grace for all." Belief in his doctrines and obedience to his precepts was, for Śûdra and Dasyu as for the Brahman, the only and the wide door to the order of "the perfect." By the lower castes, whom the Brahmans had first arbitrarily degraded and then superciliously despised, such teaching would naturally be welcomed as a timely deliverance from the spiritual, intellectual, and social despotism of the higher classes. For them, evidently, and the despised aboriginal tribes, it was most specially adapted, and among such it was sure to find its widest acceptance.

Accompanied by his disciples, Gautama wandered about from place to place, principally in Gangetic India, subsisting on the offerings placed in his alms-bowl, or the provision afforded him by his wealthier converts, teaching men the emptiness and vanity of all sensible things, and pointing out the paths that led to *Nirvâṇa* or final quiescence, "the city of peace," scarcely, if at all, distinguished from annihilation. After 45 years thus spent, Śâkya Muni died in the north of Gorakhpur district, in Bengal. His disciples burnt his body and collected his relics, which were distributed among eight different cities, where they afterwards became objects of worship.

Springing as it did from Brahmanism, of which it might be regarded as only a modification, or one of its many sects or schools, Buddhism did not at first separate from the older religion so as to assume a position of hostility to it, insult its divinities, or disparage its literature. It grew up slowly, and many of its earlier and most distinguished converts were Brahmans. Though its founder had made many disciples during his lifetime, and sent them out to propagate his religion, it was not till the conversion of the great emperor Aśoka that it acquired any political importance; under his royal favour and patronage it spread widely. He is represented as having lavished the resources of his realm on the Buddhist religion and on buildings in honour of its founder, who by that time had become almost mythical in his wonderful travels and teaching, the number of his discourses being reckoned at 84,000, and nearly every place in India having some legend of his having visited it.

The Buddhist traditions are full of the name of Aśoka as the founder of vihâras or monasteries, stûpas or dâgobas, asylums, and other religious and charitable works. "At the places at which the Vanquisher of the five deadly sins (*i.e.* Buddha) had worked the works of his mission," says the Ceylon Chronicle,[1] "the sovereign (Aśoka) caused splendid dâgobas to be constructed. From 84,000 cities (of which Râjagriha was the centre) despatches were brought on the same day, announcing that the vihâras were completed." After a great council of the Buddhist priesthood, held in the 17th year of his reign, 246 B.C., missionaries were sent out to propagate the religion in the ten following countries, whose position we are able, even now, to ascertain with very tolerable precision from their existing denominations:—(1) Kâsmîra; (2) Gandhâra or Kandahâr; (3) Mahisamaṇḍala or Maisûr; (4) Vanavâsi in Kanara; (5) Aparântaka—'the Western Country' or the Konkaṇ,—the missionary being Yavana-Dharmarakshita;—the prefix Yavana apparently indicative of his being a Greek, or foreigner at least; (6) Mahâratta or the Dekhan; (7) The Yavana country,—perhaps Baktria; (8) Himâvanta or Nepal; (9) Suvarnabhumi or Burma; and (10) Ceylon. His own son Mahendra and daughter Sanghamitrâ were sent with the mission to Ceylon, taking with them a graft of the Bodhi tree at Buddha Gaya under which Buddha was supposed to have attained the supreme knowledge.

In two inscriptions from Sahasrâm and Rupnâth, recently translated,[2] Aśoka mentions that in the 33rd year, "after he had become a hearer of the law," and "entered the community" (of ascetics)

---

[1] Turnour's *Mahâvanso*, p. 34.

[2] Dr. Bühler in *Ind. Ant.*, vol. vi. p. 149, and vol. vii. pp. 141–160.

he had exerted himself so strenuously in behalf of his new faith, that the gods who previously "were considered to be true in Jambudbipa" had, in the second year afterwards (B.C. 226–5), been abjured.

To him, as already mentioned, the first Buddhist structures owe their origin. These were principally *stûpas* or *dâgobas*, that is, monumental shrines or receptacles for the relics of Buddha himself, or of the Sthaviras, or patriarchs of the sect,—consisting of a cylindrical base, supporting a hemispherical dome, called the *garbha*. On the top of this was placed a square stone box, commonly called a Tee, usually solid, covered by a series of thin slabs, each projecting over the one below it, and with an umbrella raised over the whole. These *stûpas* were erected, however, not only as monuments over relics, but set up also wherever any legend associated the locality with a visit or discourse of Buddha's—which practically came to be wherever there were a few Buddhist Bhikshus desirous of securing an easy livelihood from the neighbouring villagers :—for legends are easily invented in India. Aśoka erected many of these over the length and breadth of his extensive dominions and raised great monolithic pillars, inscribed with edicts, intended to promulgate the spread of Buddhism. Edicts were also incised on rocks at Kapurdigiri near Peshâwar, at Mount Girnâr in Kâṭhiâwâr, in Orissa, Ganjam, and the Upper Provinces. The stûpas or topes at Bhilsâ, Sârnath near Banâras, Manikyâla in the Panjab, and elsewhere, are examples of that class of monuments, of which there are also gigantic specimens in Ceylon, erected by Devânâmpriya Tishya, the contemporary of Aśoka, and his successors. But these belong rather to a general history of Indian architecture than to a work especially devoted to the caves.[1]

The Buddhist Bhikshus thus soon became very numerous, and possessed regularly organised monasteries, or *Vihâras*, in which they spent the rainy season, studying the sacred books and practising a temperate asceticism. "The holy men were not allowed seats of costly cloth, nor umbrellas made of rich material with handles adorned with gems and pearls, nor might they use fragrant substances, or fish gills and bricks for rubbers in the bath, except, indeed, for their feet. Garlic, toddy, and all fermented liquors were

---

[1] For an account of the stûpas at Sânchi and Amrâvati, see Fergusson's *Tree and Serpent Worship*, and Cunningham's *Bhilsa Topes*; also Fergusson's *Indian and Eastern Architecture*, pp. 54, 60–65, 71–72, 92, 105; and for Sarnâth, *ibid.* pp. 65, 68, 173, and Sherring's *Sacred City of the Hindus*, p. 230 ff.

forbidden, and no food permitted after midday. Music, dancing, and attendance upon such amusements were forbidden."[1] And, though seal rings or stamps of gold were prohibited, they might use stamps of baser metal, the device being a circle with two deer on opposite sides, and below the name of the vihâra.

Buddhism, after this, flourished and spread for centuries. Chinese pilgrims came to India to visit the spots associated with the founder's memory, to learn its doctrines, and carry away books containing its teachings. In the seventh century of our era it had begun to decline in some parts of India; in the eighth apparently it was rapidly disappearing: and shortly after that it had vanished from the greater part of India, though it still lingered about Banâras and in Bengal where the Pâla dynasty, if not Buddhists themselves, at least tolerated it extensively in their dominions.[2] It existed also at some points on the West coast, perhaps till the eleventh century or even later. It has been thought that it was extinguished by Brahmanical persecution, and in some places such means may have been used to put it down; but the evidence does not seem sufficient to prove that force was generally resorted to. Probably its decline and final extinction was to a large extent owing to the ignorance of its priests, the corruptions of its early doctrines, especially after the rise of the Mahâyâna sect, the multiplicity of its schisms, and its followers becoming mixed up with the Jains, whose teachings and ritual are very similar, or from its followers falling into the surrounding Hinduism of the masses. Except in the earliest ages of its existence it probably never was predominant in India, and alongside it, during its whole duration, Śaivism continued to flourish and to hold, as it does still, the allegiance of the majority of the lower castes.

Rock temples and residences for Buddhist ascetics are early referred to. Mahendra, the son of Aśoka, on his arrival in Ceylon, erected a vihâra on the summit of the Mihintala mountain, where he caused 68 cells to be cut out in the rock, which still exist at the Ambustella

---

[1] Mrs. Speirs' *Life in Ancient India*, p. 317.

[2] The date of the Pâla dynasty has not been ascertained with accuracy. Abul Fazl in the *Ayin Akbari* assigns 689 years to their 10 reigns, which, however, is evidently too much. The most complete list is that inserted by General Cunningham in his *Reports*, vol. iii. p. 134, based on a comparison of the written authorities, with their existing inscriptions on copper and stone. He represents them as 18 kings, reigning from 765 to 1200, A.D., which is probably very near the truth.

dagoba.[1] We find also at Barabar (near Gâya) in Bihâr, several caves with inscriptions upon them, with dates upon them of the 12th and 19th years of Aśoka himself, or in 251 and 244 B.C.[2]

We have no means of knowing what the primitive religion of the Dravidians was before their country was colonised by the Brahmans of the north, who imported with them the worship of Śiva and Vishṇu and all the multitudinous Gods of the modern Hindu Pantheon. It is probable that before that time, the Dravidians did possess a Pantheon distinct from that of their northern neighbours, but so little has the comparative mythology of India been hitherto studied, that it is impossible now to say how much of the present religion of the country is a foreign importation, how much an indigenous local growth. Śiva is, and apparently as far as our information goes, seems always to have been, the favourite deity in the South, and his name and that of his consort is mixed up with so many legends, and these extend so far back, that it almost looks as if his worship sprung up there. On the other hand, the earliest authentic mention of Śiva is by a Greek author, Bardasanes, who describes him as worshipped in a cave not far from Peshawur in the early part of the third century, under the well-known form of the Ardhanâri, or half man half woman.[3] He is also found unmistakeably represented on the coins of Kadphises[4] with his trident and bull, before the Christian era, and it is not clear whether these are fragments of mythology left there by the Dravidians, dropped like the Brahui language, on their way to India, or whether it is a local northern cult which the Brahmans brought with them into India, and finally transported to the south.[5]

Though the worship of Vishṇu is as fashionable and nearly as extensively prevalent in modern times, in the south, as that of Śiva, it certainly never arose among the Dravidian races. It is essentially a cultus that could only have its origin among the same people as those from whom the Buddhist religion first took its present form. It is in fact at the present day only a very corrupt form of that religion, so corrupt, indeed, that their common origin is

---

1 Turnour's *Mahâvano*, pp. 103, 123; Emerson Tennent's *Ceylon*, vol. ii. p. 607.

2 *Jour. As. Soc. Ben.*, vol. vi. p. 671. Cunningham *Reports*, vol. i. p. 44 ff.

3 Stœbus' *Physica*. Gainsford edition, p. 54.

4 Wilson's *Ariana Antiqua*, Plate X.

5 See Kittel's *Lingacultus*.

hardly to be recognised in its new disguise,[1] but still undoubtedly springing from a cognate source, though very far from emulating either the virtue or the purity of its elder sister faith. Borrowing apparently a cosmogony from Assyria, Vishnuism separated itself from Buddhism, attracting to itself most of the local superstitions that had crept into that religion, and finally becoming fused by the all powerful solvent of the *Vedas*, it forms a powerful element in the modern Brahmanical religion as now existing in India.[2]

It is only now that we are beginning to see, dimly it must be confessed, the mode in which all the conflicting and discordant elements of the present Hindu religion were gathered from 1,000 sources, and fused into the present gigantic superstition. The materials, however, probably now exist which would enable any competent scholar to reduce the whole to order, and give us an intelligible account of the origin and growth of this form of faith. The task, however, has not been attempted in recent times. When Moor's[3] and Coleman's[4] works were written, sufficient knowledge of the subject was not available to enable this to be done satisfactorily, but now an exhaustive work on the subject could easily be compiled, and would be one of the most valuable contributious we could have, to our knowledge of the ethnography as well as of the moral and intellectual status of the 250,000,000 of the inhabitants of a land teeming with beauty and interest.

CHRONOLOGY.

As the Buddhists were beyond all shadow of doubt the earliest excavators of caves in India, and also, so far as we now know, the first to use stone as an architectural building material in that country, it will be sufficient for the purposes of this work to confine our researches in Indian chronology to the period subsequent to the reigns of the two kings Bimbasara and Ajâtaśatru. It was in the 16th year of the first-named king that Śâkya Muni, then in

---

[1] How Buddhism may be transmogrified may be learnt from the tenets and practices of the Ahyantra sect in Nepal.

[2] The facts referring to the ethnography and religion of India are stated more fully than it is necessary to do here in the introduction to my *History of Indian Architecture*, 1876, to which the reader is referred for further information.—J. F.

[3] *Hindu Pantheon*, 4to., Plates, London, 1810.

[4] *Mythology of the Hindus*, 4to., Plates, 1832.

his 35th year, attained Buddhahood, B.C. 526, and died in the 8th year of the reign of the last-named king, 481 years B.C.[1]

From this point down to the Christian era there is no great difficulty with regard to Indian chronology, and it may be as well, in so far as the first part of this work is concerned, to confine our investigations to these limits. Certain it is that no architectural cave was excavated in India before the Nirvâṇa, and no king's name has even traditionally been connected with any cave in Eastern India whose ascertained date is subsequent to the Christian era. Indeed, in so far as the Bengal caves are concerned, we might almost stop with the death of Vrihadratha, the last of the Mauryans, 180 B.C., all the names connected with any caves being found among the kings of the earlier dynasties, if at all.

When we come to speak of the western or southern caves, in the second part of this work, it will be necessary to pursue these investigations to more modern dates, but this will be better done when we come to describe the caves themselves, and then try to ascertain the dates of the local dynasties to which each individual series of caves practically owes its origin.

As a foundation for the whole, and for our present purposes, it will probably be sufficient to state that the Buddhist accounts generally are agreed that Śâkya Muni, the founder of their religion, died in the 8th year of Ajâtaśatru, king of Magadha or Bihâr, and that 162 years elapsed between that event and the rise of the Maurya dynasty. This dynasty, as is well known, was founded by Chandragupta, the Sandrakottos of the Greeks, to whose court Megasthenés was sent by Seleucus as an ambassador, and who, taking advantage of the unsettled state of India after the invasion of Alexander of Macedon, had, by the aid of an astute Brahman, named Vishnugupta Drâmila,[2]

---

[1] When previously writing on this subject, I have always adopted the Ceylonese date 543 B.C. as that of the Nirvana as the most likely to be the correct one, according to the information then available. I was of course aware that so long ago as 1837 Turnour had pointed out (*J.A.S.B.*, vol. vi. p. 716 *et seq.*) that there was a discrepancy in the pre-Mauryan chronology of Ceylon, of about 60 years. But how that was to be rectified he could not explain. I do not yet despair of some new solution being found, but meanwhile the discovery of the Rupnâth and Sahasrâm inscriptions—both of the time of Aśoka—point so distinctly to the date of the Nirvana given in the text, 61 or 68 later than the usually accepted date, that for the present at least it seems impossible to adopt any other.—J. F.

[2] He is often designated by the patronymic Chanakya, or by the epithet Kautilya "the Crafty." *See* Wilson's works, vol. xii. p. 127 *et seqq.*

raised himself to the throne of Northern India somewhere between 320 and 315 B.C.[1] This connexion with western history, therefore, enables us to place the date of the Nirvâṇa of Buddha between 482 and 477 B.C. Again, Aśoka, the third king of the Maurya dynasty, in the 12th year of his reign, in an inscription, mentions the names of the Greek kings Antiochus of Syria, Ptolemy of Egypt, Antigonos of Macedon, Magas of Cyrene, and Alexander of Epirus,[2] and as Antiochus only came to the throne in 261 B.C., and it must have been engraved some time subsequent to that event, possibly about 252 B.C.[3] the first year of Aśoka may have been 263 B.C. Chandragupta had ruled 24 years, and Bindusâra, the father of

---

[1] The ascertained chronology of the time and the references of classical writers ought to enable us to fix this date within very narrow limits. Wilford (*Asiat. Res.* vol. v. p. 279 ff., and ix. p. 87) placed the commencement of Chandragupta's reign in 315 B.C. Prinsep (I. A. *Us. Tab.* p. 240), Max Müller (*Hist. Sans. Lit.* p. 298), and most other writers have agreed to this. Lassen (I. A. II. 64) seems to hesitate between the years 317 and 315, but finally decides for the latter (II. 67, 222, 1207). Cunningham (*Bhilsa Topes*, p. 90) arrives at 316 B.C.; Dr. H. Kern (*Over de Jaartelling*, p. 27) assumes 322, Rhys Davids (*Anc. Coins of Ceylon*, p. 41) B.C. 320.

There is no hint, however, that Chandragupta rose to power before the death of Porus, who by the partition at Triparadeisus, B.C. 321, was allowed to retain his kingdom, while Seleucus Nicator obtained the satrapy of Babylon. Between 320 and 316 "Seleucus was laying the foundation of his future greatness" (Justin. xv. 4), and in 317 Eudemus, who had put Porus to death (about 319), left the Panjâb with a large army to assist Eumenes, affording an opportunity for the revolt of Chandragupta and apparently the occasion alluded to by Justin. Then the expeditions of Seleucus to Bactria and afterwards to India took place about 303–302 (Clinton, *F. H.* vol. iii., p. 482); the alliance with Chandragupta and the embassy of Megasthenēs were at a later date (conf. Plutarch, *Alex*, 62), possibly after the battle of Ipsus, B.C. 301, when Seleucus was finally confirmed in his kingdom; and as Megasthenēs resided perhaps for several years at the court of Chandragupta (Arrian *Exp. Alex.* V. vi. and 2; Solinus *Polyhistor.*, c. 60; Robertson's *India*, p. 30), we are forced to allow that the latter was alive *after* B.C. 300, so that his reign must have begun *after* 323; possibly it was dated from the death of Porus between 320 and 317 B.C.: no earlier date seems reconcileable with our information.—J.B.

[2] The accession and death of each of these kings are placed as follows;—

Antiochus Theos - - -	B C. 261 to 246
Ptolemy Philadelphus - - -	285 to 247
Antigonus Gonatas - - -	283 to 239
Magas - - -	301 to 258
Alexander II. of Epirus - -	272 to 254

[3] If we assume that the arrangement alluded to by Aśoka was made with all these kings at the same time, the latest date available would be B.C. 258, which would place Asoka's *abhisheka* in B.C. 270, the death of Chandragupta in 302, and his accession in 326 B.C., while Alexander was still in India. But agreements of the kind

Aśoka, 28 years; but the latter was not inaugurated till the 4th year after his father's death, or 218 years after the Nirvâṇa. There is some doubt about the precise duration of his reign, depending on whether we are to reckon its commencement from his father's death (cir. 267 B.C.), or as is usual with the Hindus, from his *abhisheka* or inauguration four years later. Assuming the later to be the correct mode, the following table will give the early chronology of Buddhism to the death of Aśoka—liable possibly to some modifications to the extent possibly of some 4 or 5 years, for the determination of which we must await further discoveries[1]:—

B.C. 560 Gautama Buddha born at Kapilavastu.
531 „ became an ascetic.
526 „ assumed Buddhahood in his 35th year.
481 Buddha died, the era of the Nirvâṇa and date of the first Buddhist Council.
381 The second Council held in the 10th year of the reign of Kâlavarddhana.

---

were most probably made first with the nearer kings of Syria, Egypt, and Cyrene, and afterwards with the more remote rulers of Macedon and Epirus, while the embassy on its way back through Persia may have renewed the arrangements which were not finally reported in India till as late as 252 B.C.

[1] The following list of contemporary events may enable the reader to realise the importance of the period between Buddha and Aśoka, and to fix these dates in the memory:—

B.C. 560 Nerighssar king of Babylon.
548 Cyrus overthrew Crœsus on the Halys.
530 Cambyses king of Persia.
480 Xerxes defeated at Salamis.
400 Socrates put to death.
321 Partition of the conquests of Alexander at Triparadeisus.
317 Eudemus left the Panjab with a large force to aid Eumenes.
316 Seleucus fled from Babylon to Egypt to escape from Antigonus.
312 „ returned to Babylon. Era of the Seleucidæ, 1st Oct.
306 „ assumed the regal style, and pushed his conquests to the north and east.
303 „ invades Bactria and India.
301 Battle of Ipsus; Seleucus confirmed in the East.
283 Ptolemy Philadelphus succeeds to the throne of Egypt, and Antigonus Gonatus in Macedon.
280 Seleucus slain by Antiochus Soter, who sent Daimachus on an embassy to Amitrochates (Bindusâra), son of Sandracottos.
256 Bactria revolted under Diodotus.
250 Arsaces founds the Parthian empire.

B.C. 327 Alexander's invasion of India; Philip made satrap.
326 Alexander left Pattala after the rains; Philip murdered by the mercenaries.
323 Death of Alexander.
321 Porus allowed to retain the Panjâb; Seleucus obtains Babylon.
319 Chandragupta founds the Maurya dynasty.
295 Bindusâra succeeds and rules 28 years.
267 Bindusâra's death.
263 Aśoka's abhisheka or coronation.
259 Aśoka converted to Buddhism in his 4th year.
257 Mahendra, the son of Aśoka, ordained a Buddhist priest in Aśoka's 6th year.
246 The third Buddhist Council held in his 17th year.
245 Mahendra sent to Ceylon in his 18th year.
233 Death of Aśoka's queen, Asandhimitrâ.
227 Aśoka became an ascetic in the 33rd year after his conversion.[1]
225 Death of Aśoka in the 38th year of his reign.

After the death of Aśoka, the Pauranik chronology of his successors stands thus:—

B.C. 225 Suvâśas.
215 ? Daśaratha.
200 ? Sangata, Bandupâlita.
195 ? Indrapalita, Śâliśûka.
185 ? Somaśarma.
183 ? Saśadharma.
180 Vṛihadratha.

The last of the Mauryas was overthrown by his general, Pushyamitra, who established the Sunga dynasty, which probably lost hold of many of the southern provinces of the Maurya empire at an early date. The Pauranik chronology, however, stands thus, the dates being only approximate and liable to adjustment to the extent of from 10 to 15 years throughout:—

B.C. 175 Pushyamitra.
160 Agnimitra.
134 Vasumitra.

---

[1] If Aśoka's whole reign extended to only 38 years, this and the preceding six dates should be altered to four years earlier.

B.C. 122 Badraka or Ârdraka.
110 Pulindaka,
100 Ghoshavasu?
90 Vajramitra?
75 Devabhûti.

The next dynasty of the Purâṇas is the KÂṆVAS, who are said to have ruled 45 years, say B.C. 70 to 25. These, again, are represented as followed by the ÂNDHRABHṚITYAS, who ruled only over the Dekhan. From the character of the inscriptions on the western caves and on their coins, however, it may be doubted whether they were so late as the Pauranik statements would place them, and it may yet turn out that they were contemporary, to some extent, with both the Śunga and Kâṇva dynasties. The Pauranik chronology enumerates about thirty kings from Śipraka or Śiśuka to Pulomâvi III., the dynasty extending over about 440 years,[1] but no great dependence can be placed in their accuracy.

There is in fact very little difficulty with regard to the chronology of the five centuries just enumerated. The great uncertainty prevails anterior to the advent of Buddha, and the great confusion began with the accession of the later Ândra or Andrabhṛitya dynasty, about the beginning of the Christian era. For 10 centuries after that time there are very few epochs which can be fixed with absolute certainly and very few kings whose dates are beyond dispute. By means of inscriptions and a careful analysis of Chinese documents we are now beginning to see our way with tolerable certainty through this wilderness, but it still is indispensable to state the grounds on which each date is founded before it can be used to determine the age of any cave or building on which it is found. Even then the dates can only be taken as those most probable according to our present information, and subject to confirmation or adjustment by subsequent discoveries. Still the sequence is no where doubtful, and the relative dates generally quite sufficient for the purposes of an architectural history of Mediæval India.

---

[1] See Second *Archæological Report*, pp. 131 ff; see also p. 265 (Part II.) below for Pauranik list and dates.

Architecture.

It is fortunate that in the midst of all these perplexities and uncertainties there is still one thread which, if firmly grasped, will lead us with safety through the labyrinth, and land us on firm ground, on which we may base our explorations in search of further knowledge. India is covered with buildings from north to south, and of all ages, from the first introduction of stone architecture in the third century B.C. down to the present day. With scarcely an exception, these are marked with strongly developed ethnographic peculiarities, which are easily read and cannot be mistaken. Many of these have inscriptions upon them, from which the relative dates, at least, can be ascertained, and their chronological sequence followed without hesitation. In addition to this, nearly all those before the Moslem conquest have sculptures or paintings, which give a most vivid picture of the forms of faith to which they were dedicated, and of the manners and customs, as well of the state of civilisation of the country at the time they were erected.

As mentioned above, the history of Buddhism as a state religion begins with the conversion of Aśoka, in the third century B.C., and as it happens, he was the first to excavate a cave for religious purposes. He also was probably the author of the sculptures on the Buddha Gaya rails,[1] but whether this is certain or not, we have in the wondrous collection of sculptures found by General Cunningham at Bharhut a complete picture of Buddhism, and of the arts and manners of the natives of India in the second century before Christ.[2] The tale is then taken up with the gateways at Sanchi, belonging to the first century of our era, which are equally full and equally interesting.[3] To these follow the rails at Amrávati[4] in the fourth century, showing a considerable technical advance, though accompanied with a decline of that vigour which characterised the earlier

[1] General Cunningham's *Archæological Report*, vol. i., Plates VIII. to XI., and Babu Rajendralala Mitra's *Buddha Gaya*, Plates XXXIV. to XXXVIII., and one photograph, Plate L. As none of these plates, which are lithographs, are satisfactory, it is to be hoped that the whole may some day be photographed, like the last. There is no monument in India more important for the history of Art than this rail, which is probably the oldest example of Hindu sculpture we possess.

[2] *Description of the Stupa at Bharhut*, by Gen. A. Cunningham, 4to., London, 1879.

[3] Illustrated in the first 45 plates of *Tree and Serpent Worship*, 2nd Ed. 4to., London, 1873.

[4] Illustrated in the 55 remaining plates of that work.

examples. From the fourth century, to the decline of Buddhism in the seventh, there exist a superfluity of illustrations of its progress, in the sculptures and painting at Ajaṇṭâ and in the western caves, while the monasteries of Gandhara, beyond the Indus in the north-west, supply a most interesting parallel series of illustrations. These last were executed under a singularly classical influence, whose origin has not yet been investigated, though it would be almost impossible to overrate its importance.[1]

We have thus either carved in stone or painted on plaster as complete a series of contemporary illustrations as could almost be desired of the rise, progress, and decline of Buddhism during the whole of the 1,000 years in which it existed as an important religion in India. We have also a continuation of the series illustrating the mode in which the present religious forms of India grew out of former faiths, and took the shapes in which they now exist in almost every part of India.

Were all these materials either collected together in museums or published in such a form as to be easily accessible to the public,[2] we would possess a more vivid and more authentic picture, not only of the ethnography, but of the ever varying forms of Indian civilisation, than is to be obtained from any books, or any other form of evidence now available.

The one defect in this mode of illustration is that it does not extend far enough back in time, to be all that is wanted. Neither in India, nor indeed anywhere else, were the Aryans a building race, nor did their cultivation of the fine arts ever reach that point at which it sufficed for historical illustration. They chose and throughout adhered, to the phonetic mode of expression, as both higher and more intellectual, and in this they were no doubt right in so far as all the higher forms of human intellectual expression are concerned. But books perish, and may be changed and altered,

---

[1] Neither the Ajanta frescoes nor the Gandhara sculptures have yet been published. The latter exist in the museums of Lahore, South Kensington, and Gen. Cunningham's possession. Photographs of nearly all the known specimens are in my possession.—J. F.

[2] This could easily and speedily be done, as almost all these antiquities are public property, and nine-tenths of them have been photographed, and the negatives exist, generally in the hands of the Government. The only obstacle is the apathy and indifference of the public, and of those who might be expected to take most interest in the matter.

and after all do not present so vivid and so permanent an illustration of contemporary feelings as those which may be expressed by buildings in stone, or by forms, in carving or in colour.

Be this as it may, it is in consequence of this peculiarity of the Aryan mind, that the history of art in India begins with the upheaval of the Turanian element, and the introduction of Buddhism as a state réligion under Aśoka in the middle of the third century B.C., and it is consequently with that king's reign that our illustrations drawn from Indian architecture practically begin.

When this fact was first announced, now some forty years ago, the evidence on which it rested was to some extent negative. No building had then been found which could pretend to an earlier date, nor has any one been discovered since; but till we can feel sure that we know all the buildings in India, there is no absolute certainty that some earlier example may not be brought to light. At present, however, with the solitary exception of Jarasandha-ka-Baithak, to be described presently, no building is known to exist nor any cave, possessing any architectural character, whose date can be extended back to the time when Alexander the Great visited India. It may, of course, be disputed whether or not it was, in consequence of hints received from the Greeks that the Indians first adopted stone for architectural purposes; but the coincidence is certain, and in the present state of our knowledge may be looked upon as an established fact. At the same time though it is almost equally certain that stone was used in India as a building material for engineering purposes and for foundations, yet it is quite certain that nothing that can properly be called architecture is to be found there till considerably after Alexander's time.[1]

Besides the negative evidence above alluded to, we now have direct evidence of the fact in a form that hardly admits of dispute. We

---

[1] Even in Alexander's time, accodring to Megasthenes (Strabo p. 702), the walls of the capital city, Palibothra, were constructed in wood only, ξύλινον περίβολον ἔχουσαν. A portion of the fortifications of minor cities were probably of the same convenient though combustible material. Notwithstanding this, Babu Rajendralâla Mitra in his work on *Buddha Gaya*, p. 167, and 168, asserts that the walls of this city were of *brick*, and as his authority for this, quotes the passage from Megasthenes above referred to. Besides being in brick, he adds (p. 168), apparently on his own authority, that they were 30 feet in height. In so far as the testimony of a trustworthy eye witness is concerned, this statement of Megasthenes is entirely at variance with the Babu's contention, for the use of stone generally, for architectural purposes in India before Alexander's time; and *Protanto* confirms the statements made above in the text.

have caves like this one at Bhâjá, which was excavated certainly after Aśoka's time, in which not only every decorative feature is directly copied from a wooden original, but the whole of the front,

No. 1. Front of the Cave at Bhâjâ, from a Photograph.

the ribs of the roof, and all the difficult parts of the construction were originally in wood, and a good deal of the original woodwork remains in the cave at the present hour. But more than this, as will be observed in the woodcut, the posts dividing the nave from the aisles all slope inwards. In a wooden building having a circular roof, the timber work of which was from its form liable to spread, it was intelligible that the posts that supported it, should be placed sloping inwards, so as to counteract the thrust. No people, however, who had ever built or seen a stone pillar, would have adopted such a solecism in the rock when copying the wooden halls in which their assemblies had been held and their worship had previously been performed. In order to follow the lines of these sloping pillars, the jambs of the doorways were made to slope inwards also, and there is no better test of age than the extent to which the system is carried. By degrees the pillars and the jambs become more and more upright, the woodwork disappeared as an ornament, and was replaced by forms more and more lithic, till long before the last caves were excavated we can barely recognise, and may almost forget, the wooden forms from which they took their origin.

Though therefore it is more than probable that the Indians borrowed the idea of using stone for architectural purposes from the Greeks, or to speak more correctly, from western foreigners bearing the Greek appellation of Yavanas, it is equally certain that they did not adopt any of the forms of Greek architecture or any details from the same source. It is indeed one of the principal points of interest in this style, that we see its origin in the wood, and can trace its development into stone, without any foreign admixture. It is one of the most original and independent styles in the whole world, and consequently one of the most instructive for the philosophic study of the rise and progress of architectural forms.

While asserting thus broadly that stone architecture commenced in India only 250 years before Christ, there are two points that should not be overlooked, not that they are likely to disturb the facts, but they may modify the inferences to be drawn from them. The first of these is the curious curvilinear form of the Śikharas or spires of Hindu temples, which cannot at present, at least, be traced back to any wooden original. It is true the earliest example whose date can be fixed with anything like certainty is the great temple at Bhuvaneśwar,[1] which was erected in the 7th century of our era. It is however then complete in all essentials, and though we can follow its gradual attenuation down to the present day, when it becomes almost as tall, in proportion, as a gothic spire, we cannot advance one step backwards towards its origin. My impression is, that it was originally invented in the plains of Bengal, where stone is very rare indeed, and that the form was adopted to suit a brick and terra-cotta construction for which it is perfectly adapted.[2] But it may also be derived from some lithic form of which we have now no knowledge, but be this as it may, the uncertainty that prevails regarding the origin of this form prevents us from saying absolutely that there were no original forms of stone architecture in India anterior to the time of

---

1 *History of Indian Architecture*, page 422, Woodcut 283.

2 *Ibid.*, page 223, Woodcut 124.

the Greeks. Whether, however, it was derived from wood or brick or stone, it may be the elaboration of some Dasyu form of temple of which we have now no trace, and regarding which it is consequently idle to speculate. But till we can more nearly bridge over the 7 or 8 centuries that elapsed between the first Buddhist caves and the earliest known examples of Hindu architecture, we cannot tell what may have happened in the interval. For our present purposes it is sufficient to say that if there is no evidence that the temples of the Hindus were derived from a wooden original, there is as little that would lead us to suspect that the form arose from any necessity of stone construction.[1]

Even, however, though it may be proved to demonstration that stone was not employed for architectural purposes before the age of Aśoka, we must still guard ourselves from the assumption that it was either from want of knowledge or of skill that this was so. They seem deliberately to have preferred wood, and in every case where great durability was not aimed at, and where fire was not to be dreaded, they no doubt were right. Larger spaces could far more easily be roofed over with wood than with stone, and carvings and decoration more easily and effectually applied. They think so in Burmah to the present day, and had they not thought so in India in the third century B.C., it is clear, from what they did at Bharhut and Buddha Gaya, that they could as easily have employed stone then, as they do now. At Bharhut, for instance, the precision with

---

[1] In a recent number of the *Journal of the Asiatic Society of Bengal*, vol. xlvii., Part I., for 1878, Mr. Growse, of the B.C.S., expresses astonishment that I should perceive any difficulty in understanding whence the form of these temples was derived. There are at Mathura several abnormal Hindu temples erected during the reign of the tolerant Akbar, the śikharas of which are octagonal in plan, and with curved vertical outlines, from which Mr. Growse concludes that the form of the Hindu śikharas unquestionably originates in the Buddhist Stûpas. I have long been personally perfectly familiar with these Mathura temples, and knowing when they were erected, always considered them as attempts on the part of the Hindus of Akbar's day to assimilate their outlines to those of the domes of their Moslem masters which were the most charactirestic and most beautiful features of their architecture. If these outlines had been derived from stûpas, the earliest would have been those that resemble these Buddhist forms most, but the direct contrary is the fact. The earliest, like those at Bhuvaneśwar are the squarest in plan, and the most unlike Buddhist forms that exist, and it is strange that the similarity should only be most developed, in the most modern, under Akbar. The subject I confess appears to me as mysterious as it was before I became acquainted with Mr. Growse's lucubrations.—J.F.

which architectural decorations are carved in stone 150 years B.C. has hardly been surpassed in India at any time, and whatever we may think of the drawing of the figure sculptures, there can be no hesitation as to the mechanical skill with which they are executed. The same is true of what we find at Buddha Gaya, and of the gateways at Sanchi. Though the forms are all essentially borrowed from wooden constructions, the execution shows a proficiency in cutting and carving stone materials that could only be derived from long experience.

As hinted above, the only stone building yet found in India that has any pretension to be dated before Aśoka's reign is one having the popular name of Jarasandha-ka-Baithak,[1] at Rajgir. It is partially described by General Cunningham in the third volume of his *Archæological Reports*, but not with such detail, as he no doubt would have bestowed upon it, had he been aware of its importance. As will be seen from the annexed woodcut, it is a tower about 85 feet square at base and sloping upwards for 20 or 28 feet[2] to a platform measuring 74 feet by 78. It is built wholly of unhewn stones, neatly fitted together without mortar; and its most remarkable peculiarity is that it contains 15 cells, one of which is shown in the woodcut. They are from 6 to 7 feet in length, with about half that in breadth. Their position in height is not clearly marked in General Cunningham's drawing, but Mr. Broadley describes them as on the level of the ground, and adds that they are inhabited up to this day, at times, by Nágas or Sâdhus, Jogis whose bodies are constantly smeared with

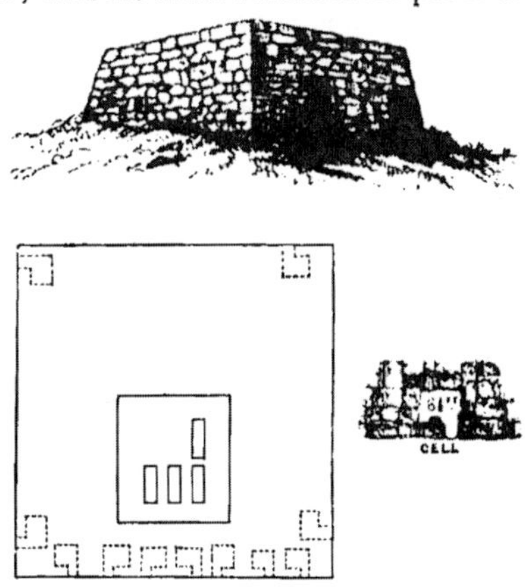

No. 2. View and Plan of Jarasandha-ka-Baithak, from Cunningham.

---

[1] There is another erection bearing the same name at Giryek, about 7 or 8 miles eastward of Rajgir; that however is a brick stûpa of comparatively modern date, and probably as General Cunningham suggests, the Hansa Stûpa or goose tower, and derives its name from a very famous Buddhist Jataka which he quotes. *Reports*, vol. i. p. 18, Plate XV.

[2] Broadley in *Indian Antiquary*, vol. i. p. 72.

ashes.[1] Immediately behind this Baithak General Cunningham discovered a cave, which he unhesitatingly identifies the Pipala Cave, where, according to Fahian, Buddha was accustomed to sit in deep meditation after his mid-day meal.[2] It is a rude cavern some 25 by 28 feet, the roof of which has partially fallen in. It seems, at one time to have been partially lined with brick, but is otherwise quite rude and unornamented. The General considers it undoubtedly the quarry hole from which the stones were taken to build the Baithak, and either it, or the tower in Hiuen Thsang's time bore the name of the palace of the Asuras.[3]

The interest of this group, for our present purposes, rests principally on the three following considerations:—

First, we have a cave with which Buddha's name seems inseparably connected. It is rude and unhewn, like all those which, so far as we at present know, are assigned to his age.

Secondly, we have the earliest vihara or monastery yet found in India, built of unhewn stones, and wholly unornamented from an architectural point of view. Originally it may have been three storeys in height, and with steps leading to each, but these are gone and probably cannot now be recovered.[4]

Thirdly, though this at present may be considered as purely speculative, the arrangements of the Baithak point almost undoubtedly to Assyria as the country from which its forms were derived, and the Birs Nimrud,[5] with its range of little cells on two sides, seems only a gigantic model of what is here copied on a small and rude scale. Without attempting to lay too much stress on the name Asura,[6] the recent discovery by General Cunningham of a procession headed by a winged human-headed bull,[7] points beyond all

---

1 Broadley in *Indian Antiquary*, vol. i. p. 72.

2 Beal's *Fahian*, clxxx. p. 117.

3 Julien's *Hiuen Thsang*, iii. p. 24.

4 In Bengal at the present day in remote villages, the inhabitants construct three-storeyed pyramids in mud, when they have no permanent temples, and generally plant a Tulsi plant on the top. These temples are of course Vaishṇava.

5 *History of Architecture*, vol. i., woodcuts 47 and 48, p. 153.

6 I have always been of the opinion of Buchanan Hamilton (*Behar*, p. 21), that the term Asura really meant Assyrian; but these nominal similarities are generally so treacherous that I have never dared to say so. Recent researches, however, seem to confirm to a very great extent the influence Assyria had in Magadha anterior to the advent of Buddha.

7 Cunningham, *Reports*, vol. iii. p. 99, Plate XXVIII.

doubt to an Assyrian origin, and fifty other things tend in the same direction with more or less distinctness. This is not the place, however, to insist upon them, as they have very little direct bearing on the subject of this work. It is well, however, to indicate their existence, as Assyrian architecture, in the form in which it is found copied in stone at Persepolis, is the only style to which we can look for any suggestions to explain the origin of many forms and details found in the western caves, as well as in the Gandhara monasteries.

When the various points hinted at above are fairly grasped, they add immensely to the interest of the caves to be described in the following pages. More than this, however, as the Buddhists were beyond doubt the earliest cave excavators in India, and the only ones for more than a thousand years after the death of the founder of that religion, these rock-cut temples form the only connecting link between the Nirvâṇa and the earliest Buddhist scriptures which have reached our times, in their present form.[1] Whether looked on from an ethnological, a historical, or a religious point of view, the Buddhist caves, with their contemporary sculpture and paintings, became not only the most vivid and authentic, but almost the only authentic record of the same age, of that form of faith from its origin to its decline and decay in India. If it is also true—which we have at present no reason for doubting—that the Buddhists were the first to use any permanent materials for building and sculptural purposes in the caves, combined with the few fragments of structural buildings that remain, they have left a record which is quite unique in India. It is, however, a representation which for vividness and completeness can hardly be surpassed by any lithic record in any other country, of their feelings and aspirations during the whole period of their existence.

Although the Brahmanical and Jaina caves, which succeeded the Buddhist, on the decline of that religion in the sixth and subsequent centuries, are full of interest, and sometimes rival and even surpass them in magnificence, they have neither their originality nor their truthfulness. They are either inappropriate imitations of the caves of the Buddhists, or copies of their own structural temples, whose

[1] The *Mahawanso* and other Ceylonese scriptures were reduced to the present form by Buddhaghosa in the beginning of the 5th century A.D. It was then, too, that Fa Hian, the earliest Chinese pilgrim, travelled in India.

details were derived from some wooden or brick original, and whose forms were designed for some wholly different application, without the least reference to their being executed as monoliths in the side of a hill. Notwithstanding these defects, however, there is an expression of grandeur, and of quasi eternity, in a temple cut in the rock, which is far greater than can be produced by any structural building of the same dimensions, while the amount of labour evidently required for their elaboration is also an element of greatness that never fails to affect the mind of the spectator. Taken by themselves it may be true that the later series of caves, notwithstanding their splendour, are hardly equal in interest to the earlier ones, notwithstanding their simplicity. It is, however, when looked at as a whole, that the true value of the complete series of rock-cut temples in India becomes apparent. From the rude Pippala cave at Râjgir in which Buddha sat to meditate after his mid-day meal, to the latest Jaina caves in the rock at Gwalior, they form a continuous chain of illustration, extending over more than 2,000 years, such as can hardly in its class be rivalled any where or by any other nation. It is too, infinitely more valuable in India than it would be in any country possessing a literature in which her religious forms and feelings and her political history had been faithfully recorded, in other forms of expression. As in India, however, the written record is so imperfect, and so little to be relied upon, it is to her Arts, and to them only, that we can turn to realise what her position and aspirations were at an earlier age; but this being so, it is fortunate they enable us to do this in a manner at once so complete and so satisfactory.

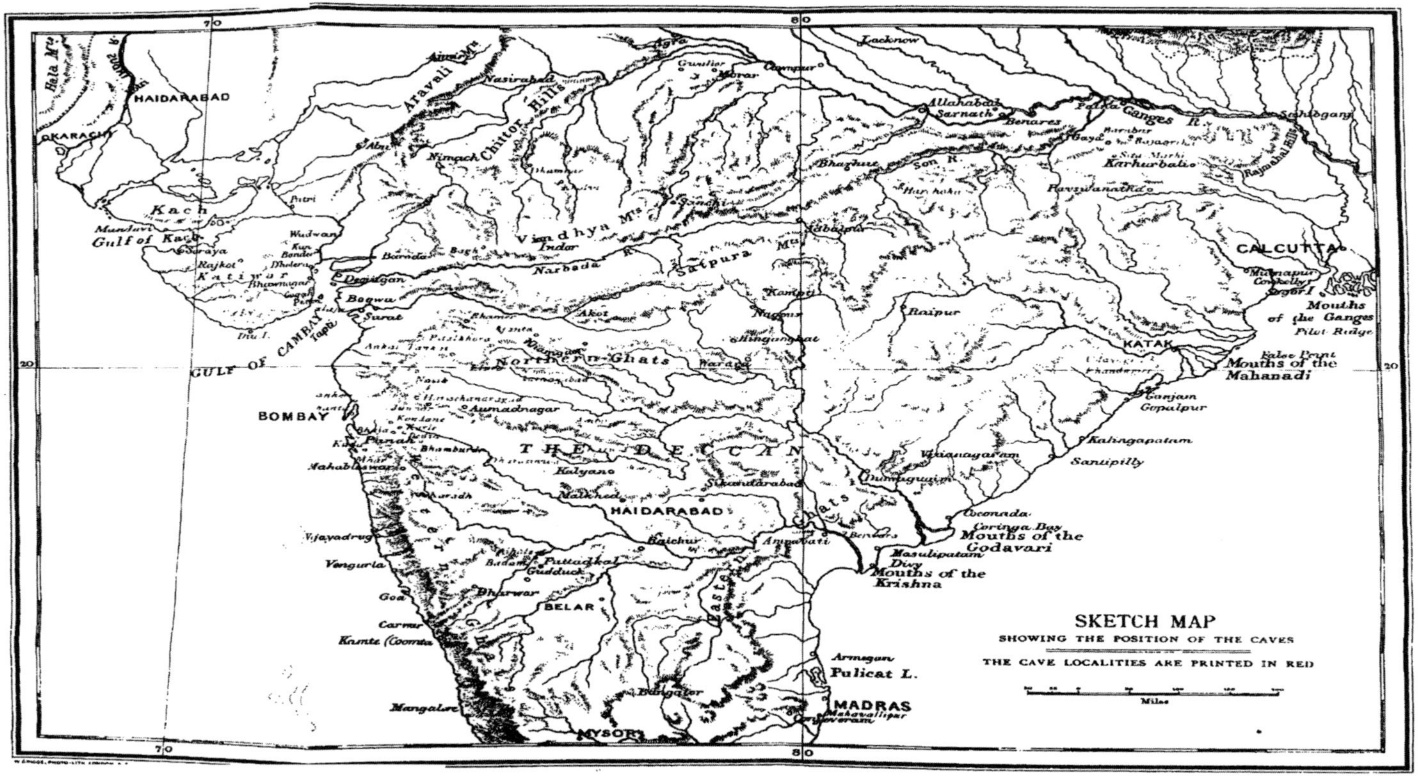
SKETCH MAP
SHOWING THE POSITION OF THE CAVES
THE CAVE LOCALITIES ARE PRINTED IN RED
Miles
HAIDARABAD
KARACHI
Kach
Gulf of Kach
Katiwar
GULF OF CAMBAY
BOMBAY
Aravali Ms
Chitor Hills
Vindhya Ms
Narbada R.
Satpura Ms
Northern Ghats
THE DECCAN
HAIDARABAD
BELAR
MYSORE
MADRAS
Pulicat L.
CALCUTTA
KATAK
Ganges R.
Son R.
Allahabad
Benares
Lucknow
Agra
Raipur
Nagpur
Surat
Goa
Mangalore
Mouths of the Ganges
Mouths of the Mahanadi
Mouths of the Godavari
Mouths of the Krishna

EASTERN CAVES.

CHAPTER I.

BARABAR GROUP.

Although this work is principally intended to illustrate the splendid series of caves in Western India, there are four or five groups in the Bengal and Madras presidencies a knowledge of which, if not indispensable, is at least extremely useful to enable us to understand the history of the cave architecture on the Bombay side of India. It is true that with the exception of the Mahâvallipur group they cannot pretend to rival the western caves either in splendour or extent, but the Katak caves present features of great beauty and are interesting from their originality. The greatest historical interest, however, centres in the Behar series, which, though small, are important for our purposes, having all been excavated during the existence of the Great Mauryan dynasty, and being, therefore, the earliest caves, so far as we at present know, excavated for religious purposes in any part of India.

The Barabar caves are situated in an isolated range of granite hills on the left bank of the Phalgu river about 16 miles due north from the town of Gaya. They are seven in number, and though differing in plan, are all similar in character and evidently belong to same age. Their dimensions are inconsiderable. The largest, called the Nagarjuni cave, is a plain hall with circular ends measuring 46 feet by 19 feet 5 inches, and though two others, the Sudama and Lomas Rishi, are nearly as large, they are divided into two apartments, and consequently have not the same free area.[1]

Fortunately there is no difficulty whatever with regard to the date of these caves; six out of the seven have inscriptions upon them, all

1 Plans of all the caves are given by General Cunningham in vol. i. of his *Reports*, Plate XIX., and also by Kittoe, *J.A.S.B.*, for May 1847, Plate VIII. There is no essential difference between these two sets of plans of these caves. The inscriptions were all copied by General Cunningham, and engraved, in facsimile, on Plate XX. of the same work, with translations, pp. 47, *et seq.*

in the oldest form of the Pali alphabet, identical with that found on Aśoka's lâts. More than this, the inscription on the Sudama cave states that it was excavated in the 12th year of that monarch or B.C. 252, and is therefore the earliest here. The latest is the Gopi or Milkmaid cave, in the Nagarjuni hill, which is dated in the reign of Daśaratha, the grandson of Aśoka, in or about B.C. 214. The whole group is therefore comprehended within about 40 years, and was commenced apparently within 80 years after Alexander's visit to India.[1]

The only cave in this group that has no ancient inscription upon it is the Lomas Rishi, but it is not difficult to see why this was the case. It is the only one which has any architectural magnificence externally, and was consequently selected by two kings, Sârdula Varmâ and Ananta Varmâ, sons and grandsons apparently of Yajña Śri of the Andra dynasty in the third or fourth century of our era, to adorn it with their inscriptions and to announce its conversion to the purposes of the Brahmanical faith.[2] Before doing this they no doubt carefully obliterated the more ancient inscription, which at that time was in all probability perfectly legible and easily understood. Whether this is, or is not the true explanation of the absence of an inscription in the lât characters in this cave, is of very little importance. It is so absolutely identical both in dimensions and disposition with the Sudama cave, which we know was excavated in the 12th year of Aśoka, that there can be no doubt as to its age. Its architecture alone, if it may be so called, would be sufficient to settle this point. As may be seen from the annexed woodcut it is as essentially wooden as any other cave façade in India. Whether it is more so than the cave at Bhâjâ quoted above (woodcut No. 1), is difficult to determine on its merits alone. If we had any Chaitya caves in

---

[1] When Hiuen Thsang was journeying from Patna to Gaya, in 637 A.D., he visited these caves, as I pointed out in 1872, in my paper on his travels in the *Journal of the R. A. S.*, vol. vi., new series, p. 221, *et seq.* He, however, found them nearly deserted, only a few monks (*quelques douzaines*) remained, who acted as guides to show him the localities. . . . When I wrote that paper I was obliged to rely on the account in the life of the pilgrim, by Hoei li. Julien's translation of the Si-yu-ki, on which General Cunningham principally relied, having a misprint of "200 *pas*" instead of "200 *li*" for the pilgrim's first journey from Patna. The Rev. Mr. Beal, who is translating the work, assures me this is so, and that I consequently was quite justified in rejecting the General's conjecture, and insisting on the fact that the pilgrim did visit these caves. Julien's *Translation* of the Si-yu-ki, vol. i., p. 139; vol. ii., p. 439, *et seq.*

[2] These inscriptions were first translated by Wilkins in the 1st vol. *Asiatic Researches*, afterwards by Prinsep, *J. A. S. B.*, vol. vi, p 671, *et seq.*

No. 3. Façade of the Lomas Rishi Cave, from a Photograph.

Behar which admitted of direct comparison it might be possible to do so, but when these eastern caves were excavated, the bold expedient had not occurred to any one of sinking a cave at right angles to the face of the rock, deep into its bowels, and leaving one end entirely open for the admission of light. All the Behar caves have their axis parallel to the face of the rock, and their entrances are placed consequently on one side, so as to act as windows to light their interiors as well as for entrances. Another peculiarity of the eastern caves is that no real woodwork was used in their decoration, while all the early Chaitya caves in the west, were adorned with wooden ribs internally, whose remains are to be seen at this day, and their façades were, as at Bhâjâ, entirely constructed in teak wood. It may be that the roofs of the buildings copied in the caves at Behar were framed in bambu, without wooden ribs, like the huts of the present day, and consequently they could neither be easily repeated nor imitated in the rock. But be this as it may, these differences are such that no direct comparison between the styles adopted in the two sides of India, could be expected to yield any very satisfactory results. It is consequently fortunate that in Aśoka's time, as we know from the example at Bharhut, it was the fashion to inscribe everything. At Bharhut there is hardly a single person, nor a Jataka, or historical scene, which has not a name or a description attached to it, and this seems also to have been the case with these caves. Before the time when the gateways at Sanchi were erected, in the first century of our era, this good custom seems to have died out. All the rails there are inscribed with the names of their donors, but they are earlier than the gateways. They too, however, have also the names of their donors engraved on them, but unfortunately nothing to help us to discriminate what the subjects are which are represented in the sculptures.

One characteristic which is constant both in the early caves in the eastern and western sides of India is that all the doorways have jambs sloping inwards. This could only have arisen from one of two circumstances: either it was, as at Mycenæ and in all the early Grecian buildings in pre-Hellenic times, for the sake of shortening the bearing on the lintel. The Pelasgi had no knowledge of the principle of the radiating arch, and used only small stones in their architecture generally. It consequently, though awkward, was a justifiable expedient. In India it arose, as already pointed out, from a totally different cause. It was because the earliest cave diggers were copying wooden buildings, in which the main posts were placed sloping inwards, in order to counteract the outward thrust of their semicircular roofs. Though tolerable, however, while following the main lines of the building, the sloping jambs of the doorways were early felt to be inappropriate to stone constructions, and the practice in India died out entirely before the Christian era.[1]

Although so differently arranged that it is difficult to institute

---

[1] General Cunningham and his assistants, like too many others, call these doorways "Egyptian," though such forms are not known in that style of architecture except in the cockney example in Piccadilly. The truth is, even as early as the times of the Pyramids (B.C. 3700) the Egyptians had learned to quarry blocks of any required dimensions, and had no temptation to adopt this weak and unconstructive form of opening, and as they never, so far as we know, used wooden architecture, they must always have felt its incongruity. If we expect to find such forms in Egypt we must go back some thousands of years before the time of the Pyramids, and I doubt much if sloping jambs could have existed in that country even then.

In Greece, on the contrary, wherever the Pelasgic or Ionian race remained, they retained these sloping jambs from that curious veneration for ancient forms which pervades all architectural history, and leads to the retention of the many awkward contrivances when once the eye is accustomed to them. The sloping jamb, it need hardly be said, is never found associated with the Doric order, but was retained with the Ionic as late as the age of Pericles in the Erechtheum at Athens. See *History of Architecture*, vol. i. pp. 234 to 240, and 286, *et seq.*

In niches, and as a merely decorative form, the sloping jambs were retained in the monasteries of Gandhara to the west of the Indus, till long after the Christian era, but never, so far as I know, in constructive openings.

any direct comparison between them and the western Chaitya or Church caves, it seems almost certain that none of the Barabar caves were meant as residences, but were intended for sacred or ceremonial purposes. The one most like a Vihara, or residence, is the Nâgarjuni cave, called "the Milkmaid's cave," but even there a great hall 46 feet long, with rounded ends, and only one small door in the centre of one side, seems too large for the residence of one hermit, and it has none of those divisions into cells which are universally found in all western Viharas.[1] At the same time it must be confessed that our knowledge of Buddhist ceremonial in the age of Aśoka does not enable us to say what kind of service would be appropriate to such a hall. It may, however, have been a Dharmaśâlâ or hall of assembly for the congregation; a form of building which was probably usual with the Buddhists in all ages of their supremacy.

The case is somewhat different with the Karna Chopar cave, a rectangular hall measuring 33 feet by 14, which was excavated in the 19th year of Aśoka. But here a vêdi or stone altar at one end clearly indicates a sacred purpose. On the other hand, there can be no doubt but that the Sudama and Lomas Rishi caves, which are so nearly identical in form, were real Chaityas. Instead, however, of the circular dagobas, which in all instances occupy the centre of the apsidal inner termination of the western caves, its place is here taken by a circular chamber evidently meaning the same thing. It is difficult for us now to decide at the present day whether it was inexperience which prevented the early cave diggers from seeing their way to leave a free standing dagoba in their halls, or

No. 4. Lomas Rishi Cave. Scale 50 feet to 1 inch.

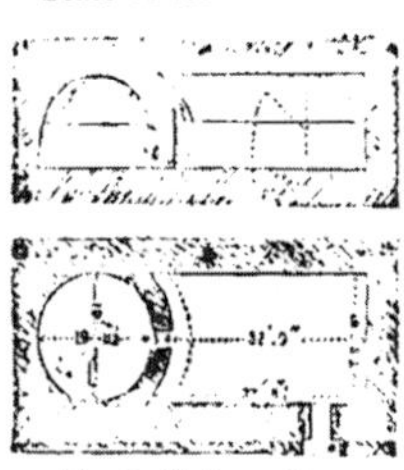

No. 5. Sudama Cave.

[1] The only erections I know of, at all like this cave in plan, are the residences of the Nâgâ chiefs, in the hills south of the Asam valley. Two of these are represented in Plate II. of the *Journal of the Asiatic Society of Bengal*, vol. xli. for 1872, which with these rounded ends seem to resemble this so-called Milkmaid's cave in many respects. The mode in which the ridge poles are thrust through the roof occurs frequently in the sculptures at Bharhut and elsewhere.

[2] At Kondiwtê in the Isle of Salsette there is a very old cave, very similar to those at Barabar, except that it is sunk perpendicularly into the hill side. It has a circular

whether it was that in structural buildings of that age a wooden or metal dagoba or relic shrine stood in a circular chapel, and they copied that.[2] But be that as it may, there seems no doubt that the circular chambers in these two caves, were the sanctuaries which contained the object to be worshipped, whatever that was, and constituted their claim to rank as chapels, not residences.

The remaining two are so small and insignificant as hardly to deserve notice, but one, the Vapiya or Well Cave, seems to have got its name from a sacred well close by. It is a square cell with an antechamber, and is attached to another, called the Vadathi, which is the last of the series. General Cunningham seems to think there was a Stûpa, or some sacred edifice, erected in brick or stone above these two caves, and that they formed only, as it were, its lower storey.[1] This on the whole seems so probable that it may be adopted without hesitation, though it will only be by careful examination on the spot that it can be determined with certainty.

Though the caves of this group are among the smallest and the least ornamented of any to be found in India, it still must have required a strong religious impulse to induce men to excavate even caves 30 and 40 feet in length in the hard granite rock, and to polish their interiors to the extent that some of these are finished, and all probably were intended to have been. Both internally and externally, however, they are so plain that but for their inscriptions we should hardly know to what age to assign them, were it not for the fortunate circumstance that a façade was added to the Lomas Rishi Cave. When it, however, is compared with the caves at Bhâjâ, (woodcut No. 1), or with any of the pre-Christian caves of the western side of India, it is found to possess all the more marked peculiarities of their architecture. It has, as all the earlier caves have, the two great posts sloping inwards, and supporting in mortices, on their heads, the two great longitudinal ribs of the roof. It has, too, the

Scale 50 feet to 1 inch.

No. 6. Kondiwtê Cave, Salsette.

chamber at its inner end, like that in the Lomas Rishi cave, but in it stands a stone rock-cut dagoba, certainly of the same age as the cave itself. This makes it extremely probable that the Barabar chambers were occupied by dagobas in wood or metal, but no other similar chamber is known to exist in the West. The circular chamber evidently is unmeaning, and its use was abandoned as soon as it was seen how much better the cave was without it.

[1] *Reports*, vol. i. p. 49.

open framework of wood between them, which was equally universal, and the rafters and little fashion pieces which kept the lower parts of the roof in its place. In fact we have here in stone every feature of those wooden façades which the earlier excavators of caves copied so literally in the rock. It is unfortunately, however, only in stone, and we cannot even now feel quite certain how the roof was covered, when erected as a building standing free. It looks as if formed of two thicknesses of wooden planks, one bent, and the other laid longitudinally, and with a covering of metal; it could hardly have been thatch, the thickness is scarcely sufficient, and when men were copying construction so literally, it would have been easy to have made the outer covering 9 inches or a foot in thickness instead of only the same as the other two coverings.[1] Be this as it may, the age of the façade is not doubtful, and so far as we at present know it is the earliest architectural composition that exists in any part of India, and one of the most instructive, from the literal manner in which it its wooden prototypes are copied in the rock.[2]

---

[1] The whole thickness of the roof so far as I can make out from the photographs is only 9 or 10 inches.

[2] The buildings now existing in India, that seem most like these primitive caves in elevation, are the huts or houses erected by the Todas on the Nilagiri hills. They are formed of bambu neatly bound together with rattans. Their section is nearly the same as that of the caves, and they are covered externally with a very delicate thatch. For an account of them see *An Account of the primitive Tribes and Monuments of the Nilagiris*, by J. W. Breeks, M.C.S., published by Allen & Co. for the India Office in 1873, Plates VIII. and IX.

CHAPTER II.

RAJGIR.

Râjâgṛiha, or Râjgir as it is now popularly called, was the capital of Magadha or central India during the whole period of Buddha's ministrations in India. It was the residence of Bimbasara, during whose reign he attained Buddhahood, and of Ajâtaśatru, in the 8th year of whose reign he entered into Nirvâṇa, B.C. 481, according to the recently adopted chronology (*ante*, p. 24, 25). It is quite true that he resided during the greater part of the 53 years to which his mission extended at Benares, Śravasti, or Vaisaka (Lucknow[1]), but still he frequently returned to the capital, and the most important transactions of his life were all more or less connected with the kings who then reigned there. Under these circumstances it is hardly to be wondered at that Râjgir was considered almost as sacred in the eyes of his followers, as Jerusalem became to the Christians, and that such pilgrims as Fa Hian and Hiuen Thsang, naturally turned their steps almost instinctively to its site, and explored its ruins with the most reverent care. Long before their time, however, the old city had been deserted. It never could have been a healthy or commodious city, being surrounded on all sides by hills, which must have circumscribed its dimensions and impeded the free circulation of air to an inconvenient extent. It consequently had been superseded long before their time, in the fifth and seventh century, by a new city bearing the same name but of much smaller size just outside the valley, to the northward. This, however, could never have been more than a provincial capital. The seat of empire during Aśoka's reign having been transferred to Palibothra (Patna) on the Ganges, which we know from the

---

[1] I state this deliberately, notwithstanding what is said by General Cunningham in the *Ancient Geography of India*, p. 401, *et seq.*, though this is not the place to attempt to prove it. Hiuen Thsang, however, places Vaisaka 500 li or 83 miles S.W. from Śravasti which can only apply to Lucknow, and Fa Hian's Sa-chi, measured from Canouge or Śravasti, equally points to Lucknow as the city where the "tooth-brush tree" grew. Neither of the pilgrims ever approached Ayodhya (Fyzabad), which had been deserted long before Buddha's time. If the mounds that exist in the city of Lucknow were as carefully examined, they would probably yield more treasures than even those of Mathura.—J.F.

accounts of Megasthenes was an important city in the days of his grandfather Chandragupta. At the same time, any ecclesiastical establishments that might have been attracted by the sanctity of the place, must have been transferred to Nalanda, between 6 and 7 miles due north from the new city, where there arose the most important monastic establishment connected with Buddhism that, so far as we know, ever existed in India.[1] Fortunately for us Hiuen Thsang has left us a glowing description of the splendour of its buildings, and of the piety and learning of the monks that resided in them. With this, however, we probably must remain content, inasmuch as some excavations recently undertaken on the spot have gone far to prove that all the remains now existing belong to buildings erected during the supremacy of the Pâla dynasty of Bengal (765 to 1200 A.D.). The probability is that all the viharas described by Hiuen Thsang were erected wholly in wood, which indeed we might infer from his description, and that the monastery was burnt, or at least destroyed, in the troubles that followed the death of Sîlâditya in 650 A.D.,[2] and they consequently can have no bearing on the subject we are now discussing.

Under the circumstances above detailed leading to the early desertion of Rajgir, it would of course be idle to look now for any extensive remains of the buildings, if it ever had any, in stone or any permanent material, and equally so to expect any extensive rock-cut Viharas or Chaitya caves in the immediate vicinity of such an establishment as that at Nalanda. Practically we are reduced for structural buildings to the Jarasandha-ka-Baithak, above described (woodcut No. 2), and for rock-cut examples to one cave, or rather pair of caves, known as the Son Bhandar or Golden Treasury.

The larger of these two caves is very similar in plan to the Karna Chopar cave at Barabur and nearly of the same dimensions, being 34 feet by 17 feet.[3] Its walls are perfectly plain to the height of 6 feet 9inches, and thence rise to 11 feet 6 inches in the centre of a slightly pointed arch. The doorway is towards one end and has the usual sloping jambs of the period, the proportion between the lintel and sill being apparently as 5 to 6, which seems to be somewhat less

---

[1] See *History of Indian Architecture*, vol. i., p. 136.

[2] Hiuen Thsang, vol. i., p. 151.; Ma-twan-lin, *J. A. S. B.*, vol. vi., p. 69.

[3] Cunningham, *Reports*, vol. v., Plate XIX.

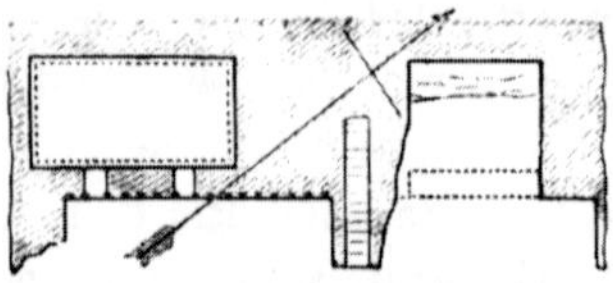

No. 7. Plan Son Bhandar Caves.
Scale 50 feet to 1 inch.

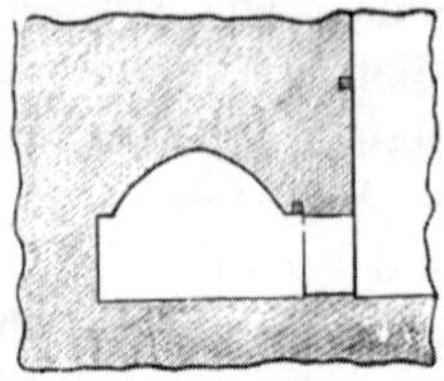

No. 8. Section Son Bhandar Caves.
Scale 25 feet to 1 inch.

From Cunningham's *Report*, vol. iii.

than the proportion at Barabar.[1] This doorway is balanced towards the other end of the cave by a window nearly 3 feet square, which is

No. 9. Front of Son Bandhar Cave, from a Photograph.

a decided innovation, and the first of its class known to exist in India. A still greater advance in cave architecture is the existence of a verandah 8 feet deep, extending along the front, and at one end some way beyond the cave. It existence is quite certain from the mortice holes still remaining in the rock into which the ends of the rafters were inserted, as shown in the woodcut. Its having been added here is specially interesting, as it certainly is, like the window, an improvement, and almost as certainly an advance on the design of the Barabar caves, and as clearly anterior to that of the Katak caves, where the verandahs are, as a rule, cut in the rock, with massive pillars in stone forming part of the original design.

As will be explained in the subsequent pages of the work, nearly

---

[1] The greater part of the information concerning this cave is taken from General Cunningham's *Reports*, vol. iii. p. 140, Plate XLIII., but his drawings are on too small a scale and too rough to show all that is wanted. Kittoe also drew and described it, *J. A. S. B.*, September 1847. It is also described by Broadley, *Indian Antiquary* vol. i., p. 74.

all the ornamentation of the Chaitya caves in the West down to the Christian era was either a literal copy of wooden construction, or was executed in wood itself, generally teak, attached to the rock and in very many instances, as at Bhâjâ, Bedsâ, Karlê, and elsewhere, the actual woodwork still remains where it was fixed some 2,000 years ago. From the representations of buildings at Buddha Gaya and at Bharhut and from the front of the Lomas Rishi cave quoted

No. 10. Representation of a Hall, from Cunningham's Stupa at Bharhut.

above (woodcut No. 3) we know that precisely the same mode of decoration was employed in the eastern caves, that was usual in the western ones, but in none of the Behar caves have we any evidence of wood being so employed except in the verandah of this cave and in one or two doubtful instances at Katak. One example may not be considered as sufficient to prove a case, but as far as it goes, this seems to be a first attempt to remedy a defect that must have become apparent as soon as the Barabar caves were completed. With very rare exceptions all the caves on both sides of India have verandahs, which were nearly indispensable, to protect the openings into the interior from the sun, but in nearly all subsequent excavations these were formed in stone, and became the most ornamental parts of the structure.

The other Son Bhandar cave is situated at a distance of 30 feet from the larger one and in all respects similar except that its dimensions are only 22 feet by 17. The roof has almost entirely fallen in, and only one mortice hole exists to show that it had a wooden verandah similar to that in front of the other cave.

Between these two caves a mass of rock is left standing in order to admit of a flight of steps being cut in it, leading to the surface of the rock above the roof of these two caves. Whether this led to an upper storey either in woodwork or brick, or whether there was not a dagoba or shrine on the upper platform, can only be ascertained when some one visits the spot after having his attention specially directed to this object, from its analogy with what is found in other places. From the arrangements of some of the Katak caves, I would rather expect to find the remains of an upper storey. But it may be very difficult to determine this, for whether it was a stûpa or dwelling, if in brick, it may have been utilised long ago. As before mentioned, General Cunningham seems to think that a vihara in brick, but with granite pillars, existed in a corresponding situation above the Vapiya and Vadathi caves at Barabar.[1] If he is right in this, which seems very probable, it would go far to establish the hypothesis of the existence of a second storey over the Son Bhandar cave.

There seems to be nothing except its architecture by which the age of this cave can be determined. Kittoe, indeed, says "there are some rude outlines of Buddhas carved upon it," and there is also a handsome miniature Jain temple much mutilated,[2] which he gives a drawing of. The Buddhas I fancy are much more likely to be Jaina Tîrthankaras, which are so easily added when there is so much plain surface, and as the "temple" shows that the cave was afterwards appropriated by the Jains, nothing is more probable than that they should ornament the walls by carving such figures upon them. Broadley is more distinct. "Outside the door," he says, "and 3 feet to the west of it, is a headless figure of Buddha cut in the rock, and close to it an inscription in the Ashoka character."[3] But as neither Cunningham nor Kittoe saw either, and they do not

---

[1] *Reports*, vol. i. p. 49. [2] Kittoe, *J. A. S. B.*, Sept. 1847, Plate XLII.
[3] *Indian Antiquary*, vol. i. p. 74.

appear in Peppe's photograph from which the woodcut is taken, we must pause before accepting his statement. On the whole, therefore, taking the evidence as it stands, there seems no good reason for doubting that the Son Bhandar caves belong to the Great Mauryan dynasty, B.C. 319 to 180. At the same time the whole evidence tends to show that they are more modern than the dated caves at Barabar, and that they were consequently excavated subsequently to the year 225 B.C.

We are fortunately relieved from the necessity of discussing the theory, so strongly insisted upon by General Cunningham, that the Son Bhandar cave is identical with the Sattapanni cave, where the first convocation was held,[1] from the fortunate discovery by Mr. Beglar of a group of caves which almost undoubtedly were the seven caves that originally bore that name (Sapta parna, seven leaved).[2] On the northern side of the Vaibhâra (Webhára) hill

[1] Cunningham, *Arch. Report*, vol. iii. pp. 140 to 144.

[2] Although we may not be able to fix with precision either the purpose for which the Son Bhandar caves were excavated, nor their exact date, it is quite clear they are not the Sattapanni cave, near which, according to all tradition, the first convocation was held immediately after the decease of the founder of the religion. In the first place, a hall, only 34 feet by 17, about the size of an ordinary London drawing-room, is not a place where an assembly of 500 Arhats could assemble, and the verandah, 8 feet wide, would add little to the accommodation for this purpose. It is hardly worth while attempting to refute in any great detail the various arguments brought forward in favour of this hypothesis, for there is no proof except the assertion of modern Ceylonese and Burmese authorities, who knew nothing of the localities, that the convocation was held in a cave at all, and everything shows that this was not the case. The Mahawanso (p. 12) states that it was in a splendid hall like to those of the Devas at the entrance of the Sattapanni cave. Mr. Beal's *Translation of Fa Hian* (p. 118) makes exactly the same assertion, but with an ambiguity of expression that might be construed into the assertion that it was *in* and not *at* the cave that the convocation was held. But Remusat's translation, as it is in strict accordance with the more detailed statements of Hiuen Thsang, is at least equally entitled to respect. He says :—"Au nord de la montagne, et dans un endroit ombragé, il y a une *maison de pierre* nommé Tchheti, c'est le lieu où après le Nirvana de Foě, 500 Arhans recueillirent la collection des livres sacrés."[1] Hiuen Thsang makes no mention of a cave, but describes the foundations which he saw of "une grande maison en pierre," which was built by Ajâtaśatru for the purpose in the middle of a vast forest of bambus.[2] Even the Burmese authorities, who seem to have taken up the idea of its having been held in a cave, assert that the ground was first encircled with a fence,—which is impossible with a cave,—and within which was built a magnificent hall.[3] The truth seems to be

[1] Foě Kuě Ki, 272. [2] Julien, vol. iii. p. 32. [3] Bigandet, *Life of Gaudama*, p. 354.

there exists a group of natural caverns, six in number, but there is room for a seventh, and evidence that it did originally exist there. As unfortunately Mr. Beglar is not an adept at plan drawing, his plan and section (pp. 92 and 96) do not make this so clear as might be desired, in fact without his text, his plans would be unintelligible. With their assistance we gather that owing to some abnormal configuration of the rocks there are at this spot a series of fissures varying in width as 4, 6, 8, and 10 feet, and ranging from 6 to 12 feet in depth (p. 96). What their height is is not stated, nor can the fact be ascertained from the drawings, it is not however of much importance.[1] The real point that interests us most in this instance is, that as in the Jarasandha-ka-Baithak (*ante*, p. 33) with its 15 cells, we have the earliest known example of a structural Vihara in India, so here we have the earliest known instance of a rock—we can hardly add—cut Vihara with 7 cells, and for both of which we have historical or at least traditional evidence, to show that they existed contemporaneously with, if not before, the lifetime of Buddha himself. Like all those, however, which have any claim to an antiquity earlier than the age of Aśoka (B.C. 250), it is a mere group of natural caverns without a chisel mark upon them, or anything to indicate that they were not rather the lairs of wild beasts than the abodes of civilised men.

There are still two other caves or groups of caves at Rajgir, which are of considerable interest from their historical, though certainly

that the modern Buddhists, like the mediæval Christians in Palestine, thought everything was, or at least ought to have been, done in a cave, but when read with care, there is certainly nothing except in the most modern writings to indicate that this was the case in this instance, and there certainly is no cave in Rajagriha which is fitted or ever could have been made suitable for such a purpose. The convocation was in fact held in one of those great halls of which we have several instances among the western caves. The last woodcut, however, representing one from the rail at Bharhut, 150 years B.C., and one at Kanheri shown in plan, Plate LIV., with the examples to be described hereafter at Mahâvallipur and probably also the Nagarjuni cave at Barabar just described, show us the form of Dharmaśâlâs that were in use among the Buddhists in that age, and were perfectly suited to the purposes of such an assembly. It probably was a building measuring at least 100 feet by 50, like the cave at Kanheri, with a verandah of 10 feet all round. With the knowledge we now have of the architecture of Aśoka's time there would be no difficulty in restoring approximately such a hall, and in a general history it might be well to attempt it, but it has no direct bearing on the history of cave architecture.

[1] Beglar on *Cunningham's Reports*, vol. viii. pp. 89 to 99.

not from their artistic value. The first is known as the house or residence of Devadatta, the persistent enemy of Buddha. It is only a natural cavern situated at the foot of the hill in the north-eastern corner of the city at a spot marked M in General Cunningham's map (Vol. III., Plate XLI.), but not described by him nor by Mr. Beglar,[1] but as it is merely a natural cavern this is of little consequence, except as affording another example of the primitive form of all the earlier caves. In front of it is still to be seen the rock which, according to tradition, Devadatta rolled down from the mountain athwart Buddha's path and wounded a toe of his foot.[2]

The other group of caves is on the Gridharakuṭa hill, about 3 miles north-east from the city, is of still greater interest, as it is described minutely by both the Chinese pilgrims as a place much frequented by Buddha and his companion Ânanda. The elder pilgrim describes it in the following terms: "The peaks of this mountain are picturesque and imposing; it is the loftiest of the five mountains that surround the town. Fah Hian having bought flowers, incense, and oil and lamps in the new town, procured the assistance of the aged Bikshus to accompany him to the top of the peak. Having arrived there he offered his flowers and incense, and lit his lamps, so that their combined lustre illuminated the glories of the cave; Fah Hian was deeply moved, even till the tears coursed down his cheeks, and he said, Here it was in bygone days that Buddha dwelt . . . . . Fah Hian, not privileged to be born at a time when Buddha lived, can but gaze on the traces of his presence, and the place which he occupied."[3]

Neither General Cunningham nor Mr. Broadley ascended the peak high enough to reach these caves; the hill may be 100 to 150 feet in height. It was consequently reserved for Mr. Beglar to make the discovery. He followed the causeway that led to them a few hundred yards further, and hit at once on two about 50 feet apart, which seem to answer to Buddha's meditation cave, and the Ânanda cave as described by the Chinese pilgrims. They are both natural caverns, the larger measuring 12 feet by 10, of irregular shape, but, the irregularities slightly reduced by filling in with brickwork on which are some traces of plaster, and inside there are now found some

---

1 *Archæological Report*, vol. viii. p. 90.

2 Fah Hian, *Beal's Translation*, p. 115; *Julien*, vol. iii. p. 27.

3 *Ibid*, vol. iii., p. 20.

fragments of sculpture lying about, but evidently of a much more modern date. As Mr. Beglar's map is nearly as unintelligible as his drawings, we are left to conjecture which of the two caves marked upon it are those just referred to, nor how many more exist on the spot. The text says 7, 2+5, but only four are shown, and the other buildings he describes cannot be identified on it.[1] Enough, however, is shown and said to make it quite clear that these are the caves referred to by the Chinese pilgrims, and to prove to us that, like all the caves connected by tradition with the name of Buddha, they are mere natural caverns untouched by the chisel, though their irregularities are sometimes smoothed down with brickwork and plaster, and that the latter may, in some instances at least, have been originally adorned with paintings.

SITA MARHI CAVE.

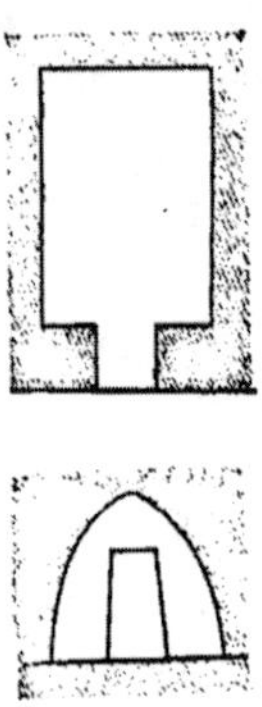
No. 11. Plan and Section Sita Marhi Cave.

Before leaving this neighbourhood there is still one small cave that is worth mentioning as the only other known of the same age as those of Barabar and Rajgir.[2] It consists of a chamber rectangular in plan, and measuring 15 feet 9 inches, by 11 feet 3 inches, which is hollowed out of an isolated granite boulder lying detached by itself, and not near any other rocks. Inside it is as carefully polished as any of those at Barabar, except the inner wall where the surface has peeled off.[3] Its principal interest, however, resides in its section (woodcut, No. 11), which is that of a pointed arch rising from the floor level, without any perpendicular sides, which are

[1] The information regarding these caves is not to be found in the body of Mr. Beglar's report, vol. viii., but in a prefatory note, pp. xv to xxi, which makes no reference to the text, which it contradicts in all essential particulars, or to Map XXII., which is equally ignored in the body of the work. In fact, it is very much to be regretted that the manner in which these reports are put together is not creditable to any of those concerned in their production.

[2] It is situated at a place called Sita Marhi, 14 miles south of Rajgir, and 24 east from Gaya, as nearly as I can make out from the map attached to Mr. Beglar's report, but the spot is *not* marked, though the name is.

[3] Mr. Beglar, from whose report (viii. p. 106) these particulars are taken, mentions some pieces of sculpture as existing, and now worshipped in the cave, but whether they are cut in the rock or detached is not mentioned, and is of very little consequence, as they are evidently quite modern.

universally to be found in the other caves here. The jambs of the doorway also slope inwards nearly in the ratio of 3 to 4, from both which peculiarities I would infer that this may be the oldest cave in the neighbourhood. We must however have a more extended series of examples before we can form a reliable sequence in this direction, but it is only by quoting new examples as they turn up that we can hope to arrive at such a chronological scale; in the meantime, however, we may feel sure that this hermitage belongs to the great Mauryan age, but whether before or after Aśoka's time must be left at present undetermined; my impression at present is that it is the oldest thing of its class yet discovered in India.

On the banks of the Sona river, above Rohtasgarh, there are several excavations, some of them apparently of considerable extent, but they have never yet been examined, so far at least as I can learn, by anyone who could say what they were, nor of what age. We must consequently wait for further information before attempting to describe them. Further up, in the valley of the same river, at a place called Harchoka, there are some very extensive excavations, regarding which it would be very desirable some more information could be obtained. The place is situated in latitude 23° 51′ 31″, longitude 81° 45′ 34″, as nearly as may be 110 miles due south from Allahabad, and as it is only 70 miles south-east from Bharhut, it seems a pity it was not visited by General Cunningham, or one of his assistants, while exploring that country in search for fragments of that celebrated stúpa. What we know of it is derived from a paper by Captain Samuells in Vol. XL. of the *Journal of the Royal Asiatic Society*, p. 177 *et seq.*, which is accompanied by a plan and section very carefully drawn, but the latter unfortunately on so small a scale that its details are undistinguishable. As Captain Samuells does not profess to be an archæologist his text does not afford us much information, either as to the age of this excavation, nor as to the religion to which it was dedicated. If an opinion may be hazarded, from the imperfect data available, I would suggest that this cave is contemporary with the late Brahmanical caves at Elurâ, and consequently belongs to the 7th or 8th century, and that the religion to which it was dedicated was that of Siva.[1]

---

[1] In the year 1794 Captain Blunt visited two extensive sets of caves at a place called Mârâ, in the neighbourhood, and described them in the seventh volume of the *Asiatic*

It may at first sight appear, that more has been said in the preceding pages, with reference to these Behar caves than their importance justifies. Looked at from an architectural point of view, this is undoubtedly the case, but from their being the oldest caves known, and their dates being ascertained with all desirable precision, a knowledge of their peculiarities forms a basis for what follows, without which our knowledge would still rest on a very unstable foundation.

From the experience gained by our examination of these caves we gather, first:—

That all the caves with which Buddha's name or actions are associated were mere natural caverns unimproved by art, except in so far as some of them have been partially lined with brickwork, but in no instance are they entitled to be called rock-cut.

Secondly. That the earliest rock-cut examples were, even internally, plain unornamented chambers with polished walls, their roofs imitating the form of woodwork, or it may be that of bambu huts.[1] That what ornament was attempted externally, as in the Lomas Rishi cave, was a mere copy of a wooden construction, and that any extension that was required, as in the Son Bhandar cave, was actually executed in wood.

Thirdly. That all the jambs of the doorways slope inward, following the lines of the posts supporting the circular roofs, which were made to lean inwards to counteract the thrust inherent in that form of construction.[2]

Lastly. That all the rude unknown caves may be considered as anterior to the age of Chandragupta, and all those, in Behar at least, with sloping jambs may be assumed to be comprehended within the duration of the Mauryan dynasty, which ended about 180 B.C.; the angle of rake being probably the best index yet obtained for their relative antiquity.

Researches. Captain Samuells seems also to have visited them, but as he does not describe them he probably thought them of less importance than those at Harchoka.

[1] In no instance is it possible to conceive that they were copies of constructions either on stone or brick.

[2] I shall be very much surprised if it is not found that the walls in the Barabar caves do also lean inwards; but they have not yet been observed with sufficient accuracy to detect such a peculiarity.

CHAPTER II.

KATAK CAVES.

Introductory.

To the artist or the architect the group of caves situated on the Udayagiri hill in Orissa is perhaps even more interesting than those in Behar just described, but to the archæologist they are less so, from the difficulty of fixing their dates with the same certainty, and because their forms have not the same direct bearing on the origin or history of the great groups of caves on the western side of India. Notwithstanding this, the picturesqueness of their forms, the richness of their sculptures and architectural details, combined with their acknowledged antiquity, render them one of the most important groups of caves in India, and one that it is impossible to pass over in such a work as this, without describing them in very considerable detail.

The caves in question are all situated in a picturesque and well wooded group of hills that rise out of the level plains of the Delta of the Mahânaddi, almost like islands from the ocean. Their composition is of a coarse sandstone rock, very unusual in that neighbourhood, but which from that circumstance offered greater facilities for their excavation than the laterite rocks with which the country everywhere abounds. Their position is not marked on any of the ordinary maps of the country, but may easily be fixed, as their bearing is 17 miles slightly to the east of south from Katak, and 4 miles north-west from Bhuvaneśwar. The great Saiva temple of that city, one of the oldest and finest in India, being easily discernible from the tops of the hills in which the caves are excavated.

Besides the facilities for excavation, there were probably other motives which attracted the early Buddhist hermits to select these hills as their abode and continue to occupy them during three or four centuries at least. We may probably never be able to ascertain with accuracy what these reasons were, or how early they were so occupied. We know, however, that Aśoka about the year 250 B.C. selected the Aśwatama rocks, near Dhauli, about 6 miles south-east from these hills, as the spot on which to engrave one of the most complete and perfect sets of his series of edicts,[1] and he hardly would have chosen so remote a corner of his dominions for this purpose, had the place not possessed some previous sanctity in the eyes of his co-religionists. Unfortunately we are not able to fix with anything like certainty the site of Danta-puri, the city in which the celebrated Tooth Relic was enshrined, and where it remained till carried off to Ceylon in the beginning of the fourth century of our era.[2] It certainly was not far from this, and may have been in the immediate vicinity of the caves, though the evidence, as it at present stands, seems to favour the idea that it was at Puri where the famous temple of Jagannâth now stands, some 30 miles south of the caves. The fact, however, that it is recorded by the Buddhists that the Tooth Relic was brought to this neighbourhood immediately after the cremation of his body, and the certainty of its being chosen by Aśoka B.C. 250 to record his edicts, is sufficient to show that early in the history of that religion this neighbourhood was occupied by Buddhists. There is however no record or tradition of Buddha himself ever having visited the locality, or of any event having occurred there that gave rise to the erection of any Stûpa or other monument in the neighbourhood, and even Hiuen Thsang, when passing through the country in A.D. 640, does not mention any spot as sanctified by the presence or labours of Buddha or of any of his immediate disciples.[3]

There are some 16 or 17 excavations of importance on the Udayagiri hill, besides numerous little rock-cut hermitages—cells in which a single ascetic could dwell and do penance. All these belong to the Buddhist religion and there is one Buddhist cave in the Khandagiri hill—the Ananta. The others there, though large and important, are much more modern and all belong to the Jaina form of faith. There is also a modern Jaina temple built by the Marâthas on the top of that hill, and I cannot help believing that Kittoe was correct when he says that there has been a large circular building on the corresponding summit of the Udayagiri rock;[4] but I have not been

---

1 *J. A. S. B.*, vol. xii. p. 436, for *Kittoe's* plates and description of the locality.

2 *J. R. A. S.*, vol. iii. new series, pp. 149 *et seq.*

3 *Julien*, vol. i. 184; iii. 88.

4 *J. A. S. B.*, xii. p. 438. In a private letter from Mr. Phillips, the joint magistrate of the district, he informs me "there are the remains of some building above the Rani ka nour, *i.e.*, on the top of the Udayagiri." It probably would require excavation to ascertain its character.

able to ascertain for certainty whether the foundations still to be seen there are either ancient or in the form of a dâgoba.

These caves were first noticed and partially described by Stirling in his admirable account of Cuttack, in the 15th volume of the *Asiatic Researches* published in 1824, and that was the only authority existing when I visited them in 1836. At that time, however, all the more important caves were occupied by Fakîrs and Bairagis who violently resented intrusion on their premises, and besides my time was too limited for any elaborate examination of the whole. In 1838 they were visited by Lieut. Kittoe, and his account, with the drawings that accompanied it, published in the seventh volume of Prinsep's *Journal* for 1838, still remains the best account of these caves yet given to the world. His visit, however, like mine, was too hurried to enable him to make plans and draw details, while in his time, as in mine, the caves were still inhabited; otherwise with more leisure and better opportunities he would have left little to be done by his successors. Since then the caves have been photographed by Col. Dixon, Mr. Murray, and others, but without descriptions or plans, so that they are of very little use for our present purposes.[1]

---

[1] Some 10 years ago an opportunity occurred, which had it been availed of, would have gone far to remedy the deficiency of former explorers, and to supply an exhaustive account of these caves. In 1868–69 Babu Rajendralâla Mitra conducted an expedition for that purpose, accompanied by a staff of draughtsmen and students in the school of art at Calcutta, who were to be employed in making drawings and casts of the sculptures. Their labonrs, however, were almost exclusively directed to the temples at Bhuvaneswar, he himself making only personal notes of the caves. In consequence of this, mainly, if not wholly, in consequence of reclamations, made by me on the subject, a second expedition was sent down by the Bengal Government in the cold weather of 1870–71. This was conducted by Mr. C. C. Locke of the Government school of art, and resulted in his bringing back plans of all the principal caves and casts of all the more important sculptures. These were placed in Babu Rajendralâla's hands for publication, which, however, he has not yet found it convenient to carry into effect, but meanwhile I have received photographs from the casts, and plans of the caves from Mr. Locke, and these form the basis of all our real knowledge of the subject, and what is most relied upon in the following descriptions. (Two of the plans were published in my *History of Indian Architecture*, woodcuts 70 and 72, and five of the casts in my *Tree and Serpent Worship*, Plate C., published in 1873).

Through the kindness of his friend, Mr. Arthur Grote, late B.C.S., I have been permitted to see the corrected proofs of the first 56 pages of the 2nd volume of Babu Rajendras' *Antiquities of Orissa*, which contains his account of these caves, with the accompanying illustrations, but under a pledge that I would not make any quotations from them, as it is possible the Babu may yet see fit to cancel them, or at all events modify

In attempting to investigate the history of these caves, it is tantalizing to discover how narrowly we have missed finding in Orissa a chronicle of events during the whole Buddhist period as full, perhaps even more so, than those still found in Kashmir, Ceylon, or any other outlying provinces of India. It is true that the palm leaf records of the temple of Jagannâth at Puri, in which alone the fragments of this history are now to be found, date only apparently from the 10th century, and it would be idle to look in a work compiled by Brahmans at that time for any record of the acts, even perhaps of the names, of Buddhist kings of that country, still less of their building temples or excavating caves, devoted to the purposes of their—to Brahmans—accursed heresy. Notwithstanding this, if we possessed a continuous narrative of events occurring in the province we might be able to interpolate facts so as to elucidate much that is now inexplicable and mysterious.[1]

What these palm leaf records principally tell us is, that from a period vaguely contemporary with Buddha, *i.e.*, from 538-421 B.C. till 474 A.D., in fact, till Yayati Kesari finally expelled the Buddhists and established the Brahmanical religion in Orissa, the country was exposed to frequent and nearly continuous invasions of Yavanas generally coming from the north-west.[2] Who these Yavanas were

---

them to some extent before publication. This, for his own sake, I trust he will do, for as they now stand they will do him no credit either as an archæologist or a controversialist, and he will eventually be forced to retract nearly all he has said in the latter capacity. So far as I am capable of forming an opinion on the subject, the conclusions he arrives at as to the age of the caves are entirely erroneous, and he does not pretend that his explanations of the sculptures are derived either from local traditions, or Buddhist literature, merely that they are evolved from his own inner consciousness. Others may form a different opinion from that I have arrived at regarding his interpretation of the scenes depicted in them; to me they appear only as an idle waste of misplaced ingenuity and hardly worthy of serious consideration.—J. F.

1 These chronicles were very largely employed by Stirling in his *History of Orissa and Cuttack*, in the 15th volume of the *Asiatic Researches*, and still more extensively by Mr. Hunter in his *Orissa*, published in 1872, vol. i. pp. 198 *et seq.* They were also further investigated by a Calcutta Brahman Bhawanicharan Bandopadhyaya, in a work he published in Bengali, in 1843, entitled *Purushottama Chandrika*, which was very largely utilised by W. W. Hunter in his last work on Orissa, vol. i. p. 198 *et seq.*

2 The following chronological account of Yavana invasions is abstracted from Mr. Hunter's *Orissa*, vol. ii. p. 184 of the Appendix :—

B.C. 538–421. Bajra Deva.—In his reign Orissa was invaded by Yavanas from Marwar, from Delhi, and from Babul Deś, the last supposed to be Iran (Persia) and Cabul. According to the palm leaf chronicle the invaders were repulsed.

it is nearly impossible to say. The name may originally have been applied to Greeks or Romans, but it afterwards was certainly understood as designating all who, from an Indian point of view, could be considered as foreigners or outside barbarians, and so it must be understood in the present instance.

The account of these Yavana invasions in the Puri Chronicle looks at first sight so strange and improbable that one might almost be inclined to reject the whole as fabulous, were it not that the last of them, that under Rekta Bahu, which Stirling looked upon as so extraordinary and incomprehensible,[1] has by the publication by Turnour of the Daladawansa,[2] been elevated to the dignity of an established historical fact,[3] and there seems no difficulty in believing that the others may be equally authenticated when more materials are accumulated for the purpose.

It is of course impossible to form an opinion as to what reliance

---

B.C. 421–306. Narsingh Deva.—Another chief from the far north invaded the country during this reign, but he was defeated, and the Orissa prince reduced a great part of the Delhi kingdom.

306–184. Mankrishna Deva.—Yavanas from Kashmir invaded the country, but were driven back after many battles.

184–57. Bhoj Deva.—A great prince who drove back a Yavana invasion, and is said to have subdued all India.

Here follows the usual account of Vicramâditya and Śâlivâhana, and we hear no more of the Yavanas till—

A.D. 319–323. Sobhan Deva.—During this reign of four years, the maritime invasion and conquest of Orissa by the Yavanas under Rekta Bahu, the Red-armed, took place. The king fled with the sacred image of Jagannâth (the Brahmanical synonym for the tooth relic), and with those of his brother and sister Balbhadra and Subhadra, and buried them in a cave at Sonpur. The lawful prince perished in the jungles, and the Yavanas ruled in his stead.

323–328. Chandra Deva, who, however, was only a nominal king, as the Yavanas were completely masters of the country. They put him to death 328 A.D.

328–474. Yavana occupation of Orissa 146 years. According to Stirling these Yavanas were Buddhists.

474–526. Yayati Kesari expelled the Yavanas and founded the Kesari or Lion dynasty. This prince brought back the image of Jagannâth to Puri, and commenced building the Temple City to Śiva at Bhuvaneswar.

After this we hear no more of Yavanas or Buddhists in Orissa. The Brahmanical religion was firmly established there, and was not afterwards disturbed till the invasion of the Mahomedan Yavanas from Delhi, repeated the old story in 1510 A.D.

[1] *Asiatic Researches*, vol. xv. p. 263.

[2] *J. A. S. B.*, vol. vi. p. 856 *et seq.*

[3] *Journal R. A. S.*, New Series, vol. iii. p. 149 *et seq.*

should be placed on the facts narrated in these palm leaf records till we see what the text is, in which they are imbedded.[1] All that at present can be said regarding them, is that they are curiously coincident with what we know, from other sources, of the introduction of Buddhism into Orissa, and with the architectural history of the province. In the present state of our knowledge it is equally difficult to say how far we may place any dependence on the tradition that immediately after his death, the relics of his body were rescued from the funeral pyre and distributed to eight different cities in India.[2] According to these accounts the left canine tooth fell to the lot of Orissa, and was received by a king named Brahmadatta, whose son named Kâśi and grandson Sunanda continued to worship and hold it in the greatest possible respect.[3] These names, however, do not occur in any lists that have come down to our time, and the first, as king of Benares (Kâśi), occurs so frequently in Buddhist legends and jâtakas that no reliance can be placed in any tradition regarding him or his acts, as being authentic history. The second name looks like the name of his capital, and the third as one of the many Nandas who figure in the history of Magadha before the time of Aśoka. Be this, however, as it may, it seems tolerably certain that a tooth, supposed to be that of Buddha, was enshrined in this province in a magnificent Chaitya, in a city called Dantapura from that circumstance, before Aśoka's time, and remained there till the beginning of the fourth century A.D., when it was conveyed to Ceylon under the circumstances narrated in the Daladawansa, and where it now remains the palladium of that island under British rule.[4]

What we gather, from all this practically is, that Yavanas from

---

[1] A golden opportunity for effecting this was presented by Babu Rajendralâla's mission to Katak in 1868–69. As a Brahman he had access to the temples and their treasures to an extent that could not be afforded to any Yavana inquirer, and indeed he seems to have intended to have transcribed and translated them (Hunter's *Orissa*, vol. i. p. 198, note), but his ambition to be considered an archæologist of the European type, led him to neglect a task for which he was pre-eminently fitted, and to waste his time instead, in inventing improbable myths to explain the sculptures in the caves.

[2] *Journal Asiatic Soc. of Bengal*, vol. vii.; p. 1014; Foë Koué Ki, 240.

[3] Turnour's account of the Daladawansa, *J. A. S. B.*, vol. vi., p. 856 *et seq.*

[4] I have already detailed so fully the circumstances under which the transfer took place in a paper on the Amrâvatî tope, which I read to the Asiatic Society in 1847 *J. R. A. S.*, vol. iii. N.S., pp. 132 *et seq.*), that I may be excused repeating what I then said. The particulars will also be found, *Tree and Serpent Worship*, pp. 173 *et seq.*

the north-west, probably bringing Buddhism with them, invaded Orissa before the time of Aśoka, and consequently before the first rock-cut temple was excavated. It seems also nearly certain that Orissa remained Buddhist, and the tooth relic was honoured there —intermittently it may be by the kings—but certainly by the people, down to the year 322 A.D.[1] when it was transferred to Ceylon, and subsequently to this, that the province remained Buddhist under the last Yavana dynasty, 328 to 474 A.D., when that religion was finally abolished by the Keśari dynasty of kings.

There is no evidence that this last dynasty excavated any caves, and as there are no remains of any structural buildings belonging to the Buddhist religion, in the province, our history halts here, and there is at present nothing to lead us to believe that any of the caves were excavated within even a century before 322. The architectural history of the province, in Buddhist times is consequently, it must be confessed, very incomplete, and all that remains to be done is to try and find out when the earliest cave was excavated, and then to trace their development, so far as it can be done, till the time when cave digging ceased to be a fashion in Orissa.

As just mentioned, history will hardly help in this. Such records as we have, were written, or rather compiled, by Hindus, haters of Buddhism, and not likely to mention the names of kings belonging to that sect, and still less to record any of their actions or works. Inscriptions hardly give us greater assistance. It is true about one half of the caves at Udayagiri do bear inscriptions, but none of them have dates, and none of the names found in them have yet been identified with those of any king who figures in any of our lists. What they do tell us, however is, from the form of the characters employed that all the inscribed caves are anterior to the first century B.C. Unfortunately, however, the two principal and most interesting caves, the Râni kâ Nûr and the Ganesa Gumpha, have no contemporary inscriptions, so that this class of evidence for their age, is not available. There remains consequently only the evidence of style. For that, fortunately, the materials are abun-

[1] There is a discrepancy here of about 10 years between the dates in the Orissan chronicles and those derived from the Mahâwanso according to Turnour. On the whole I am inclined, from various collateral pieces of evidence, to place most reliance on that derived from the Puri chronicles.

dant, and the testimony is as complete as could well be expected. We have at least three monuments, whose date we may say is known with sufficient certainty for our purposes, and which, as we shall presently see, were almost as certainly contemporary with these caves.

The first of these is the rail which Aśoka (B.C. 250) is said to have erected round the Bodhi tree at Buddha Gaya. Very little of it remains, and none of it *in situ*, still there is enough of it existing to show exactly what the style of sculpture was at that age. Unfortunately, however, it has never been photographed, or at least no photographs of it, except of one fragment, have reached this country, and the drawings that have been published are very far from being satisfactory. The best set of drawings yet made were by Major Markham Kittoe, more than thirty years ago. They are now in the library at the India Office, but have never been published. Those in General Cunningham's "Reports" are far from complete,[1] and by no means satisfactory, and the same may be said of the set engraved by Babu Râjendralâla Mitra, in his work on Buddha Gaya,[2] just published. Fortunately the latter does give one photograph of one gate pillar (Plate L.), but whether taken from a cast or from the stone itself is not clear. Whichever it is, it is the only really trustworthy document we have, and is quite sufficient to show how little dependence can be placed on General Cunningham's representation of the same subject, and by implication on the drawings made by A. P. Bagchi for the Babu's work, which are in no respect better than the General's, if so good. It would of course be a great advantage if a few more of the sculptures had been photographed like the pillar represented on Plate L., but it, though it stands alone, is quite sufficient to show what the style of sculpture was which prevailed in the third century B.C., when it was erected.

The Bharhut Tope, which is the second in our series, has been much more fortunate in its mode of illustration. All its sculptures have been photographed by Mr. Beglar and published with careful descriptions by its discoverer, General Cunningham.[3] The date, too, has been assumed by him to be from 250 to 200 B.C. on data

---

1 *Reports*, vol. i. Plates VIII. to XI.; vol. iii. Plates XXVI. to XXX.

2 *Buddha Gaya*, Plates XXXIII. to XXXVIII.

3 *The Stupa of Bharhut*, by General A. Cunningham, London, 1879.

which are generally supposed to be sufficient for the purpose. I would suggest, however, that as this date is arrived at principally by calculating backwards at a rate of 30 years per reign from Dhanabhûti II., and as 16 years on the average is a fairer rate, it may be placed by him at least 50 years too early; the more especially as even that king's reign is only determined from a slight variation in the form of the letters used in the inscriptions, which is by no means certain.[1] On the whole I fancy 200 to 150 B.C. is a safer date to rely upon in the present state of our knowledge. For myself I would prefer the most modern of these two dates as the most probable. It is, at all events, the one most in accordance with the character of the sculpture, which is, as nearly as may be, half way between those of the rail at Buddha Gaya, and those found on the gateways at Sanchi.[2]

---

[1] *The Stupa of Bharhut*, pp. 15 and 16.

[2] From the great similarity that exists between the alphabetical characters found at Bharhut, and those employed by Aśoka in his numerous inscriptions, General Cunningham was no doubt perfectly justified in assuming that the stupa's age could not be far distant from that of his reign. At the same time, however, almost as if to show how little reliance can be placed on Palæographic evidence alone, where extreme precision is aimed at, and no other data are available, he quotes an inscription found at Mathura recording some gifts of a king of the same name, whom he calls Dhanabhûti II., and joins the two together in his genealogical list, with only one name, that of Vâdha Pâla, between them. (*Stupa at Bharhut*, p. 16.)

When General Cunningham first published this Mathura inscription (*Reports, III.*, p. 36, Plate XVI.) he placed it in a chronological series, between one dated Samvat 98 and another dated Samvat 135, and from the form of its characters he was no doubt correct in so doing, more especially as in Plate XIV. of the same volume, he quotes another inscription of Huviskha dated Samvat 39, where the alphabet used is very little, if at all earlier. If the Samvat referred to in these inscriptions was that of Vikramâditya, as the General assumes, this would place this second Dhanabhûti about A.D. 50 or 60. But as it seems certain this era was not invented at that time, it must be Saka, and accordingly he could not have reigned before the end of the second century of our era, and his connexion with the Bharhut stupa is out of the question.

Another point that makes the more modern date extremely probable, is that the sculpture on the Mathura pillar represents the flight of the prince, Siddhârtha, with the Gandharvas holding up the feet of his horse in order that their noise might not awaken the sleeping guards (*Stupa at Bharhut*, p. 16). As General Cunningham knows, and admits, no representations of Buddha, are found either at Bharhut or Sanchi (*Stupa at Bharhut*, p. 107), and this legend, though one of the most common among the Gandhara sculptures, does not occur in India, so far as is at present known, before the time of the Tope at Amrâvatî in the fourth century (*Tree and Serpent Worship*, Plate LIX.

The Sanchi Tope, which forms the third of the series, has also been illustrated with all the detail requisite for a proper understanding of its historical and artistic position. In the first place we have General Cunningham's work on the subject published in 1854, which is the foundation of our historical knowledge of this tope, to which may be added an extensive series of photographs by Captain Waterhouse, made in 1862. We also possess a beautiful series of drawings by Colonel Maisey; and in addition to an exhaustive transcript of its sculptures, by Lieutenant Cole,[1] there are also the casts he brought home, and copies of which are now in the South Kensington and Edinburgh Museums.

From all these data the date of this monument has been ascertained with sufficient precision for our present purposes at least. The southern gateway, which is the earliest, seems to have been erected by a king who reigned between the 10th and the 28th year of the Christian era, and the other three gateways during the remaining three-quarters of that century.[2]

There is still a fourth building equally important for the general history of architecture in India, though not bearing so directly as that of the caves in Orissa as the other three. The principal sculptures of the tope at Amrâvatî were executed during the course of the fourth century of our era,[3] and are perhaps the most beautiful and perfect Buddhist sculptures yet found in India, and as such full of interest for the history of the Art. It cannot, however, be said that any of the sculptures in the caves at Udayagiri are so modern as they are, but this being so, marks at all events the limit beyond which the Orissan caves cannot be said to extend. On the other hand, with our imperfect knowledge of the Buddha Gaya rails it is

---

fig. 1.), and consequently this sculpture cannot certainly be earlier than the second century A.D., and may be much more modern. It is just possible, no doubt, that it may not be integral, but may have been added afterwards when the larger rails were inserted, which cut through the inscription. This, however, is hardly probable, but until this is explained all the evidence, as it now stands, tends to prove that this Mathura inscription is much more likely to be 200 years after Christ instead of 200 before that era, as General Cunningham seems inclined to make it.

[1] All these have been utilised, and form the first 45 plates of my *Tree and Serpent Worship*, published in 1873, second edition.

[2] *Tree and Serpent Worship*, p. 99.

[3] *Tree and Serpent Worship*, Plates XLVI. to C. (For dates *see* p. 178,) probably from about A.D. 322 to 380.

not easy to determine whether any of these caves are really so old as the time of Aśoka. From a comparison of their details we may, however, feel certain that some of these caves are certainly contemporary with the rail at Bharhut, others with the gateways at Sanchi. Although, therefore, we cannot fix the limit either way with absolute certainty, we may feel confident that all those which are most interesting from an architectural point of view, were excavated during the three and a half centuries which elapsed between the years 250 B.C. and 100 A.D. Some of the smaller and ruder examples may be earlier, but none of them have any characteristics which would lead us to assign them to a more modern epoch than that just quoted.

CHAPTER III.

HATHI GUMPHA.

All who have written on the subject are agreed that the Hâthi Gumpha or Elephant Cave, is the oldest that exists in these hills. It is, however, only a natural cavern of considerable extent, which may have been slightly enlarged by art, though there is no distinct evidence that this was so. At all events there is certainly no architectural moulding or form, to show that it was ever occupied by man and not by wild animals only, except a long inscription in 17 lines engraved on the smoothed brow of the rock above it. It is consequently of no value whatever in an architectural object, and from an archæological point of view its whole interest resides in the inscription, which, so far as is at present known, is the earliest that has yet been found in India.

A very imperfect attempt to copy this inscription accompanies Mr. Stirling's paper on Cuttack in the 15th volume of the *Asiatic Researches*, but so badly done as to be quite illegible. The first real copy was made by Lieutenant Kittoe in 1837, and though only an eye sketch was done with such marvellous exactness, that Mr. Prinsep was enabled to make a very correct translation of the whole, which he published in the sixth volume of the *Bengal Asiatic Journal* (pp. 1080 *et seq.*). From the more matured and priestly style of composition with which it commences, he was inclined to consider it more modern than the edicts of Aśoka, and assumed the date to be about 200 B.C., a date which I, and every one else, was at the time, led to adopt in deference to the opinion of so distinguished a scholar. It has since, however, been more carefully re-examined by Babu Rajendralàla Mitra, by personal inspection on the spot, and with the aid of photographs. For reasons which seem to me sufficient to establish his conclusion, he places it about a century earlier, B.C. 300 or 325. One of the more important data for the earlier date is the occurrence in the 12th line of the name of Nanda, king of Magadha, of which Mr. Prinsep does not seem to have been aware; and as it is used apparently in the past tense, it looks as if the king Aira who caused this inscription to be written, came after these predecessors of the Mauryan dynasty. It may, however, be that he was only contemporary with the Nandas and with the first Mauryan kings. At the same time all the historical allusions which this inscription contains seems to show that he must have lived before the time when Aśoka carved his edicts at Dauli.

The Hathi Gumpha inscription represents the king as oscillating between the Brahmanical and the Buddhist forms of faith, and though he finally settled down to the latter belief, the whole tenor of the narrative is such, that we are led to believe that the Brahmanical was the prevalent faith of the country, and that he was, if not the first, at least one of the earliest converts to Buddhism. This could hardly have been the case had Aśoka's inscriptions at Dauli—almost in sight of this cave—been in existence when it was engraved, and he could hardly have failed to allude to so powerful an emperor, had he ruled in Orissa before his time. Altogether, it seems from the contents of the inscription so much more probable that Aira should have ruled before the rise of the great Maurya dynasty, than after their establishment, that I feel very little hesitation in coming to the conclusion that 300 B.C., or thereabouts, is the most probable date for this inscription.[1]

In so far as the history of cave architecture is concerned the determination of the age of this inscription is only a political question, not affecting the real facts of the case. As it is avowedly the earliest thing here, if its date is 200 B.C., all the caves that show marks of the chisel are more modern, and must be crowded into the period between that date, and the epoch at which it can be ascertained that the most modern were excavated. If, on the other hand, its date is about 300 B.C., it allows time for our placing the oldest and simplest caves as contemporary with those just described in Behar, and allows ample time for the gradual development of the style in a manner more in conformity with our experience of cave architecture in the west of India.

---

[1] It seems that the vowel marks in the word which Prinsep read as "Suke" in the first line are so indistinct, that it is more probable the word ought to be read Saka; and if this is so it may lead to an interesting national indication. I submitted the passage to Professor Eggling, of Edinburgh, and in reply he informs me that the passage may very well be read "By him who is possessed of the attributes of the famous Saka (race)." If this is so, he may have been either one of those Yavanas who came from the north-west, or at least a descendant of some of those conquerors.

Though I am myself strongly of opinion that the true date of this inscription is about 300 B.C., the question may very well be left for future consideration. The important lessons we are taught by the peculiarities of the Hathi Gumpha are the same that we gathered from the examination of those in Behar. It is that all the caves used by the Buddhists, or held sacred by them anterior to the age of Aśoka, are mere natural caverns unimproved by art. With his reign the fashion of chiselling cells out of the living rock commenced, and was continued with continually increasing magnificence and elaboration for nearly 1,000 years after his time.

Before proceeding to describe the remaining excavations in these hills, it may be as well to advert to a peculiarity we learn as much from the sculptures of the Bharhut Tope as from the caves of Behar. It is, that during the reign of Aśoka, and for 100 years afterwards, it was the fashion to add short inscriptions to everything. Not only as already pointed out are all the Behar caves inscribed, but almost all the Bharhut sculptures are labelled in the most instructive manner, which renders these monuments the most valuable contribution to Buddhist legendary history that has been brought to light in modern times. By the time when the gateways of the Sanchi Tope were erected, the fashion had unfortunately died out. It still continued customary for donors of pillars, or of parts, to record their *Danams* or gifts, but no description of the scenes depicted, nor is any other information afforded, beyond the name and condition of the donor, who generally, however, was a private person, and his name consequently of no historical value.[1]

Bagh and Sarpa, or Tiger and Serpent Caves and smaller Cells.

Guided by these considerations and the architectural indications, it is probable that we may assume the Tiger and Serpent caves to be the oldest of the sculptured caves in these hills. The former is a *capriccio* certainly, not copied from any conceivable form of stone architecture, nor likely to be adopted by any people used to any so in-

[1] In the old temple of Pâpanâth, at Pattadkal, this fashion seems to have been revived, for once at least, for all the sculptures on its walls are labelled in characters probably of the fifth century. *Arch. Survey of West. India*, 1st Report, p. 36.

tractable material as stone in their constructions. It is, in fact, a mass of sandstone rock fashioned into the semblance of the head of a tiger. The expanded jaws, armed with a row of most formidable teeth, form the verandah, while the entrance to the cell is placed where the gullet in a living animal would be. There is a short inscription at the side of the doorway, which according to Prinsep reads "Excavated by Ugra Aveda" (the anti-vedist), which looks as if its author was a convert from the Brahmanical to the Buddhist religion. Before the first letter of this inscription there is a well-known Buddhist symbol, which is something like a capital Y standing on a cube or box, and after the last letter is a swastika.[1] These two symbols are placed at the beginning and end of the great Aira inscription in the Hathi Gumpha, though there their position is reversed, the swastika being at the beginning, the other symbol at the end. The meaning or name of this last has not yet been ascertained, but it occurs in conjunction with the swastika very frequently on the earliest Buddhist coins.[2] The probability, therefore, is that these two inscriptions cannot be far apart in date, and as the jambs of doorway leading into the cell of the Tiger cave slope considerably inwards, there seems no reason for doubting that this cave may not be only slightly more modern than the Aira inscription in the Hathi cave here, and contemporary with the Aśoka caves in the Barabar hills.

No. 12. Tiger Cave, Udayagiri, from a drawing by Capt. Kittoe.

The same remarks apply to the Sarpa or serpent cave. It is only, however, a small cubical cell with a countersunk doorway with jambs sloping inwards at a considerable angle. Over this doorway, in a semicircular tympanum, is what may be called the bust of a three-headed serpent of a very archaic type. It has no other sculptures. Its inscription merely states that it is "the unequalled chamber of Chulakarma."

There is a third little cell called the Pavana, or purification cave,

---

[1] *J. A. S. B.*, vol. vi. p. 1073.

[2] *J. A. S. B.*, and Thomas's *Prinsep*, vol. i. Plates XIX. and XX.

which bears an inscription of the same Chulakarma,[1] but is of no architectural significance. All these, consequently, may be of about the same date, and if that is the age of Aśoka, it makes it nearly certain that the Hathi Gumpha with its Aira inscription must belong to the earlier date ascribed to it above. If for no other reason at least for this, because after carving these, and a great number of small neatly chiselled cells, apparently of the same age, which exist in these hills, some inscribed, some not, it is impossible to fancy any king adopting a rude cavern, showing no marks of a chisel, as a suitable place on which to engrave his autobiography.

Besides these smaller caves which, though numerous, hardly admit of description, there are six larger Buddhist caves in these hills, in which the real interest of the group is centred. Their names and approximate dates may be stated as follows:—

The Ânanta, on the Khandagiri hill } 200 to 150 B.C.
The Vaikuntha. Two-storeyed - }

The Swargapuri } No inscriptions. 150 to 50 B.C.
Jaya Vijaya - }

Râni kâ Nûr. Two storeyed; no inscription; first century B.C.[2]
Ganeśa. One storey; no inscription; first century A.D.

ANANTA.

Though small, the Ânanta is one of the most interesting caves of this group.[3] As will be seen from the annexed woodcut it is somewhat

---

[1] These inscriptions and with the information here retailed, are abstracted from Prinsep's paper in the sixth volume of his *Journal*, pp. 1072 *et seq.*, and Plates LIV. and LVIII.

[2] In his work on Buddha Gaya, just published, Babu Rajendralâla Mitra, at p. 169, assigns these caves to "the middle of the fourth century before Christ," say 350 B.C., or about three centuries earlier than I place it.

[3] When I was at Khandagiri this cave was not known, nor does Kittoe seem to have been aware of its existence. Even now I have been unable to procure a photograph of it, nor any drawing of its details, many of which would be extremely useful in determining its peculiarities. We must wait till some one who knows something of Buddhism and Buddhist art visits these caves before we can feel sure of our facts. I wrote on April last to Mr. Locke, who made the casts of its sculptures, asking for some further particulars, but he has not yet acknowledged the receipt of my letter. I have, however, through the intervention of my friend Mr. W. W. Hunter, B.C.S., been able to obtain from the Commissioner at Katak nearly all the information I require. He instructed

irregular in plan; its greatest length internally is 24 feet 6 inches, with a depth of only 7 feet. Its verandah measures 27 feet on its inner side, but is only 5 feet in width. Its age, we may say, can be determined with precision from the fact of its architectural ornaments, and the character of its sculpture, being nearly identical with those of the Bharhut Stupa (B.C. 200 to 150). The frieze, for instance, consisting of a pyramid of steps, with a lotus between each, (Plate I., figs. 1 and 2) being common to both, and is found nowhere else in the same form that I am aware of, nor in any other age. It runs round the whole of the coping of the rail of the Stûpa, and is extended interruptedly across the front of this cave. The other sculptures in this cave show so marked a similarity in character to those at Bharhut as hardly to admit of doubt of their being executed about the same time. The jambs too of its doorways slope inwards, at what angle I have been unable to ascertain, but sufficiently so to show that the age of this cave cannot be far removed from that I have ascribed to it.

No. 13. Plan of Ananta Cave. Scale, 50 feet to 1 inch.

This cave was originally divided from its verandah by a wall pierced with four doors, but the pier between two of these having fallen away has carried with it two of the semicircular tympana which invariably surmount the doorways in these caves, and which in the earlier ones are the parts which are usually adorned with sculpture. In Mr. Locke's plan it is the left one that has fallen, but according to the photographs of the casts (Plate I.) the two end ones are complete, and it is the centre pier that has been removed. This, however, is of very little consequence. Of the two that remain one contains a sacred tree within its rail, and a man and woman on either side worshipping it, and beyond a boy and a girl bring offerings to their parents. This tree, as is well known, is the most common object of worship, and occurs at least 76 times on the gateways at Sanchi,[1] we ought not, therefore, to be surprised to find it here. The other remaining tympanum contains an image of the goddess Śrî or Lakshmî, but whether as the Goddess of Wealth or the wife of some fabled previous avatâra of Vishṇu, is not clear. As I

the joint magistrate, Mr. Phillips, to visit the caves, and answer my questions, which he has done in a most satisfactory manner, and a good deal of what follows depends on the information thus afforded me.—J.F.

[1] *Tree and Serpent Worship*, page 105.

pointed out before, she occurs at least ten times at Sanchi in exactly the same attitude, standing on a lotus with two elephants, on lotuses also, pouring water over her.[1] General Cunningham has since pointed out another in the centre of the gateway of another tope, at Bhilsa,[2] and she occurs on a medallion on the Bharhut Rail, precisely as she is represented here. She is, in fact, so far as I can ascertain, the only *person* who was worshipped by the Buddhists before the Christian era, but her worship by them was, to say the least of it, prevalent everywhere. As a Brahmanical object of worship she first occurs, so far as I know, in the caves of Mahavallipur, and in the nearly contemporary kailasa at Elurâ, in the eighth century, but afterwards became a favourite object with them, and remains so to the present day.[3]

From our knowledge of the sculptures of the Bharhut Tope we may safely predicate that, in addition to the Tree and the image of Śrî, the two remaining tympana were filled, one, with a representation of a wheel, the other, of a dâgoba, the last three being pratically the three great objects of worship both there and at Sanchi. At the latter place, as just mentioned, the worship of the tree occurs 76 times, of dâgobas 38, wheels 10 times, and Śrî 10, which is, as nearly as can be ascertained from its ruined state, the proportions in which they occur at Bharhut, and there is consequently

---

[1] Loc. cit.

[2] Notwithstanding this, General Cunningham (*Bharhut Stupa*, p. 117) states "that the subject is not an uncommon one with Brahmanical sculptors, but I am unable to give any Buddhistical explanation of it." Unfortunately the General considers it necessary to ignore all that has been done at Sanchi since the publication of his book on that Tope in 1854. He has not consequently seen Colonel Maisey's drawings, nor Capt. Cole's exhaustive transcripts, nor was he aware of the Udayagiri image published in the second edition of my *Tree and Serpent Worship*, Plate C. It is not, therefore, surprising he should not be aware how essentially it is a Buddhist conceit adopted long afterwards by the Brahmans. It occurs frequently in the Buddhist caves at Junnar and Arungabad.

[3] One of the most curious representations of this goddess occurs on a tablet, Mr. Court calls it "*symbole*," which was found by that gentleman at Manikyala, and was lithographed by Mr. Prinsep from a drawing by him and published as Plate XX. vol. V. of his *Journal*. The drawing probably is not quite correct, but it is interesting, as it represents the goddess with her two attendants and two elephants standing on a band containing eight easily recognised Buddhist symbols, such as the vase, the swastika, the wheel, the two fishes, the shield, and the altar. If the drawing is to be depended upon it may belong to the fourth or fifth century. It is not known what has become of this tablet.

every reason to suppose would be adopted in a contemporary monument in Orissa. Whether any remains of the dagoba or wheel are still to be found in the ruined tympana remains to be seen. I fancy they are, but they have not yet been looked for.

Scholars have not yet quite made up their minds what these three great emblems are intended to symbolise, but I think there is now a pretty general concensus that the Dagoba represents Buddha in the Buddhist trinity. It is always simulated to contain a relic of him, or of some of his followers when not otherwise appropriated, or to commemorate some act of his, or memorial of him, and may consequently be easily substituted for his bodily presence, before images of him were introduced.[1] The Wheel, almost all are agreed, represents Dharma, or the law, and if this is so, it seems almost impossible to escape the conviction that the tree is the real, as it would be the appropriate representation of the Sangha or congregation.

No. 14. Triśula from Amrâvati.

Above the tympanum containing the sacred tree is the triśula ornament, General Cunningham calls it the tri-ratna or three jewels, which may be as correct a designation, though the former may be preferable as involving no theory. It is essentially a Buddhist emblem,[2] and I fancy symbolises the Buddhist trinity, Buddha,

---

[1] General Cunningham admits "that even in the later sculptures at Sanchi which date from the end of the first century A.D., there is no representation of Buddha, and the sole objects of reverence are Stûpas, wheels, and trees" (*Stûpa at Bharhut*, p. 107). It is true he overlooks the representation of him at Sanchi on Plate XXXIII., *Tree and Serpent Worship*, but this might be expected. There he appears only as a man, before he attained Buddhahood, not in the usual conventional attitude in which he was afterwards worshipped. He may consequently have been overlooked; but barring this, the General's testimony as to the limitation of objects of worship is most important. Babu Rajendralâla Mitra also admits that no image of Buddha is to be found among these early sculptures. *Buddha Gaya*, p. 128.

[2] General Cunningham, at p. 112 of his *Stûpa at Bharhut* claims the credit of having been the first, in his work on the *Bhilsa Topes*, published in 1854, to have pointed out the resemblance between this triple emblem as used at Sanchi (*Tree and Serpent Worship*, Plate XXX.) and the emblematic Jagannâth with his brother and sister as now

Dharma, Sangha, when used as it is here singly and by itself, but frequently it is found in combination with other emblems. Sometimes, for instance, with three wheels on the three points, but the most common combination seems to be with the shield ornament, as in the annexed illustration from the gateways at Sanchi. What the shield represents has not yet been explained. It occurs under the Swastika in the Hathi Gumpha, and is the pendant to the triśula in this cave, being placed over the image of Śrî, and occurs in similar positions in the Ganeśa cave and elsewhere.

No. 15. Triśula and Shield from Sanchi.

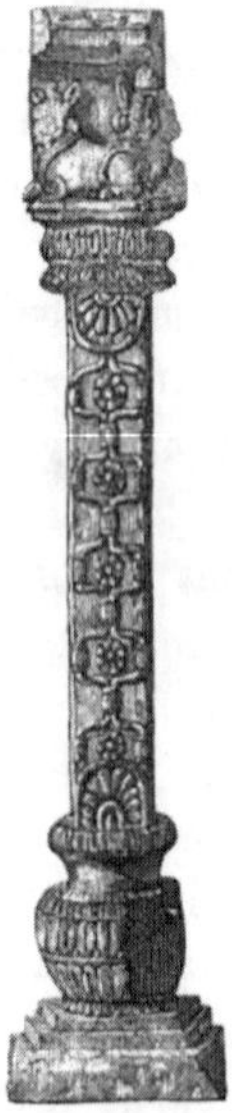

No. 16. Pilaster from Ananta Cave.

In the Ananta cave (Plate I.) these two emblems are shown in connexion with two three-headed snakes, which form the upper member of the decoration of these doorways.[1] In that one over the

worshipped at Puri. At p. 139 of my work just quoted, on the first occasion when I had an opportunity of so doing, I fully admitted, in 1873, the justice of this claim, and it was consequently hardly necessary for him in 1879 to refer indignantly to the "able though anonymous reviewer of my work," to substantiate a claim no one ever disputed. I have always maintained that Vishnuism is practically only a bad and corrupt form of Buddhism, but the subject requires far more full and complete treatment than has yet been bestowed upon it by anyone.

[1] It would be curious to know what the two emblems are that adorned the two other tympana, and it is probable that enough remains to ascertain this, but our information regarding this cave is extremely limited and imperfect.

tree there is a frieze of twelve geese or Hansas, bearing lotus buds in their beaks, which may be of any age, but over the other there is a fantastic representation of men struggling with lions and bulls, which so far as I know may be unique, though something like both these subjects occurs in two lâts at Sanchi,[1] and in a very much more modern form at the base of the outer rail at Amrâvati.[2]

The pilasters that adorn the sides of the doorways are of a curious but exceptional class, and more like some of those found in early caves in the west than any others found on this side of India. They are evidently copied from some form of wooden posts stuck into stone vases or bases, as is usual at Karlê, Nasick, and other western caves. Here, however, in addition to the usual conventional forms, the surface is carved to an extent not found elsewhere, and betrays a wooden origin indicative of the early age to which I would assign the excavation of this cave.

Taking it altogether, the Ananta is certainly one of the most interesting caves of the group. Even in its ruined state it presents a nearly complete picture of Buddhist symbolism, of as early an age as is anywhere to be found, excepting, perhaps, the great Stûpa at Bharhut, with which if not contemporary, it was probably even earlier, and of which its sculptures may be considered as an epitome. As such it is well worthy of more attention than has yet been bestowed upon it.

VAIKUNTHA.

This is the name popularly applied to the upper apartment of a small two-storeyed cave. The lower ones, however, bear the names of Pâtalapura and Yomanapura. Though small and comparatively unadorned, it is interesting as being the prototype of the largest and finest cave of the series known as the Râni kâ Nûr or Queen's palace. When I visited the place it was inhabited, the openings built up with mud and brick, and no access allowed. All consequently I could do was to make a sketch of its exterior, which was published as "a view of the exterior of a Vihara on the Udayagiri Hill."[3]

---

1 *Tree and Serpent Worship*, Plate XXXIX.

2 Loc. cit., Plates XLVIII. and LVII.

3 Plate I. of my *Illustrations of Rock-cut Temples of India*, folio, London, 1845.

There are inscriptions in the old Lât character on each of the divisions of this cave. One on the lower storey of the principal or Vaikuntha cave describes it as "the excavation of the Râjas of Kalinga, enjoying the favour of the Arhats" or Buddhist saints. Another as "the cave of the Mahârâja Vira, the lord of Kalinga, the cave of the venerable Kadepa," and a third as the "cave of Prince Viduka." But as none of these names can be recognised as found elsewhere, this does not help us much in our endeavours to ascertain its age.

There is, or rather was, a long frieze, containing figures of men and animals, extending across the whole front, but these are so time worn, and are so nearly undistinguishable, that no attempt was apparently made by Mr. Locke to take a cast of them, or even to bring away a photograph, so that there are really no materials available for a more perfect description of this cave.

Jaya Vijaya and Swargapuri Caves.

The first named of this group was drawn by Capt. M. Kittoe,[1] under the title of Jodev Garbha, and the sculptures between its two doors were cast by Mr. Locke and appear on Plate I., fig. 3. The sculpture here is not in the tympanum above the doors, as in the earlier examples, but between them in the manner always afterwards adopted. It represents a tree worshipped by two men, one on either side, attended by two women, bearing trays with offerings, and beyond the tympanum on either side are two men or giants, also bearing offerings. The whole character of the sculpture is, however, a very much more advanced type than that of the Ânanta cave, and more nearly resembles that found at Sanchi than anything to be found at Bharhut. The centre pier of the verandah has fallen away, but at either end of it there is a figure carved in high relief, standing as sentinel to guard the entrance, one a male, the other a female. These, however, are of a comparatively modern type.

This cave is two storeys in height, the two being perpendicular the one over the other, not like the Vaikuntha and Râni kâ Nûr, where the upper storey recedes considerably behind the lower.

Attached to this cave, on the right hand as you look at it, is the Swargapuri cave. It has a plain but handsome façade, that apparently

[1] *J. A. S. B.*, vol. vii., Plate XLII.

was never covered by a verandah, at least in stone. Externally it consists of a single doorway of the usual type, surmounted by a tympanum, which may originally have been ornamented by some carving, but nothing is now visible,—in the photographs at least. Above it is a rich and well sculptured band of foliage of the same type as that in the adjoining cave. On the right hand two elephants are seen approaching from a forest, represented by a single well sculptured tree, and a similar group seems to have existed on the left. The rock, however, has fallen away, and the front of only one elephant is now visible.

There is no inscription found on any part of this group of caves, and we are left wholly to the character of the sculptures for the determination of their age. From this, however, we can have little hesitation in saying that they are very considerably more modern than the Ananta, how much more so we may be able to fix more exactly when we have examined the remaining sculptures. At present it may be sufficient to say that their date cannot be far from the Christian era, but whether before or after that epoch it is difficult to determine.

Rani ka Nur.

The excavation known popularly as the Râni kâ Nûr, or the Queen's Palace, is by far the finest and most interesting of those in the Udayagiri hill. Even it, however, is small when compared with the Viharas on the western side of India, and it owes its interest more to its sculpture than to its architecture. As will be seen from the accompanying plans of its two storeys, it occupies three sides

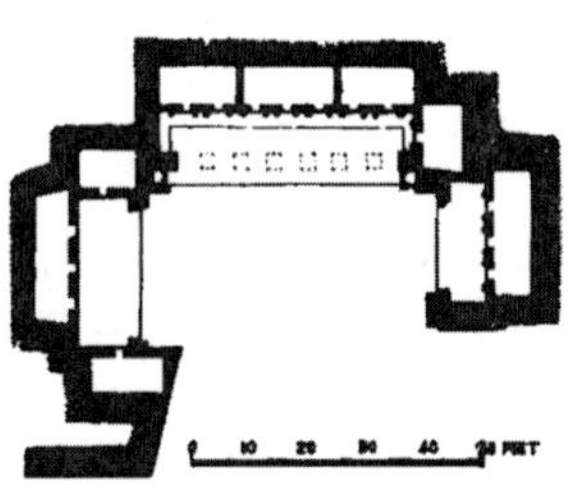

No. 17. Lower Storey, Râni kâ Nûr, from Plan by C. C. Locke.

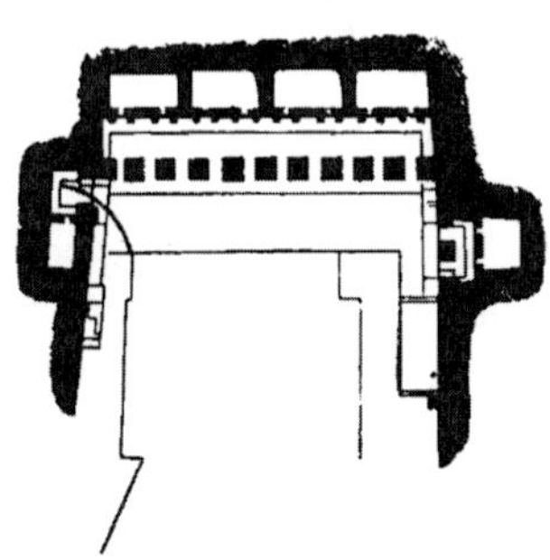

No. 18. Upper Storey, Râni kâ Nûr. Scale 50 feet to 1 inch.

of a square courtyard. The principal "corps de logis," facing the west, consists of two storeys, not exactly over one another, as in the Elurâ caves and elsewhere, but the upper receding behind the other, as shown in the diagram on the next page.

This practice of setting back the upper storey may have been introduced here from the nature of the rock, and been intended to give more strength to the lower storey by relieving it from the pressure of the upper. My impression however is, that it was adopted in consequence of the Buddhist Viharas of that age—as will hereafter be explained—being, when of more than one storey in height, of a pyramidal form, each storey being consequently less in diameter than the one below it. This cave and the Vaikuntha are evidently intended to represent three sides of a structural Vihara turned inside out, to accommodate them to the nature of the material and situation in which they are excavated, all the dimensions, both in plan and section, being consequently reversed. If the wings could be wheeled back 180 degrees to first side—the principal one now standing—they would with it, form the three sides of a free standing Vihara. It is impossible to represent the fourth side or back, from its situation, in a rock-cut example. Supposing this to be the *motivo* of the design it appears to explain all the peculiarities of this cave. It is only necessary to assume that it is a copy of a structural Vihara, 63 feet square at its base or lower storey, with 43 in the upper storey, and intended to have a third probably of 20 or 23 feet square. In this case the two little highly ornamented pavilions in the angles of the lower storey (shown in the plan), would represent the angle piers in which I fancy the staircases were situated in structural examples. All this, however, will be clearer when we come to describe the Raths at Mahavallipur, which are the only examples we possess showing what the external form of Viharas really was in ancient India.

The verandah in the upper storey is 63 feet in length, and opens into four cells of somewhat irregular form, by two doors in each, making eight doorways altogether. The lower verandah is only 43 feet long, and opens into three cells, the central one having three doors, the lateral ones only two each. In a structural Vihara these dimensions would of course be reversed; the upper storey being of course the smallest. Of the pillars in the upper verandah only two now remain out of nine that originally existed, and these are very much ruined, but their forms can easily be recovered from the antæ at either end. None of the pillars of the lower verandah now exist, nor can I learn if any, even of their foundations, are to be found *in situ.* Certain it is, however, that whether as a part of the original design, or in consequence of an accident, the roof of this lower verandah was at one time framed in wood, as shown in the diagram.[1]

It will be observed that the upper part of the rock forming part of the roof of the upper verandah has fallen, and carried away the pillars that at one time supported it, and the fall of such a mass may at the same time have broken through the roof of the lower verandah and caused it to be replaced in wood. Except from the form of the two antæ at either end of the range of columns, I would be inclined to believe it was originally of wooden construction; but they are so essentially lithic in their forms that the wood seems to be a later adaptation. In the earlier Vaikuntha, which, though on a smaller scale, seems to have been the model on which this one was formed, the whole is in stone, which to some extent favours the idea that this wooden verandah was a subsequent repair. In consequence, however, of its decay and destruction, which was sure to happen early in such a climate, the lower range of sculptures have from long exposure become so weather-worn as to be nearly undistinguishable. They may also have suffered from the original fall of the rock, while the upper sculptures are still partially protected by its projection, and consequently are much more perfect, and in them, as just mentioned, resides the main interest of the cave. They are in fact the most extensive series of sculptured scenes to be found in any rock-cut examples of their age. In the western caves such scenes or ornaments as are here found, were either painted on plaster or

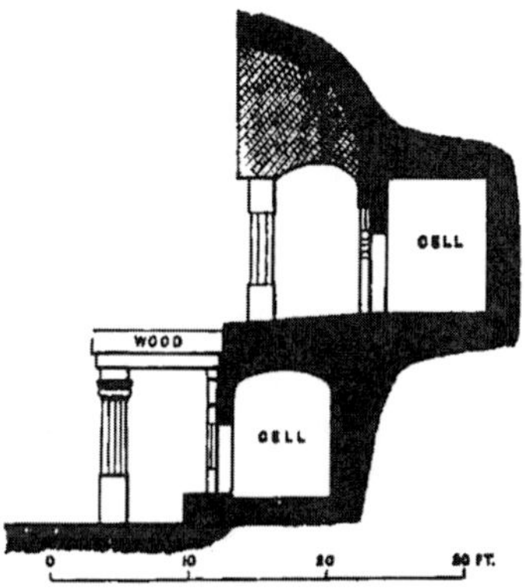

No. 19. Diagram Section of the Râni kâ Nûr.

[1] The diagram is compiled by me, from Mr. Locke's two plans and the photographs, and must not therefore be considered as quite correct, though sufficiently so to explain the text.—J. F.

carved in wood, but on this side of India, we know from what is found at Buddha Gaya and Bharhut, the prevailing fashion in that early age was to execute these things in stone, and consequently these sculptures, even in their ruined state, are full of interest to the history of cave architecture. They are far more extensive than in any of the caves of this group previously examined, and unlike them, instead of being confined to the tympana over the doors, are placed between them, so as to form a nearly continuous frieze, merely interrupted by the semicircular heads of the doorways.

The first question that arises on examining these sculptures is, Are they Buddhist? If they are, they are in some respects unlike any others belonging to that religion we are acquainted with. We do not, of course, at that early age expect to find any conventional representation of Buddha himself, nor even to be able to detect such scenes from his life as that represented on the Sanchi Tope.[1] But there is an almost total absence of all the Buddhist symbols, or objects of worship, which we find in the Ânanta, the Jaya Vijaya, or Vaikuntha caves, and with which we have become so familiar from the sculptures at Bharhut or Sanchi. I fancy I can detect the Triśula and Shield over two doorways,[2] but there certainly are no dagobas, no wheels, nor are there any trees as objects of worship, and Śrî too is absent. In fact, there is nothing essentially Buddhist about the cave; but if this is so, it is equally certain that there is nothing that savours of the Brahmanical religion. There are no many-armed or many-headed figures, and no divinities of the Hindu Pantheon can be recognised in the sculptures, nor anything that can indicate that the caves were Jaina. We are consequently forced to the conclusion that they must represent scenes from the Buddhist Jâtakas, or events occurring among the local traditions of Orissa. The latter is, however, so improbable, that my conviction is that the solution will be found in the Jâtaka; but out of the 505 births therein narrated only a few have been published, and these with so many variants that it is frequently very difficult to recognise the fable, even when the name is written over it, as is so frequently the case at Bharhut, and it consequently

---

1 *Tree and Serpent Worship*, Plate XXXIII.

2 The casts made by Mr. Locke are generally divided at the apex of the arch over the doorways, where these emblems are usually found. I cannot, therefore, feel certain that what I have taken for the Triśula and Shield emblems may not be, after all, mere architectural ornaments.

becomes almost impossible to do so when we have no such indications to help us.[1]

In a monograph of the caves in Katak, it might be expedient to describe the sculptures of the Râni kâ Nûr in detail, but even then it would hardly be possible to render their story intelligible to others without publishing at the same time the photographs from the casts made from them by Mr. Locke in 1871-2. These have been entrusted to Babu Rajendralàla Mitra for publication,[2] and when given to the world it may be worth while to go more carefully into the subject. At present it may be sufficient to indicate their general character.

The frieze occupying the upper part of the verandah of the upper storey is divided by the heads of the eight doorways into seven complete and separate *bassi rilievi* with two half ones at the ends. The latter, which are about the best protected from the weather, are occupied by two running figures with their faces turned towards the centre; the one on the left bearing a tray, apparently with offerings, while the corresponding figure at the other end carries a wreath, such as that which forms the frieze of the outer rail at Amrâvatî,[3] only of course on a much smaller scale.

The first bas-relief between the doors represents three very small elephants issuing from a natural rocky cavern, apparently to attack a man (query, giant), who is defending himself with an enormous club, worthy of Hercules. On his right hand in front of him is a Yakkhinî, known by her curly locks, standing on end, and behind him are a number of females either seeking shelter in various attitudes of consternation, or by their gestures offering to assist in repelling the attack. If this is meant for history, it probably represents some episode in the story of the conquest of Ceylon by Vijaya, which is a very favourite subject with Buddhist artists, and where elephants with

---

[1] I have shown the photographs from the casts of the bas-reliefs to Messrs. Fausböll, Rhys Davids, Sénart, and Feer, who are perhaps the four persons who at the present day are most competent to give an opinion on such a subject, but none of them have been able to offer any plausible suggestions on this subject.

[2] As the plates of this work have been complete for several years, and the text printed, it is much to be regretted that the Government did not entrust their publication to Mr. Locke or someone else, so that the public might have the advantage of the information obtained at their expense. I am afraid there is very little chance of their being published by the Babu within any reasonable time.

[3] *Tree and Serpent Worship*, Plates LVI. and XCII.

Yakkhos and Yakkhinîs always perform important parts. It is one too of the most likely subjects to be depicted in these caves, as it is always from this country of Kalinga that the conquest of that island is said to have originated.[1] But it may be some Jâtaka to whose interpretation we have no clue, and regarding which it is consequently idle to speculate.

The second bas-relief (Plate I., fig. 4) is certainly the most interesting of the series, not only because it is one of the best preserved, but also because it is repeated without any variation in the incidents, though in a very different style of sculpture, in the Ganeśa cave, to be next described. This bas-relief contains eight figures, four males and four females, in four groups. The first represents a man apparently asleep in the doorway of a hut, and a woman sitting by him watching. In front of these is a woman leading a man by the hand apparently to introduce him to the first pair. Beyond these, on the right, a man and woman are engaged in mortal combat with swords of different shapes, but both bearing shields of very unusual form, which I have never seen elsewhere. Beyond these, on the extreme right, a man is carrying off in his arms an Amazonian female, who still carries her shield on her arm, though she has dropped her sword, and is pointing with the finger of her right hand to the still fighting pair. Here again the first suggestion is Ceylon, for nowhere else, that I know of, at least, do Amazons figure in Buddhist tradition. But they are represented as defending Ceylon against the invasion from Kalinga in the great fresco in Cave XVII. at Ajaṇṭâ, engraved by Mrs. Speir in her *Ancient Life in India*, and repeated further on in a woodcut in the second part. It is by no means impossible that this bas-relief may represent an episode in that apocryphal campaign. It may, however, from its being repeated twice in two different caves, be some local legend, and if so the key will probably be found in the palm leaf records of the province, whenever they are looked into for that purpose, which has not hitherto been done. If not found there, or in Ceylonese tradition, I am afraid the solution may be difficult. It does not look like a Jâtaka. At least there is no man in any of these four groups whom we can fancy could have been Buddha in any former birth. But nothing is so difficult as to interpret a Jâtaka without a hint from some external source.

---

[1] Turnour's *Mahawanso*, chap. vi. p. 43, *et seq.*

The third compartment I have very little doubt contains a representation of one of the various editions of the Mṛiga or Deer Jâtaka; not exactly that narrated by Hiuen Thsang,[1] nor exactly that represented at Bharhut,[2] but having so many features in common with both, that it seems hardly doubtful the story is the same. The principal figure in the bas-relief is undoubtedly a king, from the umbrella borne behind him and the train of attendants that follow him. That he is king of Benares is also probable, from his likeness to the king represented at Sanchi in the Sama Jâtaka.[3] The winged deer is almost certainly the king of the herd, who was afterwards born as Buddha, but whether the second person represented is the king repeated, or some other person,—as would appear to be the case at Bharhut,—I am unable to guess. The deer at his feet is probably the doe who admitted that her turn to be sacrificed had come, but pleaded that she ought to be spared in consequence of the unborn fawn she bore in her womb, whose time had not yet arrived. I am unable to suggest who the woman in the tree may be. I know of no Dêvatas or female tree divinities elsewhere, though there may have been such in Orissa.

The fourth, which is the central compartment, is the only one in which anything like worship can be traced, but at its right hand corner, though much injured, I think we can detect something like a miniature dagoba or relic casket with some one praying towards it, and above a priest or some one seated in the cross-legged attitude afterwards adopted in the statues of Buddha. To the left of these is a figure in an attitude sometimes found at Amrâvatî, bearing a relic.[4] It is difficult to say who the great man or woman is who is seated further to the left and surrounded with attendants. He or she is evidently the person in whose honour the puja or worship in the right hand corner is being performed, but who these may be must be left for future investigation.

The next compartment is so completely destroyed that no cast was taken of it, and its subject cannot of course be ascertained. The following one, however, containing three couples with possibly a fourth—for the right-hand end is very much ruined—at once calls to

---

[1] Translated by Julien, vol. ii. p. 355.

[2] *The Stupa at Bharhut*, Plate XXV. Fig. 2.

[3] *Tree and Serpent Worship*, Plate XXXVI. Fig. 1.

[4] *Ibid.*, Plate LI., Fig. 1.

mind the scenes depicted at Sanchi on Plate XXXVIII. of *Tree and Serpent Worship*. The first pair are seated on a couch, the gentleman with his arms round the lady's waist, and a wine bottle on the ground in front of them. In the second group the lady is seated on the gentleman's knee, and there is a table with refreshments before them. The third it is difficult to describe, and the fourth is too nearly obliterated—if it ever existed—for anything to be made out regarding it.[1]

The seventh bas-relief is partially destroyed and was not cast.

As it at present stands, the evidence derived from these bas-reliefs is too indistinct to admit of any theory being formed of much value regarding their import. It looks, however, as if the first, the third, the fifth and seventh were Jâtakas, while the even numbers—the remaining four—represented local legends or scenes in the domestic life of the excavators of the cave.

Several of the reliefs on the front of the lower storey were cast by Mr. Locke, but they are so fragmentary and so ruined by exposure to the weather, that no continuous group can be formed out of any of them, nor can any connected story be discerned either of a legendary or religious character. Whether on the spot in the varying lights of the day, anything could be made out of them it is impossible to say, but neither the photographs nor the casts give much hope of this being done. They seem to represent men and women following their usual avocations or amusements, and certainly nothing can be discerned in them that illustrates either the religion of Buddha, or the history of the country.[2]

This fortunately cannot be said of the sculptures on the right-hand wing, where they are perfectly well protected from the weather by a verandah 8 feet in depth. This leads through three doors into an apartment measuring 7 feet by 20, on the front of which there is consequently space for two full and two half compartments, which are filled with sculptures. In the left-hand half division, a man and his wife are seen approaching the centre with

---

1 A similar scene occcurs at Buddha Gaya. *See* Cunningham's *Reports*, vol. i., Plate X., Fig. 33. Rajendralâla's *Buddha Gaya*, Plate XXXIV., Fig. 3. It is most unmistakably a love scene.

2 They have all been lithographed for Babu Rajendralâla's second volume, so that when that is published the public will have an opportunity of judging how far this account of them is correct,

their hands joined in the attitude of prayer. Behind them is a dwarf, and before them a woman bearing offerings. In the corresponding compartment at the other end of the verandah, three women—one may be a man—and a child are seen bearing what may also be offerings. The left-hand full compartment is occupied by a woman dancing under a canopy borne by four pillars, to the accompaniment of four musicians, one playing on a flute,[1] another on a harp, a third on a drum, and a fourth apparently on a Vina or some guitarlike instrument. In the other full division are three women, either sitting on a bench with their legs crossed in front, or dancing. My impression is that the latter is the true interpretation of the scene, from two women in precisely similar attitudes being represented as Boro Buddor, in Java,[2] but there so much better executed that there is no mistake as to their action. Whether, however, these women represent the audience, or are actually taking part in the performance, it is quite certain that the sculptures on this façade are of a wholly domestic character, and represent a Nâch and that only. As such they would be quite as appropriate to a Queen's palace—as this cave is called—as to the abode of cœnobite Priests, to which purpose it is generally supposed to have been appropriated.'

Besides the *bassi rilievi* just described, there are throughout these caves a number of single figures in *alto rilievo*. They are generally life-size and placed at either end of the verandahs of the caves, as dwârpâlas or sentinels. They are generally dressed in the ordinary native costume, and of no especial interest; but in this cave there are two which are exceptional, and when properly investigated may prove of the utmost value for the history of these caves. These two are situated at the north end of the upper verandah of this cave. The first is of a singularly Bacchic character, and is generally described as a woman riding astride on a lion, and is certainly so represented in Captain Kittoe's drawing.[3] From Captain Murray's photograph, however, the stout figure of the rider appears to me very much more like the Silenus brought from Mathura and now

---

[1] This, as in all the ancient sculptures in India, is the "Flauto Traverso," supposed to be invented in Italy in the 13th or 14th century.

[2] *Boro Buddor*, 4 vols. folio, published by the Dutch Government at Batavia, vol. i. Plate CX., Fig. 189.

[3] *J. A. S. Bengal*, vol. vii. Plate XLI.

in the Calcutta Museum, and the animal is as likely to be a tiger as a lion.[1] It is, however, too much mutilated to feel sure what it may represent.

Behind this group stands a warrior in a Yavana costume, (woodcut No. 22), which, so far as I know, is quite unique in these caves though something very like it occurs at Sanchi.[2] There, as here, the dress consists of a short tunic or kilt reaching to the knee, with a scarf thrown over the left shoulder and knotted on the right. On his left side hangs a short sword of curiously Roman type, and on his feet he wears short boots, or hose reaching to the calf of the leg, whether they are bound like sandals as at Sanchi is not quite clear, but the whole costume is as nearly that of a Scotch Highlander of the present day as it is possible to conceive. Those wearing this costume at Sanchi are known from their instruments of music and other peculiarities to be foreigners, though whence they came is not clear, and this one, we may safely assert, is not an Indian, and his costume not such as was adapted to the climate, or ever worn by the people; nor is it found in any of the bas-reliefs just described. Bearing in mind what we learn from the palm leaf records of the Yavana invasions of Orissa, there seems little doubt that these two figures do represent foreigners from the north-west, or at least a tradition of their presence here. In the present state of our knowledge, however, it is impossible to form even a plausible theory as to who they were, nor to guess at what time they may have been present in this country, beyond what we gather from the age of the caves in which they are represented.

Ganesa Gumpha.

The Ganeśa Gumpha is the only other cave of any importance on the Udayagiri Hill, which remains to be described. It is popularly known by the name of that Hindu divinity, in consequence, apparently, of the two elephants holding lotus buds in their trunks, who flank on

---

[1] There is a second figure of Silenus presented to the Calcutta Museum by Col. Stacey, brought also from Mathura, with female attendants, the whole of which, with the trees behind, was certainly sculptured in India about the period to which I assign this cave. There is also the patera brought by Dr. Lord from Budakshan, now in the Indian Museum, representing Silenus in a chariot, drawn by panthers, also of Indian workmanship.

[2] *Tree and Serpent Worship*, Plate XXVIII. Fig. 1.

either side, the steps leading up to its verandah. It is a small cave divided into two cells, opening into a verandah about 30 feet in length by 6 in width. Originally it had five pillars in front, but two of these have fallen away. The remaining three are of the ordinary type of nearly all those in these caves, square above and below, but octagonal in the centre, and in this instance with a small bracket capital evidently borrowed from a wooden form. There are four doorways leading from the verandah into the cells, and consequently room for three complete and two half reliefs. Two only are, however, sculptured. The end ones and the centre compartments are filled only with the ordinary Buddhist rails. One of the remaining two (Plate I., fig. 5) contains, as already mentioned, a replica of the abduction scene, which forms the second in the Râni kâ Nûr. There are the same eight persons, and all similarly employed in both, only that in this one the sculpture is very superior to that in the other, and the attitudes of the figures more easy and graceful, more nearly, in fact, approaching those at Amrâvatî, than even to the sculptures at Sanchi.[1]

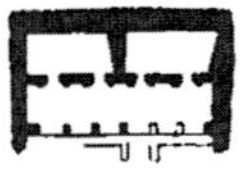

No. 20. Ganesa Gumpha. 50 feet to 1 inch.

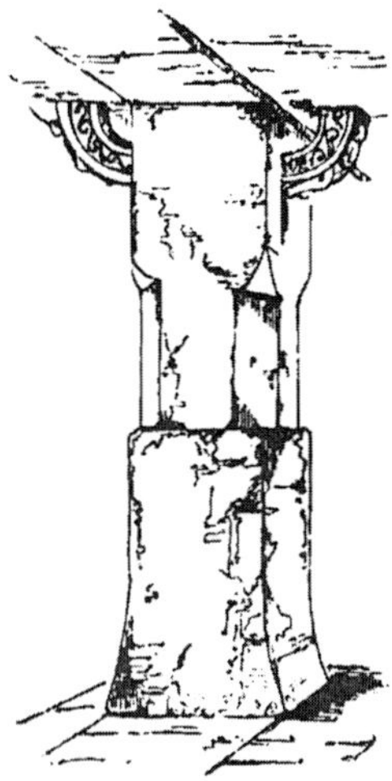

No. 21. Pillar in the Ganesa Gumpha, from a sketch by the Author.

At one time I was inclined to believe that the stories represented in the sculptures here and in the Râni kâ Nûr were continuous and formed part of one connected history. A more careful study, however, of the matter, with the increased knowledge we now possess, has convinced me that this is not the case, and that each division in the storied bas-reliefs must be treated as a separate subject. In this instance it seems the sculptor purposely left the centre compartment blank in order to separate the two so completely that no one should make the mistake of fancying there was any connexion between them. And the introduction of elephants, in

[1] It was well and carefully drawn by Kittoe, and lithographed by Prinsep, *J. A. S. B.*, vol. vii. Plate XLIV.

the second bas-relief the difference of costume, and the whole arrangement of the subject seems to point to the same conclusion.

This bas-relief contains sixteen persons, of whom eleven or twelve may be males and four or five females, but apparently of a totally different character, and with different costumes, from those in the preceding sculpture. Instead, however, of being arranged in four groups, with two persons in each, as in the preceding bas-relief, there are here five groups of three persons each, with one, apparently a slaughtered man, who does not count. The stone in which it is carved, however, is so soft and so weatherworn that it is extremely difficult to follow the action and make out the details. One thing, however, is quite certain, which is, that it is a totally different scene from that which follows the abduction scene in the Râni kâ Nûr, proving clearly that neither here nor there do these bas-reliefs represent a continuous history. Instead of a king or kings on foot shooting deer, we have here a party of soldiers on foot, dressed in kilts, pursuing and slaying a man in a similar dress, who is prostrate on the ground. In front of him are three persons on an elephant, the hindermost of whom is seizing either the severed head or the helmet of the fallen soldier, it is impossible from the state of the sculpture to make out which, while the principal person on the elephant shoots a Parthian shot from his bow at the pursuing soldiers, and they then escape from the wood in which the action takes place.[1] The remaining half of the bas-relief is made up of three groups of three persons each. In the first the elephant is kneeling, and the three persons, who apparently were those on his back in the first part, are standing behind him in the second. A little further to the right is another group of three persons, a man, a woman, and a boy, but whether they are the same as the elephant riders or not, is not clear. From the costume of the man, which differs considerably, it is probable they are not. In the last group of three the lady is sitting disconsolate on the ground, the man consoling her, and the boy, more than half concealed by the doorhead, holding the bow which he carried on the elephant.

Without some hint from some external source, it seems idle to try

[1] From Mr. Phillips' letter above referred to, it seems that the third person on the elephant is a man, and not a woman, which from the cast he might be mistaken for, and that he holds the head of the fallen man by the hair. It also appears that the head is quite severed from the body, which in Kittoe's drawing is certainly not the case.

and find out what this bas-relief really is intended to represent. It may be a story from some Yavana conquest of Kalinga, or it may be a scene from some popular legend connected with some of the earlier Princes of the land, or, lastly, it may be a Jâtaka, representing some action that took place in one of the earlier births of Śâkya Muni. In fact it may be anything, and as I know of nothing at all like it or that affords any hint of what the story may be, either in this or in its companion bas-relief, the abduction scene, I must be allowed to relegate it for further investigation when we possess more knowledge of the local and traditional history of Kalinga Deśa.

Like the Râni kâ Nûr, this cave is without any inscription[1] that can give us any hint as to the age when it was excavated, and we are consequently left wholly to the style of architecture and sculpture to enable us to fix its age in so far as it can be done, in the present state of our knowledge.

The only Buddhist emblems that can be detected in this cave are the triśula and the shield, but they are most distinctly shown in the upper part of the semicircular framework over the doors. They are there, however, connected with foliaged ornaments of so much more refined and elegant a character than the corresponding ornaments in the Râni kâ Nûr, that there can be no hesitation in ascribing them to a more modern date. The same is true of the figure sculptures in this cave. It is not only very much better than that at Bharhut, but approaches so nearly to that of Amrâvatî in some respects, that it seems difficult to carry it back even to the age of the gateways at Sanchi, with which, however, it has perhaps, on the whole, the nearest affinity. The foliaged ornaments that are found surrounding the semicircular heads of the tympana over the doorways are so nearly identical with some ornaments on the gateways at Sanchi[2] that they cannot be far removed in age. Similar ornaments are also found on the jambs of the door of the Chaitya cave at Nasik (Plate XXV.), and elsewhere, which are either a little before or a little after the Christian era, so that altogether the date of this cave can hardly be considered as open to question.

[1] In Prinsep's plates, *J. A. S. B.*, vol. vi. Plate LIV., there is an inscription said to be found in this cave, though even that is doubtful; but supposing it to exist, as I pointed out in my original paper, *R. A. S.*, vol. viii. pp. 31, 41, it is in so modern a character that it is absolutely impossible it could be coeval with the date of the excavation, though it might mark its appropriation by the Hindus at a long subsequent age.

[2] *Tree and Serpent Worship*, woodcuts 17 and 18, p. 114.

Still the inferiority in technical merit of the sculptures in the Râni kâ Nûr, and their more distinctly Indian character as compared with those in this cave, for a long time made me hesitate before coming to a positive conclusion as to which was the earliest of the two. As a rule, the history of art in India, as I have frequently pointed out, is written in decay. As we trace it backwards, not only are the architectural details more elegant and better executed in each preceding century, but the figure sculpture improves in drawing and dramatic power, till, at least, we reach the age of the Amrâvatî Tope in the fourth century. There was perhaps as much vigour in those of the Sanchi gateways in the first century of our era, but they lack the technical skill, and now that we know what was done at Bharhut and Buddha Gaya, two or three centuries earlier, we can state with confidence that there was distinct progress in sculpture from the age of Alexander to that of Constantine. The highest point of perfection was apparently reached in the fourth or fifth century, the decay, however, set in shortly after, and has unfortunately continued, with only slight occasional oscillations towards better things, to the present day. With this knowledge there can be little hesitation in placing the sculptures of the Râni kâ Nûr as earlier than those of the Ganeśa cave, though at what interval it is difficult to say. There is, however, still one point in the architecture which points most distinctly in the same direction. All the jambs of the doorways in the Râni kâ Nûr slope inwards, not to such an extent as is found in the Behar caves, or even in the earlier ones here, but still most unmistakeably, and to such an extent as is not found in any cave either in the east or west of India after the Christian era. No such inclination of the jambs can be detected in the photographs of the Ganeśa cave, and, in fact, does not exist; and this, with the superior elegance of the sculpture, and delicacy of the architectural details, is more than sufficient to prove that the excavation of the Ganeśa cave must, according to our present lights, be placed at an age considerably more modern than that assigned to the Râni kâ Nûr, whatever that may be.

From what we now know of the sculptures of the Topes at Bharhut and Sanchi, we ought not perhaps to be surprised to find no scenes that can be directly traced to the legends of the life of Buddha in the sculptures in these caves; nor till the whole of the Jâtaka stories are translated can we wonder that we cannot interpret the sculptures from that vast repository of improbable fables. Still, having recognised beyond doubt the Wasantara, the Sama, and other Jâtakas at Sanchi, where no descriptive inscriptions exist,[1]—and the inscribed ones at Bharhut show how favourite a mode of illustration they were at the age of these caves,—we ought not to despair that they may yet yield their secrets to future investigators. A more remarkable peculiarity of this group of caves is the total absence of any Chaitya caves, or of any sanctuary in the Viharas, which could ever have been appropriated to worship in any form. In all the western groups, such as Bhâjâ, Bedsâ, Nâsik, Ajaṇṭâ, everywhere in fact, the Chaitya, or church cave, seems to have been commenced as early as the Viharas or monasteries to which they were attached, The two in fact being considered indispensable to form a complete monastic establishment. Here, on the contrary, though we have Aira in his famous inscription boasting that he had "caused to be constructed subterranean chambers and caves containing a Chaitya temple and pillars,"[2] we find nothing of this sort anywhere. No traces of such excavation, have been found, and the Viharas also differ most essentially from those found on the western side of India. There in almost every instance the Vihara consists of a central hall, round which the cells are ranged; nowhere do the cells open directly,—except in the smallest hermitages,—on the verandah, or on the outer air.

The only means that occur to me of accounting for these differences, which appear to be radical and important, is by supposing that in Behar and Orissa there existed a religion—Buddhist or Jaina—using the same forms, and requiring the same class of constructions, that were afterwards stereotyped in the caves. If this were so there probably existed, before Aśoka's time, halls of assembly and monasteries—constructed in wood of course—which were appropriate for this form of worship, and they continued to use these throughout the whole Buddhist period without, as a rule, attempting to imitate them in the rock.

---

[1] *Tree and Serpent Worship*, Plates XXXVI. and XXXVIII. The identification of these jâtakas at that time was one of the most important discoveries made in modern times for the authentication of the Buddhist scriptures. Before that many were inclined to believe that the Jâtakas were mere modern inventions. Then for the first time it was proved that before the Christian era they existed, and very nearly in the same form as at the present day.

[2] *J. A. S. B.*, vol. vi. p. 1084.

If we knew exactly when it was that Buddhism was first practically established in the west, it might aid in determining this point. As before mentioned, it (*vide ante*, p. 17) is probable that it was not known there before the arrival of the missionaries sent by Aśoka after the third convocation held in the 17th year of his reign, B.C. 246. If this is so, it is unlikely that any suitable places of worship were found there, or any habit of constructing them, while as these missionaries found everywhere a rock admirably suited to the purpose, they may at once have seized the idea of giving permanence and dignity to the new forms by carving them in the imperishable rock. It is true, it may be objected, to this view that this almost necessarily presupposes the idea of the inhabitants of the country having used caves as habitations, of some sort, anterior to the advent of the Buddhists, while, as none such have been found, it seems strange the habit should have become at once so prevalent. If, however, any such earlier caves did exist, they must have been only rude unsculptured caverns, like the Hathi Gumpha and the rude caves in Behar, and would be undistinguishable from natural caverns, and it would be impossible now to determine whether they had ever been used by man for any purpose. Be this as it may, I know of no other mode of accounting for the general prevalence of Chaitya caves in the west and their non-existence in the east of India than by supposing that on the one side of India they always had, and continued to use, wooden halls for this purpose, while on the other side, having no such structures, they at once adopted the idea of carving them in the rock, and finding that so admirably adapted for the purpose they continued to use it ever afterwards.

As I hope to be able to show, in describing the Raths at Mahâvallipur, a little further on, the Viharas of the Buddhists as originally constructed consisted of a square hall, the roof of which was supported by pillars, and with cells for the residence of the monks arranged externally round, at least, three sides of the hall, on the upper storeys, at least. In some, perhaps most instances, it was two or three or more storeys in height, each diminishing in horizontal dimensions, and the cells being placed on the roof of the lower storeys of the structure, which thus assumed a pyramidal form like the Birs Nimrud near Babylon. If any such monasteries existed in Katak they probably continued in use during the whole Buddhist period, and so have been preferred as residences to others cut in the rock. Whether this was so or not, it is clear that the eastern caves are not such direct copies from structural Viharas as those on the west, where the central hall, surrounded with cells on three sides, with a portico or porch on the fourth, was as nearly a direct copy as could well be made in the rock. In the east they proceeded on a different system. The hall was entirely omitted, and the cells open either directly on the outer air or into the verandah, while, as explained in describing the Râni kâ Nûr (*ante*, p. 78) all the other arrangements of the structural Vihara were turned topsy turvey. The difference probably arose from the fact the Udayagiri group of hills is literally honey-combed with little cells, of about 6 or 7 feet square, just sufficient for the residence of a single hermit. Most of them probably had a verandah in wood or shelter of some sort over the doorway to prevent the inmate being baked alive, which without such protection he certainly would have been. Some of the earlier carved caves, such as the Tiger cave, the Bhajana cave, and the Ânanta, are still only single cells, with verandahs of greater or less magnificence. Some, like the Jaya Vijaya and Ganeśa, are only two cells with verandahs to protect both, and others, like the Vaikuntha and Râni kâ Nûr, contain three or four cells arranged in two storeys. Still these are only an assemblage of hermitages without any common hall or refectory, or any of the monastic arrangements which were so universally adopted in the western caves. At the same time it may be remarked that there being no halls in the eastern caves, accounts for the absence of any internal pillars at Udayagiri, though they form a marked and important feature in all the western caves of any pretension to magnificence.

The absence of a Dagoba either in or about these caves may perhaps be acccounted for, as before hinted, by the Tooth relic being probably the great object of worship in this province during the Buddhist period, and it may have been preserved in a Dagoba or shrine of some sort, on the top of the Udayagiri hill, if this was Dantapuri. The local traditions, it must be confessed, tend rather to show that Dantapuri was where the temple of Jugannâth now stands at Puri on the sea shore, but the evidence is conflicting on this point. But be this as it may, it is quite certain, unless Kittoe is right about the remains on the Udayagiri hill, that there is no material evidence of a Dagoba, either structural or rock-cut, existing in connexion with these caves. On the other hand, it may probably be asserted with equal confidence that in western India there is no group of caves, of anything like the same extent, which has not one or more of these emblems, either rock-cut or structural.

There are several minor peculiarities pointing however to essential differences between the caves on the east and west of India, which will be described in the subsequent chapters of this work, when describing the western caves, but which it is consequently not necessary to anticipate at the present stage of the investigation.

No. 22. Yavana warrior from the Râni kâ Nûr.

CHAPTER IV.

UNDAVILLI CAVES ON THE KRISHNA RIVER NEAR BEJWARA.

The caves of this group are not in themselves of any great interest, but the locality in which they are situated was one of great importance in early Buddhist times. It was in fact, so far as we at present know, the only place in Southern India where the Buddhists had any important establishments, or, at all events, no Buddhist remains have been found south of Kalinga, except those in this neighbourhood. This was probably owing to the fact, that it was from some port in the vicinity of the mouth of the Krishnâ and Godaveri that Java and Cambodia were colonised by Buddhists, and we know from the classical authorities that it was hence that communication was kept up between India and the Golden Chersonese at Thatun and Martaban. If no other evidence were available the existence of the Amrâvatî Tope within a few miles of Bêjwârâ is quiet sufficient to prove how numerous and wealthy the Buddhist community must have been in the fourth and fifth century. While the account given of it by Hiuen Thsang in the seventh shows how much of its previous importance, in Buddhist eyes, it retained even then.

Under these circumstances we might well expect that besides the Amrâvatî Tope, other remains might still be found there, and they probably will be when looked for. This, however, has not hitherto been the case. The knowledge we do possess may be said to have been acquired almost accidentally, no thorough or scientific survey of the country having yet been attempted.

Bêjwârâ was the capital of the country of Dhanakacheka when Hiuen Thsang visited the place in 637 A.D., and he describes two great Buddhist establishments as existing in its immediate neighbourhood. One, the Purvaśila Sangarâma, as situated on a hill to the east of the city, where its remains can still be traced. To the westward of the city he describes the Avaraśila monastery, in his eyes a far more important establishment, and by which there seems little doubt he intended to designate the Amrâvatî Tope, situated on the opposite bank of the river, about 17 miles higher up. This was first explored by General Mackenzie in 1817-21, afterwards by Sir Walter Elliot, and recently by Mr. Sewell of the Madras Civil Service, and the results of their labours, except of the last named, are described in the second part, and last 56 of the plates of my *Tree and Serpent Worship.* Though it may not have been the most sacred, it certainly is, in an artistic point of view, the most important Buddhist monument that has yet been discovered in India, and is quite unique in the part of the country where it is situated. Its magnificence, and the length of time it must have taken to execute its sculptures, prove that for a long period the Buddhists must not only have been all powerful in this part of India, but also the possessors of immense wealth, and it is consequently probable that other remains of the same class may still be found, and more especially that contemporary caves may still exist in the sides of the hills in its neighbourhood. Those that have hitherto been discovered, hardly answer to the expectations thus raised, while such as have been described belong to a much more modern age, and to another religion. It will, consequently, only be when some contemporary series of caves is discovered that we can expect to find anything that is worthy to be classed with the sculptures of the Amrâvatî Tope.[1]

---

[1] In a paper read to the Royal Asiatic Society on the 17th of November last, Mr. Sewell adheres to the opinion he expressed in his original report to the Madras Government, that the Avaraśila Sangarâma of Hiuen Thsang was not identical with the Amrâvatî Tope, but was a "rock cut" vihara situated on the side of a hill immediately overhanging the city of Bêjwârâ. He admits that there are no remains of any structural buildings on that hill, which could have belonged to ancient times, and no trace of the "caverns" mentioned by the pilgrim. All he contends for is that there are platforms cut here and there in "the rock," on which he thinks the buildings of the monastery may have been erected.

Although it may fairly be admitted that the language of Hiuen Thsang may bear the interpretation Mr. Sewell puts upon it, it is so deficient in precision that it may with equal fairness be argued that the expression which he considers descriptive of the monastery in reality applies to the road. The "Via Sacra," with its statues and rest places, which its founder constructed to lead from the city to the sacred spot. As the case now stands we have before us the substantial fact of the existence of the Amrâvatî Tope, which from our knowledge of the sculptures found in the Gandhara monasteries we know was "adorned with all the art of the palaces of Bactria," and very similar in style to them. On the other hand we have only a hill side which has in some places been cut down to afford platforms for buildings, but of what form and of what age we

The principal cave that has yet been discovered in this neighbourhood is situated in a small isolated hill about a mile from the town of Bejwâḍâ (the Bejwara or Bezwara of the maps), and is a four or rather five storeyed Vaishṇava temple, dedicated to Anantasena or Nârayaṇa. It has been suspected of having been originally excavated as a Buddhist Vihara; but there is certainly no sufficient evidence to justify such a supposition. It is entirely Brahmanical in all its arrangements, and very similar to the contemporary caves belonging to that religion at Bâdâmi and Elurâ, and can from the character of its sculptures hardly date further back than the 7th or 8th century of our era. It probably should be attributed to some of the Châlukya kings of Vengi, who like the elder branch of that family ruling at Bâdâmi, and later at Kalyaṇa, were worshippers of Vishṇu.

No. 23. View of the Undavilli Cave, from a Photograph.

The great interest of this cave for our present purposes, lies in its

have no suggestion. Under these circumstances, and with the knowledge we now possess of Buddhist cave architecture, it is probably safe to assert, that no such combination as Mr. Sewell suggests, of rock cut with structural buildings exists in India, and till some such are discovered I must be excused if I decline to register these "platforms" among the "Cave temples of India," or to believe that Hiuen Thsang did not mention the Amrâvatî Topé under the designation of the Avaraśila Sangharama.

enabling us to carry one step further back our researches into the external appearance of the structural Buddhist Viharas, which have disappeared from the land. In describing the Râni kâ Nûr, at Udayagiri (*ante*, p. 78) it was pointed out that the upper storey there, and in the Vaikuntha cave were set back, not so much from constructional motives, as in imitation of the forms of the structural Viharas of the period. Here we have the same system carried out through four—possibly five—different storeys. It is true the exact section of the cave may, to some extent, have been adapted to the natural slope of the hill, but it hardly seems doubtful that the successive terraces are adaptations to rock forms of the platforms which formed essential features of pyramidal Viharas of the Buddhists, and which became afterwards the fundamental idea of the Dravidian style of architecture, in the hands of the Brahmans of the south.

As already mentioned the Undavilli cave is four storeys in height one above the other, but there is a fifth storey in front, shown in the view, woodcut No. 22, to the right, a little detached, but which may have been intended to be connected with and made part of the original design. The lowest of the four connected storeys is so entirely unfinished, and we cannot even guess what form it was ultimately intended to take, and how far it might be extended towards a lower one still, which certainly was commenced to the right, and may have been intended to extend across the whole front.

When describing the Râni kâ Nûr at Udayagiri, it was suggested that the three sides of the court were really intended to represent the three sides of a pyramidal Vihara turned inside out. If this cave at Undavilli is carefully examined, it seems almost certain that it equally represents three sides of a similar building, its centre being three intercolumniations in width. The sides on the second storey having, or being intended to have, five, which was a greater number than it was possible to give to the centre from its situation, flattened out on the rock. In the third storey they were all reduced to three intercolumniations, and the uppermost storey of all was only the dome which all the Viharas had, flattened out. These storeys in a structural Vihara would be in wood. The lowest only, if I am correct, in stone, and consequently more solid, and not admitting of the same minute sub-divisions. To all these points we shall have occasion to revert presently when describing the Mahâvallipur Raths, but this cave is almost equally interesting, as a copy of a pre-existing form of building, but not being carved out of an isolated block, it is flattened out into a façade, which is not at first sight so obviously a copy of a Vihara as they are. Notwithstanding this, however, it seems hardly to admit of any doubt, that though so essentially Brahmanical in its dedication, this cave is intended for as literal a copy as could well be made, in the rock, of one of the Buddhist Viharas that must have abounded in the neighbourhood at the time it was executed. Even if we did not know from Hiuen Thsang's account how essentially Bejwara was a Buddhist colony in the seventh century, the ruins at Amrâvatî would be quite sufficient to show that every form of Buddhist architecture, in all probability, existed on the spot at the time it was excavated, and, as we gather from the result, were the only models the Hindus, at that time, had to copy, when designing structures for their own intruding faith.

To these points we shall revert presently, but meanwhile to finish our description of this cave the following particulars based upon Mr. Sewell's plans and report.[1]

The front of the lower storey extends about 90 feet in length, and the excavation has been carried inward to various depths, leaving portions of three rows of massive square stone pillars partially hewn out. On this façade was carved an inscription in one line in the Vengî character "of about the seventh or eighth century."

The second floor is of much greater area, and has originally consisted of four separate apartments; a door has been broken through the dividing wall between the third and fourth, thus throwing them practically into one apartment. The façades of these four apartments represent—if my theory of the design is correct—the four fronts that would have been found in the second storey of a structural Vihara, though in that case they would have surrounded only one hall instead of four, as is the case here. The south or left side hall is about 19½ feet square, the roof being supported by two plain pillars in front and two inside, all with heavy bracket capitals. At the back is a shrine cell, 10 feet square, with a *vêdi* or altar in the centre, and a runnel for water round it, for the conveyance of which to the outside a small channel was cut under the middle of the threshold. The front of this hall is ascended to by eight steps from a platform 10½ feet broad, in front of it.

[1] Report by Mr. R. Sewell, M.C.S., issued by Government of Madras, 1st Nov. 1878, No. 1620, Pub. Dep., on which and the plans prepared by Mr. Peters, together with the notes of Sir Walter Elliot (*Ind. Ant.*, vol. v. p. 80), this account is based.

Outside is a cell in the left end of the platform, 6½ feet by 4½, and behind it a still smaller one, measuring only 3 feet by 2. On the rock above is a frieze of elephants and lions.

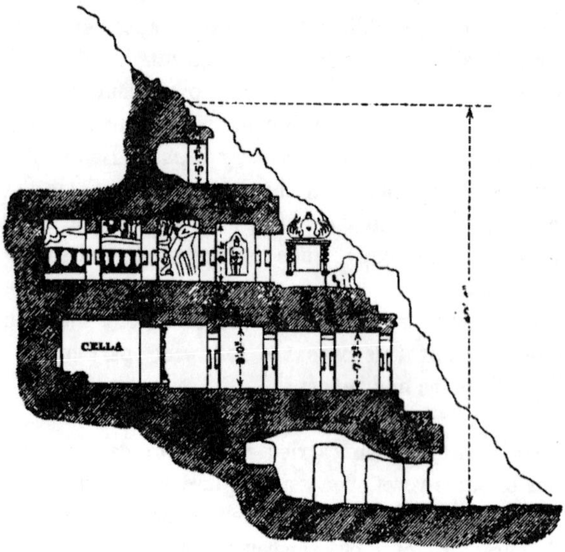

No. 24. Section of the Undavilla Cave, from a Drawing by Mr. Peters. Scale 20 feet to 1 inch.

The façade above the hall has a frieze of geese; above this is a heavy projecting member, having the *Chaitya*-window ornament; and above this a row of five protuberances too weatherworn to be recognisable; and over this, again, is a carefully carved diaper pattern on a flat band. On the rock on the north side of the platform is a long inscription, in Telugu, of the thirteenth century of the Śaka era, recording large donations to the temple. Thus showing that it was still considered sacred in the fourteenth century after Christ. Long after Buddhism had entirely disappeared from India.

To the right of this, and projecting about 10 feet further forward, is the principal or central hall of the whole, 29 ft. 9 in. wide by 31 ft. deep, and varying in height from 7 ft. 3 in. to 8 ft. The roof is supported on sixteen square pillars chamfered in the middle of the shafts, arranged in four parallel rows, with pilasters in line with each row, which are advanced from 2½ to 3½ feet into the cave. At the back is a shrine, about 13½ feet square, with an empty *vêdi* or place for an image against the back wall, as in the Râvaṇa-kâ-Khâi at Elurâ. On each side the shrine door are two standing figures cut in niches, one of them being Nârasiñha or the man-lion *avatâra* of Vishṇu. Over the head of the door is a roll ornament or *toraṇa* held by a pair of *makaras*, or conventional Saurians, and carrying some object in the centre which rests on the back of an animal. On the left side of the hall, at the back, is a deep niche containing a figure of Gaṇêśa, "which, like the others, has been heavily covered with plaster."

The four pillars in the back row are much weatherworn, and some of them are broken away. They have been sculptured with arabesques and lotuses, and on one a group of a man and his wife with a female attendant. The pillars in the next and front rows are almost entirely destroyed also. The bases and capitals of the second row are covered with lotuses, animal and human figures, &c., one group containing a figure of Mâruti or Hanuman. Outside, on a portion of the rock face, is an elephant, with a man supporting its trunk.

The third apartment has originally consisted of two rooms, that on the left measuring 19 ft. 9 in. wide by 17 ft. 7 in. deep, and its roof supported by four pillars bearing arabesque and lotus ornaments. At the back is a cell, 11 feet square, with a pedestal for the image. The other room was 17½ feet deep by 13½ wide, and has also a shrine, 4 feet square, with *dwârpâlas* or doorkeepers at the entrance to it. On the west wall is a sculpture (perhaps of Vishṇu in Vaikuntha) in which the principal male figure is seated on a couch with his wives and attendants, and with musical performers represented in front. The four pillars of this room have also arabesque and lotus ornaments on their capitals.

A stair in the left side of the large hall leads up to the third storey, and lands in a great hall, 52 ft. 9 in. long by 30 ft. 3 in. deep, including the verandah, which is arranged on the same plan as the Bâdâmi caves. First there is a long verandah, with six pillars and two pilasters in front; then in the back of the verandah, separating it from the hall, are four pillars in the middle, and a wall at each end extending the length of the opening between a pair of pillars, and carved in front with a *dwârpâla*. The hall itself, about 8 feet high has two rows of six pillars each from end to end. There is no shrine in the back wall, but a cell, 12 ft. 9 in. square, in the left end. The pillars that support the hall are square masses, the corners of the middle section of each having been chamfered off so as to make that portion of each octagonal. On the front sides of the upper portions of each have been sculptured the *avatâras* of Vishṇu, and other figures; the lower portions bearing elephants and *siṅhas* or lions. At the left end of the back wall, and partly on the return of the end wall, is a figure of Vishṇu, as represented in the left end of the great cave at Bâdâmi, seated on the body of the serpent Ânanta, while the hoods of the snake overshadow his head. He is four armed, holding the *śankha* and *chakra* emblems in his hands, and is attended by Lakshmî. At the sides were thirteen figures, each about 2 feet high, listening to his discourse or worshipping him, but two of them are broken away. The local Brahmans call it "Vishṇu and the Ṛishis." In the right end wall of this hall has been cut a gigantic recumbent figure of Nârâyaṇa, 17 feet long, resting on Śesha, the great serpent, whose seven hoods canopy his head (woodcut 24). At his feet are two colossal figures, 8 feet high, and above and below the extended arm of Vishṇu are attendant figures, with Brahmâ seated on the lotus that springs from Vishṇu's navel.

In front of the verandah is a platform, 48 feet long by 19½ feet broad, forming part of the roof of the storey below. On the northern half sits a fat male figure similar to what is found on some of the roofs of Kailâsa, and on the hall in front of the Dâśa Avatâra at Elurâ; on each side of him is a lion. On the southern half have been similar figures, but only the bases remain.

The upper storey is reached by a series of steps in the rock at the left or south side. It represents the circular or domical termination which crowns every square pyramidal temple, in the Dravidian style of architecture, in the south of India, without a single exception, so far as I know. Here it is of course flattened out to meet the exigencies of rock construction, but all its features are easily recognisable, and are identical with those found elsewhere. It stands on a plain platform over the roof of the verandah of the third storey with three circular cells or shrines in the back wall with a bench round each. They are apparently unfinished, but their existence here is interesting, as showing that the upper storey or domical part of these Viharas was intended to be inhabited. As it happens that at Mahâvallipur they are solid we have no other absolute proof that this was the case.

"Along the base and sides of this hill," according to Mr. Boswell,[1] "there are remains of a considerable number of rock-caves and temples, evidently of Buddhist origin." "There is a rock-temple in two storeys close to the village, which has recently been utilised as a granary." "In various places the figures of elephants and other animals in the Buddhist style of representation[2] are to be seen depicted. At one place there is a Mantapam or porch cut out of the rock and supported by stone pillars, more solitary cells, and lastly a rock temple (that of Undavilli) in four storeys of considerable proportions."

Among these it may hereafter be possible for some one thoroughly familiar with the details of Buddhist architecture to identify the "*grande caverne*" in which, according to the traditions reported by the Chinese pilgrim Hiuen Thsang, Bhâvaviveka resided awaiting the coming of Maitreya Buddha to dissipate his doubts.[3]

There is, however, nothing about this Undavilli cave that could have been considered as old in Hiuen Thsang's time, and there is no form or feature about it that could at any time be ascribed to the Buddhists, while from the nature of its plan, and its being constructed in the rock, it is impossible that all the Buddhist details—if they ever existed—could have been so altered and obliterated as to be no longer recognisable. We may say we now know exactly what the Rock-cut Architecture of the Buddhists was during the seventh and eighth centuries to which this cave certainly belongs, and it was not like this. At the same time, if the date assigned to the Raths at Mahâvallipur, to be described in the next chapter, is correct, we may feel equal confidence in asserting that we know what the style was, which the Hindus adopted in the south of India,

---

1 *Report to the Madras Government*, 1870.

2 It is difficult to say what the "Buddhist style of representation" of an elephant really is. There is a large bas-relief of an elephant at Ajaṇṭâ and two others at Kuḍâ in Buddhist caves, and many smaller ones on friezes; in the Hindu Kailâsa, at Elura, there are many in *alto-rilievo*, and two free standing; there are four or five free standing ones at Ambâ, a bas-relief at Karusâ, and there was a colossal free standing one at Elephanta, all Brahmanical; one free standing one and several in bas-relief at Mahâvallipur; and there is a free standing one and many heads, &c. in the Jaina temples at Elura, but no antiquary can show that each sect had its "style" of representing elephants. The carving of all figures varies more or less with the age in which they were executed, but "elephants" less than almost any other figure, and usually they are better carved than any other animal.

3 *Mémoires sur les Cont. Occid.*, tom. ii. p. 110. It is to be remarked that Hiuen Thsang says he "rested in the palace of the *Asuras*," not in a Buddhist temple.

at the time when these caves were excavated, and it is as nearly as may be identical with what we find here. Everything about this cave is Hindu, and belongs to that religion, and is comparatively modern—almost certainly after Hiuen Thsang's time. It is, in fact, like the Kailâsa at Elurâ, only another instance of the manner in which the Hindus about the eighth century appropriated Buddhist sites, and superseded their rock-cut temples by others belonging to their own form of faith. They, however, differ so essentially in many important particulars, that with a little familiarity, it seems impossible to mistake the one for the other. If this is so, it is clear that this Undavilli cave never could have belonged to the Buddhists. It is as essentially Brahmanical as any of the caves belonging to that sect at Badâmî or Elurâ, of about the same age, though by a curious inversion of the usual routine, its forms are as certainly copied from those of Buddhist vihâras, like the raths at Mahâvallipur, to be described in the next chapter. Proving as clearly as can well be done, that at the age when they were excavated, the Brahmins in the south of India had no original style of their own, and were consequently forced to borrow one from their rivals.

CHAPTER V.

MAHÂVALLIPUR, OR THE SEVEN PAGODAS.[1]

INTRODUCTORY.

With the exception of the caves at Elephanta and Elurâ, there is perhaps no group of rock-cut temples in India which have been so often described, and are consequently so familiar to the English public, as those known as the Seven Pagodas, situated on the sea-shore 35 miles south of Madras. From their being so near and so easily accessible from the capital of the Presidency, they early attracted the attention of the learned in these matters. As long ago as 1772 they were visited by Mr. W. Chambers, who wrote a very reasonable account of them, which appeared in the first volume of the *Asiatic Researches* in 1788. This was followed in the fifth volume of the same publication in 1798, by one by Mr. J. Goldingham. Both of these, however, may be said to have been superseded by one by Dr. Guy Babington in the second volume of the *Transactions of the Royal Asiatic Society* in 1830. He was the first who attempted and succeeded in decyphering the inscriptions found at the place, and the illustrations of his paper, drawn by himself and his friend Mr. Hudleston, are among the best and most trustworthy of any that up to that time had been published of any Indian antiquities. Before his time, however, in 1816, they had attracted the attention of the indefatigable Colonel Colin Mackenzie, and he left a collection of 37 drawings of the architecture and sculpture of the place, which are now, in manuscript, in the India Office library. Like

[1] There seems to be great difficulty in ascertaining what is the proper name of this place. In the beginning of the century it was the fashion to call it Maha Bali puram, which was the name adopted by Col. Mackenzie in his MS., and by Southey in his *Curse of Kehama*. Dr. Babington, in his paper in the second volume of the *Trans. R. A. S.*, states that in the Tamil inscriptions in the Varâhaswâmi Pagoda it is called Mahamalaipur, which he states means "city of the great hill." This is disputed by the Rev. G. Mahon and the Rev. W. Taylor, and they suggest (Carr. 66) Mamallaipur, Mahalaram, &c. I have adopted, as involving no theory, Mahâvallipur, by which it is generally known among Europeans, though far from pretending that it is the real name of the place.

most of his collections of a similar nature, they are incomplete and without any descriptive text, so as to be nearly useless for scientific purposes. These earlier accounts were, however, to a great extent superseded by "A Guide to the Sculptures, Excavations, &c. at Mâmallaipur, by Lieut. J. Braddock," which appeared in the *Madras Journal of Literature and Science* in 1844[1] (vol. xiii). As this was based on personal knowledge, and he was assisted in the task by such experts as the Reverend G. W. Mahon, the Reverend W. Taylor, and Sir Walter Elliot, it contained, as might be expected, all that was then known on the subject. Unfortunately, however, it was not accompanied by maps or plans, nor, in fact, with any illustration, so that, except to those visiting the spot, it is of comparatively little use.[2]

All these—except the Mackenzie MS.—which may be considered the scientific illustrations of the subject, were collected by a Captain Carr, under the auspices and at the expense of the Madras Government. These were published in 1869 in a separate volume, with several additional tracts, and with reproductions of such illustrations as were then available, and a map of the locality reduced from the Revenue Survey, which is the best by far that has yet been published. As a manual for reference this work is certainly convenient, but as its editor had no real knowledge of the subject, and no special qualification for the task, it adds little, if anything, to what was previously known regarding the place; while by rejecting Lieutenant Braddock's numbers, and adopting new ones of his own, scattered broadcast over his map, without any system, he has added considerably to the confusion previously existing in the classification of the various objects enumerated.

In addition to these more scientific attempts at description, the place has been visited by numerous tourists, who have recorded their

---

[1] I visited the spot in 1841, and my account of the antiquities was first published in the eighth volume of the *Journal of the Royal Asiatic Society* in 1843, and afterwards republished with a folio volume of illustrations in 1845.—J. F.

[2] The plans and sections used to illustrate this chapter are taken from a very complete set of illustrations of these Raths made for me, at his own expense, by Mr. R. Chisholm, Superintendent of the Government School of Art at Madras. They are all to a large scale—2 feet to 1 inch—and are not only correct but full of detail beautifully drawn. They are in fact a great deal more than can be utilised in a work like this, but I hope may some day form the foundation of a monograph of these most interesting monuments.

impressions of the place in more or less detail. Among these, none was more impressed with their importance than Bishop Heber, who described them with his usual taste and discrimination; and Mrs. Maria Graham, in her journal and letters, devotes a considerable space to them, and perhaps done as much as any one to render them popular with general readers.[1] Several views of them were published by Daniel in the beginning of this century. These, however, have lately been superseded by photographs, of which several sets have lately been made and published. The most complete is by Dr. A. Hunter, late Director of the Government School of Art at Madras. They were also photographed by Captain Lyon for the Madras Government. But the best that have yet been done are by Mr. Nicholas, of Madras, which are superior to any that have hitherto reached this country.

Notwithstanding all that has been said and written about them, there is no group of rock-cut temples in India regarding whose age or use it has hitherto been so difficult to predicate anything that is either certain or satisfactory. They are, in fact, like the Undavilli cave just described, quite exceptional, and form no part of any series in which their relative position could be ascertained. They certainly had no precursors in this part of the country, and they contain no principle of development in themselves by which their progress might be compared with that of any other series; one of the most singular phenomena regarding them being, that though more various in form than any other group, they are all of the same age, or at least so nearly so that it is impossible to get any sequence out of them. The people, whoever they were, who carved them seem suddenly to have settled on a spot where no temples existed before, and to have set to work at once and at the same time to fashion the detached boulders they found on the shore into nine or ten raths or miniature temples. They undertook simultaneously to pierce the sides of the hill with thirteen or fourteen caves; to sculpture the great bas-relief known as the penance of Arjuna; and to carve elephants, lions, bulls, and other monolithic emblems

[1] At the end of Capt. Carr's book two pages (pp. 230, 231) are devoted to the bibliography of the subject, which is the most original and among the most useful in his publication.

out of the granite rocks around them. But what is even more singular, the whole were abandoned as suddenly as they were undertaken. Of all the antiquities on the spot not a single one is quite finished; some are only blocked out, others half carved, but none quite complete. When, however, we come to ask who were the people who were seized with this strange impulse, and executed these wonderful works, history is altogether silent. They must have been numerous and powerful, for in the short interval that elapsed between their inception and abandonment they created works which, considering the hardness of the granite[1] rocks in which they were executed, may fairly be termed gigantic. Yet there is no trace of any city in the neighbourhood which they could have inhabited, and from whose ruins or whose history, we might get a hint of their age, or of the motives that impelled them to undertake to realize these vast and arduous conceptions.

There are, it is true, numerous inscriptions on the raths, from which, being in Sanskrit, we gather that the people who engraved them probably came from the north, but they consist only of epithets of the gods over whose images they are written, and only one name of a mortal man can be gleaned from them all. Eventually, when the numerous inscriptions in the Madras Presidency are decyphered, we may come to know who Atiranachanda Pallava may have been.[2] At present we only know that it does not occur anywhere else; but we gather indistinctly from it that the Pallavas lived before the rise of the Chôla race, in the 10th and 11th centuries of our era. Chôla inscriptions in the Tamil language, recording gifts to these temples, occur on several of the rocks in this neighbourhood,[3] and tell us at least that, at that time, they had superseded the people who executed these wonderful carvings.

In the absence of any real knowledge on the subject, the natives, who are never at a loss on such occasions, have invented innumerable fables and legends to account for what they did not understand. Some of these "guesses at truth" may be, and probably are, not far from the truth; but none of them, unless confirmed from other

[1] The proper description of the stone I believe to be quartzo-felspathic gneiss.

[2] The Pallavas are distinctly mentioned as ruling in Kânchîpura (Conjeveram) in an inscription dated 635 A.D. See *Indian Antiquary*, vol. viii., p. 245.

[3] *See* Sir Walter Elliot's paper in *Madras Journal*, vol. xiii., reprinted in Carr's compilation, pp. 132 *et seq.*

sources, can be considered as authentic history. It may also be added, that we are here deprived of one very common indication of age, for the stone out of which these monuments are carved is so hard that it shows no sign of weathering or decay, so as to give a hint of their relative antiquity from that cause; all are fresh as the day they were executed, and the chisel marks appear everywhere as if executed only a few days ago.

Under these circumstances it is hardly to be wondered at that authors have not been able to agree on any certain date for the execution of the works at Mahâvallipur. Some have been inclined to believe, with Sir Walter Elliot, that they could not well have been made later than the 6th century.[1] Others to side with the Rev. W. Taylor, who "would place them (loosely speaking) between the 12th and 16th centuries of our reckoning."[2] It was not, in fact,[3] till the publication of Mr. Burgess's account of the caves at Elephanta in 1871,[4] and of his still more important researches at Bâdâmi in 1874,[5] that the public had any real data from which to draw any conclusions. To these have been added his subsequent investigations among the Brahmanical caves at Elurâ and along the whole western coast of India, so that now our knowledge of that branch of cave architecture may be said to be tolerably complete. Hitherto attention has been mainly confined to the Buddhist caves; they were infinitely more numerous, and extending through a period of nearly 1,000 years—from B.C. 250 to A.D. 750—it was easy to arrange them in a chronometric series, in which their relative age could be ascertained with very tolerable certainty. It still, however, remained uncertain when the Brahmans first adopted the practice of carving temples and caves out of the living rock, and the data were insufficient to allow of their sequence being made out with the same clearness as existed in the case of the Buddhist caves. The discovery,

---

1 Carr's compilation, p. 127, reprinted from *Madrâs Journal*, vol. xiii.

2 *Loc. cit.*, p. 114.

3 When I first wrote on the subject, I felt inclined, for reasons given, to place them as late as Mr. Taylor (say 1300 A.D.), but from further experience in my later writings I have been more inclined to adopt Sir Walter Elliot's view. It now appears, as is so often the case, that the truth lies somewhere between these two extremes.—J. F.

4 The *Rock Temples of Elephanta or Gharipuri*, by James Burgess, Bombay, Thacker Vining, & Co., 1871.

5 *Report of Operations in the Belgâm and Kaladgi Districts in* 1874, London, India Museum, and Allen & Co., 1874.

however, of a Brahmanical cave dated in 579 A.D. at Bâdâmi[1] first gave precision to these researches, and with the dates, approximatively ascertained, of the temples at Pattadkal and Aiholê, made the fixation of that of the Kailâsa at Elurâ and other temples of that class as nearly certain as those of the Buddhist caves in juxtaposition with them. This was all-important for the fixation of the date of the rock-cut structures at Mahâvallipur, where, though the architectural forms, as we shall presently see, are exclusively Buddhist, there is not one single emblem or one mythological illustration that belongs to that religion. Everything there is Brahmanical, and executed by persons wholly devoted to that creed, and who, so far as their works there bear testimony, might be supposed never to have heard of the religion of the mild Ascetic.

Another source of information which is almost as important for our present purposes has only, even more recently been made available, by the publication of Mr. Arthur Burnell's researches in the Palæography of Southern Indian alphabets.[2] Hitherto we have been mainly dependent on those published by James Prinsep in 1838,[3] but they were compiled mainly from northern sources, and besides the science has acquired very great additional precision during the last forty years. It may consequently be now employed in approximating dates, without much fear of important errors arising from its application for such purposes, provided the geographical position of the inscription and all the local peculiarities are carefully attended to.

There are other minor indications bearing on this point which will be alluded to in the sequel, but for our present purpose it may be sufficient to state that both Mr. Burnell and Mr. Burgess agree in fixing the year 700 A.D. as a mean date about which the temples and sculptures at Mahâvallipur were most probably executed. It may be 50 years earlier or later. On the whole it seems more probable that their date is somewhat earlier than 700, but their execution may have been spread over half a century or even more, so that absolute precision is impossible in the present state of the evidence. Still until some fixed date or some new information is afforded, 650 to 700 may probably be safely relied upon as very

---

[1] *Report on Belgâm and Kalâdgi*, p. 24.

[2] *Researches in the Palæography of the Alphabets of Southern India*, by Arthur Burnell, M.C.S., 2nd edit., Trübner, London, 1879.

[3] *J. A. S. B.*, vol. vii. p. 277.

nearly that at which the granite rocks at Mahâvallipur were carved into the wondrous forms which still excite our admiration there.

If this date can be established,—and there seems no reason for doubting its practical correctness,—the first and most interesting inference we derive from it, is that as all the rock-cut structures at Mahâvallipur are in what is known as the Dravidian style of architecture of the south of India, they are the earliest known examples of that style. The proofs of this proposition are of course mainly of a negative character, and may, consequently, be upset by any new discovery, but this at least is certain, that up to the present moment no more ancient buildings in that style of architecture have yet been brought to light. No one has in writing described any one that can lay claim to an earlier date, and no photograph or drawing has exhibited any more Archaic form of architecture in the south of India, and so far at least as my researches extend, none such exist. The conclusion from this seems inevitable that all the buildings anterior to the year 700 or thereabouts, were erected in wood or with some perishable materials, and have perished either from fire or from causes which in that climate so soon obliterate any but the most substantial erections constructed with the most imperishable materials.

This conclusion is, it must be confessed somewhat unexpected and startling, inasmuch as it has just been shown from Aśoka's lâts, and from the rails at Buddha Gaya, and Bharhut, that stone was used for architectural and ornamental purposes in the north of India for nearly 1,000 years before the date just quoted, and though we might naturally expect a more recent development in the south the interval seems unexpectedly great. What makes this contrast of age even more striking is, the fact that in the neighbouring island of Ceylon stone architecture was practised in considerable perfection even before the Christian era. The great Ruanwelli Dagoba was erected by King Duttugaimani between the year 161 and 137 B.C., and the Thuparamya even earlier by King Devananpiatissa, the contemporary of Aśoka—and both these exhibit a considerable amount of skill and richness in stone ornamentation.[1] Still facts are stubborn things, and until some monuments are discovered in Dravida Deśa, whose dates can be ascertained to be earlier than the end of the seventh century, we must be content to accept the

---

[1] *History of Indian Architecture*, p. 188, *et seq.*

fact, that the rock-cut temples at Mahâvallipur are the earliest existing examples of the style, and must be content to base our reasoning, for the present at least, upon that assumption.

The rock-cut remains at Mahâvallipur may be divided into three very distinct classes. First there are nine Raths or Rathas,[1] small isolated shrines or temples each cut out of a single block or boulder of granite.

Second, there are thirteen or fourteen caves excavated in a rocky ridge of very irregular shape, running north and south parallel with the shore, at a distance of half-a-mile inland, and two more at a place called Sâluvankuppam about two miles further north.

Third, there are two great bas-reliefs,[2] one wholly of animals, and a number of statues of elephants, lions, bulls, and monkeys, each carved out of separate blocks.

No. 25. General View of the Rathas Mahâvallipur, from a sketch by the Author.

[1] *Ratha*, from a root meaning "to move," "to run," is the Sanskrit word for a wheeled vehicle, chariot, or car of a god. The Tamil word is *Têr*.

[2] Perhaps the sculpture in the Krishna Mantapan ought to be enumerated as a third bas-relief, but it is under the cover of a porch, and there are no signs of any such being intended to cover the great bas-relief known as Arjuna's penance.

CHAPTER VI.

RATHAS, MAHÂVALLIPUR.

The five principal Rathas, which are by far the most interesting objects here, are situated close together on the sandy beach, at some little distance to the southward of the hill in which the caves are excavated. They bear names borrowed from the heroes of the Mahâbhârata, but these are quite modern appellations applied from the popular belief that everything rock-cut, as in fact whose origin is mysterious, was executed by the Pândavas during their exile. In consequence of this the most southern of the Raths is called that of Dharmarâja, the next that of Bhîma, the third that of Arjuna, and the fourth that of Draupadî, the wife of the five Pândavas. These four are situated in one line, extending about 160 feet north and south, but whether cut out of a continuous ridge, and only separated by art, or whether each was a separate boulder, cannot now be ascertained. My impression is that it originally was a single ridge rising to a height of about 40 feet at its southern end, and sinking to about half that height at its northern extremity, probably with fissures between each block now formed into a Rath, but hardly separated otherwise, from each other. The fifth, called after the twins Sahadeva and Nakula, is situated a little to the westward of the other four, and quite detached.

The sixth, the Ganesa Rath[1] is situated near the northern end of the rocky ridge at a distance of three-fourths of a mile from the southern group, and near it are the remaining three, but they are merely commenced, and so incompletely blocked out, that their intended form can hardly be ascertained, and all that need be said of them is that they are in the same style, and evidently of the same age as the other six.

[1] Sometimes, but improperly, called Arjunas rath, a mistake first, I believe, made by Mrs. Graham, but especially to be avoided, as another Rath bears that name, and the confusion is quite sufficient already without this additional complication.

Ganesa Ratha.

As the Ganeśa Ratha is the most nearly finished of any, it may be as well to begin with it, though it would be rash to say it is in consequence, the earliest. It does seem probable, however, that the masons would first select a suitable block among the many that exist, on the hill, for an experiment, before attempting the much more serious undertaking of fashioning the southern ridge or group into the Rathas bearing the Pându names.

As will be seen from the annexed woodcut the Ganeśa Ratha is, though small, a singularly elegant little temple. In plan its dimensions are 19 feet by 11 feet 3 inches, and its height 28 feet. It is in three storeys with very elegant details, and of a form very common afterwards in Dravidian architecture for gopuras, or gateways, but seldom used for temples, properly so called, in the manner which we find employed in this instance.

No. 26. View of the Ganeśa Ratha, from a Photograph.

The roof is a straight line, and was adorned at either end by a triśula ornament, and similar emblems adorned four at least of the dormer windows that cut into it. It is, however, no longer the triśula of the Buddhist, but an early form of the trident of Śiva, who is the god principally worshipped in this place. Between the tridents the ridge is ornamented with nine pinnacles in the form of vases, which also continue to be the ornaments used in similar situations to the present day. The roof itself is pointed, both internally and externally, in a manner entirely suitable to the wooden construction from which it is copied. It is true that in most of the western caves the internal form of these roofs is of a circular section, but externally there always is and must have been a ridge, to throw off the rain water, so as to make the external form an ogee, and so it is always represented. In some instances, as the Son Bhandar cave at Râjgir (woodcut No. 7) and at Sita Marhi (woodcut No. 11), the internal form was also pointed, and so I fancy it generally was in the wooden structures from which these Raths were copied.

Like all the many storeyed buildings of this class with which we are acquainted, this temple diminishes upwards in a pyramidal form, the offsets being marked by ranges of small simulated cells, such as no doubt existed in Buddhist viharas on a large scale, and were thus practically the cells in which the monks resided, or at least slept. In this instance they are more subdued than is usually the case, but throughout the whole range of Dravidian architecture, to the present day, they form the most universal and most characteristic feature of the style.

The pillars in the porch of this temple are of a singularly elegant form, but so very little removed from their wooden prototypes as to be very unsuited for the position they here occupy in monolithic architecture. Their capitals, though much more slender, are of the Elephanta type, and their bases are formed by yalis or lions, which are clearly derived from some wooden originals, and are singularly unlike any lithic form (woodcut No. 29). They are, however, the most characteristic features of the architecture of the place, being almost universal at Mahâvallipur, but not found anywhere else, that I know of.

On each side of the entrance there is a dwârpâla or porter, and on the back wall of the verandah is an inscription in a long florid character, dedicated to Śiva, and stating that the work was executed by a king Jayarana Stamba,[1] but his name occurs nowhere else, and we can only guess his age from the form of the alphabet in which it is written, which, as before stated, is certainly not far removed from the year 700.

The image in the small shrine inside is not cut in the rock, but of

[1] *Trans. R. A. S.*, vol. ii. p. 266, Plate 14, Carr. pp. 57 and 201.

a separate stone, and has been brought and placed there, instead of a lingam, which in all probability, originally occupied the sanctuary.

Draupadi's Ratha.

The first or most northern of the great group of Raths bearing the name of Draupadî is the most completely finished of the five, probably because it is the smallest, and the simplest in its details.

No. 27. Draupadi's Ratha, from a Photograph.

It is square in plan, measuring only 11 feet each way, and with a curvilinear roof rising to about 18 feet in height.[1] Above this there evidently was a finial of some sort, but being formed from a detached stone it has been removed or fallen down, and its form cannot now be ascertained, unless indeed the original could be found by digging in the sand, where it now probably remains. It would, however, be very interesting if it could be found, as the Rath is now unique of its kind, but must have belonged to an extensive class of buildings when it was executed, and their form consequently becomes important in the history of the style.

[1] I have frequently been inclined to suggest that this little Ratha, which in reality only simulates a Buddhist hermitage or Pansala, contains in itself the germs from which the Hindu Vimâna or spire was afterwards formed. The square base, the overhanging roof, its curvilinear form, are all found here, and nowhere else that I am aware of. The gulf, however, that exists between such a cell as this and such a temple as that at Bhuvaneśwar, built on the same coast, and nearly at the same age, is so enormous that one hesitates before putting it forward, even as an hypothesis. All that can be said at present is, that it contains more elements for a solution, than any thing that has yet been put forward, to explain the difficulty.

There is a small cell in the interior, measuring 6 ft. 6 in. in depth from the outer wall to the back of the statue, and 4 ft. 6 in. across. At the back is a statue of Lakshmî, the consort of Vishṇu, standing on a lotus, four-armed, and bearing the chakra and other emblems in her hand. Two figures are represented as worshipping her, one on either side, and above are four Gandharvas, or flying figures, two of them with moustaches, and bearing swords.[1] On either side of the doorway are two female dwârpâlas, and there are also several similar figures in niches on either side, most of them females.

Over the doorway is a curious carved beam of a very wooden pattern, which is principally interesting here, as one nearly identical exists, belonging to the cave called Kapal Iśwara, on the rocky hill nearly opposite, proving incontestably, as in fact all its architecture does, that the cave, like everything else here, is of the same age as this Rath.

Bhima's Ratha.

In order to avoid repetition, it will probably be more convenient to pass over for the present Arjuna's Ratha, which comes next in the series locally, and to describe that in conjunction with the one bearing the name of Dharmarâja, which it resembles in every essential particular, the one being a copy of a three-storeyed the other of a four-storeyed Buddhist Vihara. If this is done the next will be that called Bhîma's Ratha, which is the largest of the group. It belongs to the same style as the Ganeśa temple just described, except that, as in the two last mentioned examples, the conditions as to size are reversed; the smaller, the Ganeśa, is a three-storeyed, while Bhîma's is a two-storeyed Dharmaśâlâ or hall of assembly.

Its dimensions in plan are 48 feet in length by 25 in breadth, and it is about 26 feet in height. As will be seen from the annexed plan, it is a little difficult to say what its disposition internally may have been intended to have been if completed The centre was occupied by a hall measuring 9 or 10 feet by 30, open certainly on one, probably on both sides, and as probably intended to be closed at both ends.

---

[1] A representation of this sculpture will be found *Trans. R. A. S.*, vol. ii. Plate X. Fig. 1. It is reproduced by Carr with the same references.

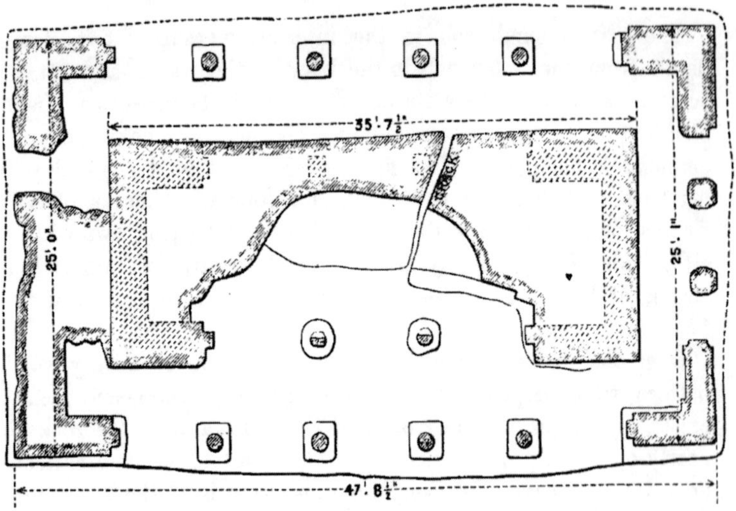

No. 28. Plan of Bhima's Ratha, from a plan by R. Chisholm. Scale 10 feet to 1 inch.[1]

It is, however, by no means clear that the eastern wall was intended to be removed and pillars substituted for it. In the account of the hall in which the first convocation was held, it is stated in the *Mahawanso*,[2] that the priest who read Bana, or the prayers, did so from a splendid pulpit at one end of the hall, but the president was seated in the centre of one side facing the assembly. The same disposition is described by Spence Hardy[3] and M. Bigandet,[4] and would exactly suit such a hall as this, supposing the wall on one side to remain solid, but would be inconvenient and unlikely, if it were removed and pillars substituted. As the *Mahawanso* was probably describing (in the fifth century) some ordinary form of Buddhist ecclesia, or hall of assembly, it seems not unlikely that this was the type of those in use at that time, and consequently that the wall on one side was solid and not pierced, except, perhaps, by doors.

This central hall was surrounded by a verandah measuring 5 feet 3 inches in the clear on the sides, but only 3 feet at the ends.

---

[1] The dotted lines on this plan represent suggested modes in which the rath might have been completed if finished as intended.

[2] Turnour's Translation, p. 12.

[3] *Eastern Monachism*, p. 175.

[4] *Life of Gaudama*, p. 354.

Assuming, however, that the hall was open on both sides, there would then be twelve pillars in the centre and two at each end. One of these is represented in the annexed woodcut, and they are all of the same pattern, which, in fact, with very slight modification, is universal at Mahâvallipur. They all have bases representing Yâlis and conventional lions, with spreading capitals, and of proportions perfectly suited to a building of the dimensions of this one, if executed in wood. So little experience, however, had the Pallavas, or whoever undertook these works, in the material they were employing, that they actually set to work to copy literally a wooden building in granite. The consequence was, that even before they had nearly completed the excavation of the lower storey, the immense mass of material left above, settled, and cracked the edifice in all directions, and to such an extent as to necessitate the abandonment of the works, while they were in even a less finished state than those connected with the other Rathas. Not only is there a crack of some inches in width, right through the rock, but several of the little simulated cells have slipped down for want of support, and give the whole a ruined, as well as an unfinished aspect.

No. 29. Pillar from Bhima's Ratha, from a drawing by R. Chisholm.

The upper storey or clerestory, as we would call it in a Gothic building, with its five windows,—one over each intercolumniation,—is so nearly complete as to enable us to realise perfectly what was the structural form it was intended to imitate, but nothing to indicate with what material the roof of the original was covered. The most probable suggestion seems to be, that it was with thatch, though the thickness seems scarcely sufficient for that purpose, and metal could hardly have been laid on without rolls, or something to indicate the joinings. On the other hand, it is hardly conceivable that they could frame carpentry so solidly. as to admit of their roofs being coated with plaster or chunam, without cracking, to such an extent as to admit the rain. As represented here it consisted of a solid mass, about a foot in thickness, formed into a pointed arch with barge boards at the ends. It may have been thatched, but judging from the construction simulated both at the ends and sides, the roof must have been strongly framed in timber, both longitudinally and transversely.[1] Its ridge was intended to be ornamented as in the Ganeśa temple, with a range of vases or kalasas, here 18 in number. All of these, however, with the two ornaments at either end—Triśuls—have all disappeared, if they ever existed. It is probable, it was intended to add them in separate

---

[1] Curiously enough exactly the same difficuly arises with reference to the Lycian tombs, which resemble the Indian rock-cut examples more nearly than any others that are known to exist elsewhere. As will be seen from the annexed woodcut, and the tombs themselves in the British Museum, they present the same close imitation of wooden construction which form so remarkable a peculiarity of the early Buddhist architecture of India. They have the same pointed form of roof, with a ridge, closely resembling the Ganeśa and Bhima Rathas, and the same rafters are shown in the gables which are so universal in the western caves. When, however, we come to inquire how the roof itself was constructed, and how covered, we are again at fault and must wait further information before deciding.

No. 30. Lycian rock-cut Tomb. from a drawing by Forbes and Spratts, Lycia.

Generally it is assumed that these Lycian tombs are ancient, at least belonging to an age immediately succeeding the conquest of the country by Cyrus and Harpagus, but this seems by no means certain. The one illustrated in the woodcut bears a Latin inscription, showing that it was either carved or appropriated for her own use and that of her sisters, by a Roman lady. It is not easy to decide which was the case, inasmuch as it is astonishing how long architectural forms continue to be employed when they become sacred, even after their use or meaning have become obsolete.

stones, like the finial of the Draupadî Rath close by this one. It would have added enormously to the quantity of cutting required, to have carved them in the rock.

Among the sculptures at Bharhut (B.C. 150) there is a bas-relief (*ante* woodcut, No. 10) which not only enables us to realise very completely the form of these halls, but to judge of the changes that took place during the nine centuries that elapsed between their execution. The pillars in the older example are unequally spaced, because on the right hand altar—if it is such—the sculptor wanted room for three hands between the pillars, for four in each of the two central compartments, and for five in that on the right. General Cunningham calls these the thrones of the four last Buddhas,[1] and he may be correct in this, though the reasons for that appellation are not quite evident. The roof of this Rath, as in the Ganeśa, has nine pinnacles, though in this instance they are not vases but mere ornaments. The two end ones are broken off.[2] It is not quite clear from the bas-relief whether the light was introduced into the interior through the dormer windows only, or whether the spaces between the pillars of the clerestory were not also at least partially open. At Mahâvallipur it is quite evident that it was through the windows alone that light was admitted to the interior of the upper storey wherever there was one.

Besides its intrinsic elegance, which is considerable, the great interest that attaches to Bhima's Rath is, as just mentioned, that it is almost certainly the type of such a hall as Ajataśâtru erected in front of the Sattapanni cave at Râjagriha, in order to accommodate the 500 Arhats who were invited to take part in the first convocation, immediately after the death of the founder of the religion. It would require the dimensions in plan of this rath to be doubled to suit it, for that purpose, but a hall 100 feet by 50 would be amply large, and in wood its construction would be a matter of no difficulty. It might be necessary to increase the number of posts supporting the superstructure, but that would improve the appearance of the building without detracting either from its convenience or the amount of accommodation it would afford.

---

1 *Bharhut Stupa*, p. 121, Plate XXXI.

2 It is not quite clear whether the peak on the right hand represents a tenth pinnacle or a finial.

As before mentioned these buildings with straight roofs are very rarely introduced in Dravidian architecture except as gopuras or gateways, but in that form they are nearly universal. Except the one in the village of Mahâvallipur, I know of no instance of this form being used for temples. The straight roofed oblong form is however, sometimes found in the north of India. There is one at Bhuvaneśwar called Kapila Devi or Vitala Dewal,[1] and another in the fort at Gwalior,[2] but they are very rare, and I do not know of any cave except the Dherwara at Elurâ (Plate LIX.) and another at Kanheri (Plate LIV.), which can fairly be said to represent such a hall as Bhîma's Rath. The Kanheri example is especially interesting, as the plan more nearly resembles that of the hall erected to accommodate the first convocation at Râjagriha (*ante* page 49) than that of any other caves now known to exist in India. The square forms of the halls of the Viharas may have been found more convenient and more appropriate to rock-cut dwellings, and thus prevented the oblong form of such a hall as this being repeated, especially in the rock, where it was impossible to enter at both ends, or to light it from both sides.

Arjuna and Dharmaraja's Rathas.

The two Rathas bearing the names of Arjuna and Dharmarâja, the second and fourth in this row, are identical in so far as their architectural ordinance and general appearance is concerned, the only difference being that the first named is very much smaller than the other. They in fact form a pair, and represent on a small scale the three and four storeyed Viharas of the Buddhists, in the same manner that the Ganeśa temple and Bhîma's Ratha may be taken as representations of the halls, or Śhâlâs, which were adapted for ecclesiastical purposes by the votaries of the same religion from the earliest times to which we can go back.

Arjuna's Ratha, though so very different in design, is very nearly of the same dimensions as that of Draupadî, which stands next to it. In plan it is a square measuring 11 feet 6 inches each way, or with its porch 11 feet 6 inches by 16 feet, and its height is about 20 feet. Inside a cell has been excavated, and though only 4 feet 6 inches by 5 feet, seems to have been the cause why the Ratha is

---

[1] *Picturesque Illustrations of Ancient Architecture in India*, Plate IV.

[2] *History of Indian Architecture*, woodcut 252, page 453.

cracked from top to bottom, and a part of its finial fallen off. The roofs both of the lower and of the first storey of this little temple are ornamented with those ranges of little simulated cells which became the distinguishing characteristics of Dravidian architecture from that day to the present hour, and it is surmounted by a dome, which is an equally universal feature, though whether it is copied from an octagonal apartment, or from a Dâgoba as at Boro Buddor, is not quite clear. There is no image in the sanctuary, though the first gallery is ornamented with 12 statues, three in each face, representing either gods of the Hindu Pantheon or mortals. Some have inscriptions above them, but none of these afford any information, we cannot gather from the statues themselves.

The Ratha bearing the name of Dharmarâja is the most southerly and is the largest and finest of the group, though like everything else about the place it is unfinished. As will be seen from the annexed woodcut its dimensions in plan are 26 feet 9 inches by 28 feet 8 inches, and its height is rather more than 35 feet. It

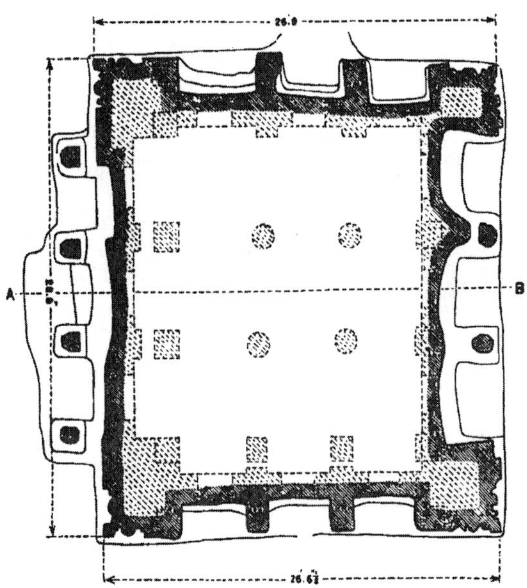

No. 31. Plan of Dharmarâja's Ratha, from a drawing by R. Chisholm. Scale 10 feet to 1 inch.

consequently occupies more than six times the area of Arjuna's Ratha, and is nearly twice as high, but even with these dimensions it can only be considered as a model. It would require to be magnified to twice or three times these dimensions to be a habitable building. The four upper storeys of the Undavilli cave (*ante*, p. 96), which resemble this Ratha more nearly than any other known building, are upwards of 50 feet in height, and they are only on the verge of habitability. The simulated cells there are still too small to be occupied by human beings.

Its general appearance will be seen from the annexed woodcut, from which it will be perceived that it is a building of four storeys arranged in a pyramidal form. The lowest storey, which was also

No. 32. View of Dharmaraja's Ratha, from a Photograph.[1]

the tallest, in the building from which this one is copied, was probably intended to be constructed in stone, as the Gopuras and temples in the south of India almost invariably are, while all the upper or pyramidal parts in them are as generally built with bricks and wood. In this instance, the upper part could only have been constructed with similar materials, and if meant to be inhabited, in wood only. The pillars of the basement all are, or were intended to be slender examples

[1] *History of Indian Architecture*, woodcut 363, p. 645.

of the Elephanta order, (woodcut No. 29), with yalis or conventional lions forming their base. The three upper storeys are all ornamented with those little simulated cells described above, in speaking of the Ganesa temple and Arjuna's Ratha, and which are so universal in the south of India,—there are 16 of these on the first story, 12 on the second, and eight on the third. The front of each of these cells with

No. 33. Elevation of Dharmaraja's Ratha, Mahavellipur. Scale 10 feet to 1 inch. From a Drawing by R. Chisholm.

their connecting links, is adorned with a representation of one of those semicircular dormer windows which are so usual in Buddhist architecture. Here each has a human head represented as if looking outwards. Behind these cells the walls are divided by slender pilasters into tall compartments, and in each of those which would have been an opening in the original building there is now placed the statue of either a deity of the Hindu pantheon, or of some now undistinguishable mortal. Among the gods are found representations of Brahma, Vishṇu, and Śiva, but without any of those extravagances which afterwards deformed the imagery of the Hindu pantheon; none of the gods have more than four arms, and except for this, are scarcely distinguishable from ordinary mortals. The Ardhanâri, a favourite form of Śiva, as half a male half female, occurs several times, and Vishṇu as Narasimha or the boar Avatâr. There is, however, no attempt at a bas-relief or any connected story, and unfortunately none of the inscriptions over these figures, though numerous and easily legible, do more than supply laudatory epithets to the gods over whose heads they are engraved.[1] At each angle of the lower storey which was meant to be solid there are two niches, one of which contains a figure of Śiva or Ardhanâri, and another apparently a Deva, or it may be only a mortal.

The whole of the three upper storeys are perfectly finished externally. But in the present state of the monument it is difficult to say how far it was intended to excavate their interiors. The upper or domical storey was probably intended to be left quite solid, like that of Bhima's Ratha. A cell was, however, excavated to a depth of 5 feet, in the third storey, and it may have been intended to have enlarged it. A similar attempt has been made in the second storey, but carried only to the depth of 4 feet, when it was abandoned. From there being six pilasters on the outside of the third storey, we gather that in a structural building its roof would have been supported by 36 wooden posts, and in like manner that the second storey would have had 64 supports (8 × 8), but of course some of these might have been omitted, especially in the centre, in actual construction, though there probably would be no attempt to copy all these in the rock. From its extreme irregularity it is not so easy to suggest what may have been the intended arrangement of the lowest, but principal storey; but from the wider spacing of its pillars externally, it is evident, that in a structural building stone, and not wood, would have been employed in its construction. From the arrangement of the exterior we gather, with almost perfect certainty, that there would have been four free standing pillars in the centre, as shown in dotted lines in the plan and section. It is not clear, however, how many of the eight piers or pillars that surrounded these

[1] *Trans. R. A. S.*, vol. ii. Plates XVI. and XVII.; *see also* Carr's compilation, p. 224, for Dr. Burnell's transliteration, unfortunately without translation.

No. 34. Section of Dharmarâja Ratha, with the suggested internal arrangements dotted in. Scale 10 feet to 1 inch.

four (woodcut No. 31) were free standing or attached as piers to the external walls. The four in the angles were almost certainly attached to the angle-pieces which in a structural building would have contained the staircases. Practically, therefore, this Ratha seems to have been designed to represent a building having on its lower storey 16 pillars besides piers, standing about 6 feet apart, from centre to centre, and being executed in some durable material. Above this the floors were supported by wooden posts less than half that distance apart. As before remarked, both these dimensions would require to be at least doubled to render them suitable for a habitable Vihâra. Be this as it may, there can be very little doubt that it was the intention of those who designed this Ratha to have excavated the whole of the lower storey. It is probable, however, that, warned by the fate that attended their operations in the case of Bhima's and Arjuna's Raths, they desisted before excavating beyond a few feet on each face; and it is fortunate they did so, for had they proceeded further inwards the mass of rock they must have left above, would certainly have crushed the four slender pillars they intended to leave in the centre, and fissures, if not ruin must have been the result. It may, however, be that some social or political revolution, of which we know nothing, was the cause why this Rath was also left incomplete. It certainly was not any physical cause which led to the abandonment of the works in the caves, or on the bas-reliefs before they were completed, as no danger of crushing existed there. In the case of the raths, however, as physical causes which we can comprehend, seem amply sufficient to account for their unfinished state, it seems hardly worth while to speculate on one of which we know nothing. Those who first attempted to carve these rocks were certainly novices at the trade when they began them, but their experience at Arjuna's and Bhima's Rathas must have taught them that wooden forms were not suited to monolithic masses, and that either they must desist from the undertaking, or must invent forms more appropriate to the material in which they were working.

Although these two last named Rathas are sufficiently interesting as examples of the patient labour which the Indians have at all times been prepared to spend on their religious edifices, their true value, in so far as the history of Indian architecture is concerned, lies in the fact that they are the only known specimens of a form of Buddhist architecture which prevailed in the north of India for probably 1,000 years before they were commenced, and they are the incunabula of thousands of Hindu temples which were erected in the south of India during the 1,000 years that have elapsed since they were undertaken.

To those who are thoroughly familiar with the development of Buddhist architecture during its whole course, few things seem more self-evident than that the upper storeys of these viharas were in wood or some perishable materials, like the Kyongs of Burmah at the present day, and that their forms were pyramidal. It is owing, however, to the first named cause, that there is so much difficulty in making either of these propositions clear to those who have not studied the style in all the countries where it has been practised. The originals having all perished we are left to the careless description of unscientific writers, or to suggestions derived from conventional copies, for our knowledge of what they once were. Still there are some indications which can hardly be mistaken. There is, for instance, Fa Hian's description of the great Dakshina vihara, cut, he says, in the rock. This building had five storeys. The lower was shaped into the form of an Elephant, and had 500 stone cells in it; the second was in the form of a lion, and had 400 chambers; the third was shaped like a horse, and had 300 chambers; the fourth was in the form of an ox, and had 200 chambers; the fifth was in shape like a dove, and had 100 chambers in it.[1] We know perfectly what is meant by the various storeys being said to be in the forms of these animals, because we find them, as, for instance, at Halabîd,[2] superimposed one over another as string courses in the basement of that and other temples in the 13th and 14th centuries. The manner in which this is done there and elsewhere makes it evident that it was a custom in earlier times to adorn the successive storeys of buildings with figures of these animals, in the order enumerated. The point that principally interests us here is, the pyramidal form this vihara is said to have assumed, as indicated by the diminished number of apartments in each storey.

The Lowa Maha Paya or great brazen monastery at Anuradhapura is said, in the *Mahawanso*,[3] to have been originally nine storeys in height, but after being utterly destroyed by Mahasena in 285 A.D., to have been re-erected by his son, but this time with only five storeys instead of nine. The forest of stone pillars, each about 12 feet in height, which once supported it still remain, measuring in plan 250 feet each way, but no remains are found, among them, either of the primitive monastery destroyed by Mahasena, nor of the subsequent erection, which was allowed to go to decay when the city was deserted. This in itself is almost sufficient to prove that the materials of which the superstructure was formed were of a very perishable nature.

It is in Burmah, however, that we see the system carried out to its

---

[1] Beal's *Fa Hian*, pp. 139, 140.

[2] *History of Indian Architecture*, p. 402, woodcut 226.

[3] *Mahawanso*, p. 163. *See also Hist. of Indian Arch.*, p. 195.

fullest extent; but even there it is now only a reflex of what it was in earlier times. There, however, all the Kyongs or Viharas, though generally supported, like the Lowa Maha Paya, on stone posts, have their superstructures, which are three, five, and nine storeys in height, constructed in wood, and all assume the pyramidal form. These differ, of course, from the earlier forms, but not more so than might be expected from their great difference of age. Perhaps, however, the best illustration, for those who know how to interpret it, is the temple of Boro Buddor, in Java. It is a nine-storeyed Vihara, converted from a residence for monks, into a temple for the reception of Buddhist images, and the display of Buddhist sculptures.[1] It is nearly of the same age, perhaps slightly more modern than these Mahâvallipur Raths, and is a perfectly parallel example. In India it is an example of an earlier form, invented for utilitarian purposes, conventionalised into a temple for the worship of the divinities of a hostile religion. In Java of one as completely diverted from its original purpose, though for the glorification of that religion for which the Viharas were originally invented.

It was evidently owing to the perishable nature of the materials with which they were constructed that no remains of any of these many-storeyed Viharas of the Buddhists is now to be found in India. The foundations of several were excavated at Sarnath, near Benares. That one explored by Lieutenant Kittoe, and afterwards by M. Thomas,[2] was apparently only of one storey, the cells surrounding an open court; and the same seems to have been the case with another discovered in cutting through a mound in making the railway near Sultangunge,[3] on the Ganges; and it is a question how far these cloister courts—if they may be so called—were the models for some at least of the rock-cut Viharas in the west. Others, however, have been excavated by General Cunningham,[4] which were evidently the foundations of taller buildings, such as those described by the Chinese pilgrims, and more resembling the Mahâvallipur Raths in design. An opportunity occurred of ascertaining what their forms were when Mr. Broadley was authorised by the Bengal Government to employ 1,000 labourers to excavate what he supposed to be the

---

[1] *History of Indian Architecture*, p. 643 *et seq.*, woodcut 363.

[2] *J. A. S. B.*, vol. xxiii. pp. 469 *et seq.* General Cunningham's *Report*, vol. i. Plate XXXII.

[3] *J. A. S. B.*, vol. xxiii. pp. 360 *et seq.*

[4] *Reports*, vol. i. Plate XXXIII. pp. 120 *et seq.*

Baladitya monastery at Nalanda.[1] He published a plan of this, said to be the result of his excavations, in a pamphlet in 1872, and a restored elevation of the building in the *Journal of the Bengal Asiatic Society* for the same year (Vol. XLI.); but in neither case is it possible to make out what he found, or what he invented, and his text is so confused and illogical that it is impossible from it, to make the one agree with the other, or to feel sure of any of the results he attained. So far as can be made out it was a five-storeyed vihara, measuring about 80 feet square according to the text, though the scale attached to the plan makes it more than 100 feet, and the two lower storeys averaging about 12 feet each, were found to be nearly entire, the height of the ruins still standing being on the different sides 30 or 40 feet. There was a portico on the east with 12 pillars, which led to a cell 22 feet square, in which was found a headless statue of Buddha 4 feet in height. The second storey, 63 feet square, was set back 8 or 9 feet from the lower one, and the whole may have made up five storeys, with a height of about 70 feet, assuming the proportions to have been about those of the Dharmarâja Ratha just described. The upper storey may, however, have assumed a more spire-like form, as was the case in Burmah, and made up the total height of 100 feet, though this is still far from the height of 200 or 300 feet, which Hiuen Thsang ascribes to the building he saw.[2]

From a photograph it appears that the base, for a height of about 5 feet, was adorned with courses of brickwork richly moulded, and above that with a range of niches 3 feet 3 inches in height, between pilasters 4 feet 6 high. These bore a cornice in moulded

---

[1] I am unable to ascertain how far these excavations are coincident with those of Captain Marshall in 1871. The latter are described by General Cunningham, vol. i. of his *Reports*, p. 33, but he does not, so far as I am aware, allude to Mr. Broadley's either in this or a subsequent Report, in his third volume published in 1874, and the dimensions he quotes in describing this Vihara by no means agree with those given by Mr. Broadley. I have since the above was in type, received from Mr. Beglar, a photograph of the part uncovered by Mr. Broadley, but unfortunately taken from so low a point of view, as hardly to assist in understanding the form of the building. It is, however, sufficient to show how utterly worthless Mr. Broadley's drawings are, and to enable us to ascertain the date of the building with very tolerable certainty.

[2] Julien's *Translation*, vol. i. p. 160; vol. iii. p. 50. If the latter dimension is assumed as the correct one, as the Chinese foot is nearly 13 English inches, the Vihara must have been as high as the cross on the dome of St. Paul's.

brick, with stucco ornaments making up altogether about 12 feet. Above this the whole exterior of the building seems to have been made up of wooden galleries attached to a plain central core of brickwork, in four or five offsets. It is now of course idle to speculate on what the appearance of these galleries may have been, and for our present purposes it is not of much consequence, inasmuch as an inscription found in its entrance, states that it was erected by Mahipâla, the third king of the Pâla dynasty, who, according to General Cunningham, reigned in Bengal from 1015 to 1040 A.D.[1]

It might at one time have been open to doubt whether this inscription was integral, and whether consequently the building was really erected by Mahipâla. The style of the architecture, however, and all the details of its ornamentation, as shown in the photograph, set that question quite at rest. The whole is comparatively modern, and must have been erected during the reign of some king who was contemporary with that dynasty of Burmese kings who built and ruled in Pagan between the years 850 and 1284.[2] This being so, although a more complete knowledge of this building would be of the utmost importance in a general history of Indian architecture, it is evident from its date, that its peculiarities can have only a very indirect and retrospective bearing on an investigation into the form of its rock-cut temples.

Though the result of this Nâlanda investigation is certainly a disappointment, there still remains the celebrated temple of the Bôdhidruma at Buddha Gaya, which might at first sight be expected to throw considerable light on the subject. It is a nine-storeyed Vihara, and so far as is known the only one that ever was erected, wholly with permanent materials, by Buddhists in India, or at all events is the only one of which any remains now exist, and had it consequently been built by natives, it could hardly have failed to be of extreme interest. It is evidently, however, of a foreign design, as there is nothing in

---

1 *Reports*, vol. iii. p. 134.

2 Yule's *Mission to Ava*, pp. 32 *et seq.*; *Crawfurd*, pp. 111 *et seq.* of vol. i., 8vo. edition. It may be observed, there is a discrepancy of from 10 to 14 years in the dates of the kings' reigns quoted by Crawfurd and Burney, and those employed at the present day. This arises, as Sir Arthur Phayre informs me, from the Burmese having recently revised their chronology, with the aid of inscriptions and other data hitherto neglected, and adopted revised lists, in many instances showing differences from the old ones to the extent just stated.

the same style in India, either before or after it, and nothing indeed at all like it, except a little temple dedicated to Târâ [1] Bodhisattwa, close alongside of it, and part in fact of the same design. When, however, the thing is looked into a little more closely, it is evident that it does not require the Burmese inscriptions found on the spot [2] to convince anyone at all familiar with the architecture of the East that the building now standing there was built by the Burmese in the 13th or 14th century of our era.[3] It need hardly be added, if this is so, that all the controversies that have recently raged about the age and form of the arches which were introduced into its construction, fall to the ground with the foundations on which they rested.[4] If the Nâlanda monasteries could be restored they would

---

[1] *Hiuen Thsang*, vol. iii. p. 51. The modern Hindus have converted this into Târâ Devî, an idea adopted by Rajendralâla Mitra, *Buddha Gaya*, p. 136, Plate XX., Fig. 1. Târâ is one of the favourite Saktis of the modern Buddhists in Nepal. She is a Mahâyâna divinity associated with the Bôdhisattwas, and figures in the Nâsik, Elurâ, and Aurangâbâd caves.

[2] These inscriptions are given at full length, and with all the necessary details and translations in Rajendralâla Mitra's *Buddha Gaya*, p. 206 *et seq.*

[3] There is some little difficulty about the exact date of these inscriptions. According to Sir Arthur Phayre, who is probably the best authority on the subject, there are two dates. The first records the repairs or rebuilding of the temple by a Burmese king, A.D. 1106. The second its final completion and dedication by a king of Arakan, 1299 A.D., 193 years afterwards, during the reign of Nasiru'd-dîn, Sultan of Bengal. It is impossible now to discriminate between the parts that may belong to each of these two dates, or whether any parts of the older erection may be incorporated in the present building, but it seems quite certain that all its architectural features belong to the two centuries that elapsed between them. *See* Sir A. Phayre's paper, *J. A. S. B.*, vol. xxxvii. p. 97.

[4] Mr. Beglar, General Cunningham's assistant, has recently sent me home an account of certain arches of construction, which he has found inserted sporadically into certain brick buildings in Bengal. So far as I can make out from his photographs, all the temples or Topes in which these are found belong to the age of the Pàla dynasty, and are consequently posterior to the beginning of the 9th century. Some of them considerably more modern. This is only what might be expected, as we know from Yule's *Mission to Ava*, Plate 9, and other authorities, that arches, round, pointed, and flat, were currently used in the brick buildings at Pagan, between 850 and 1284 A.D., and this being so, it always appeared a mystery to me that none were found in contemporary buildings in Bengal. One advantage of Mr. Beglar's discoveries is, that they tend to show that there was a considerable intercourse between Bengal and Burmah in these ages. This, however, has always been suspected though difficult to prove, and every step in that direction is consequently welcome, besides removing to a great extent, any difficulty that might be felt in believing that the Buddha Gaya temple was actually erected by the Burmese.

no doubt show a much greater affinity to those of Mahâvallipur than this one does; but its style having been elaborated in a foreign country, and under foreign local influences, we ought hardly to be surprised at it having assumed so totally different an appearance during the seven centuries that elapsed between their erection.[1] Had it been erected by Indians it probably would have taken much more of the form of the Tanjore pagoda, and the numberless examples of the Dravidian style to be found in the south of India. As it is, it is nearly a counterpart of the Bodhidruma temple at Pagan,[2] erected by King Jaya Sinha between the years 1204 and 1227.[3] The Burmese temple is, it must be confessed, a little broader in its base than that at Buddha Gaya, and its pyramid a little less steep, but this may

No. 35. Burmese Tower at Buddha Gaya, from a Photograph.

[1] In his work on *Buddha Gaya*, Babu Rajendralâla Mitra adduces the form of the temple at Konch (Plate XVIII.) in support of his theory of the Buddha Gaya temple. It would, however, be difficult to find two buildings so essentially different as these are. That at Konch is a curvilinear spire of the Northern Aryan or Bengal style; that at Buddha Gaya is a straight lined many-storeyed pyramid, deriving its form from those of the ancient Buddhist Viharas. The only advantage that can be derived from their juxtaposition is to prove that they were built by different people, at distant times, and for dissimilar purposes; there is absolutely no connexion between them.

[2] In a private letter to me Sir Arthur Phayre says that when he first saw the Buddha Gaya temple, he at once came to the conclusion, from the style of its masonry and whole appearance, that it must have been erected by the Burmese, and no one probably is a better judge and more competent than he is to give an opinion on the subject.—J.F.

[3] Crawfurd's Embassy to Ava, vol. 1, p. 117, 8vo. edition.

have arisen from the architect in India being limited to the dimensions of the temple that existed there when Hiuen Thsang visited the place, and which he described as 20 paces—say 50 feet—square, which is very nearly that of the present temple. Its height, too, is nearly the same as of that seen by the Chinese pilgrim, 160 to 170 feet, but how that was made up it is extremely difficult to say.[1] Neither the Mahâvallipur Raths, nor any other authority we have, give us a hint of how, at that age, a building 50 feet square could have been designed so as to extend to between three and four times the height of its diameter.

As these Behar examples fail us so entirely it is very difficult to ascertain what other materials may exist in India to enable us to restore the external appearance of the tall Viharas of the Buddhists with anything like certainty. If it is decided that no structural remains exist, it only makes these Mahâvallipur Raths the more valuable in the eyes of the antiquary. They certainly approach in appearance more nearly to what the ancient buildings were, from which they are copied, than anything else that has yet been discovered.

Sahadeva's Ratha.

There is still a fifth Ratha belonging to this group, which, though small, is one of the most interesting of the whole. It bears the names of Sahadeva and Nakula, the twins, but in order to avoid confusion it may be well to confine its designation to the first name only, as neither have any real bearing on either its history or use. It stands a little out of the line of the other four, to the westward, and like them it is very unfinished, especially on the east side. Its dimensions are 18 feet in length north and south, by 11 feet across, and the height is about 16 feet. Its front faces the north, where there is a small projecting portico supported by two pillars, within which is a small cell, now and perhaps always untenanted. The opposite

[1] In his work on *Buddha Gaya*, at pp. 204 *et seq.*, Babu Rajendralâla proves beyond all cavil, that the famous inscription which Sir Charles Wilkins published in the first vol. of the *Asiatic Researches* is a manifest forgery. The fable, consequently, that this tower was erected by the Brahman Amara, one of the jewels of the court of Vicramâditya in the sixth century, is shown to have no foundation in fact, and must be relegated to the company of many others which have been invented to account for the exceptional appearance of this celebrated tower. It is curious, however, that the Babu does not see how completely his learning upsets his own theories of the history of the temple.

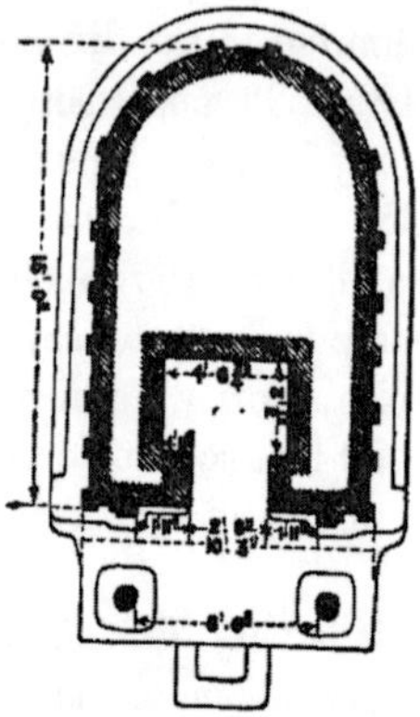

No. 36. Plan of Sahadeva's Rath, from a drawing by R. Chisholm. Scale 10 feet to 1 inch.

end is, externally at least, apsidal, and so probably if on a larger scale, its interior would have been; as it is, it is too small, being only 3 feet in depth by 4 feet 6 inches in width, to be utilised for any altar or image, and the square form is certainly more convenient in so small an apartment.

The great interest of this Ratha lies in the fact that it represents, on a small scale, the exterior of one of those Chaitya caves, which form so important a feature in all the western groups, but all of which are interiors only, and not one is so completely excavated as to enable us to judge of what the external appearance may have been, of the constructed Chaityas from which they were copied. There is one temple at Aihole dedicated to Śiva which does show the external aisle and apsidal termination, and is probably of about the same age as this Ratha.[1] Unfortunately it has been used as a fortification, and its upper storey and roof removed, so that it is of little more use to us now than an interior would be for judging of what the effect of the exterior may have been above the first storey. From the evidence of this Ratha it seems almost certain that in the larger examples there was a range of small cells in the roof of the aisles, which would naturally be much wider in constructed examples than in caves where there was no possibility of introducing light except through openings in the façade. We may also gather from the Aihole example and other indications that an external verandah surrounded the whole, and if this were so the cells would have been placed over the verandah, and the roof of the aisles used as an ambulatory.

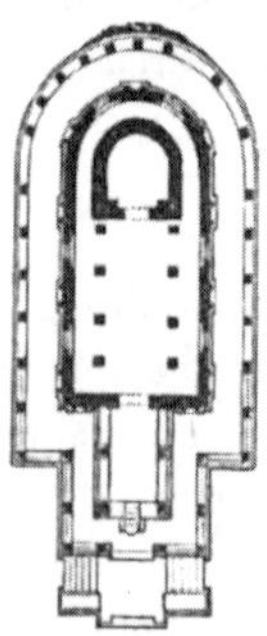

No. 37. Plan of Temple at Aihole. 50 feet to 1 inch.

One other peculiarity remains to be noticed. As will be observed from the woodcut representing the exterior, the interior of the roof is represented as semicircular, though the exterior is naturally pointed, or at least with a ridge to throw off the rain. This is the case with all the Chaitya caves in the west of India, and probably was the case with all sacred buildings. On the other hand, the evi-

[1] Burgess's *Report on Belgam and Kaladgi*, Plates LI. and LII.

dence of the Ganeśa temple and of Bhîma's Ratha here, as well as that of the Behar caves, would go far to prove that in all secular or quasi secular buildings, the form of the roof was that of a wooden framework of pointed form both externally and internally.

One of the most curious illustrations connected with this little Ratha is to be found a very long way off, in the recently excavated

No. 38. View of Sahadeva's Ratha, from a Photograph.

monasteries at Takht i Bahi and Jamalgiri in the Yusufzai country, not far from Peshawar. In both these monasteries the principal court is surrounded by a number of small cells, very similar to this Rath. In that at Jamalgiri the court is circular, 45 feet in diameter, and is surrounded by 16 cells ranging from 6 feet 2 inches across to 11 feet 8 inches; four of them, according to General Cunningham's plan and restoration, are more than 11 feet across and 20 feet in height, and consequently larger than this Rath.[1] The restoration of their façades is fortunately easy, not only from the numerous fragments found on the spot, but because of the great number of sculptured representations of them which exist there, used as frames for sculpture. One of these, with its sculptures, is shown in the woodcut below, and represents in all essential particulars just such a façade as this. The lower part quite open to the interior; the middle storey, in this instance, with lean-to roofs instead of cells, and above this an overhanging roof terminating upwards in an ogee form.[2]

[1] These particulars are taken from Gen. Cunningham's *Reports*, vol. v. pp. 23 *et seq.* 43 *et seq.*, and Plates VIII., IX., and XIV. See also *Hist. of Indian Architecture*, p. 170 *et seq.*, woodcuts 92 to 95.

No. 39. Conventional elevation of the front of a cell, from a sculpture at Jamalgiri, now in India Museum, South Kensington.

[2] One of the most interesting peculiarities of the Peshawar, or rather Gandhara sculptures, is that it would not be difficult to select from among them several that would form admirable illustrations for a pictorial Bible at the present day. One, for instance, is certainly intended to represent the nativity. The principal figure, a woman, is laying her child in a manger, and that it is intended to be such is proved by a mare with its foal, attended by a man, feeding out of a similar vessel. Above are represented two horses heads in the position that the ox and the ass are represented in mediæval paintings.

A second represents the boy Christ disputing with the doctors in the Temple. A third, Christ healing a man with a withered limb, either of which if exhibited in the Lateran, and re-labelled, might pass unchallenged as sculptures of the fourth or fifth centuries.

The scene in the annexed woodcut may, in like manner, be taken to represent the woman taken in adultery. Two men in the back ground, it will be observed, have stones in their hands ready to throw at her. The similarity in this instance is a little more farfetched than in the others, but still sufficiently near to render a comparison interesting. The study of these most interesting sculptures is now rendered impossible from the closing and dispersion of the India Museum.

Each of these 16 cells at Jamalgiri, according to General Cunningham, originally contained a figure of Buddha seated in the usual cross-legged conventional attitude. This Rath may have contained a Linga, if that emblem was introduced into the south as early as 700 A.D., or more probably a figure of Śiva in some of his manifestations, but which, not being cut in the rock, has disappeared.

The age of the Jamalgiri monasteries has not yet been settled, they are certainly earlier than the Raths at Mahâvallipur, but their distance in time cannot be very great. The Buddhism there developed is very similar to that found in the later caves at Ajaṇṭâ, and elsewhere, ranging from the fifth to the seventh century of our era, which cannot consequently be long subsequent to the date of these Peshawar monasteries, which cannot be very far removed from that of the Mahâvallipur Raths.

It may probably appear to some, that more space has been devoted to these Raths than is justified either by their relative dimensions or their artistic merits, but the fact is, that it seems almost impossible to overestimate their importance to the history of Buddhist architecture. One of its most remarkable peculiarities is, that though we have some 700 or 800 caves spread over the 1,000 years during which Buddhism flourished in India, we have not, excepting the Topes and their rails, one single structural building, and among the caves not one that has an exterior; without exception the latter are only interiors with one façade, through which the light is introduced. No Buddhist cave has even two, much less three, external sides, and not one has an external roof. Under these circumstances it is an exceptional piece of good luck to find a petrified Buddhist village—on a small scale it must be confessed—and applied to the purposes of another religion, but still representing Buddhist forms just at that age when their religion with its architectural forms were perishing out of the land where it arose. At the same time no one who has paid any attention to the subject can, I fancy, for one moment doubt that Arjuna's and Dhamarâja's Rathas are correct models on a small scale of the monasteries or vihâras of the Buddhists, that the Ganeśa temple and Bhima's Raths are in like manner models of the Sâlâs or Halls of the Buddhists, that Draupadî's Rath represents a hermitage and Sahadeva's a chapel belonging to the votaries of that religions The forms of the two last named have fallen into disuse, their purposes being gone, but the other two have been adopted by the Dravidian Hindus, and repeated over and over again throughout the south of India, and continue to be used there to the present day in all the temples of the Brahmans.

In the present state of our knowledge it is to be feared that it is idle to speculate on the mode in which these anomalous phenomena occurred, but it may fairly be inferred from them, that in the seventh century of our era there was no original and appropriate style of Hindu architecture, in the south of India. It seems also most probable that the Pallavas, or whoever carved these Raths, came from some more northern country, where they were familiar with the forms of Buddhist architecture, and that when they resolved to erect temples to their gods, in their new country, they came to the conclusion that they could not do better than adopt the forms with which they were familiar. Having once adopted it in the rock, they seem to have applied it to their structural temples, and gradually dropping those features which were either inappropriate or difficult of execution, by degrees to have developed the Dravidian style of architecture as we find it practised in the south of India from their time to the present day.

If all this is so, it may at first sight seem strange that no trace of this many-storeyed style of architecture is to be found adapted to Hindu purposes in those countries where the style first originated and had long been practised, and was consequently familiar to all classes of the inhabitants. The answer to this difficulty seems, however, not far to seek. In the north of India the Hindus early possessed styles of their own, from whatever source it may have been derived. They had temples with large attached porches, or Mantapas, and cubical cells surmounted by tall curvilinear towers, in which no trace of storeys can be detected. Having thus their own sacred forms they had no occasion to borrow from a rival and hated sect, forms which they could hardly be expected to admire, and which were inappropriate for their sacred purposes. The result seems consequently to have been that the two styles grew up and developed side by side, but remained perfectly distinct and without showing any tendency to fuse or amalgamate at any period of their existence.

CHAPTER VII.

THE CAVES, MAHÂVALLIPUR.

Although not without a considerable amount of beauty and interest in themselves, the caves at Mahâvallipur are far less important to the history of Indian architecture than the Raths just described. They have none of the grandeur, nor of that purpose-like appropriateness of design, which is so characteristic of the earlier Buddhiste caves in Western India, nor have they the dimensions or richness of architectural decoration of the contemporary Brahmanical excavations at Badâmi, Elephanta, or Elurâ. Still they cannot be passed over, even in a work especially dedicated to the more important caves of the west, and have features which are well deserving of notice anywhere.

Perhaps the most striking peculiarity of these caves is the extreme tenuity of their pillars and generally of their architectural details, when compared with those of the other groups of caves in the other parts of India. It is true, that when the Buddhists first began to excavate caves in the west of India before the Christian era, they adopted wooden forms and used details singularly inappropriate of rock-cut structures. They, however, early perceived their incongruity, and in the progress of time evolved a style of architecture of more than Egyptian solidity, which quite remedied this defect. In some of the later caves at Ajaṇṭâ, the pillars are under 4 diameters in height, including their capitals, and in such caves as the Lankeśwara at Elurâ they are little more than 2 diameters in height. At Mahâvallipur, on the other hand, 7 and 8 diameters is usual, and sometimes even these are exceeded; and generally their details are such as are singularly unsuited for cave architecture. This it appears could only have arisen from one of two causes: either it was that those who excavated these caves had no experience in the art, and copied literally the forms they found usually employed in structures either wholly, or in part, constructed with wood or other light materials; or it was, that so long an interval had elapsed between the excavation of the western caves and those at

Mahâvallipur, that the monolithic style was forgotten, and the artists had reverted to a style more appropriate to less monumental erections. These Mahâvallipur caves were consequently either the earliest or the latest among the Brahmanical caves of India, and it was at first sight very difficult to determine to which of these two categories they may have belonged. Just as in Europe it is frequently very difficult to discriminate between the details of a building belonging to the fifth or sixth century and one of the fifteenth or sixteenth; so in India, without some external evidence, it is very easy to confound details belonging to the sixth or seventh century with those of the thirteenth or fourteenth. In both cases it was either the beginning or the end of a particular phase of art, which had only a limited duration, and it is one whose history in this instance has only lately been ascertained from external sources.

Forty years ago so little was known of the history of architecture in the Madras Presidency that the more modern hypothesis seemed by far the most probable. No one then suspected that the introduction of the art was so very recent, and it seemed most improbable that these rock-cut monuments at Mahâvallipur should really be the earliest specimens of architecture known to exist in the South. Every one knew that in the north of India men had dug caves and carved stone ornamentally for at least eight or nine centuries before the date of these monuments—assuming them to belong to the seventh or eighth century of our era—and it seemed so much more likely that their very wooden forms were signs of a decadence rather than of a renaissance, that I, with most other inquirers adopted the idea that they belonged to a comparatively modern age. It was besides the one that seemed best to accord with such local traditions as existed on the spot. It now turns out, however, that the difference in style between the northern and the southern rock-cut temples is due not to chronological but to geographical causes. It is not that the inferiority of the latter is due to decay in the art of monolithic architecture, but to difference of locality. Those who carved the raths and excavated the caves at Mahâvallipur had no previous experience in the art, but under some strange and overpowering religious impulse set to work at once to copy literally and ignorantly in the rock, a form of architecture only suited to buildings of a slighter and more ephemeral nature.

If there had been a difference discernible in the style of the various monoliths at Mahâvallipur, if, for instance, we had been able to point out that one was more wooden than another, or more lithic, and exhibited the same progress from wooden to stone forms, as we find in the northern caves, this would have been detected long ago. But it is another of the marked characteristics of the place, that everything is of the same age. No one who either examines them on the spot, or compares the photographs that are to be had, can doubt that the Raths and the caves are of the same age, their details are so absolutely identical. The caves, it is true, do exhibit some slight difference in style, in parts at least, but nothing that can make out a distinct sequence. They may overlap the Raths by a few years either way, but there are no data from which a reliable sequence can be established, and the differences in parts are generally so slight that they may be owing to some individual or local caprice.

Under these circumstances it is fortunate that the sculptures with which the Mahâvallipur caves are so profusely adorned afford data from which their relative age can be ascertained with a precision sufficient at least for our present purposes. The fortunate discovery by Mr. Burgess in 1876 of a cave with a dated inscription in it, A.D. 579, at Bâdâmi, has given a precision to our knowledge of the subject not before attained, and his report on these caves has rendered us familiar with the architecture and sculpture of the sixth century of our era. By a singular piece of good fortune one of the great sculptures of the Cave No. III. at Bâdâmi[1] is practically identical with one in the Vaishṇava cave (Carr's 25) at Mahâvallipur.[2] They both represent Vishṇu as Trivikrama, or the "three stepper" in the dwarf Avatâr; practically they are the same, but with such difference that when compared with similar sculptures at Elurâ and elsewhere, we are enabled to say with tolerable certainty that the Bâdâmi sculpture is the more ancient of the two. On the other hand, we have at Elephanta and Elurâ many examples representing the same subjects of Hindu mythology as are found at Mahâvallipur, but with such differences of mythology and execution as indicate with equal certainty that the southern examples are more ancient than the northern. As these latter may all be

---

[1] *Report on Belgâm, &c.*, Plate XXXI.

[2] *Trans. R. A. S.* vol. ii. Plate VI. of Mr. Babington's paper.

dated within the limits of the eighth century, we have a limit beyond which it seems impossible to carry the date of the Mahâvallipur sculpture either way. They must be after the sixth and before the eighth century of our era, and, in so far as can now be ascertained, nearer the latter than the former date. It is, of course, impossible to speak of sculptures as affording the same precision for fixing dates as architecture is acknowledged to possess. There is so much more individuality in sculpture, and so much that depends on the taste and talent of the sculptor, and also on the material in which he is working, that a comparison with other works of the same age may sometimes lead to conclusions more or less erroneous. Architecture, on the other hand, is so much more mechanical, and its development depends so much on the progress of the school in which it was created, as seldom to lead astray. But when sculpture is combined with mythology, as it is in this instance, its indications may become almost equally reliable, and when these are confirmed by the science of palæography, as before mentioned, there is hardly room to question the conclusions that may be drawn from it. If this is so, there seems no reason for doubting that the caves as well as the Raths at Mahâvallipur were excavated subsequently to the sixth and before the eighth century, and, taking all the circumstances of the case into consideration, there seems no reason for doubting that the date above assigned to them, 650 to 700 A.D., cannot be far from the truth, and may be accepted until at least some new discovery may afford additional means for ascertaining with more precision the facts relating to their age.

As these caves are scattered promiscuously without any order, on both sides of the low ridge of hills in which they are excavated, wherever a suitable piece of rock could be found, it is extremely difficult to hit on any classification by which a description of them can be made clear and intelligible. They are all, too, so nearly of the same extent, and richness of ornament, that they do not admit of classification from their relative importance. Being all, too, as just mentioned, of the same age, with the exception of the Krishna Mandapa, or at least so nearly so, that it is impossible now to discriminate between the older or more modern, and being all unfinished, no chronological arrangement is available for their description. We are even deprived here of the division of the different caves into classes, according to religions, which is one of the most obvious means of characterising them in almost all other groups. There is not in the sculptures at Mahâvallipur a single trace of any anterior Buddhist or Jaina religion, or any feature that can be traced back to any pre-existing faith, except of course, as above pointed out, the mechanical forms of the architecture. One cave, the ninth in the following enumeration, may be said to be wholly Vaishṇava, but in all the others, representations borrowed from the religion of Śiva alternate with those relating to Vishṇu, in a manner that is most unexpected, at least to anyone accustomed to the antagonism that grew up between these two religions after the rise of the Lingayets in the ninth century. This, however, is only a further proof, if any were requisite, that it was before that time that these caves were excavated.

Under these circumstances the best mode will probably be to begin at the southern end of the ridge, nearly opposite the great group of Rathas above described, and take each cave, as nearly as can be done, in sequence as we proceed northward. Following this plan, we find—

1. At the south end of the ridge is a very neat cave in excellent preservation known as Dharmarâja's Mandapa,[1] measuring 17 feet by 12½, with four pillars, two in front and two in the middle, square above and below and octagonal in the middle. In the back wall are three empty shrines with steps ascending to their doors. Along the back wall is a moulded base, and the central door has had dwârpâlas, now hewn off.

2. Just behind the southern sculptured rock is another cave[2] with two pillars in front, but the work has been little more than begun.

3. To the north of the first is the Yamapuri or Mahishamarddani Mandapa, a fine lofty cave[3] 33½ feet long by 15 feet deep. In front it had originally four round pillars (the second is quite destroyed) and two pilasters. These pillars have a thick torus capital surmounted by a spreading cima recta, carrying a square tile. This upper portion

---

[1] Carr's No. 44; Braddock, p. 103 (?).

[2] Carr's map, No. 46.

[3] Carr, No. 32; Braddock, No. 19, p. 96, *see also* pp. 7, 32, 49, 149, 208.

is cut away from the third column, and from the manner in which this is done it would seem as if it was intended to remove the pillar entire, as was probably the case with its fellow. A short square block carrying a wide bracket rises above the capitals of all these pillars. They have also moulded bases, and two belts of florid work round the shafts. Above the façade is a range of small simulated cells similar to those on the Raths, and such as are found on nearly all the cave façades here; but in this instance they are even more unfinished than usual, and it requires a practised eye to detect the intended design. There is a porch to the shrine advanced into the middle of the floor, with two pillars rising from yalis or sârdûlas at the corners of a platform.

On the left or south wall is a large bas-relief of Nârâyana or Vishṇu, reclining upon the snake Sesha, with his head to the east. Below are three worshippers or attendants. The third is a female; their headdresses are of the Elephanta type with regal mukutas or tiaras, and above two Gandharvas, a male and female. At Vishṇu's feet are two giants struggling with each other, one said to be the partisan of Nârâyana, and the other of Mahishâsurâ, the buffalo demon.[1]

At the other end of this hall is a sculptured tableau 12¾ by 8 feet, representing the strife between Mahishâsura and Durgâ, the female counterpart of Śiva. This group merits special attention, because of the spirited character of the style in which it is sculptured; as Mr. Babington states he "has no hesitation in pronouncing this to be the most animated piece of Hindu sculpture he had ever seen."[2] The demon is represented with the head of a buffalo, a minotaur in fact, and not as is often done in later sculptures as a buffalo itself. He holds a huge club with both hands, has a long straight sword by his side, and wears the *mukuta* or tiara of a king with the *chhatra* or umbrella borne over it. Between his feet is a human head; behind him are four figures, two with round shields, and one of them with a sword, while one seems to have fallen. In front of him is a fifth also with shield, while a sixth is represented falling headlong upon a female who is fighting with a crooked sword just at his foot. Durga is mounted on her lion, her eight arms girded

---

[1] *See* the legend, p. 99 of Carr's compilation.

[2] *Trans. R. A. S.*, vol. ii. p. 261; Carr, 49.

for the strife and armed with bow, sword, club, *śankha*, axe, gong, &c., and canopied by the *Chhatra*, and attended by eight *pramathas*, some with bows and others with swords.

In the back are three cells, with male dwârpâlas by the doors of each; the central one is a shrine (called by the villagers Kailâs), with a *linga* in the middle of the floor, and on the back wall is a sculpture of Śankara or Śiva and Pârvatî seated together, she with Karttikaswâmi or Mahâsena on her knee. Behind them is seen a figure of Vishṇu, and to the left is Brahmâ, and below the seat is the bull Nandi and a female. This sculpture is exceedingly badly executed, and the style of headdress much higher than in either of the other sculptures.

Immediately above this cave is the fragment of a structural temple, which forms one of the most conspicuous objects in the landscape from whichever side it is seen.[1] It is not, however, centred exactly on the rock-cut portico below,[2] and is evidently the erection of a later age, though probably intended to complete what the original cave excavators had left, like everything else in this place unfinished. Its dimensions are 22 feet by 16 feet in plan, and its height 16 feet.[3] What its interior dimensions are cannot now be ascertained, as its roof has fallen in.

4. To the west of this at the foot of the hill is a temple of Varâha Svâmi, or the boar *avatâra* of Vishṇu, but being still used for worship it is not now accessible to strangers, and its contents are only known by hearsay, and from what can be seen from the outside. The rock excavation has four pillars and a shrine at the back. It contains (by report) the usual four-armed figure of Varâha holding up Prithvî, a four-armed Śaktî, figures known as Râja Hariśekhara and his two wives; Śri as Gaja Lakshmî (attended by elephants); Mâruti worshipping Râma; and others. In front of this rock-cut temple a modern mandap has been built, lighted only from the door, which now prevents the interior being seen.[4]

---

1 *Lord Valentia's Travels*, vol. i. Plate opposite p. 380.

2 *Rock-cut Temples*, folio, 1845, Plate XVII.

3 Carr's compilation, quoting Braddock, p. 96.

4 On the rock to the left, but partly covered by the end wall of this erection, is a long inscription dated "in the ninth year of Koppari Kesarwarmâ, also called Uḍaiyâr Śri Râjendra Devar, who having taken the whole of Iraṭṭaippâḍi seven lakhs and a half, having intimidated Âhavamalla in battle, &c." Another inscription at Gangondaram

5. Râmânujya Maṇḍapa.—This has been a small cave 18½ feet by 10, with two pillars standing on lions' heads, well cut, with octagonal shafts in front. There are three cells at the back with some sculptures on the walls, but the back wall and divisions between the cells have been cleared away, and the sculptures hewn off the walls.

At each end outside is a niche for an image surmounted by a little simulated cell like those found on all the Rathas, and in front a verandah supported on six pillars has been erected.

On the threshold is an inscription in three lines, of an old florid character. The façade of this cave has a bold projecting drip, and is ornamented above with dormer windows similar to those found on the structural or rock-cut Chaityas. The style altogether is very like that of the third or Bhima's Ratha.

The Chakra and Śankh of Vishṇu are carved on the returning walls at the end of the verandah, and at each end stairs ascend to the top where is the plain rubble temple, called by the natives Velugoṭi Singama Nâyaḍu's Maṇḍapa. Below in the valley is a stone couch, and near the front of the cave lies the top of the dormer window of a Ratha. The Ratha itself has been totally quarried away.[1]

6. Maṇḍapa to the west of Oḷakkaṇṇeśwaraswâmi's Temple.[2]

This is an unfinished cave with four lion pillars blocked out in its front.

7. Krishṇa's Maṇḍapa.—Proceeding northward the next in order locally, is Krishṇa's Choultry, which cannot be passed over in a

---

on the Kâverî speaks of "Ko-Virâja Keśarwarmâ named Râjendra Deva" as "having intimidated Âhavamalla of Kudala Sangama" (Bilhana's *Vikramakâvya*); and a third inscription at Anigiri in Dharwad mentions the invasion of the Karnatic by Râjendra Chôla.[1] Now Someśvara Deva Âhavamalla the Chalukya ruled the Karnatic from Śaka 962 to 991, A.D. 1040 to 1069, and Râjendra Chôḷâ succeeded his father Râjarâja Chôḷa in Śaka 986, A.D. 1063, and his reign was a very long one.[2] The grants, for there are two, are thus fixed to belong to A.D. 1072, but unfortunately they only record donations to the temple, which was probably excavated in a much earlier age.—J.B.

[1] Quarrying operations are going on on a very extensive scale among these caves at the present time, and it will be nothing new if the finest of them are sacrificed without a thought.

[2] No. 30 in Carr's map, where it is placed much to the west of its real position.—Not mentioned by Braddock.

---

[1] Conf. Caldwell, *Gram.* int. pp. 135, 136.

[2] *Ind. Ant.* V. 321.

description of the caves at Mahâvallipur, though it has very little claim to be considered as a cave, or as a rock-cut temple. It is quite exceptional here, and its structural arrangements belong to a different age from all those surrounding it. It probably was erected at the same time as the structural Vimana over the Yamapuri Cave described above, and may probably belong to the time of the Cholas, in or about the eleventh century of our era.

It consists of a large Maṇḍapa or porch 48 feet by 23, with twelve structural columns in three rows erected in front of a great bas-relief in a recessed portion of the rock. Six of the pillars have Śârdûlas or Yalis at the bottom, and the rest are square with carving upon them, but all have the drooping bracket capital so common in modern buildings in the south of India. The roof is formed of large slabs of gneiss laid over the lintels, which join the heads of the pillars.

The sculptured decoration of the cave consists of one long bas-relief following the sinuosities of the rock some 45 feet in length and from 10 to 11 feet in height in the centre. It represents Krishṇa holding up the hill of Govarddhana. To the left is Balarâma leaning on another male figure, and on each side are numerous Gopalas and Gopîs with cows, calves, and a bull. On the return of the wall are lions and other animals. The sculpture of all these is much more developed than those in the Daśa Avatâra and Kailâsa at Elurâ, and is almost certainly of later date, thus confirming the comparatively modern date of this hybrid temple, which, except from its locality as one of a series, is hardly worthy of much attention.

On the top of the hill, but like the Vimana over the Yamapuri cave placed unsymetrically with this porch, a very splendid structural Gopura has been commenced in the style of architecture prevalent in the eleventh or twelfth century, and evidently a part of some great design. It had not, however, been carried up higher than the sub-basement, and then like everything else at this place, abandoned and left unfinished.

8. The Maṇḍapa of the Pâncha Pâṇḍavas.[1]—A few yards north of the last, and adjoining the great sculptured rock, is a large but unfinished cave, 50 feet wide in front, and about 40 feet deep at the right end, and 33 feet at the left. It has six octagonal pillars in front rising from Śârdulâ bases (one is broken) with broad square

[1] No. 15 on Carr's map; Braddock's No. 12, p. 92; *see also* pp. 4, 205.

abacuses, and, in place of brackets, three rampant Śârdûlas, one on each side of the architrave. The second row of pillars are plain octagons standing on simple plinths, and behind them the front of the shrine occupies the width of four pillars or about 23½ feet. The shrine itself is an irregular small cell, unfinished, as are also the side aisles, in each of which three pillars are roughly blocked out. Over the façade, the rock is hewn into little models of cells, as on the Rathas and the fronts of the other caves.

9. Vaishṇava Cave.—Near to the isolated monolithic temple of Ganeśa described above (p. 114) is a very neat excavation on the left of the pathway and facing west.[1]

In front it has two pilasters and two octagonal pillars rising from *śârdûlas*, the shafts half covered with minute florid work. The capitals have a thick heavy torus over a few members, forming an astragal round the neck, and above a cima recta spreads out under a plain square tile, and the brackets are separated from this by a square block, as in the third cave described above.[2] The eaves above are ornamented with six Chaitya dormer windows enclosing rosettes, and above, the façade is carved as in the Rathas.

The hall measures 19½ feet by 9½ with a single shrine at the back which projects into the hall. In the left or north end is a sculpture of the four-armed Varâha or Boar Avatâra and Prithivî,[3] or the earth, who, according to the legend, he had rescued from the deluge in which it or she had been submerged at the churning of the ocean in the previous Avatâra. This sculpture is not unlike the figures in two of the Bâdâmi caves, but showing so much difference in style, and such general inferiority of design and execution, as to leave little doubt that this is the most modern example of the two. The geographical distance, however, of the two localities prevents any exact determination of the chronological interval that may have elapsed between the execution of the two examples.

In the Mahâvallipur example Varâha's right foot is placed on the head of the seven-headed snake Śesha. To the left are two male figures one of them with a long crook. Behind is a four-armed figure with a bag or bottle in one of his left hands, and addressing

---

[1] Carr, 25; Braddock, No. 9, p. 81 Carr's Plates V. to IX., and pp. 6, 49, 205.

[2] Carr's 32; Braddock's 17.

[3] *Trans. R.A.S.*, vol. ii., Plate V.; *see also* Carr's plate with the same number.

another figure, perhaps a female, and above them in the corners are two smaller figures of Gandharvas.

On the back wall adjoining this Varâha sculpture is a singularly interesting representation of Śrî or Gaja Lakshmî, seated on a lotus flower, with her feet on the sepals of it, and two elephants above receiving pots of water from two female attendants on each side and pouring it on the goddess. The execution of this sculpture does not seem remarkable for its excellence. The interest lies in the fact of its being the first known example of this Goddess appearing in a Hindu garb. As above pointed out (p. 72) we know of some 20 examples of her appearance in Buddhist monuments from the time of the Tope of Bharhut B.C. 150, to 6th or 7th century in the Panjab. From this time to the present day she is one of the most frequently represented deities of the Hindu pantheon, but does not afterwards, so far as is known, appear on Buddhist monuments.

To the right of the shrine is a somewhat similar sculpture, but perhaps it may rather be considered as a representation of Durgâ; though the Śankha and discus rather belong to Lakshmî, four armed, with umbrella over her head, a deer over her left shoulder, and a tiger over the other, while four gana, one with a sword, attend her. Below to the right is a suppliant, and on the left a man grasping his long hair with one hand and a long sword with the other, as if about to cut off his locks.[1]

On the right or south end of this cave is a representation of the result of the Wâman, or dwarf Avatâra, differing from similar sculptures at Bâdâmi inasmuch that the suppliants are omitted before the principal figure, which represents Vishnu with eight arms as Trivikrama or the three stepper, taking the first step by which according to the legend he deprived Maha Bali of the dominion of the earth. The local pandits regard the figure seated at the right foot of Trivikrama[2] as Maha Bali, and the one behind him as his minister Śukrâchârya. On the return of the wall and on each side of the shrine are male dwârpâlas or doorkeepers, but inside there is only a bench without any figure or image in it.

10, 11. These two caves are close together on the west side of the rocks and face W.N.W. towards the last-mentioned pair of Rathas. The northern one is an unfinished cave about 36 feet long

---

[1] Carr, Plate VIII., Fig. 1.

[2] Carr, Plate VII. Fig. 1.

and 10 deep, with four lion pillars blocked out in front (similar to Cave 6) which is not far to the south of this. A large recess is also roughly hewn out in the back.

The other (11) is about 34 feet in length by 15 feet deep, and has four square and octagon pillars in front, with a second row inside, 16 sided, with capitals similar to those of the Raths, with brackets above, but no abacus over the torus.

In the back are five cells, three of them with steps leading up to the doors, which have male dwârpâlas by their jambs. Over the doors is a projecting cornice with a drip on which are carved Chaitya window ornaments each with a head within it.

All the cells have had *lingams* in them, which are now removed.

12. Kotikal Mandapa.[1]

One hundred and twenty yards to the north-east of the last is a third cave on this west side of the rocks. Like the last, the two pillars in front are square below and above, and octagonal in the middle with brackets only roughly blocked out. It has only one shrine which is empty; but the door has a female dwârpâlas on each side, indicating that (like Draupâdî's Ratha) it was dedicated to a goddess or Śaktî. Over the door is a plain drip, no frieze but with small square holes countersunk in the rock as if a wooden verandah were once intended and perhaps executed.

At first sight the style of this cave, externally, looks older than the others, and it may be so, but can hardly be removed from them by any great interval, and the contrast between the outer and the inner rows of pillars as in Cave 11 seems to be in favour of its being of about the same age. If its outer appearance only were taken into account it would be difficult not to believe that it was the oldest cave here.

13. Kapul Iśwara.—Proceeding from this to the north-east, we reach three shrines joined together cut in the face of the rock, with slender pilasters at the sides of their doors, and by each are dwârpâlas with high, peaked caps; those to the left are bearded. The cornice or drip is ornamented with Chaitya-window sculptures, each containing a head, and the façade above is carved in the usual Ratha style. On the rock to the right or south of these is an eight-armed Durgâ, standing on a buffalo's head.

[1] Carr, No. 52.

Above this niche is a richly carved lintel, so absolutely identical with the one over the doorway of Draupadî's Rath (woodcut No. 27). that there hardly is any doubt that they are of the same age, almost, it might be supposed, that they were carved by the same sculptor.

In the left shrine is Śiva, four-armed, wearing a deep necklace of large beads, rather balls, crossing on his breast, attended by two worshippers and two of his dwarf gaṇa, one with a sword and the other with an offering. The central shrine is sculptured in nearly the same way, and the third contains Vishṇu, similarly accompanied. Or was it intended that the first should be Brahmâ? If so, it would only be another instance of a favourite habit at that age of representing the triad, as manifested in the Lankeśwara cave in the flank of the rock of Kailâsa at Elurâ and elsewhere.[1] In front of this cave is a great stone bowl.

On the east side of this same rock are carved an elephant, about 5 feet high, a monkey, and a peacock, with the heads of three smaller elephants.

Quarrying operations are now going on quite close to this, if they have not already destroyed these shrines.

13. The above exhausts the caves in the ridge, but to the south of the "Shore pagoda" are two rocks, each with a recess hewn in its west side. The northern one is surrounded by Yâlî or Śârdûla heads, like the one at Śaliwankuppam, to be described hereafter, and the other has one great Yâlî face above, and other figures round the front. Before it lies a large lion couchant on a stone, and on the back of the rock is carved a horse, and a great elephant's head with a small cell over it as at Śaliwankuppam. The carving inside is so abraded as to be unrecognisable.

North from the structural pagoda is another little shrine or cell in a rock.

Śaliwankuppam.

Three miles north from the last, among the sand on the sea beach, some rocks crop up, in two of which cells have been cut.

One is a cave-temple called the Atichandéswara Maṇḍapa, but

---

[1] Col. Mackenzie made three careful drawings of these figures, which are in his volume on the Antiquities of Maha Bali Puram in the India House Library, Nos. 15, 16, and 17. There seems little doubt that they are intended to represent the Hindu triad but in a very pure and simple form.

it is entirely filled up with sand which drifts into it from the shore. It contains some inscriptions; on the end walls are two copies in different alphabetical characters of one agreeing generally with that in the Ganeśa temple, but differing in the fifth Śloka, which reads:—

"Atiraṇachaṇḍra, lord of kings, built this place called Atiranachandeswara."

On the frieze above the entrance, also in each of the two alphabetical characters, is the word—"Atiranachanda-Pallava."

This Atiranachanda-Pallava was in all probability one of the Pallava kings of Kâñchî (Konjiveram); but until some advance has been made in translating the inscriptions with which the Madras Presidency abounds we must remain in ignorance of his date. Vinayâditya Satyâśraya in 694 A.D. claims to have subjugated them.[1] Dr. Burnell (*Pal.*, 2nd ed. p. 37 and Plate XII.) ascribes the elder character to A.D. 700, *i.e.*, the *Ratha* character, but the style of the characters in his grants differs from either of Atiranachanda's inscriptions, and it was only in the eighth or ninth century, according to Ellis,[2] that the country was conquered by the Chôlas to whom the Pallavas were afterwards tributary.

The cell contains a lingam.

Not far from this is an inscription on a rock, dated "in the 37th year of Tribhuvana-Viradeva," otherwise called Vira Chôla

No. 40. Front of Cave at Saliwankuppam, from a Photograph.

---

[1] *Ind. Ant.* VII. 303; also II. 272; III. 152; V. 154.

[2] *See also* a paper by E. Burnouf in *Journal Asiatique*, 2nd vol. of 1828, p. 241.

Deva (p. 140), which is believed to coincide with A.D. 1116, or thereabouts.

The other cave is more accessible than that mentioned above. It is only a small cell cut out of a rock, with nine *simha* or Yâlî heads round the front of it (woodcut No. 40), and small *simhas* rampant in front of each jamb.

It is a curious development of the idea of the Tiger cave at Katak (woodcut No. 12). There can be no doubt that the same fantasy governed both, but the steps that connect the two have been lost during the seven or eight centuries that elapsed between their excavation.

To the left of it are two miniature cells over elephants' heads.

GREAT BAS-RELIEF.

There still remains to be described one of the most remarkable antiquities of the place, which, though rock-cut, can neither be classed among the temples nor the caves. It is, in fact, a great bas-relief carved in two great masses of rock, and extending nearly 90 feet north and south, with an average height of about 30 feet. It is popularly known as Arjuna's penance from the figure of Sanyasi standing on one leg, and holding his arms over his head, which is generally assumed to represent that hero of the Mâhâbharata, but without more authority than that which applies his name with that of his brothers and sister to the Rathas above described.[1]

The most prominent figure in the southern half of the rock is that of a god four-armed, probably Śiva, but his emblems are so defaced that it is difficult to feel sure which god is represented; but the attendant gana and generally the accompaniments make this nearly certain. On his left is the emaciated figure of a man doing penance, just referred to. Below him is a small one-storeyed temple, not unlike Draupadî's Ratha, but further removed from the original utilitarian type, and of a more architectural design. In the cell is seen an image apparently of Vishṇu, to which an old

[1] The bas-relief is very fairly represented in the *Trans. R.A.S.* vol. ii. in Plates I. and II., Fig. 1, that accompany Dr. Babington's paper. They are reproduced in Carr's compilation under the same numbers. I possess besides numerous photographs of it by Dr. Hunter, Capt. Lyon, Mr. Nicholas, and others, which enables me to bear testimony to the general correctness of Dr. Babington's drawings.

devotee on the left hand, said to represent Dronachárya, is offering worship, with another a little lower on the right. Besides these there are some 13 or 14 human beings, men and women, life size, represented in this southern half, some six or seven gaṇa or dwarfs, usually attendant on Śiva, as many gandharvas or harpies, flying figures, the upper part of whose bodies are human, the lower extremities those of birds with claws.[1] In addition to these there are lions, deer, hares, monkeys, and birds; and if the lower part of the rock had been complete--like everything here, it is left unfinished —it would have contained a whole menagerie of animals.

The upper part of the right half bas-relief contains some 20 figures of men and women with the same admixture of animals, gandharvas, and gaṇa, like those on the southern half, all hurrying towards the centre, where the principal object of worship was evidently placed. The lower part of this half is occupied by two elephants, a male and female, life size, with four young ones, which are as perfect representations of those animals as were probably ever executed in stone.

In the centre on a projecting ledge, between these two great masses of rock, once stood the statue of the great Nâgâ Raja, who was the principal personage for whose honour this great bas-relief was designed. The upper part of the figure, above 5 feet in height, was that of a man overshadowed by a great seven-headed serpent hood (woodcut No. 41), below the figure was that of a serpent. The upper part has fallen, but still remains on the ground,[2] the lower part is still attached to the rock. Below him is his wife, about 7 feet in

---

[1] These occur frequently at Sanchi (*Tree and Serpent Worship*, Plates XXV., XXVI., XXVII., XXVIII., and *passim* XXIV., Figs. 1 and 2, and in all Buddhist sculptures, though generally in a different form from those here represented. Also in the wall paintings in the Ajaṇṭâ Caves; they are called Kinnaras.

[2] It was evident that the head of the Nâgâ Râja had fallen from the accident of its position, the artists having placed it in the centre, where it could have a shadow behind it, but where it had no support. I consequently wrote to my friend Dr. Hunter to try and find it. With the assistance of the then Madras Government he removed the sand, and found it lying where it fell. I afterwards made application to the Government to have it replaced, which could easily be done, and so give meaning to the whole bas-relief. This, I understood from my friend Mr. Campbell Johnstone, who took out my application, was also sanctioned and ordered to be carried out, but from photographs recently received it appears not only that this has not been done, but that the bust has been removed from where it originally stood after its recovery.

height, but with a hood of only three serpent heads, and below her again a simple head of a cobra. On either hand are other figures with serpent hoods, and men and animals, among which may be remarked a cat standing on its hind legs, and all doing homage to the great Nâga Râja.

No. 41. Head of Nâgâ Râjâ from Great Bas-relief at Mahâvallipur.

Even if this great bas-relief does not afford us much information regarding the rock-cut architecture of Eastern India, it has at least the merit of fixing almost beyond cavil the age of the various objects of interest at Mahâvallipur. The sculptures, for instance, of Cave No. XXIV. at Ajaṇṭâ, are so nearly identical that their age cannot be far apart. We have in these the same flying figures, male and female, the same Kinnaras (harpies), the same style of sculpture in every respect,

No. 42. Capital from Cave XXIV. at Ajaṇṭâ, from a Photograph.

and such as is not found either before or afterwards. As this Ajaṇṭâ cave is only blocked out, and only finished in parts, it is probably the latest excavation there, and may therefore with certainty be assumed to belong to the seventh century of our era, and most probably the latter half of it. The sculptures, too, at Elurâ and elsewhere, whose age has been ascertained, when compared with this bas-relief, so fully confirm this, and all we learn, from other sources, that the date of rock-cut monuments at Mahâvallipur can hardly now be considered as doubtful.

If it were not that this work is expressly limited to the rock-cut examples of Indian architecture, few things would be more instructive for the history, of Dravidian architecture at least, than to describe also the structural examples of this place. The temple on the shore is not only one of the most elegant but one of the oldest examples of the style.[1] It is small, measuring only about 60 feet east and west and about 50 feet in height, and simulates a five-storeyed Vihara, though with considerable deviation from the forms originally used by the Buddhists and copied so literally in the Raths at this place. Its details had become at the time it was erected so far conventionalised that it is not at first sight easy to detect the wooden original in all parts, and the general outline had become taller and more elegant than in the Raths. It has also the advantage, so rare in the south, of being all in stone. In nine instances out of ten only the lower storey, which is always perpendicular, is in stone. The upper or pyramidal parts are in brickwork plastered or in terracotta or some lighter material. In this example the whole is in stone, and though weather worn from its being within the reach of the surf, it still retains its outline with sufficient sharpness to show what its original form must have been.

Its age probably is about the 8th or 9th century, and if so is the earliest known structural temple in the Dravidian regions. It certainly is older than the Krishna Mantapa or than the frustum of a Vimana above the Yamapuri cave, at this place, and very considerably older than the present village temple, which is still used for worship by the inhabitants of Mahâvallipur.

This last probably belongs to the 12th or 13th century, and though comparatively modern, is an unusually elegant specimen of the class, and if illustrated, with the other antiquities of the place, would afford a complete history of the style during the six or seven centuries in which it flourished in the greatest perfection. As before mentioned it is one of the few temples that adopt the straight ridged form of Bhima's Rath, instead of the domical termination of the pyramid as exemplified in the Arjuna and Dharmarâja Raths. It has, however, a smaller temple alongside of it in the same enclosure, which follows the more usual patterns. Together they make a very perfect pair of temples, and notwithstanding their difference in age their details are

---

[1] A view of it will be found in my *Picturesque Illustrations of Indian Architecture*, Pl. XVIII., with description.

so little altered that there is no difficulty in tracing all their forms back to the Raths from which they were derived.

KULUMULU.

At a place called Kulumûlu, half way between Tinnevelly and Strivelliputtar, about 30 miles distant from each, there exist a number of rock-cut sculptures and temples, which if properly examined and described might prove of considerable interest. At present they are only known from Capt. Lyons' photographs,[1] and as no dimensions are given and the inscriptions are still untranslated, it is difficult to say much about them.

On one side of the hill they all belong to the Jaina religion, and consist (photos. 337, 338, and 339) of a great number of Jaina figures of various sizes, and differently accompanied which were originally intended to be protected by a wooden roof, which has now disappeared. They are not of great beauty or antiquity, probably the 11th or 12th century. Indeed they are of so little interest, that the place would hardly be worth mention, were it not that on the other side of the hill there is a little rock-cut temple dedicated to Śiva which is a gem of its class. It is almost a counterpart of the upper part of the Śikhara of the Kailas at Elurâ, and consequently probably of the same age. It is, however, even more elaborately sculptured than even that famous temple, and taken altogether it is perhaps, as far as it goes, as fine a specimen of its style as is to be found in India. It is, however, like most things in the south, unfinished, and its cell untenanted. Still it is so beautiful that it is to be regretted that more is not known about it, especially as it probably is not unique, but other specimens of the class may be found in that neighbourhood when looked for.

CONCLUSION.

Although it is evident from the preceding investigation that these Eastern caves cannot compete—as previously hinted—either in extent or in magnificence, with the rock-cut temples found on the Western side of India, still it results from an examination of their peculiarities, that they are far from being devoid of interest in

---

[1] *Photographs of Ancient Arch. in Southern India*, Nos. 337 to 342.

themselves, and are, in some respects, of almost equal importance for the general history of architecture in India, as their rivals in the West. Notwithstanding their comparative insignificance, the evidence derived from the Behar caves, proves more distinctly than anything else that has yet come to light, at what time, and in what manner, caves were first excavated in India for religious purposes. They also afford direct and positive proof, that before Aśoka's time, in the middle of the third century before Christ, all the caves used by Buddhists were mere natural caverns very slightly, if at all, improved by art. They also tend, by inference, to confirm the postulate, that before Aśoka's time stone was rarely, if at all used in India for purely architectural purposes. If what has been said above, is borne out by subsequent investigations, it results that the Pipala cave at Râjgir, and its accompanying Baithak, are not only the oldest buildings known to exist in India, but the most characteristic of the state of architectural art in the pre-Mauryan age. If this is sustained, its importance can hardly be overrated, as affording a firm basis for all further investigations into the origin of stone architecture and cave excavation in India. On the whole from the evidence, on these points, obtained from an examination of the Eastern caves is more complete than any derived from those in the West.

The Orissa caves are not so important in a historical point of view, but they seem to illustrate Buddhist art at a period when such illustrations are most valuable, and they supplement what is found in the Western caves in a manner that is most satisfactory. Taken together they afford a picture of the arts of architecture and sculpture as they existed in India immediately before and after the Christian era, which is full of interest, but which could hardly be considered as complete without the information to be derived from these Eastern examples.

The greatest interest, however, of these explorations among the Eastern rock-cut temples, arises from the discovery at Mahâvallipur of what may fairly be called a petrified Buddhist village. The great difficulty that has hitherto been experienced in investigating the history of Buddhist architecture in India has arisen from the fact that though we have hundreds on hundreds of caves and rock-cut examples, we have—with the exception of one or two topes—not one single structural example in the length and breadth of the land, and it consequently was most difficult to realise the external appearance of the buildings. By the aid, however, of the Mahavallipur Raths, and the clumsy attempt to copy a Buddhist vihara in the cave at Undavilli, we are now enabled to understand to a very great extent, not only the appearance but the construction of all the varied forms of Buddhist architectural art. The Raths belong, unfortunately, to a late age, it must be confessed, but still before it had entirely passed away.

Another almost equally important result for the general history of Indian Architecture, is obtained from a knowledge of the forms of the Raths at Mahavallipur and of the caves at Undavilli. It may now be said with confidence that we know for certain the origin of the Dravidian style of architecture, and the date when it was first introduced in the South, and we can also explain whence its most characteristic features were derived, and why they were adopted. All these points were little known before, and still less understood.

It may be said, with some truth perhaps, that there is very little that is new in all this; but a good deal of it was known only very hazily. The great advantage obtained from these investigations into the Eastern caves is, that we may now feel confident that we know exactly how and when Buddhist architecture was first introduced, and with the assistance of the Western caves can follow its progress step by step till its decline and extinction in the seventh or eighth century, after an existence of nearly 1,000 years. It is something too, to be able to say that we know when and how the Dravidian style arose, though we have not and never had any difficulty in tracing its history from the seventh or eighth century till the present day. It is true we have not yet been able to discover the origin of the curvilinear Śikhara or spire of Indo-Aryan style of the north of India, with its accompanying peculiarities. When, however, so much has been done, we may feel confident that before long, that last remaining obscurity that still clouds the history of Indian Architecture may, too, eventually disappear.

PART II.

CAVE TEMPLES OF WESTERN INDIA.

PART II.

CHAPTER I.

INTRODUCTION.

If there had been no other examples of Cave Temples in India than those described in the preceding pages, the subject of its rock-cut architecture, though interesting to local antiquaries and those specially connected with Indian matters, would hardly have been deemed of sufficient importance to attract attention in Europe. The caves in Behar are too small and insignificant to claim especial notice, except from their bearing on the general history of the subject. Those in Orissa, though larger and more elaborately finished, are too much isolated in their character to be of much value, except when studied in connexion with more extensive groups; while those in the Madras presidency are interesting more from their bearing on the past history of Buddhist architecture in the north, and on the future of the Dravidian style in the south, than from any peculiar merit of their own. When, however, these eastern caves are taken in connexion with the whole subject, as we now know it, they become invaluable, as throwing light on the general history of cave architecture in India, and receive a reflected light from the western caves, which increases their importance to an extent they could hardly claim for themselves. When we turn to the Western caves the case is widely different. We there find at least one thousand excavations of various sorts and dimensions. Some of great size and of the most elaborate architecture, and all having a distinct meaning and bearing on the general history of architecture. When their story is carefully examined it appears that they are spread pretty evenly over more than 1,000 years of the darkest, though most interesting, period of Indian history, and throw a light upon it as great or greater than can be derived from any other source. In addition to these claims to attention the western caves afford the most vivid illustration of the rise and progress of all the three great religions that prevailed in India in the early centuries of our era and before it. They show clearly how the Buddhist religion rose and spread, and how its form afterwards became corrupt and idolatrous. They explain how it consequently came to be superseded by the nearly cognate form of Jainism and the antagonistic development of the revived religion of the Brahmans. All this too is done in a manner more vivid and more authentic than can be obtained from any other mode of illustration now available.

With all these claims to attention it is hardly to be wondered at that the western caves have attracted the attention of the learned both in India and in Europe from a very early period of their connexion with the East, and that a detailed statistical account of them may still be considered as a desideratum, which it is hoped this work may to some extent at least supply.

It is not easy at first sight to account for the extremely rapid extension of Cave architecture in the West of India as compared with that in the East. Behar was the cradle of the religion that first adopted this monumental form, not any part of Western India, while it will probably be admitted the Buddhists were the first to introduce this form of architecture on both sides of the country. At the same time there seems no reason for supposing that Buddhism in any form existed in the West before missionaries were sent there by Aśoka, after the convocation held by him in the seventeenth year of his reign, as detailed above (ante, p. 17). Before this time there is certainly no evidence to show that the inhabitants of the Western Ghâts were dwellers in caves or used the rock for any monumental or religious purpose, but immediately afterwards they seem to have commenced excavating it and continued to do so uninterruptedly for a long series of years.

It has been suggested that as the Egyptian rock-cut temples are principally in Upper Egypt above the Cataract and in Nubia, that their comparative proximity to India may have been the cause of this form being adopted there. The distance of date, however, between the latest Egyptian and earliest Indian examples quite precludes this idea. Besides the fact that no similarity of any detail can be traced between them, and there seems no other country which could have influenced India in this respect. On the whole the explanation of the phenomenon is probably the prosaic fact that the trap rocks which overlie the country and form the hill sides everywhere in the West are exceptionally well suited for the purpose. They lie everywhere horizontally. Are singularly uniform in their conformation, and have alternating strata of harder and softer rocks which admit of caves being interpolated between them with singular facility, and they are everywhere impervious to moisture.

With such a material it is little wonder that once it was suggested, the inhabitants of the Western Ghâts early seized upon the idea of erecting permanent quasi eternal temples for the practice of the rites of their new religion, in substitution for the perishable wooden structures they had hitherto employed, and once the fashion was adopted we ought not to be surprised it became so generally prevalent nor that it continued in use so long.

At the same time it may be observed that under the circumstances the amount of labour expended in excavating a rock-cut temple in so suitable a material is probably less than would be required to erect a similar building in quarried stone. If we take, for instance, even such an elaborate temple as the Kailasa or Elurâ, it will be found that the cubic contents of the temples left standing is about equal to the amount of material quarried out of the pit in which it stands. It is at the same time evident that it would be much less expensive to chip and throw out to spoil this amount of material, than to quarry it at a distance and carry it to the temple, and then hew it and raise it to the place where it was wanted. The amount of carving and ornament being, of course, the same in both cases. It is not so easy to make a comparison in the case of a Chaitya cave or a vihara, but on the whole it is probable that excavating them in the rock would generally prove cheaper than building them on the plain. If this is so, it is evident that the quasi eternity of the one offered such advantages in such a climate over any ephemeral structure they could erect elsewhere, that we ought not to be surprised at its general adoption. The proof that they exercised a wise discretion in doing this, lies in the fact that though we have in the west of India nearly a thousand rock-cut temples belonging to the Buddhist, Brahmanical, and Jaina religions, we have only one or two structural examples erected in the same region at the very end of the period of time to which these caves belong.

There are in Western India upwards of fifty groups of rock-excavations, belonging to the three great sects,—Buddhists, Brahmans, and Jains,—and of these the great majority are within the limits of the Bombay Presidency, or on its immediate borders. Besides these there are a few insignificant groups in Sindh, the Panjâb, Beluchistân, and Afghanistân.

Geographically the Cave-Temples are distributed very irregularly, but the principal localities in which they exist may be enumerated as follows:—

1. In the province now known as Kâṭhiâwaṛ—the ancient Saurâshṭrâ, forming the peninsular portion of Gujarat, between the Gulfs of Khambay and Kachh,—there are about half-a-dozen groups of caves scattered along the ranges of hills that run parallel to its southern coast. In these groups there are about 140 separate excavations.

2. In the islands of Salsette and Elephanta close to Bombay there are at least 130 caves,—all within 9 miles north or south of the head of the Bombay harbour at Trombay, where stood the old town of Chêmula—probably the great mart known to the early Alexandrian merchants as Semylla or Timula.[1]

3. Not quite 80 miles from Bombay as the crow flies, a little to the north of east, is the old city of Junnar—probably the Tagara of Ptolemy and the *Periplus*,—round which are several groups containing not less than 120 separate caves, while at Harischandragaḍ, Pulu Sonala, and Nânâghat, about 16 miles to the west of it, there are together about 25 more.

4. About 50 miles east of Bombay and 42 south-west of Junnar is Kârlê, where there exists one of the finest Buddhist Cave Temples in India, and within a radius of little more than 20 miles from it are about 60 caves, several of them of special interest.

5. A line drawn southwards from Poona nearly parallel to the Western Ghâṭs or Sahyâdri Hills, passes through groups at Śirwal Wâi, and Karhâḍ, embracing about 80 caves.

6. Along the Konkan, on the western side of the same range, between the hills and the sea, at Kuḍâ, Mhâṛ, Chipalun, &c. the number of caves may be estimated at 60 more.

---

[1] Ptolemy (*Geog.* VII. i. 6; VIII. xxvi. 3) writes Σίμυλλα, and (I. xvii. 4) Τίμουλα; and the author of the *Periplus Mar. Æryth.* (§ 53) Σημύλλα; see below, p. 205.)

7. Within a distance at most of 50 miles from the railway leading from Bombay to Nagpur, and lying almost in a straight line between Nasik and Pâtur, 20 miles east of Akola, are the important groups of Nâsik, Ankai, Elurâ, Aurangabad, and Ajaṇṭâ, with others of less note, numbering about 150 caves.

8. About 250 miles E.S.E. from Bombay, and 130 W.N.W. from Haidarabad is the small village of Karusâ, where, and at Dhârasinwâ, 40 miles to the west, and Kalyâna—the old Châlukya capital 30 miles south-east from it,—there are about 120 caves, some of considerable dimensions, though others are small and insignificant.

9. On the north of the Narmadâ in Malwa are the groups at Bâgh, Dhamnâr, and Kolvi—neither of great importance; and, lastly, far to the south, on the banks of the Malaprabhâ in Beḷgaum district are the caves of Bâdâmi and Aiholê, architecturally among the most interesting Brahmanical groups in India, especially as affording a fixed date, by which that of others can be compared.

This brings up the total to about 900 caves, and there are a few of little note scattered in ones and twos over the same area, so that we may safely estimate the total of known caves in the West at over 900; besides many which have not yet been visited by any European, and of which consequently no record exists.

These are divided primarily into three classes according to the sects by whom or for whose use they were hewn out, viz., Buddhists, Brahmans, and Jains. The earliest examples we have belong to the Buddhists, and date from the middle of the third century B.C., but excavations belonging to this sect, extend from that date down to near the end of the seventh century of our era, thus ranging through between nine or ten centuries. They are also the most numerous class, fully 75 per cent. of the whole being Buddhist caves.

The next, in order of time, are those of the Brahmans, whether Śaiva or Vaishṇava, which range from about the fourth to the eighth century of our era, or perhaps later. Of the whole, about 18 per cent. of the excavations are Brahmanical, but a large proportion of them are of very considerable dimensions, but, except at Karusâ, and some scattered caves in the Sâtârâ district, few of them are small, whereas among the early Buddhist caves there are many which are insignificant.

Lastly, there are the Jaina Cave-Temples, which are much less numerous than those of either of the preceding sects, and of which the earliest may belong to the fifth or sixth century, and the latest perhaps to the twelfth, they are the least numerous of all, not exceeding four per cent. of the whole.

We may thus estimate their numbers as follows:—

Buddhist excavations	about	720
Brahmanical	„	160
Jaina	„	35[1]

If to these we add the Eastern caves, described in the first part of this work, it may safely be assumed that the Rock-cut Temples of India, known at the present day, amount to more than a thousand separate excavations.

All such excavations, it will be understood, were for religious purposes, some being temples—Chaityas, or Halls devoted solely to worship, others monasteries, or Vihâras consisting of a hall for assembly, sometimes with an inner shrine for worship, and with cells for monks; some were Dharmaśâlâs, with or without cells, where councils or assemblies were held; while in the more complete Buddhist establishments there were, first, the temple; secondly, one or more monastic halls with surrounding cells; and occasionally also separate dwellings, or hermitages for ascetic monks.

For purposes of description, these works may be classified as follows:—

I.—Buddhist Cave-Temples may be divided into two great classes: first, those which were executed, so far as can be judged from style or inscriptions, before the Christian era or during the first century after it. These belong to the Hinâyâna sect and are generally plain in style, and are devoid of images of Buddha for worship.

II.—Buddhist Cave-Temples belonging to the Mahâyâna sect of a date subsequent to the year A.D. 100, after which images of Buddha first began to appear. These images gradually in the course of time supersede the earlier dâgoba or relic-shrine, until, in the latest examples, the personages represented become numerous, and the pre-eminence of Buddha himself seems to have been threatened by the growing favour for Avalôkitêśwara Bôdhisattwa, who, in

[1] The Jaina excavations in the rock at Gwalior extend down to the 14th and 15th centuries, but as these are not included in the limits of the Bombay Presidency, they are omitted in the above enumeration, but will be noticed further on, after those in the west have been described. They consist of upwards of 50 separate excavations, but all of very modern date.

Nepal, under the better known name of Padmapâni, had become the favourite divinity of the populace.

III.—The Brahmanical Caves: The Brahmans were probably first led to excavate Cave-Temples in imitation of the Buddhists, and as a means of pressing their candidature for a larger share of popular favour. Their works are very similar to the later Buddhist Vihâras, only without the side cells for monks—such being unnecessary in what were meant only as places of public worship for a religion in which monasticism was not an element. The shrine is usually in the back wall of the Vaishṇava temples, but in those of the S'aiva sect it is generally brought forward into the cave with a *pradakshiṇâ* or passage for circumambulation round about it.

IV.—The Jaina Caves are the least numerous, but among them are one or two very fine ones. They also are on the plan of the Buddhist Vihâras, sometimes with cells in the walls, but more distinguished by numerous figures of their Tîrthaṅkaras or Jinas, who hold the same place in their system as the various Buddhas do in that of the Buddhist sect. The Jains are now divided into two sections; the Svetâmbaras or white-robed community, who are of more recent origin than the Buddhists,[1] and the Digambaras or naked Jains, who are generally understood to be an older sect than the followers of Buddha. It is to this latter division that all the Jaina caves belong, and as yet, with the exception of a small late group in the extreme south of the Peninsula, they have been found only in the Dekhan and Rajputana, or in the region ruled over by the Râṭhoṛs or Balharâs and Châlukyas.

Classification of Buddhist Monuments.

The various objects of Buddhist architecture may be catalogued as consisting of:—1. Stûpas or Topes; 2. Ornamental Rails, which however are found only in connexion with *stûpas*, pillars, sacred trees, and temples; 3. Stambhas or Lâts; 4. Chaitya-halls or temples; 5. Vihâras or monasteries (including Bhikshu-gṛihas or hermitages); and 6. Poṅḍhis or cisterns.

1. Stûpa, from a root meaning "to heap," "to erect," is applied to any pile or mound, as to a funeral pile, hence it comes to be applied to a Tumulus erected over any of the sacred relics of Buddha, or on spots consecrated as the scenes of his acts. Such

[1] Stan. Julien's *Mem. sur les Cont. Occ.* I., 163, 164.

were the Stûpas erected by Aśoka all over northern India, and the great Dâgobas raised in Ceylon in early times.[1] But not only for Buddha himself, but also for the Sthaviras or Thêros,—the elders of the Buddhist religion, were stûpas erected; and, in later times, probably for even ordinary monks. Moreover, when the relics of Buddha became objects of worship, as they did even before the time of Aśoka, it became necessary that they should be exhibited in some way to the congregation, on some sort of altar or receptacle called a *dhâtugarbha* or *dhâtugopa*, abbreviated into Dâgaba or Dâgoba and Dâgopa.[2] *Stûpa* has been corrupted into the Anglo-Indian word "Tope," which is generally applied to such of those monuments as are structural and outside caves,—as Dâgoba usually denotes those in caves or attached to them, and hewn out of the solid rock.[3]

---

1 The origin of the domical form of all the stupas in India, has never yet been satisfactorily explained. It is not derived from an earthen tumulus, like the tombs of the Etruscans, or it would, like them, have been a straight-lined cone. Nor was it from a Dome of construction, as none such existed in India when the earliest examples were erected. It could, apparently, only be copied from such models as the tents of the Tartars or Kirghiz, which all, so far as we know, always were domical, and with a low circular drum, very like those of the Topes (see Yule's *Marco Polo*, vol. i., woodcuts, pp. 247, 395).—J. F.

2 Turnour derives this word from *dhâta*, a relic, and *gabban*, a casket, receptacle, or shrine; Wilson (*As. Res*, vol. xvii. p. 605) from *deha*, "the body," and *gopa*, "what preserves." The *Chaitya*, or the form of Stûpa usually found in the Caves, consists of a short, wide cylinder or plinth, supporting a high dome, on which stands a square neck, usually carved on the four sides, surmounted by a capital consisting of a number of flat tiles, each overlapping the one below it, and on this stands the *chhatri*, or umbrella. The most important feature is the dome called the *garbha;* the neck or *gala* represents a box to contain a relic, and at Bhâjâ it is quite hollow; the capital or *toraṇa* forms the lid of this box, and served the purpose apparently of a small table or shelf, on which relics were displayed in small crystal caskets, over which hung the umbrella. In Nepal the *gala* is always marked with two eyes, or a face, and over the capital rises a spire called *chûḍamaṇi*—"the crest jewel"—of thirteen grades, typical of 13 *Bhuvanas*, or heavens of the Buddhists, and the *palus* or finial which terminates it represents the Akanishṭha Bhuvana, or highest heaven of Adi Buddha. In Burma the finial of the spire is called *Hti*, and popularly "Tee," a term which has frequently been applied to the capital of any *chaitya* (see Woodcut, No. 43, page 227).

3 The Dâgoba is the symbol of Buddha, just as the Tree or Lion and the Wheel are probably the symbols of the Assembly and the Law—the *triratna* or "three precious things" of the Bauddha creed. In some instances we find the *tree* apparently substituted for the Lion or *Siṅha* (*e.g.*, see figs. 38, 39, Fergusson's *Ind. and East. Archit.* pp. 101, 102). "The *Parinibhan Suttan* states that *Chaityas* or *Stûpas* 'originated' upon the death of Gautama, when 'eight *thûpas* were built over the corporeal relics, a ninth over the

2. ORNAMENTAL RAILS. Though from their nature of difficult application to Caves, and comparatively of little importance in their architecture, ornamental rails are among the most original and important features of the earliest Buddhist architecture that have come down to our times; and on them in some cases the most elaborate sculpture was lavished. They were employed round the sacred trees, stûpas, pillars, and occasionally round temples. The smaller ones, however, have so far as we know all disappeared, and it is only some of those round the stûpas that have come down to our time. The most remarkable are those of Bharhut, Sânchi, and Amrâvati, and the rectangular one at Buddha Gayâ,—perhaps originally enclosing a temple. In the cave temples examples are hardly to be looked for, yet a form of them does occur in the caves of the Ândhra dynasty, as at the great Chaitya Cave at Kâṇhêri, and at Nâsik. The simplest form of rail consists of square pillars set at little more than their own breadth

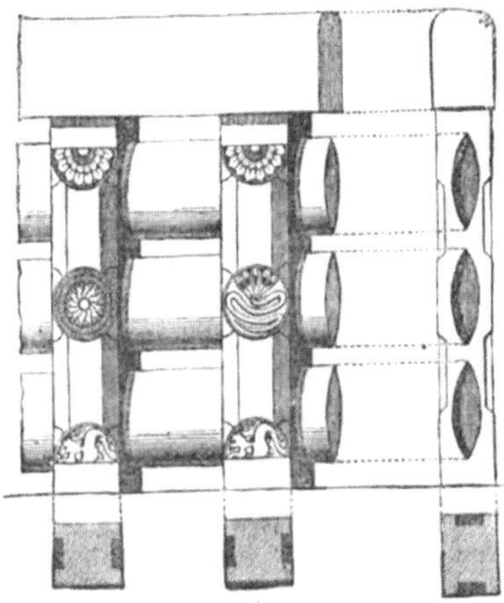

(Fig. 42.) Rail from Sanchi, Tope No. 2.[1]

kumbhan, and a tenth over the charcoal of his funeral pile' (*Jour. As. Soc. Beng.* vol. vii. p. 1014). And it would seem from the same *Suttan* that *Chaityâni* existed in several parts of the Madhyama deśa even during the lifetime of Gautama. The *Atthakathâ* explains that the *Chaityâni* were not 'Buddhistical shrines,' but *Yakkhattanâni*, 'erections for demon worship,' . . . . Gautama himself repaired to the *Chêpâla Chaitya* for rest, and there expatiated on its splendour, as well as that of many others (*J. As. S. Beng.* vol. vii. p. 1001). It was doubtless from a contemplation of the busy throng of religious enthusiasts who crowded these monuments of worship, that Gautama gave his sanction for the erection of the *thûpas* over his own relics and those of his disciples. Gautama's words were (*Parinibhan Suttan*), 'If in respect of *thûpas* any should set up flowers, scents, or embellishments, or should worship (*them*), or should (*by such means*) cause their minds to be purified (*pasâdessanti*), such acts will conduce to their well-being and happiness . . . . Ananda, many thinking that "this is the *thûpa* of the adorable, the sanctified, the omniscient, supreme Buddha," compose their minds; and when they have caused their minds to be *cleansed*, they, upon the dissolution of the body after death, are born in a glorious heavenly world.'"—Alwis, *Buddhism*, pp. 22, 23.

[1] From Fergusson's *Ind. and East. Archit.*, p. 93.

apart, and joined by three thin broad bars rounded on the sides and placed near to one another and to the head rail which joins the tops of the pillars. In more ornamental examples the pillars are carved with a circular disc in the centre, and semi-circular ones at the top and bottom, usually carved with rosettes, but sometimes with animals, &c., and the interspaces chamfered. This is well exemplified in the rail round Tope No. 2 at Sanchi (Woodcut No. 42). Mr. Fergusson remarks that "the circular discs may be taken as representing a great nail meant to keep the centre bar in its place in the original carpentry forms; the half discs, top and bottom, as metal plates to strengthen the junctions—and this, it seems, most probably, may really have been the origin of these features."

In other rails a disc is also added on each bar, and the head rail carved with festoons. Copies of such rails are also employed as friezes, and the member under it is then sometimes carved with a line of animal figures in festoons. (*See* Plate XXII.)

3. Stambhas or Lâts are pillars, usually erected in front of a temple, whether Śaiva, Vaishṇava, Jaina, or Bauddha, and carrying one or more of the symbols of the religion to which it was dedicated; the Buddhist Stambhas bearing the wheel representative of *Dharma* or the law, or Lions. The Śaiva ones bear a *triśula* or trident; the Vaishṇava a figure of Garuḍa; the Jaina a *Chaumukha* or fourfold Tîrthaṅkara. Some of the finest Buddhist Lâts, erected by Aśoka, are not apparently in connexion with any temple, but bear his edicts or other inscriptions; they may, however, have been erected in connexion with wooden or brick buildings which have disappeared ages ago.

4. Chaityas. Like *Stûpa*, the word *Chaitya* is also derived from a root (*chitâ*) signifying "a funeral pile," "heap," and hence means "a monument" and "an altar," and in a secondary sense it is used by Jains and Buddhists to indicate "a temple containing a *Chaitya*." In Nepal and Tibet, and in Buddhist Sanskrit literature, the word is applied to the model of a stûpa placed in the temples and to which we have applied the term Dâgoba. These Chaityas or Dâgobas are an essential feature of chapels or temples constructed solely for purposes of worship and which may therefore be appropriately called Chaitya-Caves. Such temples never have cells for residence in their side walls. One or more of them is usually attached to every set of Buddhist caves. Their earliest form in

the rock in Western India is an oblong room, about double as long as wide, entered from one end, and with the *Chaitya* or dâgoba near the other. This, in some of the earliest examples, is connected with the roof, by a slender shaft representing the staff of the umbrella or *chhatri*, the flat canopy of which is carved upon the roof. Sometimes this is omitted, and the thin flat members which form the capital are attached to the roof. The end of the chamber behind the dâgoba was at first square, but very early came to be cut in the form of a semi-circular apse, leaving a *pradakshiṇâ* or passage for the circumambulation of the *Chaitya*. The flat roof, however, was early replaced by a semicircular one, and then a side aisle was cut quite round, separated from the central nave by a row of plain octagonal shafts arranged close together, while the Dâgoba was left to stand free, surmounted by an umbrella (or three of them) in carved wood and sometimes in stone. This last plan seems to have fully met the requirements of the worship, for, with the addition only of more ornamentation, it continues down to the latest example.

When this form of temple became enlarged, however, the lighting became a difficulty, for it was necessary that a strong light should be thrown on the *Chaitya*. To effect this, the front, instead of being left in the rock with only a large door, was cleared quite out; the façade surrounding the arched opening thus formed was ornamented with carving, in which the "Buddhist-rail" pattern, the dâgoba, and the horse-shoe arch were repeated of every size and in every variety of arrangement. The opening itself was in the oldest caves occupied by a wooden front, of which we have no example left; but its chief features, as it once existed at Kondâṇê, Bhâjâ, and Pitalkhorâ, can be easily recovered from what we still find at Ajaṇṭâ, Kârlê, and Beḍsâ, where the wood is partly replaced by the rock over the doors and between them, leaving a large horse-shoe formed window above, partly screened by lattice-work, in wood. From the mortices left in the rock, we know that this once existed in all the older caves. At Kârlê the original woodwork still remains entire, and fragments of it have been found in other caves.

5. Vihâras.—These were for the accommodation of Buddhist Bhikshus, or mendicant monks living together in communities. The earliest form of vihâra or monastery cave seems to have been that of one or more (*grihas*) cells with a verandah (*padaśâla*) or porch in

front. In many instances the cells were small; in others they consisted of two apartments, the inner having a stone bench or bed (as in several instances at Junnar). This bed is a constant feature of all the earlier cells, but disappears in those excavated after the second century after Christ. A permanent spring or stream of water close by, or a cistern (*pôṅdhi*) cut in the rock, usually beside or under the cell, was an indispensable accompaniment. The number of these cells at one place was often considerable.[1]

The next step in Western India was to introduce a square hall for assembling in, probably copied from some wooden and structural erection that existed before any rock-cut excavations were attempted, and often also used as a school: this must have been a very early accompaniment of every group of *Bhikshu-gṛihas* or monks' cells. At first this room perhaps had no cells, but it would soon be evident that the walls of a large hall offered special facilities for excavating cells all round it, and, for purposes of worship, a larger cell was afterwards cut out in the back wall, containing a dâgoba to serve in place of a separate chapel. At first, too, the smaller halls or *śail-agṛihas* might have been formed without pillars to support the roof, — the tenacity of the rock being assumed to dispense with the necessity of any prop between the side walls. Afterwards, however, when the size was increased, it was found that this was unsafe, and that, owing to flaws and veins, large areas of roofing, if left unsupported, were liable to fall in. Pillars were then resorted to, as in the ordinary wooden buildings of the country, arranged either in rows running round the *śâlâs* or halls, separating the central square area from the aisles, or disposed in equidistant lines, as in Cave XI. at Ajaṇṭâ, and probably in the vihâra at Pitalkhorâ.

Little sculpture was at first employed in any of the caves; but in later examples the pillars came to be elaborately carved; and, though Buddha did not preach idol-worship, in course of time the plain dâgoba ceased to satisfy the worshippers of certain sects, and the shrine came to be almost invariably occupied by an image of Buddha seated on a sort of throne, called a *Siṅhâsana*, or 'lion-seat,' because the ends of it rested on lions carved in bas-relief,—and

---

[1] Groups of caves are often called *Lêṇâs*, a word which Dr. J. Wilson derived from Sansk. *layanam*, "ornamentation"; but *layana*, "a place of rest, a house," from the root *lî*, "to adhere," seems a more natural derivation, for the name of "an abode."

usually with an attendant on each hand bearing a *chauri* or fly-flap. Eventually this representation came to be repeated in all parts of the caves; while in still later times, when the *Mahâyâṇa* sect became popular and influential, other beings were associated with him, first as attendants, and then as distinct and separate objects of adoration. Such were the Indras, Bodhisattwas, Padmapâni, and Manjuśrî.

This idolatry appears at first sight quite antagonistic to the principles taught by their great sage, for, having entered *Nirvâṇa*, or perfect quiescence, he can no more hear or be in any way influenced by the worship of his followers. But they hold that this does not detract from the efficacy of the service, for the act is in itself an *opus operatum*, and that as the seed germinates when it is put into the earth without any consciousness on the part of the elements relative to the vivifying influence they exercise, so does merit arise from the worship of the images of Buddha, though the being they represent is unconscious of the deed. And this merit is, in like manner, spontaneously and without the intervention of any intelligent agent, productive of prosperity and peace. For the same reason they worship the *bodhi* or *bo* tree, under which he attained to Buddhahood, and the relics of the sage and of his disciples, enshrined in dâgobas, &c.

In the Vihâra-caves there is frequently in front of the shrine an antechamber forming the approach to it, and with two pillars and corresponding pilasters separating it from the great hall. All the Vihâras have a verandah, or *padáśâla*, as it is termed, in front, frequently with cells or chapels opening from the ends of it; and some are of two and three storeys.[1]

6. PÔṆḌHÎS or cisterns are almost invariable accompaniments of mendicants' houses and Vihâras, and are cut in the rock, usually near or at the entrance, and often extending partly under the caves. The water was brought to them by numerous small runnels cut in the rock, by which it was carried over the façade of the cave and otherwise collected from the face of the hill in which the excavations occur.

---

[1] The Vihâras of Nepâl at the present day are formed with an open court in place of the hall, surrounded by cloisters of one or two storeys, with a shrine or temple at the back of two or three storeys, usually containing an image of Sâkya Muni, Dipankara Buddha, or of Padmapâni. In the smaller side cells are images of Bodhisattwas and Dêvîs, while in the upper rooms live the priests and devotees.

The entrance to the cistern is usually by a square opening[1] in the floor of a small recess; and on the back wall of this recess, or on the face of the rock over it, is frequently an inscription. Sometimes, but seldom, the jambs of the recess are carved with pilasters.

In addition to the foregoing may be quoted the IMAGES OF BUDDHA found in so many of the Western Buddhist Caves, but perhaps in none earlier than the fourth or fifth century. These images[2] when found in the shrines are always represented as seated, though oftentimes attended by standing figures bearing fly-flaps. The seated figures are distinguished by Buddhists according to the position of the hands. The most usual attitude of the great teacher is that in which he is represented as seated on a throne, the corners of which are upheld by two lions, with his feet on a lotus blossom and his hands in front of his breast holding the little finger of the left hand between the thumb and forefinger of the right. This is known as the *Dharma-chakra mudrâ*, or attitude of "turning the wheel of the law," that is of teaching. He is also sometimes represented standing, or with his legs doubled up under him and his hands in this *mudrâ* or attitude.

The next most common attitude of Buddha is that in which the Jaina Tîrthaṅkaras are always represented, viz., with their legs doubled under them in a squatting attitude, and the hands laid one on the other over the feet with the palms turned upwards. This position of meditative absorption is called the Jñâna or *Dhyâna mudrâ*. A third attitude in which he is sometimes represented, as when under the Bodhi tree, where he is said to have attained to Buddha-hood, is called the *Vajrâsana* or *Bhûmisparśa mûdra*, when the left hand lies on the upturned soles of the feet, and the right resting over the knee, points to the earth. He is also figured on the walls standing with the right hand uplifted in the attitude of blessing, or with the

---

[1] This was probably fitted with a square wooden cover to keep insects, leaves, &c. out of the water.

[2] The Singhalese and Chinese Buddhists have a legend that a Pilima image of Gautama was made during his lifetime by the King of Kosala. The Tibetan scriptures (*Asiat. Res.* vol. xx. p. 476) speak of Buddha having lectured on the advantages of laying up his image; and the *Divya Avadâna* of Nepal gives a story (Speir's *Life in Ancient India*, p. 272) of his having recommended Bimbisâra to send his portrait to Rudrayâna, King of Roruka; but all these stories are doubtless like very much besides in Buddhist literature, the invention of later times. The earliest mention of images in Ceylon is in the Mihintali inscription of 241 A.D.—Alwis, *Buddhism*, pp. 19, 20.

alms bowl of the Bhikshu or mendicant, or, lastly, resting on his right side with the head to the north, in the attitude he is said to have lain at his death or *Nirvâṇa*. Behind the head is often represented a nimbus (*Bhâmandala*), or aureole, as in mediæval figures of the saints. This occurs in the earliest sculptured and painted figures of Buddha, probably as early as the third century and possibly even earlier.

On each side the principal image we usually find attendants, standing with *chaurîs* or fly flaps in their hands. These are varied in different sculptures; in some they are Śakras or Indras with high regal headdresses; in others Padmapâṇi[1] holding a lotus by the stalk is on one side, his hair in the *jaṭâ* or headdress of a Bhikshu, and Manjuśrî or Vajrapâṇi,—another Bodhisattwa, on the other.[2]

On the front of the seat, when the feet are turned up, is usually sculptured a wheel (*chakra*) turned "edgewise" to the spectator with a deer couchant on each side of it, and sometimes behind the deer are a number of kneeling worshippers on each side (Plate XXXV.) In more modern *reliefs* Buddha is often represented seated on a lotus, the stalk of which is upheld by Nâga figures—people whose heads are canopied by the hoods, usually five, of a cobra.

To what has already been said respecting Buddhism generally, it may here be added that the Buddhists are divided into two sects, the Hinâyâna and Mahâyâna or of the Lesser and Greater Vehicle. The original or Puritan Buddhists belong to the Hinâyâna or Lesser Vehicle, whose religion consisted in the practice of morality and a few simple ceremonial observances. The thirteenth[3] patriarch, Nâgârjuna, a native of Berar, who lived 400, or according to others, 500 years[4] after Buddha, and shortly before the time of Kanishka,[5] was the founder of the new school of the Mahâyâna,

---

[1] In China Padmapâni is called Kwan-yin, and is usually, though not always, represented as a goddess—of mercy: he is the Kanon of the Japanese.

[2] Ânanda and Kaśyapa are frequently placed on the right and left of Buddha in Chinese temples.—Edkins, *Religion in China*, p. 45.

[3] Vassilief, *Le Bouddisme*, p. 214; Lassen makes him 14th; *Ind. Alt.* II. 1203.

[4] Vassilief, p. 31; *Jour. As. S. Beng.* vol. v., pp. 530 ff.; vol. xvii. pt. ii. pp. 616, 617.

[5] Kanishka was a king on the North-west frontier of India in the first century of the Christian era, and is said to have been converted to Buddhism by Âryaheva the pupil of Nâgârjuna. Vassilief, p. 76.

which soon became very popular in the Dekhan; it taught an abstruse mystical theology which speedily developed a mythology in which Buddha was pushed into the background by female personifications of Dharma or the *Prajnâ Pâramitâ*, and other goddesses or *śaktis*, by Jñânatmaka Buddhas, or forms of the senses, &c. From all this, as might be expected, we find a very considerable difference between the sculptures of the cave temples of the earlier and later periods of Buddhism. This does not, however, become very early marked, and it is only after the fifth century that we have any very decidedly Mahâyânist sculptures—as in the later caves at Ajaṇṭa, Elurâ, Aurangabad, and in one cave at Nâsik.

As already stated, the earlier temples in the West are the plainest in style. The Chaitya Caves are sculptured indeed on their façades, but the ornaments consist almost solely of the "rail pattern" and models of the horse-shoe arch which formed the front of the temple; human figures are rarely introduced. The sculpture, however, as will be indicated below, grows more abundant and varied as we descend the stream of history, and perhaps in the century preceding the Christian era, the custom began of introducing sculptures of the kings with their wives who executed the works. In the Assembly Halls, as well as in the Chaitya-Caves, the only object of worship was the Dâgoba, to which offerings of flowers and salutations were made, and which was circumambulated by the worshipper repeating short prayers and *mantras*. The Dâgoba, be it remembered, was the emblem by which the memory of Buddha was represented, hence the step was an easy one to substitute the image of Buddha himself. But first with the dâgoba was associated in a subordinate way the *sinhastambha* and *chakrastambha* or Lion and Wheel pillars, in front of the Chaitya-Caves. And when the image of Buddha came to be substituted in the Vihâras for the Dâgoba, he was seated on a *sinhâsana* or Lion throne, and the Wheel was placed under the front of it. This, however, does not seem to have taken place till considerably after the Christian era. Indeed no image of Buddha in the caves of Western India can belong to an earlier period than the fourth century; possibly some of the wall paintings may however be older. The time that separates the older from the later style may be drawn approximately at the second century after the Christian era. Somewhere about that date, under the Ândhrabhritya dynasty whose power extended southward from the Tâptî or perhaps the Narmadâ river, probably to the northern boundary of Maisur and the Penâr river, sculptured figures and paintings began to assume great prominence in the Cave Temples.

Chronology of Buddhist Caves.

The dates of the various groups of Buddhist caves, especially of the earliest ones, have not yet been ascertained with sufficient precision to admit of their being presented in anything like a tabular form. Their relative dates can generally be fixed, and their position in the sequence is sufficiently obvious, but till the chronology of the period is determined with more certainty than it is at present, epochal dates can hardly be attached either to the groups or to individual caves without the risk of their being upset by subsequent investigations. It is probable, however, that before long this state of affairs may be altered for the better. All the more important caves are inscribed, and when these inscriptions are re-examined by competent scholars, with the additional light that can now be thrown upon them, it seems more than probable that the uncertainty that now hangs on their dates may be removed. It unfortunately happens, however, that the names in these inscriptions are either those of private individuals, whose personality affords no information, or, if of royal personages, they are of kings whose date has hitherto been only approximately ascertained. If we could depend on the Pauranik lists they would nearly suffice to remove the difficulty, but they have not yet been brought sufficiently into accord with the numismatic and paleographic evidence to be implicitly relied upon, though the discrepancies seem gradually disappearing.

As a rule, the inscriptions are devoid of epochal dates, and when such exist the era from which they are calculated is in no instance specified.[1] If it should turn out, as is more than probable, that no era was used, at that age, in Western India, except that of Saka (A.D. 78–9), one great source of uncertainty would be removed. But even then, till a greater number of dated inscriptions than are at

---

[1] In his *Ancient Geography of India*, Gen. Cunningham has quoted one, at page 533, as dated in the year 30 of the Sakaditya Kala, and repeats this at page xxi. of the introduction of his *First Annual Report*. Unfortunately, however, neither Lieut. Brett's copy of this inscription (*J. B. B. R. A. S.*, vol. v. No. 10, p. 22) nor Mr. West's more exact transcript, vol. vii. of the same Journal, No. 39, p. 9, bear out the General's translation, which cannot consequently be relied upon.

present known are found in these caves, they do not suffice to enable us to arrange them all in chronological order.

Under these circumstances we are forced to rely a great deal more than is desirable on palæographic evidence. In relative dates the varying progressive changes which the alphabetic forms assume are invaluable, and generally a safe guide; but for epochal dates they are comparatively useless. The local or geographical position of the place where an inscription is found is often a cause of greater change in the characters employed, than distance of time. It is only when the characters are compared within a certain limited area that they can be successfully employed for the purposes of chronology. Even then the results derived from such indications can only be considered as approximative, and never as capable of any great precision.

The architectural character of the caves is a far more distinct and constant characteristic than the alphabetic form of their inscriptions. All the caves have architectural features, and these, as in all true styles, all over the world change according to a certain law of progression that can never be mistaken when sufficient materials exist for comparison. In Europe it has of late years been allowed to supersede all other evidence in ascertaining the age of mediæval or classical buildings, and in no single instance has an appeal from its decision been sustained. If, for instance, we take such a cave as that at Bhâjâ (woodcut No. 1), the whole of the front of which was constructed in wood, and where the pin holes still exist, by means of which the wooden ornaments were originally attached to the rock. Where the wooden ribs of the roof still remain *in situ*, and where the rock-cut pillars of the nave slope inwards in imitation of wooden posts, we may feel sure that we are at the very cradle of stone-cut architecture, and cannot get much further back without reaching a state of affairs where wood and wood only was employed. When on the other hand we compare this with the façade of the Lomas Rishi cave in Behar (woodcut No. 3), which we know was excavated by Aśoka B.C. 250, we find the two so essentially identical, in style, that we may fix the date of the Bhâjâ cave at least as early as 200 B.C., and in doing so we may feel certain we do not err by many years, or in ascribing it to too ancient a date.

If starting from this point we take a series of four such Chaitya caves as those of Bhâjâ, Bedsa, Kârlê, and Nasik—to be described hereafter—and allow 50 years interval between each, we bring our history down nearly to the Christian era. When we look at the extent of the changes introduced, and the quantity of examples we have to interpolate, it seems improbable to allow a less period between each, nor that the position of any of these milestones can be shifted more than ten or a dozen years without a violation of the surest principles of archæology.

After the Christian era, it is not quite so easy to arrange the sequence of the caves, not from any change in the principles in which this should be done, but from the variety of the features in the examples, and the distance from each other of the localities in which they are found. It also appears that after the earlier centuries of our era there seems to have been a pause in cave excavations. After the fifth and sixth centuries, however, when they were resumed, there is no longer any difficulty in ascertaining the age of any cave with almost as much precision as can be desired.

The science of numismatics opens another source from which we may hope to obtain a considerable amount of precise information as to the age of the caves at some not distant date. In Gujarât and the cave region north of Bombay a great number of coins have been found belonging to a dynasty generally known as the Sah, kings of Saurâshṭra. Most of these bear dates from some unspecified era. The earlier coins are not dated, but the second series range from 102 to 271 at least,[1] while the number of kings who reigned was certainly not less than 25 or 26.[2]

Unfortunately numismatists have not yet been able to make up their minds as to the era from which these dates are to be reckoned. Mr. Newton assumes that it was the era of Vicramaditya, 56 B.C., but without stopping to inquire if that era had then been established. Mr. Thomas and others assume that they commenced earlier; but on the whole it seems most probable that the era was that of Saka, A.D. 78–9, and if this is so we have a thread extending through our cave history down to the year 350 A.D., which eventually may be of the greatest use in enabling us to fix the dates of the caves belonging to that period of history.

When all these various sources of information come to be

---

1 Newton on *J. B. B., R. A. S.*, vol. viii. p. 27, *et seq.*

2 Thomas in *Burgess, 2nd Report.* p. 44.

thoroughly investigated there can be little doubt that we shall obtain the dates of all the caves with all the precision that can be desired. But when actual dates are not available it is probable we must still to a great extent depend on the indications obtained from palæography and architecture. The first, as just mentioned, may be used as a useful guide to relative dates where no other or better materials are available. The latter have been found in Europe, and still more in Asia, to be infallible, yielding results that admit of no dispute, and which are more generally relied upon by antiquaries than those derived from any other source.

Pending this being done, as an approximately chronological arrangement, the several groups of Buddhist Caves may be placed in the following order:—

1. The oldest caves at Junâgadh, the groups at Sânâ, Talâjâ, and other places in Kâthiâwar, may be considered as varying from 250 B.C. to the Christian era.

2. A number of groups in the Konkan and Dekhan, all to the south of Bombay, and all bearing a general character of small plain dwellings for Bhikshus, with flat-roofed shrines for the Dâgoba and Vihâras. The chief groups in the Konkan are at Kuḍâ, and in the neighbourhood of Mhâṛ and Kol; those in the Dekhan on the other side of the Sahyâdri Hills or Ghâṭs are chiefly at Karâḍh, about 30 miles south of Sâtârâ, and at Wäi and Śirwal, north of the same town. These range perhaps from 200 B.C. to A.D. 50.

3. Almost due east of Bombay, in the Ghâṭs, and close to the line of railway leading to Poona, there are important groups of caves at Kondâṇê, Bhâjâ, Bêḍsâ, and Kârlê, each with a Chaitya cave of some architectural importance; and with these more notable groups may be taken those at Śailarwâḍi, Ambivlê, &c., all in the same neighbourhood. These may be placed within the three and a half centuries that elapsed between B.C. 250 and A.D. 100.

4. A fourth group may be formed of the caves at Junnar, about 50 miles north of Poona, the Nâsik Buddhist Caves, about 50 miles north of Junnar, the Pitalkhorâ Buddhist Caves, 84 miles E.N.E. from Nâsik, and the earliest of the Ajaṇṭâ Caves, 55 miles east of Pitalkhora. These are of various ages, the oldest Cave at Nâsik being about 100 B.C., and the later ones there belonging to the second or third century A.D., while there are some that have been excavated or altered by

the Mahâyâna sect at as late a date as the seventh century. The Junnar groups contain no excavation of note later than the second, or early in the third century, A.D., and many of the caves are perhaps one or two centuries earlier, while the earliest of those of Ajaṇṭâ may range from B.C. 150 to the end of the first century of the Christian era.

5. The fifth section will include those at Marôl or Kondivtê, and the earlier portions of the great series at Kâṇhêri, in the island of Salsette, at the head of Bombay harbour, which may be ascribed to the period between B.C. 100 and A.D. 150.

These bring us down to nearly the end of the second century of the Christian era, and include all the known examples belonging to the first or Hinâyâna division of Buddhist Caves of Western India. These, when looked at as a whole, are easily to be distinguished from the more modern examples, first from their greater simplicity in ornament, and it may also be said by their grandeur of conception, as well as from the total absence of figures of Buddha or of Saints as objects of worship.

The second or more recent series of Buddhist Caves belonging to the Mahâyâna sect, extending from the fourth to nearly the eighth century, comprises the following groups:—

1. A cave or two-storeyed hall in the Uparkoṭ or Fort of Junâgadh, in Kâṭhiâwâṛ probably of about A.D. 300; and,

2. Ajaṇṭâ, the later members of the group, A.D. 250–650 or even later; and with these may be joined the small group known as Ghatoṭkach, near the village of Jinjâlâ, about nine miles from Ajaṇṭâ, and which date from about 500 to 600 A.D.

3. The caves at Aurangâbâd in the north-west of the Nizam's territories, are so much like the later ones at Ajaṇṭâ in general style, though the arrangements differ, that we may refer them to about the same age, though they belong to a different school of Buddhists. They principally belong to the seventh century. Some are even later than 650 A.D.

4. Nearly as important as either of these, is the well known Buddhist group at Elurâ. Though somewhat overshadowed by the splendour of the Brahmanical and Jaina caves which succeeded them in the same locality, they are both extensive and interesting. They may be considered as ranging from A.D. 450 to 700.

5. In the south of Mâlwâ, near the village of Bâgh, is a group of Buddhist Caves belonging to one of the purer schools of the Hina-

yâna sect. There is no Chaitya Cave in the series as it now exists, but several caves have fallen in. This group may be placed about A.D. 350 to 450.

6. Many of the Salsette Caves at Kaṇhêri and Magathana in Bombay harbour are of comparatively recent date, and their range is very extensive. They may be placed between A.D. 150 and 850.

7. A small group of caves at Ḍhânk, in the same province, circa A.D. 700.

8. The Buddhist Caves at Dhamnâr and at Kholvi, must extend down to A.D. 700 at least, if not to even a later date.

It is hardly probable that any subsequent researches will disturb this chronology, to any material extent. A thorough revision of the inscriptions, however, especially if it should result in enabling us to fix the dates of the Andhrabhritya kings with certainty, would give the list a precision in which, it must be confessed, it is in some instances deficient at present.[1]

---

[1] Before leaving this branch of the subject, it may be interesting to allude to the curious similarities that exist betweeen some of the Buddhist forms just referred to, and many of those which are found in Europe in the middle ages.

The form of the Chaitya caves and the position of the altar and choir must strike anyone who compares these plans with those of early Christian churches, but the essential analogy that exists between the dâgoba and the altar is even more striking. Every dâgoba had a relic in or on the table under the umbrella. There are evidences of this in every known instance, while no mediæval altar was an altar, in a religious sense, until a relic had been put into it or under it. This is, in fact, what constitutes it an altar.

The monasteries too, though existing before the Christian era, are in their forms and institutions so like those afterwards adopted in Europe, that their investigation opens up numerous important questions, that ought to interest, but can hardly be entered upon in a work like the present..

CHAPTER II.

CAVE TEMPLES &c., IN KATHIAWAR.

Introductory.

The peninsula of Kâṭhiâwâṟ in Gujarat, the Saurâshṭra of earlier times and the Ânarta of the Pauranik legends, with its Kôlîs, Rabârîs, Ahîrs, and other non-Aryan or mixed tribes, seems to have become, at a very early date, a great stronghold of Buddhism, just as in the present century it has so largely embraced the doctrines of Nârâyan Svâmi. Its famous Mount Rêvati or Ujjayanta, now Girnâr, was, in all probability from the earliest times, looked upon as an abode of the gods—the Olympus of the pastoral inhabitants of the surrounding plains. As early as Aśoka's time it had attracted the attention of the Buddhists, and at its foot he caused to be incised, on a mass of rock, his famous edicts in favour of Buddhism. The first opens thus:—

"This is the edict of the beloved of the gods, the Râja Priyadarsi:—The putting to death of animals is to be entirely discontinued, and no convivial meeting is to be held, for the beloved of the gods, Râja Piyadarsi, remarks many faults in such assemblies, &c."

In the second tablet he states that, in his whole kingdom and in neighbouring countries, the kingdom of Antiochus, the Grecian, &c., a system of care for the sick, both of men and beasts, has been established. In the third, that "in the twelfth year of his inauguration in the conquered country" it was ordained to hold quinquennial expiations for the enforcement of moral obligations. In the fourth he proclaims the *dharma* or religious duty, including the sparing of animal life, the gentle treatment of all creatures, respect for relatives, Brahmans, monks, obedience to parents, &c. In the fifth, dated in his thirteenth year, Dharma Mahâmatra or great officers of morals are appointed. In the sixth he speaks of official inspectors of public places, &c. In the seventh, that ascetics are not to be molested. In the eighth, that himself leaves off hunting and takes delight in charity. In the ninth he decries all superstitious observances to bring luck, declaring that the performance of social duties, respectfulness, self-control, and charity, constitute true piety, and alone are meritorious. In the tenth he resigns all ambition, except the observance of moral duty; and in the eleventh he praises *dharma* or religious virtue and charity; but in the twelfth declares peace as more precious than beneficence, and proclaims that intrinsic worth is founded on discretion of speech, so that "no man may praise his own, or condemn another sect, or despise it on unsuitable occasions; on all manner of occasions respect is to be shown. Whatever of good a man confers on any one of a different persuasion tends to the advantage of his own, but by acting in an opposite way he injures his own and offends the other sect also." The thirteenth tablet is a long one, and very unfortunately the repairers of the road that leads towards Girnâr, some 60 years ago, seem to have broken off a large piece from the base of the stone, and so damaged what remains that it scarcely admits of translation; and the unsatisfactoriness of the copies hitherto made of the Kapur-di-Giri version has rendered them insufficient to make up the loss. The remaining words, too, make us regret this; for the thirteenth says "And the Yona King besides, by whom the *chattaro* (four) kings, Turamayo (Ptolemaios), Antikona (Antigonos), Maga (Magas of Cyrene), and Alixasunari (Alexander II.) both here and in foreign countries, everywhere (the people) follow the doctrine of the religion of Devanampriya wheresoever it reacheth."[1]

The presence of this important inscription, we may naturally suppose, was not the only indication of Buddhism here, and that it was soon followed, if not preceded, by Vihâras and other works. The remains of one *stûpa* is known to exist in the valley at the foot of Girnâr, and possibly careful exploration might bring others to light.

The same stone that bears the Aśoka inscription has also a long one of Rudra Dâman, one of the Kshatrapa dynasty of kings who seem to have ruled over Malwa and Gujarat during the second, third, and fourth centuries. Previous to them, if not of their race,

---

[1] The date of these kings has already been discussed at length, *ante*, p. 23. The inscriptions themselves have repeatedly been published. Recently in an exhaustive manner by General Cunningham, in his *Corpus Inscriptionum Indicarum*, Calcutta, 1877, but unfortunately without noticing Mr. Burgess' recent most accurate impression from the rock itself, and his transcript, with the translations and emendations by Professor H. Kern, of Leyden, and others, as set forth in his *Second Report*, 1876, pp. 96 to 127.

at Ujjain reigned a dynasty, calling themselves Kshaharâta Kshatrapas, (satraps) of which the principal king known to us was Nahapâna, variously placed from B.C. 60 to A.D. 120. The dates in his inscriptions are 40 to 42, and if these are in the Śaka era, which seems hardly doubtful, they fix his age about A.D. 118–120.

Ushavadâta, the son of Dînika, the son-in-law of Nahapâna, is mentioned in several inscriptions, but we do not know that he ruled. Gautamîputra I., a powerful Ândhra king of the Dekhan, in an inscription at Nâsik, says he entirely destroyed these Kshaharâtas. The succeeding kings, apparently descended from Bhadramukha Svâmî Chashṭana, assume the title of Mahâkshatrapas, though often erroneously styled by antiquaries as Sâhs. The early chronology of this dynasty as gathered from inscriptions and coins stands thus :—

	Dates in A.D.[1]
Chashṭana, son of Ysamotika - - -	cir. 122
Svâmî Jayadâman, his son - - - -	„ 135
Svâmî Rudra Dâman, his son, date 72[2] - -	„ 150

[1] This assumes that they dated from the Śaka era, A.D. 78.—J. B. I entirely concur in this assumption. In the first place because I can find no trace of any king Vicramâditya in the first century B.C., from whom the only other known era could be derived. His name does not occur in any inscription nor on any coin. He is not mentioned in lists in the Pauranas or elsewhere. He was avowedly a king of the Brahmans, whereas the whole country from the Bay of Bengal to the Western Ocean was, as we know from the caves, Buddhist in the first century B.C., and, lastly, the mode in which his history is narrated is so improbable as to prove its absurdity.

He is said to have established his era 56 B.C., and 135 years afterwards to have defeated the Buddhist Śaka king in the battle at Karour, so giving rise to the establishment of that era 78–79 A.D., and this last was the only era used by the defeated Buddhists afterwards during the whole of their supremacy.

My conviction is that the great Vicramaditya of Ujain did defeat the Śakas in a great battle in or about A.D. 544, and that afterwards the Brahmans in the eighth or ninth century, wishing to establish an era antecedent to that of the Buddhists, chose a date 10 cycles of 60 years each or 600 years anterior to that event, and fixed on 56 B.C.,—544 + 56,—as the one, which they afterwards employed.

I embodied my reasons for this conviction in a paper I intended to publish, in 1875, in the *Journal of the Royal Asiatic Society*, but was deterred from doing so by hearing that Dr. Bühler had found Vicramâditya's name in one of the Pauranas, and I consequently thought it better to print it for private circulation, which I then did.

As nothing has come of Dr. Bühler's discovery, and I have since seen no reason for modifying my conclusions, I now intend to publish them.—J. F.

[2] On the Girnâr inscription. For Rudra Dâman's inscription, see *Ind. Ant.* vol. vii. p. 257 *ff*; and for further information, *Archæological Survey of Western India, Rep.*, vol. ii. p. 128 ff.

		Dates in A.D.
Svâmî Rudra Siñha, his son, dates 102, 117	-	cir. 180
Svâmî Rudra Sêna, his son, dates 127, 140	-	„ 200

Coins carry down the series of nearly twenty kings till about 170 years later, or to 350 to 370 A.D., but until they are more carefully examined, the lists cannot command entire confidence. Rudra Dâman was probably the most powerful prince of the dynasty, and pushed his conquests both westwards and southwards.

The next great dynasty whose coins are found in Kâthiâwâṛ is that of the Guptas; it is not perfectly certain as yet from what era they date, and hence their position may be considered as doubtful; but until we have better information, we may retain for the chronology of this race the epoch of A.D. 318-319, as given by Albîrûnî,[1] and represent the dynasty thus:—

		Probable dates.[2]
1. Gupta	-	cir. A.D. 318
2. Ghaṭotkachha	-	„ 335
3. Chandragupta I.	-	„ 355
4. Samudragupta	-	„ 380
5. Chandragupta II., dates 82, 93	-	„ 395

[1] Reinaud, *Fragments arabes et persans*, pp. 142, 243; *Archæol. Surv. W. Ind.*, vol. ii., p. 28; Tod's *Rajasthan*, vol. i., p. 801 (Mad. ed., p. 705); Cunningham's *Bhilsa Topes*, p. 140; Prinsep's *Essays*, vol. i., p. 268 ff.

[2] It by no means follows that this era was established either to commemorate the rise or fall of the Guptas, or from any political event whatever. On the contrary, it seems almost certain that it only represents four cycles of 60 years each from the Śaka era—78-9+240=318, 319, and was adopted by the Guptas and the Ballabhis as more convenient than a longer one, of which they do not seem to have appreciated the advantage.

The Śaka era I believe to have been established by the Śaka king Kanishka, either at the date of his accession to the throne (*Burgess' Report*, 1875, p. 24), or to commemorate the third—or, as it is sometimes called—the fourth convocation held in his reign, and everything that has recently come under my notice has tended to confirm me more and more in this conviction.

While stating this so strongly, I ought perhaps in fairness to say that I have lately seen a private letter from General Cunningham, in which he states that he has recently found several double-dated Gupta inscriptions. That is, with dates in the cycle of 60 years, and with others in a cycle of months, and their differences or agreement will, he hopes, enable him to see the controversy about Gupta dates for ever at rest, and not in the manner assumed above. I need hardly add that the General calculates all the Mathura inscriptions and others of that class, as dating from the Vicramâditya Samvat, B.C. 56 (*Reports*, vol. iii. pp. 30, 41). When he publishes his Gupta discoveries we shall be in a better position to judge of their value and importance. At present the materials do not exist for doing so.—J. F.

	Probable dates.
6. Kumâragupta, 90, 121, 129 - -	cir. A.D. 415
7. Skandagupta, 130, 136, 138, 141, 146	" 449
8. Mahendragupta - - -	" 470
9. Buddhagupta, 155, 165, 182 -	" 474
10. Bânugupta, 191 - - -	" 510

If this chronology be correct, it was during the reign of Chandragupta II. that the Chinese pilgrim Fa-hian travelled in India (399–413 A.D.). From the donations of this king to the stûpa at Sânchi, he appears to have been favourably disposed to the Buddhists though probably himself a Hindu—as we might infer from other inscriptions on the Allahabad and Bhitari Lâts. In 428 and 466, Ma-twan-lin records embassies from Yueï-'aï (*i.e.* Chandrapriya) King of Kia-pi-li (Kapila) in India, who, however, can scarcely be one of these kings, but some petty prince in the north. But in 502 Kio-to (Gupta) King of India, sent presents to the Emperor Wu-ti; this was probably one of the later Gupta princes, who in his letter to the emperor calls himself a keeper of the law.[1]

They seem to have ruled over Central and Upper India. Kâṭhiâwâṛ is said to have been conquered by Chandragupta II., and placed under *Senâpatis* or lieutenants. Bhaṭârka, one of these, afterwards seized the province; his eldest son, Dharasena, however, still had only the title of *Senâpati*. A second son, Droṇasiñha, is said to have been crowned "by the Supreme Lord, the Lord Paramount of the whole earth."[2] Kumâragupta's coins are found in such abundance in the province that we might suppose that he, or some of his successors, was this "Lord Paramount."[3] This was, however, probably only a title of flattery bestowed on some much later and less powerful Gupta prince, such as Bânugupta, and with this the dates of both dynasties harmonise. We have copper-plate grants of Dhruvasena, a third son of Bhaṭârka, dated 207, 210, 216: and, if these are in the Gupta era, they place him a century later than Kumâragupta. A later Valabhî king, however, is mentioned by Hiuen Thsang (cir. A.D. 635–640) as Dhruvapaṭu, and we find a grant of S'îlâditya Dhruvabhaṭa, dated 447. If these could be shown to be the same, this would place the initial date of the Valabhî era about

---

1 Pauthier, *Examen Méthodique des faits qui concernent le Thian-Tchu*, pp. 30–33; St. Julien in *Jour. As.*, ser. iv. tom. x. pp. 99, 100.

2 *Ind. Ant.* vol. i. p. 61., vol. iv. p. 106; *Second Archæol. Sur. Rep.*, p. 80.

3 It also happens that Skandagupta's coins are almost exclusively found in Kachh.

A.D. 195, but the evidence is not sufficient to justify the acceptance of this, and we must suppose that Dharasena IV., or his father Dhruvasena II. was the king mentioned by the Chinese traveller. The dynasty then, for the present, stands thus :—

	Copper Plate dates.	Dates from Valabhi era, A.D. 319.
1. Bhaṭârka, *Senâpati*	—	500
2. Dharasena I., *Senâpati*, son of Bhaṭârka.	—	515 ?
3. Dronasiñha *Mahârâja*, 2nd son of Bhaṭârka.	—	520 ?
4. Dhruvasena I., 3rd son	207–216	526
5. Dharapaṭṭa, 4th son	—	535 ?
6. Guhasena, son of Dharapaṭṭa	236	555
7. Dharasena II, son of Guhasena	252–272	570
8. Śîlâditya I, Dharmâditya, 1st son	286	598
9. Kharagraha I, 2nd son	—	610 ?
10. Śrî Dharasena III, 1st son of Kharagraha.	—	618 ?
11. Dhruvasena II, Bâlâditya, 2nd son	310	627
12. Dharasena IV, *Chakravartin*, son of Dhruvasena.	322–330	640
13. Dhruvasena III, grandson of Śîlâditya I.	332	650
14. Kharagraha II, Dharmâditya, brother	335	563
15. Śîlâditya II, nephew	348	660
16. Śîlâditya III, son	372–376	685
17. Śîlâditya IV, son	403	710
18. Śîlâditya V, son	441	740
19. Śîlâditya VI, Dhruvabhaṭṭa, son,	447	765

Some of these kings must have been powerful, and are said to have extended their sway over Kachh, Gujarât, and Mâlwâ, and in Hiuen Thsang's time (A.D. 640) Dhruvapaṭu or Dhruvabhaṭṭa was son-in-law to the great Harshavardhana of Kanauj.[1] Several of the earlier kings in the above list patronised Buddhism and Buddhist monasteries. The dynasty probably perished through some internal revolution; tradition hints that the last S'îlâditya was arbitrary and oppressive, and provoked his subjects to call in a foreign invader.[2]

[1] For further information, see *Archæol. Reports*, vol. ii. pp. 80–86; vol. iii. pp. 93–97.

[2] Were these the Arabs ?—J. F.

Although the Buddhist caves in this province are among the most ancient to be found in India, as well as the most numerous, they are far from possessing the same interest that attaches to many of the other groups found elsewhere. There is not among the 140 caves in this district one single Chaitya cave that can for one instant be compared with the great caves of this class that exist on the other side of the Gulph of Cambay. There are numerous cells, which may be called chapels, 15 to 20 feet in depth, containing Dagobas, but in most cases without internal pillars or ornament of any sort.[1] The Vihâras, too, are generally either single cells or small groups of cells, with a pillared verandah, but seldom, if ever, surrounding a hall, or forming any important architectural combination. Sometimes, indeed, its excavations are expanded into halls of considerable dimensions, 50 or 60 feet square, but then generally without cells or pillars. They seem, in fact, to have been plain meeting houses or dharmaśâlâs, and such ornament as exists in them is of the plainest kind, and what sculpture is found upon them, of the rudest and most conventional kind.

This marked difference between two groups of monuments situated so near one another, and devoted to the same purpose, must evidently have arisen from some ethnographic or other local peculiarity distinguishing the people who excavated them. There seems no reason for believing that any form of Buddhism existed in the province before Aśoka's missionaries were sent here to convert the people immediately after the convention held by him, B.C. 246. If they were the same people we might expect they would adopt the same richly sculptured forms we found in Orissa, or the same architectural grandeur which was displayed in the same age in the Sahyâdri Ghâts. No contrast, however, can be greater than that which exists between the caves at Udyagiri, described above (pp. 69 to 94), and these Kathiwar caves. Though their dimensions and mode of grouping are nearly the same, and their age is nearly as possible identical, the eastern group is profusely adorned with sculpture, and everywhere affects ornament of an elaborate character, and in a style quite up to the mark of its age. All this is as unlike as possible to what is

[1] The cave at Junâgarh, marked F on Plate II., can hardly be said to be an exception, though its dimensions are 20 feet by 26. It has no dagoba, and it is not clear if it ever had.

found in the western caves, where no figure sculpture anywhere exists, and the ornamentation is rude and unartistic beyond anything we find elsewhere belonging to the period. When we know more of the ethnography of the province we may be able to explain why, in this country, they adopted so puritanical a form of religious architecture. At present we can only note the fact, and leave the cause for investigation in the future. It may, however, be remarked that when Buddhism disappeared from the province, it was succeeded not so much by the wild and extravagant forms of Hinduism as by the soberer and more cognate religion of the Jains. It is not, of course, intended to assert that the Ṡaiva and Vaishṇava religions did not prevail at Somnath and Dwarka in the interval between the decline of Buddhism and the Mahomedan conquest or subsequently. The most marked feature, however, in the religious history of Kathiawar seems to have been a persistence in an ascetic atheism, antagonistic to the wild polythism of the Hindu religion. It may have been the prevalence of some such feeling among the early inhabitants of the province that led to the puritanical simplicity in the forms and the almost total absence of ornament that characterise the early groups of caves in Kathiawar.

From indications still everywhere observable on the spot, it is evident that at early times large monasteries existed both at Junâgaṛh and on Mount Girnâr. Of those on the hill scarcely a trace now remains, and even their site has been built over by the Jains. But at Junâgaṛh, though many rock-excavations had been quarried away since the Muhammadans took possession of the place 400 years ago, there were still many chambers on the outskirts of the fort, even in the first quarter of the present century, in which Colonel Tod remarked inscriptions in the same character as that used in the Aśoka inscriptions. These have been almost entirely quarried away since, except a few fragments just under the scrap of the Uparkôṭ or fort, and at Naudurgâ close by. These were probably the oldest caves in Kâṭhiâwâṛ,—or perhaps in India, with the exception of those at Barabar (*ante*, p. 37), which were excavated during the reign of Aśoka himself, but with which, some of these may be contemporary. Next to them, probably comes the upper range of caves on the east side of the town, but within the walls at Bâwâ Pyârâ's Maṭh or Monastery. But here, as elsewhere, the process of excavating fresh cells probably went on at intervals for a long period, and the lowest in the sloping rock are perhaps the latest, though even they belong to an early date. A quarry has been opened behind them, and is wrought close up to and under the oldest of them: how many have been quite cut away no one can tell.

These caves are arranged in three lines (see plan Plate II.), the first and third nearly parallel and facing south, and the second, at the eastern ends of the other two, faces east. The upper range, on the north, consists of a larger cave at the west end and three smaller ones in line. The hall of the larger cave (A, Plate II.) measures 28 feet by 16, and has two plain square pillars (perhaps originally three) in line supporting the roof; at the west end it has a chamber (B), 17 feet by 6 screened off by two plain square pillars; and at the back are three cells, each about 11 feet square. The front is partly destroyed, but has still three square pillars, chamfered at the necks. On the façade is the only fragment of carving, a semicircular arch in very low relief with a cross bar across its diameter,—forming, perhaps, the earliest example of the "chaitya-window ornament," that in later times became so fashionable as an architectural decoration.

The three smaller caves (D, Plate II.) each consist of a verandah, 13 to 16 feet long, by 4½ to 5½ wide, with two pillars in front, and a cell inside. These caves may belong to the second century B.C., or even to age of Aśoka.

To the south-east of these is an open court (E, Plate II.), about 50 feet long, on the west side of which is a verandah, 39 feet long, and nearly 8 feet wide, in the back wall of which are three doors, the central one, 5 feet wide, leading into a room 20 feet wide (F, Plate II.), and fully 26 deep, to the extremity of an apse at the back. It is flat-roofed, but apparently had four square pillars supporting it; if this cave was a Chaitya, as it seems most probably to have been, the dâgoba must have been structural. The other two doors in the back wall of the verandah lead into cells. The verandah has six square pillars, each with a strut to the projecting drip, the struts being carved into the form of lions or *śârdûlas*—mythological animals with the bodies of lions, and having horns; and at each end of the verandah one of these figures is carved in low relief on the wall. The façade of the verandah is also carved with rude chaitya-window ornaments, similar to the one on the first range.

At the north end of the court, and at a higher level, approached by steps, is a verandah (H.), 19 feet 7 inches by 6 feet 10 inches, which gives access to two rooms at the back of it, each about 9¾ feet square.

These caves also seem to belong to an early date. But on the east side of the court are two cells, each with a small verandah in front, and the commencement of a third—which seem to have been an after-thought, and the rock in which it was attempted to cut them was too low to allow of their execution without lowering their floors below the level of the court outside, which would have rendered them damp. In the court just in front of these is the base (*a*) of a square stone pillar, and beside it was found a loose slab, bearing part of a Kshatrapa inscription on its edge. Unfortunately it was of soft calcareous sandstone, and many of the letters indistinct. It belongs to the time of Swâmi Jayadâman's grandson—probably Rudrasinha, the son of Rudradâman, whose inscription is on the back of the rock, bearing the inscriptions of Aśoka; and from the occurrence of the word *Kevalijnâna*, in what is left of it, Dr. Bühler conjectures that it is Jaina; and it may be, that these princes did favour Jainism and bestow on that sect this old Buddhist monastery. Outside this court to the south is a cave with a small sunk area in front (J, Plate II.). The cave consists of a verandah and two cells (K). On the doors are some roughly executed carvings, and over one of them is the *swastika*, and other Buddhist symbols (Figs. 1 and 2, Plate III.). These are certainly the rudest sculptures that have yet been found in any cave in India, and though it is hardly safe to compare things so far apart, we would probably be justified in assuming that they are consequently earlier than anything now existing in Orissa. If this is so, the first series of caves here (A to D) being certainly older must be carried back at least to the time of Aśoka, and this group (F to L) is the earliest complete Buddhist establishment we have, and most probably was excavated during the existence of the Mauryan dynasty. The emblems above the doorway (Fig.1, Plate III.) shows that it was strictly Buddhist, though of a very primitive type.

Next to this is another small cave with a bench round the small outer court. The door has a sort of arch traced over it, and the cell inside, though partially filled up with earth, is considerably lower in the floor than outside.

The third line of caves begins at the back of this, and runs west-north-west, but are noways interesting, being perfectly plain, the only peculiarity being that in the second and largest of them (O, Plate II.) there is a single octagon pillar in the centre of the floor supporting the roof. The base of it is too much damaged to allow of its shape being determined; but the capital consisted of an abacus of three thin members with the inverted water-jar form under it, as in the oldest caves at Nâsik and Junnar.

The remaining three caves are quite plain, consisting of verandahs with door and two windows, separated by square pillars, and two cells each inside, except the middle cave which has only one cell.

The rock in which these caves are cut slopes down considerably to the south, so that the roofs of the last line are considerably beneath the level of the floors of the first.

In the waste overgrown space inside the north wall of Junâgaṛh, at Mai Gadêchi, under an old Hindu or Jaina temple, long since converted into a Muhammadan mosque, is another rock excavation, 26 feet 8 inches wide and 13 deep, with a cell in one end. It has two octagonal pillars inside, with capitals that have been sculptured, but have been defaced by the Muhammadans. In the front it has two square pillars with *śârdûla* struts or brackets. It is not clear, however, that this has been a monastic abode, and from some points of likeness to another excavation in the Uparkoṭ it seems probable that this may have been a garden retreat with a bath in front, now filled up, and built over by the *sthân* or shrine of a Muhammadan saint. Its age is also uncertain, but it is undoubtedly very old.

Two-Storeyed Rock-cut Hall at Junagaḍh.[1]

About 1869, some rock-cut apartments were discovered at the bottom of a descent on the north of the Jama' Masjid on the Uparkoṭ or fort of Junâgaṛh. They are of considerable interest, for though somewhat defaced, they manifest a high style of art. Few bases for example, could be found anywhere to excel in beauty of design and richness of carving those of the six pillars in the lower hall.[2]

---

[1] This cave is described here because locally it forms one of the group, but from its age, probably belonging to the fourth century, it belongs to the second division of Buddhist caves according to the classification adopted above (p. 185).

[2] See Plates XXIII. and XXIV. in *Second Archæological Report.* Quite close to these excavations on their south side the ground sounds hollow, and there is a line of wall cropping up, exactly similar to those round the tops of the two openings which led to the discovery of those excavated.

The excavations (Plate IV.) opened up consist of a deep tank or bath (E) about 11 feet square, with a covered verandah on three sides of it; that on the west side is occupied with a built seat like the *ásana* for an idol, possibly for laying the garments upon while bathing. The pipes for the water come down the wall from the surface, pass the front of this seat, and enter a small cistern near the entrance door at the south-west corner. The water must have been raised from some well in the neighbourhood and conveyed to the supply pipe; and the small cistern may have been formed to assist in filtering the water pure into the bath.

The corridor on the south side is supported by two columns with spiral ridges on their shafts, octagonal plinths, and carved bases and capitals. The shafts of two corresponding attached pilasters on the north wall are divided into three sections each, having the grooves or ridges running in opposite spirals.

Over the bath the roof is open, and round the opening a wall still stands a foot or so above the ground-level.

In the north side over the bath is a large aperture or window into the next chamber. This apartment is entered from the north-east corner of the bath-room. It is a large chamber, 35 feet 10 inches long by 27 feet 10 inches wide, with six columns supporting the roof; the area between the first four of these, like that in the bath-room, is open to the air above, with a surrounding wall on the surface of the rock. It is also open to a hall below; and the four columns have been connected by a thin low parapet wall, about 20 inches high and 6 inches thick, now entirely destroyed. The rest of the area is occupied by the corridor on three sides, and by the space on the north where the remaining two pillars stand. In the walls on the north east, and west sides are stone bench recesses divided into long compartments, with a base moulded in architectural courses below, and a frieze above, ornamented with Chaitya-window and chequer carvings. The four pillars round the open area are square, the other two are 16-sided, and have been carved with animal figures on the abaci.

In the north-east corner a door leads into a small apartment which has a hole in the roof blackened with smoke, and which may have been used as an occasional cook-room, to prepare warm drinks, &c. for those who had been enjoying the bath. By the side of this apartment a door leads to a stair descending to the entrance of the hall below.

This lower room measures 39½ feet by 31 feet, and had evidently been filled up long before the one above it, and is consequently in a better state of preservation. It has been elaborately and very tastefully carved.[1] On entering it we come on a platform on the left side, slightly raised and nearly square, with two short pillars on its west side, supporting a frame above, descending from the roof. What this was meant for is hard to say, unless the depression within was intended to be filled with cotton or other soft substance to form a dais or a seat.

Except on the west side, the remainder of the walls is surrounded by bench recesses, divided at regular intervals, as in the apartment above. Over these recesses the frieze is ornamented with Chaitya-windows having the Buddhist rail in the lower part of the opening, and two figures looking out of each; in many cases two females with something like "ears" on their head-dresses, but too indistinct to distinguish what they represent (Fig. 4, Plate III.).

The four columns in the south end of this hall are larger than the two in front of the supposed dais, but the bases of all are alike, and the bodies of the capitals are similar. The rich bases have been already alluded to, and the drawing (Fig. 3, Plate III.), where the original pattern has been truthfully restored from the different fragments still left entire, will give a better idea of them than could be done by any description.

The abaci are carved with lions couchant at the corners, and in the middle of each is a lion, facing outwards, with a human figure on each side of it. The body of the capital consists of eight divisions round, indicated by the breaks in the ledge at the bottom, on which the human figures of the different groups stand. Most, if not all, of the figures are females, nearly nude, and some standing under foliage. They have been cut with considerable spirit, and in high, almost entire, relief: unfortunately, many of them have been much damaged,—some even since the room was excavated. In the two smaller columns, the principal member below the body of the capital is carved with the heads of animals, mostly elephants and goats or rams. On the larger columns the corresponding member is not so deep, and is a serrated torus. At the back or west side of this hall

---

[1] For drawings, &c., see *Second Arch. Report*, p. 142, and plates xxi. to xxiv.

are two small rooms; that on the south with a single door, the other with three entrances between jambs slightly advanced, and with a projecting frieze.

On the north side of this is an irregular excavation, in a corner of which there seems to be a shaft of a choked-up well; but the whole excavation here is more like the work of Mahmûd Bîgarah's quarry-men in the fifteenth century[1] than any portion of the original,—though it is quite probable that other chambers have been quarried away.

These rooms could have been no part of a monastic establishment; and the example of the old Mehal, just to the north of this, suggests that they may have been either a sort of garden-house belonging to the palace, or possibly the bath and pleasure-house of another palace now interred under the débris that covers the whole of the Uparkoṭ. The style of carving is not unlike much that has been found about Maṭhurâ, and which I feel disposed to attribute to about the fourth century A.D.

OTHER CAVES IN KATHIAWAR.

About 30 miles north-west from Junâgaṛh is Ḍhânk, in early times an important city, and a few miles west from Ḍhânk, towards the village of Siddhsar, in a ravine called Jhinjuri-jhar, are five plain caves cut in calcareous sandstone. Probably there have been others further up the ravine; but, if so, the decay of the rock has destroyed all trace of them. The furthest to the south has been a verandah facing east, with two cells.

The third has two octagonal pillars in front, with square bases and capitals. The pillars are connected below with the pilasters by a low screen, carved in front with the Buddhist rail of a large pattern. This is the only trace of ornament about these caves.

The last to the north is much larger, and has had six square pillars in front of a narrow verandah. It had an open area inside measuring 13 feet by 20, from which the roof had been cut out, similarly to what remains of a very extensive excavation known as Khengar's Palace at Junâgaṛh. Around this central court it appears to have had a number of cells with a corridor in front of them. In

[1] Mahmûd Bîgarah of Ahmadâbâd subdued Maṇḍalika the last of the Chuṛâsamâ kings of Junâgaṛh, and took the fort in 1469–70 where he erected the great Jama' Masjid. *Arch. Sur. W. India*, vol. ii. pp. 144, 165.

another ravine to the west of this, and running into it a little to the north-west, are other caves, but they are so plain that we need not occupy space describing them.

At the village of Ḍhânk itself there is also a group of small caves, but of much later age. They are the only caves in Kâṭhiâwâṛ that have any mythological sculptures in them ; but they are of a very rude description and probably of late date.[1] And, again, to the north-west of it, on the way to Jodhpur and not far from the village of Hariêsan, on the west side of the Gadhkâ hill, are some nine more caves. Like those at Siddhsar, they are perfectly plain, most of them with a verandah in front, and one or two cells at the back of it.

TALAJA.

In the south-east of the Kâthiâwâṛ peninsula, at Talâjâ, near the mouth of the Satruñji river, is an almost conical hill, called in Sanskrit Talugiri, and in modern vernacular parlance the Têkri of Talâjâ, crowned by two modern Jaina temples—one on the vertex, and the other on a sort of shoulder on the west face. The town lies on the north and west, slopes near the base, and has the Talâjâ, a small feeder of the Satruñji river, to the north of it.

On the north-west face of this Talâjâ hill are a series of Buddhist caves, about thirty-six in number, with from fifteen to twenty tanks or cisterns for water. Both have once been more numerous ; but many of them have been destroyed, probably to make way for a passage up to the Jaina temples, or their predecessors on the top. These caves appear to have been first brought to notice by Mr. Henry Young, C.S., in 1835, and are briefly described in a paper by Captain Fulljames on fossil bones of mammalia in Kâṭhiâwâṛ, written in 1841 (*Jour. B. B. R. As. Soc.* Vol. I., p. 32). Dr. J. Wilson included them in his *First Memoir* in 1850; and they were visited and described by the writer in May 1869.

One of the largest of these caves, and the only one that now presents any remains of ornamentation, is at a height of fully a hundred feet. It is locally known as the Ebhal Maṇḍapa, and measures 75 feet by 67½, and is 17½ feet high. This large hall, without any cells in its side walls, had four octagonal pillars in front, but none inside to support the roof; nor has it the wall that, at Ajaṇṭâ and elsewhere,

[1] See *Second Archæological Report*, p. 150.

usually divides such excavations into an outer verandah and an inner hall. It seems to have been constructed as a place of assembly or religious instruction, a Dharmaśâlâ in fact, where the early Buddhist missionaries preached to the simple people of the district, and taught them the new doctrines. Outside the entrance are wells or tanks on both sides, and several cells. On its façade are fragments of a modified, perhaps, a very primitive form of the horse-shoe or chaitya-window ornament, and of the Buddhist rail pattern, but this is the only sculpture now traceable among these caves.

The others are small plain caves not meriting description. In one of them is a dâgoba or stone cylinder with hemispherical top of a very simple type, the base only entire, and the remains of the toraṇa or capital still attached to the flat roof of the cave. The dâgoba and general arrangements of these caves are sufficient indications of their being Buddhist works; and though we have no very definite means of determining their antiquity, yet from the simplicity of their arrangements, and except that already mentioned on the façade of the Ebhal Maṇḍap from the entire absence of sculpture, such as is common in all the later Buddhist caves, we may relegate them to a very early age, possibly even to that of Aśoka or soon after.

The rock is of very different qualities in different parts of the hill; but where the existing caves are executed it is full of quartz veins ramified among nodules of varying degrees of hardness, and the disintegration of these under the effects of atmospheric influences has so destroyed the original surface, that if any inscriptions ever existed, they must have disappeared long ago.

SANA.

Considerably to the south-west of Talâjâ and a march from Râjulâ, is the village and hill of Lôr or Lauhar, in Bâbriâwâd, in which are some natural caves appropriated to local divinities, and a small and perfectly plain excavation, probably a Buddhist ascetic's cell. Farther west, and not far from the village of Vânkiâ, is the Sânâ hill, a wild, desolate place, without a human habitation in sight. Close to the foot of the hill is a perennial stream which aids to redeem the view, and doubtless helped to tempt the first ascetics to hew out their dwellings in the adjoining rock. The hill consists of several spurs from a central ridge, on the top of which are some old foundations of very large bricks.

The hill is honey-combed by more than sixty caves, some of them much ruined, but all of the same plain types as those at Talâjâ, Junâgaṛh, and Ḍhânk. Here, too, one of the largest, near the bottom of the hill, goes by the name of the Ebhal Maṇḍapa. It is 68½ feet by 61, and about 16½ feet high, originally with six pillars in front but none inside. About 120 feet higher up, on the face of the same spur, is a cave called the Bhîma Chauri facing the north-east; it has a verandah in front, and measures about 38 by 40½ feet, the roof being supported by four octagonal pillars, with capitals and bases of the *Lotá*, or water-pot pattern so frequent in the Nâsik and Junnar caves. Round the sides also runs a raised stone bench, a common feature in such caves. Close by is a Chaitya or chapel cave, 18 feet wide by 31 feet deep, and 13½ feet high. The roof is flat, but the inner end or back of the cave is of the semi-circular form already noticed at Junâgaṛh and common in Chaitya caves. It wants the side aisles usual in such excavations; and the dâgoba, 7 feet 10 inches in diameter,[1] is very plain and without ornament, while its capital is wanting, having been broken off by later Hindus in order to convert it into a huge *liṅga* or emblem of Śiva, and it is now worshipped as such by the people of the villages in the neighbourhood. Some of the excavations consist merely of verandahs with cells opening from them, and having recesses in the walls for sleeping places; others are halls like the Ebhal Maṇḍapa with cells arranged near the entrance, while there are two other small Chaityas similar to that mentioned above. High up the face of the hill is a cistern of excellent water; and large portions of the stairs hewn out in the rock and leading from one group of caves to another, are still pretty entire.

These caves, like those at Talâjâ, from the simplicity of their arrangements and their flat-roofed chaityas, must also be referred to a very early age, possibly as a mean date about 150 B.C., though they probably range through at least a century between the earliest and the latest excavation.

---

[1] See *Archæol. Sur. of W. India Reports*, vol. ii. p. 149, and Plate xxix.

CHAPTER III.

THE BUDDHIST CAVE TEMPLES IN THE SOUTH KONKAN.

THE Koṅkaṇ, as is generally known, is the appellation of the low-lying country between the Ghâṭs or Sahyâdri Hills and the shores of Indian Ocean, extending from Gujarât on the north, to Goa on the south. South of Bombay it is divided into the districts of Kulâba and Ratnagiri, and is much broken up by spurs and outlying hills from the Ghâṭ range. In these we find several groups of caves. The first are about 30 miles south of Bombay, in a ravine a few miles north-east of Chaul, and consist of two small plain cells without any sculptures.[1] Further south at Kuḍâ, and still further to the south-east at Mhâṛ, on the Savitrî river, are large groups to be noticed presently; and in the Ratnagiri district, at Dâbhol at the mouth of the Vaśishṭhi river, at Chipalun to the east of it, and at Sangameśwar 25 miles south of the last,[2] are cells or caves but of little importance, those at Chipalun consisting of a hall 22 feet by 15, with a dâgoba at the back, a few cells, and a water cistern. Altogether there may be about 150 separate excavations in this district. Some of them as old as any in the west of India, but none of any great beauty or interest. Though not quite so plain as those of Kathiwar they are very rarely adorned with sculpture, and what ornament is found in them, is of a very rude class. No trace of painting is to be found anywhere, nor any indications that such a mode of adornment was ever attempted. In themselves they cannot consequently be regarded as of much interest, but a description of them cannot be omitted from a work aiming at being a complete account of the known Cave Temples of India.

CAVES OF KUDA.

Kuḍên, Kuḍâ or Kuṛâ, is a small village on the shore of the Râjapûrî creek which enters the west coast about 45 miles to the south of

[1] *Jour. Bom. B. R. As. Soc.*, vol. iv. p. 342.

[2] At Wâde-Pâḍel, and at Sagwa, both near Wagotana, in the south of the district, are also some ruined cells, but they are probably Brahmanical. See *Jour. B. B. R. As. Soc.*, vol. v. p. 611.

Bombay. It lies in lat. 18° 17′ N., and long. 73° 8′ E., 6½ miles east from Râjapûrî, 17½ miles north-west from Goḍêgâṅw, the principal town of the tâluka in which it is now included, and 5 miles west from Talê. In Marâṭhâ, and even in recent English times, the tâluka went by the name of Râjapûrî,[1] and extended from the Kundalikâ river, at the mouth of which is the port of Chêṅwal (vulgo 'Chaul'), to the Habshi of Jinjirâ's territory and the tâluka of Râyagaḍh on the south. This Râjapûrî, it is not improbable, may have been Purî,—the capital of the Śilâhâras of the Konkan who claim the title of "rulers of the city of Tagara,"[2] and of whom we have the names of eleven princes from Kapardi I. in the ninth century to Chhitarâja in A.D. 1024. If, in still earlier times, as is probable, it was a place of note, it would help us to account for the numerous Buddhist excavations in its neighbourhood. The next town along the coast mentioned by Ptolemy from Simylla or Tiamula, is Hippokûra,[3] and in the *Periplus of the Erythrean Sea*, (sec. 53), we have Mandagora, which Ptolemy places further down the coast. It seems almost certain, however, that from very early times the beautiful creek which still has Murûd, Jinjîrâ, and Râjapûrî at its mouth, and villages like Tamânê and Mhaslâ at its head, must have attracted the population of a considerable town.

On the eastern shore of the northern arm of this creek, a low hill, sloping down to the north, contains a group of caves, twenty-two in number, large and small, which appear to have been first brought to notice in 1848.[4] They are all of a very plain type, only one having any sculptures, the rest being so much alike, except in size, that it does not seem worth while describing each in detail. It will only be necessary to notice the principal ones. The lowest down and furthest to the north, now used as a cattle shed, may be designated No. I. It is one of four caves here that contain

---

1 This place must not be confounded with Râjapur, a little farther south, at the mouth of the Savitrî, where the East India Company early had a factory, of which they were dispossessed before the French established themselves there in the time of Śivaji. Dellon's *Voyage to the East Indies* (Lond. 1698), p. 55 ff.

2 *Jour. R. As. Soc.*, vol. ii. p. 383; *Ind. Art.*, vol. v pp. 270-272.

3 Ptol. *Geog.*, VII. i. 6, a different place from that mentioned in VII. i. 83; VIII. xxvi. 15. Lassen places Mandagara at Râjapûrî. See *Ind. Alterth.*, III. 179, 181, 184. May not Hippokoura be Godabandar in the Ṭhâṇâ creek? Three sites near Kuḍâ seem to be named Mânḍâḍ or Mândâr—a name suggestive of Manda(*na*)gara.

4 *Jour. Bom. B. R. As. Soc.*, vol. iii. pt. ii. p. 44.

dâgobas. In front it had a verandah 22 feet by 7, with two plain octagonal pillars in front, now broken away; at the left end is a cell, 7 feet square, with a bench bed in a recess in the right wall. A door 7 feet wide leads from the verandah into the hall, which is 22 feet square, and had two octagonal pillars at the back standing on a low bench, one of them now destroyed. These separate the hall from an antechamber, 23 feet wide by 7 feet 3 inches deep, having a bench at the ends and along the back wall up to the door of the shrine. The shrine is about 15 feet wide by 14½ feet deep, and is occupied by plain dâgoba reaching to the roof.

In the end of the verandah is an inscription in late Mauryan character, in two long lines, going across it, and continued along the back wall to near the door. Though copied, this inscription has not yet been translated; from the form of the letters, however, it may be inferred that it belongs to the second century before Christ.

The next three caves are small, plain chambers in no respect worthy of especial notice.

No. V. is a large plain cave, having a verandah in front, with two octagonal pillars, a bench or seat between the pillars and the end pilasters, and two windows into the hall, which is 34½ feet wide, and nearly the same from front to back. It has no cells, only a bench round the three inner sides. Three slight recesses have been made in the back wall, but they seem to have been cut out, long after the cave was finished, for what purpose is not apparent.

This cave has an inscription in six lines in the end of the verandah, of which only a few letters are injured. The alphabet is that of the Ândhrabhṛitya age found at Nâsik and elsewhere. It reads "Hail! This cave and tank are the benefaction of the female "ascetic Paduminikâ, daughter of the female ascetic Nâganikâ, the "sister's daughter of the Ṭheras Bhadata Pâtamita and Bhadata "Âgimita, together with her disciple Bodhî and her disciple Asal-"pamitâ."[1] This cave was evidently a Dharmaśâlâ.

Cave VI. is the principal one of the group; like the two already described it may be called a Chaitya cave, that is, though flat-roofed, it has a dâgoba in the shrine (Plate V., fig. 1). The roof in front of the verandah projects nearly 8 feet, and is supported at each end

[1] Translated by Prof. Jacobi. *Ind. Ant.*, vol. vii. p. 254. It would appear from this that female ascetics were sometimes mothers of families.

by the fore part of an elephant. The verandah is about 24¼ feet long by 7 feet 8 inches wide, and has two octagonal pillars in front standing on a bench with a low back to the outside. The door into the cave is fully 6 feet wide, and on each side of it is a window. These light the cave quite sufficiently. The hall is 28 feet 9 inches wide by 29 feet 4 inches deep, with a seat surrounding the three inner sides. In the back is an antechamber measuring about 23 feet by 7, and separated from the hall by two plain octagonal pillars, between which is the entrance. These also stand on the ends of short benches, whose backs are towards the hall, and are covered with animals and *gana* along the middle, and with floral patterns above and below. *See* Plate VII., fig. 1.

At the end of the antechamber is a cell with a stone bench or bed on the right side of it, and at the back of the bench a recess 2 feet 8 inches by 5½ feet, apparently intended for storing away valuables. The shrine is 15 feet 4 inches wide by 20½ feet deep, and about 10½ feet high, containing a perfectly plain dâgoba 7 feet 3 inches in diameter, and reaching to the roof.

This is the only cave here in which there are any sculptures; but except the half elephants that support the projecting rock in front, and the carving on the rail at the back of the hall already mentioned, it appears to have all been executed after the cave had been finished. The two principal panels are at the corners on the back of the hall, and measure each about 5 feet by 6 feet 9 inches. That in the left corner contains life-sized figures of a man and woman, with a dwarf attendant. The man wears a heavy turban and large ear-jewels, and holds up his left hand. He wears no covering above the waist, but has long, heavy, tubular bracelets; his clothing is held together by a belt and round his loins is a roll of cloth. The woman has a similar abundance of head-gear, but of a somewhat different style, with a round plate on the forhead, and wears little else besides this and some bells round the lower part of the trunk, with heavy round anklets. She rests one hand on the head of the dwarf, who kneels at her left side holding up her foot as if adjusting the heavy anklets. The corresponding panel in the left corner is very similar: the male figure points upwards with his left hand; the head-dress of the female differs from that in the other sculpture; she had no wristlets; and she holds up in her right hand three flower buds. These figures bear a very striking resemblance to those in the front wall of the great Chaitya cave at Kârlê (Plate XIV., fig. 1); indeed, the figures are so alike, even in minute details, that there seems little reason to doubt that they all belong to about the same age, and that not much later than the time when these Kudâ caves were first excavated, within the first century before Christ.

On the right wall of the cave, and on the left side of the front of the verandah, are several figures of Buddha seated on the lotus, some with the legs down, and others with them doubled under him in the ascetic attitude, in one instance with the wheel below the lotus, three deer on each side, and under them two Nâga figures holding a pillar on which the wheel rests, with their wives and a number of female worshippers behind them. In another sculpture the wheel and deer are wanting, and the worshipping figures are rudely sculptured below the Nâgas and over a lotus plant, the Buddhist emblem of creation. These sculptures are of far later date than the first described; indeed they may be of the fifth or sixth century A.D., and resemble in every essential particular a similar composition inserted between the older figures on the front of the Karlê cave, as shown in the plate last referred to.

Under part of the sculpture on this right wall, and on one of the pillars in the verandah, are short inscriptions in a character approaching the Haḷa Kânaḍa, but having been but lightly incised are illegible except a few letters.

On the left or north end wall of the verandah is an inscription of seven lines in well-cut letters, each fully 3 inches in height, and in an old square character. It has not yet been translated, but the names Śivadata, Śivapâlitâ, Skandapalita, Śivabhûti occurring in it, all testify to the prevalence of the worship of Śiva alongside Buddhism.

On the south side of this is cave VII., entered by a few steps at the north end, and having two octagonal pillars in front, on a low bench, the raised back of which being to the outside is carved in the "rail pattern." But except for inscriptions this and the remaining caves are very much like those already described. Nos. VIII. and XV., like I. and VI., have dâgobas in their shrines. Nos. XVI. to XXII., in the upper terrace, stretch to the north, and are all plain Vihâra caves, or verandahs with cells at the back, and some water cisterns among them.

The whole series of the Kuḍâ caves are so plain and so similar, that, except for their inscriptions, they afford few points for comment. The inscriptions are donative, and, so far as they have yet been translated, afford no names otherwise known to us. Sulâsadata, mentioned in two of them, we have also in one of the Junnar inscriptions, and if the same person is meant in both cases, we have a chronological point of contact.

The cells of the Vihâra caves have the stone benches or beds never found in any of the later Buddhist caves.

Mhar.

On the Savitrî[1] or Bankoṭ river, 28 miles in a straight line to the south-east from Kuḍâ, is Mhâṛ, the principal town in the modern tâluka of the same name, formerly called Râyagaḍ from the hill-fort in the north of the district. Three-quarters of a mile north-west from Mhâṛ is Pâla, behind which in the perpendicular scarp of the hill is a group of 28 excavations. The first 20 are in the upper scarp, and the rest about 30 feet lower down. They have long been known to Europeans, and are probably those referred to by Niebuhr as "not far from Fort Victoria" (Bankot).[2]

Beginning from the south end of the series No. I. is perhaps one of the latest excavated. It has a verandah in front 53 feet long by 8 feet wide, supported by six pillars and pilasters at the ends, but only one pilaster at the south end and its neighbouring pillar are finished, the others are merely blocked out as square masses. The one pillar is square at the base, and to a height of 3 feet; over this is an octagonal band 6 inches high, then 3 feet 2 inches of the shaft has 16 sides, returning through another octagonal band to the square form. The pilaster has a narrow band of leaf ornament at the top, and another similar at about 3 feet from the bottom, with a line of beads or flowers over the latter.

The wall is pierced by three doors and two windows, and the hall inside measures 57½ feet wide along the front wall, and 62 feet at the back by about 34½ feet deep, with an average height of 10 feet four inches. Round all four sides of this hall runs a low bench. In

---

[1] "The vivifier," a name of the sun before his rising.

[2] "Pas loin du fort Victoire il y a (dit-on) aussi une grande pagode, taillée dans un rocher, ou, comme un autre s'exprime, 25 maisons avec des chambres taillées dans le rocher."—*Voyage*, tom. II. p. 32.

the south end four cells have been begun, but none of them finished. In the back wall, at each end, are also the commencements of four more, while in the centre is the entrance to the shrine, with a window at each side of it. The shrine measures 20 feet by 17 feet, and has a square mass of rock in the centre rising to the roof. On the front of this is sculptured an image of Buddha seated with wheel and deer beneath, *chauri* bearers at his side, and *vidyâdharas* above. On the south and north faces are other *chauri* bearers, and on the back is roughly blocked out the form of a sitting Buddha. Everything about this cave indicates that it was left unfinished.

The other caves are mostly small vihâras or *bhikshugṛihas* with one or two cells each of no note. In No. IV. was an inscription now nearly all peeled off.

Cave VIII. is one of the largest caves here and is a dâgoba cave, combining the characteristics of the flat-roofed chaitya and the vihâra as at Kuḍâ. The hall is 27 feet wide, 23 feet 9 inches deep, and 9 feet 2 inches high, and has had only two pillars with their corresponding pilasters in front. The pillars, however, are broken away, except fragments of the bases and capitals, which show that they were of the antique type found both at Junnar and Kârlê, and in some of the Nâsik caves. Round the ends and back of this runs a bench. In each end wall are three cells, while in the back are two more,—all with stone benches; and the shrine about 15 feet square, which once contained a dâgoba, as indicated by the umbrella left on the roof and the rough surface of the floor, but it has been entirely hewn away.

It has an inscription also in pretty perfect condition, but not yet translated; the character, however, seems to belong somewhere about the Christian era.

In No. XV. is a dâgoba in half relief 4 feet in diameter and 6 feet 2 inches high. The drum is surrounded at the upper edge by a plain rail pattern, and the tee is crowned by five thin slabs, the uppermost one joining the roof of the recess in which it stands.

Cave XXI. is the first on the lower scarp and is a small room or shrine, in the middle of which stands a plain dâgoba 4 feet 8 inches in diameter, the top of the capital touching the roof. Its only ornament is a band in the "rail pattern" round the upper edge of the cylinder. On the north wall is carved a figure of Buddha seated with his legs down, attended by *chaurî* bearers and *vidyâdharas*, the latter holding a mitre over his head. Over this is a *toraṇa* of flowers springing from the mouth of a *makara* on each side. A sculpture precisely similar is to be found among the later insertions on the south half of the screen wall of the great chaitya at Kârlê, as shown in the central compartment of Plate XIV. In the south side of this cave is a cell about 7¾ feet square with a stone bed in the back of it.

On the wall outside No. XXVII. is an inscription and a small dâgoba in half relief standing on a bench ornamented with the rail pattern. Over the capital is carved an umbrella, the total height, including this, being 4 feet 2 inches.

At the foot of the hill under some trees are three fallen dâgobas, which must have stood close to where they now lie. Indeed, part of the base of the largest can be traced close behind them.

Kol, Śirwal, Wai, &c.

Kôl is a small village, across the Savitrî river to the south-east of the Mhâṛ, and in the hill behind it are two small groups of caves: the first, to the north-east of the village, consists of a few dilapidated cells of no pretensions either as to size or style. The other group, to the south-east, contains one cell, rather larger than any of the others, but all are apparently unfinished excavations, and have been much damaged by time. In this second group, however, are three short inscriptions.[1]

In a hill to the north-east of Mhâṛ, a few small cells and cisterns were found by the survey party, but they are insignificant, as is also a cell in the hill to the south near the road leading to Nâgotanâ.

Passing next to the eastern or upper side of the Ghâṭs, we have to the south of Poona a group of caves at 'Sirwal on the Nîrâ river; another near Wâî, a sacred Brahmanical town, whence the ascent commences to the Sanatarium on Mahâbale'swar Hill: 25 miles further south at Pate'swar, 6 miles west of Sâtârâ was a small group to which a Brahman Saukar, about the beginning of the century, made so many structural additions in converting them into a fane of Mahâdeva, that little is now left to show what they were originally—but probably they were Brahmanical. About 30 miles

---

[1] One reads, "A cave, the religious gift of Śeth Sagharakhita, son of Gahapati."

south of Sátárâ, at Karâḍh on the Krishṇâ is an extensive series of upwards of sixty caves; and, lastly, three miles north of the village of Pâtan, to the west of Karâḍh in the Keḍâ valley, is a flat-roofed Chaitya cave of the Kuḍâ type, with a dâgoba and a small hall with two cells.

The 'Sirwaḷ group of caves is in the territory of the Pant Sacheva of Bôr, on the north-east border of the Sâtârâ Zilla. They are between 2 and 3 miles south-west from the Śirwaḷ traveller's bangala, 4 east of Bôr, and 13 north of Wâi, or in long. 73° 59′ E., lat. 18° 8′ N., at the head of a short narrow valley on the eastern slope of a spur from the Mândhardeva range of hills,[1] which bound the Nîrâ valley on the south.

They face the north-east, and are of the same severely plain type as all the earliest caves. The first is a small chaitya cave 20 feet 3 inches by 14 feet, square at the back, with a plain dâgoba 5 feet 3 inches in diameter, having a plain capital of four 3 inch fillets. The door is 5 feet wide, but the whole floor is so silted up that no part of the interior is more than 5½ feet high.

The second excavation has been a vihâra, of which the whole front has disappeared with one of the cells on the right hand side. It has been about 26 feet square, with three cells on each side and in the back: in all, except two, are the usual stone benches. Four of them have small window openings, a foot square, with a counter-sunk margin on the outer side. Round the hall runs a bench, up to the level of the top of which the floor is filled with dry mud.

The third is, apparently, a natural cavern, 17 feet deep, irregular in shape, and only about 3½ feet high.

The remaining four in the lower tier and two in the upper are more or less irregular apartments, much ruined by the decay of the rock; one of them has two benched cells at the back, but they possess no special interest. There are also six small excavations on the south side of the ravine, filled up with rubbish.

The caves near Wâî, also in the district of Sâtârâ, are all of about the same early age as those of Kuḍâ, Mhâṛ, and Karâḍh. They are in the village of Lohârî and near Sultânpur, about four miles north from Wâî, and form a group of eight excavations, cut in soft

[1] They have been carefully surveyed by Major H. Lee, R.E., Superintending Engineer, Southern Division, on whose report and drawings this account is based. They were examined by the Messrs. West in 1854.

trap rock, running from south-east to north-west, and facing south-west. They were first described about 30 years ago by Mr. (now Sir) H. Bartle E. Frere, then Commissioner of Sâtârâ.[1] The first from the south-east is a plain Vihâra, about 27 feet by 21 feet, with three cells, and near it a tank. The second and principal cave has a hall 31 feet by 29½ and 8½ feet high, with a bench along the left side and parts of the front and back; four cells on the right side with bench-beds and small windows; while in the back are two more similar cells, with a dâgoba shrine between them, 16 feet square, originally with a door and two large windows to admit light into it. The capital of the dâgoba has been destroyed to convert it into a gigantic linga, or emblem of S'iva 6 feet 4 inches high and 8 feet in diameter—styled Pâlkeśvar or Palkobâ. To the left of the cave is another excavation, much ruined. Two hundred yards north-west from this is another vihâra, of which the hall is about the same size as the last, with a bench round the sides and back and four cells in the back and one on the left side,—also an entrance made in the right wall running up to what may have been intended for a chamber over the roof of the cave, but never finished. The roof has been supported by six octagonal pillars in two rows from front to back—with a stone joist running through the heads of each row,—but only fragments of them are left. On the right hand wall near the back are the remains of some human figures, apparently two standing females and two males seated, all now headless and otherwise mutilated. The other caves are of smaller size, and not of much interest.

Other two small excavations exist in the same neighbourhood between Panchgani and Bâwadhan, 4 miles south-east of Wâî, very difficult of access.

Karadh.

The Karâḍh caves are in the hills to the south-west of Karâḍh in the Sâtârâ district, the nearest being about two and a half miles from the town, in the northern face of one of the spurs of the Agâsiva hill, looking towards the valley of the Koinâ; the most distant group are in the southern face of another spur to the south-west of the village of Jakhanwâḍi, and from three to four miles from Karâḍh. The town of Karâḍh is probably of considerable antiquity

[1] *Jour. Bom. B. R. As. Soc.*, vol. iii. pt. ii. p. 55.

and gives name to a sect of Brahmans; but its long occupation by the Muhammadans may well account for the disappearance of all traces of early works in it.

The caves were first described by Sir Bartle Frere in 1849, and for our purposes it may be as well to follow generally his arrangement into three series,[1] viz.: I. The southern group, near the village of Jakhanwâdi, consisting of 23 caves; II. Those in the south-east face of the northern spur, about 19 caves; and III. Those facing the valley of the Koinâ, which are more scattered, 22 caves;—in all 63, besides many small excavations of no note and an abundance of water-cisterns,—often two of them to a single cave.

The absence of pillars in the larger halls, the smallness of many of the excavations, the frequency of stone benches for beds in the cells, the primitive forms of the Chaityas or Dâgobas, and the almost entire absence of sculpture in these caves, combine to indicate their early age. Unfortunately they are cut in a very coarse, soft, trap rock, on which inscriptions could not be expected to remain legible for long ages, if very many of them existed; and only a portion of one has been found, with the faintest trace of another. The letters are rudely cut, but appear to belong to the same period as most of the Kârlê inscriptions. From all such indications these caves may be placed approximately as about of the same age as those of S'ailarwâḍi, and Kuḍâ, Pâla, &c., and not far from the age of the Junnar and Nâsik caves. They were all probably excavated before the Christian era, but they are generally so much alike that few, if any, can be considered as a century earlier.

They are mostly so small and uninteresting that they need not be described in detail, only a few of the more noteworthy and characteristic being noticed. In the first group the most westerly cave, No. I., has had a verandah, perhaps with two pillars and corresponding pilasters; but the front has been built up by a modern Jogi. Beyond this is a hall, 22 feet by 11 and 7 feet high, with a bench along the back and ends of it; and at the back of this again are two cells with stone benches. Cave II. has a hall about 34 feet square, and its verandah has been supported by two square pillars.

Cave V. is a Chaitya facing south-west, and is of the same style as one of the Junnar caves, but still plainer (Plate V., fig. 2). It

---

[1] *J. B. B. A. S.* vol. III., p. 108 *et seqq.*

has a semi-circular apse at the back, and arched roof, but no side aisles, and in place of the later arched window over the door, it has only a square one. At each side of the entrance is a pilaster, of which the lower portions are now destroyed, but which has the Nâsik style of capital crowned by three square flat members supporting the one a wheel or *chakra*, the emblem of the Buddhist doctrine or law, and the other a Lion or *Siṅha*, a cognizance of Buddha himself, who is frequently designated as *Śâkhya Siṅha*, and perhaps also a symbol of the *Saṅgha* or assembly (Plate VI., fig. 3). The dome of the dâgoba inside is about two-thirds of a circle in section, and supports a massive plain capital. The umbrella is hollowed into the roof over it, and has been connected with the capital by a stone shaft now broken.

Cave VI. has had a verandah supported by two plain octagonal pillars with capitals of the Nâsik, Kuḍâ, and Pâla type. The hall is 16 feet 10 inches wide by 13 feet 5 inches deep, with an oblong chamber at each end, that on the left having a bench at the inner end, and the other a small cell. At the back is a room 12 feet wide by 18 deep, containing a dâgoba nearly 7 feet in diameter, in the front of which an image of Viṭhobâ was carved by a Gosain some 35 or 40 years ago.

Cave XI. is another rectangular Chaitya about 14 feet wide by 28 feet 9 inches long, with flat roof. The dâgoba is much destroyed below; its capital is merely a square block supporting the shaft of the *chhatri* carved on the roof. Cave XVI. is another similar shrine but smaller; the verandah supported by two perfectly plain square pillars without capital or base; the hall is lighted by the door and two windows, and has a recess 15 feet square at the back, containing a dâgoba, similar to that in No. XI., but in better preservation.

Nos. IV., IX., and XX., are the largest of the other Vihâra caves and have all cells with stone beds in them.

The second group commences from the head of the ravine, the first cave being No. XXIV., which is a Vihâra facing E.N.E., 21 feet wide by 23 deep, and 7 feet 10 inches high, with a verandah originally supported by two plain square pillars. Carved on the south end wall of the verandah, near the roof, are four small Chaitya arches, with a belt of "rail-pattern" above and below, and a fretted torus in the spaces between the arches, much in the style of Cave XIV. at Nâsik and Cave XII. at Ajaṇṭâ. Below this the wall has been divided into panels by small pilasters, which were perhaps carved with figures now obliterated. On the north wall were three Chaitya arches, the central one being the larger, and apparently contained a dâgoba in low relief, as at Kondâṇê. Below this is a long recess as for a bed, now partly fallen into the water-cistern beneath. From the hall four cells open to the right, three to the back, and one to the left, each (except the centre one in the back) with a stone latticed window close to the roof, and about 15 inches square. In No. XXIX., originally two caves, of which the dividing wall has been broken through, are similar windows into four cells.

Cave XXX. is a ruined Vihâra, 36½ feet by 19, with eleven cells round the hall and a twelfth entered from one of these. The next excavations are situated about three-quarters of a mile from this, Nos. XXXI. to XXXV. of which are no ways noteworthy. Cave XXXVI., about 100 yards west from XXXV., consists of an outer hall about 17 feet by 13, with a cell in each side wall, and through it a second smaller hall is entered which has six cells and two bench bed recesses.

The third series is divided into two groups, the first facing northwards, and the second in a ravine further west, and facing westwards. It consists of Caves XLII. to LXIII., few of them deserving of detailed mention. No. XLVII. consists of a room with a bench in each end, an unfinished cell at the back, and two others at the left end, on the wall of one of which is the only inscription of which many letters are traceable, ending in the usual *lena deya dhanaṁ*, "religious gift of a cave" by some one. A few indistinct letters are just traceable also on the right hand side of the entrance, and near them the faintest trace of "the rail-pattern." No. XLVIII. (Plate VI., fig. 1) is a range of five cells with a verandah in front, supported on three square pillars and pilasters, the central cell, 27 feet by 11 feet 3 inches and 10¾ feet high, contains a dâgoba still entire, the upper edge of the drum and the box of the capital—which has no projecting slabs over it—being carved with the rail-pattern. The umbrella is carved on the roof and attached to the box by a shaft. In front of this against the right hand wall is the only figure sculpture in these caves, and though much defaced, appears to have consisted of three human figures in *alto rilievo* about 5 feet high, the left one, a male, with high turban and front knob, similar to some of the older figures at Kârlê and on the capitals at Beḍsâ, holding some objects in each hand. He wears a cloth round his neck, and another round his loins, which falls down in folds between the legs. His right hand is bent upwards towards his chin, and over the arm hangs a portion of the dress. He also wears armlets and bracelets. To his left a slightly smaller figure appears to be approaching him with some offering. Above this latter is a third, perhaps a female. At the right hand of this excavation is another cell, approached from outside.

The rest of this group ending with LV. are small and uninteresting, and the cells are not so frequently supplied with stone beds as in those previously described. From No. LV. it is about a mile and a half to LVI., which has a verandah 25 feet 4 inches by 11 feet 9 inches, with two plain square pillars in front. The hall is about 24 feet square with ten cells, three in each side, and four at the back, several of them unfinished. Cave LX. is almost choked with earth, but is 38 feet long by 13 feet 10 inches wide, with a semi-circular apse at the extreme end and arched roof similar to the Beḍsâ Vihâra. Outside and above the front, however, are traces of a horizontal row of Chaitya window ornaments, so that, though there is no apparent trace at present of a dâgopa having occupied the apse, the cave may have been a primitive form of Chaitya with a structural dâgoba. From the ease with which such structures could be removed, we ought not perhaps to be surprised that none such have been found. But as the evidence now stands, it seems probable that a dâgoba of masonry or brickwork may frequently have been introduced in the early caves in the West.

CHAPTER IV.

THE CAVES IN THE VICINITY OF KARLE AND THE BOR GHAT.

The next great division into which the older Buddhist caves of Western India naturally group themselves is one to which unfortunately no specific name can well be applied. They are not all situated together like houses in a street, as are the caves at Ajaṇṭâ or Elurâ, nor scattered like villas in close proximity to one another as at Kanheri or Junnar. Though generally situated near the head of the Bor Ghâṭ, through which the railroad passes from Bombay to Poona, they consist of small detached groups, containing a Chaitya cave with a few subordinate and detached cells, complete in itself, and having no appparent connexion with any other establishment. It might be possible to designate it as the Karlê group, from the name of its principal and most characteristic cave, but that would be misleading if applied to Kondânê, and especially to Pitalkhora, which is at some distance, and there is no district or geographical name that would include the whole. Perhaps The Great Central Group of Western Caves would be the most descriptive term that could be employed, and would be perfectly applicable. They are situated in the very centre of the cave region, and are in many respects the most remarkable of the whole.

Notwithstanding this want of geographical definitiveness, the leading characteristics of this group are easily defined when carefully studied, and their difference from other groups easily perceived. In all of them the Chaitya is the most marked and leading feature to which the Vihâra is always subordinate. Among them we have the Chaitya at Bhâjâ (woodcut, No. 1), which is probably the oldest and consequently one of the most interesting of the class, and we have also the Great Cave at Karlê, which is the largest and finest Chaitya in India. But the Vihâras that are grouped with these cannot be compared in any respect with those of Nasik or Ajaṇṭâ, and other groups where, as a rule, the monastery is the main feature and the church less prominent.

The difference becomes at once apparent if we compare this group with the two principal ones already described. If we describe the Kathiawar group as the unornamented, the Orissa as the sculptural, and this one as the architectural, we at once grasp practically the leading features of each. The first two have no Chaitya caves, which form the leading features of the third, and though the last cannot boast of the exuberant richness of decoration which prevailed in Katak, it avoids the puritanical plainness of the first. It hits a happy medium between the two, and its productions may consequently be compared as specimens of architecture with the very best that have been produced in India at any age. As a rule they all belong to an early and pure school of native art, before it became the fashion to overload its productions with a superfluity of minute ornamentation utterly destructive of the simple grandeur, which is characteristic of this great central group.

The differences between these groups are the more remarkable, as all three belong to the same age. They all begin with the age of Aśoka, B.C. 250: None can be said to be older, and they extend down to the Christian era. Some examples—but not important ones—may be more modern, but the principal caves are spread tolerably evenly over these two centuries and a half, and all emanate from the impulse given to the diffusion of the Buddhist religion given by the convocation held by that monarch on his conversion in the third century before the Christian era.

Whatever may have been the cause, whether the proximity of a large city, or something merely historical or traditional,[1] the head of the Bôr Ghâṭ, between Bombay and Poona, seems to have been the centre of a large number of Buddhist establishments. Konḍâṇê, Jambrug, and Ambivlê are in the lower scarps of the Sahyâdri range and are within a few miles from Karjat station at the foot of the Ghaṭ; Bhâjâ, Beḍsâ, and Kârlê in the spurs that strike out from the same hills into the table-land on the east. They all lie within short distances of the railway which passes up the Bôr Ghâṭ from Bombay to Poona. Kârlê is near the village of the same name and not far from Lanoli station[1]; Bhâjâ is on the opposite or

[1] Dr. J. Wilson suggested that the name of the village of Lanâvali, not far from the caves of Kârlê and Bhâjâ, might be a corruption of Lenâvali, the Grove of the Lena or Caves, noted even in recent times for its botanical peculiarities,—and which may have been a Buddhist town.

south side of the railway and about a mile from it; Bêḍsâ is on the south side of the hills in which Bhâjâ is, and the others are scattered about among the hills around.

Kondane.

About four miles from the Karjat station, on the Great Indian Peninsula Railway, and at the base of the old hill fort of Râjmâchî, is the Kondâṇê group of caves, first brought to notice about 30 years ago by the late Vishṇu Śâstri, and soon after visited by Mr. Law, then collector of Thâṇâ.[1] They are in the face of a steep scarp, and quite hidden from view by the thick forest in front of them. Water trickles down over the face of the rock above them during a considerable part even of the dry season, and has greatly injured them. So much so indeed that it is now difficult to determine whether they or the caves at Bhâjâ are the earliest. They must be nearly, if not quite contemporary, and as they must have taken some time to excavate, their dates may overlap to some extent. The Vihârâ at Konḍânê (Plate VIII., figs. 1 and 2) certainly looks more modern, while the Chaitya (Plate VIII., fig. 3), which is very similar in plan and dimensions to that at Bhâjâ, is so much ruined that it is impossible now to decide which may have been first completed.

They face north-west, and the first to the south-west is a Chaitya-cave of very considerable dimensions, being 66½ feet from the line of the front pillars to the extremity of the apse, 26 feet 8 inches wide, and 28 feet 5 inches high to the crown of the arch. The nave in front of the dâgoba is 49 feet in length by 14 feet 8 inches, and the dâgoba 9½ feet in diameter, with a capital of more than usual height, the neck—representing the relic casket—being, as at Bhâjâ, of double the ordinary height, and representing two coffers, one above the other, carved on the sides with the Buddhist rail pattern. The fillets that covered this are decayed, as is also the whole of the lower part of the dâgoba. The bases with the lower parts of all the thirty columns that surrounded the nave, as well as that of one of the two irregular columns that once ornamented the front, have also decayed, and positions only of most of them can now be ascertained. Between these two latter pillars a wooden screen or front originally filled the opening to a height of about 10 or 12 feet, in

[1] Dr. J. Wilson's Memoir in *Jour. B. B. R. As. Soc.*, vol. iii. pt. ii. p. 46. They have also been fully described by W. F. Sinclair, Bo. C.S., *Ind. Ant.*, vol. v. p. 309.

which were the doorways leading to the interior and it was fixed to them, as seems to have been the case with all the earlier caves. The Chaitya Cave at Bhâjâ and that at Kondane had similar fronts constructed in wood. The caves at Bedsa and Kârlê are apparently among the earliest, where these screens were carved in the rock instead of being erected in the more perishable material.

There are still, however, remains of seven pillars on the left side of the cave, and six on the south, which rake inwards, as do also those at Bhâjâ and Beḍsâ, to be described hereafter—a proof of the early date of the work;[1] those behind the dâgoba and six near the front on the right side have disappeared entirely. On the upper portion of one column on the left is a symbol or device somewhat resembling a dâgoba, with a rude canopy over it. (Plate VII., fig. 2.) The arched roof has had wooden rafters as at Kârlê and elsewhere, but they are gone, and the only remains of the woodwork is a portion of the latticed screen in the front arch. The façade bears a strong family likeness to that at Bhâjâ. On the left side is a fragment of sculpture in *alto rilievo*—part of the head of a single figure about twice life-size. The features are destroyed, but the details of the head-dress show the most careful attention to finish of detail. Over the left shoulder is an inscription in one line in Mauryan characters of perhaps the second century B.C., or it may be earlier, which reads—

Kaṇhasa antevâsinâ Balakena kataṁ,

which Dr. Kern translates—"Made by Balakena, the pupil of Kaṇha (Kṛishna)."

Over this head, at the level of the spring of the great arch in the façade, is a broad projecting belt of sculpture: the lower portion of it is carved with the rail pattern; the central portion is divided into seven compartments, filled alternately, three with a lattice pattern and five with human figures—one male in the first, a male and female in each of the third and fifth, and a male with a bow—and two females in the seventh. Over these is a band with the representations of the ends of tie-beams or bars projecting through it, and then four fillets, each projecting over the one below, and the upper half of the last serrated. The corresponding belt of carving on the right side of the façade is much damaged by the falling away of the rock at the end next the arch.

---

[1] Fergusson, *Ind. and East. Archit.*, p. 110.

A little to north-east is No. II., a Vihâra, of which the front of the verandah is totally destroyed except the left end. This verandah was 5 feet 8 inches wide and 18 feet long, with the unique number of five octagon pillars and two antæ. (See plan and section, Plate VIII., figs. 1 and 2.) In the end of this verandah is a raised recess, and under a Chaitya arch is a small dâgoba in half relief,—apparently the only object of worship when these caves were excavated. Inside, the hall is 23 feet wide by 29 deep, and 8 feet 3 inches high, with 15 pillars arranged about 3 feet apart and 3½ feet from the side and back walls, but none across the front. The upper portions of these pillars are square, but about 1½ feet from the top they are octagonal: the bases of all are gone, but they also were probably square. The roof is panelled in imitation of a structural hall with beams 19 inches deep by 8 thick, 3½ feet apart, running across through the heads of the pillars, and the spaces between divided by smaller false rafters, 5 inches broad by 2 deep. There are three wide doors into the hall, though most of the front wall is broken away, and on each side six cells—18 in all, each with the monk's bed in it, and the first on each side with two. Over the doors of 14 of these cells are carved Chaitya or horse-shoe arches, connected by a string course projecting 6 or 7 inches and carved with the rail pattern. (Plate VIII., fig. 1.)

No. III. is a plain Vihâra with nine cells, much ruined, especially in front, but it had probably three doors.

No. IV. is a row of nine cells at the back of what now looks like a natural hollow under the cliff. Beyond them is a tank, now filled with mud, then two cells under a deep ledge of over-hanging rock, and, lastly, a small cistern.

In a scarp over the village of Hal Khurd, eight miles south of Karjat, Mr. Sinclair describes a very plain Vihâra, consisting of a hall, 12 feet by 11 feet, surrounded by six cells, two of them double-bedded. One on the left of the entrance has been converted into a shrine for Bhairava, for whose further convenience, or that of his worshippers, the front wall of the Vihâra has been demolished within living memory. It is said to have borne an inscription.[1]

North from these, at Kothalgaḍh or Pêṭh, are other excavations

---

[1] *Ind. Ant.*, vol. v. p. 310.

which, owing to the difficulty of reaching them, have not been examined by any European.

BHAJA.

Bhâjâ or Bhâjê is a small village, about two miles south of Kârlê village and at the foot of a spur of the hill, which is crowned by the old Isâpur hill-fort. The cave temples just above the village are first referred to by Lord Valentia,[1] but were not examined by himself or any of the Europeans that accompanied him. They face the west, and, counting upper storeys, &c., they may be reckoned as eighteen excavations altogether.

Commencing from the north, the first is apparently a natural cavern, 30 feet long, slightly enlarged. The next ten are plain vihâras, with but little particular about them. No. VI. is an irregular vihâra, much dilapidated and half full of silt. The hall has been irregular, but about 14 feet square, with two cells on each side and three in the back, and with Chaitya-window ornaments all round over the cell doors, as in Cave XII. at Ajaṇṭâ, and again here, on the back wall of No. IX., where is a frieze projecting 2 feet 2 inches with four Chaitya arches connected by the rail-pattern ornament. There has been a verandah in front of this excavation, of which a fragment of the base of one of the pillars is left, and a broken capital with animal figures upon it, showing that the style was somewhat similar to that of Cave VIII. at Nâsik.

The Chaitya Cave of the group No. XII. is one of the most interesting in India, and certainly one of the most important to be found anywhere for the history of Cave architecture. It is hardly worth while to waste much time in the inquiry whether it or the caves at Koṇḍânê are the earliest. They are so like one another in all essential respects that there cannot be much difference in their age. They are certainly both as early or earlier than 200 B.C., and neither can claim to have been excavated before the time of Aśoka, B.C. 250. Be this as it may, if we had only the Koṇḍânê Cave, it is so ruined that we should hardly be able to understand from it, the peculiarities

---

[1] *Travels*, vol. ii. pp. 165, 166. They are noticed also in the *Jour. Bom. B. R. As. Soc.*, vol. i. pp. 439–443; vol. iii. pt. ii. pp. 51, 52; Fergusson's *Ind. and East. Archit.*, p. 110.

of the cave architecture of the age, while the Bhâjâ caves excavated in a better material are still so perfect as to explain every detail.

A view of the front of this cave has already been given (woodcut, No. 1, page 30), which sufficiently explains its general appearance. The wooden screen that originally closed its front is, of course, gone, but we can easily restore it, in the mind's eye, from the literal copies of it in the rock which we find at Bêdsâ, Kârlê, and elsewhere, aided by the mortices cut in the floor and at the sides, showing how the timbers were originally attached to the rock. When this is realised it seems impossible that anyone can look at these caves and not see that we have reached the incunabula of stone architecture in India. It is a building of a people accustomed to wooden buildings, and those only, but here petrified into the more durable material. There is not one feature nor one detail which is not essentially wooden throughout, or that could have been invented from any form of stone construction, or was likely to be used in lithic architecture, except in the rock. What is equally interesting, and equally conclusive on this point, is, that for 1,000 years after its date, we can trace the Indians slowly but steadily struggling to emancipate themselves from these wooden trammels, and eventually succeeding in doing so. Unfortunately, however, it was when too late for the Buddhists, who were the inventors of the style, to profit by its resultant conversion into a perfected lithic style of architecture.

From the Plan and Section, Plate IX., it appears that the Chaitya is 26 feet 8 inches wide and 59 feet long, with a semi-circular apse at the back, and having an aisle 3 feet 5 inches wide, separated from the nave by twenty-seven plain octagonal shafts, 11 feet 4 inches in height. These rake inwards about 5 inches on each side, so that the nave is 15 feet 6 inches wide at the tops of the pillars, and 16 feet 4 inches at their bases. The dâgoba is 11 feet in diameter at the floor, and the cylinder is 4 feet high; the *garbha* or dome is 6 feet high, and the box upon it, like that at Kondâṇê, is two-storeyed, the upper one being hewn out 19½ inches square inside, with a hole in the bottom 20½ inches deep and 7 inches diameter, sunk down into the dome for the purpose of securing the shaft of the umbrella that once surmounted the dâgoba. The upper portion of this box or capital being of a separate stone and hewn out, indicates very distinctly that it was the receptacle of some relic. The usual thin flat members that surmount the capital are entirely wanting in this and in other instances to be noticed below. Whether they were once supplied here in stone or in wood, we have no means now of knowing. On four of the pillars are carved in low relief seven ornaments or Bauddha symbols. On the seventh and eighth columns respectively, on the left side are the figures 9 and 10,[1]—the second apparently a conventional posy of sacred flowers, the first formed of four *triśûlas* round a centre, which perhaps contained a face, with buds and leaves at the corners. On the eighth pillar on the right side are the flowers 11, 12, and what appears to be a fan—13, and on the right-hand face the wreath represented fig. 14.

The roof is arched in the usual way, the arch rising from a narrow ledge over the triforium, 7 feet 5 inches above the tops of the pillars, and attaining a height of 26 feet 5 inches from the floor. This is ribbed inside, as at Kârlê and elsewhere, with teak girders, the first four of which, and portions of some of the others, have given way, or been pulled down.[2] The front must have been entirely of wood, and four holes are chiselled in the floor showing the positions of the principal uprights. There are also mortices cut in the arch, showing where one of the main cross beams must have been placed, probably to secure the lattice-work in the upper part of the window. Almost the only difference in detail between this and the Chaitya at Kondâṇê is, that in the latter the irregular pillars immediately in front of the nave, and nearly in line with those dividing off the aisles, were of stone, here they were of wood; both temples are equally simple and almost identical in the styles of their façades, and only the difference just remarked seems to indicate that this Bhâjâ example is rather the earlier of the two. This gains support also from the introduction of columns into the hall of the Vihâra at Kondâṇê—in none of the Vihâras here are they so employed.[3]

The fronton of the great arch is full of pin holes in three rows, about 170 in all—which indicate, beyond doubt, that some wooden

---

[1] *See* drawings, Plate VII.

[2] Application having been made to the Government of Bombay to prevent the villagers from pulling down more of the woodwork, and to fix what seemed to be in danger of falling, the engineer entrusted with the work inserted new ribs wherever he thought one had been pulled down; in fact attempted a restoration.

[3] I am strongly of opinion for these and other reasons, which can only be explained by an attentive study of the photographs, that Bhâjâ is the earliest of the two, but the difference in age cannot be very great.—J. F.

and probably ornamental facing covered the whole of it in the manner shown in all the faces of similar arches at Udayagiri (Pl. I.) and at Bharhut, several of which are seen in Woodcut No. 10, and numberless examples in General Cunningham's work on that Stupa. The only pieces of figure sculpture are—a female figure high up on the left side of the front, much weather-worn, but with a beaded belt about the loins; two half figures looking out at a window in the projecting side to the right of the great arch, and on the same side the heads of others in two small compartments in the façade, and on a level with the top of the arch. These figures bear a close resemblance to those on the façade at Kondâṇê. The struts or brackets cut in entire relief and the whole style of every detail in the front is so like wood-work, that there can be no doubt it was copied from an example in that material, and is without exception the closest copy we have. Next to it stand the cave No. IX. at Ajaṇṭâ, and the Kondâṇê and Bêdsâ Chaityas; plainer caves into which pillars were not introduced, nor any attempt made to ornament their fronts in imitation of wooden examples, belong generally to an earlier age.

By the side of this Chaitya, but with the line of its front coming forward to the south at an angle of 25° (see Plate IX), is a Vihâra No. XIII., the front (if ever it existed in stone, which is very doubtful) has been quite destroyed, but it is probable that it must originally have been of wood. It is 30 feet long by 14½ feet deep, with a cell in each of the back corners standing out into this area. Each of these has a latticed window; that on the left side has a fastening on the door jamb as if for a lock or bolt; that on the right has an arched door, and contains a stone bench. In the back of the hall are three more cells, the side ones with a single bench, and the central one with two, and with a small recess under each. Over the doors of all these cells is the Chaitya arch, connected by a frieze of "rail pattern." Over the front, also, are ornamental arches and a double course of "rail pattern."

Next to this, and facing a little more to the north, is Cave XIV., 6 feet 8 inches wide and 25½ feet deep, with one cell at the back and three on each side; the front ones have double beds with a recess under each; the second, on the left side, has no bed, but a square window; and the third, on the right, also wants the bed, but leads into an inner cell with the usual stone bench.

Cave XV. is above XIII., and with No. XVI. is reached by a stair to the south of No. XIV. It is a small Vihâra, 12½ feet wide by 10 feet deep, with a bench on the right side, and two semi-circular niches, 2 feet 8 inches wide, with arched tops, surmounted by the Chaitya arch. At the back are two benched cells. The front wall has been thin, and is destroyed; the terrace in front was about 5 feet wide, and probably, as indicated by holes in the roof, framed in wood-work and projecting forwards: the façade above this and the next cave is carved with three Chaitya-arches and the rail pattern.

Descending from these caves we come to Cave XVII., which has been a small Vihâra, 18½ feet long by 12½ feet deep, with three cells at the back and two at the right side, one of them with a bench in it. There is also a bench in the left end of the hall, and an irregular recess or cell. On the right side, beside the door of the second cell, is an inscription in two lines in early characters, of which the first is damaged. Near this are two wells in a recess, and over them an inscription, also in two lines.

At some distance along the scarp, is a large excavation, containing a group of fourteen chaityas or dâgobas of various sizes cut in the rock.[1] All have the Buddhist-rail pattern round the upper portion of the drum. The five under the rock vary in diameter from 6 feet 3 inches to 4 feet 8 inches, and the front two have the relic box only on the dome, as in the great cave, while the three behind them have also heavy capitals, the largest on the left joined to the roof by the stone shaft of the *chhatri* or umbrella, while over the other two the circle of the chattri is carved on the roof with a hole in the centre, over a corresponding one in the capital, evidently for the insertion of a wooden rod. Of those outside, the first to the north has a handsome capital, 3 feet 8 inches high, very elaborately carved; (Woodcut No. 43), most of the others are broken, so that it is not easy to say how they have been finished, except that the eighth, and possibly others, were of the

No. 43. Capital or Tee of Rock-cut Dâgoba at Bhâjâ, from a photograph.

[1] See upper part of Plate IX. on the right hand.

simple box form without any cornice. In four of the capitals under the roof there are holes on the upper surface as if for placing relics on them, and in two cases there is a depression round the edge of the hole as if for a closely fitting cover. On some of them are the names of *Theras*, but nearly obliterated.

Still farther along the scarp is a small chamber with a cell at the right end, much filled up with earth, but with a frieze, ornamented by caryatides and dâgobas alternately in high relief, supporting a moulding with dâgobas in half relief and with an arched roof, only half of which remains, the rest having fallen away. On the walls are some curious sculptures in the Sânchi style; but it has not been excavated.

Under the first waterfall is a small empty circular cell; under the second is a large square room with three cells at each side, partially filled with debris and much ruined; under the third is a small circular cell with a dágoba in it.

Rock-Temples of Bedsa.

The caves of Bêḍsâ—also known as Karunj-Bêḍsâ, from the two villages, near the foot of the Supati Hills, where they are— lie 5½ miles in a straight line, east of Bhâjâ, and 4½ south of the station of Kaṛkaḷâ, on the Great Indian Peninsula Railway. They are in a spur from the south side of the same range of hills as the Bhâjâ group, but look down upon the valley of the Pavnâ river, and are at

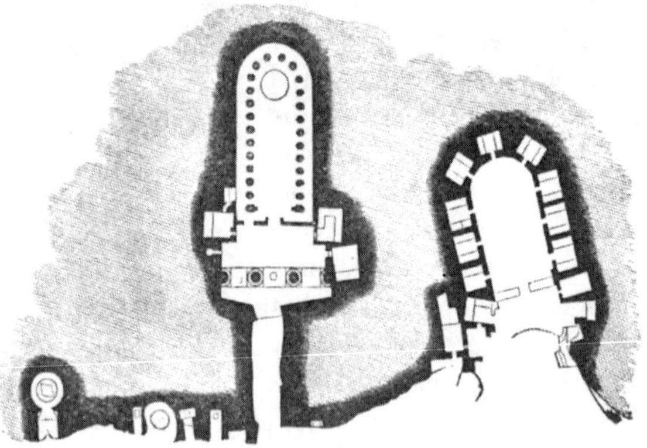

No. 44. Plan of the Beḍsâ Caves. Scale, 50 feet to 1 in.[1]

[1] From Fergusson's *Ind. and East. Archit.*, p. 113.

a height of about 300 feet above the plain, or 2,250 above the sea-level. They form one of the smallest groups, consisting only of a Chaitya-cave and Vihâra with some dâgobas, wells, and cells, and were first described by Professor Westergaard.[1]

The first excavation is a small circular chamber, containing an unfinished Dâgoba. Eight yards north of it is a well with the remains of a dâgoba on its north or right side, behind which is an inscription in two lines. Close to this is a second and third well, over the second of which is another inscription in three lines.

Four yards from this is the entrance to the Chaitya-cave, which is reached by a passage 12 or 13 yards in length, cut through the rock, left in front of it in order to get sufficiently back to obtain the necessary height for the façade. This mass of rock, on both sides the entrance, hides the greater portion of the front. A passage, 5 feet wide, has been cleared between them and the front of the two massive octagonal columns (3 ft. 4 in. thick), and two demi-columns that support the entablature at a height of about 25 feet. Their bases are of the *lotâ* or water-vessel pattern, from which rise shafts, slightly tapering and surmounted by an ogee capital of the Persepolitan type, grooved vertically, supporting a fluted torus in a square frame, as at Junnar, over which lie four thin square tiles, each projecting over the one below. On each corner of these last crouch

No. 45. Capital of Pillar in front of Cave at Bedsa (from a photograph).[1]

[1] *Jour. Bom. B. R. A. Soc.*, vol. i. p. 438; see also vol. iii. pt. ii. pp. 52-54; and vol. viii. p. 222; *Orient. Chr. Spectator*, Jan. 1862, pp. 17, 18; Fergusson, *Ind. and East Archit.*, pp. 112-114.

elephants, horses, bullocks, sphinxes, with male and female riders executed with very considerable freedom, as shown in the Woodcut, No. 45, on the preceding page.

The verandah or porch within these pillars is nearly 12 feet wide and in front 30 feet 2 inches in length, with two benched cells, projecting somewhat into it from the back corners, and one in the right end in front, having an inscription in one line over the door; the corresponding cell in the opposite end has only been commenced.[1] Along the base of the walls, and from the level of the lintels of the cell-doors upwards, the porch walls are covered with the rail-pattern on flat and curved surfaces, intermixed with Chaitya-window ornaments, but without any animal or human representations. This and the complete absence of any figure of Buddha is one of the most decisive proofs of the early and Hinayâna character of these caves. As remarked by Mr. Fergusson, the 'rail ornamentation' "becomes less and less used after the date of the Bhâjâ and Beḍsâ "Chaitya caves, and disappears wholly in the fourth or fifth cen-"turies, but during that period its greater or less prevalence in "any building is one of the surest indications we have of the rela-"tive age of any two examples."[2] The rood screen is introduced in stone in front, from which we infer that it is later than Kondâṇê and Bhâjâ, but it must follow pretty closely after them.

The door-jambs slant slightly inwards, as do also the pillars inside,—another indication of its early age. The interior is 45 feet 4 inches long by 21 feet wide. The gallery, in the sill of the great window, extends 3 ft. 7 in. into the cave, which, beside the two irregular pillars in front, has twenty-four octagonal shafts, 10 feet 3 inches high, separating the nave from the side aisles, 3½ feet wide. Over the pillars is a fillet, 4 inches deep, and then the triforium, about 4 feet high. All the wood-work has disappeared within the last twenty years, for Westergaard (in 1844) describes it as ribbed, and a writer in the *Oriental Christian Spectator*, about 1861, found fragments of the timber lying on the floor. On the columns, as late at least as 1871, could be distinctly traced portions of ancient painting, chiefly of Buddha with attendants; but a

---

[1] A view of this porch from a photograph will be found in Fergusson, *Ind. and East. Architecture*, p. 114, woodcut 51.

[2] *Ind. and East Archit.*, pp. 115, 116.

local official, under the idea of "cleaning" this fine cave, had the whole beslobbered with whitewash, and obliterated all the paintings.

On five of the pillars on the right side, near the dâgoba, are roses and other Bauddha emblems—the *dharmachakra*, shield, triśula, lotus, &c. (*See* Plate VII., figs. 3, 4, 5, 7, 8, and 11.)

The dâgoba has a broad fillet of "rail ornament" at the base and top of the cylinder, from which rises a second and shorter cylinder, also surrounded above with the rail ornament. The box of the capital is small, and is surmounted by a very heavy capital, in which stands the wooden shaft of the umbrella,—the top has disappeared. This cave faces the east.

Leaving this and passing a well not far from the entrance, at a distance of eighteen yards, we reach a large unfinished cell, in the back of which is a water-cistern. Close by this is the Vihâra, Plate X., quite unique in its kind, having an arched roof and circular at the back like a Chaitya. How it has been closed in front is not very clear (see Woodcut 44), but probably by a structural wall with some sort of window in the arch, as in the Chaitya caves. Outside are two benched cells, one on each side the entrance, which is 17 feet 3 inches wide, with a thin pilaster, 3 feet 5 inches broad on each side. Within this it is 18 feet 2 inches wide and 32 feet 5 inches deep to the back of the apse, and has 11 cells, all with benches or beds. Their doors are surmounted by Chaitya-arches connected by a string-course of "rail-pattern," and in line with the finials of the arches is another similar course. The cell-doors have plain architraves, and outside each architrave a pilaster, a portion of which has the arrises taken off, after the style of the earlier forms of pillars. In the walls between the doors mock grated windows are carved. The whole has been plastered, and probably painted, but it is now much smoked,—some devotee having made his asylum in it and carved his patron divinity on the back wall, to which *pûjâ* is done by the villagers when they visit or pass the place.[1]

Beyond this, and under steps that lead up to the left, is a small cell, and in the stream or *nala* beyond is a small open tank, 3½ feet by 7, with sockets cut in the rock. A dozen yards farther is another plain room, about 14 feet 8 inches square, with a door 7 feet wide.

---

[1] It has also been carefully whitewashed by an over zealous official, so as to vulgarise it entirely and to obliterate all its more important features.

Karle.

The caves now to be described have received the name they go by among Europeans from the neighbouring village of Kârlêṅ or Kârlâ, on the Poona road, where there used to be a staging *banglá* or rest-house; but they are much nearer and belong to the village of Vêhargaum to the north of Kârlê. They are in the west flank of the spur just above the village, and consist of a large Chaitya and several Vihâras—some of the latter much ruined.

This Chaitya is, without exception, the largest and finest, as well as the best preserved, of its class. It has been so fully described by Mr. Fergusson,[1] that I shall here quote most of his account. As he remarks, it "was excavated at a time when the style was in its greatest purity. In it, all the architectural defects of the previous examples are removed; the pillars of the nave are quite perpendicular. The original screen is superseded by one in stone ornamented with sculpture—its first appearance apparently in such a position—and the architectural style had reached a position that was never afterwards surpassed."

In and about the cave there are many inscriptions and fragments of inscriptions, but they have not yet been investigated by competent scholars so to enable us to arrive at any very definite conclusions regarding their age. One, however, reads:—"Peace! By Ushabhadâta, the son of Dînika, the son-in-law of Râja Kshahârâta Kshatrapa Nahapâṇa."[2] And as Nahapâṇa's and Ushabhadâta's names also occur at Nâsik and Junnar, with dates ranging from 40 to 42. If we may assume them to be in the same era as the Kshatrapa dynasty, and that they were dated according to the Śaka reckoning, we have A.D. 120 as a limit, at least on one side. But from the position and character of the letters used in this inscription we may fairly infer that the Chaitya was executed some time previously. Two inscriptions, one in very large letters, of an earlier form, immediately above the elephants in the left side of the porch as we enter, and another on the great pillar in front, mention the great king Bhutapála and his son, Agnimitra, as establishing "this rock mansion, the most excellent in Jambudwîpa." In the Paurâṇik lists (ante p. 25), Agni-

[1] *Ind. and East Architect.*, p. 117ff. See also *Rock-cut Temples of India*, *J. R. A. S.*, vol. viii. p. 30, *et seqq.*

[2] *Second Archæol. Report*, p. 42.

mitra appears as the second of the Śunga dynasty about 170–160 B.C., and one Devabhuti, who has been supposed to be the Bhuti or Bhûtapâla of these inscriptions, and was the last of the same dynasty about B.C. 70; but as Bhûtapâla is probably only an epithet for a great sovereign, we cannot trust much to this identification. From the form of the letters used in these last inscriptions, as well as from the style of its architecture, we shall probably not be far wrong in placing the excavation of this cave slightly anterior to the Christian era. It belongs more probably to the first half century before that time, rather than to any period after it, but it cannot be far distant from the beginning of our reckoning either way.

" The building," continues Mr. Fergusson, as will be seen from the plan and sections (Plate XI.) " resembles to a great extent an early Christian church in its arrangements, consisting of a nave and side aisles, terminating in an apse or semi-dome, round which the aisle is carried. The general dimensions of the interior are 124 feet 3 inches[1]

No. 46. View of the Interior of the Chaitya Cave at Kârlê (from a photograph).[2]

[1] These measurements have been corrected in accordance with those determined by the recent survey.—J. B.

[2] From Fergusson's *Ind. and East Architecture*, p. 120.

from the entrance to the back wall, by 45 feet 6 inches in width. The side aisles, however, are very much narrower than in Christian churches, the central one being 25 feet 7 inches, so that the others are only 10 feet wide, including the thickness of the pillars. As a scale for comparison, it may be mentioned that its arrangements and dimensions are very similar to those of the choir of Norwich Cathedral, or of the Abbaye aux Hommes at Caen, omitting the outer aisles in the latter buildings. The thickness of the piers at Norwich and Caen nearly corresponds to the breadth of the aisles in the Indian temple. In height, however, Kârlê is very inferior, being only 46 feet from the floor to the apex."

"Fifteen pillars on each side separate the nave from the aisles; each pillar has a tall base, an octagonal shaft,[1] and richly ornamented capital, on which kneel two elephants, each bearing two figures, generally a man and a woman, but sometimes two females,[2] all very much better executed than such ornaments usually are. (See Plate XII., figs. 2, 3, and 4, and Plate XIV., figs. 2 and 3). The seven pillars behind the altar are plain octagonal piers without either base or capital, and the four under the entrance gallery differ considerably from those at the sides. The sculptures on the capitals supply the place usually occupied by frieze and cornice in Grecian architecture; and in other examples plain painted surfaces occupy the same space. Above this springs the roof, semicircular in general section, but somewhat stilted at the sides, so as to make its height greater than the semi-diameter. It is ornamented, even at this day, by a series of wooden ribs, almost certainly coeval with the excavation, which prove beyond the shadow of a doubt that the roof is not a copy of a masonry arch, but of some sort of timber construction which we cannot now very well understand."

"Immediately under the semi-dome of the apse, and nearly where the altar stands in Christian churches, is placed the dâgoba"—in this instance a plain dome on a two-storeyed circular drum, similar to that at Beḍsâ, the upper margins of each section surrounded by

---

[1] The eighth pillar on the right is 16-sided, having, in *basso-rilievo*, on the central north face a small dâgoba; on the right, a wheel on a support, with two deer at the foot; and on the left, adjacent side, a small representation of the lion-pillar. See Plate XII., fig. 1.

[2] On the sides, next the aisles, are horses with single riders on each; but, as is usually the case with the horse, they are badly proportioned and ill executed.

the rail ornaments, and just under the lower of these are a series of holes or mortices, about 6 inches deep, for the fastenings of a covering or a wood-work frame, which probably supported ornamental hangings. It is surmounted by a capital or tee of the usual form—very like that at Beḍsâ, and on this stands a wooden umbrella, much blackened by age and smoke, but almost entire. The canopy is circular, minutely carved on the under surface, and droops on two sides only, the front and rear; the seven central boards are as nearly as possible in one plane, and those towards the front and back canted each a little more than its neighbour. The accompanying plate (Plate XIII.) shows the amount as well as the beautiful character of the carving on the portion of it which is left.

In the top of the capital, or tee near the north-west corner, is a hole about 10 inches deep, covered by a slab, about 10 inches square and 4 inches thick,—doubtless the receptacle for the relic, which, however, has been removed. Round the upper edge of the capital are mortice holes—eight in number, or three to each face—by which some coronet, metal umbrellas, or other ornament was attached.

"Opposite this," to resume Mr. Fergusson's account, "is the entrance, consisting of three doorways under a gallery, exactly corresponding with our rood-loft, one leading to the centre and one to each of the side aisles; and over the gallery the whole end of the hall is open as in all these Chaitya halls, forming one great window, through which all the light is admitted." In this instance, as will be observed from the last woodcut, the screen is cut in the rock as at Beḍsâ, and not in wood as at Bhâjâ or in the Chaitya at Kondânê. The great window above the screen is formed in the shape of a horse-shoe, and exactly resembles those, used as ornaments, on the façade of this cave, as well as on those of Bhâjâ, Beḍsâ, and at Kondânê, and which are met with everywhere at this age. Within the arch is a framework or centering of wood standing free, shown in the woodcut in the following page.

This, so far as we can judge, is like the ribs of the interior, coeval with the building;[1] at all events, if it had been renewed,

[1] A few years ago I reported that this screen was leaning out, and in danger of falling. Mr. Fergusson wrote me to endeavour to have it restored, and after some delay this was effected under the superintendence of Colonel Goodfellow, R.E., Executive Engineer of the District. Mr. Fergusson remarks, "It would be a thousand pities if this, which is the only original screen in India, were allowed to perish."—J. B.

No. 47. Facade of Chaitya Cave at Karle, from a sketch by J. F.

which is most improbable, it is an exact copy of the original form, for it is found repeated in stone in all the niches of the façade, over the doorways, and generally as an ornament everywhere, and with the Buddhist 'rail,' copied from Sanchi, forms the most usual ornament of the style.

The presence of the wood-work in the forms here found is an additional proof, if any were wanted, that there were no arches of construction in any of these Buddhist buildings. None indeed are found in any Indian buildings, anterior to the Mahomedan Conquest, except as mentioned above (p. 133), some few almost furtively introduced into some brick buildings of the Pâla dynasty in Bengal, when they were borrowed apparently from the Burmese. They are the only examples known to exist in purely Hindu architectural buildings before the reign of Akbar (1556 A.D.).[1]

[1] As this is the finest Chaitya cave in India, a quotation from my original paper on the architectural ordinance of these caves may not be misplaced.

"However much they vary in size or in detail, their general arrangements are the

"To return however to Kârlê, the outer porch is considerably wider than the body of the building, being 52 feet wide," by 15 feet

---

same in every part of India, and the mode of admitting light, which is always so important a piece of architectural effect, is in all precisely identical.

"Bearing in mind that the disposition of parts is exactly the same as those of the choir of a gothic round, or polygonal apse cathedral, the following description will be easily understood. Across the front there is always a screen with a gallery over it, occupying the place of the rood-loft, on which we now place our organs: in this there are three doors; one, the largest, opening to the nave, and one to each of the side aisles; over this screen the whole front of the cave is open to the air, one vast window the whole breadth and of the same section, stilted so as to be more than a semicircle in height, or generally of a horse-shoe form.

"The whole light, therefore, fell on the Dâgoba, which is placed exactly opposite, in the place of the altar, while the aisle around and behind is thus less perfectly lit, the pillars there being always placed very closely together, the light was never admitted in sufficient quantities to illuminate the wall behind, so that to a person standing near the door in this direction, there appeared nothing but 'illimitable gloom.'

"It does not appear whether the votary was admitted beyond the colonnade under the front, the rest being devoted to the priests and the ceremonies, as is now the case in China, and in Catholic churches, and he therefore never could see whence the light came, and stood in comparative shade himself, so as to heighten its effect considerably. Still further to increase this scenic effect, the architects of these temples have placed the screens and music galleries in front, in such a manner as to hide the great window from any person approaching the temple, though these appear to have been omitted in later examples, as in the Viswakarma of Elurâ, and the two later Chaitya caves at Ajanta, and only a porch added to the inner screen, the top of which served as the music gallery; but the great window is then exposed to view, which I cannot help thinking is a great defect. To a votary once having entered the porch the effect is the same, and if the space between the inner and outer screen was roofed, which I suppose it may have been in the earlier examples, no one not previously acquainted with the design could perceive how the light was admitted. Supposing a votary to have been admitted by the centre door, and to have passed under the screen to the right or left, the whole arrangements were such that an architectural effect was produced certainly superior to anything I am acquainted with, in ancient or modern temples.

"Something of the same sort is attempted in the classic, and in modern Hindu temples, where the only light admitted is by the door directly facing the image, which is thus lit up with considerable splendour, and the rest of the temple is left in a rather subdued light, so as to give it considerable relief. The door, however, makes but a clumsy window compared with that of the Buddhist cave, for the light is too low, the spectator himself impedes a portion of it, and, standing in the glare of day, unless he uses his hands to shade his eyes, he can scarcely see what is within. In the Hypæthral temples, this was probably better managed, and the light introduced more in the Buddhist manner; but we know so little of their arrangements, that it it is difficult to give an opinion on a subject so little understood.

"Almost all writers agree that the Pantheon at Rome is the best lit temple that antiquity has left us. In one respect it equals our caves, that it has but one window, deep, "and is closed in front by an outer screen, composed of two stout octagonal pillars, without either base or capital, supporting what is now a plain mass of rock, but which was once ornamented by a wooden gallery, forming the principal ornament of the façade. Above this, a dwarf colonnade or attic of four columns between pilasters admitted light to the great window, and this again was surmounted by a wooden cornice or ornament of some sort, though we cannot now restore it, since only the mortices remain that attached it to the rock, which are not sufficient for the purpose."

Considerable modifications have been made at some subsequent period in the sculptures in the porch: originally the fronts of three large elephants standing on a base carved with the "rail pattern" in each end wall supported a framed frieze, also ornamented with the "rail"; but on both ends this second "rail" has been afterwards cut away to insert figures of Buddha and his attendants, of which no representations existed when the cave was first executed. Above this was a thick quadrantal moulding, and then another "rail," the return of which forms the sill of the great window. On this stand miniature temple fronts, crowned with the Chaitya window, and between them pairs of figures similar to those described at Kuḍâ (*ante*, p. 207), some of them among the best sculptures of the kind in India. Above this, the Chaitya arch and "rail pattern" are repeated again and again to the top.

On the front wall of the cave both the "rail" at the bottom and that on a level with the heads of the doors, has been cut away in later times to make room for images of Buddha and his attendants —Padmapâni, &c., and in doing so the older inscriptions have also been mercilessly hewn away. The pairs of large figures on each side of the doors alone appear, like those at Kâṇheri, to have belonged to the original design. In the middle of the space between the central and right-hand doors is inserted a sculpture which must be of a very

---

and that placed high up; but it is inferior, inasmuch as it is seen to every one in the temple, and that the light is not concentrated on any one object, but wanders with the sun all round the building.

"I cannot help thinking that the earlier Christian architects would have reïnvented this plan of lighting had they been able to glaze so large a space; but their inability to do this forced them to use smaller windows, and to disperse them all over the building so as to gain a sufficiency of light for their purposes; and a plan having once become sacred it never was departed from in all the changes of style and detail which afterwards took place."—J. F. in *J. R. A. S.*, vol. viii. pp. 61-2.

late date: Buddha is there attended by Padmapâni and perhaps Manjûśri seated on the *sinhâsana* with his feet on the lotus over a conventionalised wheel, supported by two deer, and under the wheel is a supporting pier held by Nâga figures, while over Buddha's head two *vidyâdharas* hold a tiara. (Plate XIV.)

In front of the outer screen stands the Lion-pillar (*sinhastambha*), a plain, slightly tapering, 16-sided shaft, surmounted by a capital of the same style as those in the portico at Beḍsâ. On this stands four lions, their hinder parts joined, but there is no hole or mortice to lead us to suppose that any emblem in metal or wood was raised over them. The pillar stood on a raised circular basement or drum, carved with the rail-pattern, but now defaced. There are indications that show that, as at Kaṇhêri and Kailâsa at Elurâ, there was a corresponding pillar at the opposite side, the base of which is covered by the modern Śaiva temple. The cap of the existing pillar is connected with the screen-wall by an attachment of rock, in which is cut a large square mortice; and over the modern temple, on the south side, there remains two-thirds of a corresponding attachment with a similar mortice, as if to hold a beam horizontally across 18 inches in front of the screen. This other pillar doubtless supported the *chakra* or wheel, the emblem of the law.

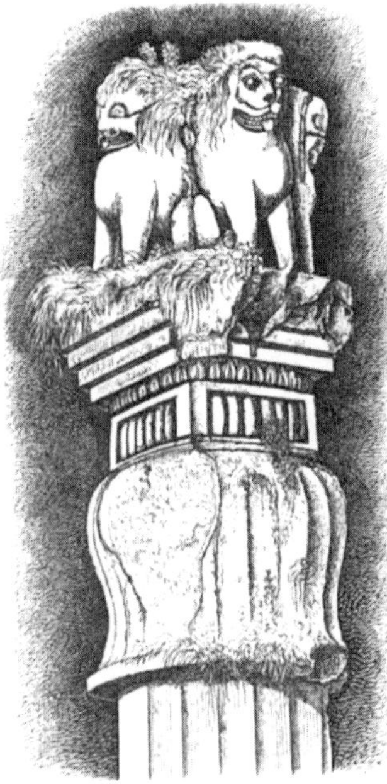

No. 48. Lion Pillar at Kârlê, from a drawing.

" The absence of the wooden ornaments of the external porch," says Mr. Fergusson, " as well as our ignorance of the mode in which this temple was finished laterally, and the porch joined to the main temple, prevents us from judging what the effect of the front would have been if belonging to a free-standing building. But the proportions of such parts as remain are so good, and the effect of the whole so pleasing, that there can be little hesitation in ascribing to such a design a tolerably high rank among architectural compositions.

"Of the interior we can judge perfectly, and it certainly is as solemn and grand as any interior can well be, and the mode of lighting the most perfect, one undivided volume of light coming through a single opening overhead at a favourable angle, and falling directly on the altar or principal object in the building, leaving the rest in comparative obscurity. The effect is considerably heightened by the closely set thick columns that divide the three aisles from one another, as they suffice to prevent the boundary walls from ever being seen, and, as there are no openings in the walls, the view between the pillars is practically unlimited.

"These peculiarities are found more or less developed in all the other caves of the same class in India, varying only with the age and the gradual change that took place from the more purely wooden forms of these early caves to the lithic or stone architecture of the more modern ones. This is the principal test by which their relative ages can be determined, and it proves incontestibly that the Kârlé cave was excavated not very long after stone came to be used as a building material in India."

On the north-west of the lion-pillar are some cells, and a water-cistern, into which a dâgoba that had stood on the roof of it has fallen. North from this is a large excavation, more than 100 feet in length, but very irregular; it has been apparently two or three Vihâras, in which all the dividing walls have been destroyed. At the north end of it are several cells, still nearly entire, three water-cisterns, and a small dâgoba.

Above these is a Vihâra, about 28 feet by 27, and 8 feet high, with four cells in each side and five in the back, six of them with benches or beds of stone, as in most of the older Vihâras, and in one is a ladder up to a stair leading to another cave above. The front of this cave, however, has given way. Still higher in the rock, and reached by a stair from the preceding, is another Vihâra, 34 feet 6 inches by 48, but not quite rectangular, and 8 feet 11 inches high. It has three cells in the right end and five in the left, with six in the back. Across the left end is a raised platform, about 8½ feet broad and 18 inches high, along the front of which there seems to have been a wooden railing or screen. On the east and south walls are two sculptures of Buddha, evidently of much later workmanship than the cave. The front wall is pierced with four openings; and the verandah, 40 feet 10 inches long, 7 feet wide, and 12 feet 3 inches high, has a low screen-wall in front, on which stand four columns between pilasters. Outside this screen, at the north end, is a water-cistern, and along the front a balcony.

Further north (the lower part of the stair broken away) is another Vihâra above those first mentioned. It is about 38½ feet long and 17 feet deep, with two cells in each end and four in the back, five of them with stone-beds. In the front wall are a door and two windows, but the corridor of the verandah has given way. On the east wall of this cave is an inscription fairly legible. From the character of the alphabet employed it may belong to the 2nd century of the Christian era.

To the south of the Chaitya there are also a number of excavations, the first being an unfinished hall, about 30½ feet wide by 15½ feet deep. The next is a small room, of which the front is broken away, with a figure of Buddha on the back wall. Close to this is a water-cistern, and beyond it a Vihâra, about 33 feet square and 9 feet 5 inches high, with four cells (without beds) in the back, three in the left end, and two unfinished ones in the right, all having their floors about a foot higher than that of the hall. On the middle of the back wall is a figure of Buddha, seated with his feet resting on a lotus, under which is the wheel between two deer, and behind are two small worshipping figures. On each side are *chauri* bearers, the one on his right holding a lotus stalk in his left hand; and over their heads are *vidyâdharas*. This hall bears evident marks on the floor, ceiling, and side walls of having been originally only 21 feet 6 inches deep, but afterwards enlarged.

The front wall is pierced by a door and two windows; and the verandah has a cell at the north end and two octagonal pillars between pilasters in front, each pillar being connected with its adjacent pilaster by a low parapet or screen, which forms the back of a bench on the inside, and is divided outside into four plain sunk panels, similar to several at Mhâṛ, Cave VI. at Ajantâ, and others.

Beyond this is a small unfinished room; and at the turn of the hill facing south is another, with a bench along part of the east wall. The front has gone, but on the wall under the eaves is a fragment of an inscription.

A little to the east, and above the footpath, is another small cave, with a cell in the left wall having a bench or bed. And beyond this is a small water-cistern.

In the hills near to Kârlê there are a number of cells and rock-cisterns. Thus in the hill above the village of Dêvagaḍh, a little to the south-west of Kârlê, is a half-finished Vihâra cave, with two roughly-hewn square columns in front having bracket capitals; and in the back of the cave a door has been commenced as if for a shrine. In a rising ground, east of the village, is a rock-cut tank and some cuttings, as if intended for the commencement of a small cave with a cistern.

Again, on the south side of the village of Śeletanâ there is a large covered rock-cistern, originally with six openings; and high up the hill to the north is a large cavern under a waterfall. In the north side is a round hole which has been fitted with a cover, and was perhaps intended for storing grain in. Beside this is a small circular chamber which may have contained a structural dâgoba. The roof of the cave has fallen in, and there has been a great flaw in the rock, which, perhaps, led to its never being finished.

At Tâṅkwê, still farther east, are two rock-cisterns; and above Walak, in the face of the scarp, is a small round cell as if for a dâgoba, and near it a cave without front, slightly arched roof, and a cell at the back, with a round hole near the entrance, possibly a place for holding stores. A flaw in the rock has also destroyed the back of this excavation.

At Ayarâ, to the east of Bhâjâ, and in several places to the north-east of Kârlê, there are also excavations, mostly single cells for hermits.

Pitalkhora Rock Temples.

The next group of caves are those of Pitalkhorâ or the Brazen Glen, about a mile and a half from the deserted village of Pâtnâ,[1] which lies about twelve miles to the south of the railway station of Châlisgaum in Khândêsh district,[2] and at the foot of the Indhyâdri

---

[1] Pâtnâ is mentioned by Bhâskarâchârya under the name of Jaḍviḍ. His grandson Changadeva established a Maṭh or college here in 1206 A.D. to teach the Achârya's works.—*J. R. A. S.*, N.S., vol. i., p. 410.

[2] Long. 75° 2′ E., lat. 20° 21′ N.

range which separates the Nizam's territories from the British. The long deserted village contains several ruined temples with inscriptions of the Yâdava dynasty of Devagaṛh of the 12th and 13th centuries.[1] In the vicinity are also Brahmanical and Jaina caves. The Buddhist caves alluded to are near the head of a narrow ravine to the south-east of the ruined village, and consist of a Chaitya cave and some vihâras in a very ruinous condition, arising apparently from the nature of the rock in which they are excavated. Were it not for this they present features that would render them one of the most interesting of the minor groups in the west. The capital of the pillars, for instance, in the vihâra (Plate XVI.) are quite exceptional, and unlike any others yet found in India. They have a strangely foreign look, as if copied from some Persian or even Assyrian examples, originally, of course, executed in colour, though here the painted forms are reproduced in stone. The double-winged animals that rest upon them are found currently at Sanchi, and in the Udayagiri caves, but not with the same accompaniments.

Whoever excavated them, they form a singular contrast with the extreme plainness of the Kathiawar caves, of the same age, and form a sort of stepping stone between them and the Katak caves, though the absence of figure sculpture prevent them ranking with the eastern caves as objects of art.

The Chaitya (Plate XV., figs. 1 and 2) the whole front of which has been destroyed by the decay of the rock, is 34½ feet wide, and must have been 50 feet or more in length, and 30½ feet high to the top of the vaulted roof. The nave is 20 feet 8 inches wide, and separated from the side aisles by plain octagonal shafts 14 feet high, of which there are still left eleven shafts and fragments of fourteen others. Like those at Bhâjâ and Beḍsâ, they have a slight slope inwards. Above them the vault has had wooden ribs, as at Kârlê, Bhâjâ, &c., but only the mortices remain to show that they once existed. The side aisles have quadrantal stone ribs like those of Cave X. at Ajaṇṭâ. It appears that in excavating this cave originally, the workmen, after having made some progress, had come to a layer of very soft rock, about 4½ feet thick. This seriously interfered with their work, but they tried to meet the difficulty by building up the lower portions of 20 or more of pillars, including all those round the apse, with large blocks of stone. The walls of

[1] *Jour. R. As. Soc.*, N.S., vol. i. p. 414 ; *Ind. Ant.* vol. viii. p. 39.

the aisles, too, where this layer cut them, were built up with a facing of stone, 6 or 8 inches thick, in large slabs. These blocks have mostly fallen out now, and the dâgobas, probably also from the same cause, having been a structural one, has almost entirely disappeared, only portions of the solid basement remaining. The whole has been painted, as at Beḍsâ and Ajaṇṭâ, with figures of Buddha in various attitudes, but almost constantly with the triple umbrella over his head. This painting is, doubtless, of later age than the excavation of the cave itself, which must belong to the same age as No. X., at Ajaṇṭâ—whatever that may be—as it resembles this cave in every essential respect.

To the right of it are several groups of cells all more or less destroyed. To the left, behind a great mass of débris, is a portion of a very curious vihâra, the whole front of which has fallen. It is 50½ feet wide at the back, and appears to have been divided, like the Dâś Avatâra and Tîn Thâl caves at Elurâ, into corridors by rows of pillars parallel to the front wall, the pillars being square above and below, with the corners chamfered off in the middle, about 6 feet from centre to centre, and supporting an architrave, as in the vihâra at Kondâṇê. Crossing the corridors are thin flat rafters supporting the ceiling. (See plan and section, Plate XV., figs. 3 and 4.)

In the back wall are seven cells, five of which, at least, had stone latticed windows. Over each door and window together is a Chaitya-window arch, with three more towards the left, over the other two doors, projecting forwards as in Cave XII. at Ajaṇṭâ and in the Beḍsâ vihâra; while between each pair of these canopies, except the second and third, is the highly ornamented capital of an octagonal attached half column. The capitals are bell-shaped, of small depth in proportion to their width, each carved in a slightly different pattern, and several of them very richly. (*See* Plate XVI.) This member is surmounted by four thin, flat ones, each projecting a little over the one below it, as in the capitals of dâgobas, and the uppermost supporting a pair of couchant animals, except in one case, all of them winged. The pillar on the extreme right, between the sixth and seventh cells, supports a pair of couched Indian bulls; the next to the left is a pair of animals with the heads of camels and the bodies and paws of a feline animal having long, narrow wings attached to the legs by a band under the shoulders. The next pair are maned lions; the fourth, horses; then elephants; and between the next pair of arches are the heads and tips of the wings of a pair of deer, the remainder with parts of the arches on each side being broken away, and the door of the cell widened so as to remove all trace of any pilaster, if such ever existed here. Over the next is a pair of animals, perhaps intended for wolves, with heavy paws and grinning teeth; and lastly, in the left corner is a pair with human faces with large ears, on animal bodies, and one of them winged. Such figures as these are very uncommon in the Cave-Temples of Western India, but they are to be found on the gateways of the Sanchi Tope.

Inside the arches the semicircular areas are divided, as usual, by imitation lattice-work, the interstices of which are filled with figures of horses, elephants, lions, *makaras*, &c., accommodated to the shape of the apertures they occupy. The first cell to the left has three bench beds, the next has one, and that on the extreme right has none; the remaining four have two each—one on the left side, and the other a few inches higher across the back. The peculiarity of these cells, however, is that all their roofs are arched like Chaitya-roofs, with stone girders imitating wooden ones about 10 inches deep, overlaid by five rafters (Plate XVII., figs. 1, 2, and 3). The arch rises scarcely 2 feet, but the girders come 1 foot 10 inches down the walls as in the aisles of the Chaitya-cave.

Of the right side of the cave a part of one cell and a piece of the roof of the next only remains. On the left side is a large irregular excavation.

From the fragments of architectural ornamentation left on the rock outside above these caves it might at first sight appear that they belong to the same age as the earlier groups above described at Kondâṇê and Beḍsâ, but the rock is so friable, and the whole in so ruined a state, that the materials for comparison hardly exist. There are, besides, peculiarities about these caves which render it difficult to speak with certainty regarding them. Circular-roofed cells are, for instance, very rare in western caves, though they are common in the east as at Barabar (woodcut, No. 5), at Râjâgriha (woodcut, No. 7), and Udayagiri (woodcut, No. 19), but none of these have the wooden rafters copied in stone as at Pitalkhora.

The fact of these being in stone here would seem to indicate a more modern date than might at first sight be expected.

On the whole it seems probable that the whole belong to the first century of the Christian era. But for the slight inclination of the columns of the Chaitya this would seem quite certain, but even that peculiarity may have lingered longer in one place than in another.

Śailarwadi Caves.

About two miles south of the small town of Talêgâṅw-Dabara, near the railway and twenty miles north-west from Poona, is the Garoḍi hill, in which are a few early Buddhist excavations. They are at a height of about 450 to 500 feet above the plain, and the first, which is high up in the scarp and now almost inaccessible, consisted apparently of a single cell, of which the front has fallen away. The next is a little lower, and, like the first, faces S.W. by W. (Pl. V., fig. 3). It consists of a vestibule, 29 feet by 9¾, and 8 feet 8 inches high, opening into four cells at the back. Between each pair of doors are two pillars attached to the wall—half octagons (Fig. 1, Pl. XXIII.) with the *lotá* or water-vessel bases and capitals, and with three animals—elephants, lions, or tigers, over each, supporting a projecting frieze of "the rail-pattern." Along the ends and back, under the pillars, runs a stone bench. The cells within are perfectly plain. The cave, however, has been appropriated by the modern Brahmans, and in the third cell from the left is installed the Śaiva *liṅga*, with a small Nandi or bull in the vestibule and a *dipamálá* or lamp-pillar and Tulsi altar built outside. On the jamb of the cell door is a short, roughly-cut inscription recording the visit of a devotee and dated "1361 *Sidharthi Samvatsare, Srávaṇa Sudha.*"

North-west from this last and at some distance is a cistern, now dry; and still further along is a small cave that has apparently had a wooden front, with four upright posts going into sockets in the rock above. In the left end is a recess, and in the back is a cell. A few yards beyond this is another rock well, near which is the fourth cave. Pl. V., fig. 5. The front is entirely gone, and a thick wall has been built, to form a new front, a few feet farther in than the original, with two circular arched doors. The hall has four cells on the right, two in the back, besides a large shrine, and three on the left,—a fourth being entirely ruined. In the shrine recess has stood a dâgoba, the capital attached to the roof as in the

Kuḍâ caves,— but this has been hewn away to make room for a small low *chavaranga* or Śaiva altar.

Over this to the left is a cell, on the left end of the front wall of which is an inscription recording its excavation by a person from Dhanakaṭaka, the capital of the Ándhras. It agrees in the style of its letters with those used by the Andhrabhṛityas and is placed by Bhagvanlâl Indraji Paṇḍit between the times of Vâśishṭhîputra and Gautamîputra II.

Crossing the ridge which connects the hill with another to the west of it, there are other two small caves—monks' cells, no ways noteworthy, and scarcely accessible.

CHAPTER V.

THE JUNNAR CAVES.

Junnar is the principal town of the northernmost talukâ or division of the Puṇâ Zilla or Collectorate, and is distant from the latter city about 48 miles. The name is said to be a corruption of *Junánagara*, "the ancient city," but what special name that ancient city bore seems entirely lost: it is probable that it was the Tagara of the Greek writers and of Hindu tradition and ancient inscriptions.[1]

Round this old city in various directions are Buddhist caves nearly equally distributed in five different localities, making altogether 57 separate excavations:—

1. In the scarp of the Śivanêrî hill-fort to the west-south-west of the town.
2. The group known as Tuljâ Lenâ, to the west.
3. The Gaṇêśâ Lenâ in the Sulaimân hills, to the north of the town.
4. A second group in a spur of the Sulaimân hills, about a mile from the Gaṇêśâ Lenâ.
5. The caves in Mânmôḍî Hill south of Junnar.[2]

Like those at Talâjâ, Sânâ, Kuḍâ, Bhâjâ, and Beḍsâ, and all the older caves in the west, those of Junnar are remarkably devoid of figure ornament or imagery, in this respect strongly contrasting with the later ones, such as those at Elurâ, Ajaṇṭa, and Aurangâbâd. The dâgoba is common to all, but in the earlier caves it is perfectly plain, and in the later ones at Ajaṇṭâ it has figures of Buddha carved upon it. The ornaments are the Chaitya-window with its latticed aperture, the Buddhist-rail pattern, and the Dâgoba. Elephants,

---

[1] Ptolemy, *Geog.*, vii. i. 82; *Periplus. Mar. Eryth.*, 52; *Ind. Ant.*, vol. v. p. 280; vol. vi. p. 75; *Archæol. Survey*, vol. iii. p. 54; Elphinstone's *Hist. of Ind.*, p. 223; *Asiat. Res.*, vol. i. pp. 357, 369–375; *Jour. R. As. Soc.*, vol. ii. pp. 383–385, 396; *Trans. Bom. Lit. Soc.*, vol. iii. p. 392; Vincent's *Periplus*, pp. 373–375; *Trans. Bom. Geog. Soc.*, vol. vii. p. 153.

[2] A sketch plan showing the distribution of these caves, and their relative position, was published by Lieut. Brett in the fifth volume of the *J. B. B. R. A. S.*, p. 175.

tigers, and other animals appear on the capitals in one or two caves, the sacred tree and some other symbolical figures in others.

Although none of these caves can compare either in magnificence or interest with the Chaityas of Bhâjâ or Kârlê, or the vihâras of Nasik, their forms are still full of instruction to the student of cave architecture. The group comprises specimens of almost every variety of rock-cut temples, and several forms not found elsewhere, and though plainer than most of those executed afterwards are still not devoid of ornament. They form, in fact, an intermediate step between the puritanical plainness of the Kathiawar groups and those of the age that succeeded them.

It is not easy to speak with any great precision with regard to the age of this group. They certainly, however, all belong to the first great division of Buddhist caves. Some of the earliest as the Manmodi Chaitya, for instance, may be 100 or 150 B.C.; the other chaitya on the Sulaimâni hill may, on the contrary, be 100 or 150 A.D.; and between those two extremes the whole may be arranged from their styles without any material error being committed in so doing.

The Śivanêrî hill-fort, the birth-place of the Marâṭha champion Śivaji Bhôṅsle, lies to the south-west of the town, and going well to the south, along the east face of the hill, we reach several cells in the lower scarp, and then a cave which has originally had two columns with corresponding pilasters in front of a narrow verandah. The cave has a wide door, and is a large square cell, containing the cylindrical base of a dâgoba, coarsely hewn out. Can the top or garbha have been of wood or brick? On the sides of the scarp to the north of these excavations are several water-cisterns.

The ascent of the hill above this is peculiarly steep and difficult of ascent. On attaining the base of the upper scarp, at the south end, there is a cave of two storeys with a stair in the north end leading to the upper floor. It has been a small hall, of which the front is now entirely gone, except one pilaster at the south end. In the south wall is a small recess roughly excavated, and over it, near the roof, is an inscription, in one line, of deeply incised letters. At the beginning of it the same shield ornament occurs which marks the commencement of the Aira inscription on the Hathi Gumpha at Katak (*ante*, pp. 66 and 74, see also woodcut No. 15), and which occurs so frequently among Buddhist symbols at an early age. The character of the letters are not so old as those employed at Udayagiri, but still certainly before the Christian era.[1] The lower hall has three cells in each side wall and four in the back, several of them unfinished.

Further north, and somewhat higher, beyond a recess and a cistern with two openings into it, is a Vihâra, the whole front of which is open. It has a plain pilaster at each end, with holes in them for the fastenings of a wooden front that has at one time screened the interior. This mode of closing the fronts of these rooms seems to have been employed in several instances here, and these, so far as can be conjectured, are among the oldest caves. A bench runs round the interior walls, with an advanced dais or seat at the back, perhaps for a *sthavira* or teacher.

Next we come to some large cisterns, of which the roof has fallen in, and over the north side of them is a large vihâra with four cells in the back and two in the south end. In this, again, there seems originally to have been only a wooden front, but in its place has been substituted a stone one, of ten courses of ashlar carefully jointed, with a lattice stone window and a neatly-carved door of the style of about the tenth or eleventh century. This alteration was probably made by some Hindu sect—not Buddhist. There is a fragment of an inscription outside, at the north end over a stone bench. At the commencement is the Buddhist *triśûla* symbol; but only three or four letters in the line can be made out.

North from this are some more cells, much decayed, but which had probably all wooden fronts. There are holes in the stone for fastenings which could only have been in wood, which clearly indicate that this was the mode employed to close the front.

A difficult scramble along the face of the cliff brings us to the Bârâ Kotri—so called from a large vihâra cave with twelve cells *First*, over a cistern, broken in, is a dagobâ in half relief in front of a large cell with a stone bed in it, and having on the south side of the door an inscription in five lines of varying length.[2] Next are four cells, the last with a stone bed; *third*, three cisterns with a small hall over the last which once has had two square pillars in front and reached by a stair. *Fourth*, the vihâra that gives name

---

[1] No. 11 in the series given in *Ind. Ant.*, vol. vi., plate at p. 38.

[2] Nos. VIII. and IX. in *J. B. B. R. A. S.*, vol. v. pp. 163, 164.

to the group,—36 feet 8 inches wide by 33 feet 5 inches deep with four cells in each of the three inner walls, and a bench running quite round the hall. It has two doors, and two large windows, one of them almost 10 feet wide, grooved in the sill and sides for a wooden frame.

Beyond this are several more cells and a well, then a small vihâra with three cells in the left wall and two in the back, and with a dâgoba in half relief in a recess—a not uncommon feature in the very oldest caves: we have it at Kondâṇê, and in another form in Cave III. at Nâsik.

The next is a lofty, flat-roofed Chaitya cave. Plate XVIII., figs. 1 and 2. The front wall was probably originally pierced only for two windows and the central door, 6 feet 1 inch wide, but the sill of the south window has been cut away until it also forms a door. Inside is an outer cross aisle or vestibule, separated from the hall by two free standing and two attached pillars, with water-jar bases and capitals as at Nâsik. From the top of the abaci of these rise short square pillars, about 2½ feet in length, connecting the capitals with the architrave that runs across under the roof. The inner hall is 30 feet 11 inches in length, 20 feet 6 inches wide, and about 18 feet high. Near the back of it stands a well-proportioned dâgoba, 10 feet 3 inches in diameter, the cylindrical base 5 feet 11 inches high, and surrounded on the upper edge by the "rail pattern" with what are intended to represent the ends of bars projecting out below it. The umbrella, as in the oldest Chaityas, is carved on the roof, and connected with the capital by a short stone shaft. The ceiling has been neatly painted, and still retains large portions of the colouring: the design is in squares, each containing concentric circles in orange, brown, and white.

Outside is an inscription in three lines, which Dr. H. Kern translates—

"A pious gift of charity, designed for a sanctuary, for the common weal and happiness, by Vîrasenaka, a distinguished householder, confessor of the Dharmâ."[1] From the form of the characters employed

[1] *Ind. Ant.* vol. vi., p. 40. Dharmanigama, Dr. Kern says, he has not met with elsewhere, and supposes it to mean "one for whom the Dharma is the source of authority." This inscription was copied by Col. Sykes, *Jour. R. As. Soc.*, vol. iv. p. 289, No. 7; and a translation attempted by Mr. Prinsep, *Jour. As. Soc. Ben.*, vol. xi. p. 1045, No. 3; a copy is also given and a translation attempted by Dr. Stevenson in *Jour. B. B. R. As. Soc.*, vol. v. p. 163, No. 7.

it may have been inscribed about the Christian era, or probably a little earlier.

Beyond this cave are only some wells and fragments of cells now destroyed.

On the other side of the hill, facing the west, are a few others very difficult of access. The first from the north corner of the hill is a vihâra, 30 feet 8 inches wide by 27 feet 6 inches deep, and having two windows and a door in the front wall. Outside it has had a verandah, with four pillars in front, of which the four thin members of the abacus still remain attached to the roof, each with a hole about 2½ inches square on the under surface as if to receive the tenon of a wooden shaft. On the roof is a small fragment of fresco-painting just sufficient to show that it has been coloured in the same style as the Chaitya cave on the other side of the hill.

To the south of this is a group of five wells and a vihâra with four cells. South from these, again, are fragments of three or four others facing west-north-west, but no ways remarkable.

The Tûljâ Lêṇa group lies in a hill about a mile and a half or two miles north-west from Junnar, beyond the north end of Śivanêrî hill. They are so named, because one of them has been appropriated by the modern Brahmans as a shrine of Tûljâ Dévî, a form of Bhavânî, the consort of Śiva.

They run along the face of the cliff nearly from south-east to north-west, facing about south-west, but all the façades have fallen away. They consist of a number of cells and two small vihâras, with a Chaitya-cave of a form quite unique (Plate XVIII., figs. 3, 4). It is circular in plan, 25 feet 6 inches across, with a dâgoba in the centre, 8 feet 2 inches in diameter, surrounded by twelve plain octagonal shafts 11 feet in height, supporting a dome over the dâgoba. The surrounding aisle is roofed by a half arch rising from the wall to the upper side of an architrave 7 or 8 inches deep over the pillars. The dâgoba is perfectly plain, but its capital has been hewn off to convert it into a huge *liṅga* of Śiva, and even the dome is much hacked into, while some of the pillars have been notched and others broken. In front of this cave and the one on each side of it is a platform built by the modern voteries of Tûljâ Dêvî.[1]

---

[1] Among the sculptures at Bharhut is a bas-relief representing the exterior of a circular temple, such apparently as this. (Stupa at Bharhut, Pl. XVI., fig. 1. *See*

Over the front of one of the cells to the north-east of this are left some Chaitya-window ornamentation,—a larger one over where the door has been, the inner arch of which is filled with knotted ribbons, &c., similar to what is over the Chaitya-cave door at Nâsik; while the front of the arch is carved with flowers. (Fig. 4, Pl. XVII.) On each side of this is a smaller arch; and farther to the left is a dâgoba in half relief with the umbrella or *chhatri* over it, on each side a *Gandharva* or *Kinnara* above, and a male figure below,—that to the right attended by a female,—but all of them weatherworn. Over all is a projecting frieze carved on front with the "Buddhist-rail pattern."

Next to these are two more plain fronts, and then two with Chaitya-window heads over where the doors have been, and smaller ones between, and the "rail ornament" and quadrantal carved roll supported by slender brackets in entire relief, as at Bhâjâ.

The next group is in the hills locally known as the Gaṇêśa Pahâr[1] or Sulaimân Pahâr, about three miles north-north-east of the town, and about 360 feet above the level of it. The ascent is partly by a built stair which leads up to near the middle of the series,—to the sixth, counting from the east end,—from which, for convenience of reference, we shall number them.

No. I., at the south-east end of the range, is a monk's residence or *Bhikshu-gṛiha*, the front apartment of which is about 10 feet by 6, with a stone bench or bed at the left end, and two cells at the back, the one with stone beds. Outside has been a small verandah with two octagonal pillars supporting a projecting frieze carved with the "Buddhist-rail pattern" in front. In the east end of the verandah is a stone seat.

The next three are small caves and cells.

We then descend a short distance[2] along the face of the rock to No. V., a small vihâra, 25 feet wide by 29 deep and 8 feet 2 inches high, without any pillars. A stone bench runs round the three

---

also Hist. of Ind. and East. Arch., p. 168, woodcut 91). They probably were not far distant in age. As this one at Junnar is unique, they present an early form of temple of which few traces remain, though it probably was common in early times.

[1] This hill is said to be mentioned in the *Ganêśa Purana* under the name of *Layanâdri*.

[2] The difference of level is about 12 or 13 feet.

inner sides, and it has seven cells—three at the back and two at each side—for the resident monks. In these cells are high stone benches for their beds: on these they spread their quilt and enjoyed their rest,—simple beds for simple ascetic livers. The *śâla* or hall of this their *Śailagṛiha* or rock-mansion, which the first occupants doubtless regarded as spacious, is now used as a goat-shed. It had a door—of which the jambs are broken away—and two windows. Over the left window is an inscription in one line, preceded by a symbol of which the upper part is perhaps a sort of *triśûla* or trident, and is followed by the *swastika* or Buddhist cross.[1]

No. VI.—The next is the Chaitya-cave, facing south, and measuring inside 40 feet in length by 22 feet 5 inches wide and 24 feet 2 inches high (Plate XVIII., figs. 9 and 10). The verandah in front has two free-standing and two attached pillars of the style so prevalent at Nâsik,—the capitals consisting of an abacus of three, four, or five thin square members each projecting a little over the one below. Under this is a thick-ribbed torus, enclosed in a square cage formed by small pieces left at the corners connecting the fillets above and below. This rests on a deep member resembling an inverted water-jar. The shaft is octagonal, and the base consists of the same members as the capital, omitting the enclosed torus, but taken in reverse order. Over the abacus are figures of elephants roughly chiselled out, somewhat in the style we meet with in some of the Nâsik vihâras. The door is plain, 5 feet 9 inches wide, and lofty, and is the only entrance for light; for the arched window of the later style of Chaitya-caves is merely indicated high up in the rock, as a shallow recess with a Chaitya window finial over it, too high, indeed, to correspond with the arched roof of the cave: but its carefully smoothed area shows that it was not intended to drive it through.

Over the door is a well incised inscription in one long line, which is rendered by Dr. Kern—

"A pious gift of charity, designed for a sanctuary, by the pure-hearted Sulâsadatta, trader, son of Haraṇika."

---

[1] *Ind. Ant.* u.s. No. 2. This is No. 1 of those copied by Lieutenant Brett, and tentatively translated by Dr. Stevenson, *Jour. Bom. B. R. As. Soc.*, vol. v. p. 160; and No. 9 of Colonel Sykes's *Jour. R. As. Soc.*, vol. iv. p. 290, and *Jour. As. Soc. Ben.*, vol. vi. p. 1044, where Prinsep conjecturally reads it, "The hundred caves and the tank of Dhârmika Senî—his act of piety and compassion."

From the form of the alphabet employed it seems probable that this inscription may be subsequent to the Christian era, though to what extent is doubtful.

The nave is about 12 feet 9 inches broad, and 24 feet 6 inches up to the dâgoba, limited on each side by five columns and one engaged, 10 feet 10 inches high, similar to those in the front, except that in the capitals the torus is not enclosed. Over the capitals are lions, tigers, and elephants, as in Cave VIII. at Nâsik, fairly well cut. Thus on the first column on each side are a pair of elephants; on the second on the right a pair of tigers, and on the left a tiger, and a sphinx with human face and animal's body and legs with hoofs, (as in the verandah of Cave VIII. at Nâsik); on the third capitals on each side are elephants, on the fourth lions or tigers, and on the fifth elephants. In the apse round the dâgoba, and about 3 feet from it, are six plain octagon shafts, without base or capital. The aisle behind the pillars is 3 feet 6 inches wide, and is ribbed over, like the roof of the nave, in imitation of wooden ribs. The dâgoba is of the usual form, a plain circular drum or base, with a Buddhist-rail cornice supporting the *garbha* or dome on which stands the *toraṇa* or capital, consisting of a square block, representing a box also ornamented with the "Buddhist-rail pattern," surmounted by an abacus of five thin slab-like members, each in succession wider than the one below, until on the uppermost is a slab 5 feet 10½ inches square, and a foot thick, with a hole in the centre of it, to support the shaft of a wooden umbrella, as at Kârlê,[1] and four shallow square ones for relics; for it was on this *toraṇa*, as on an altar, that the relics of Buddha or of Bauddha saints were deposited for adoration. In some cases, as at Bhâjâ, the box under the capital was hollow, for the preservation of the relics. The face of this slab is carved with five copies of the Buddhist *trisula*, between little pyramids.[2] The whole height of this dâgoba is 16 feet 5 inches.

---

[1] Dr. Wilson, writing 28 years ago, says this dâgoba was surmounted by an umbrella; but, if so, this is only one case, among others, in which the woodwork has recently disappeared from Buddhist caves of Western India. See *Jour. Bo. Br. R. As. Soc.*, vol. iii. pt. ii. p. 62.

[2] This style of ornament we find also in Cave XII. at Ajanta, and with lotuses between the pyramids in many of the earliest Buddhist works, as at Udayagiri (Fergusson's *T. & Serp. Wor.*, Plate C., p. 267), Amarâvati (*Ind. & East. Arch.*, Fig. 40, p. 104), at Bharhut (*Ib.*, Fig. 27, p. 88, and Cunningham's *Bharhut*, Plates XII., XVII., XXXIII. Fig. 5; XXXIX. Fig. 2, and XL. to XLVIII.), &c.

Though so small, this is one of the most perfect Chaityas to be found anywhere. Its proportions are good, and all those details which were employed tentatively at Kârlê and in the earlier caves are here well understood and applied without hesitation. It is, too, the earliest instance known in which not only the ribs of the aisles but those of the nave are in stone, and nothing was in wood but the umbrella, now removed. It is, in fact, the best example we have of the perfected Chaitya of the first century of the Christian era.

Cave VII.—To the west of the Chaitya-caves an ascending stair enters under the rock and lands in the verandah of the largest vihâra cave here,—now known as the Gaṇêśa Lenâ, because this fine cave has been appropriated by some low Brâhmans in which to enshrine an image of the pot-bellied, elephant-snouted Gaṇâpati.[1] The hall is 50½ feet by 56½ feet, and 10 feet 2 inches high, with three doors and two windows in front, and a stone seat round the three inner sides. It has seven cells on each side, and five at the back—the central one altered to make a shrine for the rat-riding god, whose large image is cut out of the rock, probably from a dâgoba in *rilievo* that may originally have occupied this cell. Outside the cave is a narrow verandah, with six pillars and two attached ones, rising from a bench as in Cave III. at Nâsik. The back of this bench forms the upper part of a basement, carved with the "Buddhist-rail pattern." This cave also resembles the style of the Nâsik one, just referred to, in having animal figures over the capitals, but on the outside only, while inside rough blocks have been left out of which to carve them, and further—in both having a projecting frieze above, carved with "rail-pattern" ornamentation, and in the absence of pillars in a hall of such a large size.

The next seven are mostly small and without interest.

Cave XV. is a rectangular, flat-roofed Chaitya-cave, 21 feet 10 inches deep, by 12 feet 9 inches wide, and 13 feet 8 inches high (Plate XVIII., figs, 6 and 7), with a dâgoba standing 3 feet from the back wall, the capital of which is connected with the roof by the

---

[1] This personification of the misformed is named Ashta Vinâyaka, as being, according to the *Ganêsa Purana*, the eighth avatara of this *deva*, performed here to please his mother, Girija. He is a favourite idol of the populace, and is visited from far and near at the annual *jatra* or fair held in his honour. The shrine is taken care of by a *panch* or committee, who pay the *gurû's* wages out of a yearly endowment of Rs. 62 per annum. The *gurû* goes there daily from Junnar.

stone shaft of the umbrella; for here, as in the case of the dâgobas under the rock at Bhâjâ, and elsewhere, the canopy of the umbrella is carved on the roof. The extreme simplicity of this arrangement and of everything about this cave seem to mark it as the earliest Chaitya-cave in the group, or perhaps in any of the various groups around Junnar. The verandah in front is only 2 feet 7 inches wide by 19 feet 5 inches in length, and has had two octagonal pillars in front with two engaged in antis. Their capitals have four thin fillets in the square abacus, a thin torus, not enclosed at the corners, and the inverted water-jar, and their bases were similar.

On the left of the door, outside, is an inscription, in two lines, in the old square Pali character, and consequently probably at least 100 B.C. Dr. Kern reads and translates thus:—

"A pious gift of charity, designed for a sanctuary by Ananda, youngest son of the believer Tapala, and grandson of the believer Kapila."

Eleven or more small caves with some cisterns and inscriptions extend along the face of the cliff beyond this.

Passing round the east end of this hill, after a walk of fully a mile, or about four miles from the town, in another spur of the Sulaimân Pahâr, we reach a group of caves in the face of the hill, 400 feet above the level of Junnar, and facing S.S.W. They are usually represented as inaccessible, from the precipice in front of them being almost perpendicular; difficult of access they really are, and dangerous to attempt for any one not accustomed to climbing.

The most easterly of them is a small Chaitya-cave only 8 feet 3 inches wide, and 22 feet 4 inches in length, or 15 feet 4 inches from the door to the dâgoba, which is 4 feet 10 inches in diameter and 9 feet 4 inches high. The walls are not straight, nor the floor level. The side aisles have not been begun, and altogether no part of the interior is quite finished, except the upper part of the dâgoba. To the top of the architrave or triforium is 16 feet, and to the centre of the roof 18 feet 2 inches. Outside, the façade is carved with Chaitya-window ornaments, some enclosing a dâgoba, and others a lotus flower; while the rail ornament is abundantly interspersed in the usual way. The fronton round the window is also carved with a geometrical pattern. The details of this cave seem to indicate that it is perhaps as early as those at Bêḍsâ and Kârlê, and consequently it is among the earlier excavations about Junnar.

Next to it, but higher up and almost inaccessible, are two cells; then a well; and, thirdly, a small vihâra, with three cells, two of them with stone-beds. Some rough cutting on the back wall between the cell-doors resembles a dâgoba in low relief, but it is quite unfinished. Outside are two more cells and a chamber or chapel at the end of a verandah that runs along in front both of the vihâra and the cells.

The Mânmôdi hill lies south-south-west from Junnar, about a mile to the west of the main road. It contains three groups of excavations, the second of which is nearest to the road, and the first a considerable way along the north-west face of the hill, near where it turns to the north-east. The principal cave here is an unfinished Chaitya-cave. The door is nearly the whole width of the nave, and it has apparently had a small semi-circular aperture or window over it, but the lintel is broken away. This arch of the window, however, is not adjusted to the arch of the roof inside, which is much higher, nor does it occupy the relative position in the great arch on the façade assigned to the window in later examples at Ajaṇṭâ, Nâsik, &c. (*See* frontispiece.) Over the opening the place usually occupied by the window is divided fan-wise into seven petal-shaped compartments with a semi-circular centre, round the edge of the inner member of which is an inscription, in one line, of Maurya characters, indicating a date not later than 100 B.C. In the middle compartment of the larger semi-circle is a standing female figure with a lotus flower on each side, the next compartments have elephants standing on lotus flowers and holding water-jars, as so often represented beside the figures of Śrî or Lakshmî on old Buddhist works (*ante*, pp. 71, 72).[1] In the next compartment on each side stands a male figure, his hands joined over or in front of his head, doing *pûjâ* towards the central figure; and in the two outer spaces are females in similar attitudes, with a lotus flower and bud beside each. The style of art in which the figure of Śrî is here represented is so similar to that employed for the same purpose at

[1] Conf. Fergusson's *Tree and Serpent Worship*, pp. 108, 112, 113, 120, 242, and 268; *Arch. Sur. West. Ind.*, vol. i. p. 13, and vol. iii. p. 76, and Plate LIII; also Cunningham's *Bharhut*, p. 117.

Bharhut,[1] that there can be little doubt that they are of about the same age. The material, however, in which they are executed, and their purposes are so different, that it would be impossible, from that alone, to say which of the two is the earliest Over and outside these the façade of the great arch projects, with ribs in imitation of wooden rafters under it. On each side the finial is a male figure: that on the left holds a *chauri* and has wings, and some animal's head above his jaunty turban; the other holds some object in his right hand, and behind each shoulder are two snake-heads with their tongues hanging out. Right and left of these are dâgobas in high relief, but roughly formed; and on the right of the arch is a tree with objects hanging in it, but it has never been quite finished, parts being only outlined. On the projecting frieze over all are seven Chaitya-window ornaments, with smaller ones between their finials, and two on the faces of each jamb. Inside the cave, three octagonal pillars on the right side are blocked out, as is also the dâgoba, but without the capital. There is a horizontal soft stratum in the rock, which has probably led to the work being relinquished in its present unfinished state. This is very much to be regretted, as the whole design of this cave is certainly the most daring, though it can hardly be called the most successful, attempt on the part of the early cave architects to emancipate themselves from the trammels of the wooden style they were trying to adapt to lithic purposes. At Barabar in the Lomas Rishi (woodcut 3) they only introduced elephants and trellis work, which we know from the Sanchi gateways were probably executed in wood and could easily have been so introduced. It would, however, have been very difficult to execute such a seven-leafed flower as this, in pierced work, even in wood, but it was an artistic mistake to introduce it above the real constructive opening, on a false front, as is done in this instance. The system here begun was afterwards carried to an extreme issue in the Gandhara monasteries, where figures were introduced everywhere, and the architecture only used as a frame such as we employ for pictures (woodcut 38). Though its employment here is a solecism, this bas-relief is one of the most interesting pieces of sculpture for the history of the art, to be found in the whole range of the western caves.

[1] Stupa at Bharhut, Pls. XII. and XXXVI. *See also Hist. of Ind. and East. Arch.*, p. 88, woodcut 27.

Higher up the rock, on the east or left side of this, are four cells with neatly-carved façades, each door having a Chaitya-window arch over it, projecting about 15 inches; and between the arches are two dâgobas with *chhatris* in half relief; while over the shoulder of each arch is a smaller one as an ornament, and the Buddhist-rail pattern along the tops. There is one plain cell beyond these, and under the five are some others filled up with earth; while rather higher up on the east are four more. Under these latter is a vihâra with two cells in the back and two in the left or east side, but the front is gone. It communicates by a passage with another to the west of it, nearly filled up with mud, and west of the Chaitya-cave are two small cells high up in the rock.

Near the south-east end of the hill is the second group, consisting of an unfinished Chaitya-cave and a number of ruined cells and vihâras. This Chaitya-cave is somewhat on the plan of the Beḍsâ one—that is, it has two octagonal columns in front, supporting the entablature above the great window. These columns are of the style already described as occurring at the Gaṇêśa Leṇa, with water-pot bases and capitals; but otherwise this cave is quite unfinished: the aisles have not been commenced; the capital of the dâgoba is roughly blocked out, and portions of a square mass of rock from which to hew out the dome of it; but a great fault in the rock at the back of the cave seems to have stopped further operations. The front is quite rough, but, if finished, would probably have been similar to the Beḍsâ Chaitya cave. It is almost covered with inscriptions,[1] but from their positions and the roughness of the surfaces on which they are carved, it may naturally be inferred that they are only the work of visitors, perhaps long after the work was relinquished. Few of them can be made out with any certainty. The cave faces north by east, and the floor is much filled up with mud. At the east side of it is a cell, also deep in earth, in which is a dâgoba, the *chhatri* or umbrella carved on the roof, but the staff has been broken—evidently with a view to convert it into the usual Śaiva emblem. Beyond it are portions of other cells, and a fragment of an inscription beside some modern steps leading up to five cells above. The two at the west end are

[1] The inscriptions from the pillars in front were copied by Colonel Sykes and also by Lieutenant Brett; the latter also copied nine from the façade;—none of them are in the square Maurya character, and many of them as late as the fifth century of our era. They were also copied by the Messrs. Wests, but their copies were not published.

converted into one by cutting away the partition, and on the walls are three defaced figures perhaps of Buddha, but possibly they may be Jaina additions. This is now dedicated to the goddess Ambikâ,—a name of Pârvatî indeed, but also the *śâsanadevî* or patron goddess of Neminâtha, one of the favourite Tîrthaṅkaras of the Jains. Here we have Brahmans worshipping the mutilated image of Buddhists or Jains as a Śaiva goddess! In the outer wall of another of these cells there have been a standing and a sitting figure of Buddha, but these are now almost obliterated. They are the only figures of the kind I have met with in the caves here, and were probably added at a late period, and perhaps by Jains.

Around the Chaitya-cave are other cells and Bhikshu's houses, and some inscriptions.

The third group is round a corner of the hill to the south-east of these last, and at a considerably higher level,—some of them almost inaccessible. The first reached is a recess over a cell or cistern, with an inscription:—

Sivasamaputasa Simtabhati? ṇo deyadhama pati.

That is, "For a pious gift of charity, from Simtabhati, son of Śivasarman."

A little beyond this, on the left side of a recess over the side of a water cistern, is another inscription in three lines, of which, however, the first letters are obliterated; still we can make out that it was [constructed by] "Ayama, the minister of Mahâkshatrapa Svâmi Nahapâna."[1]

Scrambling along the face of a precipice to the south, we reach first a small vihâra without cells or carving, then another cave (Plate XVIII., fig. 8) with two octagonal pillars in the front of the verandah, and two engaged ones at the ends rising from a bench. The door is 5 feet 10 inches wide, and reaches to the roof of the hall, which has been frescoed. The back of the seat or low screen in front of the verandah is carved outside with the rail ornament;

---

[1] The mention of Nahapâna is of interest; his date is not fixed with certainty, but probably belongs to the beginning of the second century (*ante*, p.). The alphabet of this inscription is evidently of a later date than of several others in the other groups of Junnar caves, and thus far confirms our relegating these caves to the second century of our era, after which time idol worship seems to have crept into Buddhism.

the columns are of the usual Nâsik pattern, but without animal figures above: over them the frieze projects considerably, and is carved in the style of Cave IV. at Nâsik,—the ends of the rafters projecting on the lower fascia, and the upper being carved with rail pattern. Over this is a recess some 2 or 3 feet deep, with the Chaitya arch over it, but without any carving.

The hall is 33 feet deep, and about 12 feet wide; but at the back stands a mass of rock over 8 feet wide by 5½ thick, with a squatting figure roughly sketched out on the front of it. This mass is very rotten behind, and at the left side of it is a well of excellent water.

The other caves here are small and uninteresting.

CHAPTER VII.

NASIK CAVES.

About fifty miles north from Junnar, but across some of the spurs of the Sahyâdri hills, is Nâsik in the upper valley of the Godâvarî river, and only four miles from the railway leading from Bombay to Calcutta. The town is a place of great antiquity and sanctity, being associated with the legend of Râma, who is said to have spent part of his exile at Panchavatî, a suburb of Nâsik on the north side of the Godâvarî or Gaṅgâ river. It is to a large extent a Brahmanical town, and may be regarded as the Banâras of Western India. It is mentioned under its present name by Ptolemy, and situated as it is just above one of the few easily accessible passes up the Ghâṭs, and in the middle of a fertile plain interspersed with isolated hills, it must always have been a place of note. One of the oldest inscriptions in the neighbouring caves speaks of "Kṛishṇarâja of the Śâtavâhana race [*residing*] in Nâsik,"[1] which would almost seem to indicate that it was the capital of the dynasty; but it is possible this Kṛishṇarâja was only a member of the royal family.

The Buddhist caves, locally known as the Pâṇḍu Lêṇa, are in one of three isolated hills called in the inscriptions Triraśmi, close to the Bombay road, and about five miles S.S.W. from the town. They were first described by Captain James Delamaine, who visited them in 1823,[2] and afterwards by Dr. J. Wilson and the Messrs. West, the latter with special reference to the inscriptions, of which they made copies, and which have since been translated by Professor Bhandârkar.[3] These inscriptions contain the names of several kings, as—

Kṛishṇarâja of the Śâtavâhana race;
Mahâ-Hakusîri, who reigned certainly before the Christian era;

---

1 *Trans. Orient. Cong.*, 1874, p. 338.

2 *Asiat. Jour. N. S.*, vol. iii. (1830), pp. 275–288; Ritter, *Erdk.* iv. i. 652.

3 Dr. Wilson visited them in 1831 and 1840. *Jour. Bom. B. R. A. S.*, vol. iii. pt. ii. pp. 65–69; and the Wests between 1861 and 1865, *ib.*, vol. vii. pp. 37–52; *Trans. Cong. Orient.*, pp. 306–354; Fergusson's *Ind. and East. Arch.*, pp. 94, 115, 150.

Nahapâṇa the Kshaharâta Satrap; and
Ushavadâta, son of Dînika, his son-in-law;
Śâtakarṇi Gautamîputra, and his queen Vâśishṭhî;
Śrî Puḍumâyi Vâśishṭhîputra;
Yajña Śâtakarṇi Gautamîputra; and
King Vîrasena, son of Śivadata the Abhîra, who reigned on certainly in the first centuries after Christ, though at what dates has not yet been settled with certainty.

Several of these were "lords of Dhanakataka," that is, of the Andhra dynasty, and at Nânâghâṭ we have of the same race—Śâtavâhana, his son Śâtakarṇi (Vediśri), and his sons, Kumâra Śâtavâhana, Kumâra Hâkusîri, and Kumara Bhâya(*la*). At Kaṇheri we have some of the above and Sirisena Madharîputra;[1] and coins give his name as well as those of the three last Śâtakarnis in the Nâsik list. Now Ptolemy (cir. A.D. 150) mentions a Siri Polemios of Paithaṇa, who may have been the Puḍumâyi of the above list; and Rudra Dâman in the Girnar inscription some time *after* the 72nd year (probably of the Śaka era, or A.D. 150) boasts of having defeated "Śâtakarṇi, lord of Dakshiṇapatha." Which of the Śâtakarṇis this was we have no means of knowing for certain as yet, nor shall we be able to do so till the chronology of the Andrabhṛitya kings is ascertained in a more satisfactory manner than it is at present.

If the Krishnaraja of the inscriptions is the second of the Pauranik lists, as there seems little reason for doubting, it may fairly be assumed that the dynasty arose, as is generally supposed, immediately before the Christian era. If, too, Hâkusiri was the excavator of the Chaitya cave at this place, which, from the long inscription containing his name engraved on it, this seems nearly certain, we gain from its architecture at least an approximate date for the age in which he lived. It may have been excavated a few years before, but as probably a few years after, the Christain era, but cannot be removed from that epoch.

The fixation of the dates of the kings who reigned after the Christian era is more difficult, owing to the paucity of the materials available for the purpose. It is now generally admitted that the

[1] Skandasvati of the Pauranik lists preceded Yajna Śrî, and if Śivaśri is the same as Śrisena Mâdharîputra, he must be placed between these two; but we have no coins of his nor any corresponding names in the inscriptions.

Pauranik lists,[1] which are the only written document we possess bearing on the subject, cannot be implicitly relied upon. We are consequently almost wholly dependent on the inscriptions, and they are few in number, and have not yet been examined with the care requisite for reliable results being obtained from them. Now, however, that such scholars as Bühler, Burnell, Fleet, and Bhagvanlal Indraji are available for their investigation, it seems most desirable thât they should all be recopied in facsimile, so as to admit of comparison and translation. If this were done it is probable that all the difficulties that now perplex the subject would disappear.

Pending this being done, if we may assume, as was done above

---

[1] The Pauranik lists give the following names and durations of reigns :—

—	Andhrabhṛitya Kings.	*Vâyu Purâṇa.*	*Matsya Purâṇa.*	*Brahmâṇḍa Purâṇa.*
		Years.	Years.	Years.
1	Ś'ipraka, Sindhuka, or Ś'iśuka - - -	23	23	23
2	Kṛishṇaraja his brother - - -	10	18	18
3	Ś'âtakarṇi I., Ś'rîmallakarṇi, or Ś'antakarṇa -	wanting	10 (or 18)	18 (or 10)
4	Pûrṇotsanga or Paurṇamâsa - - -	"	18	18
5	Skandhastambhi or Ś'rîvasvâmi - - -	"	18	—
6	Ś'âtakarṇi II. - - - - -	56	56	56
7	Lambodara - - - - -	wanting	18	18
8	Ivîlaka, Apîlaka, or Apîtaka - -	12	12	12
9	Sangha or Meghasvati - - - -	wanting	18	18
10	Ś'âtakarṇi III. or Sváti - - - -	—	18	12
11	Skandasvâti - - - - -	—	7	7
12	Mṛigendra or Mahendra Ś'âtakarṇi - -	—	3	3*
13	Kuntala or Svâtikarṇa - - - -	—	8	8
14	Svâtikarṇi or Svatishena - - -	—	1	1
15	Paṭumat, Paṭumâvi, or Pulomâvi - - -	24	(36 ?)	34
16	Arishṭakarṇi, Gaurakṛishṇa, or Gorakshâsvaśri -	25	25	25
17	Hâla or Haleya - - - - -	1	5	5
18	Pattalaka or Maṇḍalaka - - - -	(5 ?)	5	5
19	Pravilasena or Purindrasêna - - -	21	5	12
20	Sundara Ś'âtakarṇi - - - -	1	1	1
21	Chakora Ś'âtakarṇi or Rajâdasvâti - -	½	½	6
22	Ś'ivasvâti - - - - -	28	28	28
23	Gautamîputra Ś'âtakarṇi - - - -	21	21	21
24	Pulimat, Pulomavit, or Puḍumayi Ś'âtakarṇi -	wanting	28	29
25	Ś'ivaśri Ś'âtakarṇi, or Avi - - -	"	7	4
26	Ś'ivaskaṇda Ś'âtakarni, or Skandhasvâti - -	"	7 (9)	8
27	Yajnaśri or Yajna Ś'âtakarṇi Gautamîputra -	29 ?	9 (20)	19
28	Vijaya - - - - - -	6	6	6
29	Chandraśrî Ś'âtakarṇi, Vadaśrî, or Chandravijna	3	10	3
30	Pulomarchis or Pulomâvi - - -	7	7	7

The *Vâyu Purâṇa* says there were thirty kings, but gives the names of seventeen only; the *Bhâgavata Purâṇa* also gives thirty, but with the *Vishṇu Purâṇa* names only twenty-four, while the *Matsya* has twenty-nine names. The total periods also vary from 435½ to 456 and 460 years. And the *Brahmâṇḍa Purâṇa* places the 12th, 13th, and 14th of the above list after the 21st.

(p. 189), that Nahapana's inscriptions are dated from the Śaka era, we have in 118, 120 A.D., a fixed point from which to start, and the real *crux* of the whole is to ascertain what interval must be allowed between him and Gautamiputra Satakarni, who almost certainly was the 23rd king of Pauranik lists. According to them, if the Andrabhṛityas began to reign about the Christian era, Gautamiputra must have reigned in the beginning of the 4th century and Yajnaśri, the 27th, nearly a century later. Both the inscriptions, however and the architecture of Cave No. VIII. in this place, which belongs to Nahapana, when compared with those of No. III., which was excavated by Gautamiputra, render it improbable that so long an interval as two centuries should have elapsed between these two reigns. One century is possible, indeed probable, but what the exact interval may have been must be left for future investigations.

The caves themselves are 17 in number, and though a small, are a very interesting group. The Chaitya itself is not so remarkable as some of those described above, but there are two vihâras, Nos. III. and VIII., which are very far in advance of any yet met with, and display in their façades a richness of decoration quite unlike the modest exteriors of those excavated before the Christian era. Notwithstanding this they all, except Nos. II. and XVII., belong to the Hinâyâna or first great division of Buddhist caves, being devoid of images, or any representation of Buddha as an object of worship, or in fact of any of those characteristics which marked the introduction of the Mahâyâna theosophy.

They are situated about 300 feet above the level of the plain below, have a northerly aspect, and extend about a quarter of a mile along the face of the hill. Beginning at the west end, they may conveniently be numbered eastwards. But it should be remarked that large portions of the rock among these interesting caves, and even whole excavations, have been blasted away, whether to obtain metalling and stones for the road and culverts when the neighbouring government road was constructed, or by Muhammadans at an earlier date, seems uncertain ; at the same time, I am not aware that either Hindus or Muhammadans applied gunpowder for blasting rock, until taught by our Public Works officials, and if, under their directions, these caves were so damaged 60 years ago, it is only a single instance added to others of similar vandalism.

The terrace that extends all along in front of the caves is prolonged westwards of the first excavation for several hundred feet, where there seem to have been some cisterns, and four or five places are scarped or quarried out.

Except the ornamental frieze over the front of the first excavation, no part of it is finished; it has been planned for a Vihâra, with four columns between pilasters in front of a narrow verandah, but they are all left square masses. A cell has been begun at each end of the verandah. The front wall has been more recently partly blasted away.

Cave II. is a small excavation that may have been originally a verandah, 11½ feet by 4¼ feet, with two cells at the back; but the front wall and dividing partition have been cut away, and the walls pretty nearly covered with sculpture, consisting of sitting and standing Buddhas with attendant *chauri*-bearers, in some cases unfinished. These are the additions of Mahâyâna Buddhists of the sixth or seventh century. The verandah has apparently had two wooden pillars, and the projecting frieze is carved with the "rail pattern," much weather worn, and apparently very old. On the remaining fragment of the back wall of the verandah, close under the roof, is a fragment of an inscription, which reads:—

Sidhaṁ Raṇo Vâsathiputasa sarapaḍumayasa savachhare chha (?) *the* 6 *gimapakhe pacham*(o) *divase* . . . .

"Siddham! In the sixth year of the king, the prosperous Puḍumâya, the son of Vâśishṭhî, in the fortnight of Grishma, on the 5th (?) day."

Between this and the next are a tank with two openings above it, a large scarped out place, and two decayed recesses, one of them a tank, and all along this space are blocks of rock blasted out, or fallen down from above.

Cave III. is a large Vihâra, the hall of which is 41 feet wide and 46 deep, with a bench round three sides, and eighteen cells, seven on the right side, six in the back, and five in the left, besides two opening from the verandah. (*See* plan, Plate XIX.) The central door into this is rudely sculptured in a style that at once reminds the spectator of the Sânchi gateways; the side pilasters are divided into six compartments, each filled mostly with two men and a woman, in different stages of some story which seems to end in the woman being carried off by one of the men.[1] (Plate XX.) Over the door are the three symbols, the *Bodhi* tree, the *dâgoba*, and the *chakra*, with worshippers, and at each side is a *dwârpâla*, or doorkeeper, of very ungainly proportions holding up a bunch of flowers. If the carving on this door be compared with any of those at Ajaṇṭâ, it will be found very much ruder and less bold, but the style of headdress agrees with that on the screen walls at Kârlê and Kaṇhêri, and in the paintings in Cave X. at Ajanta, which probably belong to about the same age. The verandah has six octagonal columns without bases between highly sculptured pilasters (Plate XXI., fig. 1). The capitals of these pillars are distinguished from those in the Nahapâṇa Cave No. VIII. by the shorter and less elegant form of the bell-shaped portion of them, and by the corners of the frame that encloses the torus having small figures attached (Plate XXII.); both alike have a series of five thin members, overlapping one another and supporting four animals on each capital, bullocks, elephants, horses, sphinxes, &c., between the front and back pairs of which runs the architrave, supporting a projecting frieze, with all the details of a wooden framing copied in it. The upper part of the frieze in this case is richly carved with a string course of animals under a richly carved rail, resembling in its design and elaborateness the rails at Amrâvati, with which this vihâra must be nearly, if not quite contemporary. The pillars stand on a bench in the verandah, and in front of them is a carved screen, supported by three dwarfs on each side the steps to the entrance. The details of this cave and No. VIII. are so alike that the one must be regarded as a copy of the other, but the capitals in No. VIII. are so like those of the Kârlê Chaitya, while those in the verandah of this cave are so much poorer in proportion, that one is tempted to suppose this belongs to a much later period, when art had begun to decay. The chronology, however, is merely conjectural, and it may turn out that Nahapâṇa preceded Gautamîputra by a considerable period.[2]

---

[1] It is difficult to say whether this has any relation to the abduction scene in the Udayagiri caves (*ante*, p. 82). The other groups do not seem to have any affinity with those in the east, there certainly is no fighting group nor any other incidents which can be identified.

[2] The inscriptions in the Nahâpana cave No. VIII. ascribe the execution of it too distinctly to the members of his family to allow us to suppose that they were executed

Next to this is No. IV., much destroyed and full of water to a considerable depth. The frieze is at a very considerable height, and

No. 49. Pillar in Nahapâna cave, Nâsik. (From a photograph.)

No 50. Pillar in Gautamiputra cave, Nâsik, No. III. (From a photograph.)[1]

long after its excavation. Nor does the difference of character between the inscriptions Nos. 14, 17, 16, and 18 in Cave VIII., and Nos. 25, 26, and 26*a* in Cave III. seem to warrant any great lapse of time. The workmen of Nahapâna, however, would be from the west and north, those of Gautamiputra from the south-east, and this must be allowed its weight in judging of differences of detail.

1 The differences between the architectural details of these two vihâras are so nearly identical with those, that it struck me, in comparing the Chaitya Kârlê with that at Kanheri (Rock-cut Temples, Plate XI.), that the relative dates must be nearly the same. At the same time the architecture of the Nahapana caves (No. VIII.) is so similar to that of the Kârlê Chaitya and that of Cave No. III. to that of the Kanheri Chaitya that the two vihâras cannot be very distant in date from the two Chaityas. Whether the adjustment is to be made by bringing down the age of the two Chaityas to a more modern date than is assumed in the text, or by carrying back that of the vihâras, or by separating them by a longer interval, can only be determined when the inscriptions are more carefully investigated than they have hitherto been. Their relative chronology is not doubtful, though their epochal dates are at present undetermined.—J. F.

is carved with the "rail pattern." The verandah has had two octagonal pillars between antæ, with bell-shaped capitals, surmounted by elephants with small drivers and female riders. There has also been a plain doorway and two grated windows leading into the cave, but only the heads of them remain. From the unusual height and the chisel marks in the lower part, apparently recent, it seems as if the floor of this cave had been cut away into a cistern below it, Indeed, when the cave ceased to be used as a monastery, from the breaking through of the floor into the water cistern below, the floor seems to have been quite hewn out to form a cistern. This seems to have been done in many cases here.

Cave VIII. is the second large Vihâra, and contains six inscriptions of the family of Nahapâna.[1] As already remarked, the six pillars (two of them attached) have more elegant bell-shaped Persian capitals than those in Cave III., and their bases are in the style of those in the Kârlê Chaitya, and in that next to the Gaṇêśa Lêṇa at Junnar; the frieze also, like those that remain on the other small caves between Nos. IV. and VII., is carved with the simple rail pattern. At each end of the verandah is a cell "the benefaction of Dakhamitrâ, the daughter of King Ḳshaharâta Kshatrapa Nahapâna, and wife of Ushavadâta, son of Dînîka." The hall is about 43 feet wide by 45 feet deep, and is entered by three plain doors, and lighted by two windows. It has five benched cells on each side and six in the back; it wants, however, the bench round the inner sides that we find in No. III.; but, as shown by the capital and ornaments still left, it has had a precisely similar dâgoba in *basso rilievo* on the back wall, which has been long afterwards hewn into a figure of Bhairava. Outside the verandah, too, on the left-hand side, have been two *rilievos* of this same god, evidently the later insertions of some Hindu devotee.

Cave IX. is close to the last, but at a somewhat higher level. In

---

[1] *Trans. Cong. Orient.*, No. 14, p. 336; 15, p. 341; 16, p. 334; 17, p. 336; 18, p. 331; 19, pp. 327-330. Nos. 16 and 18, however, should be read as one; line 1 of No. 18 being a continuation of line 3 of 16, line 2 of 18 completes line 4 of 16, line 3 of 18 follows line 5 of 16, and after the word *sarva* in (the printed copy, p. 334, of) line 6 of 16 comes lines 4 of No. 18. The mistake seems to have originated with Lieutenant Brett, who copied the portion of the inscription on the end wall as No. vi., and that on the back of the verandah as No. v. (*Jour. B. B. R. As. Soc.* vol. v., p. 56, pls. 10 to 12). This was followed by the Messrs. West (*J. B. B. R. A. S.*, vol. vii. p. 50), who made the same portions their Nos. 16 and 18 respectively.

the left end of the verandah is the fragment of a seat; the room inside is 11 feet 7 inches by 7 feet 10 inches, having a cell, 6 feet 8 inches square, at the left end, and another, not quite so large, at the back, with a bench at the side and back. In the front room is carved, on the back wall, in low relief, a sitting figure and attendants on a lion throne, and on the right-end wall a fat figure of Ambâ on a tiger with attendants, and an Indra on an elephant: all are small, clumsily carved, and evidently of late Jaina workmanship. An inscription in two lines states that the cave was "the benefaction of Râmaṇka, the son of Śivamitra, the writer."[1]

No. X. is a group of chambers, probably the remains of three *bhikshugrihas* or hermitages, with one, two, and three cells respectively. The first has an inscription of Râmaṇaka, mentioning an endowment of 100 kârshâpanas for "a garment to the ascetic residing in it during the rains."[2] To the left is a tank, and then for thirty yards everything has been blasted and quarried away.

No. XI. seems to be only the inner shrines of a two-storeyed cave, the whole front of which has disappeared, and the upper is only accessible by a ladder. Both have on each of their three walls a sitting Buddha with the usual standing attendants, similar to what we find in Caves II. and XVII., and in the later Ajaṇṭâ Caves. These are, apparently, Mahâyâna works. Beyond them, another fifty feet has been quarried away by blasting, which has been continued along the outer portion of the terrace of Cave XII.

Cave XII. is the third large Vihâra, though smaller than Nos. III., VIII., or XV., and has been executed close to the upper portion of the Chaitya cave. The hall measures 22 feet 10 inches wide by 32 feet 2 inches deep, and has a back aisle screened off by two columns, of which the elephants and their riders and the thin square members of the capitals only are finished. The steps of the shrine door have also been left as a rough block, on which some Hindu has carved the *shâlunkha* or receptacle for a *linga*. The shrine has never been finished. On the wall of the back aisle is a standing figure of Buddha, 3½ feet high; in the left side of the hall, 2 feet 3 inches from the floor, is a recess, 18½ feet long and 4 feet 3 inches high by 2 feet deep, intended for a seat or perhaps for a row

---

[1] *Trans. Cong. Orient.*, 1874, No. 13, p. 346.
[2] *Trans. Cong. Orient.*, p. 345, No. 12.

of metallic images; a cell has been attempted at each end of this, but one of them has entered the aisle of the Chaitya-cave just below, and the work has then been stopped. On the right side are four cells without benches. The verandah is somewhat peculiar, and it would seem that, at first, a much smaller cave was projected, or else by some mistake it was begun too far to the left. It is ascended by half a-dozen steps in front between the two central octagonal pillars with very short shafts, and large bases and capitals, the latter surmounted by elephants and their riders, and the frieze above carved with the plain "rail pattern." They stand on a panelled base; but the landing between the central pair is opposite the left window in the back wall of the verandah, to the right of which is the principal door, but to the left of the window is also a narrower one. The verandah has then been prolonged to the west, and another door broken out to the outside beyond the right attached pillar; at this end of the verandah also is an unfinished cell. An inscription [1] in three and a half lines tells us that it was the work of "Indragnidatta, the son of Dharmadeva, a Northerner, a Yavanaka (or Greek), a native of Dâttâmitrî (in the Saûvira country), as a shrine for a Chaitya in Mount Triraśmi." But inscriptions like this do not help us much as to dates, and all we can say of this cave is that it is evidently much later than the Chaitya next it, the verandah a little later in style than the Nahapâna Cave No. VIII., and the interior probably executed at a much later date, or about the early part of the sixth century A.D., when image-worship had gained full ascendancy among the Mahâyâna Buddhists.

The next, Cave No. XII., the only Chaitya cave of the group, belongs to a very much earlier date; and though none of the three inscriptions [2] on it supplies certain information on this point, yet the name of Mahâ Hâkusiri, found in one of them, helps us to relegate it to some period about or before the Christian era. The carving, however, over the door and the pilasters with animal capitals on the façade on each side the great arch, and the insertion of the hooded snake, will, on comparison with the façades at Beḍsâ and Kârlê, tend to lead us to an early date for this cave; the interior is severely simple, and there are hardly sufficient

[1] *Trans. Cong. Orient.*, 1874, p. 345, No. 11.

[2] *Trans. Cong. Orient.*, 1874, p. 343, Nos. 8, 9, 10. Prof. Bhandarkar has not attempted the mutilated inscription outside No. 7.

departures from the earlier forms in the ornamentation to lead us to

No. 51. View of exterior of the Chaitya Cave at Nâsik, from a photograph.

assign it to a much later date than the Beḍsâ and Kondaṇê Chaitya caves, and I should be inclined to ascribe it to the century before—but not distant from—the Christian era, the date to which it would seem the next cave also belongs. The doorway (shown in Plate XXV.) is evidently of an early date, and the ornament up the left side is almost identical with that found on the pillars of the northern gateway at Sanchi,[1] with which it consequently is in all probability coeval (1st century A.D.).

The carving over the doorway, which represents the wooden framework which filled all openings, of a similar class, at that age, is of a much more ornamental character than usual, or than the others shown on this façade. Animals are introduced as in the Lomas Rishi (woodcut 3). So also are the trisul and shield emblems, in a very ornamental form, but almost identical with those shown in Plate XVII., fig. 5, as existing in the Manmodi cave at Junnar, which is probably of about the same age as this Chaitya.

The interior measures 38 feet 10 inches by 21 feet 7 inches, and the nave, from the door up to the dâgoba, 25 feet 4 inches by 10 feet, and 23 feet 3 inches high (Plate XXIV.). The cylinder of the dâgoba is 5½ feet in diameter and 6 feet 3 inches high, surmounted by a small dome and very heavy capital. The gallery under the great arch of the window is supported by two pillars, which in all cases in the Chaitya caves are in such a form as strongly to suggest that a wooden frame was fastened between them, probably to hold a screen, which would effectually shut in the nave from observation from outside. Five octagonal pillars, with high bases of the Kârlê pattern but without capitals, on each side the nave, and five without bases round the dâgoba, divide off the side aisles. The woodwork that once occupied the front arch, and the roof of the nave has long ago disappeared. Whether there ever were pillars in advance of the present façade as at Beḍsâ, or a screen as at Kârlê, cannot be determined with certainty, unless by excavating largely among the débris in front. I incline to think there was something of the kind, but the Vihâras, inserted so close to it on either side, must have hastened the ruin of the side walls of it.

Cave XIV. is at a rather lower level even than the Chaitya cave, and some distance in advance of it, but the front and interior have

---

[1] *Tree and Serpent Worship*, woodcuts 17 and 18, p. 114.

been so filled up with earth as to conceal it from general view. It is a small Vihâra, 14 feet 3 inches square (Plate XXVI., figs. 2 and 3), with six cells, two on each side, filled nearly to the roof with earth, so that it is not known whether they contain stone beds or not; their doors are surmounted by the Chaitya-arch ornament connected by a frieze of "rail pattern" in some places wavy. In the front wall are two lattice windows, and in the verandah two slender square pillars, the middle portion of the shaft being chamfered to an octagonal shape. Over one of the windows is a Pâli inscription stating that the cave "was constructed by the Śramaṇa officer of Kṛishṇarâja of the Śâtavâhana race, residing in Nâsika." If there was no other Kṛishṇarâja of the Śâtavâhana race but the one mentioned in the *Purâṇas*, then, as he was the second of the Ândhrabhṛityas, if we knew his age,[1] we should be able at once to fix that of this cave; and its exceedingly plain style, and the remarkable rectangularity of all its parts, agree perfectly with what we might expect in a Vihâra of the first or second century B.C. Its close family likeness to No. XII. at Ajaṇṭâ and others at Bâjâ and Kondâṇê, all of the earliest age, would lead us to attribute it to about the same date.

Over this last and close by the Chaitya-cave, from which it is approached by a stair (being, like No. XII., at a considerably higher level) is No. XV., another large Vihâra (see plan, Plate XXVI., fig. 1), its hall varying in width from 37½ feet at the front to 44 feet at the back and 61½ feet deep. Originally it was little over 40 feet deep, but at a much later date it was altered and extended back by one "Marmâ, a worshipper," as recorded on the wall. It has eight cells on each side, one on the right rather a recess than a cell, two on the left with stone beds, while in the back are two cells to the left of the antechamber and one to the right, with one more on each side of the antechamber and entered from it. The hall is surrounded by a low bench as in Cave III., and in the middle of the floor is a low platform, about 9 feet square, apparently intended

---

[1] He is placed by Prinsep and Mr. Fergusson about the Christian era; by Jones in the 9th century B.C.; by Wilford about 200 A.D. In my second *Archæol. Report*, I accepted Prinsep's assumption from the *Purâṇas*, that the Śunga, Kânwa, and Ândhra dynasties succeeded one another in regular sequence; as already indicated, I doubt if this is correct, and suppose that the Ândhra dynasty was to some extent contemporary with the Paurâṇik Śungas and Kanwas.—J. B.

for an *âsana* or seat; but whether to place an image upon for worship, or as a "seat of the law," where the Thêra or high priest might sit when teaching and discussing, I am not prepared to say. On the right-hand side, and nearer the front, are three small circular elevations in the floor much like ordinary millstones. Are these seats also for members of the clergy, or are they not rather bases on which to set small moveable *dâgobas*, &c.? But when the cave was altered and extended backward, the floor seems also to have been lowered a few inches to form the low dais and these bases.

The antechamber is slightly raised above the level of the hall, from which it is divided by two richly carved columns between antæ. (see Plate XXI., fig. 3). On either side the shrine door is a gigantic *dwârpâla*, 9½ feet high, with an attendant female, but so besmeared with soot—for the cave has been long occupied by Bhairagis, that minor details are scarcely recognisable. These *dwârpâlas*, however, hold lotus stalks, have the same elaborate head-dresses, with a small dâgoba in the front of one, and a figure of Buddha in the other, and have the same attendants and *vidyâdharas* flying over head as we find in the later Buddhist caves at Aurangâbâd. In the shrine, too, is the colossal image of Buddha, 10 feet high, seated with his feet on a lotus flower and holding the little finger of his left hand between the thumb and forefinger of his right. He is attended by two gigantic *chauri*-bearers with the same distinguishing features as the *dwârpâla*. All this points to about the seventh century A.D. or later, as the age of alteration of this cave.

Fortunately we have an inscription of the seventh year of Yajña Sâtakarṇi Gautamîputra, stating that "after having been under excavation for many years" it was then carried to completion by the wife of the commander-in-chief.[1] Unfortunately the age of Yajña Sâtakarṇi, who was one of the later Andhrabhṛityas, has not yet been determined with anything like certainty. It must, consequently, for the present remain doubtful to what part of the cave this inscription refers. It is quite clear, however, that the inner and outer parts were excavated at widely different ages. The pillars of the verandah have the water-pot bases, and the bell-shaped capitals of those in Kârlê Chaitya. Those of the sanctuary are represented (Plate XXI., fig. 3), and belong to a widely distant

[1] *Trans. Cong. Orient.*, p. 339-40, No. 4 (misprinted "24" both on p. 339, 340); and *Second Archæolog. Report of W. India*, p. 132.

age.[1] Like No. XII. it has a side door near the left end of the verandah, and a cell in that end. The façade has four octagonal pillars between antæ, the shafts more slender than in any of the other caves, but the bases of the same pattern disproportionately large, as if the shafts had been reduced in thickness at a later date. They stand on a panelled base, with five low steps up to it between the middle pair. A low screen wall in front is nearly quite destroyed, except at the east end, where a passage led to a large irregular and apparently unfinished apartment with two plain octagonal pillars with square bases between pilasters in front, and having a water-cistern at the entrance.

About a dozen yards from this, and approached along the side of the cliff by a few modern steps, is a plain unfinished chamber, and a little farther on is No. XVI., a decayed chamber half filled with rubbish. The rock has been much blasted and quarried below this, and the path along the intervening 30 or 35 yards is over rough broken scarp to No. XVII., a large, nondescript, irregular cave, about 30 feet deep, with three shrines. To judge from the holes in the floor and roof it might be supposed that the front and partitions in it had been of wood; the whole façade, however, is destroyed. In front are several cisterns; on the floor is a raised stone bench and a circular base as if for a small structural dâgoba; and all the shrines as well as many compartments on the walls are filled with sculptures

---

[1] I speak with diffidence, never having seen these caves, and in such cases personal inspection is so valuable for determining details. But, so far as I can judge from photographs, the façade of this cave belongs to the Nahapana age, or earlier, and could not have been executed after the Gautamîputra Cave No. III., and Yajña Srî certainly came after that king. It is also a curious coincidence, that if the Pauranik date for the last-named king were correct (407 A.D.), the architecture and the imagery of the sanctuary of Cave XV. would be in perfect accordance with it. In fact, the age of these caves still remains to me a mystery. With regard to the Chaitya, and its accompanying vihara (No. XIV.), there seems little doubt they are before the Christian era. From that central point, the caves seem to spread right and left. I would place the façades of No. XV. next the Cave XII. After this the Nahapana Cave VIII. followed at a considerable interval by the Gautamîputra Cave III., and No. II. at one end and No. VII. at the other complete the series in the sixth and seventh century, and between these great landmarks the remaining caves are easily arranged. Whether this is so or not must be determined by investigation on the spot and a re-examination of the inscriptions. Meanwhile it seems at all events worth while drawing attention to this view whatever it may eventually prove to be worth.—J. F.

of Buddha attended by Padmapâni and Vajrapâni such as we have only met with here in the two shrines high up on the scarp at No. XI., but so like what is found at Aurangâbâd, Elurâ, and Ajaṇṭâ, that there can be no hesitation in ascribing it to a late age. Among the many repetitions of Buddha and attendants is a small figure on the wall that cuts off the third shrine from the larger portion of the cave, of Buddha reclining on his right side as represented entering *nirvâṇa*, much as he is found in Singhalese temples at the present day, and of which larger representations are found at Ajaṇṭâ, Kholvi, and Aurangâbâd. All these, and the female figures of Târâ, Lôchanâ, and Mamukhi found in the shrines, clearly show that this was a Mahâyâna temple. The pillars in front of the entrance to the first shrine are also of a much more modern type than in any of the other caves here.

Farther on is a small rude chamber much ruined, and 45 yards from it is a recess with an inscription over it[1] of Pulumai, the son of Vasishṭhî, twenty or 25 yards beyond, along a difficult scarp, was a small Bhikshu's house, the lower part of which, as in Nos. IV., &c., has all been quarried away. It probably consisted of a verandah with two small chambers at the back. The frieze is still pretty entire, and whilst preserving the copies of wooden forms, it is ornamented with a string of animal figures as in that of Cave I.; the ends of the projecting beams represented as bearing it, are carved with conventionalised forms of the Buddhist *triśûla* or symbol of *dharma*, the prongs in one case being changed into cats or some such animals; seated on the lower beam under the rock at the west end is carved an owl, and at each end of the ornamented "rail pattern" is a rider on a sort of female centaur,—probably a Greek idea. The inscriptions speak of a cave and two (if not three) tanks, but give no royal name.[2]

These Nâsik caves, like those at Kaṇheri, belong principally to the times of the Kshaharâta and Ândhrabhṛitya kings, the former of Central India and the latter of the Dekhan. The silver coins of the first-named dynasty have been found in abundance in Gujarât, and

---

[1] *Trans. Cong. Orient.*, p. 338, No. 3. Among the Andhrabhṛityas there was a Putumâyi, or Pulumâvi, or Pulomâvit, the successor of Gautamîputra.

[2] *Trans. Cong. Orient.*, 1874, pp. 342, 343, Nos. 1 and 2.

have been examined and described; the coins of the Ândhrabhṛityas seem to have been mostly of lead, or a mixture of that metal with copper, and have been found at Kolâpur and near the mouth of the Kṛishṇâ, where the dynasty had their capital in later times. These coins are now attracting attention,[1] and when properly examined, they, together with the numerous inscriptions in these caves, when they too are correctly copied and translated, may lead to a solution of the chronological difficulties which still hang over the reigns of the kings of these two dynasties. It is to be hoped that this may be successfully accomplished before long, for if the dates of the Andhrabhṛitya kings were ascertained there would practically be very little ambiguity about the age of any of the caves in Western India.

---

[1] *Ind. Ant.*, vol. vi. pp. 274, 277.

CHAPTER VIII.

THE AJANTA CAVE TEMPLES.

Ajaṇṭâ, as is well known, is situated at the head of one of the passages or ghâṭs that lead down from the Indhyâdri hills, dividing the table-land of the Dekhan from Khândesh, in the valley of the Tapti. Four miles W.N.W. of this town are the caves to which it gives name. Most other groups of Buddhist caves are excavated on the scarps of hills, with extensive views from their verandahs; those of Ajaṇṭâ are buried in a wild, lonely glen, with no vista but the rocky scarp on the opposite side. They are approached from Fardapur, a small town at the foot of the ghâṭ, and about three and a half miles north-east from them. They are excavated in the face of an almost perpendicular scarp of rock, about 250 feet high, sweeping round in a curve of fully a semicircle, and forming the north or outer side of a wild secluded ravine, down which comes a small stream. Above the caves the valley terminates abruptly in a waterfall of seven leaps, known as the *sát kuṇḍ*, the lower of which may be from 70 to 80 feet high, and the others 100 feet more. The caves extend about 600 yards from east to west round the concave wall of amygdaloid trap that hems in the stream on its north or left side, and vary in elevation from about 35 to 100 feet above the bed of the torrent, the lowest being about a third of the arc from the east end.

The whole of the caves have been numbered like houses in a street, commencing from the east or outer end, and terminating at the inner extremity by the caves furthest up the ravine. This enumeration, it will be understood, is wholly without reference to either the age or purpose of the caves, but wholly for convenience of description. The oldest are the lowest down in the rock, and practically near the centre, being numbers VIII. to XIII., from which group they radiate right and left, to No. I. on the one hand, XXIX. on the other.

From the difficulty of access to them, the Ajaṇṭâ caves were but little visited until within the last forty years. The first Europeans known to have seen them were some officers of the Madras army in 1819.[1] Lieutenant (now General Sir) James E. Alexander of the Lancers, on a tour which he made privately through the Nizam's territories in 1824, visited them and sent a short account of them and their wall paintings to the Royal Asiatic Society, which was published in their *Transactions*[2] in 1829. Captain Gresley and Mr. Ralph were there in 1828, when Dr. J. Bird was sent up by Sir John Malcolm to examine them. Mr. Ralph's lively notice of the paintings appeared in the *Bengal Asiatic Society's Journal* in 1836.[3] Dr. Bird's account was published in his *Historical Researches* (1847), a work in which the erroneousness of the author's opinions on Buddhism[4] is only matched by the inaccuracies of the drawings that illustrate it. An interesting and trustworthy description of them appeared in the *Bombay Courier* in 1839, from Lieutenant Blake.[5] Mr. Fergusson visited them in 1839, and in 1843 laid before the Royal Asiatic Society his paper on the Rock-Cut Temples of India, about a dozen pages of which is devoted to a critical architectural description of the Ajaṇṭâ caves and their paintings.[6]

---

[1] *Trans. Bomb. Lit. Soc.*, vol. iii. p. 520.

[2] *T. R. A. S.*, vol. ii. p. 362.

[3] *J. A. S. B.*, vol. v. pp. 557–561; see also some copies of inscriptions by the same, *ib.* pp. 348, 556.

[4] Conf. *Jour. A. Soc. Beng.*, vol. v. p. 560.

[5] This was reprinted with other papers as *A description of the ruined city of Mandu, &c., also an account of the Buddhist Cave Temples of Ajanta in Khandes, with ground-plan illustrations*, by a Subaltern (Bombay Times Press, 1844), 140 pp. cr. 8vo., with two plates.

[6] Dr. John Wilson visited them early in 1838 (*Life*, p. 278), but his account of them (*Jour. Bom. B. R. A. Soc.*, vol. iii. pt. ii. pp. 71, 72) is a mere resumé of what had previously been written by Mr. Fergusson and others. A good description of the principal caves appeared in Dr. J. Muir's *Account of a Journey from Agra to Bombay in* 1854.

About 1862 Major Gill's stereoscopic photographs of the *Rock Temples of Ajanta and Ellora* were published; and in 1864 his *One hundred Stereoscopic Illustrations of Architecture and Natural History in Western India*,—both volumes with descriptive letter-press by J. Fergusson, Esq., F.R.S. In 1863 Dr. Bhâu Dâjî published transcripts and translations of the inscriptions which he found in the caves,—*Jour. Bom. B. R. A. Soc.*, vol. vii. pp. 55–74; these require careful revision. The writer visited them at Christmas 1863, and again in 1867, and contributed his notes on them to the *Times of India*; these were also printed separately (16mo. pp. 58) as *The Rock-cut Temples of Ajanta, &c.* Another visit was paid to them in May 1872 (*Ind. Ant.*, vol. iii. pp. 269–274). An account of the wall-paintings, &c. has also been printed officially by the Bombay Govern-

In consequence of the interest this created in the subject, and representations addressed by him to the Court of Directors of the East India Company, Captain Gill, of the Madras Army, was appointed, in 1845, to copy the paintings in these caves, and for several years afterwards sent home a series of extremely beautiful facsimile copies of the principal subjects on the walls and roofs of these caves. These paintings, all except in three or four, were unfortunately lent the Crystal Palace Company for exhibition at Sydenham, and were destroyed in the disastrous fire in 1860. Fortunately before that, tracings of several of them were made by Mr. Geo. Scharf, and reproduced as woodcuts in Mrs. Speir's "Life in India," and are reproduced further on, woodcuts 54 to 61.

Ajaṇṭâ was not visited by Hiwen Thsang, the indefatigable Chinese pilgrim of the seventh century, but after visiting Pulikêśi, the king of Maharâshtra, at his capital, probably Bâdâmi, he says, —" Sur les frontières orientales du royaume, il y a une grande montaigne qui offre des sommets entassés les uns sur les autres, des chaînes de rochers, des pics à double étage, et des crêtes escarpées. Anciennement il y avait un couvent qui avait été construit dans une sombre vallée. Ses bâtiments élevés et ses salles profondes occupaient les larges ouvertures des rochers et s'appuyaient sur les pics: ses pavillons et ses tours à double étage étaient adossés aux cavernes et regardaient la vallée.

" Ce couvent avait été bâti par le *Lo-han 'O-tche-lo* (l'Arhat Atchâra).

" Le *Vihâra* du couvent a environ cent pieds de hauteur. Au centre, s'élève une statue en pierre du *Bouddha*, qui a environ soixante et dix pieds. Elle est surmontée de sept calottes en pierre, qui sont suspendues dans l'air, sans aucune attache apparente. Elles sont séparées chacune par un intervalle d'environ trois pieds. D'a-

---

ment as *Notes on the Bauddha Rock Temples of Ajanta, their Paintings and Sculptures, &c.* During the dry seasons of 1872–73, 1874–75, 1875-76, and 1877–78, Mr. Griffiths, of the Bombay School of Art, was engaged with a staff of students recopying the frescoes, and finished most of what is left of them in Caves I. and II., with some parts of those in Caves VI., IX., and XVI., (*Ind. Ant.*, vol. i. p. 354; vol. ii. p. 152; vol. iii. pp. 25 ff.; vol. iv. p. 253). Two papers have appeared on some of these paintings, one by Râjendralâla Mitra, LL.D., " On Representations of Foreigners in the Ajaṇṭâ frescoes" (*Jour. A. S. Ben.*, vol. xlvii. pp. 62 ff.); and the other by J. Fergusson, D.C.L., F.R S., "On the identification of the portrait of Chosroes II. among the paintings in the caves of Ajaṇṭâ" (*J. R. As. Soc. N.S.*, vol. xi. pp. 155 ff.)

près les anciennes descriptions de ce pays, elles sont soutenues par la force des vœux du *Lo-han* (de l'Arhat).

" Suivant quelques personnes, ce prodige est dû à la force de ses facultés surnaturelles, et, selon d'autres, à la puissance de sa science médicale. Mais on a beau interroger l'histoire, il est impossible de trouver l'explication de ce prodige. Tout autour du *Vihâra* on a sculpté les parois de la pierre, et l'on a représenté les évènements de la vie de *Jou-laï* (du Tathâgata) dans tous les lieux où il a rempli le rôle de *Bôdhisattva*, les présages heureux qui ont signalé son élévation à la dignité d'*Arhat*, et les prodiges divins qui ont suivi son entrée dans le *Nirvâṇa*. Le ciseau de l'artiste a figuré tous ces faits dans les plus petits détails, sans en oublier un seul.

" En dehors des portes du couvent, au midi et au nord, à gauche et à droite, on voit un éléphant en pierre. J'ai entendu dire à des gens du pays que, de temps en temps, ces (quatre [1]) éléphants poussent des cris terribles qui font trembler la terre. Jadis *Tch' in-na-p'ou-sa* (Djina Bôdhisattva) s'arrêta souvent dans ce couvent."[2]

This account can only be applied to Ajaṇṭâ, and though only reported on hearsay is remarkably descriptive of these caves, but of no other group.

In some respects the series of caves at Ajaṇṭâ is more complete and more interesting than any other in India. All the caves there belong exclusively to the Buddhist religion without any admixture either from the Hindu or Jaina forms of faith, and they extend through the whole period during which Buddhism prevailed as a dominant religion in that country. Two of them, a Chaitya cave and a vihara, IX. and VIII., certainly belong to the second century before Christ, and two others, No. XXVI., a chaitya at one end of the series, and No. 1, a vihara at the other end, were certainly not finished in the middle of the seventh century, when Buddhism was tottering to its fall. Between these two periods, the 29 caves found here are spread tolerably evenly over a period of more than eight centuries, with only a break, which occurs, not only here, but everywhere, between the Hinâyâna and Mahâyâna forms of faith. Five or six caves at Ajaṇṭâ belong to the former school, and consequently to the first great division into which we have classed these monuments.

---

[1] This interpolation of M. Julien's is evidently a mistake, only two elephants are spoken of.

[2] Stan. Julien, *Mém. sur les Cont. Occident.* tome ii. pp. 151–52.

The remaining 23 belong as distinctly to the second division, and possess all the imagery and exuberance of the latter school.

PAINTINGS.

Another characteristic of these caves is that they still possess their paintings in a state of tolerable completeness. From the fragments that remain there is very little doubt that all the Buddhist caves were originally adorned with paintings, but in nine cases out of ten these have perished, either from the effects of the atmosphere, which in that climate is most destructive, or from wanton damage done by ignorant men. Forty years ago those at Ajaṇṭâ were very tolerably complete, and their colours exhibited a freshness which was wonderful, considering their exposure to the vicissitudes of an Indian climate for from 15 to 18 centuries. Since that time, however, bees, bats, and barbarians have done a great deal to obliterate what was then so nearly perfect. Enough, however, still remains or has been copied, and so saved, to show what was originally intended, and how it was carried into effect. As no such series of pictures exists now in any other series of caves, its being found here adds immensely to the interest of this group. Besides this it affords an opportunity, not only of judging of the degree of excellence to which the Indians reached in this branch of the fine arts, but presents a more vivid picture of the feelings and aspirations of the Buddhists during their period of greatest extension in India than we can obtain from any other source.

In Western India the older caves seem as a rule to have been decorated with painting,[1] while sculpture was as generally employed in the East. To receive these paintings the walls were left somewhat rough on the surface, and were then covered with a thin coating of plaster composed of fine dust, in some instances at least, of pounded brick, mixed with fibres and the husks of rice. This was smoothed and covered with a coating of some ground colour, on which the designs were drawn and then painted. The pillars being smoothed with the chisel seem to have received only a heavy ground coating to prepare them to receive the scenes or figures to be drawn on them.

In about half the Ajaṇṭâ caves there are no remains of painting, and in those that are unfinished there perhaps never was any; but

[1] A somewhat detailed account of these paintings will be found in my *Notes on the Bauddha Rock-Temples of Ajaṇṭâ, their Paintings and Sculptures, &c.*, printed by the Government of Bombay, 1879 (112 pp. 4to., with 31 plates).

in about 13 of them fragments of greater or less extent still exist, and most of these were no doubt originally covered with paintings. It is only, however, in about seven caves that the fragments left are large or of special interest; these are caves Nos. I., II., IX., X., XVI., and XVII.

Of the date of these paintings it is difficult to form a very definite estimate, nor are they all of the same age. Over the door on the inside of the front wall of Cave IX. is a fine fragment, which probably belongs to an earlier date than the major part of the paintings in Caves I., II., &c.; while again on the front wall of Cave I. are two large fragments that seem probably to be of a later date than the others. There are, moreover, in Cave IX. some portions of one layer of painting over another, of which the lower must be the older, probably a good deal older than the upper, or indeed than most of the painting in the other caves. We shall probably not be far wrong if we attribute the generality of the paintings in Caves I., II., XVI., XVII., &c. to the sixth century, which we may gather from the style of alphabetical character used in a few painted inscriptions and names of figures is the date of these paintings. The later pictures may then be attributed to the seventh century, and the earlier ones, in Caves IX. and X., may possibly date even as far back as the second—in the time of the Andhrabhritya kings, the great patrons of Buddhism in the first three centuries of our era.

The scenes represented are generally from the legendary history of Buddha and the *Jâtâkas*, the visit of Asita to the infant Buddha, the temptation of Buddha by Mârâ and his forces, Buddhist miracles, the Jâtâka of king Śibi, Indra and Sachî, court scenes, legends of the Nâgas, hunting scenes, battle pieces, &c. Few of these pictures have ever yet been identified, because no visitor has had the time to spare on the spot and the books at hand to refer to, in order to determine which story each represents. The scenes depicted, too, separately cover a much larger space, and are more complicated, than would at first sight appear to be the case. They are divided, too, into separate acts or sections in a way that is sometimes perplexing. The copies hitherto made are often only of parts of a whole story, while large portions have been destroyed,—and this must be borne in mind by those who use them in attempting to read their contents.

Certain parts of the pictures are always represented conventionally and it is necessary to note this before further examination. For example, whenever the scene of any picture is intended to be among the Himâlayas or other mountains, this is indicated by the background being chequered by what might seem to represent bricks, usually with one or two sides of a dark or bluish green and the other light; these are the rocks, presented with a conventionalism worthy of Chinese artists. To interpret the meaning, however, there are frequently represented on these blocks, figures of birds and monkeys, and sometimes of Bhill or other wild tribes of bowmen and the fabled inhabitants of the hills—Kirâtas, Guhyakas, and Kinnaras; the latter are the musicians to the mountain gods with human busts and the legs and tails of birds. Torrents and trees are also occasionally depicted.

It may be remarked that this mode of representing mountain scenery is employed also in the sculptures,—especially in the favourite one in Brahmanical caves where Râvana is represented under Mount Kailâsa trying to carry it off.

Rivers and the sea are equally fantastically drawn, and sometimes with rocky shores. But the fishes, *śaṅkhas*, &c. in them and a boat, generally interpret the representation at once.

Doors and gateways are represented always in one form, as an entrance between two jambs surmounted by a semi-circular coping terminating in the Chaitya window ornament at either end; usually a *dwârapâla*, *darwân*, or *chokidâr* is represented standing in or near it, but in many cases some other figure is passing in or out and connecting the scene inside with that in the court, street, or champaign.

The palaces or buildings are represented by a flat roof over the heads of the figures, supported by slender pillars, often with blue capitals, and commonly dividing the area within into a central hall and two side aisles or verandahs.

The dresses are very various but pretty clearly distinctive of the classes represented. The great ones, Dêvas, Râjas, Diwâns, and nobles wear but little clothing, at least above the waist, but much jewellery, armlets, necklaces, fillets, and high crowns or *mukuṭas*. Men of lower rank are often more covered, but have little or no jewellery. Bhikshus and monks usually are clothed by their *śelâ* or robe, which leaves only the right shoulder bare. Râṇîs and ladies of distinction, and perhaps also their more personal servants, wear much jewellery on their persons but of different sorts according to their rank. The Rânis are frequently, if not always, represented almost as if they were nude; very close examination, however, shows that that is not intended, but that they are dressed in—

" A wondrous work of thin transparent lawn."

—so thin indeed that the painter has failed to depict it, and has usually contented himself by slightly indicating it in a few very light touches of whitish colour across the thighs, and by tracing its flowered border, and painting the chain by which it was held up round the waist.

Dancing women are represented much as they would be now in an abundance of flowing coloured clothing. *Dâsîs* and *Kañchukinîs* —household slaves or servants—wear boddices or *cholîs* and a *sâri* round the loins, usually of striped cloth.

Thirty years ago there were some fine fragments of painting on the walls of Cave X., the few portions of which now remaining have all been scribbled over by natives. These paintings are of a very early date, the figures, Plate XXIX., differing in costume from those in the other caves; the dresses of the human figures belong to the age of the Śâtakarṇis, and can hardly be attributed to a later date than the latter half of the second century A.D. They were mostly in outline, but the drawing was strikingly bold and true; on the left wall was a procession of men, some on foot and others on horseback, variously dressed and armed, some with halberts, and with them groups of women, who appear to have formed part of a procession, one carrying what appears to be a relic casket, with an umbrella borne over it, or over a râja who stands before it. In another place is the *Bodhidruma* or sacred tree hung with offerings, and people worshipping it, as is so frequently represented in the sculptures at Sanchi and elsewhere. There are also two drawings of a gateway, which at once remind us of those at the great tope of Sânchi in Bhopal, as well as of the marriage *toranas* still set up in wood in Mâlwâ. Elephants and people in procession covered a portion

No 52. Chhadanta Elephant from Cave XVI.

of the right wall, and among the former was one with six tusks (*chhadanta*).[1] To the right of them was a building with peacocks, &c. about it; then a king and his râṇî, seated with attendants and approached by two figures, one of them carrying some objects hung from the ends of a pole. In the next scene the same two men were saluting or supplicating the râja and his consort; again, apparently the râja stands addressing her seated in an attitude betokening sorrow; and still behind, to the right, were other figures.

The paintings between the ribs of the aisles of Cave X. are of much later date, and in one case at least there is a more modern inscription painted over the older work on the walls. Near the front, on the left wall, however, is a painted inscription in much older characters, like those of the inscription of Vâśishṭhîputra on the right side of the great arch.[3]

In these and in the other old portions, the dresses, jewellery, &c. all remind us most vividly of the style of the early sculptures at Sânchi, in the verandah and capitals of the Kârlê Chaitya-cave, on the capitals at Bêḍsâ, in the vihâra of Gautamîputra I. at Nasik, and in the oldest discovered sculptures at Mathurâ. A broad heavy neck-chain is usually prominent, with large oblong discs or jewels slipped over it; large earrings, sometimes oblong, and apparently resting on the shoulders; many heavy rings on the wrists and legs of the females, who also have the hair covered in front in a peculiar style, and have a circular yellow disc or *tilaka* on the forehead; a sort of high turban with a knob in front is worn by the males, and the upper classes of neither sex wear much clothing except jewellery above the waist. Soldiers are armed with halberts, spears, and bows and arrows.

Between the ribs of the arched roof there are figures of Buddhas, rosettes, &c., but they are not of earlier date than the sixth or seventh century.

---

[1] Mrs. Speirs's *Life in Ancient India*, p. 266, from which the woodcut is taken. Mâya on the conception of Buddha is said to have dreamed that she saw a *six-tusked* white elephant descend through space and enter her right side (Beal's *Romantic Hist. of Buddha*, p. 37). The Ceylon books say she dreamed that an elephant from Chadanta (in the Himâlayas, famous for its breed of elephants) rubbed her side. Rajendralâla Mitra thinks it must have been the *Hippopotamus sivalensis*: (*Buddha Gayâ*, p. 214).

[2] In the *Illustrated News* (vol. xv. p. 173), Sept. 8, 1849, are small woodcuts of two of these wall scenes.

[3] *J. B. B. R. A. S.*, vol. vii. p. 63.

Early Buddhist Caves.

As mentioned above, five, probably six, of the caves at Ajaṇṭâ belong to the first division of Buddhist Caves, and consequently to the older or Hinâyâna sect. The remaining twenty-three belong to the more modern class of caves of the Mahâyâna sect, and will be described in the next book which is their proper place.

Although the older caves cannot boast among them of any Chaityas so magnificent as that of Kârlê, nor any vihâras to compare with Nos. III. and VIII. at Nasik, they form a very compact group. They are too of considerable interest, as being part of a series of caves so complete in themselves as those at Ajaṇṭâ, and as illustrating in a marked manner the differences between the earlier and later forms of Buddhist art.

The lowest down of the whole, and probably the oldest, is No. VIII., a small vihâra, with a hall 32 feet 4 inches wide by about 17 in. deep and 10 feet high. There are two cells at each end, and two at each side of the antechamber to the shrine. The latter is entered by a low door, and contains only a low stone bench at the back, but no trace of an image. The whole of the front of this cave has fallen away, and it was so choked up with earth that it was only lately that it could be examined, and very little architecture remains by which its age could be determined. Its position, however, so low down in the rock is an almost certain indication of its antiquity, and it holds exactly the same relative position to No. IX., the oldest Chaitya here, which the Cave No. XIV. does to the Chaitya Cave at Nasik (*ante*, p. 274), that there can be little doubt that the two bear the same relation to one another, and whatever the age of No. IX. is determined to be, that of No. VIII. follows as a matter of course, as its satellite.

Cave IX. may for many reasons be considered not only the oldest Chaitya in Ajaṇṭâ, but as one of the earliest of its class yet discovered in the west of India. It is probably not so old as that at Bhâjâ (woodcut, No. 1.), for the whole of its front is in stone, with the single exception of the open screen in the arch, which was in wood, as was the case in all the early caves of Hinâyâna class. There is, however, no figure sculpture on the front, as at Karlê and Kondâṇê, and all the ornaments upon it are copied more literally from the wood than in almost any other cave, except that at Beḍsâ, which it very much resembles. Another peculiarity indicative of age is that its plan is square (Plate XXVIII.), and the aisles are flat roofed and lighted by windows, and the columns that divide them from the nave slope inwards at an angle somewhere between that found at Bhâjâ and that at Beḍsâ.

In many respects the design of its façade resembles that of the Chaitya at Nasik, but it is certainly earlier, and on the whole there can be little hesitation in classing it with the caves at Beḍsâ, and consequently in assuming its date to be about 100 B.C., and more probably rather a few years years earlier than a few later.

This Chaitya is 45 feet deep by 22 feet 9 inches wide and 23 feet 2 inches high. (Plate XXVIII., figs. 3 and 4, p. 98.) A colonnade all round divides the nave from the aisles, and at the back the pillars form a semicircular apse, in the centre of which stands the *dâgoba*, about 7 feet in diameter; its base is a plain cylinder, 5 feet high, supporting a dome 4 feet high by about 6 feet 4 inches in diameter, surmounted by a square capital about 1¼ feet high, and carved on the sides in imitation of the "Buddhist railing." It represents a relic box, and is crowned by a projecting lid, a sort of abacus consisting of six plain fillets, each projecting over the one below. This most probably supported a wooden umbrella, as at Kârlê. Besides the two pillars inside the entrance, the nave has 21 plain octagonal columns without base or capital, 10 feet 4 inches high, supporting an entablature, 6 feet 8 inches deep, from which the vaulted roof springs, and which has originally been fitted with wooden ribs. The aisles are flat-roofed, and only an inch higher than the columns; they are lighted by a window opening into each. Over the front doorway is the great window, one of the peculiar features of a Chaitya-cave: it is of horse-shoe form, about 11½ feet high, with an inner arch, about 9¾ feet high, just over the front pillars of the nave. Outside this is the larger arch with horizontal ribs, of which five on each side project in the direction of the centre, and eleven above in a vertical direction. The barge-board or facing of the great arch here is wider than usual, and perfectly plain. It probably was plastered, and its ornamentation, which was in wood at Bhâjâ, was probably here reproduced in painting. On the sill of this arch is a terrace, 2¼ feet wide, with a low parapet in front, wrought in the "Buddhist-rail" pattern; outside this, again, is another terrace over the porch, about 3¾ feet wide, and extending the whole width of the cave, the front of it being ornamented with patterns of the window itself as it must have originally appeared, with a wooden frame of lattice-work in the arch. At each end of this, on the wall at right angles to the façade, is sculptured a colossal figure of Buddha, and on the projecting rock on each side there is a good deal of sculpture, but all of a much later date than the temple itself, and possibly of the fifth century. The porch of the door has partly fallen away. It had a cornice above supported by two very wooden-like struts, similar to those in the Bhâjâ Chaitya-cave.

The paintings in this cave consist principally of figures of Buddha along the left wall, where there are at least six, each with a triple umbrella, and some traces of buildings. On the back wall is a fragment, extending nearly its whole length, containing figures of Buddha variously engaged, disciples, worshippers, a dâgoba, &c.[1] This is probably of older date than the generality of the paintings found in the other caves, but it may fairly be questioned whether it is of so early an age as the fragments on the walls in Cave X. It is of high artistic merit, however, which makes us the more regret that no more of it is left.

On the front wall over the left window a layer of painting has dropped off, laying bare one of the earliest fragments left, possibly a version of the *Jâtaka* of Śibi or Siwi Râja, who gave his eyes to Indra, who appeared to him in the form of a mendicant to test him.[2]

Close to this is a Vihâra No. XII., most probably of the same age. and one of the oldest here. Its front has fallen away with the verandah which in all probability covered it. What remains is a hall (Plate XXVII.) about 36¼ feet square, with four cells in each of the three inner sides,—eleven of them with double beds having raised stone pillows. There are holes in the sills and lintels of the doorways for pivot hinges, and others in the jambs for fastenings. The upper portion of the walls are ornamented over the cell doors with canopies representing the Chaitya window, with others in the interspaces; below these is a string course wrought in the "Buddhist

---

[1] This has been copied by Mr. Griffiths in four sections, marked A, B, C, D, of 1874–75, and are probably at South Kensington.

[2] For the Jâtaka, see *Jour. Ceylon B. R. As. Soc.*, vol. ii. (1853), pp. 5, 6; Spence Hardy's *Eastern Monachism*, pp. 277, 278, 279; or *Notes on Ajaṇṭâ Rock-Temples, &c.*, p. 76; conf. Fergusson, *Tree and Serp. Worsh.*, pp. 194, 225.

rail pattern," as in Cave XIV. at Nâsik, which this cave resembles in almost every respect except dimension, this being by far the finest and largest of the two. Their details, however, are so similar that there can be little doubt that they are not distant in age, as may be seen by comparing the elevations of their sides, Plates XXVI., fig. 3, and XXVII., fig. 1.

Close to this is Cave XIII., which may be as old as anything at Ajaṇṭâ, but it is almost wholly without architectural form, and its front has fallen away like that of No. XII., so that it is impossible to say what its original form may have been. It is only a *Layana* or Bhikshu's room, such as one may fancy to have been the residence of some holy man with his disciples, whose sanctity may have attracted others to the spot, and so have given rise to the excavation of this series of caves.

The hall here is 13½ feet wide by 16½ deep and 7 feet high, and has seven cells,—three on the left side and two on the back and right sides,—in all which are stone couches or beds, which are characteristic of all the cells of an early age.

Cave X. is the second and largest Chaitya of the group, and must have been when complete a very fine cave. There is some little difficulty in speaking of the date with confidence, as the façade has entirely fallen away (Plate XXVII., figs. 1 and 2), and the pillars inside are plain octagons, without either bases or capitals, and having been at one time plastered and painted there are no architectural details by which its age can be ascertained. There is, however, one constructional feature which is strongly indicative of a comparatively modern date. The roof of the nave was adorned with wooden ribs, like all the caves described above, though all these are now gone; but the aisles here are adorned with stone ribs carved in imitation of wood. In the next group of caves we have to describe—the Mahâyâna caves—all have stone ribs, both in the nave and aisles, and this seems a step in that direction, but so far as is known the first.[1]

Another circumstance indicative of a more modern date is the position of this cave in the series. It is higher up in the rock, and very much larger than No. IX. (*see* Plate XXVII.), and it seems most improbable that having a large and roomy Chaitya they should

---

[1] A view of the interior of this cave will be found in my illustration of the *Rock-cut Temples*, folio, London 1845, Pl. III.

afterwards excavate a smaller one close along side of it on a lower level, and in a more inconvenient form. The contrary is so much more likely to be the case, as the community extended, and more accommodation was wanted, that it may fairly be assumed, from this circumstance alone, that No. X. is the more modern of the two Chaityas, though at what interval it is difficult to say in consequence of the absence of architectural details in the larger cave.

It measures 41 feet 1 inch wide, about 95½ feet deep, and 36 feet high. The inner end of the cave, as well as of the colonnade that surrounds the nave, is semi-circular, the number of columns in the latter being thirty-nine plain octagons—two more than in the great Chaitya at Kârlê,—but many of them are broken. They are 14 feet high, and over them rises a plain entablature 9½ feet deep, from which springs the arched roof, rising 12½ feet more, with a span of about 23½ feet. Like the oldest Chaitya caves at Bhâjâ, Kârlê, Beḍsâ, Kondâṇê, &c., it has been ribbed with wood. The aisles are about 6 feet wide, with half-arched roofs, ribbed in the rock. The *chaitya* or *dâgoba* is perfectly plain, with a base or lower drum, 15½ feet in diameter; the dome is rather more than half a sphere, and supports the usual capital, consisting of an imitation box, covered by a series of thin square slabs, each projecting a little over the one below it. There is an inscription on the front of the great arch at the right hand side, which reads:—

Vâsiputasa kaṭahâ dito gharmukha danam.

"The gift of a house-door (front) by Vasithiputra."

If we could be certain that this was the Puḷumavi Vâśishṭhîputra of the Nâsik inscriptions, we might at once refer this one to the second century A.D., and the alphabet would support such a date. But then does it mean that Vâśishṭhîputra *began* the excavation and carved out the façade? or does it only imply that he inserted, in a Chaitya cave already existing, a new front? Now, in excavating the floor under the great arch, I found that a wall had been built across the front of immense bricks of admirable texture and colour, several tiers of which still remain *in situ.* This may have been Vâśishṭhîputra's work, and the cave itself may be of an earlier date.

The whole of this cave has been painted.

Both these Chaitya Caves still retain a great deal of the fresco paintings with which they were at one time completely adorned. Those in number IX. have been minutely described by Mr. Griffith in a report to the Government (not published), and many of them copied by him, and are in this country, but from the closing of the India Museum there is no place where they can be exhibited. They are, as just mentioned, of various ages, and none of them probably coeval with the cave.

Those in Cave X. may possibly be of the age of Vâsishṭhîputra, who certainly was one of the Satakarnis and contemporary with the Andhrabhritya, and possibly with the excavation of the cave. Their general character may be judged from Plate XXIX. Both figures and costume are very different from anything found in any of the other caves, but they resemble—as far as sculpture can be compared with painting—the costumes found among sculptures at Sanchi [1] in the first century of our era. They certainly are not Aryans, but are more like the Bhills and Brinjaris, and other low caste quasi aboriginal tribes of the present day.

Cave XI.

The verandah of this cave is supported in front by four plain octagonal columns with bracket capitals and square bases, raised on a panelled base or parapet, similar to what we find in one of the Vihâras at Kârlê and elsewhere. The roof also projects considerably in front of the pillars, and has been very elaborately painted with flowers, birds, and geometrical patterns. The verandah has a cell at either end, that on the right entering in by the side of the hall, whilst the end wall itself is sculptured in three compartments, two with seated Buddhas, attendants, and worshippers, and one with a standing Buddha with *chamara*-bearer and attendant. The door is plainer than in other Vihâras, and the windows are each divided by two pillars into three openings. The hall is 37 feet wide by 28 deep and 10 high, and is supported by four octagonal columns of a more than usually clumsy and primitive style (Plate XXX., fig. 1), from which it has been inferred that this is one of the earliest examples of the introduction of pillars in Vihâras. None earlier are known to exist anywhere, and the mode in which they are introduced here is so exceptional that the inference seems, to say the least of it, extremely probable. There is a sort of seat along the right side of the cave such as we find so frequently in the older caves, and three cells on the left side, also in the back two to the left and one to the right, of the sanctuary,

[1] *Tree and Serpent Worship*, first 45 plates.

which opens directly from the cave, and is about 12 feet wide by 19¾ deep, with the statue of Buddha separate from the back wall and seated on a *siṅhâsana* with two well-cut deer on each side of the *chakra* or wheel, and lions behind them. There are no attendant *chaurî*-bearers, but above are flying figures or *gandharvas*. In front of the image is a charmingly natural figure of a man kneeling in adoration, or holding an alms-bowl, the face and hands unfortunately damaged, and probably wilfully. This was perhaps intended to represent the excavator of the cave. High up in the wall, and scarcely visible, is an aperture on the left side of the sanctuary, opening into a secret cell.

It depends wholly on whether the age of Cave XI. is to be determined from its architecture or from its sculpture to know whether it is to be classed among those of the first or Hinâyâna division, or to belong to the second or Mahâyâna class of caves. Its architecture certainly looks old, certainly much more so than the two great Vihâras at Nâsik, and can hardly be brought down below the first century of our era; but there is an image of Buddha, unfinished, in the sanctuary, and *bassi relievi* at either end of the verandah containing seated images of Buddha. These last, however, are so like those figures which are avowedly late insertions on the front of the Kârlê cave that they cannot be considered as integral, and the same may be said of the image in the sanctuary. The probability is that this cave, like XV. at Nasik, was remodelled at some period long subsequent to its original excavation, and that all its sculptures belong to a much later date than its architecture. If this is so it probably belongs to the same age as the Chaitya Cave No. X., and was excavated as its companion. From its position and its appearance this seems most probable. If this is so, the date of these two caves may be the first century A.D., or it may be even in a slight degree more modern.[1]

[1] I am responsible for the arrangement and dates of these six caves. Mr. Burgess and I are perfectly agreed as to the age of the group, but differ slightly as to their relative position *inter se*. I have consequently in his absence, when there was no opportunity of consulting him, been obliged to arrange them in the manner which, according to the latest lights, seems to me on the whole, most probable.—J. F.

BOOK II.

CHAPTER I.

LATER OR MAHAYANA CAVES AT AJANTA.

The preceding six chapters have been devoted to the description of the various groups of caves known to exist in Western India belonging to the Hinâyâna sect, or the first division of Buddhist caves. They are so numerous that it has been impossible to describe them all, but enough has probably been said to make their characteristic features known, and to explain the limits within which further investigations are either promising or desirable.

The caves belonging to the second division, or the Mahâyâna sect, are much less numerous than those belonging to the first, owing principally to there being no Bhikshugrihas or hermitages among them. The monks were no longer content to live apart by themselves, or with only one or two companions in rude caves, but were congregated into large and magnificent monasteries, richly adorned, and which, in that climate and at that age, may have been considered as replete with every comfort, it may almost be said, with every luxury.

The great and most essential change, however, which took place between these two classes was in the forms of worship which was characteristic of them. The Dâgoba or relic shrine, which was so generally revered in ancient times, disappears almost entirely from the Vihâras, and is only found in the Chaitya caves, and even then it always has an image of Buddha attached to it in front, and personal worship of him evidently, in these instances, replaced that of the symbol under which he had previously been adored. It is indeed this multiplication of images of Buddha which is most characteristic of the caves of the Mahâyâna sect. Not only do figures of Buddha, as objects of worship, take the place of the Dâgobas in the sanctuaries of the Viharas, but the insignia of the Bodhisatwas are given to his *Chauri*-bearer, and these are increased in later times from two to four, and sometimes even to eight or more. In addition to these figures of Buddha with the Bodhisatwas, which are multiplied almost everywhere on the walls of the caves, and they are frequently accompanied by female figures or *Sâktîs*, such as Târâ, Mârmukhî, Lóchana, and others. In fact, a whole system of idolatry is introduced into them, at total variance with the simpler form of faith that characterized the earlier caves.

The architecture of the later caves belonging to the Mahâyâna sect exhibits almost as great a change as their imagery. The grandiose design, and simple detail of the early caves, gives place to façades and interiors crowded with pillars, carved or painted with the most elaborate and minute ornaments. The animal figures disappear from the capitals, and are replaced by brackets richly ornamented and filled with figures and mythological representations of the most varied kind. The doorways of the caves too are occasionally marvels of elaborate decorations. The change is, in fact, quite as great as that which took place between the early English style that prevailed in this country betweeen the reigns of Henry II. and Henry III., and the decorated style introduced by Edward III., and which prevailed till the time of Richard III. The change was perhaps even greater, and accompanied, in India certainly, by a far greater change of ritual than was introduced into England with the change of architectural style.

It is not at present possible to state with precision the exact period at which the transition from the Ḥinâyâna to the Mahâyâna sect took place. As stated above, the last caves of the Hinâyâna are those at Nâsik, and their age depends on our being able to ascertain when Gautamîputra excavated No. III., and what Yajñaśrî really did in No. XV. Even then the uncertainty that hangs over the lists of the Andhrabhrityas prevents our being able to fix these dates with certainty. It is probable they reigned in the third century, but nearly as probable, that the last-named king flourished in the fourth. Be this as it may, there seems to have been a pause in the fashion of excavating caves after the disappearance of these Śâtakarnis. We have no cave that can with certainty be dated in the fifth century, probably not one in the latter half of the fourth, but with the sixth century the practice was resumed with vigour, and during the next century and a half nearly all the Mahâyâna caves were excavated.

It certainly seems to be the case that all or nearly all the remaining 21 caves at Ajaṇṭá were excavated between the years 500 and 650, with a very little margin either way before or after these dates.[1]

When we pass over the gulf, and it is a vast one, that separates the older from the more modern caves, at Ajaṇṭâ we come first on a very small and somewhat abnormal group, consisting of only two caves, Nos. VII. and VI., which, whatever their other characteristics may be, most distinctly belong to the Mahâyâna school.

Cave VII. is a Vihâra somewhat differing in type from any yet described. In front of the verandah were two porches, each supported by two advanced octagonal pillars with capitals somewhat like those in Cave II. and at Elephanta. The frieze above is ornamented with the favourite Chaitya-window device. The verandah measures 62 feet 10 inches long by 13 feet 7 inches wide and 13 feet 6 inches high. There is no hall, but in the back wall are four cells and the antechamber leading to the shrine; and at each end of the verandah are rooms at some height above the floor with two pillars in front, each again opening into three cells, about 8½ feet square. The shrine is an unequal four-sided room, in which Buddha is

---

[1] One of the most curious results obtained from recent discoveries in Afghanistan is the apparent certainty of the prevalence of Mahâyâna doctrines on the Indus, and beyond it, long before their introduction in India. Near Ali Musjid a tope has recently been excavated by M. Beglar, and photographs of it have been sent to me by General Cunningham—but not yet published—with a letter in which he informs me it contains coins of Vasu Deva, and he considers that it certainly belongs to his age. Inscriptions of this king have been found at Mathura (Cunningham, *Reports*, vol. iv. pp. 34 and 35), dated Samvat 83 and 98. Now, assuming these to be dated from the Saka Samvat, which there seems no reason for doubting was the case, this would only bring his reign down to 162–177 A.D., and there is nothing in the architecture of the tope to contradict this date. It is adorned with the bell-shaped capitals so common in India at about this date, and they are surmounted by the double animals as usual. The sculpture, however, is wholly of the Mahâyâna school. There are not only one, but dozens, it may almost be said hundreds, of figures of Buddha in all the usual conventional attitudes, and of a type that does not appear in India till at least two or three centuries afterwards. It may be a question for future investigation whether we ought to bring the date of the Afghanistan topes further down, or whether we ought to carry the introduction of Mahâyâna further back; the evidence of the caves seem to indicate the latter as the most probable alternative. I am strongly impressed with the idea—from the evidence as it at present stands—that the bulk of the Gandhara topes were erected between the age of Constantine and that of Justinian, but we must wait for further information before this can be determined.—J. F.

seated at the back on a low *Sinhâsana* or lion-throne, having in front of the seat two lions at the ends, and two antelopes facing each other, with a small wheel or *chakra* between them, with his legs crossed under him, his right hand raised in the *asiva mudrâ* or attitude of blessing, and the left holding his robe, and with high *mukuṭa*. From behind Buddha a *makara's* head projects on each side; there is a figured halo behind his head, and much carving round about him; a male *chaurî*-bearer stands on either side behind the *makara's* head; and in the corners above their heads are *Gandharvas*, *Vidyâdharas* or Buddhist cherubs. The projection of the *siñhásana* is carried round the sides of the room, and carved in front with eight squatting Buddhas on each side. Upon this projection stand three tall Buddhas on each side, also with nimbi behind their heads; those next the central image are of smaller stature, but the other two are gigantic figures; each holds up his left hand, with the edge of his robe in it, up to his breast, whilst the right hangs by his side with the palm turned out. Between these figures are other small cross-legged ones. The sides of the antechamber are entirely covered with small Buddhas sculptured in rows of five to seven each, sitting or standing on lotuses and with lotus leaves between them (*see* Plate XXXI.). The stalk of the lowest central lotus is upheld by two kneeling figures with regal headdresses, canopied by the many headed *nâga* behind each, on the left is a kneeling figure and two standing Buddhas, and on the right a Buddha is behind the *nâga*, and behind him three worshippers with presents. The door into the sanctuary has four standing and three sitting Buddhas on each side, carved in alternate compartments of the architrave, and eight sitting ones above, while at the foot of the architrave is a lion's head and paws. The pilasters outside the architrave are supported by dwarfs, and divided into three compartments each, containing a standing Buddha in the lower and cross-legged ones in the compartments above, whilst over the capitals a female figure stands under foliage and on a *makara*. Beyond this the wall is divided into three nearly square compartments, each ornamented with small pilasters at the sides, and all except the two upper ones on the right having *gandharvas* in the corners over the large cross-legged Buddhas which occupy them; these have all aureoles behind their curly-haired heads, except the upper one on the right, which has the protection of the snake with seven heads.

Cave VI. is of two storeys, Plate XXXII. The whole of the verandah has fallen away from the lower part. The outer wall is panelled under the four large windows which light a hall, 53 feet 4 inches wide and 54 feet 10 inches deep, the front and back aisles being about 71 feet long with chambers 8 feet by 10 at the ends of each. Having been occupied by natives who used to light their fires in it, this cave is much ruined, and has a very dilapidated appearance. The columns are arranged in four rows of four each, 16 in all, but only seven are now standing with four thin pilasters in the lines of the rows on each wall. Five columns have fallen within the last 40 years. Between the pilasters are three chambers on each side, each fully 8 feet by 9, and all with niches in their back walls. The pillars are about 13 feet high, plain octagons to about three-fourths of their height, above which they are 16-sided, without bases, and having a cincture under a 16-sided fillet at the top; imitation beams only 2 or 3 inches deep run from one pillar to another. The columns in front of the antechamber are somewhat similar in character to those in the porticoes of Cave VII. The antechamber is 13 feet 4 inches deep, and the sanctuary is 10 feet by 15¼; the figure of Buddha, which has apparently been painted blue, is seated in the *dharmachakra-mudrá*, on a pedestal 3 feet high, with wheel and small deer in front and supported at the corners by lions; the usual attendants are wanting. It is quite separate from the back wall, along the upper part of which is a recess. Over the door to the sanctuary is an ornamental arch, with *makara toraṇas* at the spring of it, and a *Nâga* figure with two attendants under the centre of it.

The stair in the front aisle, leading to the upper storey, has been broken away below. It lands in the verandah above. This verandah has been supported by four columns and two pilasters; but only one of the latter now remains, which is a particularly fine one. Above the stair landing are many small Buddhas carved on the walls and two dâgobas. Outside the verandah there are small chapels with sculptured Buddhas. There are also at each end of the verandah open chambers with carved pillars, and inside these chambers there are rooms 11 feet by 9. The entrances have plain mouldings, and over them are figures in bas-relief of Buddha and the Dâgoba. Plate XXX., fig. 2, represents the one in the right end of the aisle. The hall is 53 feet wide by 50 feet deep and 11¼ high, supported by 12 plain columns, enclosing the usual square area. The pillars have square bases and octagonal shafts, changing to square under the bracket capitals, which are sculptured with figures of Buddha in small recesses. Opposite the central interspace of each side, and at the end of the left aisle, are chambers or chapels with pillars in front, each leading to an inner cell. There are also three cells on each side, and one at the end of the right aisle. Over the chapel on the left of the entrance the frieze is carved with elephants, spiritedly cut, one of them killing a tiger.

The antechamber is 16 feet by 8½, and has colossal figures on each side of the shrine door, and others in the ends of the room. The shrine contains the usual statue of Buddha, with two antelopes on the front of the throne. The cave has been painted, but it has almost entirely disappeared. It has also a larger number of sculptured figures of Buddha than any other Vihâra at Ajaṇṭâ, some of them probably carved after the cave was occupied.

There is very little except their local position in the series that enables us to speak even hesitatingly regarding the age of these two caves. Their disposition is abnormal, the one being the only two-storeyed cave in the group, and the other, with its two porches and no hall, are quite unlike any others, and their architecture, too, is of type not exactly found elsewhere. It is still sufficiently similar in character to enable us to say that they are earlier than the five caves that follow them to the end of the series, V. to I., and are separated by a vast interval from the earlier group, Nos. VII. to XIII., described above; 450 A.D. is certainly the earliest date that can be assigned to them, and 500 is as likely to be nearer than that date, or even perhaps 550 A.D.

The next, which may be considered as the great central group of Ajaṇṭâ caves, is perhaps the most interesting of any. It consists of seven caves, Nos. XIV. to XX., and although XIV., XV., XVIII., and XX. are not very remarkable, though they might be considered so elsewhere, the remaining three,—two Vihâras, XVI. and XVII., and the Chaitya cave No. XIX.,[1] are, both from their architecture

[1] Views of the interiors of Caves XVI. and XVII., and of the interior and exterior of No. XIX., will be found in my illustrations of the *Rock-cut Temples of India*, folio, 1845, Plates IV., V., VI., and VII., and woodcut illustrations of them, *Hist. of Eastern and Indian Architecture*, woodcuts 60 and 61, 84, 85, 86.

and their paintings, as full of beauty and of interest as any caves in the West of India.

Cave XIV. is just over XIII., and is reached by a rough ascent over the rock from No. XII. The verandah is 63 feet long by 11 feet 1 inch wide and 9 feet high, with six pillars and two pilasters in front of it, differing in style from any other here, being square piers, divided by two slightly sunk, fluted bands about 11 inches broad. The body is vase-shaped, with a flat inverted shield on each side, and a plain abacus above. Into the cave, which has never been nearly finished, there is a very neat central door and two side ones, with two windows. It was intended to be 61 feet wide by 25½ deep, with a row of six columns and two pilasters running along the middle of it, but only the front half has been partially finished. This is probably a comparatively late excavation.

Cave XV.—The next is a few yards farther on. The verandah is about 30 feet long inside by 6½ wide, and had two columns and two pilasters; but the front has fallen away, a fragment of one pillar lying in the verandah, showing that they had a torus and fillet at the base, above which they were octagonal, changing to 16 sides, and thence to 32 flutes. The architrave of the door is plain, but the pilasters beyond it are similar to those in other caves. On the upper member of the frieze are carved four birds in low relief. The hall inside has no columns, and is nearly square, 34 feet each way by 10 feet 2 inches high. It has four cells on each side and one at each end of the verandah; the antechamber has two plain pilasters in front and two columns with square bases, then octagonal and 16-sided shafts returning through the octagon to square heads. The shrine contains an image of Buddha with the feet turned up on a *siṅhâsana*, having only the wheel and lions in front. It stands against the wall, and is without attendants, but with small flying *gandharvas* above. In the hall, to the left of the antechamber, are two pieces of carving, representing Buddha and attendants. The roof of the antechamber retains only a fragment of painting.

Cave XVI.

Nos. XVI. and XVII., though not the largest, are certainly the finest and most interesting Vihâras at Ajaṇṭâ. They are both nearly of the same age, and were excavated at about the same time with No. XIX., which is the best finished Chaitya cave of the series. If to these then we add No. XX. beyond the last-named, we have a group of four caves, all of about the same age, and whether looked at from an architectural or pictorial point of view they are superior to any at Ajaṇṭâ, or indeed perhaps any similar group in any part of India.

Of these four No. XVI. is certainly the earliest and in some respects the most elegant. Its verandah (Plate XXXIII., fig. 1), 65 feet long by 10 feet 8 inches wide, had six plain octagonal pillars with bracket capitals and two pilasters, of which all are gone except one. The cave has a central and two side doors with windows between. The pilasters on each side the principal door are surmounted by female figures standing on the heads of *makaras*. The front aisle is longer than the cave, measuring 74 feet; whilst the body of the hall is 66 feet 3 inches long, by 65 feet 3 inches deep, and 15 feet 3 inches high, supported by twenty octagonal shafts. The middle pair in the front and back rows, however, have square bases, and change first to eight, and then to 16 sides on the shafts, with square heads and bracket capitals. The roof of the front aisle is cut in imitation of beams and rafters, the ends of the beams being supported by small fat figures as brackets, in the two central cases single, in the others by two, and in one or two by male and female figures of *Kinnaras*,

No. 53. Front aisle in Cave XVI. at Ajaṇṭâ.

&c. This curiously wooden construction of the roof will be best explained by the preceding woodcut (53) from a photograph.[1] It is in fact the mode of framing floors and roofs still in use in India at the present day, and what is here carved in the rock is only painted in Caves XII., II., and I., with flowers and other ornaments to fill the interspaces.

There are six cells in each side, two in the back wall, and one in each end of the verandah. The adytum or shrine is entered direct from the hall and has a chamber on each side, separated from it by a screen of two pillars and pilasters. The gigantic statue of Buddha sits with the feet down and the hands in what is called the *dharma-chakra mudrâ* or teaching position, that is, he holds the little finger of the left hand between the thumb and forefinger of the right, with the other fingers turned up. There is a passage quite round the image; and on each side are octagonal pillars screening off side aisles, entered by small doors from the hall, and further lighted by small square windows near the roof.

At the left end of the façade of this cave is an inscription of about 27 lines, unfortunately mutilated, but partially translated by Dr. Bhâu Dâjî. It begins—"Having first saluted (Buddha who is renowned) in this world for the removal of the intense fire of misery of the three worlds......... I shall relate the genealogy of the King Vindhyaśakti, whose power extended over the great," &c. It then goes on to mention six or seven other kings of the Vâkâṭaka dynasty; but most of the names are more or less mutilated; they mostly appear, however, in the Seoni copper-plate grant deciphered by Mr. J. Prinsep,[2] being—

Vindhyaśakti, cir. 400 A.D.
Pravarasena I.
Dêvasena.
Rudrasena I., grandson of Gautamî, the daughter of Bhavanâga.[3]

---

[1] From Mrs. Manning, formerly Mrs. Speir's, *Ancient and Mediæval India.* We are indebted for this and the following eight woodcuts to the kindness of Miss Manning, who was left literary executor to her aunt.

[2] *Jour. As. Soc. Beng.*, vol. v. pp. 726–731. For another inscription of this dynasty, see my *Notes on the Rock Temples of Ajaṇṭâ*, p. 54 ff.

[3] Cunningham gives a list of a Nâga dynasty of Narwar (*Archæol. Surv. Rep.*, vol. ii. p. 310), which he considers to have been tributary to the Guptas. If, as we suppose,

Pṛithivisena.
Rudrasena II.
Pravarasena II., son of Prabhavatî Guptâ, daughter of the great King of Kings Śrî Deva Gupta.[1]

Of this Vindhyaśaktî or Vâkâṭaka[2] dynasty we know but little; it was probably a subordinate kingdom, extending over Berar and parts of the Narmadâ and Central Provinces in the fifth century; and from the style of architecture of this cave and the character of the alphabet used in the inscriptions, we may with very considerable probability assign it to a date very near to 500 A.D.

A stair leads down from the front of this cave, and turns to the left into a chamber, on the back wall of which was found, on excavating it, a figure of Nâga Râja seated upon the coils of the snake whose hoods overshadow his high flat topped *mukuta* or tiara. A door leads out from the front of the room towards the river, to which a stair must have descended. This door is flanked outside by two elephants in relief, but much damaged.[3]

In this Cave (XVI.) very little of the painting now remains in the verandah, but there are still some very noteworthy pieces in the hall. On the left wall is a picture that has attracted much attention, representing, it is supposed, the death of a princess.[4] A lady of rank sits on a couch leaning her left arm on the pillow and an attendant behind holds her up. A girl in the background places her hand on her breast and looks towards the lady. Another. with a sash across her breast, wields the *pankhâ*, and an old man in white cap looks in at the door, while another sits beside a pillar. In the foreground sit two women. In another apartment are two figures; one with a Persian cap has a vessel (*kalasa*) and a cup in the mouth of it; the other, with negro-like hair, wants something from him. To the right two *kanchukinîs*, or household slaves, sit in a separate

---

the Guptas ruled from the 4th to the 6th century, this Bhavanâga may have been one of these Nâgas.

[1] This may have been one of the latest Guptas, about the end of the 5th or the beginning of the 6th century A.D.

[2] There is a Bâkaṭaka mentioned as a district apparently, in Rudra Deva's inscription at Warangol, *Jour. As. Soc. Beng.*, vol. vii. p. 903.

[3] Can these be the *two* elephants referred to by Hiwen Thsang (*Mem. sur les Cont. Occid.*, t. ii. p. 153)? S. Julien says, "ces (quatre) éléphants," but Mr. Beal informs me the Chinese text speaks only of two.

[4] See *Ind. Ant.*, vol. iii., p. 25 ff., where a drawing of this scene is given.

apartment. Mr. Griffiths very justly remarks on this picture that "for pathos and sentiment and the unmistakeable way of telling its story this picture, I consider, cannot be surpassed in the history of art. The Florentines could have put better drawing, and the Venetians better colour, but neither could have thrown greater expression into it."

"The dying woman with drooping head, half closed eyes, and languid limbs, reclines on a bed, the like of which may be found in any native house of the present day. She is tenderly supported by a female attendant, whilst another, with eager gaze, is looking into her face, and holding the sick woman's arm as if in the act of feeling her pulse. The expression on her face is one of deep anxiety as she seems to realise how soon life will be extinct in the one she loves. Another female behind is in attendance with a *pankhâ*, whilst two men on the left are looking on with the expression of profound grief depicted in their faces. Below are seated on the floor other relations, who appear to have given up all hope, and to have begun their days of mourning, for one woman has buried her face in her hand and apparently is weeping bitterly."

No. 54. King paying homage to Buddha.

On the same wall is Buddha represented with the begging dish (*patra*) in his hand, while a râja with rich diadem kneels and pays him reverence.[1]

Again he is represented teaching in a vihâra[2] (woodcut No. 55). On the same wall he is represented as seated on a throne, of which the seat is upheld by lions that bear a strong family resemblance to some Assyrian figures. On the back wall is a large scene with elephants ridden by râjas, with attendants bearing musical instruments and soldiers with long blue curved swords. In another scene Buddha sits enthroned teaching a great assembly of crowned princes. On the right wall were several interesting scenes

---

[1] From Mrs. Speir's *Life in An. Ind.*, p. 305.

[2] The woodcut is from Mrs. Speir's *Life in Anc. India*, p. 197. The eight woodcuts, Nos. 54 to 61, are from the same source. They were reduced by Mr. George Scharf from Major Gill's copies at the Crystal Palace, for Mrs. Speir's work.

No. 55. Buddha Teaching, from a wall painting in Cave XVI.[1]

from the legend of the Buddha, such as Asita with the infant Buddha in his arms, Siddhârtha at school, drawing the bow, &c.,

No. 56. Asita and Buddha.[1]

No. 57. The young Siddârtha drawing the bow.[2]

but many of them have been ruined within the last few years by a native official at Ajaṇṭâ.

---

[1] From Mrs. Speir's *Life in An. Ind.*, p. 248. For the story see p. 257, and *Lalita Vistara;* also *Ind. Ant.*, vol. vii. p. 232 ff.; *Jour. As. S. Beng.*, vol. vii. p. 801; Beal's *Rom. Leg. of Buddha*, p. 56 ff.

[2] From Mrs. Speir, *u. s.* p. 279, and see p. 258, *Rom. Leg. of Buddha*, p. 88 ff.

Cave XVII.

The next is another fine Vihâra cave similar to the last (Plate XXXIII.), and apparently executed at no distant date from the other. Still there is so much difference in the architecture of these two caves, and so much progress shown in the style of painting, that some interval must have elapsed between the time when they were excavated. The form of the characters used in the long inscription on its verandah, when compared with the Vindhyaśakti inscription in Cave XVI., shows such an advance that, though it may safely be assumed that they were both excavated within the limits of the sixth century, there may be an interval of 50 years between the two.

Outside to the left, over a cistern and under an inscription, is a triple compartment of sculpture; in the centre Buddha squats under an ornamental arch or *toraṇa*, with *Vidyâdharas* above, and wheel, deer, and lions below. On each side is a Buddha standing on a lotus with worshippers below. At the right end opposite this several rows of squatting Buddhas have been sculptured on the rock, a piece of which has broken and fallen away, leaving a higher portion to slide down into its place.

The verandah has been supported by six plain octagonal columns with bracket capitals and neat bases resembling the Attic base, but without its lower torus. The hall is entered by a central door, resembling that in No. XVI., with a row of painted Buddhas over it, and by two side doors. It is further lighted by two windows. This apartment is 63¾ feet wide by 62 feet deep, and 13 feet high, its roof being supported by twenty octagonal pillars,—all plain, except the two in the middle of the front and back rows, which have square bases, shafts partly octagonal and partly sixteen sided and more ornamented.

The antechamber is small with two figures in front,—but the shrine is 17¾ feet wide by 20 deep, and in front of the great image there stands on the floor two figures, one holding the alms-bowl of the *Bhikshu*, the other damaged. There are also two attendants on each side of the Buddha and two *chaurî*-bearers.

Besides the two in the verandah, this cave contains sixteen cells. At the right end of the verandah there is a small hole in the floor into a fine cistern of water, the entrance to which is up a flight of steps between this cave and No. XVI.

There is an inscription at the left end of the verandah, outside, of about the same length as that on Cave XVI. Dr. Bhau Dâji's translation of it gives us the names of certain princes of Aśmâka,—

Dhritarashṭra;
Hari Samba, his son;
Kshitipala Sauri Samba, his son;
Upendragupta; and
Skacha, his son.

Of these we know nothing more; they may have been petty râjas of the sixth century.

This cave is sometimes called the Zodiac cave, from its containing at the left end of the verandah a circular piece of painting, divided into eight compartments by radii from the centre. This has been much injured by visitors attempting to remove parts from the wall.[1] The compartments have been filled with human figures, variously employed, and it may possibly have been a *saugata maṇḍala* or mystic circle representative of existence. In one a man is represented alone; in another he is accompanied by animals; in the next utensils are introduced; then buildings, streets, &c., with numerous men and women variously engaged. The rim of this circle is divided into sixteen compartments containing symbols, and is upheld by a pair of long green arms. To the left of it, on the return of the front wall, is painted a large yellow spotted snake bent in a semicircle with rocks on the outer side, and many figures on the other carrying various sorts of burdens.[2]

No. 58. Figures flying through the air.

---

[1] In 1828 Lieutenant Blake counted 73 figures in three divisions of this shield, varying from 5 to 7 inches in height, and apparently only about a third of it was then wanting; Dr. Bird is believed to have removed some of the figures from it, and a mere fragment now remains.

[2] Is this a representation of the *snake-like* stream hemmed in by *rocks*, with the

Below the great circle is a green râja-like figure labelled *Mânibhadra*, and to the left of it a painting of the Litany now much defaced. On the upper part of the back wall is a good deal of painting in fragments. To the right a group of three female and one male figure floating through the air accompanied by two swans (woodcut No. 58).[1] It is not easy to feel sure what this picture is meant to represent. It looks like three Apsarasas bearing or rather accompanying the soul of a deceased saint to heaven, or it may be merely a Gandharva accompanied by Apsarasas. Such flying figures are very usual, in pairs, in Buddhist sculptures of this age. Be this as it may, however, whether we look at its purity of outline, or the elegance of the grouping, it is one of the most pleasing of the smaller paintings at Ajaṇṭâ, and more nearly approaches the form of art found in Italy in the thirteenth and fourteenth centuries than any other example there. The easy upward motion of the whole group is rendered in a manner that could not easily be surpassed. Towards the right end of the verandah and partly on the end wall is the scene in which Devapatta tries to get Buddha destroyed by an enraged elephant, which however kneels at Buddha's feet (woodcut 59).[2]

No. 59. Buddha and the Elephant.

The ceiling of the verandah is still pretty entire, and was copied by the late Major Gill, his copy being at South Kensington.

This cave contains more remains of painting than any other,

Sangha bringing offerings to the Ajaṇṭâ Bhikshus? A sketch of it is given in my *Notes on Ajaṇṭâ Temples and Paintings*, Plate XVI.

1 From Mrs. Speir's *L. in An. Ind.* p. 370.

2 From the same, p. 290. This scene occurs also in the Amarâvati sculptures; Fergusson's *Tree and Serpent Worship*, 2nd ed., Plate LXXXII., Fig. 2. For the story see Bigandet's *Legend of Gaudama*, 2nd ed., p. 250; conf. *Vie de Hiouen Thsang*, p. 153; *Mém. sur les Cont. Occid.* t. ii. p. 16.

though even here much has been wilfully destroyed [1] since they became known to European visitors.

In the hall the paintings are tolerably entire, but so smoked and dirty that little or nothing can be seen over large areas. On the wall of the left aisle are two large and interesting scenes, whose story might be made out if we had only copies of them. On the left end of the back wall is a very large one. So much of which, as was transferred from Major Gill's copy, is given in the accompanying woodcut from Mrs. Speir's *Ancient India.*[2] In it a king is re-

No. 60. Wall painting in Cave No. XVII. Ajaṇṭâ, from Mrs. Speir's *Life in Ancient India.*

[1] Mr. Griffiths proposed years ago that doors and shutters should be employed to shut out bats and nest building insects from the few caves that contain much painting, but this excellent suggestion was only carried out in the case of Cave I. Were these caves anywhere else but in India they would be most carefully looked after.

[2] P. 313.

presented seated on his throne, with his usual female attendants behind him, and his prime minister seated on a low stool in front. A crowd in front of him are either lodging a complaint against one who seems to be brought up as a criminal, or it may only be bringing intelligence about a lion who appears to be the hero of the story. On the right of the palace court in which he is seated are the stables. On his left the office or court of justice in which a culprit is being beaten and led off to prison. Below this the king issues from the palace gate with a large sowari on a hunting expedition, accompanied by dogs and huntsmen. The centre of the picture, on the left, represents a forest in which a lion is seen licking the feet of a man who is asleep, and above as his companion. Above this the same lion is seen apparently worshipped by the villagers; but also as attacked by the same king and with the same party which, in the lower part of the picture, are seen issuing from the city gate. Whether this has any reference to the legend of Siṇha or Siha as narrated in the Mahawanso is not quite clear. It is there said that a king of Vanga, Eastern Bengal, had a daughter named Supradêvî, whose mother was a princess of Kalinga. She is said to have eloped with the chief of a caravan, but he and his party were attacked by a lion (*Siṅha*), who carried her off and hunted for her support. In course of time she bore a son, Siñhabâhu, and a daughter Siñhasîwalî. When these grew up they escaped with their mother, but the lion soon after began to ravage the country. The king offered a large reward to any one who would kill it, and Sîhabâhu, against the wishes of his mother, accepted the offer. When the lion saw him it only fawned upon him with delight, and he soon destroyed his putative father.[1]

If this picture has any connexion with this legend it must refer to some earlier passage in the life of Siṇha, not to the abduction of the princess nor to his tragic end. The legend is a favourite one with the Buddhists, as the son of this Sîhabaha was Vijaya who afterwards conquered Ceylon, and gave it the name of Sîhalâ from his lion ancestors. Whether this identification can or cannot be maintained there is little doubt that most of the other pictures in this cave do

[1] *Mahâvânso*, pp. 44–46, and conf. introd. p. lxxxvi. The details vary in different accounts; conf. Stan. Julien, *Vie de Hiouen Thsang*, pp. 194–198; *Mém. sur les Cont. Occid.* t. ii., pp. 125–130: Laidlay's *Fa Hian*, pp. 336–338; Beal's *Travels of Bud. Pilg.*, p. 149; Mrs. Speir, p. 300.

refer to the conquest of Ceylon by Vijaya. The lion licking the feet of a man apparently asleep occurs elsewhere also among the paintings.

To the right of this picture is another in which about a dozen soldiers are attacking a tall crowned râja who is coming out of his palace, and represented in the act of throwing a javelin at his enemies, of whom two lie slain.

In the left end of the antechamber is a fine scene in which a great assembly or *sangha* of râjas and their attendants, among whom are several in Persian dress, attend Buddha on his right hand, while on his left are his beloved Bhikshus.

On the wall of the right aisle were some scenes in which Râkshasîs—female demons with tusks and long dishevelled hair—are represented devouring their human victims, attacked by men, or

No. 61. Landing of Vijaya in Ceylon and his coronation, from Cave XVII.

otherwise employed. And below is an animated scene, which almost certainly represents the landing of Vijaya in Ceylon,[1] and the

[1] Mrs. Speir's *Ancient Life in India*, p. 303.

conquest of its Râkshasî inhabitants.[1] Fortunately a very reduced copy of this scene has been preserved in the accompanying woodcut, No. 61. It is rapidly being destroyed by the native official who has done so much mischief also in Cave XVI. The march, the landing on elephants and horses from boats, with the struggle on the shore, and the *abhishekha* or anointing of the king, are vividly portrayed.

Though on too small a scale to do justice to them, the two last woodcuts (Nos. 60 and 61) are probably sufficient to convey an idea of the mode in which historical subjects are treated in these caves. The grade of art and the mode of treatment is very similar to that shown in the nearly contemporary hunting scenes at Takt-i-Bostan in Persia.[2] As nearly at least as sculpture, which is there employed by Chosroes, can be compared with painting, which is the mode of representation here adopted. Neither can be said to be the highest class of art, but they are wonderfully graphic, and tell their story with a distinctness not often found in works of a higher order of design.

In the front aisle Indra appears as an aged mendicant before Śibi Râja and his queen, begging for an eye. Here we are at no loss, for Śibi and Indra appear twice over, with their names written on them.[3] Besides these there are many interesting scenes depicted on the walls of this fine cave.

Cave XVIII. is merely a porch, 19 feet 4 inches by 8 feet 10 inches, with two pillars, apparently intended as a passage into the next cave.

Cave XIX.—This is the third of the Chaitya caves, and differs only in its details from Nos. IX. and X. As will be seen from the plan, Plate XXXVII., fig. 1, it is 24 feet wide by 46 feet long and

---

[1] According to the legends Vijaya Siñhalâ went to the island of Ceylon with a large following; the Râkshasîs inhabiting it captivated them by their charms, but Siñhalâ warned in a dream escaped on a wonderful horse. He collected an army, gave each soldier a magic *mantra*, and returned. Falling upon the Râkshasîs with great impetuosity, he totally routed them, some fleeing the island, and others being drowned in the sea. He destroyed their town and established himself as king in the island, he gave it the name of Siñhalâ. Conf. Stan. Julien, *Mem. sur les Cont. Occid.*, t. ii. pp. 131–139; Laidlay's *Fa Hian*, note by Landresse, p. 338; Mrs. Speir, p. 301.

[2] Ker Porter, *Travels in Persia*, vol. ii. p. 64.

[3] This *Jâtaka* is also represented in the Amarâvati sculptures, *Tree and Serp. Worship*, pp. 194, 225, and Plate LXXXIII., Fig. 1, and see above, p. 285.

24 feet 4 inches high. But whereas the former two were perfectly plain, this is elaborately carved throughout. Besides the two in front, the nave has 15 columns 11 feet high. These pillars are square at the base, which is 2 feet 7 inches high with small figures on the corners; then they have an octagonal belt about a foot broad, above which the shaft is circular, and has two belts of elaborate tracery, the intervals being in some cases plain and in others fluted with perpendicular or spiral flutes (*see* Plate XXXVIII., fig. 2); above the shaft is a deep torus of slight projection between two fillets, wrought with a leaf pattern, and over this again is a square tile, supporting a bracket capital, richly sculptured with a Buddha in the centre and elephants or śârdûlas with two riders or flying figures, on the brackets. The architrave consists of two plain narrow fascias. The whole entablature is 5 feet deep, and the frieze occupying exactly the same position as a triforium would in a Christian church, is divided into compartments by rich bands of arabesque, and in the compartments are figures of Buddha—alternately sitting cross-legged and standing (Plate XXXVI.) The dome rises 8 feet 4 inches, whilst the width of the nave is only 12 feet 2 inches, so that the arch is higher than a semicircle, and is ribbed in stone. Between the feet of every fourth and fifth rib is carved a tiger's head.

The *Chaitya* or *dâgoba* is a composite one; it has a low pedestal, on the front of which stand two demi-columns, supporting an arch containing a *basso-rilievo* figure of Buddha. On the under part of the capital above the dome there is also a small sculpture of Buddha, and over the *chûḍamaṇi*, or four fillets of the capital, are three umbrellas in stone, one above another, each upheld on four sides by small figures. These may be symbolic of Buddha—"the bearer of the triple canopy—the canopy of the heavenly host, the canopy of mortals, and the canopy of eternal emancipation," or they are typical of the *bhuvanas* or heavens of the celestial Bôdhisattwas and Buddhas.

The roof of the aisles is flat and has been painted, chiefly with ornamental flower scrolls, Buddhas, and *Chaityas*, and on the walls there have been paintings of Buddha—generally with attendants, the upper two rows sitting, and in the third mostly standing, but all with aureoles behind the heads.

There is but one entrance to this cave. The whole is in excellent preservation, as is also the façade and the lower part, the accumulated materials that had fallen from above have now been removed, and display entire what must be considered one of the most perfect specimens of Buddhist art in India. Over the whole façade of this Chaitya temple projects a bold and carefully carved cornice,—broken only at the left end by a heavy mass of rock having given way. In front has been an enclosed court, 33 feet wide by 30 feet deep, but the left side of it has nearly disappeared. The porch and whole front of the cave is covered with the most elaborate and beautiful carving, which it is impossible to describe.

There is no inscription on this cave by which its date could be ascertained, but from its position and its style of architecture there can be little doubt that it is of about the same age as the two Vihâras, XVI. and XVII., which are next to it, and consequently it may safely be assumed that it was excavated near the middle of the sixth century—a few years before or after 550 A.D.

Beside the beauty and richness of the details, it is interesting as the first example we meet with of a Chaitya cave wholly in stone. Not only are the ribs of the nave and the umbrella over the Dâgoba, but all the ornaments of the façade are in stone. Nothing in or about it is or ever was in wood, and many parts are so lithic in design that if we did not know to the contrary, we might not be able to detect at once the originals from which they were derived. The transformation from wood to stone is complete in this cave, and in the next one we meet. The Viswa Karma at Elura the wooden type is still further left behind.

Outside to the left, and at right angles to the façade of the cave, is a sculpture representing a Nâga râja and his wife (Plate XXXIX.). He with a seven-headed cobra hood. She with one serpent's head behind her. At Sanchi in the first century when the Naga kings first appear the serpent has only five heads,[1] but the females there are still with only one. At Amrâvati the heads of the serpent were multiplied to 21,[2] and in modern times to 100 or 1000. Who these Nâga people were has not yet been settled satisfactorily. They occur frequently on the doorways and among the paintings at Ajaṇṭâ, and generally wherever we find Buddhism there we are sure

---

[1] *Tree and Serpent Worship*, Plate XXIV.

[2] *Loc. cit.*, LXXVI.

to find Nagâs when looked for. They were also adopted by the Jainas and Vaishnaves, but their origin is certainly Buddhist, and they must represent some class of the Dasya people who, as mentioned above, were those who first adopted Buddhism. Whether the Nâga tribes in Sylhet and Asan have any affinity with them beyond the name is not clear. They certainly belong to the same race, and their locality is favourable to the idea that they had some connexion with the serpent worshipping races in Cambodia,[1] but no reverence for serpents has been traced among their religious observances.[2]

On the other side opposite this image of the Nâga Râja is a porch, with two pilasters in front, which probably was a *châwaṛi* or place of rest for pilgrims. It has a room at each end, about 10 feet by 8 feet 4 inches. The capitals of the pillars in front of it are richly wrought with mango branches and clusters of grapes in the middle of each.

On each side the great arch is a large male figure in rich headdress, that on the left holds a bag, and is Kubêra, the god of wealth, a favourite with the Buddhists. The corresponding figure on the right is nearly the same, and many figures of Buddha sitting or standing occupy compartments in the façade, and at the sides of it.

Cave XX. is a small Vihâra with two pillars and two pilasters in front of its verandah. One pillar is broken, but on each side of the capitals there is a pretty bracket statuette of a female under a canopy of foliage. The roof of the verandah is hewn in imitation of beams and rafters. There is a cell at each end of the verandah and two on each side of the hall, which is 28 feet 2 inches wide by 25 feet 4 inches deep and 12½ feet high, and has no columns. The roof is supported only by the walls and the front of the antechamber, which advances 7 feet into the cave, and has in front two columns in antis, surmounted by a carved entablature filled with seven figures of Buddha and attendants. The statue in the shrine has probably been painted red, and is attended by two large figures of Indras,

---

[1] *Loc. cit.* p. 50. *Indian and Eastern Architecture*, p. 664 *et seqq.*

[2] It is to be regretted that no one has yet read my work on *Tree and Serpent Worship*, who was capable of carrying the subject further, and of expressing an opinion regarding it. No one, at least, has done so yet. These many headed serpents occur so frequently, and in such prominent positions, that their classification would certainly result in important mythological and ethnological discoveries.—J. F.

with great tiaras, bearing *chauris* and some round object in the left hand, while on the front of the seat, which has no lions at the corners, are carved two deer as *vâhana*, with a *chakra* or wheel between them. The painting in this cave has now almost entirely disappeared.

The probability is that this cave should not be considered so much as a Vihâra or a Dharmaśâlâ as the vestry hall or chapter house of the group. If this is so these four caves, XVI. to XX., form the most complete Buddhist establishment to be found among the Western caves. Two Vihâras, one Chaitya, and one place of assembly. Hitherto it has generally been supposed that the halls of the Vihâras formed the place of meeting for the monks, and so that probably it did, each for their convent, but it seems probable that besides this there was a general hall of meeting attached to each group, and that this was one of them.

CHAPTER II.

LATEST CAVES AT AJANTA.

The third group of twelve caves, into which the Ajaṇṭâ excavations naturally divide themselves, is the largest; consisting of the first five caves from the western end and the last seven at the other extremity. In some respects also it is the most magnificent. Caves I. and IV. being the largest Vihâras here, and also the most elaborately ornamented, and XXVI. the richest, though not the largest of the Chaityas. They have not, however, the same beauty of design and detail which characterises the central group, and show evident symptoms that the art was tending towards decay.

There are no inscriptions from which their age can be ascertained with precision, but their architectural details and other indications are sufficient to enable us to feel confident that nearly the whole of them belong to the seventh century, as those of the central group belong certainly to the sixth. Some of them it is true may have been commenced in the sixth, but none were finished before the following century, and the works, some of them, such as those from XXII. to XXIV., which are unfinished, were probably continued till nearly the end of it. They certainly were not abandoned before 650, and may have been continued 20 or 30 years after that time.

Cave I. is one of the finest Vihâras of its kind. Certainly no Vihâra at Ajaṇṭâ has been so handsomely ornamented as this one. Its façade is the only instance here of a Vihâra decorated with sculpture. In front of the verandah there has been a porch (Plate XL.), supported by two advanced columns, of which only fragments of the bases and elegant capitals remain; at each end, outside the verandah, there is a room whose open front is supported by two pillars, the floors being raised a few steps in order that the elaborate entablature of the façade might be carried round the whole front at the same level. The room on the east opens into another nearly 13½ feet square, and all but perfectly dark; that on the left opens into two others somewhat smaller. In the verandah are six columns and two pilasters (Plate XLI.) The pair in the middle, which originally formed part of the porch, like all the others, have square bases and elaborately carved bracket capitals. Above the bases they are first octagonal, then there is a belt of 16 faces, above which they are fluted with bands of beautifully elaborate tracery up to the thick compressed cushion between two fillets, on which rests the carved fascia under the capital. The next pillars on either side are similarly rich in carving, but have narrower bands of tracery round the upper portion of the fluting, and their flutes are spiral. Outside these are two octagonal pillars with three bands of tracery round them, supporting a very deep square carved fascia under the bracket capital. The pilasters beyond these have short fluted necks with tracery above and below them, more like what we should work in metal than attempt in stone. The central compartment in each capital has its own group of human figures.

The architrave all along the front is sculptured; (Plate XLI.) above each column there is a compartment containing human figures only; at the corners are terminal figures apparently intended for lions or *śârdûlas;* and the remaining spaces are filled principally with elephants in every variety of attitude, and cut with great spirit and correctness.

The part over the front of the porch has been mostly destroyed when the pillars gave way, but from a fragment that remains, the lower frieze or architrave seems to have been filled with groups of figures, possibly scenes from the life of Buddha. The left side is carved with elephants fighting, and with the figure of a rider on a *śârdûla* at the corners. Continuing the same member along the façade to the left, after the usual corner *śârdûla*, we have representations of two figures beating drums and one playing on some sort of flute followed by others with Nepalese swords, oblong shields, three figures on horseback, one blowing a long trumpet, then three elephants and another horse with their riders. The next to the left is an in-door scene, a râja and his wife in earnest converse with three attendants. Outside, a saddled horse is being led out towards a tree, and to the left is a little figure carrying a bag on his back towards two figures sitting and talking under foliage with birds in it. Beyond these a male elephant stands facing a man sitting at the foot of a tree with a stick in his hand. Then comes another in-door scene, in which the wife has her arms round her husband's neck and two female household servants (*dâsîs*) stand by. Outside are four elephants, the first butting against a tree, the next, a young one, following its dam, who is pinning a tiger to the ground; the fourth is behind, and has apparently turned tail. Then come two buffaloes fighting, a man behind each urging it on. To the left are other two human figures in front of the corner *śârdûla.*

This band is continued across the front of the left side chapel. To the left of the *śârdûla* are four figures, a woman, a man with a stick or sword, another with a shield, and a figure sitting on the ground. Towards these comes Buddha in his chariot with two horses and the driver. Next is a royal figure seated on a seat in a garden under a tree, while a woman plays on a musical instrument to him, and another waits on him behind. A palm tree separates this from the next scene, in which Buddha is driving to the left, and passing a plantain tree, meets an aged man with a staff. Behind him is Buddha in his car again, and just before some men carrying a dead body and a woman wailing by it. The rock is here broken, but to the left we have a royal figure seated again on an *âsana* with attendants, and a horse looking at him; beyond is a man walking out, and, after another defaced piece, a horse with an attendant beside it. This sculpture then represents the so-called predictive signs[1] which led to Siddhârtha, afterwards the Buddha, becoming an ascetic, and his escape.

On the right side of the porch, the sculpture is a representation of a hunt of the wild ox, spiritedly carved. On the front of the façade, to the right of it, is another hunting scene, perhaps of deer; the first horseman on the left is spearing one, and by the side of the next runs a dog or cheetah. Behind are three elephants with riders, followed by a fat ill-proportioned figure, bearing some load at the ends of a pole over his shoulder. In the next compartment is a domestic scene, a stout squatting figure with a cup in his hand, caressed by his wife, behind whom stands a servant with a flagon.

To the right of this is an out-door scene, first an elephant, before whom a man sits as if feeding it or addressing it, while beyond him another stands with a staff in his left hand. A woman proceeds to the right with a vessel on her left hand towards a man who squats under a tree addressing another woman, who kneels before him in an attitude of supplication. Behind her is a dwarf with a bag on

[1] Beal's *Rom. Leg. of S. Buddha*, pp. 117 ff.

his back, and beside it a man leading a saddled horse, behind which stands another man holding an umbrella, probably the attendants of the kneeling woman. Another small compartment to the right of this represents a râja and his wife seated together attended by two female servants. The next contains six wild elephants, the first two fighting and the next dragging a huge snake in his trunk; then a *śârdûla* terminates the front.

Over the right side chapel the continuation begins as usual with the *śârdûla*, in front of a group of cattle, behind which are two figures seated, and beyond them is seen the head of a bearded old man. Then, under trees, are two more men with beards and their hair done up in the *jaṭâ* style of devotees; behind them a third head is seen. One has a bottle, and beside the other the same vessel is hung in the tripod stand represented in front of the dying Buddha in Cave XXVI. (Plate L.), and elsewhere. Another bearded ascetic is leaving these, with something like a club in his right hand and a bent rod over his left shoulder. He is meeting a man who appears to address him, but to the right is another with an uplifted sword as if about to strike this last. To the right is a plantain tree and a saddled horse led by a man. The second compartment is a small interior scene in which a man sits listening to a lady attended by two female servants. The last compartment is broken, but began with a kneeling figure offering some present to a portly man seated.

Above the entablature is a projecting band, carved with representations of the Chaitya window, each containing a human head; then comes a frieze, ornamented with compartments, containing human pairs in different attitudes, attended by female servants. These are separated by spaces filled with figures of the sacred goose (*hanśa*), in varieties of position, with the wings extended into elaborate floriated tracery so as to fill the spaces, a device well known in works of about the sixth century in Northern India and in Singhalese art; and on the Buddhist carvings of Ceylon we find the elephant and the *hanśa* constantly occurring, whilst the latter also figures on the standard of Burma. Above this frieze is a line of tigers' heads, then a dentilated fillet, then another with a line of string tracery, surmounted by a belt, containing human heads within miniatures of the Chaitya window, each with the hair represented as if a sort of heavy wig. The specimen given in Plate XLI., being the left-half of the façade, will illustrate the style of these sculptures.

The wings of the brackets of the columns are ornamented with *gandharvas* and *apasarasas*, the central panels with figures of Buddha and his worshippers; but on the sixth pillar it is apparently a version of the temptation of Mâra. On his left are two females. On his right, a man is shooting at him with a bow, another above, in a peaked cap, is in the attitude of throwing a stone at him.

The verandah is about 64 feet long by 9¼ wide and 13½ high, and has a chamber at each end (*see* Plate XL.), A wide door in the centre, with elaborately carved jambs and entablature, leads into the great hall, and there are smaller doors near each end and two windows. The great hall, or *śâlâ*, is nearly 64 feet square, and its roof is supported by a colonnade of 20 pillars, leaving aisles of about 9½ feet wide all round. The columns are about 5½ feet apart; but the middle ones on each side of the square are 6¼ feet asunder. Their bases are about 2¾ feet square, and with the four pilasters in continuation of the front and back row are mostly very richly carved.

The front of the brackets in the first row of columns in the hall and the inner sides of all the rest are sculptured; the inner side of the front row and those that face the side and back aisles have been painted with similar figures.

The sculptures on the other sides of these brackets are of some interest. The wings of the brackets are very much alike: of those facing the front aisle, the two central and two corner pillars have *śârdûlas* or horned lions with riders; the other two pillars have elephants with two riders on each of those that face the inner area of the hall; the two central ones on each side have an *apsarasa* and *gandharva;* and the others a human figure coming out of the mouth of a *makara*, except that the first column on the left side has two fat figures on each wing, and the fourth *Vidyâdharas*. The central panels are more varied. In the two middle pillars in the front row are figures worshipping a *dâgoba;* in the pair outside these is a small fat figure (in one case carrying a load) under an arch (*toraṇa*) thrown over him between the mouths of two *makaras;* in the corner pair is Buddha seated in the usual fashion between two *chauri*-bearers; in the middle area of the hall the two central columns on the right hand have, in this position, four deer so arranged that one head serves for any of the four (Plate XXXVIII., fig. 3), a curious conceit which seems to have been in favour with the early Hindu sculptors, as we find similar combinations elsewhere; the panels of the brackets on each side these have elephants fighting. The left central pillar on the left hand has a râja, his wife and child, diwân, two *châmara* bearers and an attendant, perhaps Suddhodana and Mahâprajâpti with the infant Buddha; and on the right hand one, two râjas seated, with attendants, much as in the two chapels of Cave II. The first pillar in the left row has an eight-armed fat dwarf attended by two others, one of them probably a Nâga figure; in the fourth, two Nâga râjas are worshipping the *dâgoba* (Plate XLII., fig. 2). In the back row, the two central columns have Nâga figures with their *Nâgakanyâs*, worshipping richly decorated dâgobas; on the first pillar, to the left hand, are two half human figures with a lotus flower between them, and on the fourth, two deer with the wheel between them—the usual *chinha* or cognizance of Buddha.

The most elaborate description would convey but a faint idea of the rich tracery and sculpture on the shafts of the back row of pillars; above the base they are ornamented by mythological *makaras* or dragons; the upper part of the shaft is encircled by a deep belt of the most elaborate tracery, in which are wrought medallions containing human figures; the fascia above is supported at the corners by dwarfs.[1] Again on the left side, on the corners of the bases, we find the *makara* and dwarf together, and on eight facets round the upper part of the columns are pairs of rampant antelopes, bridled by garlands held in the mouths of grinning faces between each pair. The corner pillars have three brackets each. On each side of the cave there are five cells or *gṛihas* for the monks, and in the back four, two on each side of the shrine.

In the middle of the back wall are two pillars with brackets of human figures, and between these we pass into an antechamber, about 10 feet by 9, leading into a shrine, about 20 feet square, in which is a colossal statue of Buddha, with a figure of Indra at each side as his supporters, wearing rich headdresses (*mukuṭas*), and their hair in curls. That on Buddha's left has the *vajra*, or thunderbolt, in his left hand. The wheel in front of the throne is set edgewise, as with the Jainas, between two deer, with three worshippers on Buddha's left and five on his right, behind the deer. The shrine door (Plate XLII., fig. 1) is one of the most elaborate

[1] One of these pillars is represented, Plate XLII., fig. 2.

in these caves. At the bottom on each side is a dwârpâla, with a five-headed snake hood, above which are four compartments, with a male and female figure in each, and beyond and outside these two female figures standing on the head of pillars representing—it is generally understood—the rivers Ganges and Jumna. The figure so sculptured is of considerable elegance, but is surpassed as in these later caves, by the sculptured foliage with which it is interwoven, which is here of great beauty.

The whole of this cave has been painted, though near the floor it has entirely disappeared. Within the last fourteen years much of the painting in all the caves has either fallen off or been wantonly defaced; yet there are some as interesting fragments in this as in any other cave, and most of what does remain has been copied by Major Gill and Mr. Griffiths. The ceiling of it has been copied in about a hundred separate panels.[1] Mr. Griffiths thus describes it:— "Having divided the ceiling into a number of panels, with a circle for variety in the central division, we find these panels filled with ornaments of such variety and beauty, where we have naturalism and conventionalism so harmoniously combined as to call forth our highest admiration. For delicate colouring, variety in design, flow of line, and filling of space, I think they are unequalled. Although every panel has been thought out, and not a touch in one carelessly given, yet the whole work bears the impression of having been done with the greatest ease and freedom, not only freedom of execution, but also freedom of thought, as a reference to the copies made will testify.

"The ornament in the smaller squares is painted alternately on a black and red ground. The ground colour was first laid in, and then the ornament was painted solidly over this in white. It was further developed by thin, transparent colours over the white.

"In order fully to appreciate the copies of the paintings, it is necessary to bear in mind that the originals were designed and painted to occupy certain fixed positions and were seen in a subdued light. Many of the copies of the panels, on close inspection, appear coarse and unfinished; but seen at their proper distance (never less than 7 feet from the spectator) apparent coarseness assumes a delicate gradation."

On three of the panels of this ceiling a striking group of figures

[1] These are now at the India Museum.

recurs:[1] This is a Persian figure apparently of a king attended by his queen and servants. Râjendralâl Mitra has called attention to these panels,[2] but describes them as Baktrian figures. Mr. Fergusson more correctly identified them as Iranian, and, taking them in connexion with the reception of an embassy painted on the front wall, supposes that they represent Khosru Parwiz and his queen the fair Shirín.[3] (Plate XLIV., fig. 1.) The reception of an embassy on the front wall is evidently of a later date than those on the other walls, or by a different artist, but the ceiling may be of the same date with it. It represents a pale-skinned râja seated in Darbâr on a cushion placed on a dais, higher than usual, with a semicircular canopy of green over the middle of the back of it, just behind his head, and having a gilt border with little *vidyâdhara* figures on each side of it, and *makara's* mouths at the corners of the back. From the right three fair, bearded men, in Iranian costume, with peaked caps and completely clothed, approach him in crouching attitude; the first bearing a string of pearls,[4] the second a jug or bottle (of wine perhaps), and the third a large tray filled with presents. Behind the third stands another figure near the door in white clothing, perhaps the porter, with a stick in his hand and a dagger in his belt, apparently speaking to another Iranian in the doorway, also bringing in some present. Behind the porter is another foreigner in full white clothing, with stockings, curled hair, and peaked cap, holding a vessel in his hands, and with a long straight sword at his back.

Behind the throne stands an attendant and a female with *châmara;* to the right of her a reddish fair figure in blue clothes; and beside him one still fairer with a rich headdress and striped loin-cloth holding a green stick. In front of him again is a stool, broad at the upper and lower ends (*bhadrâsana*); and to the right are a red and a fair man—the latter with his arms crossed on his breast and wearing a red turban. In front of this last is a reddish skinned man, his left hand on his knee, while he bends forward and holds up the fingers of the right hand as if addressing some information to the

---

[1] It was probably repeated again in the centre of the fourth quarter, but it has almost entirely fallen off.

[2] *Jour. A. Soc. Beng.*, vol. xlvii. (1878), pp. 68–72.

[3] See *Jour. R. As. Soc.*, vol. xi. pp. 155–170.

[4] And some object in his left hand supposed to be a letter.

râja: probably he is the interpreter. Beyond him, to the right, are other two figures, one having in his hand a dish, perhaps with fruit, and a spear with a small flag attached to it.

In front of the three Iranians sit three royally dressed figures, perhaps members of the royal family (*Râja kumâras*), the reddish one in the centre, possibly the Yuvarâja. To the left of them is a man with a basket, and in front of the throne a woman sits with a *châmara*, and beside her is an elegantly chased spittoon.

On the left (at the proper right side of the throne) sits another lady with richhead dress, a "breast-band," a basket beside her, and some object in her lap. Behind her is a short female or dwarf, of red complexion, with blue earring, and not so richly dressed. Behind these two again is a third richly dressed young woman with breast-band also, and looking towards the râja. Above is a fourth with a *châmara*, while a fifth face looks over the back of the throne on the râja's right.

Outside the palace, to the right, an Iranian, like the one seen in the door, appears speaking to a green man with a stick in his hand. Behind are several horses, and in front of them a *sipâhi* or soldier, with a sword. A portion to the left of this interesting memento of some embassy from Persia, probably in the seventh century, is completely destroyed.[1]

On the left end of the antechamber is the representation of Buddha beset by the emissaries of *Mâra*, a favourite subject with the Buddhists.

This picture when complete occupied the whole left wall of the antechamber to the sanctuary, 12 feet 9 by 8 feet 4½; but a portion has been entirely destroyed, *i.e.*, 1 foot from the top and 3 feet 5 inches from the bottom.[2] Even as it is, however, it forms one of

---

[1] Mr. Fergusson ingeniously points out that Khośru Parwiz, the Chosroes II. of the Greek writers, who reigned 591–628 A.D., was not only contemporary with Pulikeśi (A.D. 609–640), the king of Mahârâshṭra, but appears from Tabari to have had relations with him; Zotenberg's *Tabari*, t. ii. pp. 328 ff. In the Arabic version of Tabari there is even a letter from Pulikeśi to Shiruyieh, the son of Khosru.—*J.R.A.S.* (N.S.), vol. xi. pp. 165, 166.—J.B.

[2] This is marked "X" among Mr. Griffith's copies made in 1875–76, and now at South Kensington, and a photograph from his copy forms Plate II. of Babu Rajendralalâs work on Buddha Gaya. For a detailed account of the attack of Mâra, see Beal's *Rom. Leg. of S. Buddha*, pp. 205–224; Bigandet's *Gaudama* (2d ed.), pp. 80 ff.; and S. Hardy's *Manual of Buddhism.*

the most complete and graphic representations of that celebrated episode in Buddha's life that is known to exist anywhere. The scene is, however, so varied and so strange that it is impossible to convey any correct idea of its appearance by mere words, and it is of the less importance to attempt this here, as a bas-relief of the same subject, with only a little less detail, is found in Cave XXVI., and represented in Plate LI., so as to convey a fair notion of the strange accompaniments with which the Buddhists in the seventh century had invested the legend.

On each side of the shrine door are fragments of figures of Indra and his consort Sachî, with attendants. The right hand wall of the antechamber is covered with numerous painted Buddhas, with the *bhâmaṇḍala* or aureole round their heads, mostly seated, but some standing on lotus flowers, the leaves and stalks filling all the vacant spaces. Mr. Griffiths remarks that "the delicate foliage which fills in the spaces between the figures will give some idea of the power of these old artists as designers, and also of their knowledge of the growth of plants."

Between the front of the antechamber and the first cell-door to the right, is a scene in a mountain[1] represented in the usual conventional style. In the centre is a colossal figure of a râja with richly jewelled *mukuṭa* or crown, holding a flower in his right hand and leaning his left on the shoulder of an attendant, whose left hand passes through a black leather strap which comes over his shoulder and supports a long straight sword at his back, the ends of the strap being fastened by a buckle. This man has a chain about his neck. Behind him is a tall female figure, perhaps a *châmara*-bearer, and above to the right is part of a sitting figure with his legs crossed.

At the râja's right side is—perhaps the Yuvarâja, or heir-apparent (distinguishable by his crown), bringing forward and offering a trayful of flowers. Between the râja and him, a bald-head is thrust forward from behind—perhaps that of a eunuch (*kanchuki*), who is richly dressed, and rests his chin upon his right hand. In front of him, and to the left, are two ladies in the dress of *râṇîs*, with coronets on their heads, leaving the presence, one with a tray of flowers, looking wistfully back.

To the right of this and over the two cell doors is a large indoor

---

1 Mr. Griffiths' copy of this is in the India Museum at South Kensington.

scene in which a snake charmer is exhibiting a large cobra before a râja and his court.

Below this, and between the cell-doors in this wall, is another very interesting and animated indoor scene (see Plate XLIII.)[1] The two prominent figures in it are a Nâga Râja, on the left with the five-hooded snake overshadowing his head, and on the right another royal personage, seated on a large draped couch, talking interestedly. The Nâga Râja seems to be speaking, and to the left is a female with *châmara.* Her hair and that of the two principal figures are all bound with fillets. Behind the Nâga King is a dark red attendant with a straight sword, the richly-jewelled hilt held up, and then a female holding a chased casket in her left hand and a jewel with a string of pearls depending from it in her right. She has a serpent at the back of her head, and may therefore be considered of the same race and rank as the seated figure, probably his wife. Next to her, and behind the second speaker, is a man with blue and flowered gold robe, and an Iranian headdress, also holding a sword with a blue hilt. To the left of the Nâga Râja sits a female in blue and white striped kirtle, the face turned up and the left hand stretched forward as if speaking or calling attention to something she had to say. She, too, has a serpent at the back of her head. Behind the other râja one female is handing a tray with flowers in it to another, and in front of the second a third brings in another flat vessel covered with flowers and leans forward as if listening. Behind this last stands an old man, very fair skinned, with wrinkled brow, and white hair. In front, on the left, are two ladies seated and listening with interest. Most of the females in this picture have their hair hanging in ringlets.

Outside the doorway, to the left, a râja is departing with high *mukuṭa* on his head and the *chhatra* or state umbrella borne over him, and with him is another figure with a large five-hooded snake canopy (*pañcha-phaṇa nâga chhatra*) over his head. Beyond them are two elephants, one with a rider holding an *ankuśa* or driving hook in his hand.

"Parts of this picture," Mr. Griffiths remarks, "are admirably executed. In addition to the natural grace and ease with which she is standing, the drawing of the woman holding a casket in one hand

[1] This is the picture of which Mr. Griffiths' copy is indicated by the letter "N."

and a jewel with a string of pearls from it in the other, is most delicately and truly rendered. The same applies to the woman seated on the ground in the left-hand corner. The upward gaze and sweet expression of the mouth are beautifully given. The left hand of the same woman, which, by the way, I did not discover until I had been at work for some weeks, is drawn with great subtlety and tenderness."

To the right of the second cell-door is a picture that seems to be related to the last.[1] The dresses are very nearly, if not quite the same, and some of the figures seem to be identical. It is also a palace scene, in which four of the seven figures left have the snake hood over their heads, three females, each having one serpent, and another one with five heads. Their hair falls down in ringlets, held back in some cases by a fillet. On the left is the Nâga Râja, and beside him sits another without the snake-hoods, but over his head a bearer behind holds the *chhatra.* A Nâga figure, with a single hood and loose hair, stands a little behind and seems to be receiving a long straight sword of state from a female still more to the right and also with a Nâga hood and long ringlets, who holds it up by the scabbard, whilst apparently speaking to the others. Before, and either kneeling or sitting, is a lady of rank, looking importuningly at the face of the râja. Behind her is still another *Nâgakanyâ*, and in front of her is a portion of one more. "The porch behind," as Mr. Griffiths remarks, "with the partly open door, is a very fair piece of perspective."

These Nâga paintings are of especial interest here, as they are the only representations we have of that interesting people in colour. In stone they abound at Bharhut, Sanchi, and Amrâvati. They occur everywhere in Ceylon, and still more so in Cambodia. They are found at Kârlê, and in all the later sculptures in the western caves; in fact wherever Buddhism exists in India or the neighbouring country. It is only, however, from these paintings that we learn that in feature, in colour, and in dress they do not differ from the other races with whom they are mingled. Whoever they were we gather not only from their sculptures and paintings, but from all Buddhist tradition that they were the most important of all the races that adopted that religion. If consequently their origin and affini-

---

[1] Mr. Griffiths' copy of this is designated by "Q." *Report*, 1874–75.

ties could only be ascertained it would probably throw more light on the peculiarities of that religion than can be obtained from any other source that now remains open to us. Only one attempt[1] has yet been made to investigate this question, and that being manifestly not sufficient it is hoped it may soon be taken up by those who are competent to the task.

The painting on the right wall is so destroyed by holes made in it by bats as almost to defy description.

Above, between the second and third cell-doors, and cut off from the next portion by a white gateway is a large scene much destroyed. Above are eight elephants. In front have been numerous soldiers, one on horseback, one green-skinned,[2] dressed in striped *dhótis* and armed with the long crooked Nepalese swords. Three figures have deep collars round their necks, and all advance towards the left after some elephants without any housings. Other scenes may also be more or less distinctly made out.

Cave II.

Cave II. is another Vihâra, similar but smaller than the preceding, and somewhat different in the style of its front columns. The verandah (Plate XLIV., fig. 2), is $46\frac{1}{4}$ feet in length, supported in front by four pillars and two pilasters, all of the same style, having a torus and fillet at the base, but no plinth; to about a fourth up they have 16 sides, above that they have 32 flutes with belts of elaborate tracery. The capitals are flower-shaped, along which the flutes of the column are continued as petals: first there is a deep calyx, widest near the bottom and terminating in a double row of petals; then, above a very small fillet, is a thick projecting torus, surmounted by a bell-shaped flower of about the same depth as the torus, and on this rests a thin abacus. Over them runs a plain architrave on which the roof rests, and beyond which it projects very considerably, with indications of the patterns in which the under side of it was once painted.[3] At each end of the verandah are chambers similar to those in Cave I. (*see* plan, Plate XLIV.),—the architrave above the pillars

---

[1] *Tree and Serpent Worship*, quarto, London, 1873.

[2] Can it be that these green people are intended to represent the lower castes?

[3] A view of this verandah forms Plate IX. of my picturesque illustrations of the *Rock-cut Temples of India*, folio, London, 1845.—J. F.

in front of them being filled with carving. In the central compartment of the façade of the chapel, in the right end of the verandah, is a Nâga Râja and attendants. In that on the left end is a female and child. The side compartments in both are occupied by fat male figures. Each chapel opens into an inner cell. At the left end of the façade in a niche, is Buddha squatting in the *dharmachakra mudrâ*, and over each shoulder is a smaller one. The cave has two windows, and a fine central door with an elaborate architrave, at the bottom of which are *dwârpâlas* with five hooded snake-canopies, each apparently holding a flower; above this, the compartments on each side are filled with pairs of standing figures, male and female, in varied attitudes; above the door the figures are sitting ones, with a single fat one in the centre compartment. Outside the architrave are three members of florid tracery, then a pilaster, similar in style to the columns, and surmounted by a female figure standing under the foliage of a tree and leaning on a dwarf. (Plate XLV., fig. 2.) Over the upper architrave is a line of prostrate figures with what resembles a crown in the centre.

The hall inside is 47 feet 7 inches wide, by 48 feet 4 inches deep, and is supported by twelve pillars, similar to those in the last cave the most highly ornamented being those just in front of the sanctuary. These pillars are very similar to those in Cave I. Those in the front row and the central pair in the back row have little fat dwarfs with four arms supporting the corners of the abaci. The central pairs of pillars in the back and front rows are the richest in carving, and the corner ones have flutes running in spirals up two belts of the shaft. The brackets have *Vidyâdharas* and *Apsarasas* on the projections. In the central panels of the brackets in the back row are numbers of people worshipping the dâgoba; in those of the right side row are single fat figures canopied by *toraṇas* rising from the mouths of *makaras*, and in the rest a fat râja, his wife and other female attendants. The pilasters are beautifully carved.

In a line with each side aisle, in the back wall, is a chamber with two pillars and pilasters in the front. In the chamber on the right or east side of the sanctuary, are sculptured a pair of portly sitting figures, both with rich headdresses: the woman holds a child on her knee, apparently amusing it with a toy held in her right hand; to the right and left of them are female slaves with *chaurîs*, whilst one behind holds a parrot and fruit. Below are eleven small figures, some of them making rams butt, others wrestling, and some playing on musical instruments for the child's amusement. This is probably intended to represent the infancy of Buddha nursed by his mother Mayâdêvî (or Mahâprajâpate) with a peculiar round headdress, who sits by his father, Suddhodana. In the upper corners are representations of a holy man giving instruction to a woman and her child; and of Buddha attacked by a four-armed demon with skull, necklace, club, snake, &c.

In a corresponding apartment on the other side there are two fat male figures with elaborate headdresses, neck-chains, and armlets, the one holding an egg-shaped object in his hand. The frilled back to the headdress on the right-hand figure is of the style in vogue in sculptures of about the sixth or seventh century A.D. Female slaves with *chaurîs* stand on either side, and *Gandharvas* or Buddhist cherubs with large wigs appear in the upper corners. Below are two semicircular representations; but whether intended for vegetable food or not, is uncertain. Over the fronts of these side chapels in the back wall are also groups, the central one over the left chapel having a Nâga Râja and his family in it.

The shrine itself is about 14 feet by 11; but, owing to the cave being only 11 feet 5 inches high, it is very dark, and smells strongly of bats. The Buddha squats in the *dharmachakra mudrâ* with the wheel and two deer in front, and behind them, to the right, a female in the attitude of adoration before a male, with a long object like an empty bag; to the left is a female kneeling with a long-twisted object, and behind her a kneeling male worshipper. The right *châmara*-bearer is richly dressed with *mukuṭa* and nimbus; the left one is Avalôkitêśvara; he has the *jatâ* headdress, and in his left hand a bottle-shaped object. The other has a rich headdress.

The doorway to the shrine (Plate XLV., fig. 1) is a rich and elegant specimen of its class, though hardly of so pleasing a design as that of Cave No. I. (Plate XLII.). The inner pilaster consists of five panels, each containing two figures, a male and a female, the male is in the lowest compartment, being represented by a dwarf. The outside face equally consists of five panels, but only with single figures in each, all except the top one males with five-headed snake hoods. The lintel is adorned with seated figures in pairs, with three figures in the central compartment. The figure sculpture on this doorway seems to be superior to that in Cave No. I., but the architectural ornaments are certainly inferior both in the design and execution.

A good deal of the painting still remains in this cave. In the verandah, so much of the beautifully decorated ceiling is left that the pattern can be completely made out. When entire it must have been remarkably beautiful both in colour and design. The few fragments that remain on the wall indicate that it also was of a very high order as regards design, drawing, and colour.

Inside, the ceilings of the great hall and aisles, the antechamber, shrine, and chapels are all admirably designed, and though (especially in the hall) blackened with smoke,[1] they contain many striking examples of floral decorations, Nâga and flying figures, and others with human and animal heads, but the lower extremities ending in scroll work.

It is the only cave that retains any fragments of painting in the shrine, the ceiling being especially fine. "On entering the sanctuary with a light," says Mr. Griffiths, "the effect produced is one of extreme richness, the floating figures in the spandrils standing out with startling effect. These figures are bringing their gifts of flowers to present to the gigantic Buddha below. The wreath of flowers is admirably painted, and the band of black and white with its varied simple ornament is a most happy idea, giving additional value to the rest of the design. The eye would have been satiated by the amount of colour were it not for the relief it derived from the imposition of this band."

The painting in the two chapels is of a yellower tone than most of the other wall paintings, and is filled with standing figures, many of them females, some with aureoles round their heads, and is possibly of later date than the rest, probably of the seventh century. On the right wall of the hall is one of the most interesting groups of pictures now left, of which it is to be regretted

[1] It is to be regretted that some precautions have not long ago been taken for preserving these interesting relics, for the bats have recently attacked the ceilings and will soon ruin them unless shut out. "What would be the effect," says Mr. Griffiths, "if a few hundred of them were allowed to flutter over Michael Angelo's fresco on the ceiling of the Sistine Chapel, or among the paintings of the greatest of the Venetians in the Camera di Collegio in the Ducal Palace? . . . I am fully convinced that they have been one of the principal agents in hastening the destruction of the paintings."—*Report*, 1872–73, p. 11.

no copy has yet been made. It would occupy too much space to describe the whole, even if it were possible to do so intelligibly without some sort of copy of it. In one of the scenes, between the second and third cell doors below, is the retinue of a râja. He goes out on a large elephant with the umbrella of state over his head. and the *ankuśa* or goad in his hand; behind him is an attendant with the *chhatra;* at his side goes a smaller elephant, with a rider now defaced, and before it walks a man with some load in a bag on his back. In front (to the left) five horses (two of them green) advance; the men on the green horses looking back to the râja. There are also fourteen men on foot, of whom eleven seem to be soldiers, some carrying oblong shields, and three round ones with a great grinning Gorgon face painted on the front of each. Two above on the extreme left have swords in scabbards, nine others have Nêpal swords known as *khukharîs* or *dabiyas*, but very long; other two men play flutes, and one beats a drum (*ḍâk*).

Between the first and second cell doors is represented, with a conventionalism worthy of the Chinese, a river with many fish and shells in it. A boat with three masts, a jib sail, and an oar behind, and filled towards the stern with ten *matkâs* or earthenware jars, carries a man in it with long hair, who is praying. In the heaven behind Chandra, the Moon, a figure with a crescent behind him, is represented as coming to him, followed by another figure. A Nâga Râja and his wife in the water seem to draw the boat back; and below is represented in the water another similar figure with a human head and long tail. On the left, to which the boat is going, is Buddha on the shore and a figure worshipping him. On the shores rocks are conventionally painted.

The upper part of this wall is covered with interesting scenes, and much remains on the other walls also well deserving of publication.

Cave III.

This is a small Vihâra higher up on the face of the rock, but quite unfinished. The verandah is 29 feet by 7, and supported by four pillars and two pilasters, only blocked out. An entrance has been made for the hall, but little of it has been excavated. There is also a commencement of an under-storey to this cave.

Cave IV.

We now come to Cave IV. (Fergusson's No. 3), the largest *Vihâra* of the series (*see* plan on Plate XLVI.). The verandah is about 87 feet long, 11¾ wide, and 16 feet high, supported by eight octagonal columns with plain bracket capitals. There is a room 10 feet by 8½ at each end, entered by a small door with three steps. The cave has had a façade outside, carved with *chaitya*-window ornaments containing figures of Buddha.

The windows are surrounded by neat tracery with a female and attendant at the bottom of each jamb. The hall is entered by one central and two side doors, and has two windows between the doors. The large door, though considerably damaged for about two feet above the floor, to which depth the cave was long filled with earth, is one of the most elaborate to be found here; generally it resembles that of Cave II., but no mere description can convey an idea of its details, which can be better studied from the drawing (Plate XLVII.) than from any verbal account. The *dwârapâl* were *as* females attended by dwarfs. The upper compartment of the architrave on the right contains a bull, lying much as the Nandi does before Śaiva temples; and on the upper member of the cornice, at the extreme right, two monkeys are carved. The frieze is ornamented by five models of the chaitya window, three containing Buddhas, and the end ones pairs of human figures. At the upper corners of the door are figures somewhat like goats rampant (*śârdûlas*) facing each other, and which have had riders, but they are broken.

To the right of the door, and between it and the architrave of the window, there is a large compartment sculptured with a variety of figures at the side, and in the middle a large one of Padmapâni, the Bôdhisattwa of Amitâbha, the fourth *Jñânî*, or divine Buddha, and who is supposed to be incarnate in the Dalai Lama of Lhasa. The arms are both broken, but the figure of Amitâbha Buddha is on his forehead. The head is surrounded by a nimbus, and the remains of the lotus may be traced in his left hand. The compartments, four on each side,[1] represent the Bauddha Litany. This

[1] In China Padmapâni, known as Kwan-yin, "who saves from the eight forms of suffering," is usually represented as a female. The principal seat of his (or her) worship is at the island of Puto.—Edkins, *Religion in China*, (2nd ed.,) pp. 100, 101.

may be regarded as an evidence of the later age of this cave, probably contemporary with those of the Ḍheṛwâṛâ at Elurâ and Cave VII. at Aurangâbâd,[1] where this litany is also found. There are also pieces of sculpture very similar to this behind one of the dâgobas in the vihâra to the right of the chaitya, and in some of the smaller caves at Kaṇhêri, and there are two copies outside the façade of Cave XXVI. here, as well as a painted one in Cave XVII. Above this is a small horse-shoe shaped compartment with a Buddha sitting inside. The pillars inside are plain octagons, except two in the middle of the back row (Plate XLVIII.), which are richly decorated.

There is no painting in the cave, except traces of a small fragment in very brilliant colours on the roof of the verandah to the right of the central door. Portions of the roof inside appear as if a layer of the rock had fallen off, near the front, and the workmen had begun to smooth it again from the back. It was, however, never finished.

The antechamber is 21 feet by 13. On each side the shrine door is a large standing Buddha, and on each end wall of the antechamber are two similar figures, but, with the shrine and cells, it is much infested with bats. The Buddha in the shrine is in the usual *dharmachakra mudrâ*, the left-hand attendant holding a lotus in his left hand. The wheel and deer are in front, and quite a group of worshippers at each corner of the throne. The hall is 87 feet square, and is supported by 28 columns, 3 feet 2 inches to 3 feet 3 inches in diameter, of the same style as in the verandah, plain, and without the elaborate tracery in Caves I. and II., but with a deep architrave over them, as at Ghatoṭkach, which raises the roof of the cave considerably. The front aisle is 97 feet in length and has a cell at each end.

We descend to the next by a rough rocky path.

Cave V.

Cave V. is only the commencement of a *vihâra*, the verandah of which is 45½ feet by 8 feet 8 inches; but of the four pillars, only one is nearly finished, and it is of the same style as the

[1] See *Archæological Survey of Western India*, vol. iii. Plate LIII.

last, only shorter and with a square base. The door has an architrave round it, divided into six compartments on each side, and each filled by a pair of standing figures in various attitudes. In the lintel are nine divisions, the central one with Buddha and attendants and the other with pairs of seated figures. Two very neat colonettes support the frieze in which are five *chaitya*-window ornaments. Outside is a roll-pattern member and a border of leaves; but at the upper corners these are carried outwards so as to surround a female standing on a *makara* under foliage of the Aśoka and Mango trees, and attended by a small dwarf.

The left window is also richly carved, but scarcely any progress has been made inside.

Cave XXI.

On leaving No. V., which is the last of the latest Mahâyâna caves of the North-western group, and passing over the 15 caves already described, we reach No. XX., from which we descend and then ascend again by a steep path for a considerable distance along the face of the scarp to No. XXI. Its verandah has fallen away, but the elaborately carved pilasters at each end, in the style of Cave I., Plate XLIX., fig. 2, indicate that it was probably finished with the same richness of ornamentation. At each end is a neat open chapel like those in Caves I. and II., separated from the verandah by two pillars of elegant design with the corresponding pilasters (Plate XLIX., fig. 1), in these the falling leaf is introduced probably for the first time over the bowl of the capital. The frieze above this is divided into three compartments by dwarf pilasters, ornamented by what is called "jewel pattern," which is one of the most usual and typical of all the ornaments used in the seventh century. It occurs everywhere in caves and buildings of that age. The hall is 51½ feet wide by 51 feet deep, and has chambers with pillared fronts in the middle and at the ends of the side aisles, each leading into an inner cell, besides which there are four other cells on each side of the cave. The pillars in front of the cells at the back are surmounted by some very good carving and devices. The roof of the hall is supported by twelve columns, ornamented in a style similar to those in Cave II. The entrance to the adytum is unfinished, and the image sits cross-legged, has huge ears, and is attended by *chauri*-bearers, holding fruits or offerings in their hands, and with high ornate tiaras; they are perhaps intended to represent Indras or Śakras. The paintings on the left wall are much destroyed since first known to Europeans.

Cave XXII.

The next[1] is a very small Vihâra, about 16½ feet square and 9 feet high, with four unfinished cells, no window, a very pretty door, and a narrow verandah, of which both the pillars are broken, ascended by two steps. The sanctuary opens directly from the cave, and contains an image with its feet on the lotus, the Buddhist emblem of creative power. On front of the *siñhâsana* or seat is the *chakra*, the *chinha* or cognizance of Śakya, with two small deer as *vâhana* or supporters. To his right, beyond the *chauri*-bearer, is Padmapâni, and on the left another attendant. On the right side, under a row of painted Buddhas, are their names:—"Vipasyi, Śikhi, Viśvabhu, . . . Kanakamuni, Kâsyapa, Śâkya Muni, Maitre(ya)," the missing name being Krakutsanda or Kakusanda, the first Buddha of the present *kalpa* or regeneration of the world; for the Buddhists believe that the world is destroyed and regenerated at the end of immensely long periods or *kalpas*; and that each *kalpa* has one or more Buddhas, thus in the third past regeneration Vipasyi was the Buddha in the last Śikhi and Viśvabhu; and in the present Krakuchchhanda, Kanakamuni, Kaśyapa, and Śâkya Muni or Gautama have already appeared as Buddhas whilst Arya Maitreya, the last, is yet to come, 5,000 years after Śâkya. These are also known as the "*mânushya* or earth-born Buddhas." Below the names is painted:—"The charitable assignation of Śâkya Bhikshu . . . May the merit of this . . . be to father and mother and to all beings . . . endowed with beauty and good fortune, good qualities and organs, the bright . . . protectors of light . . . thus become pleasing to the eye."

Cave XXIII.

This is another twelve-pillared Vihâra, 50 feet 5 inches wide by 51 feet 8 inches deep, and 12 feet 4 inches high. The four columns of the verandah are all entire. They have bases, 2¾ to 3 feet square;

[1] High up in the rock above the scarp, between Nos. XXI. and XXII. and almost inaccessible, is another small Vihâra, numbered XXVIII. in this arrangement.

the shafts are circular, the end ones fluted, and on the torus of the capital are four dwarfs, upholding the corners of a square tile under the brackets. The door has small *dwárpálas*, canopied by the many-hooded snake. There are chapels at the ends of the verandah and of the left aisle, but the sanctuary is only commenced. There is no trace of painting in this cave.

Cave XXIV.

Cave XXIV. was intended for a 20 pillared vihâra, 73¼ feet wide by 75 feet deep, and if completed it would probably have been one of the most beautiful in the whole series, but the work was stopped before completion. The verandah was long choked up with earth, and of the six pillars in it only one is now standing; the rest appear to have fallen down within the last thirty years. The bracket capitals still hang from the entablature, and the carved groups on them are in the best style of workmanship.[1] In two of the capitals and in those of the chapels at the end of the verandah the corners are left above the torus, and wrought into pendant scroll leaf ornaments. The work on the doors and windows is elaborate. Inside only one column has been finished.

Here we learn how these caves were excavated by working long alleys with the pickaxe into the rock and then breaking down the intervening walls, except where required for supporting columns. There is some sculpture in an inner apartment of the chapel outside the verandah to the left, but much in the usual style.

Cave XXV.

This is a small vihara with a verandah of two pillars; the hall is 26 feet 5 inches wide by 25 feet 4 inches deep without cell or sanctuary. It has three doors; and at the left end of the verandah is a chamber with cells at the right and back. In front is an enclosed space, about 30¼ feet by 14, with two openings in front, and a door to the left leading on to the terrace of the next cave.

Chaitya Cave No. XXVI.

This is the fourth Chaitya-cave, and bears a strong resemblance to Cave XIX. It is larger however, as may be seen from the two

---

1 Woodcut No. 42 is a representation of one of the capitals of the verandah of this cave.

plans engraved on Plate XXXVII., and is very much more elaborately ornamented with sculpture, but that generally is somewhat inferior in design, and monotonous in the style of its execution, showing a distinct tendency towards that deterioration which marked the Buddhist art of the period. It is also certainly more modern than No. XIX., though the two are not separated by any long interval. Still the works in Cave XXVI. seem to have been continued to the very latest period at which Buddhist art was practised at Ajaṇṭâ, and it was contemporary with the unfinished caves which immediately preceded it in the series. It may possibly have been commenced in the end of the sixth century, but its sculptures extend down to the middle of the seventh, or to whatever period may be ascertained as that at which the Buddhists were driven from these localities. This was certainly after Hiwen Thsangs visit to the neighbourhood in 640,[1] and it may not have been for 10 or 20 years after this time.

Once it had a broad verandah along the whole front, supported by four columns, of which portions of three still remain, and at each end of the verandah there was a chamber with two pillars and pilasters very like those in the left side chapel of Cave III. at Aurangâbâd. The court outside the verandah has extended some way right and left, and on the right side are two panels above one another, containing the litany of Avalôkiteśwara, similar to that in Cave IV., and to the right of it is a standing figure of Buddha in the *âśîva mudrâ*, holding up the right hand in the attitude of blessing. One of these panels, however, is much hidden by the accumulation of earth in front of them, and the other is entirely concealed by it. Over the verandah, in front of the great window and upper façade of the cave, there was a balcony, about 8¼ feet wide and 40 feet long, entered at the end from the front of the last cave. The sill of the great arch was raised 2¾ feet above this, and at the inner side of the sill, which is 7 feet 2 inches deep, there is a stone parapet or screen, 3¾ feet high, carved in front with small Buddhas. The outer arch is 14¼ feet high, but the inner one from the top of the screen is only 8 feet 10 inches. The whole façade, outside the great arch and the projecting side-walls at the ends of the balcony, has been divided into compartments of various sizes sculptured with Buddhas. On each side the great arch is a seated

[1] Julien's Translation, vol. ii. p. 150.

figure of Kubêra, the Hindu god of wealth, and beyond it, in a projecting alcove, is a standing Buddha. On the upper parts of the end walls of this terrace there is, on each side, a figure of Buddha standing with his *śelâ* or robe descending from the left shoulder to the ankle, leaving the right shoulder bare: these figures are about 16 feet high.

Under the figure on the left is an inscription in a line and a half, being a dedication by the Śâkya Bhikshu Bhadanta Gunâkara. On the left of the entrance is a longer inscription[1] recording the construction of the cave by Devarâja and his father Bhavvirâja, ministers of Aśmâkarâja. This is important as connecting the excavators of this cave with Cave XVII. and the large Vihâra at Ghatotkacha.

Besides the central door, there is a smaller side one into each aisle. The temple is 67 feet 10 inches deep, 36 feet 3 inches wide, and 31 feet 3 inches high. The nave—besides the two in front, has twenty-six columns, is 17 feet 7 inches wide, and 33 feet 8 inches long to the front of the dâgoba; the pillars behind it are plain octagons, with bracket capitals, and the others somewhat resemble those in the verandah of Cave II.; they are 12 feet high, and a four-armed bracket dwarf is placed over each capital on the front of the narrow architrave. The frieze projects a few inches over the architrave, and is divided into compartments elaborately sculptured. The stone ribs of the roof project inwards, and the vault rises $12\frac{3}{4}$ feet to the ridge pole.

The body of the *chaitya* or *dâgoba* is cylindrical, Plate XXXVIII., fig. 1, but with a broad face in front, carved with pilasters, cornice, and maṇḍapa top; in the centre is a Buddha sitting on a *siṅhâsana* or throne with lions upholding the seat, his *śelâ* reaching to his ankles, his feet on a lotus upheld by two small figures with *Nâga* canopies, behind which, and under the lions, are two elephants. The rest of the cylinder is divided by pilasters into compartments containing figures of Buddha standing in various attitudes. The dome has a compressed appearance, its greatest diameter being at about a third of its height, and the representation of the box above is figured on the sides with a row of standing and another of sitting

[1] *Jour. Bom. B. R. As. Soc.* vol. vii. p. 61, and my *Notes on Ajaṇṭâ*, p. 83, and Plate XXI.

Buddhas; over it are some eight projecting fillets or tenias, crowned by a fragment of a small stone umbrella. The aisles of this Chaitya-cave contain a good deal of sculpture, much of it defaced. In the right aisle there are large compartments with Buddhas sculptured in *alto rilievo*, with attendants; their feet rest on the lotus upheld by *Nâga*-protected figures with rich headdresses, and others sitting beside them. Over the Buddhas are flying figures, and above them a line of arabesques with small compartments containing groups.

On the left wall, near the small door is a gigantic figure of Buddha about 23 feet 3 inches in length, reclining on a couch (*see* Plate L.) This represents the death of the great ascetic. "It is," says Fahian, "to the north of Kusinara" (probably Kusia, between Betiya and Gorakhpur) "betwixt two *sal* trees on the bank of the river Hiranyavati (probably the Gandak) that the 'Illustrious of the Age,' his face turned to the north, entered *nirvâṇa*. There where Subhadra long after obtained the law, and where they adored for seven days in his golden coffin the 'Illustrious of the Age;' there where 'the hero that bears the diamond sceptre' (Vajrapâni) let go the golden pestle, and where the eight kings divided the *sariro* (or relics), in all these places they established Sangharâmas or monasteries which exist to this day."[1] The visitor will observe a tree at the head and another at the foot of the figure, and Ânanda, the relative and attendant of Buddha, standing under the second. This figure has also its face turned to the north. "In a great chapel erected at Kusinara," says Hiwen Thsang—writing about A.D. 640—is a "representation of the *nirvâṇa* of the Tathâgata. His face is turned to the north, and hath the appearance of one slumbering."[2]

Above the large figure are several very odd ones, perhaps representing the *dêvas* "making the air ring," as the legend says, "with celestial music, and scattering flowers and incense." Among them is perhaps Indra, the prince of the thirty-two *dêvas* of Trayastrinshas, on his elephant. In front of the couch are several other figures, his disciples or *bhikshus*, exhibiting their grief at his departure, and a worshipper with a flower in his hand and some little offerings in a tray.

---

[1] Foë Koué Ki, Chapter XXIV.

[2] General Cunningham in a private letter to me reports that he has discovered this figure, but nothing has yet been published regarding it.—J. F.

Farther along the wall, beyond a figure of Buddha teaching between two attendants—a Bodhisattva on the left and perhaps Padmapâni on the right—there is a large and beautiful piece of sculpture that has perplexed every one who has attempted to explain it. (Plate LI.) To the left a prince, Mâra, stands with what appears to be a bow and arrow in his hands and protected by an umbrella, and before him—some sitting, others dancing—are a number of females, his daughters Tanhâ, Ratî, and Rangâ, with richly adorned headdresses. A female beats the three drums, two of which stand on end which she beats with one hand, and the other lies on its side while she almost sits on it and beats it with the other hand. Mâra appears again at the right side, disappointed at his failure. Several of the faces are beautifully cut. Above are his demon forces attacking the great ascetic sitting under the Bodhi tree, with his right hand pointing to the earth and the left in his lap (the *bhûmisparśa mudrâ*), while the drum of the *dêvas* is being beat above him. This is the same subject that is represented in painting in Cave No. I. above alluded to. The painting contains more detail, and a greater number of persons are represented in it, than in this sculpture, but the story and the main incidents are the same in both. On the whole this sculpture is perhaps, of the two, the best representation of a scene which was so great a favourite with the artists of that age. Besides this it is nearly entire, while a great deal of the plaster on which the other was painted has pealed off, leaving large gaps, which it is now almost impossible to fill up.[1]

[1] One of the most interesting results obtained from a study of the sculptures in this cave is the almost absolute certainty that the Great Temple of Boro Buddor in Java was designed by artists from the west of India, and almost as certainly that it was erected in the last half of the seventh century, or it may be somewhat later, as such a temple must probably have taken nearly 100 years to complete. The style of execution of the figure sculptures in the two temples resemble each other so nearly that we might almost fancy they were carved by the same individuals, and the "jewelled pattern" and other architectural ornaments are so nearly identical that they must be of the same age, or very nearly so. The Mahâyâna doctrines, as portrayed at Boro Buddor, are somewhat more advanced than anything found at Ajaṇṭâ, especially in the upper storeys, but that may have arisen from the time the works were in progress.

The time and manner of the Buddhist migration to Java have hitherto been a complete mystery. In the beginning of the fifth century Fa Hian, who resided there five months, confesses that there "heretics and Brahmans flourish, but the law of Buddha "is not much known."[1] It probably, however, was not long after that time that they

* Beal's Translation, p. 169.

CAVES XXVII. to XXIX.

Cave XXVII. is the last accessible vihâra. The front is broken away and a huge fragment of rock lies before the cave, which is about 43½ feet wide and 31 deep, without pillars. It has never been finished, and the antechamber to the shrine is only blocked out. There are three cells in the left side, two in the back, and one in the portion of the left side that remains.

Cave XXVIII. is the beginning of a Chaitya cave high up on the scarp between Nos. XXI. and XXII.; but little more than the top of the great arch of the window has been completed.

Cave XXIX. is the verandah of a vihâra beyond XXVII., supported by six rough-hewn pillars and two pilasters. No. XXVIII. is very difficult of access, and XXIX. is inaccessible.

CAVES OF GHATOTKACH.

The caves of Ghaṭotkach are situated in a gorge near the village of Jinjâlâ, about eleven miles west from Ajaṇṭâ and three south-west of Gulwâḍâ, and consist of two Buddhist excavations, a larger and a smaller cave. They were first brought to notice by Captain Rose and described by Surgeon W. H. Bradley.[1]

The larger Vihâra (Plate LII.) in plan closely resembles Caves VI. and XVI. at Ajaṇṭâ: it is a twenty-pillared hall, with the front aisle somewhat longer than the width of the cave, the corner and two middle pillars on each side being of one pattern, square bases changing into octagon, sixteen-sided, and then 32 flutes, returning through the sixteen and eight-sided forms to the square under the plain bracket capitals. The remaining two pillars on each side have octagonal shafts, square heads, and brackets. There are pilasters on the side

migrated there in sufficient numbers to build Chaityas and Vihâras, for there is a certain local character and indigenous looking details at Boro Buddor, which it must have taken some time to assimilate. But from the identity of the figure sculpture and the general similarity of design, it seems nearly certain that it was not till the end of the seventh century that they were in sufficient numbers and with sufficient wealth to contemplate such an undertaking as that great temple, certainly the most magnificent temple of the Buddhists now, at all events, existing. The migration to Cambodia seems to have been undertaken later. The temples there are hardly Buddhist at all, that religion being there overwhelmed and buried in local superstitions and serpent worship, so as to be barely recognizable, if, in fact, it pre-existed at all.—J. F.

[1] *Jour. B. B. R. A. Soc.*, vol. v. p. 117.

walls in line with the front and back rows of pillars, those behind being richly carved, and the front left side one bearing a figure of Buddha with an inscription over it in rather badly formed characters. It is merely the Baudda creed. In the middle of the back wall is an antechamber with two pillars in front, and behind it is the shrine containing a figure of Buddha with his legs doubled under him, hands in the teaching *mudrâ*, with gigantic *chauri* bearers, and *vidyâdharas* on clouds. In front of the throne is the usual wheel, on each side of which are couchant deer, and behind them on either side two kneeling figures in entire relief and four others in half relief from the throne.

In the back wall on each side the shrine and in the middle of each side wall is a chapel with two pillars in front, and three of the chapels with inner cells. There are also four cells in the right side and six in the left.

In the extension of the front aisle to the right there is a dâgoba in half relief, and on the other two walls of the same recess are a number of standing and squatting Buddhas all cut into the wall, and possibly of later date than the excavation.

In the front wall are three doors, a central one and two at the ends, and two windows, the central door carved in the style of most of the doors in the caves at Ajaṇṭâ, but at the upper corners the female figures stand on boars instead of *makaras*, and the windows and side doors are ornamented with the Chaitya arch containing figures of Buddha, with globular forms on the finials. At the ends of the verandah are two small chapels each with two pillars between pilasters supporting their fronts, similar to those in the chapels of Caves XXIV. and XXV. at Ajaṇṭâ. On the back wall of the verandah at the north end (the cave faces south-west) is an inscription of the Aśmaka princes much defaced, but originally cut in small well formed letters, each line containing one *śloka*.

The whole front of the verandah is ruined, not a vestige of a pillar being left.

The second was a small cave, the front supported by two pillars and two pilasters, but now almost entirely destroyed, the bracket of one pillar and pilaster only remaining, and in the middle compartment of the bracket of the pillar is a representation of four deer with one common head as in Cave I. at Ajaṇṭâ.

CHAPTER III.

KANHERI CAVES.

The Island of Salsette, or Shaṭshâshṭhi, at the head of the Bombay harbour, is peculiarly rich in Rock-Temples, there being works of this kind at Kâṇhêri, Marôl, Magathana, Maṇḍapêśwar, and Jogêśwari. The most extensive series is the group of Buddhist caves at Kaṇhêri, a few miles from Thâṇâ, in which are about 109 separate caves, mostly small, however, and architecturally unimportant.

From their position, within easy access from Bombay and Bassein, they early attracted attention, and were described by Portuguese visitors in the 16th century,[1] and by European voyagers and travellers like Linschoten, Fryer, Gemelli Careri, Anquetil, Du Perron, Salt, and others.[2]

They are about six miles from Ṭhâṇâ, and two north of the Tulsi lake, recently formed to increase the water supply of Bombay, and, as described by Mr. Fergusson,[3] "are excavated in one large bubble of a hill, situated in the midst of an immense tract of forest country. Most of the hills in the neighbourhood are covered with the jungle, but this one is nearly bare, its summit being formed by one large rounded mass of compact rock, under which a softer stratum has in many places been washed out by the rains, forming

---

[1] Diogo de Couto (1603), *Da Asia* Dec. vii., liv., iii., cap. 10 (Ed. Lisboa), tom. vii. Translated in *Jour. Bom. B. R. A Soc.*, vol. i. pp. 34–41.

[2] J. H. Van Linschoten (1579), *Discourse of Voyages*, Book I., ch. xliv. p. 80; Fryer (1673), *New Account of East India and Persia*, Let. ii. ch. ii. pp. 72, 73; Gemelli Careri (1693), *Voyage* (Fr. ed. 1727), tom. ii. pp. 51–75; A. Du Perron, *Zend Avesta*, Prel. Disc. cccxciv., ccccxiii., ccccxix.; Hunter in *Archæologia*, vol. vii. pp. 299–302; S. Lethieullier, *ib.*, pp. 333–336: H. Macneil, *ib.*, vol. viii. pp. 251–263; Salt, *Trans. Bom. Lit. Soc.*, vol. i. pp. 46–52; Erskine, *ib.*, vol. iii. p. 527; Wilson *Journ. Bom. B. R. A. Soc.*, vol. iii. pt. ii. pp. 39-41; Stevenson, *ib.*, vol. iv. pp. 131–134; vol. v. pp. 1 ff.; West, *ib.*, vol. vi. pp. 1–14, 116–120, 157–160; Bhau Dâji, *ib.*, vol. viii. pp. 227 ff.; Bird, *Jour. A. S. Beng.*, vol. x. p. 94; *Histor. Res.*, pp. 10, 11; Hamilton's *Desc. of Hindustan*, vol. ii. p. 171; Heber's *Journals*; Fergusson, *J. R. A. Soc.*, vol. viii.

[3] *Rock-cut Temples*, p. 34.

natural caves; it is in the stratum again below this that most of the excavations are situated."[1] The rock in which the caves are is a volcanic breccia, which forms the whole of the hilly district of the island, culminating to the north of the caves in a point about 1,550 feet above the sea level.

In so large a group there must be considerable differences in the ages of some of the excavations. These, however, may generally be at least approximatively ascertained from the characters of the numerous inscriptions that exist upon them. Architectural features are necessarily indefinite where the great majority of the excavations consist of a single small room, usually with a little verandah in front, supported by two plain square or octagonal shafts, and stone-beds in the cells. In the larger and more ornate caves they are, of course, as important here as elsewhere. Their style is certainly primitive, and some of these monks' abodes may date from before the Christian era. One small cave of this type (No. 81) in the ravine, consisting of a very narrow porch, without pillars, a room with a stone bench along the walls, and a cell to the left, has an inscription of Yajña Śri Śâtakarṇi[2] of the Andrabhritya race, whose date is still undetermined (*ante*, page 265), and it is probable that numbers of others in the same plain style may range from the second to the fourth century. Others, however, are covered inside with sculpture of a late *Mahâyâna* type, and some have inscriptions which must date as late as the middle of the ninth century.

The existence of so many monastic dwellings in this locality is partly accounted for by the neighbourhood of so many thriving towns. Among the places mentioned as the residences of donors to them, occur the names of Surpâraka, the Supara of Greek and the Subara of Arab writers, the ancient capital of the northern Koṅkaṇ; Kalyâṇ, long a thriving port; Chemûla,[3] the Samylla of Greek

---

[1] *J. B. B. R. A. Soc.*. vol. vi. pp. 171, 172.

[2] Bird's Plate XLIV., No. 14; Stevenson, *J. B. B. R. A. Soc.*. vol. v. p. 23, and No. 13 of Brett's copies; West's No. 44, *J. B. B. R. A. S.*, vol. vi. p. 10.

[3] It is mentioned as Chemulî in a grant of the Silâhâras of 1095, A.D. Mas'ûdi (*Murûju'l Zahab*) says he visited Seymûr in A.D. 916, which was one of the dependencies of the Balharâ, and the ruler of the port was called Janja; now we find a Jhañjha, one of the Śilâhâra princes, mentioned in copper-plate inscriptions found at Ṭhâṇâ and the neighbourhood (*J. R. As. Soc.*, vol. iv. p. 109; *Asiat. Res.*, vol i. p. 358; *Ind. Ant.*, vol. v. pp. 276, 279) who must have been alive at this very date, his grandfather having been alive in 877 A.D. under Amoghavarsha, the Rashṭrakuṭa king (*J. B. B. R. A. S.*, vol. xiii. pp. 11, 12.); see also *Ind. Ant*, vol. vi. p. 72.

geographers, on the island of Trombay; and Vasya perhaps Vasâi or Bassein. Śrî Staânaka or Ṭhâṇâ itself, and Ghoḍabandar were also doubtless thriving towns.

Chaitya Caves.

The cave first met in the way up the hill, and the most important one in the whole series, is the great Chaitya cave, Plate LIII., so often described. On the jamb of the entrance to the verandah of it is an inscription of Yajña Śrî Śâtakarṇi or Gautamîputra II., the same whose name we have just mentioned as found on No. 81; indeed, the inscription here being much mutilated, it is only by help of the other that we can hope to make it out.[1] It seems, however, to be integral, and it is consequently not improbable that the cave was excavated during his reign.

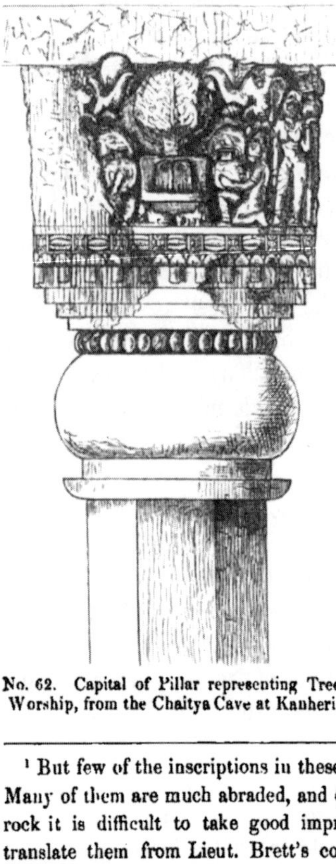

No. 62. Capital of Pillar representing Tree Worship, from the Chaitya Cave at Kanheri.

Till, however, the dates of the reigns of the Andhrabhritya kings are determined with more precision than they are at present,[2] the exact date of their excavation must remain for future investigation. The fact is we meet here exactly the same problem that prevented our being able to fix the dates of

[1] But few of the inscriptions in these caves have yet been satisfactorily deciphered. Many of them are much abraded, and owing to the weatherworn uneven surface of the rock it is difficult to take good impressions of them. Dr. Stevenson attempted to translate them from Lieut. Brett's copies (*Jour. B. B. R. A. Soc.*, vol. v. pp. 1–34), but they were inaccurate. A better series of copies were taken by E. W. West, Esq. (*J. B. B. R. A. S.*, vol. vi. pp. 1–14), but some of them were lithographed on much too small a scale. Bhagwanlâl Indraji Pandit has given a good transcript and translation of Mr. West's No. 19 from Cave 36 (*J. B. B. R. A. Soc.*, vol. xi. p. 407), contain the name of Madarîputra, one of the Andra kings; and also versions of Nos. 15 and 42, *ib.*, vol. xiii. p. 11.

[2] See list of the Andhrabhritya kings, page 265, *ante*.

the Nâsik caves within any narrow limits. From the style of the architecture we are able to state with certainty that the Cave XII. at Nâsik is contemporary, or nearly so, with the great Chaitya at Kârlê, and that the Nahapana Cave there (No. VIII.) is more modern than No. XII., but at no great interval of time. The Gautamîputra Cave No. III. succeeded to these after a considerable lapse of time, but which we are not at present in a position to measure, while anything that Yajña Śri may have done there must, of course, have been executed within a short interval of time after that. On the other hand, whatever its date may be, it is certain that the plan of this Chaitya Cave (Plate LIII.) is a literal copy of that at Kârlê (Plate XI.), but the architectural details show exactly the same difference in style as is found between Caves XII. and III. at Nâsik. If, for instance, we compare the annexed woodcut 62, representing one of the capitals in this cave, with those

No. 63. Screen in front of Chaitya Cave at Kanheri.

shown in Plate XII. we find the same degradation of style as is exhibited in woodcuts No. 49 and No. 50, page 269.[1] The screen,

[1] When I first saw these caves I was so struck with the vast inferiority of style in this cave that I was inclined to believe that the interval between these two Chaityas was much greater than it now seems possible to make it, and in my folio volume of plates I drew the pillars in each (Plate IX.) in order to explain why I did so. On architectural grounds I do not even now see any reason for doubting that the interval between them may be at least four centuries, and though the reading of the inscriptions seems at present unfavourable to this view, nothing would surprise me less than that the opinion I have recently advocated (*Ind. and East. Arch.*, p. 129) should prove correct, and it turn out that this cave was excavated in the first years of the fifth century.—J. F.

too, in front of this cave (woodcut 63), though very much weather-worn and consequently difficult to draw, is of very nearly the same design that is in the Gautamîputra Cave at Nâsik, and in its complication of discs and animal forms seems almost as modern as what we find at Amrâvati, which there seems little reason for doubting belongs to the fourth or fifth century after Christ.

This temple is 86½ feet long by 39 feet 10 inches wide from wall to wall, and has thirty-four pillars round the nave and the dâgoba, only 6 on one side and eleven on the other having bases and capitals of the Kârlê Chaitya-cave patterns, but not so well proportioned nor so spiritedly cut, while fifteen pillars round the apse are plain octagonal shafts. The dâgoba is a very plain one, nearly 16 feet in diameter, but its capital is destroyed; so also is all the woodwork of the arched roof. The aisle across the front is covered by a gallery under the great arched window, and probably the central portion of the verandah in front was also covered, but in wood. At the ends of this verandah are two colossal figures of Buddha, about 23 feet high, but these appear to be considerably later than the cave itself. The sculpture on the front screen wall is apparently a copy of that in the same position at Kârlê, but rather better executed, indeed, they are the best carved figures in these caves; the rock in this place happens to be peculiarly close grained, and the style of dress of the figures is that of the age of the great Śâtakarṇis. The earrings are heavy and some of them oblong, while the anklets of the women are very heavy, and the turbans wrought with great care. This style of dress never occurs in any of the later caves or frescoes. They may, I think, with confidence be regarded as of the age of the cave. Not so with the images above them, among which are several of Buddha and two standing figures of the Bodhisattwa Avatokitéśwara, which all may belong to a later period. So also does the figure of Buddha in the front wall at the left end of the verandah, under which is an inscription containing the name of Buddhaghosha, in letters of about the sixth century.

The verandah has two pillars in front, and the screen above them is carried up with five openings above. In the left side of the court are two rooms, one entered through the other, but evidently of later date than the cave. The outer one has a good deal of sculpture in it. On each side of the court is an attached pillar; on the top of that on the west side are four lions, as at Kârlê; on the other are three fat squat figures similar to those on the pillar in the court of the Jaina Cave, known as Indra Sabhâ, at Elurâ; these probably supported a wheel. In front of the verandah there has been a wooden porch.

On the left of the court is a small circular cell containing a solid Dâgoba, from its position almost certainly of more ancient date than this cave. On the right also, and pressing very closely upon it, is a long cave, now open in front, and which contained three dâgobas, one of them now broken off near the base. These also are probably older than the Chaitya cave, which seems to have been thrust in between these two caves at a later date; but this long room has been so much altered at different times that it is not easy to make out its original arrangements. On the rock surrounding the dâgobas are sculptures of Buddha, a litany, &c., but all these are probably of later date.

South of the last is another Chaitya cave, but quite unfinished and of a much later style of architecture, the columns of the verandah having square bases and compressed cushion-shaped capitals of the type found in the Elephanta Cave. The interior can scarcely be said to be begun. It is probably the latest excavation of any importance attempted in the hill, and may date about the ninth or tenth century after Christ.

Darbar Cave.

To the north-east of the great Chaitya cave, in a glen or gully formed by a torrent, is a cave bearing the name of the Mahârâja or Darbâr Cave (Plate LIV.), which is the largest of the class in the group, and, after the Chaitya Caves, certainly the most interesting. It is not a Vihâra in the ordinary sense of the term, though it has some cells, but a Dharmaśâlâ or place of assembly, and is the only cave now known to exist that enables us to realise the arrangements of the great hall erected by Ajâta Śatru in front of the Sattapanni Cave at Râjâgriha, to accommodate the first convocation held immediately after the death of Buddha. According to the Mahâwanso (page 12), "Having in all respects perfected this hall, he had invaluable carpets spread there, corresponding to the number of priests (500), in order that being seated on the north side the south might be faced; the inestimable pre-eminent throne of the high priest was placed there. In the centre of the hall, facing the east,

the exalted preaching pulpit, fit for the deity himself, was erected."
t is described nearly in the same words by Spence Hardy in his *Eastern Monachism*, p. 175, and Bigandet in his *Life of Gaudama*, p. 354, after even a fuller description, adds, "The seat of the President was placed opposite, in the northern part.[1] In the centre, but facing the east, a seat resembling a pulpit was raised," &c. If from this we turn to the plan of the cave, Plate LIV., it will be observed that the projecting shrine occupies precisely the position of the throne of the President in the above description. In the cave it is occupied by a figure of Buddha on a siñhâsana, with Padmapâni and another attendant or chauri-bearers. This, however, is exactly what might be expected more than 1,000 years after the first convocation was held, and when the worship of images of Buddha had taken the place of the purer forms that originally prevailed. It is easy to understand that in the sixth century, when this cave probably was excavated, the "present deity" would be considered the sanctifying President of any assembly, and his human representative would take his seat in front of the image. In the lower part of the hall, where there are no cells, is a plain space, admirably suited for the pulpit of the priest who read Bana to the assembly. The centre of the hall, 73 feet by 32, would, according to modern calculation—5 square feet to each individual—accommodate from 450 to 500 persons, but evidently was intended for a much smaller congregation. Only two stone benches are provided, and they would hardly hold 100, but be this as it may, it seems quite evident that this cave is not a Vihâra in the ordinary sense of the term, but a Dharmaśâlâ or place of assembly like the Nagarjuni Cave, Barabar (p. 41), Bhima's Ratha at Mahâvallipur (p. 118), and probably Cave XX. at Ajaṇṭâ. The Mahârwâdi Cave at Elurâ, to be described hereafter, is probably another of this class, and others may be found when they are looked for.[2]

---

[1] There is some confusion here between the north and south sides of the hall, but not in the least affecting the position of the President relatively to the preacher. From what we know, *ante*, page 50, it seems, as might be expected, the Mahâwanso is correct. The entrance to the hall would be from the north, and the President's throne would naturally face it.

[2] It is curious that this cave should retain a popular name, which is a translation of the original correct designation.

There are two inscriptions in this cave,[1] but neither seems to be integral, if any reliance can be placed on the architectural features, though the whole cave is so plain and unornamented that this testimony is not very distinct. The pillars of the verandah are plain octagons without base or capital, and may be of any age.[2] Internally the pillars are square above and below, with incised circular mouldings, changing in the centre into a belt with 16 sides or flutes, and with plain bracket capitals. Their style is that of the Viswakarma temple at Elurâ, and even more distinctly that of the Chaöri in the Mokundra pass.[3] A Gupta inscription has lately been found in this last, limiting its date to the fifth century, which is probably that of the Viswakarma Cave, so that this cave can hardly be much more modern. The age, however, of this cave is not so important as its use. It seems to me to throw a new light on the arrangements in many Buddhist Caves, whose appropriation has hitherto been difficult to understand.[4]

Directly opposite to it is a small cave[5] with two pillars and two half ones in the verandah, having an inscription of about the 9th or 10th century on the frieze. Inside is a small hall with a rough cell at the back, containing only an image of Buddha on the back wall.

The next, on the south side of the ravine, is also probably a comparatively late cave. It has two massive square pillars in the verandah, with necks cut into sixteen flutes as in the Darbar cave and some of the Elurâ Buddhist caves, it consequently is probably of the same age. The hall is small and has a room to the right of it, and in the large shrine at the back is a well cut dâgoba.

---

[1] One (West's No. 15) is dated Śaka 775 in the time Kapardi, a Śilâhâra feudatory of Amoghavarsha, the Râshṭrakuṭa or Balharâ sovereign. Another (No. 42) is dated in Śaka 799 (A.D. 877) in the time of the same princes.

[2] A view of the exterior of this cave forms Plate XIII. of my illustrations of the *Rock-cut Temples*, folio, 1845. The dotted lines in the plan, Plate LIV., which is taken from a plan by Mr. Arthur A. West, show the position and size of a small rough cave under the front of the large cave. In the same plate the excavations opposite and lower down the stream are also shown.

[3] *Picturesque Illustrations of Ancient Architecture in Hindostan*, page v.

[4] I am responsible for the indentification of this cave as a Dharmaśâlâ, and consequently for the above description.—J. F.

[5] No. 78 in Dr. Bhau Dâji's numeration, which is an unfortunately awkward one, no system having been followed, but as the numbers are painted on the caves, and have been used by Messrs. West and others, it does not seem desirable to change them now

The next[1] consists of a small hall, lighted by the door and a small latticed window, with a bench running along the left side and back and a cell on the right with a stone bed in it. The verandah has had a low screen wall connecting its two octagon pillars with the ends. Outside, on the left, is a large recess and over it two long inscriptions.[2] Close to this is another cave[3] with four benched chambers; possibly it originally consisted of three small caves, of which the dividing partitions have been destroyed; but till 1853 the middle one contained the ruins of four small dâgobas, built of unburnt bricks. These were excavated by Mr. E. W. West, and led to the discovery of a very large number of seal impressions in dried clay, many of them enclosed in clay receptacles, the upper halves of which were neatly moulded somewhat in the form of dâgobas, and with them were found other pieces of moulded clay which probably formed *chhatris*[4] for the tops of them, making the resemblance complete.

Close to the dâgobas two small stone pots were also found containing ashes and five copper coins apparently of the Bahmani dynasty, and if so, of the 14th or 15th century. The characters on the seal impressions are of a much earlier age, but probably not before the 10th century, and most of them contain merely the Bauddha creed: "Yê dharma hêtu prabhava hetuṅ teshân Tathâgato hyavadat-têshân cha yo nirodha evam vâdî Maha-Śramaṇa."

The next cave[5] on the same side has a pretty large hall with a bench at each side, two slender square columns and pilasters in front of the antechamber, the inner walls of which are sculptured with four tall standing images of Buddha. The shrine is now empty, and whether it contained a structural *siñhâsana* or a *dâgoba* is difficult to say.

Upon the opposite side of the gulley is an immense excavation[6] so ruined by the decay of the rock as to look much like a natural cavern; it has had a very long hall, of which the entire front is gone, a square antechamber with two cells to the left and three to the right of it.

---

[1] No. 12. [2] No. 16 of West's copies. [3] No. 13.

[4] The supposed "earrings" of brass, may have been metal *chhatris* for others, only they were found in a ball of ashes. *Jour. B. B. R. A. Soc.*, vol. vi., Plate VIII., Fig. 19, and p. 160.

[5] No. 14. [6] No. 83.

The inner shrine is empty. In front has been a brick dâgoba rifled ong ago, and at the west end are several fragments of caves; the fronts and dividing walls of all are gone.

Some way farther up is a vihâra[1] with a large advanced porch supported by pillars of the Elephanta type in front and by square ones behind of the pattern occurring in Cave XV. at Ajaṇṭâ. The hall door is surrounded by mouldings, and on the back wall are the remains of painting, consisting of Buddhas. In the shrine is an image, and small ones are cut in the side walls, in which are also two cells. In a large recess to the right of the porch is a seated figure of Buddha, and on his left is Padmapâni or Sahasrabâhu-lokeśwara, with ten additional heads[2] piled up over his own (*see* Plate LV., fig. 2); and on the other side of the chamber is the litany with four compartments on each side. This is evidently a late cave.[3]

Altogether there are upwards of 30 excavations on both sides of this ravine,[4] and nearly opposite the last-mentioned is a broken dam,[5] which has confined the water above, forming a lake. On the hill to the north, just above this, is a ruined temple, and near it the remains of several stûpas and dâgobas. Just above the ravine, on the south side, is a range of about nineteen caves,[6] the largest of

---

No. 64. Padmapâni, from a Nepalese drawing.

[1] No. 21.

[2] *Notes on Ajaṇṭâ, &c.*, p. 100.

[3] This representation of Padmapâni with many heads is a very favourite one with the modern followers of the Mahâyâna sect in Nepal, and is found also among the ruins of Nakon Thom in Cambodia (Garnier, *Atlas*, p. viii) and probably elsewhere. So far as I know it is not found in Java, and one would hardly expect to find it here in a cave which from its architecture can hardly be later than the eighth or ninth century (see *Picturesque Illustrations of Rock cut Temples*, fol. , Plate XIV.), but it is interesting to be able to trace these strange aberrations even so far back as that, in India. When their gods were represented with 11 heads it is evident the Buddhist could no longer reproach the Hindus for their many-headed and many-armed divinities, and that the simplicity and purity which sustained it in its early days had long since passed away.—*J. F.*

[4] These are numbered 5 to 23, 98, 97, 96, 95, 94, 93, and 78 to 87.

[5] Said to have been destroyed by the Portuguese.

[6] These are awkwardly numbered from west to east thus:—29–33, 34, 77, 76, 75, 74, 73, 99, 44, 43, 42, 72, 71, 70, 69. In six of these there are inscriptions.

which is a fine vihâra cave, with cells in the side walls. It has four octagonal pillars in the verandah connected by a low screen wall and seat, and the walls of the verandah, and sides and back of the hall, are covered with sculptured figures of Buddha in different attitudes and variously accompanied, but with so many female figures introduced as to show that it was the work of the Mahâyâna school. There is reason, however, to suppose that the sculpture is later than the excavation of the cave.

Behind and above these is another range,[1] in some parts double, three near the east end[2] being remarkable for the profusion of their sculptures, consisting chiefly of Buddhas with attendants, dâgobas, &c. But in one[3] is a fine sculptured litany (Plate LV., fig. 1), in which the central figure of Avalôkitêśwara has a tall female on each side, and beyond each are five compartments, those on the right representing danger from the elephant, lion, snake, fire,[4] and shipwreck; those on the left from imprisonment (?) Garuḍa,[5] Sitalâ or disease, sword, and some enemy not now recognisable from the abrasion of the stone.

In another is a similar litany representing Buddha seated on the Padmasana, or lotus throne, supported by two figures with snake hoods, and surrounded by attendants in the manner so usual in the Mahâyâna sculptures of a later age in these caves (Plate LVI.). There are more figures in this one than are generally found on these compositions, but they are all very like one another in their general characteristics.

Over the cistern and on the pilasters of the verandah are inscriptions which at first sight appear to be in a tabular form and in characters met with nowhere else; they are in Pehlavi.

Lastly, from a point near the west end of this last range, a series of nine excavations[6] trend to the south, but are no way remarkable.

What strikes every visitor to these Kâṇheri caves is the number of water cisterns, most of the caves being furnished with its own cistern at the side of the front court, and these being filled all the

---

1 This includes Nos. 35, 49, 48, 47, 46, 45, 56 to 68.

2 Nos. 64, 66, and 67. 3 No. 66.

4 Oddly enough represented as a flame with a face in the middle of it.

5 The supplicant for deliverance in this case is a Nâga figure, conf. Boyd's *Nágánanda*, art. iv.

6 Nos. 90, 91, 50, 51, 37, and 52 to 55.

year round with delicious pure water. In front of many of the caves too there are holes in the floor of the court, and over their façades are mortices cut in the rock as footings for posts, and holdings for wooden rafters to support a covering to shelter the front of the caves during the monsoon.[1]

All over the hill from one set of caves to another steps are cut on the surface of the rock, and these stairs in many cases have had handrails along the sides of them.

Passing the last-mentioned group and advancing southwards by an ancient path cut with steps wherever there is a descent, we reach the edge of the cliff and descend it by a ruined stair about 330 yards south of the great Chaitya cave. This lands in a long gallery extending over 200 yards south-south-east, and sheltered by the overhanging rock above. The floor of this gallery is found to consist of the foundations of small brick dâgobas buried in dust and débris, and probably sixteen to twenty in number, seven of which were opened out by Mr. Ed. W. West in 1853.[2] Beyond these is the ruin of a large stone stûpa, on which has been a good deal of sculpture, and which was explored and examined by Mr. West. In the rock behind it are three small cells also containing decayed sculptures, with traces of plaster covered with painting. Beyond this the floor suddenly rises about 14 feet, where are the remains of eleven small brick stûpas; then another slight ascent lands on a level, on which are thirty-three similar ruined stûpas buried in débris. Overhead the rock has been cut out in some places to make room for them. On the back wall are some dâgobas in relief and three benched recesses. The brick stûpas vary from 4½ to 6 feet in diameter at the base, but all are destroyed down to near that level, and seem to have been all rifled, for in none of those examined have any relics been found.

There were other large stûpas in front of the great Chaitya cave, but these were opened in 1839 by Dr. James Bird, who thus described his operations[3]:—"The largest of the topes selected for examination appeared to have been one time between 12 or 16 feet in height. It was much dilapidated, and was penetrated from above to the base, which was built of cut stone. After digging to the

---

[1] In some of the inscriptions mention is said to be made of donations to pay the expense of these temporary erections.

[2] *J. B. B. R. A. S.*, vol. vi. pp. 116 ff.

[3] *Jour. A. S. Beng.*, vol. x. p. 94; conf. Bird. *Hist. Res.*, p. 7.

level of the ground and clearing away the materials, the workmen came to a circular stone, hollow in the centre, and covered at the top by a piece of gypsum. This contained two small copper urns, in one of which were some ashes mixed with a ruby, a pearl, small pieces of gold, and a small gold box, containing a piece of cloth; in the other a silver box and some ashes were found. Two copper plates containing legible inscriptions, in the *Lât* or cave character, accompanied the urns, and these, as far as I have yet been able to decipher them, inform us that the persons buried here were of the Buddhist faith. The smaller of the copper plates bears an inscription in two lines, the last part of which contains the Buddhist creed."

Dr. Bird, like too many other dilettanti, kept these plates in his own possession, and they are now lost, all we have to indicate their contents being a corrupt copy of his own making, which Dr. Stevenson attempted to decipher and translate,[1] making out, erroneously as it now appears, that it was dated "in the reign of Kripa Karṇa in the year 245," and that it mentions "the exalted Śrâmi Karṇa of the victorious Ândhrabhṛitya family."[2]

On the east side of the hill are many squared stones, foundations, tanks, &c., all betokening the existence at some period of a large colony of monks.

KONDIWTE.

Considerably to the south of Kâṇhêri, near Kondiwtê, and about a mile north of the village of Marôl, is a group of sixteen small Bauddha caves, four on the west and twelve or fourteen on the east side of the summit of a hill.[3] Among them is one Chaitya-cave of rather peculiar plan, resembling the Sudama cave at Barabar,[4] but with a dâgoba

[1] *J. B. B. R. A. Soc.*, vol. v. pp. 32 ff.; also Bird, *Histor. Res.*, pp. 7, 64, and Plates XLVII., XLVIII. Nos. 28, 29.

[2] It has since been ascertained that Dr. Stevenson's translation cannot be relied upon, especially as regards the names quoted above. The date, however, is quite certain, being written in words as well as in figures, and if from the Saka era, which there seems no reason for doubting, were written in 324 A.D.

[3] They have been long known to Europeans, for Mr. Wales the artist in the end of last century communicated an inscription from them through Sir C. W. Malet to Lieut. Wilford (*Asiat. Res.*, vol. vi. pp. 140, 141). The latter had no idea of even the alphabet of the inscription, as is shown by his transliteration.

[4] Fergusson, *E. and Ind. Archit.*, p. 108. For plan of this cave see above, p. 42, woodcut 6.

in the circular domed chamber at the back. It is 17 feet 4 inches wide by 9 feet 3 inches high, with side walls 29½ to 30 feet 9 inches in length; the wall in front of the dâgoba cell is only about 8 inches thick, and has a lattice window on each side the door, with an inscription over the one on the right. On the right wall is also a group of Buddhist sculpture of the usual description, the largest compartment containing Buddha on the lotus-throne supported by Nâgas and with chauri-bearers and Gandharvas. The next contains a standing figure of Buddha, similar to those on the façades of the Chaitya-caves of Ajaṇṭâ. Above are small seated and squatting figures, similar to those in the upper storey of Cave VI. at Ajaṇṭâ. All this may be of much later date than the cave itself.

Other small caves have been inserted, afterwards probably, so close on each side of this as to endanger the walls of it. Passing a number of cells to the left or south of this, we come to a regular vihâra cave, with four pillars in front of the verandah, which has a room opening from its left end. The large hall has three doors and two windows, with a stone bench nearly surrounding it. On each of the three interior sides is a chamber with two square pillars in front, the recesses in the two side walls have each three cells behind, those in the left-hand side much broken. Another cave to the south of this measures about 24 feet by 14, with numerous sockets in the side walls, and a pedestal against the back, over which is a dâgoba in bas-relief recessed in the wall, and with a number of sockets in a semicircle over it. In the verandah are four square pillars and pilasters, with low bases, standing on a platform carved with rail pattern, and in the floor are four holes into water cisterns.

Near the north end of this range is another pretty large vihâra. It is entered by steps up to a platform in front of the verandah over which the roof extends. The verandah has two pillars and pilasters in front, and three doors lead from it into the hall, the roof of which is supported by four octagonal pillars disposed in a square: these have low bases, and capitals somewhat of the type found in the first two large Buddhist caves at Elurâ. In each of the three inner walls are three cells, three of them with bench beds. The south end of the verandah has been broken into one of the cells of the neighbouring cave, which is perhaps the older of the two.

The caves on the west side of the hill are small and huddled together

Magathana.

The caves at Mágáthāṇá were also Buddhist,[1] but small and so dilapidated as not to merit much attention. They are excavated in the lower district of the island, and even in the hot season they stand in pools of water. In the back of the hall of the principal cave is a large figure of Buddha, squatted in the *Jñyána Mudra*, or attitude of abstraction, and above his shoulders are other smaller images in the same attitude. The other walls of this shrine or recess have also been sculptured with numerous figures of Buddha on the lotus throne upheld by Nágá figures, &c. Over the arched entrance to it is a fine *toraṇa* or ornamental frieze between two *makara* heads. This frieze is continued in compartments to the right and left along the side walls, and in one panel is a dágoba in bas-relief with traces of two worshipping figures beside it. The pillars are of the style of Cave VII. at Ajaṇṭá.

---

[1] Strangely enough Dr. Wilson describes them as Brahmanical.

CHAPTER IV.

THE CAVES OF BAGH.

In the south of Mâlwâ, about twenty-five miles south-west of Dhâr, and thirty miles west of Mându, is the village of Bâgh, three miles to the south of which is a group of Vihâras, now much ruined, from the rock in which they are cut being stratified and having given way in many places; indeed, one, if not more, of the caves have fallen in altogether. Some of them are so entirely in possession of wild bees that it is difficult getting access to them.

They were first described by Lieutenant Dangerfield in the *Transactions of the Bombay Literary Society*,[1] 1818, and more in detail by Dr. E. Impey in the *Journal of the Bombay Branch Asiatic Society*,[2] in 1854.

The first cave from the east is a large Vihâra, about 82 feet by 80, with twenty pillars in the square, or six in each face counting both the corner pillars, and four additional pillars in the centre introduced to support the rock, which is too much stratified to sustain a bearing of any considerable length. The pillars have bases consisting of a plinth and two toruses; the four in the middle have round shafts with spiral ridges, and taper to the necks, changing through 16 and 8-sided bands to square under the brackets. Of the others, two in front and back are square to about a third of their height, then change through 8 to 12 sides and to circular with spiral ridges, then by bands of 24 and 12 sides to the square; the rest have sections of 8, 16. and 8 sides only, between the lower square portion of the shaft and its head. There are seventeen cells in the hall, four of them in the back. The antechamber has two twelve-sided pillars in front. The walls of this room are adorned with sculpture; on each end is a standing image of Buddha between two attendants, one of whom seems to be Padmapâni, but not of so late and fully-developed a type as we find at Ajaṇṭâ, Elurâ, and Aurangâbâd. On the back

---

[1] Vol. ii. pp. 194–201, with three Plates.

[2] Vol. v. pp. 543–573; *see also* vol. iii. pt. ii. pp. 72, 73.

wall are two more tall standing figures in arched recesses, one Padmapâni and the other probably some Bôdhisattva, with a bottle or water-gourd in his hand. The faces and hair of some of these figures are really well cut; but a Jogi, who has taken possession of the cave, is rapidly besmearing them with soot from his fires.

In the shrine is a *Chaitya* or dâgoba, 14½ feet high and 10 feet 3 inches in diameter at the plinth of the octagonal-moulded base, which is 4 feet high; it then becomes round for 3 feet 9 inches, with a diameter of about 7 feet, also moulded. This supports the dome, about 4¾ feet high—being considerably more than a hemisphere. The box above is a mere short neck to the five overlapping slabs which crown it. This form of *Chaitya* we find again repeated in the third cave.

In the back of a cell in the east side is an aperture which leads into another cell, and from that into an area, much choked up with fallen rock, but which is the corner of another Vihâra, of which the whole roof has fallen in.[1]

No. II. seems to have been left unfinished, and is much ruined. It has had four pillars in a front hall, of which two are gone. Behind this another hall has been roughly blocked out with two rows of four pillars each across it. In the sides of the front hall are apartments with two pillars in front, and inside what appears to be a small shrine in the middle and two cells at each end.

No. III. is known as "the painted cave," from its having been covered with fresco painting, apparently quite as good as any at Ajaṇṭâ, but somewhat different in the subjects and arrangement. The roof has been in compartments as at Ajaṇṭâ, and about 4 feet of the upper portion of the walls covered with intertwined vegetable patterns, while below were figures and scenes, Buddhist Jâtakas, &c., now very much injured by the fall of much of the roof, as well as from natives having scribbled their names over it, and from decay.

The hall is a magnificent one, about 96 feet square, with twenty-eight pillars round it, having high square bases, but a band of soft earth just at the bottom has ruined many of them; inside there is an octagon of eight round pillars, within which again are four square built piers. The rock in which the cave is cut is stratified, the diffe-

[1] In Captain Dangerfield's plan a series of six cells are represented in line one behind another: the first two only exist as shown, the others are in the wall of the cave which is entered beyond the second.

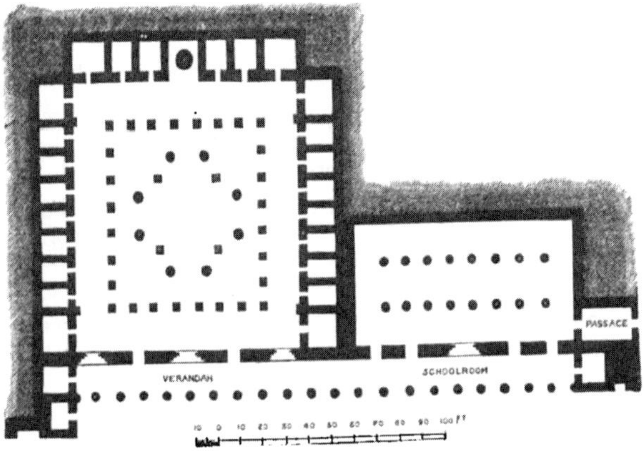

No. 65. Great Vihâra at Bâgh. (From a plan by Dr. Impey.)[1]

rent layers varying from a light ochrey tint to a dirty dark grey, and apparently a portion of the roof inside the octagon had given way while the work was being executed. The piers were then introduced, and the damaged portion of the roof was hewn out, leaving the central area higher than the rest of the cave; the architraves forming the inner sides of this, are carved with a double row of Chaitya window ornaments.

This hall has nine cells on each side and six in the back—twenty-four in all, while in the middle of the back wall is the shrine having a *Dâgoba* or *Chaitya* precisely similar to that in No. I. The whole hall is filled up half way to the roof with fallen rock.

No. IV. is entered from the same verandah as No. III., and is a plain room, 94 feet by 44, with two rows of eight pillars, each running from left to right. Mr. Impey calls it "the shala or schoolroom," but it evidently is a Dharmaśâlâ like the Darbar cave at Kanheri and not unlike it in dimensions, though the pillars are differently arranged. From it a passage leads into the next cave. which with two or three beyond are much ruined, and scarcely worth detailed description.

These two caves have a common verandah 220 feet in length, and which once had twenty pillars, but they have all fallen. The back wall of this was adorned with a series of very beautiful frescoes, rivalling in excellence those at Ajaṇṭâ. Processions on elephants

[1] From Fergusson's *I. and E. Archit.*, p. 160.

and horseback, musical entertainments, and the like, form the principal subjects, and the number of women considerably exceeds that of the men.[1]

There are no inscriptions to help us either with historical names, or even the style of their characters, to the age of these caves. From the simplicity of their sculptures we may perhaps be justified in relegating them to about A.D. 450 to 500, and regarding the wall paintings as belonging to the sixth century.

---

[1] See my *Notes on the Rock-Temples of Ajaṇṭá*, pp. 94 ff.

CHAPTER IV.

THE BUDDHIST CAVES AT ELURA.

The largest and most varied group of Cave Temples in India are certainly those at Verûlê, Elorâ or Elurâ,[1] about twelve miles east of Aurangâbâd, in the Nizam's territory, consisting as they do, of some of the largest and finest examples of the works of all the three sects—Buddhists, Brahmans, and Jains.

The caves are excavated in the face of a hill, or rather the scarp of a large plateau, and run nearly north and south for about a mile and a quarter, the scarp at each end of this interval throwing out a horn towards the west. It is where the scarp at the south end begins to turn to the west that the earliest caves—a group of Buddhist ones—are situated; and in the north horn is the Indra Sabhâ or Jaina group, at the other extremity of the series. The Brahmanical group is situated between the two, and the ascent of the ghâṭ passes up the south side of Kailâsa, the third, and over the roof of the Dâś Avatâra, the second of them. Sixteen caves lie to the south of Kailâsa, fourteen being Buddhist,—and nearly as many to the north—Brahmanical and Jaina, but scattered over a greater distance.

From their great extent and magnificence the Elurâ caves have attracted considerable attention,[2] and were described by Theve-

---

[1] The Brahmanical name for the modern shrine at the village of Elurâ is Ghṛishṇeśwara, *Archæol. Sur. Rep.*, vol. iii. p. 82. It is one of the twelve sacred tîrthas, containing *Lingas* of Śiva, the others being,—Somnâth in Kâṭhiâwâṛ; Mahâkâla at Ujjain; Oṁkâra on an island in the Narmadâ; Tryambak near Nâsik; Nâganâth in the Nizam's territory, east of Ahmadnagar; Vaidyanâth in the Dekhan; Bhîmasankar at the source of the Bhîma, north-west of Poona; Kedareśwar in the Himâlayas; Viśwânâth in Banaras; Mallikârjuna, on Śriśaila mountain in the Karnatic; and Râmeśwar in the extreme south on an island opposite to Ceylon.

[2] The earliest mention made of them seems to be that of Masu'di. In B. de Meynard's translation we read:—"Nous avons décrit les temples de l'Inde consacrés aux idoles qui ont la forme de *bodrah* (sans doute *pradjapati*) c'est-a-dire du germe qui parut dans l'Inde à l'origine des temps; le grande temple nommé *Aladra* [الادري for الاوري Alura], où les Indiens se rendent en pèlerinage des régions les plus éloignées, le temple a une ville entière a titre de foundation pieuse et il est entouré de mille cellules où vivent les dévots qui se consacrent á l'adoration particulière de cette idole," tom. iv. p. 95. I owe this reference to Mr. E. Rehatsek. Ferishtah also refers to them.

not,[1] Anquetil du Perron in 1758,[2] by Sir Charles W. Malet[3] in 1794. Colonel Sykes[4] visited them about 1820, and many others have since then visited and described them.[5]

In 1803 Thomas Daniell published 24 views of these caves in folio, accompanied by plans made under his direction by James Wales, which are by far the most splendid and accurate account of these caves, as a whole, which has yet been published.

Beginning at the extreme south end of the series, where the oldest are situated, we find a group of Buddhist caves, apparently ranging from about A.D. 350 to 550, and popularly known as the Dhêṛawâṛâ, or low caste's quarter. It is not clear whether this term was applied out of contempt for the Buddhists by the modern Hindus, or is a corruption of Thêrawâṛâ or quarter of the Thêras[6] or teachers, or, from their having in later times been occupied by Ḍhêṛs.

The first cave is much filled up with earth. It is, however, of no great interest, except as perhaps one of the oldest here, and probably attached to the next. It was a Vihâra or monastery with eight cells inside for monks, four in the back and four in the south side. It is 41 feet 6 inches wide and 42 feet 3 inches deep. The front has all

---

[1] *Voyage des Indes*, pp. 221–223.

[2] *Zend Avesta. Disc. prel.*, pp. ccxxxiv–ccxlix. He calls the place Iloura; R. Gough's *Comparative View*, pp. 60 ff.

[3] *Asiat.* Res., vol. v. pp. 382–424, with nine plates, and plan of Kailâs, but exceedingly inaccurate.

[4] *Trans. Bomb. Lit. Soc.*, vol. iii. pp. 265–323, with thirteen Plates, and two sheets of inscriptions. The drawings are by no means correct, but they are much better than Malet's.

[5] Capt. J. B. Seeley visited them in 1810, and wrote an octavo volume of 560 pages, entitled *The Wonders of Elora*, &c. (published in 1824), giving a long inflated account of these temples, and of his own adventures, &c. The frontispiece, plan of Kailâs, and two other plates, are evidently copied from those in Malet's paper without acknowledgment, and signed "J. B. S. delt." For other notices *see* Bird's *Historical Researches*, pp. 18–30; *Trans. R. As. Soc.*, vol. ii. pp. 326, 328, 487; Sykes, *Jour. R. As. Soc.*, vol. v. pp. 81–90; Fergusson, *ib.*, vol. viii. pp. 73–83, or *Rock-cut Temples*, pp. 44–54; and *Ind. and East. Arch.*, pp. 127, 163, 262, 334–337, 445; Buckley, ... *Calcutta Rev.*, vol. xxi. p. 457; Wilson, *ib.*, vol. xlii.; *J. B. B. R. A. Soc.*, vol. iii. pt. ii. pp. 80–84; Muir, *Notes of a Trip*, &c., pp. 53–63; *The Rock Temples of Elurâ or Verul*, by J. Burgess (Bombay, 1877).

[6] There was a Buddhist school called Therawâdîs, conf. Oldenberg's *Vinayapiṭakam*, Int. p. xli.

fallen, except one pillar near the south end. Outside, in the south end of what may have been a verandah, is another cell or room.

The second is a large and interesting cave, and was, doubtless, a chapel or hall for worship. It is approached by a flight of steps leading to the top of a stylobate, the front of which has been carved in compartments with fat *gaṇa* or dwarf figures, often in grotesque attitudes. On this, four pillars, with pilasters at the ends, once supported the roof of the verandah, but this is now entirely gone (*see* plan, Plate LVII., fig. 2).

At the north end of the verandah is a fat squatting figure with a high and elaborate headdress or *mukuṭa*, a jewelled cord over his breast, and a bouquet of flowers in his right hand, attended by a *chauri*-bearer with his fly-flap. Right and left are small figures of Buddha sitting, with attendant *chauri*-bearers. On the south was probably a similar female figure, but only the attendant is left, and a *gandharva* or cherub holding a garland over her head. These figures are often met with, and may be conventional representations of the prince who executed the cave, and his wife, or possibly Suddhodana and Mayâdêvî, or (as in the Ajaṇṭâ paintings) of Śakra or Indra,—a favourite divinity with the Buddhists and Jains, and represented as almost a servant or attendant on Buddha,—with his wife Sachî or Ambâ.

Two tall guardians or *dwârpâlas* stand by the door with lofty head-dresses and aureoles, *gandharvas* or cherubs over their shoulders, and a female figure with an aureole or *nimbus* behind her head, standing between the *dwârpâla* and the door.

The front wall is pierced by a door and two windows, and much of the remaining wall, together with the jambs of the windows, is covered with sculptures of Buddha. The cave is peculiar in having lateral galleries along each side, and, exclusive of these, measures nearly 48 feet square. The roof is supported by twelve massive columns arranged in a square, with elegant cushion capitals and high square bases, of the type found at Elephanta, standing on a platform raised about 18 inches above the front and side aisles, which are about 17 feet high. Except the four in the back row, they have little dwarf figures on the upper corners of the square portions of the shafts; above these they are circular and fluted, while the spaces between the dwarf figures and a belt below them are covered with rich and varied arabesques (*see* Plate LVIII., fig. 1).

The side galleries have each four pillars in front, of a different design, while the fronts of the galleries are carved with florid work and musicians. In the five compartments of the back of each gallery are as many Buddhas seated in the same attitude as the colossal one in the shrine, and with his usual *chauri*-bearers, the one on his right hand usually holding also a lotus-bud. These side galleries were perhaps an afterthought, for in that on the north side some of the figures are quite unfinished.

The *dwârpâlas* of the shrine are large figures, 13 to 14 feet high: that on the left or north side is Padmapâni, very plainly dressed, with his robe fastened round the waist by a string; his headdress is the *jaṭâ* of plaited hair worn by ascetics; he has a small image of Amitâbha Buddha as a crest on the front of it, and holds a *mâlâ* or rosary in his right hand, and a lotus-stalk in his left. The other (on the south side) perhaps Indra,—as is almost always the case – has a very richly jewelled headdress, with a small dâgoba on the front of it, bracelets, armlets, a thick jewelled Brahmanical cord or *janvi*, and a small bouquet of flowers in his right hand. Both are attended by two pairs of flying *gandharvas* above, while about midway up the wall are others with curly wigs, bearing garlands. Between each *dwârpâla* and the door is a female worshipper with a flower in her right hand.

The shrine contains a colossal Buddha seated on a throne borne up at the corners by lions. His feet rest on a nearly circular plinth; his hands are in the *dharmachakra mudrâ*, and through the palm of the left hand passes the corner of his robe. This attitude, as well as a few others, are repeated scores of times, and is that of the Teacher enumerating, like Socrates, the points of his argument or lecture on his fingers. His head, always represented as covered with small knobs as of short-cut curly or woolly hair, and with a pile of them on the top, is surrounded by the usual *nimbus*. On each side of it are *gandharvas*. At each end of his throne stand his attendant *chauri*-bearers, who are just the duplicates of the warders outside. And on each side wall is a colossal standing figure of a Buddha. His right hand hangs down, and has the palm turned out; the left is bent upwards, and holds a part of his robe. In the corners next to these are four worshipping figures, one above the other. This cell is dark, but one of the least damaged of the sort here. The nose of Buddha has been broken off, probably within the last few years.

On each side of the shrine is a double cell in line with the side aisles. In the outer of these, and all over the front wall, are many figures of Buddha in different attitudes, with his attendants—the largest figure, however, being of a female on the front wall, right opposite to the north *dwârpâla* of the shrine, and with similar head-dress, lotus, &c., attended by two smaller females with lotus flowers. It is difficult to say who this may represent. It may be Mâyâ, the mother of Buddha, or his wife Yaśodharâ, or probably Târâ—a female counterpart of Avalôkiteśwara or Padmapâni,—all of whose symbols she possesses. In other places, too, we find Padmapâni attended by a female, and frequently by two.

The horse-shoe-shaped arch, representing the window of a *Chaitya* cave, the Buddhist-rail pattern, and the dagobâ in bas-relief, which are almost the sole ornaments in the early Buddhist caves at Bhâjâ, Beḍsâ, Kondânê, and Nâsik, have in this, and in the other caves here, almost entirely disappeared; we find only two small dâgobas in relief over an image of Buddha in the cell on the south of the shrine, and a third on the end of the south gallery. This and the profusion of imagery would seem to indicate a late date for the cave. Moreover, though evidently intended, like the Chaitya caves, solely as a place for worship, it has not the arched roof so general in such caves. It is very difficult to fix an age for it, but it may have been begun in the fifth or sixth century, while the carving may have been continued down to the seventh.

Proceeding northwards; between the last cave and the third is a water cistern, now filled up with earth.

The third cave, somewhat lower down in the rock, is a Vihâra or monastery, and belongs to about the same age as the second; it is probably the older of the two, but, like it, never seems to have been perfectly completed. The south half of the front wall is now entirely gone, as is also the verandah before it. It measures nearly 46 feet square and about 11 high, the roof being supported by twelve square columns with drooping ears falling over circular necks,— a sort of Indian Ionic. Three of them on each side are only blocked out, with octagonal necks. The cells for the monks have been twelve,—five on each side and two in the back,—but the front one on the south side is now broken away. Between the two cells in the back is the shrine,—smaller than in the last cave, and the figures more abraded, but otherwise almost exactly the same; the uppermost of the four supplicants in the corners, however, has no attendants. *See* plan, Plate LVII., fig. 3.

On the north wall of the cave are two small sculptures (one of them just begun) of Buddha and attendant *chauri*-bearers.

There is a window in the front wall, north of the door, which has been divided by two colonnettes, both broken. It is bordered outside by a neat florid pattern. In the north end of the verandah is a chapel containing a Buddha with his legs crossed in front, and, as usual in most of the caves, with his hands in the teaching *mudrâ*. He is seated on a lotus, the stalk of which is supported by small figures having snake or *nâga*-hoods over their heads,—the males usually with three, five, or seven hoods, and the females with one or three. This sort of seat is known as a *padmâsana*, or lotus-throne. Buddha is attended, as usual, with two *chauri*-bearers, the one on his left having a *jaṭâ* or headdress of plaited hair, with long locks hanging over the front of his shoulders, and a lotus in his left hand. Above their heads are *gandharvas*, or Indian cherubs.

On the right of this apartment is a much damaged copy of the pictorial litany described in No. VII. of the Aurangâbâd caves, but on a much smaller scale.

The next four or five caves are somewhat difficult to arrange satisfactorily; indeed, they are so damaged that it is not easy to say how many of the apartments were separate caves, or how many belonged to one. We shall, however, take first the lower floor of the next as No. 4, Plate LVII. It is much ruined, the whole of the outer half of it having disappeared. It measured 35 feet wide by 39 deep up to two pillars and pilasters with capitals having drooping florid ears, the shafts square below, and the necks having 32 flat flutes. Behind these is a cross aisle, and at the left or north end of it is a prominent figure of Lôkeśwara seated like Buddha, with high *jaṭâ* headdress, a small image of Buddha as a crest on the front of it, and his locks hanging down upon his shoulders, a deer-skin over his left shoulder, a *mâlâ* or rosary in his right hand, and clasping a lotus to his left thigh. He is attended by two females, one on his right hand with a rosary, the other holding a flower bud. Above the first is a standing Buddha, and over the latter another seated cross-legged on a lotus, with his right hand raised and the left down.

In the wall are doors to two cells and the shrine. The *dwârpâlas* are carved with elaborate headdresses, and a dwarf stands between each and the door. In the shrine Buddha is seated in the usual teaching attitude with a *nimbus* behind his head, and the foliage of the sacred Bo or Bodhi-tree rising from behind it. The *chauri*-bearers in this case stand behind the throne, and are only in *bas-relief*. The tall attendant on his left is richly dressed, and wears a jewelled cord like the Brahmanical *jânvi* across his breast; the other is destroyed.

In a cell on the south side of this cave is some sculpture. The west side is broken away, and blocked up by a mass of rock that has slipped down from above. The figures are principally Buddha with attendants, and a female with a rosary, &c.; but to the west of the door is a Padmapâni, and half of what has been already described in the last cave as a sort of litany, only that here there are two supplicants in each case, and that a smaller flying figure of Padmapâni is represented before each group.

The Mahârwâḍâ cave.[1]—Ascending a few steps we enter the fifth excavation, a very large Vihâra cave, about 117 feet deep by 58½ wide, exclusive of two large side recesses, Plate LIX. The roof is supported by twenty-four pillars with square shafts, and capitals of the type found at Elephanta, and in the second cave here, having a thick torus or compressed cushion as the chief feature of the capital. They are arranged in two rows extending from front to back, and the space between is divided into three passages by two low stone benches, similar to those found in the Darbar cave at Kanheri (Plate LIV.). Their presence here at once suggests that this cave may have been used for the same purposes. That in fact it was the Dharmaśâlâ of the group, though, it must be confessed, it is not so easy to demonstrate its appropriateness for that purpose, as in the case of the Kanheri cave, nor to reconcile its disposition with the descriptions of Buddhist authors. Its arrangements generally do not seem well adapted to a hall of assembly, but it must be recollected that it is a very late cave of the sixth,

---

[1] There is some confusion about the name of this cave. In 1803 it was called the Dherwara by Daniell, and has since generally borne that name. Mr. Burgess, however, is quite certain that that appellation belongs to the caves represented on Plate LVII., and that this cave was properly called by natives on the spot "Maharwara."—J. F.

possibly of the seventh, century, and we ought not to be surprised at any vagary the Buddhist architects indulged in at that period. It has been suggested that it was a refectory, but solid tables that you cannot get your legs under, nor get close to while squatting, are not a likely arrangement, nor one adapted to the simple fare of ascetic monks; besides these tables are very much in excess of the accommodation required for the 20 monks this cave might accommodate. Till therefore some better explanation of its peculiarities is brought forward, we are probably justified in assuming that it was the chapter house, or hall of assembly, of this group of Buddhist caves.

At the entrance of the left aisle is a chapel which contained a sitting figure of Buddha, now quite destroyed. In the shrine at the back is a large seated Buddha with attendants, and on each side the door, in arched recesses, as at a Bâgh, are attendants separately; Padmapâni, on the north side, attended by two small female figures with headdresses resembling royal crowns. The other figure is more richly bejewelled and similarly attended, while above *gandharvas* or cherubs on clouds bring garlands and presents to them.

Connected with this cave on the south side is another shrine, over the Cave No. 4, Plate LVII., but the rock having fallen away it is inaccessible without a ladder. This shrine contained the usual image of Buddha and attendants: also a female figure holding a lotus-stalk, with her attendants. Round it was a passage or *pradakshiṇa* for circumambulation, as in Hindu temples. From this passage and the vestibule in front several cells were entered. The half of the shrine, however, has slid down, and now blocks up the west side of the front cell of the Cave No. 4 just below it.

Northwards from this we enter a hall with a stair landing in it from the cave below. This hall, of which the west side is entirely gone, is 26 feet from north to south, and 28¾ from east to west. On the east side it has three cells, and on the north has been separated from a still larger and very lofty hall by two pillars and their corresponding pilasters, of which only one pillar and pilaster remain. The central hall was 26½ feet wide and about 43 feet in length, exclusive of the antechamber at its east end, cut off from it by two pillars and their pilasters, as was also another hall on the north, 27 feet by 29, similar to that on the south, with three cells in the back, and as many in the east end, all with very high steps (*see* Plate LX., fig VI.).

The antechamber in the front of the shrine is filled with sculpture. On the north end is a female dressed exactly in the garb of Padmapâni. On the south end is a similar female figure, supposed to represent Sarasvatî, the goddess of learning, with a peacock at her left hand; below it a pandit reading. Neither of these are seen in the Plate No. LXI., which represents this façade. In it on the left, or north side, of the cell door is Padmapâni with his usual attributes, and two *gandharvas* above, and a male and female attendant below. It is not so clear who the corresponding figure of a dwârpâla on the right may represent, probably Manjuśrî. Both are tall, carefully executed in all their details, and the figures by which they are accompanied, and the foliage above their heads, are of very considerable elegance. The frame work of the door of the cell is simpler than is generally found at that age, and in better taste than in most examples of its class.

In the shrine is a large image of Buddha seated, with the usual attendants. On the side walls are three rows containing, each, three Buddhas with their feet turned up, while below them on each side are worshippers and others.

On the north side of the front hall, a passage, divided from a balcony or small cave by two pillars, is the only way of access now left to a shrine which we may call the ninth cave. This has a well-carved façade, as seen from the south, which it faces. It consists of a small outer balcony and an inner covered portico, separated by two pillars, square below, octagonal above, and with drooping-eared capitals. On the back wall are two deep pilasters or attached column, with the compressed cushion capitals of the Elephanta cave style. These divide the wall into three compartments: in the centre one is a seated Buddha with four *gandharvas* above; in the left one is Padmapâni with two female attendants and two fat *gandharvas* above; in the east one is Buddha's other usual attendant, whether Indra, Manjuśrî, or Vajrapâni, with two females, &c.

Returning now through No. VI. to the stair, we descend into the seventh, a large plain Vihâra, 51½ feet wide by 43½ deep, the roof supported by only four square columns. It has five cells in the back, and three on each side, but is no ways interesting, and appears never to have been finished.

The eighth may be entered from the last by a roughly-cut passage, or perhaps unfinished cell, in its north wall, and may be described as consisting of two rooms and the shrine, with its circumambulatory passage. The inner hall is 28 feet by 25, with three cells on the north side, and is cut off by two pillars and pilasters at each end, on the east from the shrine, with its surrounding *pradakshiṇa*, and on the west from the outer apartment.

The shrine has the usual *dwârpâlas* and their attendants at the door; and inside is the seated Buddha with his attendants, but in this case Padmapâni has *four* arms, holding the *châuri* and the lotus in his left hands, and over his shoulder hangs a deer-skin. At his feet are small figures of devotees, and behind them is a tall female figure with a flower in her left hand, and a *gandharva* over her head. The other tall male attendant has a similar companion on his left, with a lotus flower and a rosary in her hands.

On the wall, at the south entrance to the *pradakshiṇa*, is a sculpture of Saraswatî, somewhat similar to the one in the cave above. Opposite is a cell, and in the passage two more, while behind the shrine is a long, raised recess with two square pillars in front.

The outer room is 28 feet by 17, with a slightly raised platform filling the west end of it. On the north side is a chapel on a raised floor with two slender columns in front, on the back wall of which is a seated Buddha, with attendants dressed nearly alike, with Brahmanical cords, necklaces, and armlets, but no *chauris*, the one on Buddha's left holding in his hand a three-pronged object, which is half of what we shall find as his frequent cognizance in other caves,—the *vajrâ* or thunderbolt, whence he may be styled Vajrapâni. On the west wall is Padmapâni with the female figure that we find so frequently associated with him.

Coming out of this by the large opening on the south side, just under the ninth cave, we find on the face of the rock to the west, but partly broken away, a sculptured group of a fat male and female, the latter with a child on her knees, and attendant, which we find in other caves,[1] and have supposed to represent the parents of Buddha, and himself as an infant, in fact, a Buddhist Holy Family.

There is now a break in the continuity of the caves, and we have to go some way northwards to the next and probably most modern group of all the Buddhist caves.

---

[1] In Cave IV. at Ajaṇṭâ and Cave VII. at Aurangâbâd for example.

Viswakarma Cave.

The next cave is locally known as the Sutâr ka jhoprâ or Viśwakarma, and is much frequented by carpenters who come to worship the image of Buddha as Viśwakarma, the patron of their craft. It is the only Chaitya cave here, the cathedral temple of the Buddhist caves. And, though not so magnificent in its proportions, or severe in its decoration, as the great cave at Kârlê, it is still a splendid work, with a large open court in front surrounded by a corridor, and a frieze above its pillars carved with representations of the chase, &c. The inner temple, consisting of a central nave and side aisles, measures 85 feet 10 inches by 43, and 34 feet high. (*See* plan, Plate LXII.) The nave is separated from the aisles by 28 octagonal pillars, 14 feet high, with plain bracket capitals, while two more square ones, just inside the entrance, support the gallery above, and cut off the front aisle. The remote end of the nave is nearly filled by a high dâgoba, 15½ feet in diameter, and nearly 27 feet high, which, unlike older examples, has a large frontispiece, nearly 17 feet high, attached to it—as on that in the Caves Nos. XIX. and XXVI. at Ajaṇṭâ—on which is a colossal seated figure of Buddha, 11 feet high, with his feet down, and his usual attendants, while on the arch over his head is carved his Bodhi-tree, with *gandharvas* on each side.

The arched roof is carved in imitation of wooden ribs, each rising from behind a little *Nâga* bust, alternately male and female, and joining a ridge piece above. The triforium or deep frieze above the pillars is divided into two belts, the lower and narrower carved with crowds of fat little gambolling figures (*gaṇas*) in all attitudes. The upper is much deeper, and is divided over each pillar so as to form compartments, each usually containing a seated Buddha with two attendants and two standing Buddhas or Bôdhisattvas. The inner side of the gallery over the entrance is also divided into three compartments filled with figures.

At the ends of the front corridor, outside, are two cells and two chapels with the usual Buddhist figures repeated. From the west end of the north corridor a stair ascends to the gallery above, which consists of an outer one over the corridor, and an inner one over the front aisle, separated by the two pillars that divide the lower portion of the great window into three lights. The pillars of these

No. 66. Façade of the Viśwakarma Cave at Elura.[1]

corridors are generally of great elegance, having tall square bases changing into octagons, and then to 16 and even more sides, and under the capitals returning to the square by the "vase and falling leaf pattern" (*see* Plate LXIII.). The most remarkable feature, however, of the façade of this cave is that instead of the great horseshoe window, which is characteristic of the Chaitya caves, from the earliest at Bhâjâ to the latest at Ajaṇṭâ, we here find it cut up into three divisions, like a modern Venetian window, with an Attic window over the centre opening. Then for the first time we begin to lose all trace of the wooden forms with which we have so long been familiar,

[1] From Fergusson's *I. & E. Archit.* p. 128.

and find at last Buddhist architecture assuming lithic forms, from which all trace of their origin would soon disappear, but as this cave is the last of its class that is known to exist, we are unable to say what the next change would be, but we may safely predict that it would be even more appropriate to stone architecture than even this façade.

From the outer area, four small chapels are entered, each containing sculptures of Buddhist mythology, and where the very elaborate headdresses of the females of that period may be studied. Over the chapel to the right of the window is a remarkable group of fat little figures (*gaṇa*), similar to those in the Rameśwara Brahmanical cave near by; and the projecting frieze that crowns the façade is elaborately sculptured with pairs of figures in compartments.

High up on each side are two small chapels, difficult of access, and not specially interesting.

From the developed state of the mythological sculptures on the balcony and dâgoba, the ornate headdresses of the figures, and the very marked departure in architectural style in this from the other Chaitya caves, we can hardly assign it a date earlier than first half of the seventh century A.D. Much later we can hardly venture to place it, because after that period we have little evidence that works of the kind were executed by Buddhists.

THE DO THAL.

A little further north is the cave known as *Do Ṭhâl*, because it has for long been regarded as consisting only of two storeys. In 1876 the excavation of the earth from what was then the lower floor revealed the landing of a stair from a cave below. This was partially excavated in 1877, and laid open a verandah, 102 feet in length by 9 feet wide, with two cells and a shrine behind, in which is Buddha with Padmapâni and Vajrapâni or Indra as his attendants, the latter with the *vajra* or thunderbolt in his right hand.

The stair leads into a similar verandah above, with eight square pillars in front, the back wall pierced with five doors. The first, at the stair landing, is only the commencement of a cell. The second, to the south, leads into a shrine with a colossal Buddha, his right hand on his knee, and the left in his lap. In front of the throne, rising from the floor, is a small female figure holding up a water-jar, and to the right another sitting on a prostrate figure. Buddha's left-hand attendant has a flower stalk by his left side, and over the bud is a *vajra* or thunderbolt—a short object with three prongs on either end. On the same (or right) wall are three other tall standing males. The one next Vajrapâni has a similar flower-stalk supporting an oblong object which strongly resembles a native book tied up with a string; this may perhaps be Manjuśrî. The next holds a lotus-bud, and the last a pennon. On the return of the wall is a tall female figure with a flower. On the north side are also three figures, one of which holds a very long sword; and on the return of the wall on this side a fat male figure, adorned with garlands and necklaces, with a round object like a cocoanut in his right, and perhaps a money-bag in his left hand—possibly meant to represent the excavator. Above these figures on either side are seven figures of Buddhas, the foliage of the peculiar *Bodhi*-tree of each extending over his head like an umbrella. The central door leads into a small hall with two square pillars, and partially lighted by two small windows. Behind it is a shrine with a Buddha on a *siñhâsana*, or throne supported by lions, his feet crossed in front of him, his right hand hanging over his knee—in the *Bhumisparśa* or *Vajrâsana mudrâ*. Vajrapâni here holds up his *vajra* in his right hand.

The fourth door has a carved architrave, and leads into a shrine very similar to the corresponding one on the other side the central area. Buddha, as usual, with his attendants Padmapâni, bejewelled and wearing a thick cord or necklace, and Vajrapâni with three tall figures on either side, the one next to Vajrapâni having a book on the top of the flower-bud he holds, the strings by which it is held together being distinctly visible. There are seven squatting Buddhas above, with the foliage extending over their heads; and on the inside of the front wall, on the north, a fat male figure with garlands and necklaces, a round object,—perhaps a cocoanut—in his right hand, and in his left what appears to be a purse from which coins are dropping out; on the south side stands a female with a flower in her left hand: these again possibly represent the patron and patroness of the cave. The last door leads into a cell.

At the north end of the verandah the stair ascends to the upper storey. It requires little description: it was intended to have three shrines as below; the south one, however, has not been commenced; the north one contains a squat, and the central a sitting Buddha with two attendants only. On the walls are many small Buddhas, a Padmapâni with four arms, females with lotus-buds, &c.

There are several cells in the court; but, as it has not been cleaned out, and is deep in silt, only one of them is accessible, containing a headless image of Buddha, a seated Lokeśvara, and other sculptures.

THE TIN THAL.

The court of this fine cave has been thoroughly cleaned of the silt that filled it, and thus (thanks to the Nizam's Government) its ample area and great depth is now shown off to advantage. The labour in originally excavating such a court alone out of the solid rock must have been enormous. (*See* plan, Plate LXIV.)

Like the last, it is of three storeys, the first entered by a few steps ascending from the court. It has eight square columns with bases, and plain brackets in the front, the upper portion of the central pair being covered with very pretty florid ornamentation. Behind the front row are other two lines of eight pillars each, and in the area that recedes back in the centre are six more columns, making thirty in all.

In a large compartment on the back wall, to the left of the approach to the shrine, is a sculpture in nine squares: in the centre Buddha with *chauri*-bearers; to his right and left Padmapâni and Vajrapâni; and, above and below, the six figures found in the shrines of the Do Ṭhâl, with book, sword, flag, buds and flowers. This sculpture is repeated over and over again in different parts of this cave. In the corresponding position on the south side has been a seated Buddha, now quite destroyed. In three cells in the north side are stone couches for the monks. In central recesses right and left of the vestibule to the shrine are Buddhas squatting on *siñhâsanas*, the left attendants having different flowers in each case.

On each side the shrine door is a fat, seated guardian, with flower-stalks, that on the south side having the book laid over a bud.

The shrine contains an enormous squat Buddha, over 11 feet from the seat to the crown of the head. High up on each side wall are five squat Buddhas, and below are larger sitting figures: to the left, 1*st*, Padmapâni with his lotus; 2*nd*, a figure with something very like a crozier; 3*rd*, one with a sword over a flower; and, 4*th*, with fruit and a flag. On the right, 1*st*, Vajrâpâni, defaced; 2*nd*, a figure with a flower; 3*rd*, one with flower-stalk and book; 4*th*, with lotus bud. On the inside of the front wall are—on the north a squatting female with a belt over her breasts; and on the south, one with four arms, a bottle, and a flower.

From the south end of the front aisle the stair ascends, and from the first landing a room is entered on the south side of the court, with two pillars in front. On the back wall is a Buddha on a high throne with his usual attendants; and on the west side is Padmapâni seated between a male and female—the latter, perhaps, his wife. There are many smaller figures, four-armed Devîs, &c., in this room.

From this the stair leads up to the first floor. It has a long open verandah in front, and a large central entrance divided by two square pillars leads into the hall. There are also entrances from near each end of the verandah. These lead into a long hall, 11 feet 5 inches high, divided into three aisles by two rows of eight pillars each. On the ends of the central vestibule are many sculptures,—among them Padmapâni seated between two females (one of them with a bottle), a *dâgoba*, figures of Buddha, females, &c.

The shrine door has two fine *dwârpâlas*. Padmapâni on the north side holds a fully blown lotus and a rosary or *mâlâ*, and the other his *vajra;* both have jewelled belts, &c. Inside is an enormous squatting Buddha, and in front of the low throne is a female holding up a *loṭâ*, and opposite her a smaller one standing over a prostrate figure. At the ends of the throne are large figures of Padmapâni and Vajrapâni with their emblems, and on each side wall four figures —while on the front wall are the usual male and female, which I have supposed to represent the patron of the cave and his wife. Above are seven squatting Buddhas on shelves.

In the north end of the verandah is Buddha sitting with the wheel between his heels, and two deer on the ground in front. On each side are his usual attendants and a standing Buddha—coarsely executed. From this point the stair ascends, and in the jamb of the window at the first landing is a figure on horseback with two attendants; above is a female with a flower.

The upper floor is the most striking among the Buddhist caves. It is divided into five cross aisles by rows of eight pillars, which with two in front of the shrine, are forty-two in all, perfectly plain square columns (*see* Plate LXV). In recesses at the ends of the aisles are large figures of Buddhas seated on thrones, with their usual attendants. At the south end of the back aisle the Buddha is on a *sinhâsana* with the wheel in the middle, and lying in front two finely-cut deer, unfortunately broken by some barbarian. Possibly this may be intended as an allusion to Buddha's teaching in the Mṛigadava or deer-park at Banâras--which seems to have been a favourite resort of his. In the north end of the same aisle Buddha is represented in a squatting attitude, his feet drawn up in front of him, and his hands in the teaching *mùdrā.* He sits on a throne with a lion in the centre, but, instead of his usual attendants, on either side of him are (1) a squatting Buddha with hands in his lap, in the act of ascetic meditation, by which he attained Buddhahood ; (2) above this is Buddha soaring to the heavens to preach his law to the gods; and (3) Buddha dying or entering *nirvâṇa*—everlasting, undisturbed, unconscious repose. These are the great scenes in his life as a Teacher.

To the right of this figure, on a raised basement, along the back wall, extending from the corner to the vestibule of the shrine are seven large squat meditative Buddhas, all perfectly alike, except that each has the foliage of a different *Bodhi*-tree represented over his head springing from behind the *nimbus* or aureole. These are the seven human or earth-born Buddhas, painted also in Cave XXII. at Ajaṇṭâ with the name below each, as Vipasya, Sikhi, Viśwabhu, Krakuchchhanda, Kanaka Muni, Kaśyapa, and Śâkya Siñha.

On the south side of the vestibule is a similar row of seven meditating Buddhas,[1] being perhaps the representations of the same personages, only with umbrellas over their heads, as symbols of dominion, instead of the *Bodhi*-trees.

The vestibule of the shrine contains two tall *dwârpâlas* with crossed arms and lofty headdresses; on each end wall are three female

[1] The Jñâni or divine Buddhas are only five :—(1) Vairochana, (2) Akshobhya, (3) Ratna Sambhava, (4) Amitâbha, and (5) Amogha Siddha—the mental creations of Adi Buddha, and each of whom respectively produced a Bódhisattwa, viz. (1), Sâmanta Bhadra, (2) Vajrâpâni, (3) Ratnapani, (4) Padmapâni, and (5) Viśwapâni. Had there been *seven* Jñâni Buddhas we might have supposed that this second group represented them.

figures seated on a high basement, with the right foot down and resting on a lotus, and the left turned under her. The one next the corner on each side has four arms, and holds a *mâlâ* or rosary and a crooked rod; she is, doubtless, the counterpart of some Hindu Dêvî, like Lakshmî or Saraswatî, introduced into the Buddhist mythology. On the back wall on each side are three similar figures, but all with two arms, and each holding some symbol, as a flower, *vajra*, &c. They sit on *padmâsanas*, or lotus-thrones, supported by *nâga*-canopied figures, standing among lotos leaves, fish, birds, &c. They are perhaps Lochanâ, Târâ, and Mâmukhî, female counterparts of the Bôdhisattwas we have already met with in the shrines. Above all are four Buddhas on each division of the back wall, and five on each end wall.

In the shrine is the usual very large squat Buddha, which the natives persist in worshipping as Râma. His nose and lips have long been wanting, but these as well as mustachios are supplied in plaster, and whenever they fall or are knocked off, their place is speedily restored by fresh ones. On his left is Padmapâni or Avalôkiteśwara, with a *chauri*, and, as usual, a small figure of Amitâbha Buddha on the front of his cap; next to him is a figure with a bud; then one with a long sword on his right, with a flower in his left hand; a fourth with a fruit and flower or small *chauri*, and the fifth with some unrecognisable object and a branch or flower. On Buddha's left are Vajrapâni and four other similar figures. On the inside of the front wall are a male and female—the male with a purse and money. Above, on each side, are squatting figures of Buddha.

In the north side of the court of this cave is a small one with two pillars in the east face, and containing a water-cistern.

This is the last of the Buddhist caves here; it bears decided evidences of belonging to the latest form of the *Mahâyâna* sect in India, and was perhaps one of the latest executed—probably not before 700 A.D.

CHAPTER IV.

AURANGABAD CAVE TEMPLES.

The group of caves at Aurangabad, though one of the smallest and least known, is far from being one of the least interesting among the Cave Temples of Western India. With the exception of a small and ruinous Chaitya, and some insignificant cells, they are all of one age, and that of the latest known. They are, in fact, the last dying effort of the style, and, like most architectural objects similarly situated, these caves display an excess of ornamentation and elaborateness of detail, which, though pleasing at first sight, is very destructive of true architectural effect. To the historian of art they are not, however, less interesting on that account, nor less worthy of attention in this place.

The hills in which these caves are situated lie to the north of the city, about a mile from the walls, and rise to a height of about 700 feet above the plains, presenting a precipitous scarp to the the south—the side in which the caves are excavated.

They may be divided into three groups, scattered over a distance of fully a mile and a half, the first and second of which are Buddhist of a late date; and the third—from their unfinished condition and the entire absence of sculpture in them, it is difficult to say to what sect they belonged.

The first group consists of five caves lying nearly due north from the city. They are reached by a footpath ascending the right side of the gorge or recess of the hill in which they are, at a level of about 300 feet above the plain. Commencing from the west end of the series, or that farthest from where the path lands, we shall number them towards the east.

Cave I., the most westerly of this group, is reached by a precipitous and difficult footpath leading up to it from the others, which are all at a lower level. The front, which is 74 feet in length, has had four advanced pillars forming a porch, and supporting a great mass of rock projecting far in advance of the pillars of the verandah.[1] A great slab of rock, however, several feet thick and more than fifty in length, has split off by a horizontal flaw, and fallen down on the platform, crushing the pillars of the porch under it.

The verandah is 76 feet 5 inches long and 9 feet wide, with eight pillars in front, each with square bases and round or polygonal shafts of four different patterns, and bracket capitals with struts under each wing of the bracket, carved mostly with female figures. The whole style of these columns is so similar to that of those of Cave I. at Ajaṇṭâ, and of others near the eastern extremity of the group, they must be assigned to the same age, while this being probably the last cave attempted here, it fixes the latest limit of this series as about coeval with or slightly subsequent to the latest at Ajaṇṭâ—say towards the middle or end of the seventh century A.D.

The back wall of the verandah is pierced for three doors and two windows. It was intended for a 28 pillared Vihâra; but the work was stopped when only the front aisle, about 9 feet wide, had been roughly cleared out.

CAVE II.—Descending now to the second cave, we find that it has been a temple intended solely for worship, and yet not of the pattern usually designated Chaitya caves, but of a form probably borrowed by the *Mahâyâna* sect of Buddhists from the Brahmanical temples. The front is quite destroyed, but it has consisted of a verandah or open hall, 21 feet 6 inches wide by 12 feet 10 inches deep, with two pillars and their corresponding pilasters in front. Behind this the floor is raised about 2 feet, and on this stand two square pillars neatly carved on the upper halves of the shafts. Inside these is an aisle, about 9 feet wide and 21 feet long, in front of the shrine, which is surrounded by a *pradakshiṇâ* or passage for circumambulation—a ceremony probably taken over, with others, from the Brahmanical religions, and employed by the *Hinâyâna* or primitive Buddhists in connexion with the *Chaitya*, and by the *Mahâyâna* or later development of the sect, as in this case, in connexion with the shrine containing the principal image.

At the doorway of this shrine stand two tall figures, each upon a lotus flower. That on the left of the door is the more plainly dressed, and from the small image of Buddha on his forehead and

[1] *Archæological Reports*, vol. iii., Bidar and Aurangabad, p. 60, Plates XL. and XLI.

the lotus stalk he grasps in his right hand, at the top of which is also a figure of Buddha, we may suppose it was meant for Padmapâni or Avalôkitêśwara, and the more elaborately-dressed one on the other side for Indra. Each is attended by a *vidyádhara* or *gandharva* and by a *Nága* figure with the five-hooded cobra. Inside is a seated Buddha, 9 feet high, his feet on a lotus footstool, and his hands in the *dharmachakra* or teaching *mudrâ*, with celestial admirers over each shoulder. On the walls are four rows of smaller figures, each with his attendant *chauri* bearers, and some in the *Jñâna* and others in the *dharmachakra mudrâ.*

The walls of the *pradakshiṇá* are also covered with multitudes of similar figures. This cave is hardly earlier than the first, but not separated from it by any long interval. They were probably excavated within the same century.

Cave III.—The next is the finest cave in the group. It is a vihâra, of which the hall is 41½ feet wide by 42½ feet deep, with twelve columns, all richly carved in a variety of patterns combining the styles of Caves I. and XXVI. at Ajaṇṭâ.[1] One pillar and a pilaster on Plate LXVI. illustrate the style, but as all are varied, and some richer than even these, they convey no idea of the richness of effect produced by the elaborate and elegant decorations of this cave. On each side of the hall are two cells, and a room or chapel with two pillars in front; those on the left side are marvels of elaborate sculpture. The verandah has been 30½ feet long by 8 feet 9 inches wide, with four pillars in front, and a chapel at each end, but it is entirely ruined. The antechamber to the shrine has two pillars and pilasters in front, with struts from their capitals consisting of female figures standing under foliage. The shrine is occupied by the usual colossal Buddha, his feet down, and hands in the *dharmachakra mudrá*, but the face and one knee have been damaged. (For Plan and details, *see* Plate LXVI.)

It has one striking peculiarity, however, not noticed elsewhere, namely, two groups of worshipping figures about life-size which occupy the front corners of the shrine, seven on one side and six on the other, both male and female, some with garlands in their

---

[1] For details see *Archæological Reports*, vol. iii. pp. 64-72, and Plates XLIII. to XLVIII.

hands, mostly with thick lips and very elaborate headdresses[1] and necklaces.

It is difficult to conjecture the age of this work, but it may be approximately placed about 640 to 650 A.D., or even later, for it is evident from an inspection of its plan that the original idea of a Vihâra as an abode of monks had almost as entirely died out, as in the latest caves at Elurâ. There are only four cells in the angles which could be used for that purpose. The back and sides are used as chapels, and adorned in the most elaborate manner, and the whole is a shrine for worship rather than a place of residence. We cannot tell how far the same system might have been adopted in the latest caves at Ajaṇṭâ. The corresponding caves there, XXIII. and IV., are only blocked out, and their plans cannot be ascertained. But this one is certainly later than No. I. there, Plate XL., which still retains all the features of a Vihârâ as completely as the Nahapana caves at Nâsik.

Cave IV.—A few yards to the east of the last is the Chaitya cave, very much ruined, the whole front being gone, and what is left filled with fallen rock, &c. Its dimensions seem to have been 38 feet in length by 22½ wide, with seventeen plain octagonal pillars and a *Dâgoba*, 5 feet 8 inches in diameter. From the primitive simplicity of this cave we can hardly suppose that it was excavated after the middle of the fourth century, and may be even earlier. If this be the case, then we must suppose that there were monks' cells and Vihâras of a much earlier type than any that now remain. These may have been enlarged, and altered into Caves II. and V., or, which seems very probable, they were to the east of No. V., where there is now a large hollow under the rock partially filled up with débris.

Cave V. appears to have been originally a small temple like No. II., but without any *dwârpâlas* to the shrine, which is all that is left. Inside it is about 8 feet square, and contains a large image of Buddha, now appropriated by the Jains of the neighbouring city, and dedicated to Pârśwanâtha.

The second group of caves is about three-quarters of a mile farther east in the same range of hills.

Cave VI., the most westerly of this second series, is considerably

[1] See *Archæological Reports*, vol. iii., Plate XLIX.

higher up in the rock than the next two. It also combines the characteristics of a Vihâra and a temple, consisting of a shrine with its antechamber in the centre, surrounded by a passage or *pradakshiṇâ*, with four cells in each side and two in the back—the latter containing images of Buddha. The front has been supported by four square pillars, of which little more than the bases are left. In front of the antechamber are two square pillars and their corresponding pilasters, with bracket capitals, standing on a step about 15 in. high. On each side the shrine door is a tall *dwârpâla* as in No. II., each accompanied by a smaller female worshipper on the side next the door. By the door jambs stand small male figures, each with the snake-hood canopy. Inside is a colossal Buddha attended by two *chauri*-bearers, 7 ft. high. Here, again, in the front corners of the shrine are worshippers, but not so large as in Cave III.,—five male figures on the right and five females on the left of the entrance.

There are traces of painting left on the roof of the front aisle of this cave in the same style as is used in the roofs of the verandahs at Ajaṇṭâ, and probably of about the same age.

Cave VII. is (after No. III.) the most interesting of this series. The front hall is about 14 ft. deep by 34 ft. in length, with four square pillars and their pilasters in front, and a chapel raised a few steps and cut off by two smaller pillars at each end. From the plan (Plate LXV.) it will be observed the arrangements of this cave make a still further step in advance towards those afterwards found in Brahmanical temples. The cells containing the image of Buddha is boldly advanced into the centre of the cave, and with a *pradakshinâ*, or procession path, round it, so that it can be circumambulated by worshippers, as the Dagobâ was in the earlier caves. The two cells at the ends of the verandah, and the two at the back of the cave, are filled with sculpture, but there are still six remaining, which are suitable for the abode of monks. Notwithstanding this, from the arrangement of its plan and the character of its sculptures, it may be considered one of the very latest caves here, and probably contemporary with the Do Tâl or Tin Tâl Caves at Elurâ, and consequently as excavated after the middle of the seventh century.

In this cave we have the *Mahâyâna* mythology full-blown, with a pantheon rivalling the ordinary Brahmanical one, but differing from it in a remarkable way. The hideous and terrible Rudra, Bhairava, and

Kâlí have not found their counterparts: its divinities are kindly and compassionate, and may be appealed to for protection. Buddha has passed *nirvâṇa*, and is unaffected by aught that takes place in the sphere of suffering humanity, but a legend has sprung up of a Bôdhisattwa of such compassion and self-denial that he has pledged himself never to seek, through *nirvâṇa*, to enter "the city of peace" until he has redeemed the whole race from ignorance and suffering. Such is Padmapâni or Avalôkitéśwara Bôdhisattwa—"the manifested lord" or "the lord who looks down"— the lover and saviour of men,—evidently borrowed from some western and Christian source.[1] To the left of the entrance into the inner cave is a large tableau in which he is represented with the *jaṭâ* headdress of the ascetic, holding the *padma* or lotus which is his cognizance in his left hand and a *mâlâ* or rosary in his right. At each side of the *nimbus* which surrounds his head is a *vidyâdhara* with a garland, and behind each an image of Buddha squatted on a lotus. At each side are four smaller sculptures, which form a pictorial litany cut in stone, executed with such simplicity and clearness that it is read at a glance. In each scene two figures are represented as threatened by some sudden danger, and praying to the merciful lord Avalôkitêśwara, are met by him flying to their deliverance. In the uppermost, on his right hand, the danger is fire; in the next, the sword of an enemy; in the next, chains; and in the lowest, shipwreck; on his left, again, the uppermost represents the attack of a lion, the second of snakes, the third of an enraged elephant, and the last of death represented by the female demon Kâlî about to carry off the child from the mother's lap.

This scene, as we have already remarked, is represented also at Ajaṇṭâ, and in painting in Cave XVII. there, as also at Elurâ and at Kaṇhéri (Plate LV).

On the other side of the door another tall figure is represented with both human and celestial worshippers. The right hand, which probably held a cognizance, is broken; but from the high and very rich headdress we may infer that it is intended for Mañjuśri, the patron of the *Mahâyâna* sect, and who is charged with the spread of the religion.

---

[1] See Prof. Cowell in *Jour. of Philology*, vol. vi. (1876), pp. 222–231, and *Ind. Ant.*, vol. viii.; Vassilief's *Le Bouddisme*, pp. 121, 125, 212, &c., and *Third Arch. Rep.*, pp. 74 ff.

The inner hall is mostly occupied by the shrine, round which there is a *pradakshiṇâ* with three cells in each side aisle, and two small shrines in the back wall, each containing a seated figure of Buddha. The front of the principal shrine is covered with sculpture, chiefly of female figures, three on each side the door, nearly life-size. The centre figure in each case stands on a lotus, has the *nimbus* behind the head, holds a lotus or other flower-bud in one hand, and, like her companions, wears a headdress of extraordinary dimensions[1] and elaboration. They probably represent Târâ—a favourite with the Nepalese,— but whether Bhṛikuta-târâ and Ugra-târâ, or only one of the forms, is not clear.* The two attendants on the right side of the door carry *chauris*, and one of them is attended by a dwarf; those on the left bear flowers, and one is attended by a bandy-legged male dwarf, the other by a female one. The two larger figures in these cases may be Mâmukhî and Lôchanâ. Above are *vidyâdharas* with garlands, and over each side passage are two figures of squatting Buddhas.

Inside is the usual colossal Buddha, with *gandharvas* and *apsarasas* on clouds over his shoulders. On the right wall are standing male and female figures with attendant dwarfs; and on the opposite side, apparently, the representation of a *nachh* or dance, with six female musicians. On the walls are many small figures of Buddha.

In the chapel, in the left end of the front hall, are represented eight figures: on the right Buddha standing, then six females, each distinguished from the other by the style of her coiffure, standing on lotuses and with *nimbi*, and, lastly, a Bôdhisattwa—perhaps Padmapâni.

In the corresponding chapel, at the east or right end, is a sculpture of a fat pair of squatting royal personages, the female with a child on her knee, a female attendant at each side, and *vidyâdharas* in the clouds above with garlands. This is probably intended to represent Suddhodana and Mayâ, the parents of Buddha, with the infant reformer.

No. VIII.—Close to the last is a large recess under the rock, probably the remains of a large ruined cave; over it is the commencement of another, the hall measuring 27 feet by 20, with some sculpture, but quite unfinished.

---

[1] See *Third Arch. Report*, Plate LIII. Fig. 2, and Plate LIV. Figs. 1, 2, and 3.

No. IX. is at a somewhat higher level, but is very much ruined, and filled up with mud. Its front hall has been 85 feet long by nearly 19 feet deep, with three smaller ones at the back, each leading into a shrine, but much of the cave has been left unfinished. On the walls are several female figures larger than life, and on the west wall Buddha is represented, 16 feet in length, lying on his right side, dying or entering *nirvâṇa*, while on the back wall, at his feet, is a four-armed image of Padmapâni—the only one of the kind here.

The other caves in the same hills are perfectly plain and some of them unfinished, with little or nothing to indicate whether they were Buddhist or Brahmanical.

DHAMNAR.

The caves of Dhumnâr or Dhamnâr,[1] near the village of Chandwâs in Rajputana, are about 75 miles north of Ujjain, 70 south of Koṭâ, and 22 miles north-west from those of Kholvi. They were first noticed by Colonel Tod who visited them in December 1821,[2] and they have since been examined by Mr. Fergusson,[3] and General Cunningham,[4] the latter of whom has given a plan of the principal group of Buddhist caves, but on rather too small a scale and with too few details to be of much service.

The flat-topped hill in which they are excavated is composed of a coarse laterite not at all favourable to the execution of the minute details of sculpture. In this hill there are four groups of caves,—two in the north-west, one at the point of a spur to the west, and the fourth and only important group in a bay to the south. Most of them are small, being merely cells, and altogether they may amount to about sixty or seventy.[5]

The principal group on the south face of the hill are all Buddhist caves, and from the style of their architectural details and their

---

[1] Tod writes "Dhoomnâr," Cunningham "Dhamnâr."

[2] *Ann. and Antiq. of Rajasthan*, vol. ii. p. 721 ff., or Madras ed., vol. ii. pp. 660 ff. Tod was misled by his Jain attendant in regarding the Buddhist caves as dedicated to he Tîrthaṅkaras.

[3] *Rock-cut Temples of India*, p. 40; and *Ind. and East. Archit.*, pp. 131–162.

[4] *Archæological Report*, vol. ii. *for* 1864–65, pp. 270 ff.

[5] Fergusson's *Rock-Temples*, p. 42; Tod says he counted "one hundred and seventy," *Rajasthan*, vol. ii. p. 721 conf. Cunningham, *Arch. Rep.*, vol. ii. p. 275.

arrangements they are evidently of a late date. Cunningham assigns them "to the 5th, 6th, and 7th centuries of our era," and there can be little doubt that some of these and in the neighbouring group at Kholvi were probably the last executed Buddhist caves in India, and can hardly be dated before the 8th century A.D., though there may, of course, be some much older caves among them, though from the extreme coarseness of the material in which they are excavated, it is impossible to speak with any confidence as to their age. Some of the detached cells may be earlier, but the larger caves are certainly of very late date.

Several of them are small caves consisting of a small verandah or outer room and one or two cells behind. Two forms of Chaitya caves occur, the one flat-roofed and the other arched. Dâgobas are also placed in cells as at Kuḍâ, &c. One known as the *Bará Kacheri* is a vihâra cave, the hall of which is 20 feet square with four pillars, with three cells on each side, and a shrine containing a dâgoba in the back. The façade is not unlike that of some of the Kânḥeri caves, being supported by two plain pillars, with the side openings closed by a stone screen, only the pillars have bracket capitals in the style of those inside the Viśwakarma cave at Elurâ. The architrave consists of plain members, and the frieze has a dâgoba in bas-relief in the centre and Chaitya-window ornaments on each side.[1]

Passing a small cave the next to the east, known as the *Chhotá Kacheri*, is an arched roofed Chaitya cave 23½ feet by 15, with a dâgoba on a moulded base 9½ feet square at the foot.

A little eastward is another hall, shown in the left of the woodcut (No. 67) on the following page, similar to the first described, but without any shrine or cells inside. To the left of the entrance, however, are four or five cells, and a dâgoba in half relief similar to what we find in the Ghatotkachh cave.

The great cave is locally known as "Bhîm Sing-kâ Bazar" and presents peculiarities of arrangement not met with elsewhere. It is in fact a Chaitya-cave surrounded by a Vihâra (woodcut No. 67).[2] The Chaitya-cave measures 35 feet by 13½, with a vaulted roof ribbed in stone, and having a porch or antechapel in front, on the walls of which are sculptured six dâgobas in half-relief. The usual

---

1 *See* sketch view in Cunningham's *Reports*, vol. ii. Plate LXXX., at p. 271.

2 From Fergusson's *Ind. and East Archit.*, p. 131.

pillared aisle is outside the walls of this cave, and encloses a corridor that runs round the west and north sides, and part of the east, from which four cells of various sizes are entered on the north side, ten on the west, mostly about 7½ feet square, and three on the east, the central and largest one being a Chaitya cell containing a dâgoba. To the left of the entrance also is a similar room; and in advance of the front are two small dâgobas 5 feet in diameter, which seem to occupy the place of the *stambhas* in the older Chaitya-caves. As

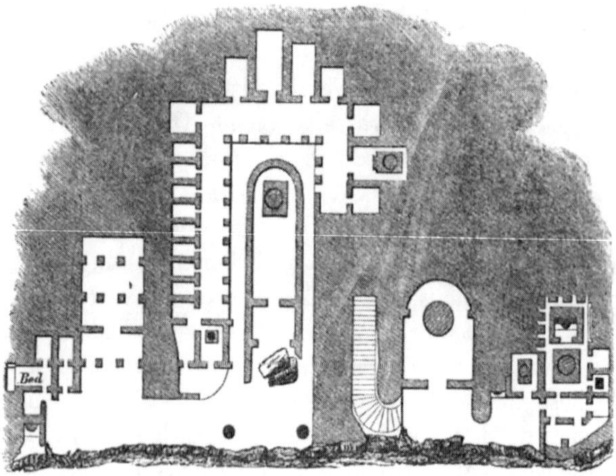

No. 67. Caves at Dhamnâr. (From a plan by General Cunningham.)
Scale, 50 feet to 1 inch.

Mr. Fergusson remarks the whole makes "a confused mass of chambers and Chaityas, in which all the original parts are confounded, and all the primitive simplicity of design and arrangement is lost, to such an extent that, without previous knowledge, they would hardly be recognisable."[1]

The next cave to this is a flat-roofed Chaitya-cave, with an apse at the back and a plain rude circular dâgoba reaching to the roof. To the east of it is a small Chaitya cell, and then a cave partially fallen in, but the inner room contained a dâgoba on a base 8¾ feet square, and behind it is a shrine with the *pradakshiṇâ* or passage for circumambulation round it, as in some of the Aurangâbâd and Elurâ caves. The shrine inside is 10 feet square and is occupied by a seated figure of Buddha 8 feet high. There are *dwârpâlas* at

[1] *Ind. and East Arch.*, p. 131.

the door 10 feet high, as in Cave III. at Aurangâbâd and in several of the Elurâ Buddhist temples; and on the walls of the *pradakshiṇâ* are standing and seated figures of Buddha, and on the right side, with "the head to the north" as in all such cases, is the Buddha reclining with his hand under his head, 15 feet in length, as he entered *nirvâṇa*.[1] On the east side of the dâgoba are two cells, one containing a small dâgoba and the other a Buddhist image.

Kholvi Caves.

As already mentioned the other group of caves in Mâlwâ is at the small village of Kholvi, in the Koṭâ territory, about 22 miles south-east from Dhamnâr and 55 miles north of Ujjain. They were first described by Dr. E. Impey in 1853,[2] and afterwards, but in less detail, by General Cunningham in 1864-65.

They are, like those of Dhamnâr, excavated in a hill of coarse laterite to the north-east of the village, and may be divided into three groups,—on the south, east, and north sides of the hill, numbering between forty and fifty excavations in all, the principal caves being in the group on the south face. The most marked feature about them is the presence of some seven *stûpas*, with square bases, in all the larger of which there are cells for images of Buddha. They are, in fact, in their arrangements more like Hindu temples than anything we have hitherto found in Buddhist architecture, though they still retain the circular plan and domical top which were the essential characteristics of the Dâgoba in all ages.[3] The first of

[1] Tod says "10 feet in length," *Rajasthan*, vol. ii. p. 723. Conf. Cunningham, *Archæol. Rep.*, vol. ii. p. 274.

[2] *Jour. Bom. B. R. As. Soc.*, vol. v. pp. 336–349; Cunningham, *Arch. Report*, vol. ii. pp. 280–288.

[3] If anything could convince Mr. Growse (*J. A. S. B.*, vol. xlvii., p. 114) how erroneous his views are as to the origin of the Hindu Sikhara, it would be the examination of these temples. There is at Dhamnar a Hindu rock-cut temple (*Hist. of Ind. and East Arch.*, p. 446) which is as complete and perfect an example of the style as the Temple at Barolli or Bhuvanêśwar. Square in plan, and with the curvilinear Sikhara and Amlika termination, in fact, all the features of the style perfected as if they had been practised for centuries. At the same time we have close by, in the same material, and at the same age, temples of the Buddhists of the same size, and used for the same purpose, but as unlike them as it is possible to conceive two classes of buildings to be. The latter retain all the circular forms of the Dâgoba both in plan and section, and show as little tendency to copy the Hindu style as the Brahmans showed to imitate them.—J. F.

these, beginning from the west, stands on a base 28 feet square. "On this base," says General Cunningham, "is raised a square plinth 8 feet high with a projection in the middle on each side, which on the east is extended into a small portico supported by two square pillars. Above this rises a second or upper plinth of 11 feet, which is circular in form," 18 feet in diameter,[1] "but with the same projections continued on the four faces. All these projections, as well as the intervening spaces, are decorated with a bold trefoil moulding with a circular recess in the middle,"—a modernised version in fact of the Chaitya-window ornament. As the top of this plinth is on a level with the summit of the hill the dome and capital must have been structural, and given it a total height when entire of about 40 feet.

The cell inside measures 6½ by 5½ feet, and 11 feet high, and contains a seated figure of Buddha in the *Jñâna mudrâ*, or attitude of abstraction, about 5 feet in height, but much abraded.

The other stûpas are smaller; the next one to this having an octagonal base 6 feet across; the third stands on a base 18 feet square, surmounted by a dome three-fourths of its diameter in height, and with a shrine inside containing the pedestal for the image, which however has been a moveable one, and is gone; the fourth is the only one that seems to have been under cover, and the side walls of the cell inside have been prolonged forward and arched over, while outside is a passage all round forming a very peculiarly shaped Chaitya cave. The fifth *stûpa* has a base 15 feet square, and 9 high, on which stands a circular drum 12 feet in diameter and 7 high, supporting a dome 7½ feet high, making a total of 23½ feet in height. On the outer face of the drum is a niche containing a seated image of Buddha. The sanctum is placed to the west of the centre, but the image has disappeared from it. On the right side of a platform immediately behind is a standing figure of Buddha upwards of 12 feet in height; and behind this platform is the largest cave in the group, 42 feet wide by 22 deep, with two rows each of four square columns running from right to left, each of the three aisles thus formed having a vaulted roof.

These caves, as already remarked, are of very late date, and are

---

[1] This is on General Cunningham's authority, but on his plan it measures 23 feet. Dr. Impey says "28 feet" (*u. s.* p. 342).

curious examples of the works of the last of the Hinâyâna school. Neither here nor at Dhamnâr are there any evidences of the worship of Bodhisattwas, or Śaktis. The Dâgoba and the great Teacher seem alone to have been venerated, and it is curious to remark that whilst in the earliest times the Dâgoba alone was regarded as a sufficient *qeblah*, and the only emblem of Buddha—the model of the monument that enshrined his ashes--the principal alteration from this, among the school that deviated least from the earlier doctrine, was the introduction of an image into the very place the relics might be supposed to occupy.

These works belong, so far as we can judge from the details we possess, to the end of the eighth century, or possibly even to a later date.[1]

It seems probable that these caves at Dhamnâr and Kolvi, if not the last, are at least among the very latest works of the Buddhists in Western India. It might indeed be expected that the religion would be found lingering in the fastnesses of Rajputana, and in a remote island like Salsette, for some time after its followers had been expelled from the fertile plains and the rich cities, in whose neighbourhood the greater number of the caves are found. It is difficult, however, to speak with precision on such a subject, for when it is looked into, it is startling to find how wholly dependent we are on the caves for our knowledge of the subject. Except from some vague hints in classical or Byzantine authors, we have no external evidence that a Buddhist community ever existed in Western India. There is not one single passage in any work by any native historian or author that mentions the fact; but for the brief account of the country by the Chinese traveller, Hiwen Thsang, we might—but for the caves—have remained ignorant of the fact. It is almost equally astonishing to find that there has not been found in the whole cave region any remains of any structural buildings belonging to the sect. The Vihâras and Chaityas, being presumably all in wood, may have perished of course; but we might expect that the foundation at least of some of the larger stûpas would yet remain. Except, however, the remains of some insignificant

[1] From their square bases, and tall forms, these Kolvi dâgobas resemble those found in Afghanistan near Jellalabad more nearly than any others found in India; but it seems impossible, at present at least, to bring down these latter to anything like the same age.

Dâgobas on the island of Salsette, nothing of the sort has been discovered.

This negative result is the less to be expected, inasmuch as we know from the erection of the Tope at Sârnâth, and the rebuilding of the Great Monastery at Nâlanda, that Buddhism flourished in Bengal under the Pâla dynasty from the 9th to the 12th century (*ante*, p. 132), and this seems no *à priori* reason why this might not have been the case in the West as well as in the East of India. There is perhaps no country in the world, however, in which it is so unsafe to rely on historical analogies as it is in India. The history of each province must be taken by itself, and, however likely or unlikely it may be, it is seldom that what may have happened in one province has so direct bearing on what may have occurred in another, that it can be used as an argument to illustrate any particular development either of religion or art.

Under these circumstances it is fortunate that in the thousand and one caves of the West, we have a complete series of perfectly authentic illustrations of the rise and fall of the Buddhist religion in that region, from the time of its introduction in the age of Aśoka, in the third century before Christ, till its extinction, when the Râthors eclipsed for a time the glories of the great Chalukya race in the eighth century. The Buddhists then disappear as suddenly as they rose, being either absorbed among the Jains, with whose faith they had many points in common, or by being converted to that of Vishnu, towards which they had long been tending, or crushed by the followers of Śiva, who in many places superseded them. During the 1,000 years, however, of their existence in the West they have left in their caves a complete record of the vicissitudes of Hinâyâna and Mahâyâna sects among themselves, and of their rise and progress till their decline and fall. As a chapter of architectural history it is one of the most complete and interesting known to exist anywhere. It is almost the only one example of a stone architecture which we can trace back with absolute certainty to its wooden original, and can follow it throughout its whole course without detecting any foreign influence in the introduction of any borrowed forms, and in which we can watch its final extinction, in the district where it arose, together with the religion to which it owed its origin.

BOOK III.

THE BRAHMANICAL CAVES.

CHAPTER I.

INTRODUCTORY.

It is sufficiently evident, from what has been said in the preceding pages, that the Buddhists were the first to appreciate the fitness of the stratified rocks of India for the construction of temples appropriate to the purposes of their religion, and as abodes for the priests who were to serve in them, and they retained a monopoly of the idea long enough to perfect a style of their own, without any admixture of elements borrowed from any other form of faith. When, however, in the decline of their religion the Brahmans were competing with them for popular favour, they eagerly seized on a form of architectural expression which evidently had gained a strong hold on the public imagination, and in the sixth and seventh centuries commenced the excavation of a number of caves which rival those of their predecessors in extent and elaborateness of decoration, though certainly not in appropriateness for the purposes for which they were designed.

With them monasticism does not occupy so prominent a place as with the Buddhists, and is not connected in any way with the popular worship, so that monastic abodes were not required, and all the Brahmanical caves copied from the Vihâras became simply temples of the new faith. Nor were the ceremonials of their rituals at all alike, and as it happened that the Chaitya form of temple was not so suitable for either the Śaiva or Vaishṇava cults, as the later form of Buddhist Vihâra; it seems accordingly to have been chosen as the first model. The side cells were, of course, dispensed with, and the walls occasionally carved with *rilievos* of their mythology, the shrine at the back was retained, and in Śaiva temples it was soon surrounded by a *pradakshiṇâ* or passage for circumambulation, it being considered a reverential and potential mode of salutation to go round the image or shrine of Śiva, keeping the *right* side towards it.

Other modifications suggested themselves by degrees: in some cases, as in the Dumar Lêṇa at Elurâ, and at Elephanta and Jogeśwari, the hall was brought more into accordance with the cruciform plan of the structural temples of the sect, and entrances excavated at the sides, while the shrine was brought out of the back into the area of the temple, and instead of the large central area and side aisles of the Buddhist caves, rows of pillars were carried across the hall, forming a succession of aisles.

As time went on other changes, both in plan and detail, were introduced, till after persevering in this course for about a century and a half the design of the Brahmanical caves had acquired a form and consistency which almost entitled them to rank as a separate style of their own. The original form of the Vihâra was almost entirely obliterated by the introduction of new features required to adapt it to the purposes of the Brahmanical faith, and in a few years more all traces of its origin might have been lost, when the progress of the style was interrupted by a revolution which changed the whole aspect of the case, but which at the same time proved to be a last expiring effort, and was ultimately fatal to the progress of cave excavations on the part of the Brahmans.

This time the revolution came from the south. When, as just mentioned, the Râthors superseded the Chalukyas in cave regions south of the Nermada; they brought with them their own Dravidian style of architecture, and instead of continuing the almost hopeless task of converting a Buddhist vihâra into a Brahmanical temple, they boldly cut the knot and at once resolved to copy one of their own structural temples in the rock. The result was the Kailâs Temple at Elurâ, an effort on a grand scale to form out of the living rock a shrine, complete in itself, with all necessary accompaniments. It was in reality a great monolithic temple hewn out of the living rock, highly sculptured outside and in, nearly 100 feet in total height, with surrounding shrines, *stambhas* or ensign pillars, gigantic elephants, corridors, &c., all in imitation of the most perfect structural examples, and forming one of the most beautiful and interesting monuments in India.

It was a daring effort, and the result has been one of the most remarkable monuments in India; but a temple in a pit, which this practically is, is an anomaly that could not be persevered in. It was only very rarely that the Brahmans could find detached boulders, or even ridges as at Mahâvallipur, out of which to hew their shrines, and when these did not exist, the proper effect of a monolithic temple cannot be obtained, as it is evidently impossible, in most cases, to remove the mountain to a sufficient extent to admit of its being properly seen. In this respect the Buddhists were more successful, because more logical than their successors. All their rock-cut temples are interiors—are caves in fact—and as such perfectly suited to the place where they are found. When, however, the inevitable logic of facts had proved to the Brahmans, after their experience in the matter, that interiors could not supply all they wanted for architectural effect, they boldly attempted to supplement the deficiency by adding the external forms they were familiar with to the small modicum of accommodation that was required for the purposes of their religion. They failed in effecting this at Mahâvallipur from their ignorance of the nature of the granite material in which they were working, and their inexperience of the forms necessary to meet the difficulties consequent on the nature of the mass. At Elura, from their long experience of the material in which they were working, they were perfectly successful, from a mechanical point of view, but artistically the Kailâsa was a mistake it was hardly probable would be repeated. So the Brahmans seem to have thought, for though their greatest effort it seems also to have been their last. There are no later Brahmanical rock-cut temples in India. What few cave temples there are after this date belong to the sect of the Jains, and except those excavated within sight of the Kailâsa at Elurâ, they are not remarkable either for their beauty or their magnificence.

It is difficult to fix with any certainty the age at which these Brahmanical temples were first constructed in the rock. It would seem, from a remarkable passage in Porphyry,[1] that there were

---

[1] Stobæus I. iv. 56; *Elephanta*, § 38, and note 58. Priaulx's *Apollonius*, p. 15.

Śaiva caves in India before the end of the second century; for, in one described, there is a distinct account of Arddhanâri, the union of the male and female forms in one body.

That Śaivism flourished all through the Buddhist period, we have ample proof even in the names of the excavators of Buddhist caves;[1] and in the great cave at Bâdâmi we have a Vaishṇava temple executed in the latter half of the sixth century. Śaiva caves are by far the most numerous, and some of them may go back as far as the second century; but it is probable that only from the fourth century did they become at all common, and nearly all the latest ones belong to this sect. It is only at Bâdâmi that we have two Vaishṇava ones, probably both of the sixth century, a single example at Elurâ, another at Undavalli (*ante*, p. 95) on the lower Krishṇâ, and there may be one or two others elsewhere.

Śaivism being the older and popular religion of the masses, was also patronised by their rulers: Vaishṇavism being of more recent origin was only favoured where it had most effectively gained the adherence of individual princely families, like the Châlukyas of Karnataka and Vengî; hence the relative disproportion in the number of the temples of the two sects. Another cause tending, perhaps, also to this result, was the extreme tolerance of the Śaivas previous to the Lingâyata movement. In temples dedicated to Śiva or his partner, with the *liṅga* or Bhavâni in the shrine, it was apparently usual to find side chapels and sculptures appropriated to Vishṇu and his Avatâras of Varâha, Vâman, Narasiṅha, &c.; and shrines in which these were prominent, like the caves known as Râvaṇa-kâ-kâi and the Dâśa Avatâra at Elurâ, or Mahâdeva's cave at Karusâ, doubtless served at once for the worshippers of Śiva and Vishṇu alike.

The age of cave excavation among the Brahmans probably passed away in the eighth century, none of any importance are known to have been excavated in the ninth. The absence of all inscriptions on their works, with the exception of that of Mangaliśa on the great cave of Bâdâmi, a few names and titles of gods and one or two late inscriptions on the Rathas at Mahâvallipur, and a quite illegible one on the Dâśa Avatâra at Elurâ,[2] leaves us entirely dependent on the

[1] For example, in the inscriptions of Kuḍâ and Junnar.

[2] Since paritally deciphered and found to contain the names of Karka, Indra, Dantidurga, and other kings of the Râshtrakûta dynasty, 660 to 850 A.D.

characteristics of their styles for any approximation to their relative ages. As already stated, all the more important temples of the Brahmans were excavated between 500 and 800 A.D., though some comparatively insignificant ones may be traced back to as early a date as the fourth century.

Liable to some transpositions we may arrange the Brahmanical caves in the following approximately chronological order:—

1. Śaiva cave at Aihoḷê in the Kalâdgi district, south of Bijâpur, A.D. 500–550.
2. Bâdâmi caves—one Śaiva and two Vaishnava caves, in Kalâdgi district, A.D. 550–579.
3. Karusâ caves, between Ausâ and Kalyâna in the Haidarâbâd territory, A.D. 500–700.
4. Jogai Ambâ Maṇḍap, a Śaiva cave near Mominâbâd in the Dekhan, and Bhamburdê cave near Pooṇâ, A.D. 550–600.
5. Dhokeswara cave, between Junnar and Ahmadnagar, A.D. 550–600.
6. Rameśwara cave at Elurâ, A.D. 600–650.
7. Râvaṇa-ka Khai and Dâś Avatâra at Elurâ, A.D. 600–700.
8. Dumar Lena and Elurâ caves, north of Rameśwara, A.D. 650–725.
9. Mahâvallipur Rathas, and caves on the coast thirty miles south of Madras, A.D. 650–700.
10. Undavalli Vaishṇava cave on the Krishnâ at Bejwâḍâ, A.D. 650–700.
11. Elephanta, Jogeśwari, and Mandapeśwara caves, near Bombay, A.D. 725–775.
12. Caves at Pâtur, in Berar, Rudreśwara, not far from Ajaṇṭâ, Pâtna, in Khândesh, and scattered caves in the neighbourhood of Sâtârâ, A.D. 700–800.
13. Kailâsa monolithic Śaiva temple at Elurâ, with its adjuncts, A.D. 725–800.
14. Dhamnâr Brahmanical caves, 750–800.

CHAPTER II.

CAVE-TEMPLES AT AIHOLE AND BADAMI IN THE DEKHAN.

A little to the north-west of the village of Aihoḷe,[1] on the Mâlaprabhâ river, in the Kalâdgi district, in the south of the Bombay Presidency, is a small Brahmanical temple, probably one of the oldest yet discovered. It consists of a hall, 18½ feet by 13½ and 8 feet 9 inches high, with two plain square pillars in front; on each side the hall is a chapel, and behind it the shrine, each raised by five steps above the level of the hall floor, and the front of each divided by two pillars with square bases and sixteen-sided shafts.[2] In front of this shrine has been an antechamber, at one time separated from it by a carved doorway built in, but now destroyed. The chapel on the right of the hall measures about 12 feet by 14, but is either quite unfinished, or, having been originally like the other, it has afterwards been enlarged. In the left side chapel is a sculpture, on the back wall, of a ten-armed Śiva dancing with Pârvatî, Gaṇêsâ, Kâlî, a horse-headed Gaṇa, Bhṛingi and others of his *gaṇa* or followers, all with very high headdresses as at Bâdâmi.

In the corners of the hall are larger figures—in one of Arddhanârî, the androgynous form of Śiva—in another of Śiva and Pârvatî with the skeleton Bhṛingi; while out of Śiva's headdress rise three female heads representing the river goddesses Gaṅgâ, Yamunâ, and Saraswatî, or the female triad of Umâ, Lakshmî, and Saraswatî.[3]

In a third corner is another form of Śiva, with cobra, &c., and in the fourth, Śiva and Vishṇu, or Hara and Hari, standing together. In the left end of the antechamber is Varâha, or the boar incarnation of Vishṇu, and in the right is Mahishâsurî, a form of Durgâ, slaying the buffalo-demon. On the roof are other carvings, and in the shrine a plain *chavaraṅga* or base for an idol.

---

[1] It is the ancient Ayyâvole, in Lat. 16° 1′ N., Long. 75° 57′ E. in the Hungund tâluka. In the seventh and eighth centuries it was a capital of the Western Chalukya dynasty.—*Ind. Ant.*, vol. viii. pp. 237, 287.

[2] See *First Arch. Report*, Plate XLVIII. and p. 38.

[3] See my *Elephanta*, § 44 and notes.

The sculptures in this cave being so simple, and the arrangement so little developed, we may perhaps be justified in placing this cave even before those at Bâdâmi.

Cave-Temples at Badami.

Bâdâmi is a moderate-sized town in the Kalâdgi Collectorate, about 23 miles south-east from the district town of Kalâdgi and nearly three from the Malaprabhâ river. It is the chief town of a tâlukâ of the same name. A little to the south of it is Bânaśaṁkarî; among the hills to the east is Mahâkûṭa; eight miles to the east and on the river is Paṭṭadkal; and another eight miles down the river is Aihoḷe — all noted for their ancient temples and inscriptions.[1] As pointed out by Mr. Fleet, there seems little doubt but that Bâdâmi was the ancient Vâtâpipurî, or Vâtâpînagari, of the Chalukya kings of the Kanarese country, and made the capital by Pulikêśî I. early in the sixth century of the Christian era. In the seventh century it is mentioned by the name also of Bâdâvi; Paṭṭadkal is the old Paṭṭadakisuvoḷal, the capital of the Sindavaṁśa chiefs about 1162 A.D.; and Aihoḷe, another early capital, is the Ayyâvole mentioned in a grant of the reign of the Châlukya king Vikramâditya the Great, 1093 A.D.

Bâdâmi is situated at the outlet between two rocky hills on its north and south-east sides, a dam to the east of the town between the bases of the hills forming a large tank for the supply of water to the town. All along the north side of this small lake are old temples, most of them built of very large blocks of hard stone, while on the hill behind them is a ruined fort that must have been a place of great strength in early times. The passages through it are cut to great depths in the rock, and are narrow, long, and winding, so that, if the gate were stormed, the besieged had their enemies far below them, and from above they could easily hurl destruction on the heads of all that could enter the pathways before any of them could reach a place of vantage. In and about this rock-fort are some temples also. But it is in the scarp of the hill to the south-east that the cave-temples are excavated. They are four in number: the lowest, on the west end of the hill, is a Śivâlaya or Śaiva cave;

---

[1] *Ind. Ant.*, vol. iii. p. 305; vol. v. pp. 19, 51, 67, 68, 71, 174, 344; vol. vi. pp. 72, 74, 85, 137, 139, 142.

the next is a Vaishṇava temple considerably higher up in the rock, and to the north-east of the Śivâlaya; the largest, also Vaishṇava, is still further to the east on the north face of the hill; and the last is a little beyond it, but is a Jaina cave, and of much smaller dimensions than the preceding three Brahmanical ones. All four are still in unusually excellent preservation, and are very rich in mythological sculpture.

Cave No. III. or Great Cave is by far the finest of the series, and one of the most interesting Brahmanical temples in India; it is also the only cave-temple the age of which is known with certainty, for it is in it that the inscription of Maṅgalîśa, the son of Pulikêśi I., the Châlukya king, who made Bâdâmi his capital, is found. Though it cannot compare with Elephanta or some of the larger caves at Elurâ in dimensions, it is still a temple of considerable size, the verandah measuring nearly 70 feet in length, and the cave inside 65 feet, with a total depth from the front of the verandah pillars to the back wall of 48 feet,—the shrine going into the rock about 12 feet further, while the general height throughout verandah and hall is 15 feet.[1] (Plate LXVII., fig. 2.) It is higher up in the rock than the other Vishṇava cave, and is entered by an ascending stair through a door in the west end of a square court in front of it, the north side of this court being formed by a large mass of rock left unexcavated there. The east and west ends are formed by old walls of masonry, that on the east entirely precluding all access from this side to the Jaina cave just beyond it, so that the Jainas must have formed a path for themselves from the shore of the lake or *taláo̩* below up to their rock-cut shrine.

The cave faces the north, and the level of the floor is eight or nine feet above that of the court outside. A narrow platform is built up outside the whole length of the front, the cave being entered by a flight of steps in the centre of it, but which have now been torn down,—probably because the long treads of the steps were found useful for some purpose or other in the village. The front of the platform has a moulded cornice, and under it a dado of blocks, many of them seven feet long, divided into more than thirty compartments throughout the length of it, and in each compartment two of those little fat dwarfs or *gaṇas* that are such

---

[1] For plan and details see *Archæol. Sur. W. Ind.*, vol. i.

favourites with the early Hindu sculptors for the decoration of basements, and which they were fond of representing in every possible attitude and in every form of grimace, or even with the heads of animals. All sects—Buddhists, Brahmans, and Jains—seem to have employed such figures in similar positions: in fact, they appear to have been conventionalities dependent more upon the taste and imagination of the craftsmen than upon the mythology of the sect for which any particular temple was constructed.

The verandah is supported in front by six pillars, each two and a half feet square, and two pilasters, with pretty deep bases and capitals,—the latter almost hid by the three brackets attached to the lower part of the capitals on the backs and sides of each, and by the eave or drip which comes down in front. The brackets on each side the pillars, in every case but one, represent a pair of human or mythological figures—a male and female standing in various attitudes under foliage, in most cases attended by a small dwarf figure; the only exception to the pair of figures is one in which Arddhanâri is represented, four armed and with two dwarf attendants. The brackets on the backs or inner sides of the pillars are all single tall female figures, each with one or two small attendants. These brackets extend from near the bottom of the capitals to the roof. The necks of the pillars below the capitals are carved with broad bands of elaborate beaded festoon work, and on each of the four sides of the lower portions of the shafts are medallions carved with groups of figures within a border.

The verandah is 9 feet wide, and is separated from the hall by four free-standing columns and two demi-columns in antis, all with high bases, the two central pillars being of that purely Hindu type, consisting of a square shaft with thin and slightly narrower slabs applied to each face: in this case two of these slabs are superimposed on each side, forming five exterior angles at each of the four corners. The two pillars outside these are octagons with capitals of the Elephanta type. There are thus left for sculptures the two ends of the verandah, and the spaces on the back between the attached pillars and the ends.

In the east end of the verandah is a large figure of Vishṇu seated on the body of the great snake Śêsha or Ananta, which is thrice coiled round below him, while its hoods—five in this instance—are spread out over and round his big *mukuṭa* or crown, as if to protect it. He is represented as four-armed (Chatturbhuj)—the front left hand resting on the calf of his leg, and the other holding up the *śaṅkha* or conch-shell, one of his characteristic emblems.[1] In the front right hand he holds some object perhaps representing wealth or fruit, and in the other his *chakra* or discus,—a sharp-edged heavy quoit, which seems to have been used as a missile instrument in early warfare by the Hindus, being thrown with force against the enemy, and recovered by a string attached to it.[2] He has three necklaces, each formed with a mass of gems in front. Round his waist is another belt of gems, while over his left shoulder and under his right arm hangs a thick cord apparently formed of twisted strands or strings of beads; and again round his loins are other richly embroidered belts; on his arms and wrists also he wears rich armlets and bracelets. At his right, below, sits Garuḍa, his *vâhana* or vehicle who carries him, and attends him also as a page. Opposite to him is a little female figure with high *mukuta*, which may possibly represent Lakshmî, the wife of Vishṇu. Above these stand two taller female figures, each holding a *chauri* or fly-flap: they have jewelled headdresses and large chignons, out of which rises a single cobra-hood overshadowing the head. These attendants remind us of the supporters we so often find under the *padmâsanas* or lotus-thrones of figures of Buddha.

This large sculpture fills the end compartment of the verandah. Under it is a plinth, the front of which is carved with little fat gambolling figures or *gaṇas*.

Turning to the right, we find on the back wall of the verandah another large sculpture, and one which in the early ages seems to have been a great favourite, for we seldom miss it in a Vaishṇava shrine. It is also repeated in several of the Śaiva rock-temples of Elurâ, and always in nearly the same form as here. It is the Varâha or boar *avatâra* which Vishṇu assumed to rescue the Earth from the Asura Hiraṇyâksha, the chief of the Dânavas, who had carried it off to the bottom of the ocean, when Vishṇu, taking the form of a boar, dived down and rescued it, after a contest of a thousand years.[3] Here he is represented again as four-armed, similarly dressed as in

[1] Wilson, *Vishnu Puràna*, 1st ed., p. 562; *Harivaṁśa*, cap. 89; Wilford in *As. Res.*, vol. viii.; Moor's *Hindu Pantheon*, p. 2'3.

[2] *Harivaṁśa*, cc. 9 and 215.

[3] Conf. *Harivaṁsa*, cc. 41, 223, 224,

the other figure, and with the *chakra* and *śaṅkha* in his up-lifted hands, but with a boar's head, standing with his left foot on the coil of a snake, the head of which is human, with five hoods behind it. In one of his left hands he holds a lotus flower, on which stands Pṛithivî, also called Bhûmidêvî or Bhûdêvî—the Earth personified —steadying herself against his shoulders.[1]

In front of Varâha's knee kneels a human figure with the five Nâga-hoods over his jewelled *mukuṭa*, and behind stands a female *chauri*-bearer with the single hood; another figure lies between Varâha's feet, holding by the long cord or *yajñopavîta* that hangs down from his shoulder. Over Varâha's shoulders are two pairs of *vidyâdharas*, each apparently with offerings.

On the pilaster by the side of this sculpture is the inscription of Maṅgaliśa, dated in Śaka 500[2] (A.D. 579).

At the west end of the verandah is another of the *avatâras*, namely, the Narasiñha or man-lion. The demon Hiraṇyakaśipu, the son of Kaśyapa and Ditî, and brother of Hiraṇyâksha, having, in consequence of severe penance, obtained from Brahmâ the boon that he should be invulnerable to gods, men, snakes, &c., became imperious, and troubled earth and heaven, when, at the desire of Prahlâda, the son of Hiraṇyakaśipu, Narasiñha bursting out of a column destroyed him, to the great joy of the *devatas*. He is here represented four-armed, one of the left arms resting on his huge club or *gadha*, besides which stands Garuḍa in human form. On the other side is a dwarf attendant, and above Narsiñha's shoulders are figures floating with garlands and gifts. Over the lion-head is a lotus, and his jewelled necklaces are elaborately carved.

On the other side of the front pilaster of the verandah from this last is a large and very striking sculpture, repeated also on a smaller scale in the other Vaishṇava cave here, in the Dâśa Avatâra cave and in other places at Elurâ, Mahâvallipur, &c. Locally it is called

---

[1] Pṛithivî is the wife of Vishṇu in his Varâha *avâtara*. She is represented in mythology as a woman with two arms, standing on a lotus-flower, and holding in one hand another lotus-blossom, with a crown on her head, her long black locks reaching to her feet, of yellow complexion, and with a *tilaka* of red paste on her forehead. Bhûmidêvi is the goddess of patience and endurance, but receives no special worship. See, however, *Manu*. iii. 85, 86; ix. 311; Colebrooke's *Essays*, vol. i. p. 137.

[2] For a full translation of this *see Ind. Ant.*, vol. iii. p. 305 ff.; or vol. vi. pp. 363 ff.; and see *Archæol. Rep.*, vol. iii. p. 120.

Virâtrupa, but there can be no doubt that it relates to Vishṇu in the fifth or Vâmana *avatâra.* He is represented in this case as eight-armed (Ashṭabhuja), with *chakra*, sword, *gadha* or club, and arrow in his right hands, and *śaṅkha*, bow, and shield in the left, while with the fourth on that side he points to a round grinning face, perhaps Râhu, to which he lifts also his left foot. Over this face is the crescent moon; beside Vishṇu's jewelled *mukuṭa* is a Varâha and two other figures, and below on his right is his attendant Garuḍa.[1] In front stand three figures, probably representing Bali and his wife, with Śukra his councillor, the first holding the pot out of which he had, against Śukra's advice, poured the water on the hands of the dwarf in confirmation of his promise to grant Vâmana's request for as much as he could compass at three strides. But scarcely was the water poured on his hands when, say the legends, "he developed all his divine form. The earth became his feet, the heaven his head, the sun and moon his eyes, the Piśâchas his toes, &c., &c. At the sight of this divine form, the Asuras, Bali's subjects, enraged dashed at him." They were of all animal and monstrous shapes, and armed with all sorts of instruments, their heads decked with diadems, earrings, &c. Vishṇu's form, however, grew as he dispersed them, until the sun and moon were no higher than his breast, and still he grew.[2]

Holding by his thigh is Garuḍa, and above the heads of the three figures before him is one with sword and shield falling down, and a half-figure behind.

Facing this at the other end of the verandah, just outside the pilaster that separates it from the first described of the sculptures, is another large one representing Vishṇu eight-armed, with *chakra*, arrow, *gadha*, and sword in his right hands, and in the left the *śaṅkha*, shield, and bow (*sarṅga*), the fourth hand placed against his loin. Behind the head a portion of the headdress is formed into a circular frill, somewhat resembling an aureole: this may be observed also both in the last described figure and in the next. He wears

---

[1] Garuḍa corresponds to the eagle of Jove; he is the *vâhana* or conveyance of Vishṇu, and is usually placed before Vaishṇava temples, as Nandi is in front of Śaiva ones.

[2] *See Harivaṁśa*, cc. 254–257. The account of the contest bears a strong likeness to that of the onset of Mâra's emissaries upon Buddha, as given in Spence Hardy's *Manual of Budhism*.

long pendant links hanging down from the ears, similar to what is found in many Buddhist images, and in the lower portion of the link is hung a heavy ear-drop that rests against the collar. From the top of his high *mukuṭa* or cap springs a figure of Narasiñha, four-armed and with *chakra* and *śaṅkha*. Whom this is intended to represent is somewhat difficult to say; as it occupies a position beside the entrance, it may be intended merely as a figure of Vishṇu in his more active and terrible form, while the next, inside, represents him in repose seated on Śesha, or it may be for Balarâma, the seventh *avatâra*. It is, like the others, well cut in a close-grained rock, and the only damage it has suffered is a piece out of the long sword, and some slight injury near the ankle. The dress is knotted behind the thighs, and round his body and thighs he wears a belt.[1]

The last large sculpture to be noticed in this cave is a figure on the back wall of the verandah, adjoining that of Narasiñha, and locally known as Harihara. This name is applied to the Ayinar of Southern India, the alleged son of Śiva by Môhinî, and who is the only male Grâmadêvata worshipped by the Tamiḷs. There is, however, another legend of Harihara as a form of Śiva assumed to contend with the Asura, called Guha.[2] Here the left side of the figure represents Hari or Vishṇu with the *śaṅkha* in his uplifted hand, the other resting against his haunch, while the earring and cap are of a different pattern from that of Hara or Śiva, on which is the crescent and a withering skull, while a cobra hangs from his ear, another from his belt, a third is on the front of his *mukuṭa*, and a fourth twines round the *parasu* or axe he holds in one hand. In the other hand he has some oval object.

The roof of the verandah is divided by cross beams into seven recessed panels, each filled with sculptures. In the central circular compartment in each of these panels is one of the favourite gods, Śiva, Vishṇu, Indra, Brahmâ, Kâma, &c., surrounded in most cases by smaller sculptures of the eight Dikpâlas, or regents of the points of the compass, the corners being filled up with arabesques.[3]

---

1 Perhaps the same as the *Bâhupaddai* of Southern India, represented as worn by sages and other holy beings when they sit.

2 *See* Foulkes's *Legends of the Shrine of Harihara*, pp. 37–41; *Harivaṁśa*, cc. 180, 181; Ward's *Hindus* (ed. 1817), vol. i. p. 242.

3 For a full description of these, see *Ind. Ant.*, vol. vi. p. 361.

The roof of the front aisle of the hall is likewise divided into compartments, in the central one of which are a male and female figure floating on clouds—the male (Yaksha) carrying sword and shield. The panels right and left of this are occupied by expanded lotus flowers. The hall roof is divided into nine panels by divisions very slightly raised from the level of the ceiling. In the central one, in front, is a Dêva riding on a ram—perhaps Agni—with a figure before him and another behind. In the other central panels are Brahmâ and Varuna; in other compartments are flying figures, &c.

Cave II. is considerably to the west of the large cave, and like it faces north. The front of it is raised a little above the level of the area before it, and the face of the basement is sculptured with *gaṇa*.[1] Three steps have been built against the middle of the front by which to ascend to the narrow platform outside the verandah. At the ends of this platform are *dwârpâlas*, each 5 feet 10 inches high. The verandah has four square pillars in front minutely carved from the middle upwards. Above them, slender *makara* or *yâli* brackets project to support the drip, which is ribbed on the under side. The central areas of the bracket capitals of the pillars are filled with sculpture.

At the left end of the verandah is Varâha, the boar *avatâra*, and at the right or west end the Vâmana *avatâra*, neither of them so large as in the great cave. The roof is divided into compartments and sculptured, and the frieze that runs all round the wall head is carved with numerous scenes from the legends of Kṛishṇa or Vishṇu.[2]

The entrance from the verandah to the cave is by three openings divided by two pillars, each 8 feet 6½ inches high, neatly carved with arabesques or figures in festoons, &c., standing on a step 7 inches above the level of the floor.

Inside, the roof is supported by eight square pillars, arranged in two rows across the hall, which is 33 feet 4 inches wide by 23 feet 7 inches deep and 11 feet 4 inches high.[3] The brackets to the

---

[1] See *First Arch. Report*, Plate XXI.

[2] See *Ind. Ant.*, vol. vi. pp. 364, 365. It is a remarkable proof of the late development of the Kṛishna cult, that so few sculptures referable to it are to be found. The series of small ones on this frieze are almost the only examples to be found in a rock-temple.

[3] *See* plan in *Second Arch. Report*, Plate XXII.

rafters are lions, human figures, vampires, elephants, &c. The shrine is approached by five steps, which raise the floor of it 3 feet above that of the hall; it measures 8 feet 9 inches by 7 feet 5½ inches, and contains a *chavaranga* or square altar, but the idol that stood in it is gone.

Cave No. I. (Plate LXVII., fig. 3) is on the north-west side of the hill, and only about 50 feet above the level of the town streets. It is entered by a few steps rising from what may have been a small court, but which the decay of the rock has carried away. Along the front on each side of the steps are the *gaṇa* of Śiva—dwarfs, with human, bovine, and equine heads, capering and posing in all sorts of attitudes. On the right or west side, above the return of this base, is a figure of Śiva, 5 feet high, with eighteen arms, dancing the *tâṇḍava*[1] or wild dance of demoniac rage which he is fabled to perform when he destroys the world—Nandi, Gaṇapati, and the drummer Nârada being the only audience. Between this figure and the cave is a small chapel[2] with two pillars in front, standing on a base or raised step, the face of which is also sculptured with rollicking *gaṇa*,—and, as at Elephanta, and on the four-armed figures that support the brackets in some of the Ajaṇṭâ caves, one of these *gaṇa* has a tortoise as a pendant to his necklace. Inside this chapel, round the ends and back, are more of these *gaṇa*. Above them, on the back wall, is a pretty perfect figure of Mahishâsurî or Durgâ as the destroyer of the buffalo-demon. On the right wall is Gaṇapati, and on the left Skanda or Mahâsena, the god of war, and the *kula*-deva of the Châlukya royal family.

At the other end of the front of the cave is a *dwârpâla*,[3] 6 feet 2 inches high, with the *triśula* of Śiva in his hand; and below is a figure composed of a bull and elephant in such a way, that when the body of the bull is hid the elephant is distinctly seen, and when the body of the elephant is covered the remainder is a bull. The front of the verandah is supported by four square pillars and two pilasters, their upper halves and brackets carefully carved with festoons of beaded work. Over the brackets against the architrave, and hidden from outside by the drip in front, are a series of

---

1 *See* my *Elephanta*, § 69, and notes.

2 *First Arch. Report*, Plates XVII., XVIII.

3 *First Arch. Report*, Plate XX., Fig. 2.

squat male figures, each different, and acting as brackets to the roof above.

Inside the verandah, at the left end, is a figure of Harihara, the joint form of Śiva and Vishṇu, 7 feet 9 inches high,[1] attended by two females, perhaps Lakshmî and Umâ, with elaborate girdles, head-gear, and bracelets. At the right end is another large sculpture —that of Arddhanârîswara.[2]

As is usually the case at Elephanta and elsewhere, the god is attended by his favourite white bull Nandi,—a form of Dharmadêva, the god of justice, who offered himself to Śiva in this form as a vehicle. Behind Nandi, with clasped hands, stands Bhṛingi—a favourite devotee, or perhaps Kâl, a form of Rudra or Śiva himself as the author of destruction,—a gaunt and hideous skeleton. At the left or female side stands a female richly decked, and bearing some flat object in her left hand.

The right side, which is always the male half, represents Śiva,—the crescent moon and skull on his headdress, a snake in his ear, another coiled round his arm, a third hanging from his belt—(the heads of them broken off),—and a fourth twisting round the battle-axe he holds in his uplifted hand; a portion of the tiger-skin, in which he wraps his person, hanging down on his thigh; with richly jewelled necklaces, bracelets, &c.

The left half, representing Umâśaktî, has a large flat earring, necklaces, belt, armlets, and bracelets of different patterns from those on the male half. The hair is made up in a sort of chignon over the shoulder, much as it is still worn by the lower classes in the Madras Presidency, and is covered with a network of pearls or gems. A cord hangs down in front of the thigh, terminating in a small flat heart-shaped end—an ornament specially noticeable on many of the figures in the Kailâsa temple at Elurâ. On the foot are two heavy anklets, and these and the very long bracelets on the wrists, and also on the female companion, cannot fail to remind the observer of the similar abundance of bone and brass rings worn by the Banjârîs and other aboriginal tribes to the present day. She holds up a flower, and with the other hand grasps one end of a stick or lute, the other end of which is held by the front hand of the male half.

---

1 *First Arch. Report*, Plate XIX. Fig. 4.

2 "Arddhanârîśvari, Arddhaneśwarî, or Arddhânârinateśwara," is the union of Śiva and Pârvatî, in a half male half female form.

The attendant female wears a loose kirtle held up by a richly jewelled belt. Her earrings are different—that in the right ear consisting of a long link hanging down to the shoulder, and in the end of it a thick jewelled ring and short pendant; the other is a broad thick disc like that known in Bengal by the name of *dheṅri*.[1] Floating overhead on each side are two figures, male and female, with offerings, and having elaborate headdresses. Her hair is done up in a very elaborate style, with a profusion of pearls over the forehead. This union of Śiva and Pârvatî in a single body personifies the principle of life and production in its double aspect—the active principle under the name of Purusha, and the female or passive under that of Prakriṭî.[2] On the male side the figure of Arddhanârînaṭêśwara is usually painted dark blue or black, and vermilion or orange on the left or female side, but sometimes the colours are white (Śiva's proper colour) and yellow.

The roof is divided by imitation beams into five compartments. In the central one is a figure of the serpent Śesha very similar to that over the antechamber in the great temple at Paṭṭadkal.[3] The head and bust are well formed, and project boldly from the centre of the coil. In a compartment to the right, on a cloud or boss 2 feet 6 inches in diameter, are a male and female well cut, the male (*Yaksha*) with a sword, and the female (*Apsaras*) drawing forward a veil that floats behind her head. In the corresponding compartment on the other side are two rather smaller figures; and in the end panels are lotuses.

The entrance to the hall itself, as in the two already described, differs from what we found in the Buddhist cave-temples. The front wall of the Vihâra with its small windows and doors admitted too little light; and so here, while retaining the verandah in front

---

[1] Râjendralâ Mitra's *Antiquities of Orissa*, vol. i. p. 98, and Plate XXVII., Fig. 118. It is to be regretted that we have no descriptive catalogue of female ornaments used in India.

[2] It embodies the central idea of nature-worship, and occurred to the early Greeks, as we see from the old Orphic hymn preserved by Stobæus, beginning

Ζεύς ἄρσην γένετο, Ζεύς ἄμβροτος ἔπλετο νύμφη.

"Zeus was a male, Zeus became a deathless damsel."

Stobæus, *Eclog. Phys.*, ed. Heeren, vol. i. p. 42; conf. Muir, *Orig. Sansk. Texts*, vol. i. pp. 9, 36; vol. iv. p. 331; and vol. v. p. 369.

[3] See *First Arch. Report*, Plate XX., Fig. 4, and Plate XL., Fig. 5. This one is also represented on the cover of Mr. Fergusson's *Tree and Serpent Worship*.

and further protecting the hall from rain and sun by projecting eaves, a large portion of the front was left open, the whole, indeed, except in front of the side aisles. In this case the entrance is 21 feet wide, divided into three by two pillars. These pillars have simple bases, square shafts, the upper part of each ornamented with arabesques, birds, &c. The capitals are circular, and so much in the style of those at Elephanta as to suggest no great difference of age,[1] and the brackets are similar to those over the back columns in Cave XVI. at Ajaṇṭâ.

The hall measures 42 feet 1 inch wide by about 24½ feet deep, the roof being supported, as in Cave II., by two rows of four columns, each parallel to the front and similar to those in the verandah. It is divided into compartments by imitation joists and rafters. In the first, immediately within the middle entrance, are a pair of figures (a *Yaksha* and *Apsarasa*), the male having sword and shield; in the next or central compartment is a lotos; and the rest are plain.

The shrine is irregular in shape, varying from 6 feet 11 inches to 8 feet 3 inches deep, by 9 feet 6 inches wide, and contains a square altar or *chavaraṅga*, with a small *liṅga* or phallic emblem of Śiva in it.

The fourth cave at Bâdâmi is the Jaina one, and will be noticed in its proper place.

---

[1] See *First Arch. Report*, Plate XX., Fig. 1.

CHAPTER III.

KARUSA CAVES.

About a quarter of a mile to the east of the village of Karusâ and about 43 miles east of Dhârasinwa, in the south-west of the Nizam's territory, is a low but steep hill of laterite, in which soft rock a range of caves are excavated; but, as may easily be supposed, the coarse conglomerate character of the rock not being favourable for the execution of fine sculptures, these have been originally but clumsily cut, and subsequent decay has in many places rendered them still worse. Owing to the circumstance, and perhaps also to their remote situation, none of this group of caves—except perhaps that known as the Mahadeva Cave—are of much beauty or interest. That one, however, would be a really fine cave anywhere if the material out of which it is excavated had been such as to admit of its design being adequately elaborated. Another cave, the Lâkola, is also of some merit, but very inferior to the other. All the others are extremely rude, but not without some interest from their peculiarities of design.

At the south end of the hill is a cave quite ruined by the fall of nearly the whole roof and front. It has been about 45 feet wide, and probably of considerable height. A little to the north, along the west face of the hill, is a small shrine with a rude imitation of a *śikhar* or low spire,—or rather pyramidal roof,—carved on the rock above it. Next is a rude cell, 12 feet by 6, with an inner one of smaller dimensions. In front is a recess in the rock about 15 feet wide, which can hardly ever have been covered; and at the north side of this, again, is a small monolithic temple measuring only 3½ feet by 3 inside, with a small door, the outside of the roof being carved into a *śikhar*, as in the previous instance.

For some distance from this, along the face of the scarp, there are no more caves; then we come to the principal group consisting of larger ones. The first of these is of irregular shape, 11 to 15 feet wide by 13 feet 2 inches to 14 feet 8 inches deep, much filled up, and with a cell or plain shrine at the back, but nothing to indicate to what sect it belonged. Above it is another small monolithic temple.

About six yards to the north of this is a second, 23 to 25½ feet wide by 16½ feet deep, with a cell in the north wall, of very irregular shape. In the south wall is also the commencement of a cell. None of the walls are straight or perpendicular. It contains a very rude image of a *Jina* or *Tirthaṅkara*, perfectly featureless, seated with his legs crossed under him as usual.

Beyond this are remains of cuttings in the rocks, as if for open courts, and perhaps a well, and a stair leading to the top of the hill; then, thirty yards from the last, we reach one of the largest of the series;—a double cave of two storeys, very irregular in plan, and roughly about 50 feet deep by 70 feet wide, divided into two halls above and below. Close to the front of the north half of the cave stands an octagonal pillar, the mouldings about the top of which, however, are almost effaced. In the top is a hole about a foot square and the same in depth, but whether it held the *triśula* of Śiva or a cresset for fire, is left to conjecture. In the floor of the north side of the excavation there have been sixteen square pillars of rough form, with rudely blocked out bracket capitals; but, except seven, all are rotted away. At the back is the shrine standing forward into the cave, and from the way the excavations terminate on each side of it, it would seem that it was intended to carry the *pradakshiṇa* quite round it. The shrine is an oblong cell with sculptures on the back wall, which are much obliterated. The central figure has lost his head, but he had a battle-axe or *paráśu* in the upper right hand, a small *triśula* or trident in the upper left, while the lower hands seemingly rested against the thighs. All this is distinctly enough applicable to Śiva. The right side figure appears to have been Vishṇu: while the left-hand one had the three faces usually assigned to Brahmâ.

The floor of the south half of this cave is about 6 feet 5 inches below that of the other hall. In front it has a screen with two pillars supporting a massive lintel; but, inside this, what may be termed the verandah, it is open above, and has a roughly fashioned *dwârpâla* or door-keeper on the south end and an unfinished one on the other. A descent of seven steps leads down to the floor of the hall, which seems to have been a very rude imitation of a Buddhist Chaitya-cave. It was evidently intended to have four square pillars on each side with aisles behind, but the left aisle ran into the other half of the cave, and spoilt the plan. The nave has a low arch with ribs across it, and the aisles are much lower. The shrine is in the back wall, but the figures are so decayed as to be nearly undistinguishable; they were probably Brahmâ, Vishṇu, and Śiva—the Hindu Triad, as in the other shrine.

At each end of the front, and in the block of rock left between these halls, is a small *liṅga* shrine.

A stair in the left wall of the north hall leads up to the apartments above. The north one, in which it lands, is somewhat in the style of the hall just described. It has three pillars on each side, with a low arched roof having a ridge pole along the centre, and rough ribs running up to it. The side aisles are narrow and low. At the back is a shrine with a larger square pillar left in front on each side and carved each with a *dwârpâla.* Behind this are two other similar blocks or pillars, each with *dwârpâlas* on the front and back. Between these last stands a large *liṅga* nearly 4 feet in diameter at the base and 3 feet 2 inches at the top. In front of it is a sort of trough in the floor.

A door in the wall leads into the south hall, about 30 feet wide by 54 feet from the front to the back wall. It has four pillars along each wall, but the roof is flat, and slopes upwards towards the back. There is a *pradakshiṇa* round the shrine, the rock in the south-east corner of which has been broken through from above, and this corner is now filled with débris. Three figures in the shrine are about 5½ feet high, were probably Vishnu, Śiva, and Brahma,—but all are much defaced.

Above the north end of the façade of this cave are some sculptures, but so worn that little can be made of them.

Adjoining the upper floor on its north side are a number of irregular apartments with a good deal of rude Śaiva sculpture.

Mahadeva's Cave.

Fifty feet north of the large cave is another, known as Mahâdêva's, having an extreme width of 60 feet by 64 feet in depth, with a fragment of a small square *maṇḍapa* in front for the Nandi or bull

D D 2

of Siva. The façade is 43½ feet long, with a low parapet wall in front, from behind which rise four square pillars with thin bracket capitals. The roof is supported by six lines of three pillars, each running from front to back,—one row on each side having five pillars, and running up the *pradakshiṇa*. There are thus twenty-six pillars in all, including the four in front, all approximately square except four immediately in front of the shrine, which stand on low octagonal plinths, and have shafts with sixteen shallow flutes, then a thick square member, and above it the capital, the lower portion of it being a conoidal frustrum fluted to the neck, and the upper part octagonal with a few simple members.[1]

The shrine is about 16 feet by 11 and 8 high, has four doors, and contains a large *liṅga* in a *śaluṇkhâ* or altar, not 2 feet above the level of the floor. The front of the shrine is carved with two rude *dwârapâlas*, each leaning on his club. The door has a narrow architrave and slender pilaster on each side, outside which are two huge snakes,—their tails are grasped by a human figure over the door, and their human heads turned up below. On the basement, on each side the steps and below the *dwârapâla*, is an elephant in bas-relief.

At the sides of the south door of the shrine are a pair of tall male and female figures, the male in each case next to the door, and leaning on a heavy club,—the female attended by a small dwarf. At the north door are similar pairs of guardians, but without the dwarfs.

The sides of the cave are covered with large sculptures, but in many places so damaged as to be almost unintelligible. Along the south or right wall they are generally Vaishṇava, while those on the north side are Śaiva. All have been at one time covered with plaster, and the appearance of the whole must have depended greatly on the manner in which this was done. Beginning on the south side,—just behind the pilaster, on the back of the front wall, —are represented a number of men with clubs or swords, as if engaged in an action, below are two elephants and several human figures some of them greatly defaced.

Beyond these and on the return of the wall are two figures wrestling, and above them other two apparently similarly engaged. The

---

[1] See *Third Arch. Report*, Plate XIV.

next figure below appears to be escaping from the next group, of which the principal figures are a tall male standing on the low narrow bench or base that runs along under all the sculptures, holding up a sort of whip in his right hand, as if about to strike with it a *Nâga* whose long tongue he holds with his left hand. The *Nâga* has a human head and bust, with his hands joined in the attitude of supplication; over his head is the five-fold snake-hood, whilst his tail is coiled up below. To his left is a smaller female *Nâganî* in a similar attitude. Some small figures below are obliterated. Above are several others: one man is seizing an animal like a horse by the mouth; another twists the head of a bull right round by the muzzle and one horn; and others are not so distinct.

The next group is the common one of Varâha or Vishṇu of the boar's head avatâra. To the left of this is a still larger group, intended to represent the contest between Vishṇu and the Âsuras, the concluding scene in the Vâmana or Dwarf Avatâra, and somewhat similar to those at Bâdâmi.

Near the east end of this wall is the Narasiṅha avatâra, or Vishṇu of the Lion-head, four-armed, holding the *chakra* and *śaṅkha* in two hands, and with the others tearing out the bowels of the impious Hiraṇyakaśipa, the brother of Hiraṇyâksha, who still grasps his sword and shield. Beside this is Vishṇu represented as a two-armed man holding up the hill of Govardhana over the herds of Vraj which are represented by some badly-formed cattle between him and Narasiṅha.

In the return of the wall, to the left of this, is the door of a small cell with a carving on the back apparently intended for Karttikeya, or Mahâsena, the god of war.

Entering the *pradakshiṇa* or circumambulatory passage, on the south side, the wall up to the door of another cell is occupied by a scene 13 feet in length. On the right, in a very rude chariot drawn by two small horses, is a figure shooting from a bow against two tall bowmen close in front. Behind them is a male with high cap, holding a female by the arm. In the chariot is a very diminutive driver, and beyond or above it are seen about seven warriors with bows and clubs, while high up on the left are two pairs, apparently interested spectators. Whether this represents a scene in the war of the Pâṇḍavas or in the story of Râma is not very clear.

On the back wall is another large tableau; below, seven figures are represented, four of whom appear to be carrying weighty objects, one is either building a pillar or sacrificing, and another is crouching below at the foot of it. Above the pillar two figures are stretched at ease looking on, and behind are two men, and a female between them. To the left, and over the first mentioned figures, are four men and a woman, apparently dancing. Above them lies a man with three women attending on him, and at his feet three men in attitudes as if hopping. To the right of these, again, is a man standing with a long bow, and a female seated with uplifted hand.

On the north of the shrine, and on the back wall, is a figure with a bow drawn against two figures struggling together. Above are five or six people, worshipping or supplicating.

On the north wall of the *pradakshiṇa* is a much-defaced group consisting, apparently, of one tall male figure and four females. On the west of this is the door of a small irregular cell, and to the left of it, again, is a large sculpture of the churning of the sea of milk,—a story frequently alluded to in sculptures.[1] In the sculpture here a solitary Daitya has got hold of the head of Vâsuki, and three others appear behind him, while at least three of the Suras have a hold of the tail, and other three stand close by. Brahmâ and another god, four-handed, are above, and on the top of Mount Mandara, used as a churning staff, Vishṇu appears helping to twirl it round.

In the cell which opens from the aisle of the cave is a figure which appears to be intended for Vishṇu.

On the north wall of this aisle are the Śaiva sculptures. The first in the direction in which we are now proceeding is Râvaṇa under Kailâsa.

A little to the left of this, Śiva and Pârvatî are represented sitting together. The bull Nandi stands in front, with the almost undistinguishable traces of gambolling *gaṇa*, monkeys, &c. round him. The next scene is Śiva in the *tâṇḍava* dance, with Pârvâtî at his left knee, and some small figures among his feet.

Lakola's Cave.

In its plan, and the general character of its sculptures, this cave so nearly resembles the three Brahmanical caves of Bâdâmi, that it

[1] For an account of this see *Third Arch. Report*, pp. 16, 17.

must be very nearly of the same age. It may consequently be safely assigned to the latter half of the sixth century, though from the coarseness of the materials out of which it is excavated, it is difficult to ascertain its date with any great precision.

A little to the north of Mahâdêva's cave is an unfinished cell, and at twenty yards from the same is a cave, locally known as LÂKOLA'S. Its entrance is reached up six or more steps. It has four pillars in front and twenty-four inside, about 2 feet square. The cave measures from 41 to 49 feet wide by about 58 feet deep to the back of the *pradakshiṇa* and about 10 feet 4 inches high. In front is a low half screen wall with a descent of four steps down into the cave.

In the cell on the south side are five female figures on the back wall, a male and female on the left wall, and Gaṇapati and a male on the right, all dancing. One of those on the back wall has a horse's head. In the back cell on the same side is a male figure with two arms, but defaced.

In the shrine is a four-armed figure of Vishṇu, 6 feet high, and formed of a different and more compact stone than the rock in which the cave is cut. In his left hand he has the *chakra* and *śaṅkha*, and in the right a huge club and some round object. He wears a high cap, with the radiated broad frill like a *nimbus* behind.

A stair leads down from the north side of this cave into the next, in which are four pillars with corresponding pilasters, but the pillars are much eaten away. It measures about 21 feet wide by 23 feet deep, and has a small shrine in the back wall. On each side the outer door has been a window in latticed stone work, now broken away.

Above this cave are two cells, one with Ganêśa roughly carved on the wall, and a small *vêdi* or altar in a shrine behind it.

Between this last and the next an elephant is rudely carved on a projecting rock, but apparently has never been finished. The next cave was probably a large one, but is entirely ruined by the fall of the rock which formed part of the roof of it. It was, perhaps, never finished, as the back wall is very irregular.

To the north of this again is a low-roofed cave, with two octagonal pillars in the hall, somewhat of the pattern of those in front of the shrine in Mahâdêva's cave. The hall is about 17 feet wide by 23 feet deep, but the *pradakshiṇa* extends to 34 feet 10 inches in length behind the shrine, the cave being irregular in form. The shrine inside is about 6 feet 9 inches square, and contains a figure of Vishṇu, cut from the rock *in situ*, and very much decayed.

Higher up on the scarp are three or four cells and small shrines. Then we come to a cave varying in width from 25½ feet in front to 43½ at the back, about 30½ feet deep and 8½ feet high. It has two pillars, with rough pilasters in front—two pillars in the second row, and four in the back one. The shrine, about 8 feet by 7, is in the back wall, there being no *pradakshiṇa*, and contains an oblong altar in which is placed a modern *liṅga* of hard stone. Still to the north are two cells, the second with Ganêśa carved on the south wall, and Mahishâsurî, the slayer of the buffalo-demon.

On the ascent of the hill, in front of Mahâdêva's cave and the two-storeyed one, are seven or eight very small monolithic temples, mostly ruined.

Round the north end of the hill are upwards of forty very small shrines, some with façades cut on the rock over them, and dedicated —some to the *liṅga*, and others to Vishṇu.

The extreme simplicity of the carving in these caves might incline us to think they were early. This however may arise from the nature of the rock in which they are excavated, and these sculptures are, at all events, sufficient to show that they were made before the rise of the Lingâyats. They are probably, as just mentioned, of about the same age as those at Bâdâmi described above.

Nine miles north from Karusâ, and as far east of Awsâ, is a solitary hill near the village of Hasagaṅw. In the east side of it were two large caves; but, owing to disintegration of the rock, they are worn almost to the appearance of natural caverns. On the west side is another, 49 feet deep by 41 wide, with a *pradakshiṇa* round the shrines. It had some sculpture right and left of the shrine door, but they are much decayed. This cave had probably twelve columns, in three rows across, but no trace whatever is left of the two immediately in front of the shrine door.

CHAPTER IV.

BRAHMANICAL CAVES IN THE DEKHAN, MOMINABAD, POONA, &c.

At Mominâbâd or Jogâi Ambâ, in the Nizam of Haidarâbâd's territory, are some Brahmanical and Jaina caves, architecturally of a very plain type, to which it is difficult to assign an age with any confidence. They are just outside the town, in two low rocky knolls. The largest (Plate LXVIII.) has an open court in front, measuring about 90 feet by 85, in the middle of which stands a low pavilion about 34½ feet square outside, with a sloping roof. Inside it is an oval platform for the Nandi or bull, the vehicle of Śiva. The roof within is supported by four perfectly plain square pillars. The hall of the cave is 91 feet long by 45 deep, and its roof is upheld by thirty-two similar pillars, 2 feet 3 inches square, each surmounted by a bracket block, 5 feet long and 10 inches deep, on which lie the architraves which run from end to end of the cave. In the back wall are three small rooms and the principal shrine, containing the faint traces of what appears to have been a Trimûrti or triple-headed image of Śiva as combining the three characters of Rudra, Vishṇu, and Brahmâ. There is another small shrine in the left end of the third aisle. Along the back wall has been a good deal of the ordinary Śaiva sculptures—the Saptamâtras, the *tândava* dance, Mahishâsurî, &c., which may be of almost any age.

In the court, at each end of the front of the cave, stand two large elephants cut out of the rock, and behind the maṇḍap are other two.

To the west of this, across a small stream, are the remains of other caves, but much destroyed by a current of water that runs through them, and overgrown by prickly-pear, &c. One of them has been fully 100 feet long by 41 deep, but its roof is almost totally destroyed. Like the Dâśa Avatâra at Elurâ, the great cave at Karusâ, and others, the walls of it have been covered with rude sculptures both of the Avatâras of Vishṇu and of the forms and feats of Śiva and his consort.[1]

---

[1] For more details and plans see *Third Archæol. Report*, pp. 50–52, and Plates XXXIII., XXXIV.

Cave-Temples of Bhamburde, Rajapuri, &c.

At the small village of Bhâmburdê to the north of Poona is another Śaiva rock-temple, very closely resembling that of Jogâi Ambâ both in style and arrangements, only that the Nandi pavilion in front is round instead of square, as may be seen from the plan, Plate LXIX., and the annexed woodcut. The shrine is advanced into

No. 68. Bhâmburdê Cave, from a drawing by T. Daniell.

the floor, instead of being a cell in the back wall. It is somewhat larger however, being 160 feet in one direction by about 100 across, and, as may be seen by comparing these plates, it is altogether of a finer and more monumental character, and hence probably of a more ancient date. The roof of the pavilion slopes, and has been hewn with ridges or ribs after the shape of an umbrella. Owing to there being no exit for the water that accumulates in the trench round this maṇḍap—for it sits quite in a pit—it stands for a large part of the year in a sheet of water that reaches from the Nandi in the centre of it to the entrance of the cave.

Râjapurî is a small village about 8 miles to the west of Wâï in the Sâtârâ district, near the source of the Kṛishṇâ.[1] The caves are in a spur of the Mahâbaleśwar range, on the south-west of the Kṛishṇâ, and at a height of 1,200 or 1,300 feet above the valley, but

[1] These caves have not been described in any detail hitherto. They were surveyed by the Messrs. West in 1853, who have kindly placed their collections at my disposal.

not difficult of access. They are cut in a soft ochrey coloured rock, just below the laterite.

The caves are irregular and rudely cut, and extend about thirty yards along the face of the cliff. The largest somewhat resembles the Dhokeśwara cave: a structural wall is inserted in front, inside which are four plain square pillars in two rows in front of the shrine which is about 7 feet square inside, but irregular in its outer form. There is also another smaller liṅga shrine in the right wall of the front area, and two cells, one unfinished, in the back of the *pradakshiṇa*. A low passage leads to the right into a room, of which the front is blocked up and which has a smaller room behind it. From the left side there is also an entrance into other two rooms, and from the front one, a low passage leads into an irregular area containing two tanks, and a cell dedicated to Bhavânî. In front is an inscription on a loose slab in an old form of Devanagari—perhaps of the 14th century A.D.

The Pâteśwara caves are a small group of some five excavations near the top of a hill about six miles south-east from Sâtârâ. They are, like the Râjapuri caves, very rudely excavated, and have been much altered and enclosed with buildings during last century, but from the number of loose liṅgas lying about, and their plans, so far as they can be made out, they appear to have been Brahmanical.

About twenty miles in a straight line to the E.S.E. of Karâdh is the town of Kandâl, in a hill near which are some 16 Brahmanical caves, mostly small, cut in a soft reddish rock, and divided into two groups, one of thirteen caves on the north-eastern face, and the other of three on the southern face of the hill. One contains traces of some rude sculptures. Like those at Pâteśwara, they have been altered and added to by building, but are probably not of very ancient date.

MALKESWARA.

Thirteen miles south-west of the Kandal caves and about 18 miles north from Kolâpur, in a hill near the village of Mâlwâḍi, is a group of seven Brahmanical caves, mostly very small. The largest has a hall about 26 feet by 21½, with four massive square pillars, having circular necks and a projecting member under the brackets resembling what we find in structural columns of the 12th and 13th centuries. This cave has an antechamber to the liṅga shrine, and also a small shrine on the right side of the hall. Like the Pâteśwara and Kandâl caves, these have also been modified in very recent times by building.

Patur.

Pâtur is a village twenty miles to the east of Akola, the chief town of Berar. To the west of the village are two caves facing east, and each consisting of a sort of double verandah, fully 40 feet in length, divided by a step with two plain square pillars and pilasters upon it. The outer verandah has also two square pillars in front, and is about 9 feet wide, while the inner one or hall is 13 to 13½ feet deep, in the back of which is a cell about 11 feet square. The southern one at least has once contained a *liṅga;* possibly the other may have been dedicated to Vishṇu, or perhaps Bhavânî; it contains a *chavaranga* or image altar, and the hall is only 31 feet by 14 feet, and 12 to 13 feet high. There are some names on the pillars in old Devanagari characters of about the ninth century. A line on one pillar has been supposed to be in Pehlvi; but it is too faint to be made out, though it was probably in Hala-Kânaḍâ.

Rudreswar.

Near the village of Gulwâḍâ (besides the Buddhist cave known as Ghatotkacha) there is a rude Brahmanical cave or small group of excavations in which are figures of Gaṇeśa, Bhairava, Narasiñha, the Saptamâtrâs, &c., but all weatherworn and dilapidated. There is nothing of architectural interest about the place, and the whole is probably of comparatively recent origin.

Patna.

On the west of the deserted town of Pâtna in Khandesh, already mentioned in connexion with the Pitalkhorâ caves, is the hill fort of Kaṇhar, and on the west side of the hill or that farthest from the ruins of the town, and up a torrent bed, is a Brahmanical cave, probably Vaishṇava, and locally known as Śriṅgâr Châvaḍi. It consists of a plain hall or shrine 19 feet wide by 17 feet 6 inches deep, and varying in height from 6 feet 8 inches in front to 8 feet at the back. The entrance door is neatly carved, with two high steps, with moulded pilasters, small standing figures, &c. at each side, much in the style of the early structural temples, such as that at Ambarnâth and the Hemâḍpanti temples of the Dekhan.

In front is a verandah about 7 feet wide, returning outwards on the right side. Besides the double pillar at the corner, this is supported by two pillars and a pilaster in front of the cave, and by one pillar and pilaster in the return. These pillars support a narrow entablature carved with arabesques, and are hidden on the outside, to fully half their height, by a curtain, carved in the style of the corresponding portions in the Kailâs temple at Elurâ, and of the first of the old Jaina temples at Belgaum, and which may belong to about the 11th century A.D. It is thus perhaps one of the latest excavated of the Brahmanical caves, and possibly the work of some local chief under the Yâdavas of Dêvagiri. Inside is an *Otâ* or seat about 2 feet high. Outside is a water-tank.

DHOKESWARA.

The Brahmanical caves of Dhokeśwara are in the east side of a hill near the village of Dhôkê, in the Pârner Tâluka, about twenty miles west of Ahmadnagar.

The principal cave (Plate LXX., fig. 1) is irregular in shape, but about 45 feet wide in front, and upwards of 50 feet deep. In front it has two massive pillars between pilasters, and 14½ feet behind them other two pillars, standing on a raised step, square below, changing above into eight and thirty-two sides, with square capitals having pendant corners, under brackets of the ordinary form. The front pair of columns have more carving on the lower halves, but are square up to the capitals.

The shrine is cut in the solid rock, with a wide *pradakshiṇa* quite round it, and with doors in front and in the right end. On each side of the front one is a *dwârpâla* with *nimbus* behind the head, holding up a flower in his right hand; his headdress is high, and in a style representing twisted locks of hair. These figures are similar to those on the sides of the shrine at Elephanta and the Dumar Lêṇa at Elurâ. Over their shoulders are *vidyâdharas*. Under the right hand of the *dwârpâla*, to the left of the shrine door, is a figure standing with folded arms and a *triśula* or trident set on his head as a cap. Other figures are carved to right and left. In the shrine is a small *liṅga*, and on an earthen platform in front, among many fragments of sculpture of all ages, is a modern hollow copper *liṅga* with a human face in front, a snake coiled round it, and the seven hoods raised over it.

On the south wall of the cave are the Mâtrâs, eight female divinities, with Gaṇêśâ at their head, and on the side of the pilaster next him a tall naked figure, probably Kâla. Varâhi, the third, has a boar's head; each has her cognizance below and a *nimbus* behind her head; they are seated under the foliage of five trees; and beyond the last is a form of Śiva. The work is of a very inferior sort. On the deep architrave over the inner pair of pillars in the centre is the common sculpture of Lakshmî and the elephants pouring water over her, and to the left some other figures.

At the north end is a chapel with two pillars in front, and on the back wall a large sculpture of Bhairava and some snake figures. Outside, at each end of the façade, is a tall standing female figure with lofty headdress, and holding an opening bud in one hand.

In a recess to the north of the shrine is a coarsely hewn out bull. In the back are three small recesses, and in the south end a raised platform with a seat at the back, at the end of which a hole has been made into a large cistern, the entrance to which is a dozen yards to the south of the cave. Between the great cave and the cistern and some way up the face of the rock, approached by a risky stair, is a small cave, low in the roof, with a built front, the original having given way. On each side of this is a sort of cell with an opening into it, about 2 or 2½ feet from the floor. In the left front corner is a trap-door into some sunk apartment partially filled up.

CHAPTER V.

BRAHMANICAL CAVE-TEMPLES AT ELURA.

As before mentioned the Buddhist group occupies the southern extremity of the crescent in which the caves of Elurâ are situated. At a later age the northern horn was taken possession of by the Jains, who excavated there a remarkable series of caves to be described hereafter. But between these two, at an intermediate age, the Brahmans excavated some 15 or 16 caves, rivalling those of their predecessors in magnificence, and exceeding them in richness of decoration. In their earlier caves the Brahmans copied to a certain extent the arrangements of those belonging to the Buddhists, though gradually emancipating themselves from their influence till the series culminated in the Kailâsa, which is not only the largest and most magnificent Rock-cut temple in India, but the one in which its authors most completely emancipated themselves from the influence of Buddhist cave architecture.

The Brahmanical caves begin at a distance of about 40 yards north of the Tîn Ṭhâl, or last Buddhist cave, the first one being a large perfectly plain room, of which the front has been destroyed by the decay of the rock, and the floor is deep in earth. It may probably have been a *dharmaśâla* or rest-house for visitors. Close to this, and to which it doubtless belonged, is the cave known as Râvaṇ-ka Khâï; and next to it, but higher up in the rock, is the Dâś Avatâra, between which and the famous Kailâsa the road passes up the hill to the town of Rozah.

To the north of Kailâsa is a deep ravine, and beyond it are four or five caves not usually distinguished by separate names. Then follow those known as Râmeśwara, Nîlakaṇṭh, a small cave, Têli-kâ Gana, Kumbârwâṛâ, Janwâsa, and the Milkmaid's cave. This last is near a high waterfall, at the north side of which is excavated the magnificent temple known as Sîtâ's Nhâni, or Dumâr Leṇâ, the most northerly of the Brahmanical series.

Fortunately the age of these caves can be ascertained within very narrow limits from the style of their architecture and local peculiarities, though there are hardly any inscriptions or traditions that tend to elucidate the matter. They certainly are all subsequent to the caves at Bâdâmi (A.D. 579), and anterior to the Kailâsa, which, as we hope presently to show, was commenced in or about 725. These are at least the extreme limits within which the age of the group is comprised, though it is hardly probable that the earliest of them overlap the Buddhist series to the extent which that would imply. Both in their plans, and in the style of their architectural details, they resemble so nearly the latest caves at Ajaṇṭâ and Aurangabad that it is probable they belong generally to the second half of the seventh century rather than the first. Their succession appears to be nearly as they are situated locally, and enumerated in the following pages—beginning with those situated nearest to the Buddhist group, and ending with the Dumâr Leṇâ, the most northern, which may be assumed to be the last excavated, anterior to the Kailâsa, which probably, however, was not completed before the end of the century.

Ravana-ka Khai.

The Brahmanical shrine locally known as Râvaṇa-kâ Khâï has four pillars in front and 12 inside the open hall, which measures 54 feet wide by 55½ to the front of the shrine. The shrine is surrounded by a wide passage or *pradakshiṇâ* for circumambulation, making the total depth of the excavation 85 feet. The central area is 14¼ feet high, and the side aisles 13 feet 8 inches (Plate LXX., fig. 2).

Two pillars in front and one inside the front aisle are gone. They have high square bases and drooping-eared florid capitals, with circular necks of varied patterns (Plate LXXI). The pilasters, fig. 2, are carved from the floor to the brackets, fig. 1. The former recall the style of decoration found in the caves at Aurangabad (Plate LXVI.) and in the latest caves at Ajaṇṭâ. This would indicate that the age could hardly be earlier than the middle of the seventh century, while the pilasters are in a style more closely resembling what was afterwards developed at Elephanta and in the Brahmanical caves of the beginning of the following century. All the compartments of the wall between the pilasters are filled with sculpture; but even within the last ten years the faces have been hacked and destroyed by Musalmans.

The south wall is covered with Śaiva sculptures; beginning at the front they are—

1. Mahishâsurî killing the buffalo-demon.

2. Śiva and Pârvatî on a raised platform playing at *chausar* or *chaupat*, a sort of chess played with dice. Gaṇapati and another attendant wait behind Śiva, and two females and a male behind Pârvatî, while between but beyond them Bhṛingi looks on at the game. Five of the faces in this compartment have been hacked within the last ten years. Below is Nandî, the bull of Śiva, and thirteen small fat *gaṇa* rollicking. This sculpture seems to be peculiar to Elurâ, where it occurs several times in different caves, but while most of the other Śaiva sculptures occur at Elephanta and elsewhere, this does not. Śiva as Mahâyogi, which is twice repeated at Elephanta, occurs at Elurâ only in the Dumár Leṇa cave, and there in a scarcely finished form.

3. Śiva dancing the *tándava*, or great dance, which he performs over the destruction of the world; three figures with drums and fifes are to his right; Bhṛingi, his skeleton attendant, is behind, and Pârvatî and two *gaṇa*—one with a cat's face—are on his left; above are Brahmâ and Vishṇu on his left, and on his right Indra on his elephant, Agni on his ram, and two others.

4. Râvaṇa, the demon king of Laṅkâ or Ceylon, proud of his immeasurable strength, got under Kailâsa, the White Mountain or heaven of Śiva, intending to carry it off; Pârvatî got alarmed on feeling the place shake, and clung to Śiva, who fixed Râvaṇa under the hill with his foot until he repented of his temerity. Râvaṇa had ten heads and twenty arms, and often on the top of his cap an animal's head is represented, some say that of an ass. Four *gaṇas* here mock him. Śiva and Pârvatî have each their attendants, and two guardians stand at the sides. The peculiar conventional mode of representing a mountain by means of brick-shaped blocks may be noted; it recurs again and again, and, as already mentioned, is employed also in the paintings at Ajaṇṭâ.

5. Bhairava, the destructive form of Śiva, his foot on a large fat dwarf, another at his side, Gaṇapati behind him, and holding up with two of his hands the elephant-hide in which he wraps himself, with other two he holds the spear with which he has transfixed his puny enemy Ratnâsura; in one is a long sword, and in another a bowl to receive the blood of his victim.

These last four are frequently represented in other caves with more or less detail.

6. In the *pradakshiṇa* on this side is a remarkable group (Plate LXXII). The first portion of it is very much in shade, but consists of three skeletons; Kâl, four-armed, with a scorpion on his breast; Kâlî, the female personification of Death; and a third kneeling. Then comes Gaṇapati eating his favourite balls of sweetmeat, beyond whom are the seven divine mothers, four-armed, each with a child, and, on the base below, her cognizance—(1) perhaps Chamuṇḍâ with the owl, (2) Indrânî with the elephant, (3) Varâhî with the boar, (4) Vaishṇavî or Lakshmî with Garuḍa, (5) Kaumârî with the peacock, (6) Maheśwarî with the bull, and (7) Brâhmî, Brâhmaṇî, or Sarasvatî with the *hansa* or goose.[1] On the return of the wall at the back is Śiva seated with the mace or axe and *damru* or small hand-drum.

On the north wall, commencing from the front, are—

1. Bhavâni or Durgâ, four-armed, with her foot resting on her tiger, holding a *triśula* or trident in her upper right hand; the others are broken.

2. Lakshmî, the wife of Vishṇu, over a mass of lotuses, in which are Nâga-canopied figures holding up water jars, and a tortoise among them. She has two arms, but her attendants on each side holding water-pots have four; one on her right also holds a *śaṅkha* or conch, one of the symbols of Vishṇu. Elephants bathe her with water from jars, as in the similar Buddhist sculptures.

3. Varâha, the boar-incarnation of Vishṇu, his foot on Śesha, the great serpent, holding up Pṛithvî, the personification of the Earth, whom he rescues from destruction. A snake-demon is between his feet, and figures with Nâga-hoods over their heads stand on each side, one supplicating.

4. Vishṇu, four-armed, in his heaven of Vaikuntha, sitting between his wives Lakshmî and Sitâ, and four attendants behind with *châmaras*. Below is Garuḍa and several males and females, some of them playing on musical instruments.

5. Vishṇu and Lakshmî seated on the same couch under a *toraṇa* or ornamental arch, with attendants behind. Below are seven dwarfs seated, four of them with musical instruments.

---

[1] See *Indian Antiquary*, vol. vi. p. 74, note ‖.

The front of the shrine has two very tall male *dwârpâlas* and a number of other figures, principally females and attendant dwarfs, fat *gandharvas* with curly wigs and garlands, &c. Inside is an altar against the back wall, and a broken image of Bhavânî or Durgâ, to whom the temple was doubtless dedicated. There are four holes, as if for fire-pits (*agnikuṇḍas*), in the floor of the hall.

The Dasa Avatara Cave.

The second of the Elurâ series, usually known as the Dâś Avatâra Cave, resembles, both in plan and in its style of architecture, the Jogâi Ambâ, Bhâmburdê, and the great cave at Karusâ, and may consequently be assumed to be of the same age, or nearly so. From the pathway to the Buddhist caves and Râvaṇa-ka Khâi there is a very considerable ascent by means of steps up the rock to it. Like the last two Buddhist caves here, the whole court has been hewn out of the solid rock, leaving a curtain wall across the front of it, and a sacrificial hall in the middle, with a number of small shrines and a cistern in the surrounding rocky-walls (Plate LXXIII.) This central hall has had a porch to the west, supported by two square pillars in front of a perforated window, over which is a long Sanskrit inscription,—nearly obliterated however (*ante*, p. 402). The entrance faces the cave on the east, and inside it has four pillars on a raised platform in the floor—possibly for a Nandi. In the back is a single round hole, perhaps a fire-pit. The outer walls have a good deal of figure-carving, and the flat roof is surmounted outside by lions at the corners, and fat human figures between, along the edges,—resembling in this respect the cave at Undavilli.

The cave itself is of two storeys, the lower being a few feet above the level of the court, supported by fourteen plain square pillars, and measuring 95 feet in length, with two cells in the back wall near each end. In the north end of the front aisle the stair ascends, and is lighted by a window at the landing where it turns to the right. On the wall of this landing are eleven compartments, each about two feet high, with bas-reliefs of Gaṇapati, Pârvatî, Sûrya or Vishṇu with a lotus in each hand and two attendants, Śiva and Pârvatî, Mahishâsurî—the head of the buffalo struck off, and the Ásura coming out of the neck; Arddhanârî, the androgynous form of Śiva, four-armed, with *triśula* and looking glass; Bhavânî, four-armed, on her tiger, with *triśula* and *damru;* Umâ or Pârvatî with water-pot and rosary, practising *tapas* or asceticism between two fires, with Brahmâ and others looking on; Kâli or Bhavânî, four-armed, with sword, *triśula*, bowl, and a piece of flesh at which a dog snatches, &c.

Another flight of steps leads into the end of the front aisle of the great hall above, 95 feet wide by 109 deep, inclusive of the vestibule to the shrine, and supported by forty-four square columns, including two in front of that vestibule (Plate LXXIV.). Those in front are richly carved with floral ornamentations, in which dwarfs, snakes, &c. are also introduced. Between the pilasters in each side wall are deep recesses filled with large sculptures, mostly in almost entire relief, and some of them cut with great boldness and power. Like the Râvaṇa-kâ-Khâi Cave, the sculptures on one side are mostly Vaishṇava, and on the other entirely Śaiva. Outside the front, at either end of the balcony, is a gigantic Śaiva *dwârpâla*.

Beginning on the north side with the Śaiva sculptures—the first from the door is Bhairava or Mahâdêva in his terrible form; and a more vivid picture of the terrific, a very diseased imagination only could embody. The gigantic figure lounges forward holding up his elephant-hide, with necklace of skulls (*muṇḍmâlâ*) depending below his loins; round him a cobra is knotted; his open mouth showing large teeth, while with his *triśula* he has transfixed one victim, who, writhing on its prongs, seems to supplicate pity from the pitiless; while he holds another by the heels with one of his left hands, raising the *damru* as if to rattle it in joy, while he catches the blood with which to quench his demon thirst. To add to the elements of horror, Kâlî, gaunt and grim, stretches her skeleton length below, with huge mouth, bushy hair, and sunken eyeballs, having a crooked knife in her right hand, and reaching out the other with a bowl, as if eager to share in the gore of the victim; behind her head is the owl (the symbol of destruction)[1] or a vampire as fit witness of the scene. On the right, in front of the skeleton, is Pârvatî; and higher up, near the foot of the victim Ratnâsura, is a grinning face drawing out its tongue. Altogether the group is a picture of the devilish; the very armlets Bhairava wears are ogre faces.

The second chapel contains Śiva dancing the *tândava;* the third

---

[1] One small species of owl is called Bhairava.

has an altar, perhaps for Bhavânî, never quite finished; the fourth contains Śiva and Pârvatî at the game of *chausar*, with Nandi and the rollicksome *gaṇa* below; the fifth is the marriage scene of Śiva and Pârvatî, in which, contrary to the usual representations, she is at his left side. Brahmâ with triple face squats below to perform the priestly functions, while above are the gods, riding on various animals as witnesses of the scene. The sixth chapel contains the usual representation of Râvaṇa under Kailâsa.

On the back wall we have, first, Śiva springing out of the *liṅga* to protect his worshipper Mârkaṇḍeya, whom Yama, the Hindu Pluto, has noosed and is about to drag off to his dark abode.

The second has Śiva and Pârvatî. Śiva holds a lock of his hair with one hand, and a rosary or *mâlâ* in the other. On his right is the bull Nandi, and beyond it is Bhṛingi; over him is an elephant, and above this a squatting ascetic. To the left of the *nimbus* round Śiva's head is a deer—one of his symbols.

We now come to the antechamber or vestibule of the shrine. On the left end of it is a huge Gaṇapati. On the floor at the back corners are lions, carved with considerable spirit. On the back wall, to the left of the shrine door, is Pârvatî with a rosary, and on each side of her musicians. She sits on a *padmâsana* or lotus seat, upheld by two figures among the leaves. The *dwârpâlas* of the shrine are four-armed, with snake, club, and *vajra*. Inside the sanctuary the *śâluṅkha*, or altar, round the *liṅga* or emblem of Śiva, is broken.

To the right of the shrine door is the favourite sculpture of Gaja Lakshmî or Śrî, with four elephants pouring water upon her, while two male attendants offer jars of water and hold the *śaṅkha*, *chakra* or discus, and lotus: she has a lotus and a *sitâphal* or custard-apple in her hands. In the south end of this vestibule is Vishṇu with his lotus and *triśula*, somewhat differing from Śiva's, and with a large bird (Garuḍa) at his right hand.

In the south side of the back wall is, 1*st*, Śiva inside a *liṅga* with flames issuing from the sides of it. Vishṇu is represented below on the right as Varâha—the boar-*avatâra*—digging down to see if he can reach the base of the great *liṅga*; having failed to do so, he is also represented as worshipping it. On the other side is Brahmâ ascending to discover the top of it, which he also failed to do, and stands as a worshipper. Thus Śiva is said to have proved to these rival divinities his own superiority to both of them.

2nd, Śiva having seized the chariot of the sun, made the four *Vedas* his horses, and Brahmâ his charioteer, is going out to war against the Âsura Târaka.

We now came to the south wall, and proceeding towards the front we have, *1st*, Vishṇu, six-armed, his left foot on a dwarf holding up the hill Govardhan to protect the flocks of Vraj from the deluge of rain that Indra sent down. *2nd*, Vishṇu Nârâyaṇa resting on Śesha, the great serpent, with a human head and five hoods; while out of Vishṇu's navel springs a lotus on which Brahmâ is seated. Lakshmî rubs her lord's feet, and seven figures are represented below. *3rd*, Vishṇu riding on Garuḍa. *4th*, a *śâḷuṅkha* or altar, which has been protected by a high screen in front. *5th*, Varâha, the boar-*avatâra* of Vishṇu, holding Pṛithvî (the Earth) on his hand, with three snake figures or Nâgas below. *6th*, Vishṇu in the Wâmana or dwarf incarnation, in which he deceived the good king Bali, obtaining from him a promise of all he could cover at three strides. The dwarf then burst into tremendous proportions, strode over earth and heaven at two strides, and, though Bali tried to appease him with a pot full of precious stones, nothing would do but a third stride, and placing his foot on Bali he thrust him down to Pâtala, or Hell. Garuḍa behind him binds a prisoner. This is the same scene that appears twice at Bâdâmi, and also at Mahâvallipur and elsewhere. *7th*, Narasiñha, or the lion-*avâtara* of Vishṇu, wrestling with his enemy, who is armed with sword and shield, but with two arms can have no fair chance with his eight-armed enemy. Plate LXXV., fig. 1. Notwithstanding its mutilated state, this sculpture shows a vigour rivalling that of the Durga bas-relief at Mahâvallipur, and so like it in style as to indicate that they must belong to the same age. The distance between the two places where they are found, and the difference of the material in which they are carved, render it difficult to say from that alone which may be the earliest of the two, but they cannot be distant in date.

RAMESWARA.

Passing Kailâsa, and four other caves at some distance to the north of it, is the cave-temple locally known as Râmeśwara,—a lofty and interesting Śaiva temple, behind a fine large platform. (Plate LXXVI.) In the court before it, on a lofty pedestal with *bas-reliefs* on the sides of it, couches the Nandi; in a chapel on the north side, with two pillars in front, is Gaṇapati; and between it and the pilaster is a gigantic female standing on a *makara*, with dwarf attendants, *chauri*-bearer, and *gandharvas*; on the south side is a similar figure on a tortoise,—both river goddesses—Yamunâ and Gaṅgâ. A screen wall, half the height of the pillars, connects the front ones. The capitals of the four in front are carved in representation of a water-vessel (*kamandala*), with plants growing out of it and drooping over on each side. To this are added struts carved with female figures standing under foliage, with their attendant dwarfs, somewhat in the style already noticed in the large cave at Bâdâmi. On the brackets above are horned monster *śârdûlas* or *grâsḍas*. The frieze above is carved in compartments of arabesques divided by fat *gaṇas*.

The hall is 15½ feet high, and measures 69 feet by 25, with a chapel at each end, cut off by two pillars with cushion-capital. Each of these chapels is surrounded by sculptures. In the south one we find,—1, on the right wall, a tall, four-armed, ghastly skeleton with a broad, short, pointed knife; another skeleton clasps his leg while it looks up to Kalî, just behind, who seizes it by the hair, while she holds a dissevered head in her left hand, and wears a snake (not a cobra) round her neck. Another skeleton, also with a snake round its neck, grins over her head. A more hideous group could not well be conceived. In front of the tall skeleton (*Kâl*) stands a figure with a sword, and overhead is a *gandharva* with an offering. 2. On the back wall is Gaṇêśa, seven four-armed dêvîs (the Saptâmâtrâ), and a musician. The *chiñhas* below are mostly rotted away. Except in the elaborateness of their headdresses they are nearly the same as already described in Râvaṇa-ka-Khâi. 3. On the east end is Śiva dancing, eight-armed, while gods riding on peacock, elephant, ox, Garuḍa, &c., appear in the clouds over his shoulders; Pârvatî and attendants, with four musicians, look on below; and a small Bhṛingi dances behind Śiva's leg.

In the north chapel are,—1. On the left end, a tall four-armed figure standing with a chick in one left hand, and holding a large bird by the neck with the other; right and left are attendants with rams' heads. On the back wall are—2. Brahmâ seated on a chair, with an attendant behind him, addressing a squatting figure with a female behind. 3. The marriage of Śiva—Brahmâ on the extreme left, with a fire before him, while a bearded figure is seated on the other side of it. Behind him are two males, one carrying a box. Then comes Pârvatî or Umâ, with a female behind her, and a male with a round jar: Śiva takes Pârvatî's hand, and in front is a small figure of Gaṇêśa, while behind Śiva is a dwarf and four other attendants, one with a *śaṅkha*. 4. Pârvatî or Umâ, the daughter of Himâlaya, as an ascetic, amidst four fires, a rosary in one hand, and rocks behind her: this *tapas* she undertook to gain the love of Śiva. Her maid kneels at her right hand, and on her left is a tall female with a box. Śiva or a Yogi approaches her with a water-bottle, and behind him are lotuses, and overhead fruits. Next, to the right, is a tall female addressing a figure,—possibly Kâmadeva or Makaradwaj, the Hindu Cupid,—with shaven crown, coming out of a *makara's* mouth; and behind him is another male figure. 5. On the base of this tableau is a most remarkable row of *gaṇas* very spiritedly carved. 6. On the east end of the chamber is Mahishâsurî slaying the buffalo-demon; a four-armed figure with a club stands in front, and one with a sword behind: above are *gandharvas*.

On each side of the approach to the shrine is a large sculpture:—1. On the north side Râvaṇa under Kailâsa, with five heads and an animal's—possibly a boar's—rising out of the top of his high cap; Śiva and Pârvatî with their attendants are represented above. 2. On the south, Śiva and Pârvatî playing at *chausar*, with Bhṛingi beyond, resting his chin and hand on his knee. Pârvatî is attended by females, one plaiting her hair. The dispute between the gamesters is here pretty well represented. Below is the bull, with the usual gambolling *gaṇa*.

In front of each pilaster of the antechamber stands a female *chauri*-bearer with dwarf attendants. The two columns here are of the Elephanta style, or with compressed cushion capitals, but in place of brackets they have deep square abaci carved with figures. The door of the shrine is also elaborately carved (Plate LXXVII.), and very similar in style to some of the later doorways at Ajaṇṭâ. Those of Cave I. (Plate XLII.) and Cave IV. (Plate XLVII.) present nearly the same architectural arrangements, and even their figure sculptures are not so diverse as might be expected to result from the difference of the two religions to which they are dedicated. This doorway, in fact, might have been applied to a Buddhist cave without any one being able to detect any incongruity in such an application, and their age is undoubtedly very nearly the same. On each side of the doorway of the shrine is a gigantic *dwârpâla* with wigged dwarf attendant, one of them with a high cap having the prongs of the *triśula* projecting from the top of it, a broad dagger, a sword, and round his loins a cobra.

The shrine contains a square *śâḷuṅkhâ* with a water-rotted *liṅga* in it. A wide and lofty *pradakshiṇa* surrounds it.

Caves North of Kailasa.

The next large cave north of Kailâsa at Elurâ is across a deep ravine, and till 1876 was filled to a depth of 6 or 7 feet with earth so that only the capitals of the pillars were visible. It was, however, well worth excavating, and has been cleared with care, and without damage to the carving. This and the next are called by the natives "Dumâr Leṇa,"—a name, however, which has been attached by Europeans to the most northerly of the Brahmanical series.

This is a Śaiva temple with three rows of four pillars from side to side: the front and back aisles being 64 feet long, and the depth up to the front of the shrine 37 feet, or over all 76 feet. In front has been a porch raised by seven or eight steps above the level of the court, on two massive square pillars, one of which is gone, and the other reduced to a shapeless mass, principally by the weather and a *pipal* tree that has taken root against one of them. Surrounding the court on three sides has been a low covered corridor with a small door in the centre of the front for ingress. Over this corridor, at each end of the façade, is a sculptured compartment: that on the south contains Brahmâ with two female attendants and two *gandharvas* on clouds: the other, probably Vishṇu, four-armed, with female attendants; a hole, broken through the lower portion of it, opens into the verandah of the next cave.

The extreme pillars of the front are plain square ones with bracket capitals; the inner pair have deep brackets on two sides, carved with female figures and dwarf attendants. The middle pair in the next row have cushion capitals with female figures, &c. as struts on their inner sides, and fat dwarfs on the corners of the high square bases; the brackets above have not been finished. The outer pillars in this and the next row are in section "broken squares," so favourite a form in later structural temples,—the form being that of a square with thin pilasters of less breadth attached to each side. The middle pillars in the next row are unlike any others here: the base is of the "broken square" pattern, with female figures carved on the principal faces, and males on the corner ones. Over this is a Drâviḍian moulding as in the pilasters of Râvaṇa-kâ-Khâi, then a belt with floral ornament in the centre, and two dwarfs at each corner. Over this is a 16-sided neck, and then the struts with female figures and attendants on three sides. These columns are too heavy to be elegant.

The shrine door is boldly moulded in the Drâviḍian style. The *dwârpâlas* have each only two hands, and hold flowers—no clubs, but each is attended by his dwarf and *gandharvas*. Inside is a large square *śâḷuṅkhâ* and rotted *liṅga*. The *pradakshiṇa* is entered by a door on each side the shrine.

The only sculptures on the walls inside are,—Mahishâsurî on the south end of the front aisle, and Gaṇapati—four-armed—on the north, both well preserved, from having been so long buried in the earth.

The second cave is close to the last, and measures 67 feet by 55 over all. It has four clumsy unfinished columns in front, and a deep recess at each end inside. At the back of the hall is a vestibule or antechamber to the shrine, 30 feet by 10½, with two pillars and corresponding pilasters in front. Some plaster, consisting of mud with vegetable fibres in it, adheres to parts of the walls and pillars of this cave, and on one of the last a few letters of a painted inscription in Devanâgarî are still visible. In the shrine is a round *śâḷuṅkhâ* set on a base, and of a different stone from the cave. In front, in the usual place for the Nandi, is a square trough: possibly an *agnikuṇḍa* or fire-pit.

Descending to a slightly lower level, a little further along the scarp, we come to a primitive-looking cave. Part of the roof has fallen in; it has not been excavated; the rain-water stands long in it, and it stinks from the bats that infest it. The front pillars have gone, and for some distance inside the entrance the cave is not so wide as it is in the middle, where four pillars on each side screen off recesses; in line with the fourth of these are four more in front of the shrine, which contains a broken *śâḷuṅkhâ* and *liṅga*. The pillars are very rude attempts at the Elephanta style, with cushion-shaped capitals.

Close to the next is another unexcavated cave, all ruined, and overgrown by underwood.

Ascending again, we come to a small *liṅga* shrine, originally with two pillars in front,—now gone, but which, as the pilasters show, were probably of the Elephanta pattern. Outside the façade on the north is Gaṇapati, and on the south Mahîshâsurî. The shrine has a wide *pradakshiṇa* round it, and in each entrance to it is a large cell with two square pillars, having octagon necks in front. Inclusive of these chambers, this cave measures 53 feet by 30 over all.

The shrine door is carved round with *veli* or creeper and roll patterns. On each side is a tall *dwârpâla*, with a smaller female figure between him and the entrance (*see* Plate LXXVIII.). This again is so like the arrangement of the front of the shrine in the Buddhist represented in Plate LXI., that we cannot doubt that they are of the same age, and are rather staggered to find they do not both belong to the same religion.

Nilakantha.

A short distance to the north from the last, and the fifth from Rameśwara, we enter a court 42 feet square, within which an ascent of three steps leads to a slightly sloping platform on which stands the Nandi Maṇḍapa—a four-doored chamber, partially ruined. On the south side of the court is a low chapel with the *Ashtâmâtrâ*, or eight divine mothers, all four-armed, and the eighth—Brahmî—with three faces. Thirteen steps lead up to the cave, in front of which, at each end, is a *dwârpâla* besmeared with paint. This excavation is 70 feet by 44, including the end chapels and vestibule of the shrine, and 12 feet high. It has four pillars in front, and two on each of the other three sides of the hall,—all square plain shafts with bases and bracket capitals. At each end is a chapel with an altar. On the walls of the vestibule are a few sculptures,—Gaṇêśa, three dêvîs,—one on a crocodile,—and a four-armed Vishṇu, or perhaps Kârttikeya. In the shrine is a round *śâḷuṅkhâ*, and a highly polished *liṅga*, still worshipped, and which the local Brahmans pretend to show blueish streaks upon: hence the name given to the cave—Nîlakaṇtha—"blue-throated," one of the names of Śiva.

On a rather higher level is a low cave consisting of a verandah (partly double) with five doors entering into small cells, one of them containing a round *śaḷuṅkhâ* and *liṅga*, with a *Trimurti* on the back wall.

Teli-ka-Gana.

Below the front of the last is a series of five low cells, known as "the Oilman's mill." They contain some small sculptures of no special interest.

A little to the north, in the course of a torrent, just where it falls over a cliff, a beginning of a cave has been made, but a flaw in the rock seemingly has stopped progress.

Kumbharwada.

The whole front of the Kumbhârwâḍâ Cave, which is the next to the north, must have been supported by six columns and pilasters, but it has fallen away. The hall, including recess, is 95 feet long, the width about 27 feet, and height 13 feet 10 inches. An image has been placed on a pedestal at the north end, and at the south is a recess with a shrine behind it containing an oblong altar. Between the front of this recess and the pilaster of the front of the cave is a fat male seated on a rich *gâdi* or seat, with a bag in his hand.

At the back of the hall are four free-standing and two attached square pillars with moulded bases. The smaller hall behind these measures 57 feet by 23, and has two pillars in the ends and two at the back, with two attached ones dividing it from the vestibule of the shrine, 30 feet by 9. On the ceiling of the vestibule is a figure of Sûrya—the Sun-god—in his chariot drawn by seven steeds, and a female at each side shooting with a bow (*see* Plate LXXXIII., fig. 2). Was this a Sun-temple? In the shrine, 15 feet square, is an oblong altar.

Janwasa.

The columns of this temple are quite of the Elephanta pattern. It has four in front, and two pilasters; and at the back two with pilasters. At each end of a spacious hall, 16 feet 6 inches high, is a chapel raised three or four feet above the floor on a moulded base. The total length, including these chapels, is 112 feet, and the depth to the back of the *pradakshiṇa* 67 feet.

In front of each pilaster of the vestibule is a female *chauri*-bearer —her hair carefully crimped—with dwarf attendant. At the shrine door are two large *dwârpâlas*, one with a flower; and stout attendants, one with a very high cap terminating in a sharp spear-point, with a skull on the right side of it. In the shrine is a large square *śaḷuṅkhâ* and *liṅga*. The *pradakshiṇa* is wide and lofty.

The Milkmaid's Cave.

This is on the south edge of a ravine that separates it from the last Śaiva cave, and over the scarp at the head of which is a fine water-fall after heavy rain. One octagonal pillar and a fragment of another are left in the verandah: it had, perhaps, two more pillars. The back wall of the verandah is pierced for a door and four windows. On this wall are a few carvings:—Lakshmî with two male attendants; Vishṇu four-armed, with club, *chakra*, and rosary; Śiva with cobra and trident; Brahmâ, three-faced, with staff, water-pot, and rosary; and Mahîshâsurî with the buffalo. In the north end is Varâha with Pṛithvî, and in the south Nârâyaṇa on Śesha, half finished. Inside is a hall 53 feet by 22, and 11 feet 8½ inches high, beyond which is a vestibule to the shrine, 23 feet by 10, with a raised floor and two short square pillars in front.

In recesses on each side the shrine door are Vaishṇava *dwârpâlas*, and inside is a long oblong altar at the back of the shrine.

It was doubtless a Vaishṇava cave, but the style of it says but little for the wealth or influence of the sect in the days when it was executed.

Under the cliff over which the stream falls are the remains of a couple of cells, and a vestibule and shrine with *dwârpâlas*—perhaps Vaishṇava—at each side of the door. Inside is the base of a square altar, and on the inside of the front wall is an eight-armed devî with attendants, still worshipped.

A footpath leading up to the plateau, on the north side of the great pit in which Kailâsa stands, passes some small caves, in the shrine of one of the first of which is a Trimurti or Triad figure, representing Śiva or Mahâdêva under the threefold aspect of the creator, preserver, and destroyer (Plate LXXV., fig. 2). Though not equal to the celebrated one in the Elephanta cave, it is a fine specimen of a class of sculpture very common at that age, in India. Being nearly uninjured it supplies some features which are not easily recognisable at Elephanta. Some way further up, and not easily discovered, are several larger cells; and about a quarter of a mile farther north, on the sides of the stream which comes over the cliff at the point we have now arrived at, is a considerable group of small shrines, the plan of a number of which is given (Plate LXXVI., fig. 2). Some of these are curious from having small open courts entered by a door with a Dravidian pediment over it, similar, on a small scale, to what we meet with at the entrance to the Jaina cave, here known as the Indra Sabhâ. Others have Trimurtis on the back walls of the little shrines, with round (instead of square) *śâluṅkhâs* for the *liṅgas*, a pretty sure indication of their late date. On the ceilings of two of them are some pieces of painting indistinctly traceable.

SITA'S NANI, OR DUMAR LENA.

In the projecting scarp on the north side of a waterfall that divides the last caves from the next is excavated one of the largest caves in the series, known as Sitâ's Nâni (or Bath), and sometimes as Dumâr Leṇa (Plate LXXIX.).

This cave is often compared with that at Elephanta or Gârapuri, to which it bears a striking resemblance, but it is larger and in some respects a finer cave. It is in fact the finest cave, of its class, known to exist in India, and probably also the oldest. The other two—that at Elephanta and the cave at Jogêśwari—show a deterioration in architectural style, and a divergence from Buddhist forms of representation in sculpture, that seem to mark the progressive steps by which the change was gradually spreading itself over the forms of two great religious faiths then prevailing.

The great hall, including the shrine, is 148 feet wide by 149 deep and 17 feet 8 inches high, but the excavation, including the entrance court, extends to more than 200 feet in a direct line north and south. Two large lions, with small elephants under their paws, guard the steps which lead into the hall from three sides. Before the west approach is a large circle for the Nandi. The hall is in the form of a cross, the roof supported by twenty-six massive pillars.

In the front aisles on three sides are large sculptures at each end. These are so like those of Elephanta, in the account of which they will be described more at length, that we need here only indicate briefly what they are. In the west aisle, south end, is Râvaṇa shaking Kailâsa, as usual, and in the north end Bhairava with two victims. In the south verandah there is a large pit opposite the landing: in the west end Śiva and Pârvatî are playing *chausar;* Nandi and the *gâṇa* are below, Vishṇu to the right of them, and Brahmâ to the left.

In the east end is the marriage, with gods and goddesses above. It is thus described by Kâlidâsa:

"E'en Brahmâ came—Creator—Lord of might,—
And Vishnu glowing from the realms of light.
* * * * * *
By Indra led, each world-upholding lord
With folded arms the mighty god adored,—
In humble robes arrayed, the pomp and pride
Of glorious deity were laid aside.
* * * * * *
Around the fire in solemn rite they trod—
The lovely lady and the glorious god;
Like Day and starry Midnight when they meet
In the broad plains at lofty Meru's feet.
Thrice at the bidding of the priest they came
With swimming eyes around the holy flame;
Then at his word the Bride in order due
Into the blazing fire the parched grain threw,
And toward her face the scented smoke she drew,
While softly wreathing o'er her cheek it hung,
And round her ears in flower-like beauty hung.
* * * * * *
'This flame be witness of your wedded life,—
Be just, thou Husband, and be true, thou Wife!'
Such was the priestly blessing on the Bride;—
Eager she listened, as the earth when dried
By parching summer sun drinks deeply in
The first soft dropping when the rains begin.
'Look, gentle Umâ,' cried her lord, 'afar!
See'st thou the brightness of yon polar star?
Like that unchanging ray thy faith must shine!'
Sobbing she whispered—'Yes, for ever thine.'"[1]

Outside the pilaster to the south of this is a gigantic *devî* with round headdress peaked in front. Above are four *munis* or sages,

---

[1] Griffiths's translation of the *Kumâra Sambhava,* or *Birth of the War-God.* (Trübner, 1879). For fully detailed accounts of these sculptures see my *Elephanta.*

and below, three females; a bird or goose pulls at her mantle; may it not be Sarasvati—"Queen of Speech"?

To the south of this is a stair descending down to the stream below.

In the north verandah is Śiva as Mahâyogî, seated on a lotus, with a club in his left hand: the stalk of the lotus (as in Buddhist caves) being upheld by Nága-hooded figures, with two worshippers behind them. This differs very markedly from the corresponding sculpture in the left side of the entrance at Elephanta, where the whole accompaniments of his asceticism in the Himálayas are indicated,—the surrounding rocks and jungle, and the approach of Umâ as described in the glowing verses of Kalidása's *Kumâra Sambhava*. Opposite to this is Śiva dancing the *tândava*, with very fat legs: Pârvatî is seated at his left, perhaps because this dance is said to be executed by him occasionally for her pleasure.

On the east wall, outside the pilaster, is a tall female figure—a river goddess—standing on a tortoise, with a single female attendant and *gandharvas*. This is in a small court on the north side of the cave, in the east of which is a low cave much silted up, with a large oblong block of stone inside.

The shrine is in the back wing or recess of the cave, and is a small square room with *liṅga* in it, with four doors, each guarded by a pair of gigantic *dwârpâlas*, each holding a flower in his right hand, and with a female attendant also holding a flower.

The headdresses are varied in almost every case. In the south *pradakshiṇa* is a square cell, and through it another is entered with a deep hole in one corner.

This is the most northerly of the Brahmanical caves here (below the great scarp); and from this we return southwards to the famous Kailâsa or Ranga Mahâl—the Painted Palace.

Kailasa or the Ranga Mahal.

The plans of all the Brahmanical caves above described are so manifestly copies of the Buddhist vihâras which they were intended to supersede, that they present very little of novelty. Their architectural details, too, are so similar that it requires a practised eye to detect the difference, and were it not for the absence of cells for the residence of monks, and the character of the sculpture by which they are replaced, it would be difficult to feel sure to which religion any particular caves might belong. It is true that after a century of perseverance in practising the style, the Brahmans began to draw away from the Buddhist originals which they had been copying, and in the Sitâ ka Nâni and in other later caves seemed on the verge of creating a new style. Before, however, they had done much in this direction their progress was stopped by a revolution of rather a startling nature. From motives we are only now beginning to understand, those who designed the Kailâsa resolved to cut the gordian knot, and instead of a temple which could in any sense be called a *cave*, determined on excavating what

No. 69. View of Kailâsa from the West, from a sketch by Jas. F.

could only be designated as a *rock-cut* temple. With the exception of the Rathas at Mahâvallipur, perhaps the first of its class that had been executed in India.

Fortunately we have now the means of perceiving with tolerable clearness how and when this revolution took place. During the struggle that took place between the Buddhist and Brahmans in the latter half of the seventh century, the Chalukyas held sway at

Kalyan, and in the country where all the principal caves are situated. Even if not very strict Buddhists themselves, they at least tolerated it, and apparently favoured it more than the rival faith. At the end of that century, however, a new dynasty known as the Râshṭrakuṭas or Râthors arose at Malkhêd—the Mulker of the maps—near Kalbarga, and 50 miles south of Kalyan, who under various names during the next two centuries eclipsed, even if they did not entirely supersede the power of the Chalukyas in these regions.[1] The fourth king of this dynasty, Dantidurga, was one of the most remarkable and powerful sovereigns of his age in that country. During his reign (725–755 A.D.) he conquered the whole of the Dekhan up to the Narmada[2] (Nerbudda), and consequently held sway over all these regions in which Elurâ and the other great cave centres are situated. As he was so powerful a king and a zealous worshipper of Śiva, nothing is more likely than that he should undertake such an excavation as that of the Kailâsa. Those among his successors who were sufficiently powerful to do so, such as Govinda III. (A.D. 785–810) and Amoghâvarsha (810), were too late for the style which we fortunately know was that which prevailed during the reign of Dantidurga. No one will probably hesitate to accept this as a fact, who is familiar with the plan and details of the great Śaiva temple at Paṭṭaḍkal near Badami, and not far from the capital of this king. The arrangements of the plan and even the dimensions of the two temples are almost identical. The style is the same, and even the minutest architectural ornaments are so alike as almost to be interchangeable.[3] In fact it would be difficult to find in India two temples so like one another, making allowance, of course, for the one being structural and the other cut in the rock, and the one being consequently one storey in height, the other two. Barring these inevitable peculiarities they both might have been erected by the same architect, and certainly belong to the same age. What that was has been ascertained from an inscription on the Paṭṭadkal Temple, which states that it was erected by the Queen of the second

[1] *J. R. A. S.*, vol. iv. p. 7, *et seqq.*

[2] Burgess's *Archæological Reports*, vol. iii. p. 23, *et seqq.*; G. Bühler, in *Indian Antiquary*, vol. vi. p. 59, *et seqq.*, where all the known details regarding these Râthors will be found.

[3] *Archæological Reports*, vol. i., Plates XXXIX. and XL., for plan and details; and *Architecture of Dharwar and Mysore*, Plates 54 to 57, for views.

Vikramâditya Chalukya in the year 733 A.D.,[1] and consequently during the reign of Dantidurga. Thus confirming the probability, in so far as architectural evidence can do so, that the Kailâsa was excavated during the reign of that monarch.

Although it is extremely improbable that the Paṭṭadkal temple is the earliest example of a structural temple in the Dravidian style in India, it certainly is the earliest to which an authentic date can be attached, and none with an older appearance have yet been found. If, however, our chronology is correct, the Raths at Mahâvallipur are at least half a century earlier, and even there the conversion of the wooden forms of Buddhist vihâras into lithic temple architecture is so complete that their intermediate forms must have pre-existed somewhere.

As the case at present stands, those Raths at Mahâvallipur are the earliest examples known to exist in India of rock-cut, as contra-distinguished from cave temples—the Kailâsa the latest, and unless some detached hills or boulders suitable for the purpose could be found,—a temple in a pit is so illogical and such an anomaly that none were probably ever executed anywhere else. Besides this both the Raths and the Kailâsa being in the Dravidian style of architecture they belong properly to the south country, where caves never were the fashion. The latter, in fact, is the farthest north specimen known to exist of the style, and is altogether so exceptional that it seems in vain to look for any repetition of it in the cave regions.

Notwithstanding the defects arising from its situation and its anomalous design, the Kailâsa is by far the most extensive and elaborate rock-cut temple in India, and, in so far as dimensions and the amount of labour bestowed upon it are concerned, will stand a comparison with those of Egypt or any other country. Now, too, that its history is practically known, it is one of the most interesting, as well as the most magnificent, of all the architectural objects which that country at present possesses.

At the Kailâsa the work, instead of being commenced as in all antecedent cave temples from the face of the rock, was begun by cutting down three mighty trenches in the solid rock, two of them

[1] *Archæological Reports*, vol. iii. p. 31.

at right angles to the front of the rock and more than 90 yards in length, and the third, connecting their inner ends, over 50 yards in length and 107 feet deep, leaving the nearly isolated mass in the middle to be carved both on the outside and interior into a great monolithic shrine with numerous adjuncts. In front of the court in which it stands, a mass of rock has been left to represent the Gopura, or great gateway pyramid, which is an indispensable adjunct of Dravidian temples. These generally are in stone only to height of one storey, above which the pyramidal part is in most instances in brick and some lighter substance. Here it is in two storeys, the lower one adorned on the outside with the forms of Śiva, Vishṇu, and their congeners, and with rooms inside it. It is not clear whether it ever was intended to carry it higher than it now is, but from the existence of a diminutive roof-formed projection in the top, cut in the rock, it is probable the intention was at all events abandoned, if ever proposed. It is besides unlikely, as it would have hid the temple entirely from the outside. This Gopura is pierced in the centre by an entrance passage (*A.*, Plate LXXXI.)[1] with rooms on each side. Passing this the visitor is met by a large sculpture of Lakshmî seated on lotuses, with her attendant elephants. There are some letters and a date on the leaves of the lotus on which she sits, but illegible, and probably belonging to the 15th century. On the bases of the pilasters on each side have been inscriptions in characters of the eighth century, but of these only a few letters remain legible.

Here we enter right and left, the front portion of the court, which is a few feet lower than the rest; and at the north and south ends of it stand two gigantic elephants,—that on the south much mutilated. Turning again to the east and ascending a few steps, we are in the great court of the temple, which measures 276 in length, with an average breadth of 154, and with a scarp 107 feet high at the back. In the front part of the court stands a maṇḍapa or shrine for the Bull Nandi (*B.* in plan LXXXI.), 26 feet square and two storeys in height; the lower one solid, the upper one connected with the Gopura, and with the Temple itself, by bridges cut in the rock. On each side of this porch stands a square pillar or dwajaśtambha or ensign staff, 45 feet in height. But to this must be added what

[1] In order that the plans of the Kailâsa may be introduced into the work without twice folding, the scale on which they are engraved has been reduced to 35 feet to 1 inch instead of 25 feet to 1 inch, which is that usually adopted for plans throughout.

remains of the trisula of Śiva on the top, making up the total height to 49 feet, as represented on Plate LXXX., fig. 1.

A little further back in this court stands the temple itself (*C.* in plan), measuring 164 from east to west, and 109 across where widest, and rising to a height of 96 feet to the top of its dome. Like the Nandî shrine, its basement is solid, and, as will be seen from the plan (LXXXI.), very irregular in form, being a curious example of symmetriphobia, which is characteristic of all the Hindu buildings of that age. This irregularity is hardly perceived in the elevation (Plate LXXXII.), which is in itself a most remarkable conception. Between a bold podium and its cornice, it is adorned with a frieze of huge elephants, *śardûlas*, or griffins, and other mythological animals. These are in every possible attitude, feeding, fighting, and tearing each other to pieces, but all executed with considerable spirit and truth to animal forms, and notwithstanding the freedom with which they are executed, all seeming to support the temple above.

Under the bridge connecting the temple with the *maṇḍapa* are two large sculptures,—on the west Śiva as Kâl Bhairava with flaming eyes and in a state of frenzied excitement, with the *Saptâmâtras* at his feet; on the other he is represented almost exactly in the ascetic attitude of Buddha—as Mahâyogi the great ascetic, with attendant *munîs* or hermits, and gods. At each side of this bridge a stair leads up to the great hall of the temple. On the outer wall of the south stair is carved, in a series of lines, the story of the *Râmâyaṇa* or war of Râma, aided by Hanuman and his monkeys with Râvaṇa, the demon king of Laṅkâ; and on the north side are some of the episodes from the other great Hindu epic—the *Mahâbhârata* or account of the great war between the Pâṇḍavas and their relatives the Kauravas. Behind these bas-reliefs the sculptures of the lofty basement of the temple commence, with its row of huge elephants, *śardûlas*, &c. This line is unbroken except on the south side, where there has been a bridge across from a balcony of the temple to a cave in the scarp, but this bridge has long since fallen. Under this is a somewhat spirited sculpture of Râvaṇa under Kailâsa. Pârvatî is stretched out clinging to Śiva; while her maid, in fright at the shaking of the ground under her feet, is represented in the background fleeing for safety (*see* Plate LXXXII.).

The interior of the temple and parts at least of the exterior, if not the whole, have been plastered over and painted, whence, perhaps, the name Ranga Mahâl, or Painted Palace, by which it is generally known among the natives to the present day. Where the painting has not very long ago peeled off, it has had the effect of preserving the stone inside from the smoke of wandering *jogis'* and travellers' fires, with which it must for ages have been saturated.

On the roof of the porch of the upper temple some bits of old fresco paintings still remain, of two or three successive coatings, that might help to give an idea of the style of decoration that at one time covered the whole of this great fane. The door of the upper temple (*C'*, Plate LXXXI A.), which rests in the solid basement just described, is guarded by gigantic Śaiva *dwârpâlas*, leaning on heavy maces. The hall (*C'*), 57 feet wide by 55 deep, has a wide central and cross aisle, while in each corner thus formed four massive square columns support the roof (Plate LXXXIV., fig. 3). The four round the central area are of one pattern, differing only in the details of their sculptures; the remaining twelve are also of one general type; while the sixteen pilasters (Plate LXXXIV., fig. 1) are more of the style of the four great central columns. At each end of the cross aisle is a door leading out into a side balcony with two pillars in front of it richly carved in florid ornamentation.[1]

The effect of this hall crowded by 16 great square piers on its floor is extremely different from what we have been accustomed to find in Buddhist vihâras. In them a large open space was always reserved in the centre for the use of the monks and the service of the shrine, and the well proportioned pillars are arranged so as to produce the best possible architectural effect, by dividing the hall into a centre and side aisles. Here, on the contrary, the 16 pillars are spread pretty evenly over the whole floor of the hall, evidently for the purpose of supporting the roof, and being square and massive they do produce an almost Egyptian effect of solidity and grandeur unlike anything else even in cave architecture known to exist in India. At Paṭṭadkal[2] the 16 pillars are even more evenly spaced over the floor, but that being a structural building they are more slender, and do

---

[1] If the details of these pillars and pilasters are compared with the pilaster represented in Plate XL., fig. 1, of Mr. Burgess' first *Archæological Report*, they will see at a glance how nearly the style of the great Śaiva temple at Paṭṭadkal resembles that of the Kailâsa. I am not aware of anything at all like them occurring anywhere else, except perhaps in the temple of Aiholê close by, and of the same age.—J. F.

[2] *Archæological Survey of Western India*, vol. i., Plate XXXIX.

not crowd it to the same extent. Perhaps it was the failure that followed from the architect not providing sufficient supports at Mahâvallipur (*ante*, p. 118), which may have induced those who designed the Kailâsa to err, if error it is, on the side of over solidity. But whatever the cause the result gained is satisfactory, beyond anything of its class elsewhere in India.

At the east end of the hall is the vestibule of the shrine (*D'*). On the roof is Lakshmî or Anna Pûrṇâ, standing on a lotus, with high *jaṭâ* headdress. Brahmâ squats at her right elbow, and perhaps Vishṇu at her left, with *gandharvas* at the corners of the sculpture. On the north wall of this vestibule *was* Śiva and Pârvatî, engaged at *chausar*, but the gods are now almost totally destroyed; on the south was Śiva and Pârvatî upon Nandî couching on a slab supported by four *gaṇa*, and a fifth at the end. Śiva has a child on his right knee, and behind him are four attendants.

The *dwârpâlas* on each side the shrine door were females,—probably Gaṅgâ and Yamunâ, one on a *makara*, and the other on a tortoise (*kûrma*), but the heads of both have been destroyed.

The shrine is a plain cell 15 feet square inside, with a large rosette on the roof. The present altar or *śâḷuṅkhâ* is a modern affair. What originally occupied it is uncertain; it was probably a *liṅga*-shrine from the first, though the female *dwârpâlas* might suggest that this "Ranga Mahâl," or Painted Palace, was dedicated to one of the forms of Pârvatî or Bhavânî.[1]

A door in each of the back corners of the hall leads to the terrace behind, on which a wide path leads quite round the outside of the shrine, which forms the base of the *vimâna*, *śikhara*, or spire. This

---

1 Tradition says that Râja Il of Ilichpur, in Berar, cleaned out and painted the Elurâ Caves, and that he was afterwards killed in battle by Sayyid Rihman Daulah in A.H. 384 or A.D. 994: this is evidently much too early a date for any Muhammadan invasion of the Dekhan. It is possibly connected, however, with part of a painted inscription still traceable under a relief of Śiva and Yama near the north corner of the west face of the great temple, beginning "Śakê 1384 (A.D. 1463), when Kailâsa at least must have been covered with a fresh coating of plaster and painted in the debased style of the age. The temples doubtless suffered severely when Alâu'd-dîn took Devagiri (now Daulatâbâd) and forced Râja Râmadeva to cede Ilichpur to his uncle Jelalu'd-dìn, cir. 1294. They were sure also to suffer at the hands of Muhammad Tughlik, when he attempted to make Daulatâbâd his capital (1325–1351) (Elliot and Dowson's *Hist. of Ind.*, vol. vii. p. 189); but tradition ascribes their final desecration and most of the destruction of the sculpture to Aurangzeb, cir. 1684.

spire rises to a height of 96 feet from the court below, and is all elaborately carved. Below are compartments between pilasters, with richly-sculptured finials over each, and the centre of each compartment is occupied in most cases by some form of Śiva, with Vishṇu. (Plate LXXXII.) On the wall above these are flying figures, and over them the horizontal mouldings of the *śikhara* begin.

On the outer side of this platform are five small shrines, in four of which are altars as if for the worship of goddesses: the fifth is empty.

Besides their value here as elegant and appropriate adjuncts surrounding the central shrine, these five cells are interesting, as illustrative of the class of cells that apparently, at one time existed on the terraces of all the pyramidal Buddhist Vihâras. At Mahâvallipur and on the great Sikâra here, they have become so diminutive that they are unfit for human habitation, and are only reminiscences of the original types, and so they remained throughout the whole Dravidian period. Here, on the contrary, they are somewhat exaggerated in the opposite direction, to convert them from the abodes of men to temples for gods. But be this as it may, it is evident that these shrines are only part of that system by which the Vihâras of the Buddhists were converted into temples in the Dravidian style of architecture, of which the Kailâsa is one of the oldest and most conspicuous examples known to exist anywhere.

Returning to the entrance of the hall we pass across the bridge outside the porch to a pavilion (*B'*.) with four doors and a broken Nandî in it—probably not the original one, for this is but a small bull. Beyond this, to the west, are a number of chambers over the entrance porch. From these there is access to the roof of the small chambers which form the screen in front of the court, and from it good views along each side of the great temple can be had.[1]

Descending to the court we may again scramble up (for the steps are broken away) into a cave under the scarp on the south side (*E'*), measuring about 37 feet by 15, with two square pillars and pilasters in front, each pillar having a tall female warder with her hair hanging in loose folds towards her left shoulder and with two dwarf

---

[1] It is from the terrace of south wing that the view in the last woodcut, No. 69, is taken.

attendants. Behind each pillar on the floor is a low square pedestal, as if for an altar; and round the three inner sides of this *yajñaśâla*, or sacrificial hall, as it is sometimes called, are the female monsters the Bráhmaṇs delighted to teach their votaries to revere as the mothers of creation. First, on the west end, comes Wâgheśwarî, four-armed, with *triśula*, and under her feet the tiger; then a second, somewhat similar figure; and next, Kâl, a grinning skeleton with cobra girdle and necklace, seated on two dying men —a wolf gnawing the leg of one,—while behind him is Kâlî, and another skeleton companion. On the back wall is (1) Gaṇapatî as usual. (2) A female, almost quite destroyed, with a child, sitting on a wolf. (3) Indrânî, also destroyed. (4) Pârvatî with a bull in front of the seat as a cognizance, her head and the child destroyed. (5) Vaishṇavî, her arms and the child destroyed, and Garuḍa below. (6) Karttikeyî, bust gone, child crawling on the knee, with peacock holding a snake as a *chinha* or cognizance. (7) A Devî with *triśula*, and having a humped bull below. (8) Saraswatî holding a rosary. (9) Another Devî, two of her four arms broken off, holding a shallow vessel. On the east end are three female seated figures without the nimbus and cognizances that mark the others, and each holding a *chauri* or fly-flap:[1] these are separated from the preceding by a fat dwarf, who sits with his back to the three. All the figures are quite separate from the wall, and form a somewhat imposing assemblage.

Descending to the court again: under the west end of the *yajña-śâla* is a small low cave (*F.*, Plate LXXXI.), the verandah divided from the inner room by a *toraṇa* or ornamental arch from two attached pillars. Inside is an altar for some idol, probably a moveable one.

Opposite the sculpture of Râvaṇa already described, the ascent to the second storey of the cave in the scarp (*G'.*) may be effected by means of a ladder. The verandah is 61 feet by 22, inclusive of the two pillars in front, and inside is a dark hall 55 feet by 34, with four heavy plain pillars,—the shrine scarcely more than begun. A stair at the west end of the verandah leads to a third storey, not shown in the plan, but almost identical in dimension and arrangement, with similar verandah and hall. It is however lighted by two windows,

[1] These three figures are sometimes named by the local Brahmans Śivakâli, Bhadra-kâli, and Mahâkâli. They and the dwarf are represented (rather too artistically) in a fine plate by Captain Grindlay in *Trans. R. As. Soc.*, vol. ii. p. 487.

besides the door, and by an opening in the roof up into a small cave that may be noticed at the roadside on the ascent of the ghâṭ; its four pillars support arches on the four sides of the central square.

Passing now to the north side of the court, nearly opposite the obelisk, we enter a corridor 60 feet long (*H.*), with five pillars in the front. At the east end is an ascent of two or three steps to a figure of Śrî or Gaja Lakshmî, the goddess of prosperity, with a lotus in each hand, and four attendant elephants[1] (Plate LXXXIII., fig. 1). The stair to the left of this is badly lighted, but ascends to a fine cave called Laṅkâ or Laṅkeśwara, 123 feet long from the back of the Nandî shrine to that of the *pradakshiṇa*, and 60 wide inside the front screen. On entering from the stair a low screen-wall, connecting the west line of pillars, faces the visitor: to the left, and directly in front of the Nandî, which occupies a large recess in this end, is the entrance into the hall.

The roof is low, and supported by 27 massive pillars, besides pilasters, most of them richly carved, and of singularly appropriate design, but evidently of a later style than the central temple. As will be seen from the plan (Plate LXXXI A.) the arrangement of the 16 pillars in the centre is identical with that of the greater temple, only that the central and central cross aisle is somewhat wider, and being open on the west and south sides the hall has a more spacious and more cheerful appearance than the porch of the temple itself, though its dimensions are nearly the same. The pillars are all varied in design,[2] no two of them being exactly alike, and, being hardly more than three diameters in height, are more appropriate for rock-cut architecture than almost any other in India (Plate LXXXIV., fig. 4), and in strange contrast with quasi wooden posts that deformed the architecture of Mahâvallipur about a century earlier.

---

[1] We have had occasion to remark the frequency of this sculpture in Buddhist works both of early and late date. Like Aphrodite, she sprang from the froth of the ocean (when it was churned) in full beauty, with the lotus in her hand. The representation of her, bathed by elephants, seems to have been an equal favourite with the Brahmans. With whom is prosperity, abundance and fortune, not a favourite?

[2] A view of the interior of this temple forms Plate XVI. of my *Illustrations of the Rock-cut Temples of India*, fol., 1845.

On the inner side each of the pillars on the south face are connected by a low screen, which, like that at the western entrance, is adorned with sculptures. They have been cut with considerable care, and the stone being in this place very close-grained the carving has been sharp, and would have stood for ages, had not the bigotry of ignorant iconoclasts spared no pains to deface the inoffensive stone. In the south-west corner was Mahîshâsurî; on the second pillar Arddhanârî,—the face and breast broken, perhaps not very long since; the third was Bhairava or Vîrabhadra, terribly mutilated; the fourth Śiva and Pârvatî—entirely gone except the feet; and the fifth, Śiva with his left foot on a dwarf, and Pârvatî at his right hand. At the end of the aisle has been a boldly executed Śiva dancing the *tâṇḍava*, with a skull withering in his head-dress.[1]

On the right-hand side of the entrance to the *pradakshiṇa* is a sculpture of Śiva and Pârvatî with Râvaṇa below, and a maid running off; in the north entrance are the same gods playing at *chausar*—the board distinctly represented, a plantain-tree behind, and the Nandî and *gaṇa* below.

On each side the shrine door is a female guardian, one standing on a *makara*, the other on a *kûrma* or tortoise,—probably Gaṅgâ and Yamunâ, as in the great temple. The *śâluṅkhâ* or altar inside the shrine has been smashed. On the back wall of the shrine, in very low relief, is a grotesque *Trimurti*, or bust of Śiva with three faces, representative of three phases of his supposed character as Brahmâ, Vishṇu, and Rudra.

In the back aisle of the cave are a series of pretty large sculptures:—1. At the east end is Vishṇu as Sûrya or the Sun-god, with two hands, holding flowers, and with male and female attendants on each side holding buds,—one with a spear and oval shield. 2. On the back wall, Varâha holding up Pṛithvî. 3. Pârvatî or Umâ performing austerity or *tapas* between two fires, four-armed, and holding up Gaṇapati as an ensign or *dwaja*. 4. In the middle compartment are three figures,—in the centre Śiva, four-armed, with *triśula* and cobra, Nandî on his left, and an attendant on right; to the left of Śiva is Vishṇu; and to the right a three-faced Brahmâ.

---

[1] This is the subject of Capt. Grindlay's fourth plate at p. 326, *Trans. R. As. Soc.*, vol. ii.

5. In the next recess is Narasiñha, the lion-*avatâra* of Vishṇu, tearing the bowels out of his victim, and supported by Garuḍa and *gaṇa*. 6. A large Gaṇapati.

On each side the recess for Nandî, in the west end of the hall, is a four-armed *dwârpâla*, with huge clubs having axe-edges protruding from the heads of them.

In a recess at the east end of the balcony in front are the Saptamâtrâ on a small scale, and some remains of grotesque paintings.

In the court below, just behind the northern elephant, is a small shrine with two pillars in front (*I.*). The back wall is divided into three compartments, each containing a tall river goddess with creepers, water plants, and birds in the background. They stand respectively on a tortoise, a *makara*, and a lotus, and must represent Gañgâ, Yamunâ, and Sarasvatî. Above this is a small unfinished cave (*I'*), which it was apparently intended to extend considerably inwards, but only the drift ways, have been excavated.

Returning now to the south side of the court a doorway at the east end of the unfinished hall (*G.*), under the fallen bridge that once led from the upper temple to the scarp, leads into the corridor which surrounds the whole back half of the court on the ground floor. On the south side (*J.*) it measures 118 feet in length. The wall is divided by pilasters into twelve compartments, each containing a large sculpture. They are as follows:—

1. Perhaps Anna Pûrṇâ, four-armed, holding a waterpot, rosary, spike or bud, and wearing her hair in the *jaṭâ* style, resembling Lakshmî. 2. Said to be Śiva as Balaji who slew Indrajît, the son of Râvaṇa, but very like Vishṇu, four-armed with club, discus or *chakra*, and conch or *śaṅkha*, with a supplicant, and a small female figure in front of his club. 3. Vishṇu, four-armed, with the *śaṅkha*, holding by the tail the seven-hooded snake Kaliya, he is armed with a sword, and has his foot on its breast. 4. Varâha raising Pṛithvi; he is four-armed, with *chakra* and *śaṅkha*, and has the snake under his foot. 5. A four-armed Vishṇu on Garuḍa, the man-eagle that carries him. 6. The Vâmana or dwarf incarnation of Vishṇu, six-armed, with long sword, club, shield, *chakra*, and *śaṅkha*, with his foot uplifted over the head of Bali holding his pot of jewels, as in the Dâś Avatâra. 7. A four-armed Vishṇu upholding the lintel of the compartment, intended to represent the base of a hill, over

the flocks of Vraj. 8. Śesha Nárâyaṇa, or Vishṇu, on the great snake, and Brahmâ on the lotus springing from his navel, with five fat little figures below. 9. Narasiñha, or the lion-incarnation of Vishṇu tearing out the entrails of his enemy. 10. A figure with three faces, and four arms trying to pull up the *liṅga*. 11. Śiva, four-armed, with his bull Nandî. 12. Arddhanârî, or the androgynous personification of Śiva, four-armed, with Nandî.

The sculptures in the 12 corresponding bays (*K.*, Plate LXXXI.), on the north side of the court are, beginning in like manner from the west end:—1. The linga of Mâha Dêva surrounded by nine heads and supported by Râvaṇa. 2. Gaurâ Pârvati, and beneath Râvaṇa writing. 3. Mâha Dêva, Pârvati, and beneath Nandî. 4. The same subject slightly varied. 5. Vishṇu. 6. Gaurâ Pârvati. 7. Baktâ (a votary of Vishṇu) with his legs chained. 8. Gaurâ Pârvati. 9. The same subject differently treated, as indeed are all the bas-reliefs, when the same deities are represented. 10. Another repetition of the same subject. 11. Vishṇu and Laksmî. 12. Bala Bhadra issuing from the pinda or linga of Mahâ Dêva.

The 19 subjects occupying the compartments (*L.*) at the east end of the courtyard, beginning from the northern end, are:—1. Gaurâ and Pârvati. 2. Bhêru with Gôvinda Râja transfixed on his spear. 3. Daitâsur on a chariot drawing a bow. 4. Gaurâ and Pârvati. 5. Kâla Bhêru. 6. Narasiñha Avatâra issuing from the pillar. 7. Kâla Bhêru. 8. Bala Bhêru. 9. Vishṇu. 10. Gôvinda. 11. Brahma. 12. Lakshmî Dâs. 13. Mahmund. 14. Narâyana. 15. Bhêru. 16. Gôvinda. 17. Bala Bhêru. 18. Gôvinda Râja and Lakshmî. 19. Krishna Dâs.[1] Showing throughout the same admixture of Śaiva and Vaishnave mythology which characterises all the Brahmanical temples, anterior to the rise of the Lingayet sect. After that time the two sects became distinct, and no such toleration of rival creeds is anywhere to be found.

While passing along these corridors the visitor has the best opportunity of studying the variety in, and effects of, the great elephant base that surrounds the central temple.

---

[1] A description of these sculptures on the north and east sides of the courtyard having been omitted from Mr. Burgess' account of this temple I have supplied them from Sir Charles Malet's description (*Asiatic Researches*, vol. vi., p. 409). The mythological determinations I have no doubt are correct, though the descriptions are not so full, nor the transliteration from the Sanskrit names may not be so perfect as Mr. Burgess might have made it.—J. F.

A door from the north corridor (*K.*) leads into a continuation of it, 57 feet long, (*M.*) but without sculptures at the back: the two front pillars however, as seen from the court, are elegantly ornamented. It is situated immediately under the Lankeśwara cave, and at one time it seems to have been intended to continue it inwards, but whether from fear of endangering the stability of that cave, or from some other cause the idea was abandoned.

Assuming the temple itself to have been excavated by Danti Durga (725–755), it is evident, both from its position in the scarp and the style of its ornamentation, that the Lankeśwara was excavated subsequently to the great temple, though at what interval of time it is impossible to say. The same may be said of this gallery (*J.*, *K.*, and *L.*), surrounding the inner side of the court on the ground floor, which, from the way the rock overhangs it, was evidently no part of the original design. The probability seems to be that these parts may have been added by the second or third Gôvindas, 765 to 810, or even by Amogha Varsha, whose reign began in the last named year.[1] In fact, we are probably justified in considering this great temple and its adjuncts occupied some 80 or 100 years in execution. Each successive sovereign of the Râṭhor or Balhara dynasty contributing, according to his means, towards its completion.

It is indeed difficult to understand how so vast a work as the Kailâsa, with its surroundings, could have been completed in less time with the limited mechanical means available at that age. Even allowing all the time this would imply, and granting that all the superfluous wealth of the Râṭhor princes was placed at the disposal of the Brahmans, to commemorate their triumph over the Buddhists, the Kailâsa must always remain a miracle of patient industry applied to well defined purpose. It far exceeds, both in extent and in elaboration, any other rock-cut temple in India, and is and must always be considered one of the most remarkable monuments that adorn a land so fertile in examples of patient industry and of the pious devotedness of the people to the service of their gods.

On the face of the hill above the scarp in which the caves from Kailâsa to Sitâ's Nâni are excavated, are a large number of small caves, scattered in groups up and down, but many of them on the stream that comes over the cliff near the last named cave. Some of

[1] *Indian Antiquary*, vol. vi. p. 72.

these are curious from their having small open courts entered by a door with a Dravidian pediment upon it; others have *Trimurtis* on the back wall of the shrines, which contain round *śâḷunkhâs* and *liṅgas* in them: the oldest *śâḷunkhâs* are square. On the ceilings of two of them fragments of paintings are still left.

Dhamnar Brahmanical Rock-cut Temple.

About the same time that the Brahmans undertook the excavation of the Kailâsa at Elurâ, they also commenced a rock-cut temple for a similar purpose at Dhamnâr. As before mentioned (*ante*, p. 392), the Buddhist caves there are excavated in the scarp of a hill of coarse laterite. On the top of this, in the centre of the caves, the Brahmans have dug a pit, measuring 104 feet by 67, in the centre of which they have left standing a mass of rock which they have hewn into a monolithic temple, 48 feet in length by 33 feet in width across the portico. This time, however, instead of being like the Kailâsa, in the Dravidian style of architecture, it is in the Indo-Aryan style of the north of India, and instead of being dedicated to Śiva it is wholly Vaishṇave, being dedicated to Chatturbhuja, the four-armed manifestation of Vishṇu. It is true, a liṅga has recently been introduced into the cell, but there is no doubt about its original dedication. Externally its architecture very much resembles that of the temple at Barrolli[1] situated about 50 miles further north, and of about the same age, though the porch at Dhamnâr is larger and somewhat differently arranged, more resembling that of the Kailâsa, though on a much smaller scale.

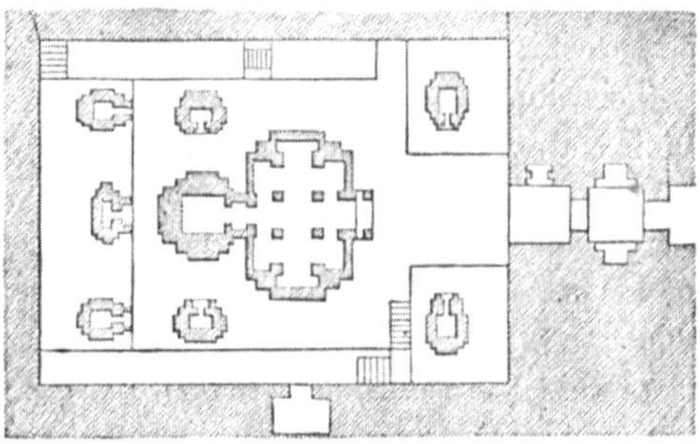

No. 70. Rock-Temple at Dhamnâr. (From a plan by General Cunningham.) Scale 50 ft. to 1 in.

As will be seen from the plan the principal temple is surrounded, like the Kailâsa, by five smaller shrines. These, however, are here

[1] *Picturesque Illustrations of Ancient Architecture in Hindostan*, folio, London, 1847, Plate VII.

quite detached, and stand by themselves on the ground, and two more are placed on the right and left of the entrance. Owing to their exiguity these small detached cells, for the display of the various manifestations of the deity, have in most instances disappeared in India, but in Brahmanical temples in Java, about the same age, the system was carried to excess. At Brambanan the central temples were surrounded by 16, 160, and even 238 small detached shrines, each containing an image of the god to whom the principal temple was dedicated, or some sculptured representation connected with his worship.[1] In India a more frequent mode of displaying these was to arrange them in a continuous gallery, such as that round the eastern end of the court of the Kailâsa, and such as are generally found in Jaina temples. Either of these plans was preferable to the Dravidian mode of crowding these cells on the successive storeys of their Gopuras or their Temples, and placing the images, or the manifestations of the God, outside in front of the cells.

A crooked passage, 282 feet long, leads from the face of the rock to the courtyard of the temple, so that it is not seen from the outside at all, and all the anomalous effects of a temple in a pit which were pointed out in speaking of the Kailâsa are here exaggerated to a ten-fold extent. Besides these defects in design, this temple at Dhamnâr is so small that it would hardly merit notice here, were it not, that like the Kailâsa it marks the final triumph of the Brahmans over the Buddhists in the eighth century, and was placed here for that purpose. In an architectural sense, however, it is valuable, as being a perfectly unaltered example of the northern, as the Kailâsa is of the southern, style of architecture as practised at an age when the idea of utilising the living rock for the purposes of architectural display was fast dying out.

---

[1] *Hist. of Indian and East. Arch.*, p. 652.

CHAPTER VI.

LATE BRAHMANICAL CAVES.

ELEPHANTA.

The island of Elephanta or Ghârâpurî, as it is called by the Hindus, is about six miles from Bombay, and four from the shore of the mainland.[1] It was named Elephanta by the Portuguese from a large stone elephant 13 feet 2 inches in length, and about 7 feet 4 inches high, that stood near the old landing-place on the south side of the island.

The great cave is in the western hill of the island, and at an elevation of about 250 feet above high-water level. It is hewn out of a hard compact trap rock, which has also been cut away on either side, leaving open areas affording entrances from its east and west sides. The principal entrance faces the north.

The accompanying ground plan (Plate LXXXV.) will convey the best general idea of the form and arrangement of the parts of the cave. From the front entrance to the back it measures about 130 feet, and its length from the east to the west entrance is the same. It does not, however, occupy the entire square of this area. As in the

---

1 The principal notices of Elephanta are in J. H. Van Linschoten (1579) *Discourse of Voyages* (Lond. 1598), Boke I. ch. xliv. p. 80; Diogo de Couto (1603), *Da Asia*, Dec. VIIma. liv. iii. cap. 11; Fryer (1673) *New Account of East India and Persia*, p. 75; J. Ovington, *Voyage to Suratt* in 1689, pp. 158–161; Capt. A. Hamilton, *New Account of the East Indies* (ed. 1744), vol. i. pp. 241, 242; Pyke (1712) in *Archæologia*, vol. vii. pp. 323–332; A. du Perron, *Zend-Avesta*, disc. prel. tom. i. pp. ccccxix–ccccxxiii.; C. Niebuhr (1764), *Voyage en Arabie, &c.*, tom. ii. pp. 25–33; Grose, *Voyage from England to India* (1750), vol. i. pp. 59–62; Dr. W. Hunter, in *Archæologia*, vol. vii. pp. 286–295; H. Macneil, *ib.*, vol. viii. pp. 270, 277; *Asiat. Res.* vol. iv. pp. 409–417; Forbes, *Oriental Memoirs*, vol. i. pp. 423, 432–435, 441–448; Erskine in *Trans. Bom. Lit. Soc.* vol. i. pp. 198–250; Fergusson, *Rock-Cut Temples*, pp. 54, 55; Dr. J. Wilson, *Calcutta Review*, vol. xlii. (1866) pp. 1–25; and my *Rock Temples of Elephanta or Gharapuri* (illustrated), Bombay, 1871.

Dumar Lenâ at Elurâ (Plate LXXIX.), which it closely resembles even in details, the porticoes on the three open sides are only about 54 feet long and 16½ feet deep. Omitting these and the back aisle, in front of three of the principal sculptured compartments, and which is of about the same dimensions as each portico, we may consider the body of the cave as a square of about 91 feet each way. It is supported by six rows of columns, six in each row, except at the corners and where the uniformity is broken on the west side to make room for the shrine or Sacellum, which occupies a space equal to that enclosed by four of the columns. The plan shows too the irregularities of the dimensions, irregularities that do not at first sight strike the eye, but, as may be observed in the ground plans, which prevail in almost all the cave-temples. By actual measurement it is found that scarcely two columns are exactly alike in the sizes of even their principal details, and often are not even square, nor three of them in a line. The angles at the corners differ considerably from right angles, and the depth of the cave as well as its height varies in the east and west sides.

The porticoes have each two pillars and two pilasters or demi-columns in front. The columns are very massy and were originally twenty-six in number with sixteen attached ones. But eight of the separate pillars have been destroyed, and others are much injured. As neither the floor nor the roof are perfectly horizontal, they vary in height from 15 to 17 feet. The aisle at the back has a chamber at each end of it 16 feet by 17½ or 18 feet. The portico on the east side opens into a court, from which an ascent of a few steps on the south leads into a smaller cave. At the other end of the great hall is also an open court, with a water cistern on the south side, of which a portion of the roof has fallen in, and with other débris now almost fills it up. At the west side of this court is a small open chapel with a *liṅga* shrine at the back.

The pillars closely resemble those of the Dheṛwâṛâ Buddhist caves, and of several of the Brahmanical caves at Elurâ, with a thick projecting cushion-shaped member as the principal feature of the capital. Imitations of wooden beams over the pillars run across the cave. (Woodcut 65.)

It is a matter of some difficulty to fix the age of this temple, and the only record that could have helped us to its solution, like too many others that have been removed from their original sites by officious or dishonest pedantry, has long been lost. Diogo de Couto, the Portuguese annalist, says:—"When the Portuguese took Baçaim and its dependencies they went to this pagoda and removed a famous stone over the entrance that had an inscription of large and well written characters, which was sent to the king, after the Governor of India had in vain endeavoured to find out any Hindu or Moor in the East who could decipher them. And the king D. Ioáo III. also used all his endeavours to the same purpose, but without any effect, and the stone thus remained there, and now there is no trace of it."[1] Architecturally we may regard it as probably belonging to the latter part of the eighth or beginning of the ninth century of our era.[2]

No. 65. Pillar in Cave at Elephanta, from a photograph.

The most striking of the sculptures is the famous colossal three-faced bust, at the back of the cave facing the entrance, called a Trimurti, or tri-form figure. It occupies a recess 10½ feet deep, and is 21 feet 6 inches in width, rising from a base about 2 feet 9 inches in height. In the corners of the opening, both in the floor and lintel, are holes as if to receive door posts, and in the floor is a groove, as if a screen had been used for occasionally concealing the sculpture, or perhaps there was a railing here to keep back the crowd.

The central face has a mild and tranquil appearance;[3] the lower

[1] De Couto, *Da Asia* (ed. Lisboa, 1778), Dec. VII. liv. iii. cap. 11. in tom. vii. p. 259.

[2] I would feel inclined to place it slightly earlier. The Dumar Lena I take to be earlier than the Kailâsa at Elura, and consequently was most probably excavated between 700 and 725 A.D. This cave seems to have followed almost immediately afterwards, and may therefore have been well advanced if not completed before 750 A.D.—J. F.

[3] The general arrangement and appearance of this sculpture may be gathered from the nearly contemporary one at Elura, Plate LXXV., fig. 2.

lip is thick; the breast is ornamented with a necklace of large stones or pearls, and below it a rich jewel breast ornament; in the left hand he holds what may represent a gourd, as the *kamandala* or drinking vessel of an ascetic Brahman or Yogi. The right hand, like the nose, has been mutilated, but when it was entire, it perhaps held the snake, the head of which still remains behind his right ear. The headdress or *mukuta* is fastened by the folds or bands that encompass the neck; it is richly wrought, and high up on the right side it bears a crescent, a peculiar emblem of Śiva. The jewel in front "is certainly," as Mr. Erskine remarks, "both for elegance of design and beauty of execution one of the finest specimens of Hindu taste anywhere to be met with."

The face to the spectator's left is that of Rudra, or Śiva as the Destroyer. His right hand comes up before his breast, and the cobra, one of his favourite symbols, is twisted round the wrist, and with its hood expanded looks him in the face, while he appears to contemplate it with a grim smile. His tongue appears between his slightly parted lips, and at the corner of the mouth a tusk projects downwards. The brow has an oval prominence in the centre, representing the third eye which Śiva has in his forehead—always represented on his images vertically as opening up the forehead.

The third face of the Trimurti, that to the spectator's right, has generally been regarded, and perhaps correctly, as Śiva in the character of Vishṇu the Preserver, holding in his right hand one of his emblems, a lotus flower. It is very tastefully sculptured with festoons of pearl pendants on the head-dress.

On each side of the Trimurti recess is a pilaster in front of which stand gigantic dwârpâlas or doorkeepers. The one to the right (at *a* on the plan) is 12 feet 9 inches high, and is now the most entire of the two. The cap, like most of those on the larger figures, is high and has round it a sort of double coronal of plates. The left arm leans on the head of a *Piśâcha*, or dwarf demon, who is about 7 feet high, and has on his head a wig with a smooth surface; he wears a necklace and a folded belt across his stomach.

The dwârpâla, on the east side, is 13 feet 6 inches high, and is similarly attended by a dwarf Piśâcha standing in a half crouching attitude, with prominent eyes, thick lips from between which his tongue hangs out.

In approaching the Trimurti we pass the shrine or *garbha* of the temple on the right. It is entered by a door on each of the four sides, each approached by six steps, which raise the level of the floor of the sanctuary 3 feet 8 inches above that of the temple. On each side the doors is a gigantic dwârpâla (woodcut No. 65) or guard, from 14 feet 10 inches to 15 feet 2 inches in height, and each standing on a low base, several of them attended by dwarfs.

The doors into the shrine have plain jambs with two plain fascias round them. Inside are the sockets of the door posts both in the floor and roof. The chamber or sacellum is perfectly plain inside, and about 19½ feet square. In the middle of the room stands a base or altar (*vêdi*) 9 feet 9 inches square, and about 3 feet high. In the centre of this is placed the *Liṅga*, cut from a stone of a harder and closer grain than that in which the cave is executed. The lower end of the Liṅga is 2 feet 10 inches square, and is fitted into a hole in the *vêdi* or base. The upper portion is circular, of the same diameter, about 3 feet in height and rounded above. This plain stone—the symbol representative of Śiva as the male energy of production, or source of the generative power in nature, as the *Yoni* or circle in which it stands is of the passive or female power—is the idol of a Śaiva temple, the central object of worship, to which everything else is only accessory or subsidiary. The *śâluṅkâ* or top of the pedestal is somewhat hollowed towards the *liṅga*, to receive the oil, ghi, &c., poured on it by the worshippers, and which are carried off by a spout or *praṇâlikâ* on the north side, but this is now broken off.

The compartment to the east of the Trimurti (marked *A* on the plan) contains many figures grouped about a gigantic Arddhanâri not unnaturally mistaken by European visitors ignorant of Hindu mythology for an Amazon. This figure is 16 feet 9 inches in height; it leans to the right, which, as usual in the representations of Arddhanâri, is the male side, and with one of its four arms rests on the bull Nandi. The headdress is the usual high one, with two heavy folds descending on the left or female side of it and reaching the shoulder, while the right side differs in ornamentation and bears a crescent. On the left side the hair falls down along the brow in a series of small ringlets, while on the right there is a line of knobs at the under edge of the cap. The female breast and pelvis on the left are much exaggerated. The back pair of hands is in fair preservation, the right holds up the *nâga* or cobra, the left a metallic mirror, and has rings on the middle and little fingers. Opposite to the upturned back left arm Vishṇu is represented riding upon Gáruḍa. Vishṇu has here four arms, the front left hand seems to have rested on his knee, the other is raised and holds his *chakra* or discus.

On the right or male side of Arddhanâri, and on a level with Vishṇu and Garuḍa, are Indra and Brahmâ, the latter seated on a lotus throne supported by five wild geese which are his *vâhana*.

In a recess between Brahmâ and the uplifted right arm of Arddhanâri is Indra the King of the Vaidik gods, the Jupiter Pluvius of the old Hindus, the god of the firmament, riding on the celestial elephant Airâvati who sends the rain from his trunk. He holds the *vajra* or thunderbolt in his left hand, and in his right what may have been the *ankúś* or goad for driving the elephant. Numerous other figures fill up the remainder of the compartment.

The compartment to the west of the Trimurti (marked *B* on the plan) is 13 feet wide by 17 feet 1 inch in height, with a base rising 2 feet 6 inches from the floor. The two principal figures are Śiva, and at his left hand his śaktî—Pârvâtî or Umâ.

The figure of Śiva is 16 feet high and has four arms; the two left ones are now broken off. As elsewhere, he has a high cap with three pointed plates rising out of the band of it, and a smaller one in front of that on the forehead. Between these is a crescent over each temple. From the crown rises a sort of cup or shell in which is a singular three-headed female figure of which the arms are broken off. It probably represents the three principal streams, which, according to Hindu geography, form the main stream of their sacred river, namely, the Gangâ, the Yamunâ or Jamná, and the Saraswatî, or it is a female triad, the mythological union of the *śáktîs* or consorts of the three great divinities; it is repeated in the Brahmanical cave at Aihoḷê.

On Śiva's left stands Pârvatî, about 12 feet 4 inches high, wearing a circlet round the brow, from under which the hair is represented in small curls round the brow. The headdress rises in tiers, and has a pointed plate in front, and behind the neck on the right side is a sort of cushion, perhaps of the back hair. Her dress comes over the right leg, the corner falling to the ankle, and then passes over the left leg, and a loose robe hangs over her right arm.

On Śiva's right, as in the last compartment, are Brahmâ and Indra. On Pârvatî's left we find Vishṇu on Garuḍa.

Passing by the south side of the shrine to the west porch, we come to the fourth compartment (marked *C* in the plan), which represents the marriage of Śiva and Pârvatî, in which she stands at his right hand, a position which the wife rarely occupies except on the day of her marriage.

Śiva wears the usual high *mukuṭa* or cap corrugated above, and which has behind it a sort of oval disc occupying the place of the nimbus or aureole.

Pârvatî or Umâ is 8 feet 6 inches high; her hair escapes in little curls from under the broad jewelled fillet that binds the brow; and behind the head is a small disc, possibly in this case a part of the dress. She wears heavy ear-rings and several necklaces, from one of which a string hangs down between her breasts and ends in a tassel. The robe that hangs from her zone is indicated by a series of slight depressions between the thighs.

At Śiva's left, crouching on his hams, is a three-faced Brahmâ who is acting the part of priest in the ceremony.

The fifth compartment is that (marked *D* on the plan) on the south side of the eastern portico. Śiva and Pârvatî are represented in it seated together on a raised floor and both adorned as in the other sculptures. Behind Pârvatî's right shoulder stands a female figure carrying a child astraddle on her left side; this is probably intended to represent a nurse bearing Karttikêya called also Skanda and Mahâsena, the war-god, the son of Śiva, born to destroy the power of Târak, a giant demon, who by penance secured such power that he troubled earth, hell, and heaven, deprived the gods of their sacrifices, and drove them in pitiable fright to seek the aid of Brahmâ. Other figures of attendants fill up the rest of the compartment.

The rock over the heads of Śiva and Pârvatî is carved into patterns somewhat resembling irregular frets disposed on an uneven surface intended to represent the rocks of Kailâsa. On clouds on each side are the usual celestial attendants or Gandharvas and Apsarasas rejoicing and scattering flowers.

On the north side of the east portice is a compartment facing the last and similar to it (marked *E* on the plan) in which Śiva and Pârvatî again appear seated together in the upper half of the recess attended by Bhṛingi, Gaṇeśa, and others. Under them is the ten-faced Râvaṇa, King of Lankâ or Ceylon, the grandson of Pulastya. According to the legend Râvaṇa got under Kailâsa or the Silver mountain that he might carry it off to Lankâ, and so have Śiva all to himself and make sure of his aid against Râma. Pârvatî perceiving the movement, called in fright to Śiva, on which he, raising his foot, pressed down the mount on Râvana's head, and fixed him where he was for ten thousand years, until his grandfather Pulastya taught him to propitiate Śiva and perform austerities, after which he was released, and became a devoted Śaiva. Râvana's back is turned to the spectator, and a sword is stuck in his waistband; his faces are entirely obliterated, and only a few of his twenty arms are now traceable.

Passing again to the west end of the cave to the compartment marked *F* on the plan, the principal figure—Kapâlabhṛit—has been a standing one about 11½ feet in height. The headdress is high and has much carving upon it, with a skull and cobra over the forehead and the crescent on the right. The face is indicative of rage, the lips set, with tusks projecting downwards from the corners of the mouth, and the eyes large as if swollen. Over the left shoulder and across the thighs hangs the *muṇḍamálá* or rosary of human skulls. A weapon seems to have been stuck into the waist cloth, of which some folds hang over the right hip. His arms were eight, but five of them with both the legs are now broken. The small human body on his left was transfixed by a short spear held in the front left hand, as in the Dâś Avatâra sculpture of the same scene. The second right hand wields a long sword, without guard, with which he seems about to slay his victim, the third left hand holds a bell as if to intimate the moment to strike the fatal blow, and the second presents a bowl under the victim to receive its blood, while a cobra twists round the arm. The third right hand held up a human form by the legs.

This is Bhairava or Kapálabhṛit, a form of Rudra or Śiva, and one of the most common objects of worship among the Marâṭha people.

The eighth compartment is that on the right side when entering the north portico (marked *G* on the plan). The compartment is 13 feet wide and 11 feet 2 inches high, raised on a low base. The figure of Śiva in the centre is about 10 feet 8 inches in height. It has had eight arms, nearly all broken. The headdress secured by a band, passing under the chin, is the usual high one.

To the left of Śiva is a female figure 6 feet 9 inches high, probably Pârvatî. She wears large ear-rings, rich bracelets, and a girdle with carefully carved drapery, but her face and breasts are defaced. Brahmâ, Vishṇu, Indra, Bhṛingi, Gaṇeśa, and others, attend on Mahâdeva as he dances the Tândava.

Facing the last (at *H* on the plan) is a compartment containing Śiva as Mahâyogi, or the Great Ascetic. Not only in the position given to the ascetic does this figure resemble that of Buddha, but many of the minor accessories are scarcely disguised copies. Śiva has only two arms, both of them now broken off at the shoulder; he is seated cross-legged on a *padmâsana* or lotus seat, and the palms of his hands probably rested in his lap, between the upturned soles of the feet, as in most images of Buddha and the Jaina Tîrthaṅkaras. The stalk of the lotus forming the seat is upheld by two figures, shown only down to the middle, corresponding to the Nâga-canopied supporters of the *padmâsana* of Buddha. The attendants of course are different, one of them being Umâ or Pârvatî.

By a flight of nine steps we descend from the eastern side of the Great Temple into a court fully 55 feet in width, which has been quite open to the north, but the entrance is now filled up with earth and stones. In the middle of the court is a circular platform only 2 or 3 inches in height and 16 feet 3 inches in diameter. It is directly in front of the shrine in the temple to the south, and also in that of the great cave to the west of it, and was most probably the position of the Nandi or great bull which always faces the Liṅga shrine, but no trace of it is known to exist now.

The temple on the south of this area is raised on a panelled basement about 3½ feet high, which again stands on a low platform 2 feet 4 inches in height. The front is about 50 feet in length and 18½ feet in height from the platform. It was divided into five spaces by four columns and two pilasters, but there are now only traces of the column in the west end of the façade.

On each side the steps leading up to this temple are bases (*n m*), on which stand tigers or leogriffs, as at the Dumar Lena.

Inside, the maṇḍapa or portico of this temple measures 58 feet 4 inches by 24 feet 2 inches. At each end it has a chamber, and at the back the *garbha* or *liṅga* shrine with a *pradakshiṇa* or passage round it. The shrine is 13 feet 10 inches wide and 16 feet 1 inch deep. In the middle of the floor stands a low square altar, in the middle of which is a *liṅga* of the same compact stone as that in the shrine of the Great Temple.

At the back of the *maṇḍapa* near the east end is a gigantic statue or dwârpâla with two attendant Piśâchas. Near the west end is a similar statue, reaching nearly to the roof, with four arms and the usual protuberance indicative of the third eye in the forehead.

At the west end of this portico is a small chapel marked *N* on the plan, 11 feet 7 inches in depth by about 27 feet 7 in width inside, and with two pillars and two pilasters in front. Inside this, at the south end, is a large figure of Gaṇeśa, with several attendants.

At the north end is a standing figure of Śiva, holding in his hands the shaft of what was probably a *triśula.* On his right is Brahmâ supported by his *hansas*, and other figures. On the left of Śiva is Vishṇu on Garuḍa, holding his mace in one of his right hands. In one of his left hands he has his *chakra*, and in the other his *śaṅkha.* On the back wall of this chapel are sculptured ten principal figures, probably the Mâtrâs or divine Mothers, with Gaṇapati—but all much defaced. Opposite this chapel, at the east end of the portico, is another also with two pillars, and two pilasters in front, but perfectly plain inside.

Besides the Great Temple there are three others at no great distance, though quite distinct from it. The first of these is towards the south-east on the same level and faces E.N.E. Its extreme length is about 109½ feet, inclusive of the chapel at the north end. The façade, however, is completely destroyed, and the entrance almost filled up with a bank of earth and débris. The front was nearly 80 feet in length, and must have been supported by a number of columns, now all perished. Inside, the portico or maṇḍapa was 85 feet long by 35 feet deep. At the north end of this is a chapel supported in front by four octagonal columns. The chapel is about 39 feet in width by 22 in breadth, and perfectly plain inside. At the back of the portico are three large chambers or liṅga shrines.

At the south end of the portico of this cave is the second detached rock-temple, still more dilapidated than the last. The width of its maṇḍapa or portico can scarcely be determined, the length inside was about 50 feet 2 inches. At each end there seems to have been a chapel or room with pillars in front, and cells at the back.

The shrine is a plain room 19 feet 10 inches deep by 18 feet 10 inches wide with a low *vêdi* or altar 7 feet square, containing a liṅga. On each side is a cell about 15 feet square entering from the portico by doors which have projecting pilasters and ornamental pediments. They are much destroyed, but the horse-shoe ornament so frequent in the Buddhist caves is repeated several times over the door and forms the principal feature.

Crossing the ravine in front of the first three caves, and ascending the opposite hill to a height of upwards of 100 feet above the level of the Great Temple, we come to a fourth excavation bearing nearly E.N.E. from it.

The portico has four pillars and two pilasters 8 feet 5 inches high and about 3 feet square at the base. The style of moulding is similar to those of the columns in the other caves, but the proportions differ; they are square to a height of 4 feet 6½ inches from the step on which they stand, and above this they are sixteen sided with the exception of a thin crowning member of 1½ inches, which is square. The maṇḍapa is 73 feet 6 inches long, and about 26½ feet wide with three cells at the back. The end cells are empty, and the central chamber is the shrine, the door into which has neat pilasters and a frieze. About 150 yards to the north of this last is another small excavation, being little more than the commencement of what was perhaps intended for three cells. Still farther on to the north-east, and just under the summit, are three wells cut in the rock, with openings about 2½ feet square, similar to the cisterns found beside many Buddhist excavations.

Jogeswari or Amboli.

A short distance to the south of the Mahâkâl or Kondivte caves, in the island of Salsette, is the Jogêśwari Cave with its appendages, excavated in a rising hummock of rock, and at so low a level that water stands in the floor of the great hall most of the dry season.

This is the third of the great Brahmanical caves of its class known to exist in India. The other two being the Dumar Lenâ, or Sitâ ka Nâni at Elurâ, and the great cave at Elephanta. It resembles them in many respects, but the hall here is square instead of being star-shaped as in them, and the sanctuary is situated exactly in the middle of the hall surrounded by an aisle separated from it by pillars equally spaced.[1] Though the hall itself is practically of the same size as that at Elephanta, being internally 92 feet square, the lateral porticoes and courts are on so much more extensive a scale as to make this one the largest of the three. The most interesting fact, however, connected with this cave is, that the mode in which these adjuncts are added, is such that we lose nearly all trace of the arrangements of the Buddhist Vihâra in its plan, and were it not for the intermediate examples would hardly be able to find out whence its forms were derived. It is on the whole so much more like the more modern structural temples, that with the details of its architecture, and the fact that it is unfinished, leave no doubt that it is the most modern of the three. If we may assume that the Dumar Lena at Elurâ was excavated in the first quarter of the 8th century, and that the great cave at Elephanta followed immediately afterwards, then this Jogêśwari Cave may safely be dated in the last half of that century. The three being thus excavated concurrently with the Kailâsa, worthily conclude the series of pillared Brahmanical caves by one in which the features of their Buddhist prototypes are almost entirely obliterated, and the elements of the succeeding styles are fast developing themselves.

The court on the south appears to have been left in a very unfinished state, though this side was doubtless intended as the front. Only a narrow winding passage on the east, leads into this partially excavated court, in which stands the verandah of the cave, supported by ten columns of the Elephanta pattern with pilasters. On the capitals of these pillars are struts, carved with a female figure and dwarf standing under foliage as at Rameśwara and in the great cave at Bâdâmi. This verandah is about 120 feet in length, and at its back has three doors and two windows looking into the great hall. This is a somewhat irregular quadrangle about 92 feet each way, with twenty pillars arranged in a square, in the middle of which stands

[1] A plan of this cave accompanied Mr. Salt's description of it in the 1st vol. of the *Transactions of the Literary Society of Bombay* in 1819, and was apparently engraved with a reprint of it in the *Calcutta Journal* of the same year. It was re-engraved by Mr. Langlès in his *Monuments de l'Hindoustan*, folio, vol. ii., Plate 77 *bis*.

the shrine, about 24 feet square, with four doors and a large *liṅga* on a square *sâḷuṅkhâ* inside, as at Elephanta and Dumar Lenâ at Elurâ.

The approach from the east is by a descending passage and a flight of steps from 10 to 12 feet wide, landing in a small court in front of a neat doorway with fluted pilasters having *śârdûla* brackets and a bas-relief under an arch over the lintel. This is the entrance to a covered porch about 36 feet long by 45 feet in width, with four pillars on each side, separating it from two apartments, the walls of which have been covered with sculptures. A similar doorway leads from this first porch into a court about 42 feet by 66. On the opposite side of this court are three entrances into a second porch 60 feet wide and 28 deep, with two rows of four columns each across it, from front to back, and from this again three other doors, one in each bay, lead into the great cave, the central door having sculptures on each side of it. The whole distance from the eastern entrance porch to that on the west, including the courts mentioned above, but excluding the passages, is thus about 250 feet in a straight line, which exceeds that of any other Brahmanical cave known, except of course the Kailâsa.

The approach on the west side is also by a descending passage cut in the rock, into a partially roofed court, whence steps lead down into a small cave with two side recesses, each with two pillars in front. From this there is a door into the great cave.

On the south side of the cave is a large cell, a *liṅga* shrine, a small one for a *devî*, and other small rough excavations.

Harischandragad Brahmanical Caves.

About 20 miles to the north of Junnar, and a few miles north-east from Nânâghât stands the great mountain of Hariśchandragaḍ, lifting its giant head considerably over 4,000 feet above the plains of the Konkan at its base, with its tremendous scarps down to them. It is the culminating point of the ridge that from it stretches eastward from the Sahyâdri hills dividing the basins of the Godâvarî and the Bhîmâ, a feeder of the Kṛishṇa. The top is somewhat triangular and is somewhat longer from north to south than across the southern and loftier end, which is about four miles in length. Its surface is very unequal, the small fort on the very summit being about 500 feet above the level of the caves which are to the west of the centre. The ascent from the south-east is steep and dangerous; from Ankôlâ on the north-east it is said to be more easy.

The caves[1] are principally in a low scarp of rock to the north of the summit, and face N.N.W., and consist of some eight or nine excavations, none of them large, and without much sculpture The pillars are mostly plain square blocks; the architraves of the doors are carved in plain facets; and there are a few sculptures of Gaṇapati, who also, as the symbol of a Śaiva temple, is represented also on the lintels of some of the doors. This marks the character of these caves, and moreover, as this symbol is perhaps of late adoption, were there no other indications it would lead us to assign a comparatively late origin to these caves. But the style of the low doorways, and of the pillars in the second cave from the east end of the range, the detached sculptures lying about, and some fragments of inscriptions, all seem to point to about the tenth or eleventh century.

The first cave at the east end of the range is about 17½ feet square, and has a low bench round three sides. The door is only 4 feet in height, with a high threshold, and has a plain moulding round the head of it. On the west side of it is a water-tank.

No. II. is eight or nine yards from the first, and is one of the largest in the group. The verandah is 23½ feet long and about 7½ wide, with an entrance into a large cell from the left end. The hall measures about 25 feet by 20, and varies in height from 8 feet 1½ inches to 8 feet 11 inches, and has one cell on the right side and two in the back with platforms, as for beds, from 6 inches to a foot high. Outside on the right is another cell leading into a larger one at the right end of the verandah. The verandah is not quite open in front, the space between the left hand pillar and the pilaster at that end being closed, and the central and right hand space only left open. The two square pillars, of which only one stands free, are 6 feet 4½ inches high with a simple base, and a great number of small mouldings on the neck and capital which occupy the upper 2 feet 7 inches of them. The door is surrounded with plain mouldings, and has a small Gaṇêśa on the lintel. Two square windows help to light the principal room.

The third is an unfinished cave, somewhat on the same plan, but

---

[1] Mr. W. F. Sinclair was the first to give an intelligible account of these caves in *Ind. Ant.*, vol. v. pp. 10, 11; and separately by the Bombay Government in *Notes on the Ant. of Parner, &c.* (*Archæol. Sur*, No. 6), 1877.

half of the front wall of the hall has been cut away, and a large image of Ganêśa is carved on the remaining half, while in a cell to the right is a *vêdi* or altar for a Liṅga.

The fourth is only an oblong cell, and the fifth in the bed of a torrent is apparently unfinished, and has a structural front inserted in it. It has a broad high stone bench round three sides. The sixth, seventh, and eighth are similar to the fourth, but a bed of soft clay has destroyed the walls of the first two. In the shrine of the sixth is a long *vêdi* as if for three images, and next to the last is a deep stone tank 10 feet square.

To the north of these caves is a somewhat lofty structural temple without any maṇḍap, but consisting only of a shrine with a spire over it in the northern Hindu style of architecture, and the west side of the court of this temple is hewn into caves, which seem never to have been used for any other purposes than for the residence of yogis attached to the temple. They are very irregular in plan and without any architectural features whatever. About fifty yards further down the ravine is a cave about 55 feet square with four columns in front, each about 3 feet square, with plain bracket capitals 9 inches deep and 6 feet 10 inches long. In the middle of the hall is a large round *śâluṅkhâ* containing a liṅga, and surrounded by four slender columns of the Elephanta type. All round these, to the walls and front of the cave, the floor is sunk fully 4 feet and is always full of water, so that the worshippers can only approach the liṅga by wading to it or swimming, and to perform the *pradakshiṇa* by swimming may have special merits. On the left end is a relief carved with a liṅga and worshippers on each side of it.

It would seem from the absence of shrines in the caves here (except some very inferior ones in one or two of them) that with the exception of the last described cave they were chiefly intended as *dharmaśâlas* or rest houses for pilgrims to the temple, and if so, must be as recent as the establishment of such a shrine. And the temple seems quite as old as the caves, so that they probably formed part of one seat of Śaiva worship here, erected in the tenth century A.D., or soon after. They are thus as much beyond the true age of cave excavating as they are beneath the preceding examples in design. They are useful here as negative proofs how completely the art and fashion of excavating temples in the rock had passed away, but are hardly worth quoting otherwise for their own sake.

Ankai-Tankai Brahmanical Caves.

Four or five miles south from the railway station of Manmâḍ to the east of Nasik and twelve miles south-east of Châṇdwaṛ is a hill—or rather two joined together by a short connecting ridge. The western hill is called Ankâi, and is crowned by the ruins of what has been a very strong Marâṭha hill-fort within the area of which are some Brahmanical caves. To the north-east of it is the Tankâi hill which has also been fortified, and on the ascent to the connecting ridge, on the south face of this hill, is a group of Jaina caves to be noticed in their place. Below them is the now almost deserted village of Ankâi.

The Brahmanical rock-temples of Ankâi are three in number, very rough and unfinished. The first is just inside the second gate on the ascent up to the fort, and is an unfinished Liṅga shrine. The entrance is 17 feet 9 inches wide, and on each side of it is a small group of sculpture just outside the pilaster, consisting of a central female figure with a *chhatri* or umbrella carried over her head by a second female, while she is also attended by a dwarf: one of two figures on the outer side of the pilaster seems to have been a male, attended by a dwarf. Behind the females is a pilaster with much carving on the face of it. From the entrance to the front of the shrine is about 13½ feet. The shrine is the usual square room with dwârpâlas on each side the door wearing high rounded headdresses and inside a base for a Liṅga inside. The *pradakshiṇâ* round it has been left unfinished, as also a chamber to the right of the entrance. There is a Trimurti on the back wall of the shrine, somewhat of the style of those in the small caves at Elurâ, and this and the style of execution of the pilasters and sculptures lead me to regard this as a very late cave, probably of the 10th or 11th century.

The other two caves are at the base of a knoll that rises on the plateau of the hill. They are without ornament or sculpture of any kind. One of them is a hall 31¼ feet wide by 48¼ deep with two plain square pillars in front. Three cells have been begun in the left wall. The area is divided by brick and mud partitions, and it has evidently been used for other than religious purposes; indeed it seems rather to have been a magazine or place for keeping stores in. The third is a very irregular excavation 32 feet wide with two rough pillars in front, and other two further back. Below the front of it is a water cistern.

Christian Cave Church at Mandapeswar.

At Mandapeswar, called by the Portuguese Montpezir, in the north-west of the Island of Salsette, there is a Brahmanical Temple of some extent, not very remarkable in itself, but worth noticing, as one of few instances of a Śaiva Cave converted into a Roman Catholic Church. This was the case when this cave was made a component part of an extensive monastic establishment founded in the 16th century by P. Antonio de Porto. The King Don John III. transferred the revenues, which sufficed to support 50 jogis, from the Temple to the Church, and built a very extensive monastery in connexion with it.[1] The cave was dedicated to Notre Dame de la Misericorde, and was converted into a church by having a wall built in front of it, as shown in the woodcut No. 72, and the Śaiva sculptures either screened off by walls or covered up with plaster. Some strange feeling of reverence seems to have prevented the priests from destroying them altogether, for now that the plaster has fallen off and the walls gone to decay they seem almost entire.

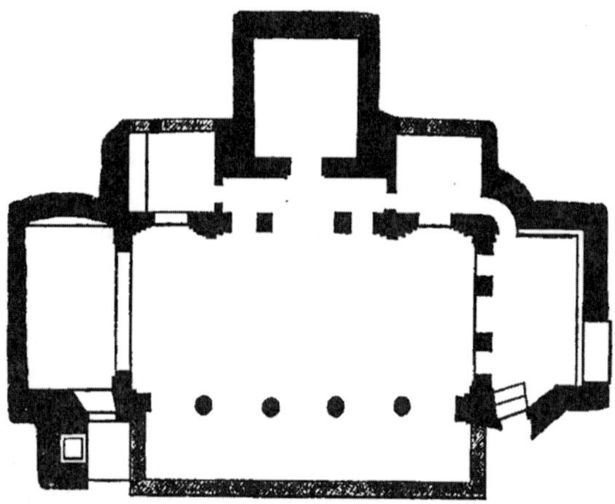

No. 72. Notre Dame de la Misericorde, Mandapeswar.

The maṇdap or hall measures 51 feet by 21 inside, with four pillars in front of the Elephanta type, but more richly ornamented, and

[1] These particulars are taken from Salt's paper in the first volume of the *Transactions of the Literary Society of Bombay*, p. 45, and from Langlès' *Hindoustan*, vol. ii. p. 201, quoting Da Couto and others.

evidently of more modern date. At each end is a smaller room, divided from the hall by two pillars and their pilasters. That to the left has been entirely screened off by a built wall, but behind the wall a large sculpture was found of Śiva dancing with accompanying figures. In the back of the hall is a small square room at each end, which led into an inner one, with two pillars in front; these are now walled up. In the middle of the back wall is the vestibule of the shrine, with two pillars in front of it. The shrine itself is about 16 feet square, but is now empty.

The cave faces the east, and is cut into a low rock. On the top of it stands a large monastic building, now rapidly going to decay; one of the many remains of the power and piety of the Portuguese when they were in possession of the island.

Concluding Remarks.

Although it must be admitted that the Brahmanical Cave-Temples are wanting in that purpose-like appropriateness which characterised the Buddhist Vihâras, from which they are derived, still they have merits of their own which render them well worthy of attentive study by those interested in such researches. Their architectural details are generally as rich, and, as mere matters of ornament, frequently as elegant and as well adapted to their purposes as any used by their predecessors; in some instances, indeed, more so. Nothing, for instance, in any Buddhist Cave is so appropriate to rock-cut architecture as the pillars in the Lankeśwara Caves, and in the Kailâsa generally. The architects seem there to have felt the requirements of cave architecture fully, and, having no utilitarian necessities to control them, used massiveness as a mode of expression in a manner that was never surpassed, not even perhaps in Egypt. If the masses thus introduced had been mere unornamented blocks, the effect might have been far from pleasing, but in nothing did their architects show better taste than in the extent of ornament used, and the manner of its application. The expression of power gained by the solidity of their forms is never interfered with, though the amount of ornament is such as in less skilled hands might easily have become excessive and degenerate into bad taste. This, however, is never the case, and though as architectural forms they are to us unfamiliar, and consequently often appear strange, the principles on which they are designed are well worthy of attentive study.

By their employment of sculpture, in preference to painting, for the decoration of their caves, the Brahmans had, for us at least, an advantage which is now very striking. Except in the caves at Katak, and some perhaps of the earliest in the west side of India, sculpture was rarely employed by the Buddhists, and for all historical and legendary purposes painting no doubt afforded them facilities of which they were not slow to avail themselves. The Brahmans, on the other hand, had no story to tell. Their mythology required only representations of single acts, or manifestations of some individual deity, easily recognised by his attributes, and consequently easily represented in sculptured groups consisting only of a few figures. These could be more easily and forcibly reproduced in a cave by form than by colour. From their greater durability, these, in most instances, remain, and, though mutilated in many instances, have not lost their value as architectural decorations, while, except in some caves at Ajaṇṭâ and at Bagh, the paintings have perished so completely that it is only by analogy that we can feel sure that they ever existed. If, however, the paintings in the Buddhist caves were as complete now, as there is every reason for believing they once were, they no doubt would afford illustrations of history and mythology far more complete than can be gathered from the more limited scope of the Brahmanical sculptures. As they, however, have so generally been obliterated, while the sculptures in the caves at Mahâvallipur, at Elephanta, and Elurâ remain so nearly complete, the Brahmanical caves do,—at the present day at least—possess an interest that hardly attaches to the earlier and more appropriate caves of their predecessors.

However these artistic questions may ultimately be decided, there is no question as to the extreme historical interest of the Brahmanical Cave Temples. They afford us a more vivid picture than we obtain from any other source of the arts and aspirations of the Hindus during the whole of the seventh century, to which nearly the whole of them practically belong.

On the disappearance of the Guptas, who, if not Buddhist themselves, at least favoured Buddhism during the whole of the fifth century, an immense impulse was given to the cultivation of Hindu literature and the revival of the Brahmanical religion by the splendour of the court of the great Vicramâditya of Ujjain, and the learning of the so-called nine jewels who adorned it. It is not clear that any overt acts of aggression against the Buddhists were attempted during his reign (A.D. 520–550 ?),[1] but at the end of that century we find the Brahmans (579) excavating caves at Bâdâmi, where, however, there is no evidence of Buddhists having previously existed, so that this can only be considered as a challenge from afar. In the following century, however, they boldly enter into competition with them at Elurâ, Dhârâsiṅwa, and along the whole line wherever they were most powerful. In the eighth century they signalize their triumph by excavating such temples as the Kailâsa and those at Elephanta and Jogêśwari. In the ninth the struggle is over, and there were no longer any motives to attempt to rival the Buddhists by excavating temples in the rock. Brahmanism reigned supreme in the length and breadth of the land, and when the curtain is again drawn up, after the dark and impenetrable night that hangs over India during the tenth century, there were no longer any Buddhists in the cave regions of the west, at least. It still lingered in Bengal till the Mahomedan conquest, but there are no caves there that throw any light on the mode in which the second struggle terminated in the final expulsion of the Buddhists from India. We have no written record of this momentous revolution, except of the preliminary grumblings of the coming storm in the works of the Chinese pilgrim, Hiwen Thsang (A.D. 630 to 644), but the record of the Brahmanical caves, as we are now able to read it, throws a clear and distinct light on the whole of the events of the period, which is invaluable to those who know how complete our ignorance otherwise would be, of the history of these dark ages in India.

---

[1] *Journal Royal Asiatic Society*, vol. iv. pp. 81, *et seqq.* See also paper on the same subject in the present April number of the same journal, where the origin of the Saka and Samvat eras is discussed by the light that recent discoveries in Afghanistan and elsewhere have thrown on the subject.—J. F.

BOOK IV.

THE JAINA CAVE-TEMPLES.

CHAPTER I.

THE JAINS AND JINAS.

The third sect that excavated cave-temples were the Jains, who have many points of belief and ceremonial in common with the Buddhists. Like them the Jains are atheists, believing in no supreme moral ruler, but in the attainment of *moksha* or *nirvâṇa* as the result of a long continued course of moral and ceremonial observances in a succession of lives. As their name implies, they are followers of the *Jinas*, or "vanquishers" of vice and virtue—men whom they believe to have obtained *nirvâṇa* or emancipation from the power of transmigration. They reject the details of Buddhist cosmogony, but have framed a system of their own, if possible more formal. They believe that the world is destroyed and renewed after vast cycles of time, and that in each of these æons or renovations there appear twenty-four Jinas or Tîrthaṅkaras at different periods, who practise asceticism and attain *nirvâṇa*. Besides the Tîrthaṅkaras of the present (*avasarpiṇî*) cycle, they name those also of both the preceding and the coming cycles.[1] Ṛishabha, the first Jina of the present cycle, is pretended to have been of immense stature, to have been 2,000,000 great years of age when he became Chakravartti or universal emperor, to have ruled 6,300,000 great years, and then to have practised austerity for 100,000 years before attaining *nirvâṇa* on Mount Śatruñjaya in Gujarât, shortly before the end of the third age of the present great cycle. At an immense distance of time, Ajitanâtha, the second Jina, appeared, was not quite so tall,

[1] Hemachandra, *Abhidâna Chintâmaṇi*, *śl.* 58–70; Briggs, *Cities of Gujarashtra* p. 349; *Ind. Ant.*, vol. ii. p. 140.

nor lived quite so long; and so with each successor—their stature age, and distance of time after the preceding diminishing in a regular progression, till we come to the twenty-third, named Pârśwanâtha, said to have been born at Banâras, married the daughter of King Prasênajita, adopted an ascetic life at the age of 30, and died at the age of 100 years while performing a fast on Samet Śikhar or Mount Parisnath in the west of Bengal, 250 years before the death of the last Tîrthaṅkara (*i.e.*, about 777 B.C.). Vardhamâna or Mahâvîra,[1] the last, began his austerities at the age of 30, and continued them for 12½ years as a *Digambara* or naked ascetic without even a bhikshu's begging dish. Finally he became an Arhat or Jina "worthy of universal adoration, omniscient and all seeing," and at the age of 72, at the court of King Hastipâla, he entered *nirvaṇa*, leaving Gotama Indrabhûti, the chief of his initiated disciples, to propagate his doctrines. Different dates are given for this event, but the majority of Jaina books place it in 526 B.C.[2]

The Jains are divided into two great sects, the *Digambaras*, "sky-clad," also called Nirgranthas, "without a bond," and Nagnâtas, "naked mendicants,"[3] and the *Swetâmbaras* or "white-robed." The first are frequently mentioned in early Buddhist literature under the name of *Nirgranthas*,[4] and seem to have been know even in Buddha's own times. They are still found both in Maisur and Rajputana, but do not appear naked in public. To them all the Jaina cave-temples appear to belong. The Swetâmbaras are probably a later sect. Hiwen Thsang seems to refer to their origin in his account of Siñhapura in the Panjab, near which he says "the founder of the heretical sect who wear white garments" began to expound his doctrine. "The law," he adds, "that has been set forth by the founder of this sect has been largely appropriated from Buddhist

---

[1] His real name seems to have been Nirgrantha Jñâtiputra; he is referred to in the Buddhist *Piṭakas* under the Pâli form of Nigaṇṭha Nâtaputta, and one of his disciples is called Makkhali Gosâla.—Bühler, *Ind. Ant.*, vol. vii., p. 143; and Jacobi, *Kalpa Sûtra*, pp. 1, 2, 6.

[2] Weber would lower this to B.C. 348 or 349 B.C. (*Über Catr. Mâhât*, p. 12).

[3] Bühler, *Ind. Ant.*, vol. vii. p. 28.

[4] Burnell, *Ind. Ant.*, vol. i. p. 310, n. §; and conf. St. Julien's *Mém. sur les Cont. Occ.*, t. i. pp. 41, 354; t. ii. pp. 42, 93; *Vie de H. T.*, pp. 224, 228; Laidlay's *Fa-Hian*, pp. 144, 145; *Jour. R.A.S.*, vol. vi. p. 267.; *J. B. B. R. As.*, vol. v., pp. 405, 407.

books, by which it is guided in establishing its precepts and rules." "In their observances and religious exercises they follow almost entirely the rule of the Srâmaṇâs" (Buddhists). "The statue of their divine master, by a sort of usurpation, resembles that of Buddha, it only differs in costume; its marks of beauty are exactly the same."[1]

All this holds perfectly true of the Jains, whose leading doctrines are:—the denial of the authority of the *Vedas*, reverence for the Jinas, who by their austerities acquired a position superior even to that of the Hindu gods, to whom the sect pays a qualified reverence; and the most extreme tenderness of animal life, which they do not distinguish from "soul," and believe to be one in gods, men, brutes, and demons, only in different stages according to its merits acquired in previous states of existence. Through the annihilation of virtue and vice it attains *nirvâṇa*. The moral obligations of the Jains are summed up in five great commands almost identical with the *pâncha śîla* of the Buddhists, care not to injure life, truth, honesty, chastity, and the suppression of worldly desires. They enumerate four merits or *dharmas*, liberality, gentleness, piety, and penance; and three forms of restraint, government of the mind, the tongue, and the person. Their minor obligations are in many cases frivolous, such as not to deal in soap, natron, indigo, and iron; not to eat in the open air after it begins to rain, nor in the dark, lest an insect should be swallowed; not to leave a liquid uncovered, lest one should be drowned; to keep out of the way of the wind, lest it should blow an insect into the mouth; water to be thrice strained for the same purpose before it is drunk, and the like.[2]

The proper objects of worship are the Jinas or Tîrthaṅkaras, but, like the Buddhists, they allow the existence of the Hindu gods, and have admitted into their worship such of them as they have connected with the tales of their saints, such as Indra or Śakra, Garuḍa, Iśâna, Śukra, Saraswatî, Lakshmî, and even Bhavânî, Hanumân, Bhairava, and Gaṅeśa, besides which they have a pantheon of Bhuvanapatis, Asuras, Nâgas, Râkshasas, Gandharvas, &c. inhabiting celestial and infernal regions, mountains, forests, and lower air.

Each Tîrthaṅkara is recognisable by a cognizance or *chinha*,

---

1 *Mém.*, t. i. pp. 163, 164; conf. *Ind. Ant.*, vol. ii. p. 16.

2 See *Ind. Ant.*, vol. ii. p. 17; *Kalpa Sûtra*, and *Nava Tattva.*

usually placed below the image; they have also their peculiar complexions or colours, though these are not often represented except in the case of Neminâtha and Pârswanâtha, whose images are often of black basalt or marble. The following is a list of the twenty-four[1] with their cognizances:—

No.	Name.	Chinha or Distinctive Sign.	Colour.	Place of Nirvâṇa.
1	Âdinâtha or Ṛishabha	Bull (*vṛisha*)	Yellow or Golden.	Mount Śatruñjaya in Gujerât.
2	Ajitanâtha	Elephant (*gaja*)	„	Samet Śikhar.[2]
3	Śambhava	Horse (*aśva*)	„	„
4	Abhinandana	Ape (*plavaga*)	„	„
5	Sumati	Curlew (*krauñcha*)	„	„
6	Padmaprabha	Lotus (*abja*)	Red	„
7	Suparśwa	The *swastika* mark	Golden	„
8	Chandraprabha	Moon (*śaśi*)	White or fair	„
9	Pushpadanta	Crocodile (*makara*)	„	„
10	Śîtalanâtha	The *Srîvatsa* mark	Golden	„
11	Śrî Anśanâtha	Rhinoceros (*khaḍgi*)	„	„
12	Vâsupûjya	Buffalo (*mahisha*)	Red	Champapuri.
13	Vimalanâtha	Boar (*Sûkara*)	Golden	Samet Śikhar.
14	Anantanâtha	Falcon (*śyena*)	„	„
15	Dharmanâtha	Thunderbolt (*vajra*)	„	„
16	Śântinâtha	Antelope (*mṛiga*)	„	„
17	Kunthunâtha	Goat (*chhâga*)	„	„
18	Aranâtha	The *Nandyâvarta* mark	„	„
19	Mallinâtha	Water jar (*ghaṭa*)	Blue	„
20	Munisuvrata	Tortoise (*kûrma*)	Black	„
21	Naminâtha	Blue water-lily (*nîlôtpala*)	Yellow	„
22	Neminâtha	Conch (*śaṅkha*)	Black	Mount Girnar.
23	Pârśwanâtha	Hooded snake (*śesha*)	Blue	Samet Śikhar.
24	Mahâvîra	Lion (*siṅha*)	Yellow	Pawapuri.

Among these, the favourites are the first, sixteenth, and three last, which are regarded as principal Jinas, and with the Digambaras the image of Gotama Swâmi the disciple of Mahâvîra is often represented, especially in Kanara and the Malabar coast, where there are several gigantic images of him.[3] He is also, with Pârśwanâtha, frequently figured in their cave sculptures, both always as naked, with creeping plants growing over their limbs, and Pârśwanâtha

[1] For a complete tabular view of the particulars relating to each of the Tîrthaṇkaras, see the Jaina work *Ratnasâra*, bhâg ii. p. 708 ff.

[2] The celebrated Mount Pârśwanâtha or Parisnath near Ramgur in Lower Bengal.

[3] One at Śrâvana Beḷgola, in Maisur, is 56½ feet in height (*Ind. Ant.*, vol. ii. p. 129 ff.; vol. iii. p. 156); another at Yênûr is about 38 feet high (*ib.*, vol. v. p. 37); and one at Kârkaḷa, twenty-four miles west from Yênûr in Kanara, is 41½ feet high, and goes by the same name, though an inscription on it calls it Bahubalin, who was the son of Ṛishabhadêva (*Ind. Ant.*, vol. ii. p. 353). See also *Hist. of Ind. and East Architecture*, p. 267 *et seq.*

usually having a polycephalous snake[1] overshadowing him with its hoods.[2]

---

[1] Dharaṇa or Dharaṇîdhara, the Nâga King, *Satruñjya Mâhat.*, xiv. 31–35; conf. Bigandet, *Legend of Gaudama* (2nd ed.), p. 99; Hardy, *Budhism*, p. 182; Delamaine, *Tr. R. As. Soc.*, vol. i. pp. 428–436.

[2] The best accounts we yet possess of the Jains and their tenets are the very brief one by Goldstücker in Chambers's *Encyclopædia*; by Colebrooke in his *Essays*, vol. ii.; and by H. H. Wilson, *Works*, vol. i.

CHAPTER II.

JAINA CAVE TEMPLES.

The cave-temples of the Jains are not of so early an age as those of either of the other two sects, none of them perhaps dating earlier than the seventh century. Nor are they numerous: there is one at Bâdâmi in the south of the Bombay Presidency, one at Karusâ, another at Ambâ or Mominâbâd, a small group at Dhârasiṅwâ north of Śolâpur, another at Châmar Lêṇâ, a few miles from Nâsik, a cave at Chândor, another at Bhâmêr, a third at Pitalkhorâ, and a group at Ankai in Khandêś. All these are comparatively insignificant, and except in a work like the present would hardly deserve much attention. It is only at Elurâ that there are any large caves belonging to this sect in Western India. Among its caves, however, there are two groups known as the Indra Sabha and Jagannatha Sabha, which, both for extent and elaborateness of decoration, are quite equal to any of the Brahmanical caves in that locality, with the single exception, of course, of the Kailâsa. At Gwalior are some excavations and large images cut in the rocks, and in Tinnevelly are some unfinished monolithic temples.

As might be expected from their later age they show all the characteristics of detail of the structural temples of the same period. They consist of halls, much like the Brahmanical cave-temples, but always with the shrine in the back wall, and in some cases with others in the sides. These halls at Elurâ are large and numerous, probably to afford as much accommodation as possible to the large *Saṅghas* or assemblies that come together at the annual pilgrimages. The doorways are richly carved with numerous mouldings and high thresholds are introduced. The pillars have the heavy bases and capitals of the age, with a triangular facet on each side, and images are introduced sometimes wherever there is space for them.

The principal images are of course the Tîrthaṅkaras, who, in the shrines always, and elsewhere generally, are represented as seated on a *siñhâsana* with their feet doubled up in front of the body, and the hands laid on their soles, one over the other with the palms turned upwards, in the *Jñâna mudrâ* position. All are perfectly alike and can only be distinguished by their *chinhas.* Pârśwanâtha is sometimes represented standing with the snakes' hoods overshadowing him, and with attendants or worshippers on each side, and sometimes, like the trial of Buddha by Mâra, he is represented immobile under the assaults of his demon foe Kamaṭha and his forces.

Badami Jaina Cave.

Besides the three Brahmanical cave-temples at Bâdâmi, there is, a little to the east of the largest one, a small Jaina cave differing perhaps little in age from its neighbours, but certainly more modern. and may therefore be considered to have been excavated about the middle of the following century, say about 650 A.D. The verandah is 31 feet long by 6½ wide, and the whole depth of the cave is only about 16 feet. In the front are four square pillars resembling the Elephanta type with bracket capitals, and in the back of the verandah two freestanding and two attached ones. Behind these the apartment that does duty for a hall is only about 6 feet deep by 25½ wide, and from it an ascent of four steps leads into the shrine, in which is a seated figure of Mahâvîra on a *siṅhâsana* against the back wall, with chauri-bearers, śârdûlas, and makara's heads in bas-relief on either side. In the ends of the verandah are figures of Gotama Swâmi attended by four snakes, and Pârśwanatha about 7½ feet high with their usual attendants. Figures of Tîrthaṅkaras are also inserted in the inner pillars, and on the walls in large numbers.[1]

Aihole.

At Aihoḷe there is another Jaina cave somewhat larger than that at Bâdâmi. It is in the face of a rocky hill west-south-west from the village, and faces S.S.W. The verandah is about 32 feet long inside by 7¼ feet wide, and supported in front by four square plain pillars. In front of them, however, a wall has been built of three courses of very large blocks of ashlar, leaving only an entrance between the central pair. The roof of the verandah is sculptured with *makaras*, frets, and flowers, and on the left end wall alto-rilievo is Pârśwanâtha Śeshphaṇi, as at Bâdâmi, attended by a male

---

[1] For a more detailed account, with drawings and a photograph, see *Arch. Sur. W. Ind. Rep.*, vol. i. p. 25.

and female Nâga figure. At the right end is a standing Jina with two female attendants, and behind him a tree with two figures among the branches of it to the left.

The entrance into the hall is 8 feet wide divided by two pillars, much of the same pattern as those in the Brahmanical cave not far off. The hall is 15 feet by 17 feet 8 inches with a chapel at each side 14 feet by 5, divided off by two pillars in front of each. The roof is carved with a large central rosette or lotus and four others at the corners, the interspaces being filled with makaras, fishes, flowers, and human heads with arabesque continuations.

At the back of the hall are two dwârpâlas with high headdresses and frill behind, as in the Elephanta sculptures, and attended the one by a male dwarf, and the other by a female. The entrance to the shrine like that to the hall is divided into three apertures by two pillars. The shrine, about 8 feet 3 inches square, a sitting figure of the Tîrthaṅkara very similar to that at Bâdâmi.

The walls of the chapel to the left of the hall are covered with sculpture consisting of Mahâvîra on his siṅhâsana on the middle of the back wall with chauri-bearers, and about a dozen other figures, some on elephants, apparently come to do him homage; the whole seems to be a sort of Jaina copy of the Râja Maṇḍala of Buddha, where the râjas and great ones come to do him homage. This sculpture, however, has never been finished.[1]

Jaina Caves at Patna.

In the west side of Kanhar Hill fort, which overhangs the east side of Patna village, near Pitalkhora, are two rock excavations known as Nâgârjuna's Kotri and Sîtâ's Nhâni.

The second of these consists of a verandah 28 feet in length with two pillars rudely blocked out, and inside an irregular room about 24 feet by 13, with two rough pillars near the middle of it. Nâgârjuna's Kotri is the same in general plan, irregular in shape, but with a good deal of Digambara Jaina sculpture. The verandah is 18 feet long by 6 feet wide at one end and about 4 at the other, supported in front by two pillars, one square and the other rhomboidal, with moulded capitals. In the left or south end of the verandah is a small room with a bench along the back wall; and outside the verandah at this end is cut in the rock a *Satî* stone,

[1] See *Arch. Sur. W. Ind., First Rep.*, p. 37.

about 6 feet high including the base, and with carvings of the usual sort upon it.

Inside, the hall is about 20 feet wide by from 14 to 16 feet deep with two irregular pillars in the middle. At the base of the left one sits a fat male figure upon a mass of uncarved rock, and with a similar mass over his head; at the base of the other is a female figure with a child on her left knee seated on a plain seat, and a tree carved over her head with squirrels, birds, and fruits among its foliage. These two figures correspond to those known as Indra and Ambâ or Indrânî in the Jaina caves of Elurâ.

On the back wall, on a slightly raised dais or throne, is an image of a Jina or Tirthaṅkara, squatted on a lotus, the back of the throne being richly carved with two elephants' heads, two standing Jinas, two chauri-bearers, *makaras*, *vidyâdharas*, &c., and over the head a conventionalised triple umbrella, with foliage hanging over it. On either side beyond and a little back from this sits another cross-legged Jina figure about 2 feet high.

On the south wall, near the back, is a life-size standing Jina, with nimbus, triple umbrella, and small attendant figures on each side of his head and shoulders. There is a small irregular cell in the back wall near the south end; and three niches in the north wall with one in the south, as if for movable images.

This cave bears a close analogy to the latest Jaina excavations at Elurâ, and is probably of the same age. Like them it may belong to the ninth or even to the tenth century A.D.

Chamar Lena.

The Châmar Lena hill lies a few miles north-west from Nasik, and contains a few excavations at about 450 feet above the level of the road which passes not far from the foot of the hill. They are late Jaina work of the 11th or 12th century, or it may be even later, cut in a coarse porous rock. There are two caves containing a good deal of rude sculpture of Jinas seated in meditation or standing in ascetic abstraction, with the usual Indras and Ambikâs.

On the wall of one of them is a small image of a Tirthankara seated on a siṁhâsana with celestial attendants, two other small Jinas at each side of his head, and nineteen more in the sculptured border around, making the 24 in all. Beside the caves is a large open excavation with a colossal bust having a snake hood over it but never finished.

BHAMER.

The fort of Bhamer in the Nizampur division of Khandesh lies 30 miles west by north from Dhulia. There is one plain monk's dwelling in the western of the two hills above the village, and two of those in the other are mere cellars, but the third is a cave or rather three of more pretensions; it has had a verandah 74 feet in length with an unfinished cell at the left end; from the verandah three doors open into as many small but dark halls, each about 24 feet by 20, with four square pillars supporting the roof, and having corresponding pilasters on each wall.

There are a number of rude sculptures on the walls, of Pârśwanâth and other Jinas, much defaced from the decay of the rock, but apparently of the same coarse rough type as those on the Châmer Lena hill.

BAMCHANDRA.

About twenty-five miles north-west from Poona and seven W.N.W. from Chakan, over the village of Bamchandra, is one small rock-temple and the commencements of two other excavations.

The cave here is now occupied as a *liṅga* shrine, but it is somewhat doubtful whether it was not excavated by Jains. The maṇḍapa or hall is only 15½ feet square, low in the roof, and supported by four massive pillars. (Plate XXIII., fig. 2.) The front wall is structural and the jambs and lintel of the door of the shrine are formed of a different stone and let in. It has very small dwârpâlas and slender pilasters. On the lintel was a *chinha*, but it has been daubed over with red lead and oil till it is quite unrecognisable. The frieze is carved with small figures—one of them with an umbrella. On the roof of the shrine is a rosette, and in the middle of the floor a modern small linga. The hall has a raised circular platform on a square one which occupies the whole central area between the pillars, a feature which, though common in Śaiva temples, is also found in Jaina ones, as for example in the principal old Jaina shrine in Belgaum fort.[1]

---

[1] *First Arch. Rep. W. Ind.*, p. 3.

CHAPTER III.

JAINA CAVES AT ELURA.

The Jaina caves at Elurâ are separated by a distance of about 200 yards from the Dumar Leṇâ, the most northerly Brahmanical temple, and occupy the northern spur of the hill, called by them Châraṇâdri. They are not numerous, consisting of only some five or six large excavations, but some of these are really extensive works, comprising several halls in one temple. They are of various ages, dating probably from the eighth to the thirteenth century.

It may be as well to take them in the order in which they occur, though by so doing two that may be the latest in the group come first.

CHHOTA KAILASA.

The most southerly of the group is a little way up the face of the hill to the south-east of the others. It has been little frequented by visitors or even by natives, and was so silted up till recently that there was considerable difficulty in getting inside it. It was, however, partially excavated in 1877 by orders of the Haidarâbâd Government. It is known as Chhota Kailâsa, and is a curious example of the imitation of the works of one sect by the votaries of another, for there can be no doubt that this was undertaken in imitation of the great Brahmanical temple of Kailâsa, but on a much smaller scale. The hall or *maṇḍapa* is 36 feet 4 inches square and like its great prototype has sixteen columns. The porch in front is about 10 feet square, and the shrine at the back measures 14½ feet by 11¼. The whole temple is situated in an excavated pit 80 feet wide by about 130 feet long, with a small excavation in each side. The outside is in the Dravidian style, but the *śikhar* or spire is low, and the workmanship stiff, while it has been left unfinished, though from what cause we have at present no means of ascertaining. Its similarity, however, to the Kailâsa in design, and the fact that the Dravidian style is not known to have been practised so far north, after the destruction of the Râshṭrakûṭas in the ninth century, would lead to the inference that these two temples cannot be far distant in date. Except the Dhamnâr Temple, which belongs certainly to the eighth century, no other temples in pits are known to exist in India. During the partial excavations some loose images were found, one of them bearing the date Śaka 1169, or A.D. 1247, which may, however, be considered as much too modern to belong to the age when this temple was first excavated.

Near to this is another excavation also unfinished and filled with earth to the capitals of the pillars. The porch is hewn out entirely on three sides from the rock, and stands in a deep excavated pit, like a structural work against a wall of rock. The pillars have "compressed-cushion" capitals, and have been carefully chiselled; those of the porch stand on a screen supported by elephants, and with water-jars in compartments as ornamention. A large portion of the earth in front has been removed, but inside it is left nearly full.

The Indra Sabha.

The Indra Sabhâ, or "Court of Indra" so called, is rather the group of Jaina caves than a single one and its appendages; in reality two double-storeyed caves and a single one, with their wings and subordinate chapels, &c. The first, however, is pretty well known to Europeans as the Indra Sabhâ, and the second as the Jagannâth Sabhâ. The court of the Indra Sabhâ proper is entered through a screen wall facing the south. Plate LXXXVII. Outside this on the east side is a chapel with two pillars in front, and two more at the back. The walls are sculptured with Pârśwanâtha on the north end, nude,—as in all cases in these caves,—with a seven-hooded snake overshadowing him, a female attendant with a snake-hood bearing a *chhatri* or umbrella over him. (*See* Plate LXXXVI.) Below the chhatri-bearer are two young nâganîs, and above a male figure riding on a buffalo, and above gandharvas and a figure playing on a conch shell. On the right side of the sculpture is the demon Kamatha riding on a lion, and below him two worshippers, apparently a male and female. The whole scene has a considerable likeness to the temptation of Mara, depicted in Plate LI., but even wilder in design, and very much inferior in execution. On the south end is Gomata, or Gotama Swâmi, also nude, with creepers twining round his limbs, with female attendants and worshippers, and in the shrine we find

Mahâvîra, the last of the Jaina Tîrthaṅkaras. These figures are remarkably like the figures of Buddha in the meditative attitude with his hands in his lap, only they are usually represented as nude, and have a drummer and other musicians over their heads. On the back is a figure, generally known as Indra, under a tree with parrots in it seated on an elephant and with two attendants; on the right side is a female divinity locally known as Indrânî, the wife of Indra, but properly it is Ambâ or Ambikâ, a favourite female divinity of the Jainas.

Entering the court; on the right side is a large elephant on a pedestal, and on the left stood a fine monolithic column 27 feet 4 inches high, with a quadruple or *chaumukha* image on the top (*see* Plate LXXX., fig. 2), but it fell over against the rock the day after Lord Northbrook visited the caves. In the centre of the court is a pavilion or *maṇḍapa* over a quadruple image,—either of Rishabanâtha, the first of the twenty-four Tîrthaṅkaras, or of Mahâvîra, the last;[1] the throne is supported by a wheel and lions, as in Buddhist temples. The style of the pavilion and of the gateway leading into the court is nearly as essentially Dravidian as the Kailâsa itself, and so very unlike anything else of the kind in the north of India that it probably was excavated during the supremacy of the Raṭhors, and is of about the same age as the Jaina cave at Badami. The details, too, of that cave have so marked a similarity to those of the Indra Sabha, that the probability is they all belong to the eighth century.

On the west side of the court is a cave or hall with two pillars in front and four inside. In the central compartment of the south wall is Pârśwanâtha, the 23rd Tîrthaṅkara; and opposite, with deer and a dog at his feet, is Gomata or Gautama. In this cave these figures are larger than those in the shrine outside the gate, and they recur again and again in these caves with only slight variations in the surrounding figures. On the back wall are Indra and Ambikâ, and in the shrine is Mahâvîra on a *siñhâsana*, with a triple umbrella over his head. Between this and the main cave, but lower, is a small chapel long partially filled up, in which the Indra and Ambikâ are peculiarly well cut, though recently the face of the latter seems to have been wilfully damaged. Over this chapel is another similarly furnished, and directly opposite is still another like it.

---

[1] A view of this pavilion, with the entrance doorway or miniature gopura, is given in my *Ind. and East Arch.*, p. 262, woodcut 147.

Entering the lower hall, we find it has a sort of double verandah, divided by a screen, beyond which is a twelve-pillared hall, few of the columns of which, however, have been entirely cut out from the rock, and the aisles are little more than begun. At the left end of the front verandah, on the pilasters, are two colossal nude images of Śântinâtha, the 16th Tîrthaṅkara, with an inscription under that on the right in characters of about the eighth or ninth century :—

Śrî Sohila brahma-
châriṇaḥ Sântibhaṭṭâ-
raka pratimeyaṁ.

"The image of Śântibhaṭṭâraka, (*made by*) Sohila, a Brahmachârin (*i.e.* paṇḍit of the Digambara Jains)."

Beyond this is a chapel with shrine and the usual sculptures. Inside the hall on one of the pillars is another large nude image, with one line underneath :—

Śrî Nâgavarmma kṛitâ pratimâ,
"The image made by Srî Nâgavarmma."

Near the east end of the verandah a stone stair leads to the upper storey, and facing the bottom of it is a chapel sculptured much as the rest,—Pârśwanâtha on the right, Gotama on the left, Indra and Ambikâ at the back, and Mahâvîra on the throne in the shrine.

The stair lands in the verandah of the grand hall, Plate LXXXVIII., once all bright with painting, of which some smoked fragments still remain, especially on the roof. Two pillars of "broken square" pattern, with their pilasters connected by a low wall, support the front; two others with boldly moulded square bases and sixteen-sided shafts and capitals, with a low partition between, form the back of the verandah, dividing it from the hall; and twelve, of four different patterns, surround the hall inside. Comparing the pillars Nos. 2 and 3 in Plate XCII., which are both about the same age, with that in the Lankeśwara caves, Plate LXXXIV., fig. 4, it will be seen how nearly identical they are, and if we are right in ascribing the last-named cave to the latter half of the eighth century, these two Jaina Sabhâs cannot be much more modern. The Brahmans and the Jainas seem to have been together in the field to share the spoils of the Buddhists, but the former were certainly the earliest to take advantage of their decline, and the most powerful at Elurâ at least, and their caves consequently the most numerous and most magnificent.

Colossal figures of Indra and Ambikâ, with their usual attendants, the one under a banyan, the other under a mango-tree, occupy the ends of the verandah, Plate XCI., fig. 1, which is 14½ feet high. The walls of the side and back aisles are divided into compartments filled with Jinas or Tîrthaṅkaras. The centre space on each end has a large Jina on a *siṅhâsana;* one on each side the shrine door is devoted to Pârśwanâtha and Gotama; and the others have two Mahâvîras each, under different *Bo*-trees, as with the Buddhas, but between the trees is a figure holding up a garland, and above him another blowing a conch, while at the outer sides are *gandharvas.* On the pilasters on each side the shrine door is a tall nude guardian and on the next pilaster a squat Mahâvîra. The door, which is richly ornamented, has two slender advanced pillars, beaten by the Brahman guides to show the reverberation, and called by them the *damru* or drum of the idol. Over and around this door is a mass of carving, represented in Plate LXXXIX. The shrine, 12 feet 3 inches high, is, as usual, occupied by Mahâvîra.

In the centre of the great hall in a sort of *śâluṅkhâ* has stood a quadruple image (*chaumukha*), now destroyed; and over it on the roof is an immense lotus-flower on a square slab with holes in the four corners and centre, as if for pendent lamps.

A door in the south-east corner leads through a cell with a sort of trough in the corner of it, and a natural hole in the roof, into a small cave on the east side of the court. The few steps leading down to it occupy a small lobby carved all round with Jinas, &c. This hall has a verandah in front, and inside are four square pillars with round capitals. Gotama occupies a recess on the right, and Pârśwanâtha another on the left. Indra, with a bag in his left and a cocoanut in his right hand, occupies the south end of the verandah, while Ambikâ faces him in the entrance,—in fact they occupy much the same places as the supposed patrons occupy in Buddhist caves. Nude Jaina *dwârpâlas* guard the entrance of the shrine, which contains the usual image. Some scraps of painting still remain on the roof of this apartment.

Returning through the great hall, a door in the north-west corner leads through a small room into the temple on the west side corresponding to the last described. It has a carefully carved façade, the sculpture still sharp and spirited. In the entrance to it on the right hand is a four-armed Dêvî with two discs in the upper hands, and a *vajra* in her left on her knee; and on the left another Dêvî,—perhaps Sarasvatî,—eight-armed, with a peacock. The hall is exactly similar in plan to that on the east, but the four central pillars have capitals with looped drooping ears, as in the great hall, and everything has been finished in the close grained rock more elaborately and sharply. Indra, Gotama, and Pârśwanâtha recur in their usual positions.

The Jagannatha Sabha.

A little beyond the Indra Sabhâ is another cave-temple, with a court in front, known as the Jagannâtha Sabhâ or Court of Jagannâtha (lord of the world): the screen, if any, and the *chaumukha maṇḍapa*, however, must have been structural, and have now disappeared; while the number of fragments of loose images that were discovered in cleaning out the court of this cave testify to the quantity of sculpture that must have been in these caves in addition to what was cut in the rock on the original execution of the work.

On the west side of the court is a hall with two heavy square pillars in front, and four in the middle area (Plate XC., fig. 1). It is sculptured like all the rest, Pârśwanâtha on the left and Gotama on the right, with Mahâvîra or some other Jina in the shrines, on pilasters, and in a few recesses. Indra occupies the left end of the verandah, and Ambikâ the right or north end. There are some inscriptions, a few letters of which are legible, on the pillars of this cave. They are in the old Canarese character, and may belong to about A.D. 800-850, though such evidence can hardly be much relied upon for the date of a cave so far from the country to which that alphabet belongs.

Right opposite to this is a chapel with a pretty large cell inside; this is carved with the usual figures also. The cave at the back of the court has been long filled with earth, and the sculpture in it is generally in a remarkable state of preservation. In the ends of the front aisle are Indra and Ambikâ under trees, with attendants, all very sharply cut, and the features as yet but little injured. The front pillars are square and fluted; those behind the front aisle, square below and sixteen-sided above; and the four in the inner area are square with drooping-eared capitals. The shrine has a vestibule entered under a *torana* or ornamental arch. Pârwśanâtha, Gotama, &c. recur as before.

To the east side of the entrance, and also facing the south, is a chapel with Mahâvîra or Śântinâtha on each end, and further back Pârśwânâtha on the left and Gotama on the right.

On the right of this is the stair leading to the upper storey, fig. 2, consisting of a great twelve-pillared hall, varying in height from 13 feet 10 inches to 14 feet 6 inches. Two columns in front and as many in the back row have square bases, and round shafts with florid shoulders: the others are square, except the neck and cushion capital, which are round but not well proportioned: all have massive bases. Two more pillars stand on the bench screen wall that forms the front of the cave. The roof has been painted in large concentric circles, and on the walls Mâhavîra is sculptured between fifty and sixty times, Pârśvanâtha perhaps nine or ten times, and over the heads of the Jinas the space has also been painted with more Jinas and their worshippers. Indra and Ambikâ are on the back wall outside the *dwârpâlas*. In the shrine is a Jinendra with four lions on the front of the throne, and a wheel upheld by a dwarf. Over the Jina is a triple umbrella, and dogs and deer lie together at the foot of the throne. A low-doored cell on the right side of the shrine, and a square hole in the floor, were perhaps for concealing objects of value.

A door in the west end of the front aisle enters a low cell, the side of which has been cut away in excavating the hall below it. Through a cell in the other end of the front aisle a hole in the wall leads into the west wing of the Indra Sabhâ.

A little to the west of the preceding is the last cave of the series. The verandah, which had two square columns and pilasters in front, is gone. The front wall is pierced for a door and two windows. Inside, the roof, 9 feet 8 inches high, is supported by four short pillars square below, with moulded bases, and having a triangular flat shield on each side—a mark of their comparative modernicity.

The right side wall has cut into a cell of the west wing of the Jagannâtha Sabhâ. Indra and Ambikâ are in compartments on the back wall, and the other figures are repetitions of those in the other Jaina caves; on the side walls Tîrthaṅkaras are represented in pairs with rich florid sculpture over their heads. One of these compartments is represented in Plate XCI., fig. 2. Having been inaccessible till 1876, when the earth that filled it was taken out, most of the sculptures in this cave are comparatively sharp and fresh.

PARSWANATHA.

Over the top of the spur in which the caves are, is a structural building facing W. by N., erected early last century by a Banyâ of Aurangâbâd over a gigantic image of Pârśwanâtha, cut in the red trap of this part of the hill. It measures 9 feet from knee to knee, and 10½ feet from the topknot to the under-side of the cushion on which it squats, and 16 feet from the snake-hoods over his head to the base of the *siñhâsana*, which has a wheel set edgewise in front.

Right and left of him are worshippers, among whom are Śiva and Bhavânî. On the cushion on which he sits is an inscription dated 1234-5 A.D., which is thus rendered by Dr. Bühler :—

" Hail! In the year 1156 of the famous Śâka era, in the year (of the Bṛihaspati cycle) called Jaya.

" In Śrî (Va)rddhanâpura was born Râṇugi.........his son (*was*) Gâlugi, (*the latter's wife*) Svarṇâ, (*dear*) to the world.

" From those two sprang four sons, Chakreśwara and the rest. Chakreśwara was chief among them, excelling through the virtue of liberality.

" He gave, on the hill that is frequented by Châraṇas a monument of Pârśwanâtha, and by (*this act of*) liberality (*he made*) an oblation of his *karma*.[1]

" Many huge images of the lordly Jinas he made and converted the Châraṇâdri thereby into a holy *tîrtha*, just as Bharata (*made*) Mount Kailâsa (*a tîrtha*).

" The unique image of faith, of firm and pure convictions, kind, constant to his faithful wife, resembling the tree of paradise (*in liberality*), Chakreśwara becomes a protector of the pure faith, a fifth Vâsudêva.[2] *Quod felix faustumque sit!* Phâlguṇa 3, Wednesday."

Below this, on the slope of the spur, are several small caves, all Jaina, but now much ruined; and near the summit is a plain cave with two square columns in front.

---

[1] *I.e.* destroyed his *karma*, which bound him to the Samsâra.

[2] Name of a class of demigods peculiar to the Jains; among the Brahmanical Hindus Vâsudêva is a name of Kṛishna.

CHAPTER IV.

JAINA CAVE-TEMPLES.

DHARASINVA.

Dhârâsiṅva is a town on the brow of the ghât that forms the western border of the Nizam's territories, and about thirty-seven miles north of Solâpur on the railway from Poona to Madras. About two miles north-east from this town, in the north side of a ravine facing the south, is a small group of Jaina caves, with some other unfinished ones on the opposite side, some of which seem to have been intended as Vaishṇava temples.

The Jaina caves are now almost deserted by the sect, and a substantial temple has been erected to Mahâdêva just in front of them, which at first, at least, must have acted as a decoy.

The caves are excavated in a soft conglomerate rock of very unequal texture, containing hæmatite, and they are greatly dilapidated through its decay.

At the west end is a small unfinished cave, but the next has been a large and handsome cave with a verandah 78 feet long by 10 feet 4 inches wide, the whole façade of which, however, has fallen. Judging from the pilaster left at one end, it must have been supported by massive square pillars with bracket capitals richly carved. Above the pillars was a frieze sculptured with Tîrthaṅkaras, and "chaitya-window" ornaments. Five doors apparently led into the hall 82 feet deep and from 79 to 85 feet wide, the roof supported by thirty-two columns arranged in a square of twenty and an inner one of twelve square columns (Plate XCIII.), with bracket capitals and some of them with floriated ornamentation. Four in front of the shrine, however, have round shafts, and "compressed-cushion capitals." Round this hall are twenty-two cells, and the shrine in the back. The image is that of Pârśwanâtha Śeshphani with the seven hoods of a snake, each head with a small crown on it, and seated on a throne in the *jṅana mudrá*. Hanging from the seat is carved the representation of rich drapery; in front of it has been a wheel set edgewise, now broken away, with antelopes at each side; and from behind his cushion appear on each side a *śârdûla* or nondescript monster, a chauri-bearer with high regal tiara, and a very fat *vidyâdhara* with coronet and moustache: the figures have all been repaired with plaster. Round this image is a *pradakshiṇa*.

There has been an open court in front of this cave as at the Indra sabhâ at Elurâ, but only the pediment of the entrance is now visible among the débris of the façade. On the left of the entrance is a water-cistern.

The front aisle is peculiar in having a gable-shaped roof with an opening in one end into a passage which runs over the water-cistern and comes out beyond it; what it was meant for is difficult to conjecture.

The third cave has a hall about 59 feet square by 11 feet 3 inches high, with twenty square columns[1] arranged in a square with six on each side, and twelve cells in the sides and back besides the shrine, which has been a copy of that in the second; there are also images in bas-relief in two of the cells in the back. The hall has five doors and the verandah is supported by six plain octagonal columns, and has an unfinished cell in the right end, with a large square block or pillar of rock in the middle of it.

The fourth is a hall 28 feet deep by about 26½ wide which has had four columns, four cells in the walls, and a shrine; but all the columns are broken, only the capitals hanging by the roof; and the shrine wall has been broken through into the cell on the right of it. The pillars in both the last two caves are of a simple not inelegant type resembling the Tuscan order, but with a neck of the Elephanta type, and a collar of ornamental carving round the upper edge of the shaft.

As to the age of these caves it is difficult to speak with much confidence; the absence of wall sculptures and the style of the pillars in all of them seem certainly to mark them as of a considerably earlier type than the Elura Jaina caves, and compared with the architectural features of Brahmanical and Buddhist caves, I am disposed to assign them to about the middle of the seventh century of our era.

---

[1] Four pillars, two on each side, are round. See *Arch. Sur. W. India*, vol. iii. Plate VII.

The other caves in the neighbourhood are all Brahmanical, much ruined, and never seem to have been of much importance, being small and almost devoid of carving. They are probably older than the Jaina ones, and may belong to the sixth century.[1]

Ankai-Tankai Jaina Caves.

At Ankâi, already mentioned, there is a group of some seven Jaina caves, small, but very rich in sculptures, though unfortunately much defaced. They face the south looking down upon the village of Ankâi, from which they are hardly a hundred yards distant.

The first is a two-storeyed cave; the front of the lower storey is supported by two pillars, with a figure at the base of each and facing one another, and occupying the place of small *dwârpâlas*. Low parapets, ornamented on the outside, join each pillar to the end walls. The door leading from the verandah into the hall is very richly sculptured, overloaded indeed with minute details and far too massive and rich for the small apartments it connects. (*See* Plate XCV., fig. 1.)

The hall inside is square, its roof supported by four columns, much in the style in vogue from the tenth to the twelfth century, the capitals surmounted by four brackets, each carved with fat little four-armed figures supporting a thin flat architrave. The enclosed square is carved as a lotus with three concentric rings of petals.

The shrine door is ornamented similarly to the entrance one, the lower portion of the jambs being carved with five human figures on each. There is nothing inside the cella.

The upper storey has also two pillars in the front of the verandah similar to those below, but not so richly carved. The hall inside is perfectly plain (*see* plan and section, Plate XCIV.).

The second cave is very similar to the first, being also two-storeyed, only the verandahs are shut in, and form outer rooms or vestibules to the halls. On the lower floor the verandah measures 26 feet by 12, and has a large figure at either end; that at the west or left end is the male figure usually known as Indra seated on a couched elephant, but instead of being reliefs in this case, the elephant and Indra are each carved out of a separate block, and set into a niche cut out to receive them. Opposite him is Indrânî or Ambâ, which the villagers have

---

[1] For a fuller account of these caves, see *Archæol. Survey W. India*, vol. iii.

converted, by means of paint, tinsel and paper, into a figure which does duty as Bhavânî Dêvî.

The door into the hall is of the same elaborate pattern as those in No. I. The hall is about 25 feet square and similar in details to the last, but more coarsely carved. There is a small vestibule to the shrine at the back. The shrine door is much plainer than those already mentioned, having a pair of pilasters only on each side and a small image of a Tîrthaṅkara on the centre of the lintel. The shrine itself is about 13 feet square and contains a seat for an image with a high back rounded at the top. It seems as if it had been intended to carry a *pradakshiṇâ* behind it, but this has not been completed.

The upper storey, reached by a stair from the right end of the front room below, has a plain door, and is also partly lighted by square holes pierced in geometric patterns. The door leads to a narrow balcony, at each end of which is a full-sized lion carved in half relief. The hall inside was apparently intended to be about 20 feet square with four pillars, but only part of it is excavated. The shrine is about 9 feet by 6, with a seat against the wall for an image.

No. III. is like the lower storey of the last, with a perforated screen wall in front, much injured by time and weather. The front room is about 25 feet long by 9 wide, the ends occupied by large reliefs of Indra and Ambâ, the former much destroyed and his elephant scarcely recognisable; he wears a high tiara of a late type, and is attended by chauri-bearers and *gandharvas*. A pilaster at each side of the compartment is crowned by a four-armed dwarf as a bracket, and supports a *makara* and a human figure. Between the *makaras* is the *tôraṇa* arch so common in such positions in modern Jaina shrines. Ambâ has also her attendants—one of them riding on a small defaced animal with a large club in his hand; another an ascetic with a long beard and carrying an umbrella. The mango foliage usually represented over this figure is here conventionalised into six sprays hung out at equal distances under the straight *toraṇa* that (with a *kirttimukh* or grinning face, in the centre) extends across the top of the sculpture.

The hall is entered by a door with only a moderate amount of ornament, and measures 21 feet by 25, the roof supported by four pillars as in the others. The lotus, however, that fills the central square is much richer and more curious than in the others. It has four concentric rows of petals, the inner and outer ones plain, but in the second, counting outwards, each of the sixteen petals is carved with a human figure, mostly females, and all dancing or playing on musical instruments; the third circle contains twenty-four petals, each carved apparently with divinities, singly or with a companion, and mounted on their *vâhanas* or vehicles—mostly animals or birds.

The whole lotus is enclosed in an octagonal border carved with a lozenge-and-bead ornament, outside which, in one corner, is a single figure standing on one foot; in the others there are three each—a larger in the centre dancing or playing, and two smaller attendants.

On the back wall, on each side the vestibule of the shrine, is a standing nude Jaina figure about life-size, with accompaniments. That on the left is one of the Tîrthaṅkaras, probably Śântinâtha, for he stands on a low basement, carved with a devotee at each end, a lion next, then an elephant on each side a central wheel, not set, (as in most cases) with the edge towards the front, but with the side; under it is an antelope (*mṛiga*), the *chinha* of the 16th Tîrthankara, with a very small worshipper at each side. The Jina has a diamond-shaped mark on the centre of the breast; and drops his hands straight down on either side to meet with the finger points some objects held up by devotees wearing loin-cloths. The sculpture has a pilaster on each side, in front of which stands Pârśwanath in the same attitude as the central figure but only about a third of the size, and distinguished by the pentecephalous snake (*pâncha-śesha-phaṇa*) overshadowing him. In a recess in the top of each pilaster on a level with Śântinâtha's head is a seated Jina; and outside the pilaster on the left is a female chauri bearer. Over the shoulders of Śântinâtha are small Vidyâdharas, above which, on projecting brackets, stand two elephants holding up their trunks towards a very small figure seated like Śrî, behind the point of a sort of crown or turreted canopy suspended over the Tîrthaṅkara's head. On each side this figure and above the elephants are four males and females bringing offerings or worshipping it. Over them is a *toraṇa* with a *kîrttimukha* and six circles in it, each filled with a sort of *fleur de lis* ornament, and above this, under the arch that crowns the compartment, are seven little figures each holding up a festoon with both hands. All this is so like what we find in Jaina temples even of the present day, that it cannot be ancient, and probably belongs to the twelfth or thirteenth century.

The Pârśwanâtha, on the other side, stands in the same stiff attitude, touching with the points of his fingers the heads of two little attendants. On the left stands a female with an offering, and on the right is a seated figure with a pointed cap. The pilasters on each side this compartment are plain, and over the snake hoods canopying Pârśwanâtha's head is an almost hemispherical formed object intended for an umbrella. Over this is a figure with his hands clasped, and two others on each side bearing oblong objects like bricks, which they seem about to throw down on the ascetic.

The door of the shrine is moulded but without figure ornament, and the sanctum is about 12 feet square with a seat for an image in the middle of it. Behind this to the right is a trap hole into a small room below, with a Tîrthaṅkara in it evidently thrown down from the shrine. The custom of providing sunk hidden rooms for these images came into vogue after the inroads of Mahmud of Ghazni; whether this one was formed when the excavation was made, or afterwards, it shows that the shrine was in use in times when all idols were special objects of Muslim iconoclasm, as they were during the bloody rule of Alau'd-dîn Khilji.

The fourth cave has two massive plain square pillars in front of its verandah, which measures about 30 feet by 8. The door is similar to that in Cave 1, with a superabundance of small members, and having a Jina on the lintel. The hall is 18 feet deep by 24 wide, its roof supported by two pillars across the middle, with corresponding pilasters on the side walls, also on the front and back, quite in the style of structural temples of the present day. They have no fat figures on the brackets which are of scroll form. A bench runs along the back wall, which serves as a step to the shrine door. The seat for the image is against the back wall, in which an arched recess has been begun but left unfinished.

On the left pillar of the verandah is an inscription scarcely legible, but in characters of about the eleventh or twelfth century.

The remaining excavations to the east are smaller and much broken and damaged; they have doors similar to those in the first and second, and in the shrine of one of them is an image of a Tîrthaṅkara (Plate XCV., fig. 2). They are partly filled in with earth and need not further detain us.

GWALIOR.

The well known fortress of Gwalior is situated on a perfectly isolated flat-topped hill of sandstone, rising like an island from the plains around it. It is nearly two miles in length, north and south, and about half a mile across in the centre where broadest. The central plateau is bounded on all sides by a perfectly perpendicular cliff some 300 feet in height, with one ravine, the Urwâhi running into it for some 2,000 feet on its western side. There are no ancient buildings in the fort, nor any evidence of its having been considered sacred by the Jains, or indeed any other sect, anterior to the 11th century. The Sasbâhu, or as it is generally called the great Jain temple, was probably erected in A.D. 1093,[1] and the others such as the Teli ka Mandar, which was originally dedicated to Vishṇu, are not very much earlier.

In the 15th century, during the reign of the Tomara Rajas, the Jains seem to have been seized with an uncontrollable impulse to convert the cliff that sustains the fort into a great shrine in honour of their religion, and in a few years excavated the most extensive series of Jaina caves known to exist anywhere. Unfortunately their date is so modern that their style of execution is detestable, and their interest, consequently, very inferior, not only to that of the group at Elurâ, but even to that of the detached caves found elsewhere, though these are comparatively insignificant in number and extent.[2]

The principal group is situated on the Urwâhi ravine, and consists of 22 colossal figures of the Tîrthaṅkaras, all of which are entirely naked. One is a colossal seated figure of Adinâth, the first of the Jain pontiffs; another, a seated figure of Neminath, is 30 feet in height, but the largest in the group—indeed of all those at Gwalior—is a standing colossus 57 feet in height. These are interspersed with smaller figures, and the niches in which they stand are ornamented with architectural details of great elaborateness, though generally in very questionable taste.[3]

---

[1] Cunningham, *Reports*, vol. ii. p. 360; *Hist. of Indian & East. Architecture*, p. 452.

[2] The following account of these caves is almost entirely based on Gen. Cunningham's account of them in the second volume of his *Reports*, p. 364, *et seqq.*

[3] Two views of this group are given in Rousselet's *L'Inde des Rajas*, pp. 369 and 371. As these are engraved from photographs they give a fair idea of the state of the art at the time the sculptures were executed.

The second great group extends for upwards of half a mile on the opposite face of the cliff, and contains 18 great statues from 20 to 30 feet in height, and at least as many more from 8 to 15 feet high. There are also some real caves on this side, but they are at present inhabited by Bairâgis, and consequently inaccessible.

There are three other smaller groups, but they contain little that is remarkable, except in that to the south-west, where a sleeping female figure is represented, 8 feet long and highly polished, and close to this a group of a male and female with a child, but there is nothing to show who these are intended to represent.

The most remarkable thing about these sculptures is, if the numerous inscriptions upon them are to be depended upon, that they were all executed in 33 years, or between the years of 1441 and 1474 A.D. As General Cunningham points out, however, the inscriptions are not all integral. Some, at least, were added afterwards, but be this as it may, there seems no reason for doubting that they all belong to the 15th century, and this is quite sufficient to account for the inferiority of style in which they are executed.

Concluding Remarks.

It would, of course, be absurd to attempt to institute any comparison between the Jaina caves in India and those excavated either by the Buddhists or the Brahmans. The Jains never were cave excavators, and it was only at the last when Buddhism was tottering to its fall, and the Brahmans were stripping them of their supremacy and power, that the Jains seem to have awakened to the idea that they, too, might share in the spoil. The consequence was that, timidly at first, in Dharwar and the Dekhan, they seem to have put in their claim to a share in popular influence, and afterwards at Elurâ boldly asserted their position as co-heirs of the expiring Buddhists. Though existing long before, this was practically the first appearance of the Jains on the public stage in India. The fact being that the Jains have left very few material evidences of their existence before the sixth or seventh centuries. A few inscriptions at Mathura and some fragments of statues[1] are nearly all that

[1] Gen. Cunningham, *Reports*, vol. iii., p. 30 *et seqq.*

recall to us that such a congregation really held together anywhere in India.

There seems, nevertheless, no reason for doubting that the Jains are as early a sect as the Buddhists, perhaps even earlier, but the teaching of Mahâvîra seems to have been wanting in some element that would successfully recommend it for general acceptance, or it may only be that his doctrines never had the good fortune to obtain the patronage of so powerful a king as Aśoka, to whom the Buddhists owe so much. From whatever cause, however, it arose, the fate of the two religions was widely different. From and after the third century before Christ, the doctrines promulgated by the Buddhists spread everywhere over India and into Ceylon, and in the first century after our era they were carried to Burmah and the Indo-Chinese provinces, and spread themselves extensively even in the Celestial Empire itself, till they became the faith of a greater number of human beings than ever before adopted the creed of any single prophet.

During the greater part of this time the doctrines of Mahâvîra remained dormant in comparative obscurity, and only flickered into a transitory brilliancy on the decline of Buddhism. Their real revival was some two or three centuries afterwards, when we find them erecting buildings of extreme beauty and splendour on Mount Abu, at Grinar, or at Palitana. Nothing in India surpasses the beauty of the temples with which the Jains adorned all their sacred sites in Gujerât during the 11th and 12th centuries; but it was not the architecture of the caves which they employed in them, or anything derived from cave architecture. It would, for instance, be difficult in India to find any architectural forms more dissimilar than those displayed in the temples of Vimâla and Tejpâla at Abu, when compared with those in the Indra and Jagannâth Sabhâs at Elurâ. The former are light and elegant to an extent hardly found in any other style in India, and their beautiful horizontal domes supported on eight pillars, which are their most characteristic features, are not found anywhere else at that time. They had, in fact, a structural style of their own, whose origin we have not yet been able to trace. Their rock-cut style was only a passing episode in their architectural history, and was evidently borrowed from that of the Buddhists and Brahmans, but it was dropped by them when it was no longer wanted, without having had any permanent influence on their own peculiar style.

Under these circumstances, though it was of course impossible to omit a description of these forms in a work like the present, it is evident that a study of the Jaina caves adds but little to our knowledge of the subject. It neither reveals to us what the architecture of the Jains was before they adopted this passing fashion, nor does it throw any light on the origin of the style they afterwards developed with such success in their structural temples. Notwithstanding this, however, the architects who excavated the two great Sabhâs at Elurâ certainly deserve a prominent place among those who, regardless of all utilitarian considerations, sought to convert the living rock into quasi eternal temples in honour of their gods.

APPENDIX.

Since Mr. Burgess' return to India in October last, a fresh cave has been discovered at Bhâjâ, which, though one of the smallest, seems to be among the oldest, and certainly one of the most interesting known to exist in India. Mr. Cousins' drawings of it, reproduced in Plates CXVI., CXVII., and CXVIII., did not, from various causes reach this country in time for a description of this cave being inserted in its proper place, along with that of the other caves of the group. This, however, is hardly to be regretted, as the cave is quite unique, and presents so many features of novelty, giving rise to fresh subjects of inquiry, that it may be as well that it should be treated apart by itself, rather than that the narrative should be interrupted by entering upon them in the middle of the work.

When first discovered, the cave was filled nearly to the roof of the verandah with mud, and a great bank of earth and débris accumulated in front of its façade, which had to be cut through before it could be cleared out. It is owing to this circumstance that the sculptures which it contains are in so remarkable a state of preservation. No wilful injury has been done to any of them, nor, indeed, to any part of the cave, except to the sides of the entrance doors, where the wall being very thin the rock has been broken away, and the sculptures on either side slightly damaged. The pillars, too, of the verandah have been broken away. This, however, is hardly to be wondered at, as they are less than a foot in diameter, and were easily broken from their exposed situation.

The cave faces the north, and, as will be seen from the plan (Plate XCVI., fig. 1), is a small vihâra, with a hall of a somewhat irregular form, measuring 16 feet 6 inches north and south, and 17 feet 6 across, in the opposite direction. There are two cells in the inner wall, one with a stone bed, the other without, and two in the east wall. There are besides these, a larger cell, with a stone bed at one end of the verandah, and two smaller, similarly provided, at the other end. The latter, however, are partially detached, their proper entrance being from the front, outside the Vihâra. At this end there is a pillar and pilaster (Plate XCVII., figs. 1 and 2), whose capitals (Plate XCVI., figs. 2 and 3) are familiar to us, the one as an example of the bell-shaped quasi Persepolitan capitals, which we find surmounting the lâts of Aśoka at Sankissa and Bettiah[1] which are certainly of his time, and which afterwards assumed the more Indian forms we find at Bedsâ (woodcut 45) and at Kârlê (Plate XII.) as well as elsewhere; the other as the original of those found at Kanheri in the great cave there, as well as in numerous vihâras, and which long afterwards bloomed into the cushion capitals of Elephanta (woodcut, p. 467). These pillars are surmounted by figures, as is so generally the case in the early caves, but in this instance they are exceptional, being fabulous animals, human female busts united to bovine bodies. Not, consequently, centaurs, but sphinxes, and, except in the Nahapâna cave at Nasik (Plate XXIII., fig. 3), nearly if not quite unique.

The eastern (Plate XCVII., fig. 3) and inner sides of the cave are very nearly similar, except that the latter is slightly more elaborate, and the jambs of its two doorways slope inwards at rather a greater angle. The west side, however, has no doorways, but their place is supplied by two niches, in one of which is an ascetic, with his hair twisted into a high top knot, and with a staff in his hand. In the other is a layman, probably a prince, and as probably the excavator of the cave, but there is nothing about him by which he can be identified with any known personage.

The sculptures in the verandah are, however, much more remarkable than those in the interior. Beginning at the east end (Plate XCVIII.) we have a prince mounted on a richly caparisoned elephant, with an attendant behind, who carries a standard, surmounted by the triśula ornament, as at Sanchi, and also what apparently was meant as the chattri or umbrella of state. He drives himself, having the ankuśa in his hand, and the elephant has apparently torn up a tree from its roots, and is brandishing it in his trunk. In front of him are several small figures, some apparently floating in the air. The most remarkable of these, however, are three:—two male and one female—with the most extraordinary head-dresses, standing on the top of a tree, of a species not seen in any other sculptures, but surrounded by a rail, and with a goose or some such bird behind

[1] *Hist. of Indian and East Architecture,* Woodcuts 5 and 6.

[2] There are figures surmounting capitals at Buddha Gaya (Rajendralâla Mitra Bud. Gaya, Plate L.) which seem to represent the same symbolism, but they are so weather worn that it is difficult to feel sure what they are intended to represent.

it. Below the tree a king, on a very much smaller scale, is seated on his morhâ, under an umbrella of state, and with a female chauri bearer and two musicians beside him. Below these again is one woman dancing, and one, or it may be two, though only two legs are seen, playing and dancing. In the centre of this lower compartment is a sacred tree, surrounded by a rail, hung with garlands and surmounted by an umbrella, but it, like the other, is of a species not represented in any other sculptures known. Beyond these, too, there is a man and a Kinnari—a woman with a horse's head. In this instance she is not quite naked, as she is represented on the rail at Buddha Gaya,[1] having a bead-belt round her waist. The rest of this portion of the bas-relief is filled with lions and monsters of various kinds preying on one another.

The first impulse on looking at this extraordinary sculpture is to assume that it is intended to represent the god Indra on his elephant Airâvata, but on the whole it seems most probable it is intended only as a glorification of the king or prince who excavated the cave. The exaggeration of his size and of that of his elephant, which is greater than in any other Indian sculptures known, may only be an attempt to express his greatness relatively to other men, and to the king his father, who seems to be the figure seated in front of him.

The bas-relief on the other side of the doorway is of a much simpler character. It represents a prince in his chariot drawn by four horses, and attended by two females with most remarkable head-dresses. One bears a chauri in her right hand, and behind the prince is a staff, which may have been intended to symbolise or support an umbrella, which has now however been entirely obliterated. Two men on horseback attend them. The most remarkable part of this group are the hideous female monsters which apparently support the chariot, and the architectural features of the cave. They are so totally unlike anything known to exist in any cave, in any age, and, so far as I know, in any mythology, that we must pause before attempting an explanation of their appearance here.

The three figures of men that adorn the front of the cave beyond and between the doorways are extremely well designed, and very remarkable for their costumes, which are unlike any others known anywhere else. The most eastern one (Plate XCVI., fig. 5) is singularly elegant and well drawn, though his head is somewhat too

[1] Dr. Rajendralâla Mitra, *Buddha Gaya*, Plate XXXIV., Fig. 2.

small for his other proportions, but the amount and character of jewels he wears is most remarkable. His gold earrings rest on his shoulders, and his arms are nearly covered with armlets of pearls (?), while the *fleur-de-lys* ornament he wears on his right arm is not only elegant but most unusual.

No inscription of any sort has been found in this newly discovered cave, which either from its purport or the form of its letters gives us a hint of what the age of this Vihâra may be. We are thus left almost wholly to rely on local and architectural evidences for ascertaining this. These, fortunately, especially the latter, are, in this case, as satisfactory as almost could be wished for, and leave little room for doubt that if not the very oldest it is at least among the most ancient excavations, of its class, that has yet been discovered in India.

The situation of this cave, as forming part of a group where all the others are old, raises at first a strong presumption that it, too, may be as ancient as the others are. The Chaitya cave here (woodcut No. 1) I have always looked upon as the oldest of its class on the western side of India, and its accompanying Vihâras (Plate IX.) are certainly of the same age. Recent researches have somewhat modified this conclusion, and it is now doubtful whether the caves at Pitalkhorâ (Plate XV.), and that at Kondânê (Plate VIII.) may not be as old, and, on the whole, there seems so very little difference between them, that it is hardly worth arguing the point. These groups may overlap each other, as to their dates, and may be considered as contemporary, till something turns up to decide the question of priority.

Though the fact of its being associated with an old group of caves may render it probable that it, too, is ancient, it is far from proving it to be so; but if any reliance can be placed on architectural evidence, this is amply sufficient to render its antiquity beyond all cavil. Any one familiar with the subject, on looking at the doorways of the interior (Plate XCVII.), will see at a glance that their form is more ancient than that of any others yet adduced in this work. Those most like them are those in the Vihâra at Bedsâ (Plate X.), but these are not so rude as in this cave, and their jambs do not slope inwards to anything like the same extent, while as mentioned above (p. 40 *et seq.*), in describing the Eastern caves, this is one of the most certain indications of their relative antiquity. The decorations of the walls of the Vihâra No. XII. at Ajaṇṭâ resemble those of this cave even more closely, as that cave has the square sinkings or niches between the doorways (Plate XXVII.) which are only found there and in this cave. The Ajaṇṭa example, though universally admitted to be the oldest cave there, has not, like the Bedsâ one, the sloping jambs nor the great posts on the sides of the doors which are so characteristic in this Bhâjâ cave and of the Lomas Rishi cave at Barabar (woodcut No. 3), which latter, we may say with certainty was excavated in the time of Aśoka.

The cave most like it in plan, is Cave No. XIV. at Nâsik (Plate XXVI.); but it is regular and formal in every respect, and, though excavated probably one or two centuries before Christ (p. 275), is evidently a much more modern example. On the whole, the cave most resembling it is, perhaps, the Vihâra at Pitalkhorâ (Plate XV., figs. 3 and 4), but even this has the sloping jambs, only in an almost imperceptible degree, if at all.

When the description of the Pitalkhorâ caves was written in the body of this work (pp. 242 to 246), there seemed no data available from which their age could be ascertained with anything like precision, while the frequent substitution of stone ribs in the roofs, instead of wooden ones, seemed to warrant their being brought down to a more modern date than we now find to be justifiable. In a letter received from Mr. Burgess, at Bombay, dated on the 28th of last month (February 1880), he informs me that inscriptions have been found on the Pitalkhorâ caves, " in the Mauryan character," from which he infers that " they must be very old." This fact, coupled with the discovery of this Vihâra at Bhâjâ, has thrown a flood of light on the history of the most ancient forms of these caves, which was not available a few months ago, and we now see our way to ascertain their dates with a degree of precision not hitherto attainable.[1]

---

[1] In his recent communications Mr. Burgess has given me the following list of these old Chaitya caves, with the dates he is now inclined to attach to them, though without insisting on them, till he has leisure to go over the whole subject with all the documents before him:—

Pitalkhorâ and Bhâjâ - -	250 to 200 B.C.
Kondânê - - - -	200 to 150 B.C.
No. IX and X. Ajaṇṭâ - -	150 to 200 „
Bedsâ and Nâsik - - -	100 to 50 „
Kârlê - - - - -	First century of our era.

Now that the age of these Pitalkhorâ caves may be said to be ascertained, it is evident that that of No. X. Ajaṇṭâ may be carried back to any age, which from other indications may be considered reasonable, but, above all, it enables us to understand the arrangement of the verandah in this Bhâjâ Vihâra which before looked very anomalous. Its form is, however, quite unique, so far as is at present known, being a quadrant of a circle, projecting forwards and externally, probably, of an ogee form.[1] Internally it was framed as if with wooden ribs, supporting horizontal rafters, all copied in stone exactly in the same manner and to the same extent as was practised at Pitalkhorâ (Plate XVII.), and with the same windows formed of cross-bars, originally, undoubtedly, in wood, but like everything else here, copied in stone. Though arising probably from a different cause, it will be observed the roof of this verandah has the same diagonal slope as is observable in the Pitalkhorâ Vihâra (Plate XV., fig. 3). Altogether there is a remarkable affinity between the two caves, which is most satisfactory now that their ages are at least approximately known, and that it is nearly if not quite certain that these two are the earliest caves, of an ornamental character, known to exist in Western India.

Whatever doubt may hang over other matters connected with this cave, or over the subjects meant to be portrayed in its sculptures, there is fortunately none as to the religion to which it is dedicated. We have been accustomed, in the caves at Katak and at Bhârhut and Sanchi to Buddhism without Buddha, but at the two last-named places we have, thanks partly to inscriptions, partly to the extent of the sculptures, been able to identify jâtakas and

---

This list appears to me to represent very correctly the present state of our knowledge of the age of these old caves. The Vihâra No. XII. at Ajaṇṭâ, which this cave so much resembles in detail, has always been admitted to be the oldest cave there, and earlier than either of the Chaityas IX. or X. at that place.

[1] There is no other instance known of this form of verandah in any other cave, but it must have been common in structural buildings of the Buddhists in that and perhaps in all ages. At least it is found repeated in all the great Dravidian buildings down at least till a century or two ago. At Vijyanagar (Captain Lyons' photographs, No. 509 *et seq.*) and at Avadea Covil (photo. 381) there are repetitions of this form almost exactly of the same dimensions and with the same ribbed construction internally. It is, in fact, the most characteristic feature of the Dravidian style, and is found in every conceivable position and of all dimensions.

legends which leave no doubt in the matter. At Katak we have not even a dâgoba, and the emblems are few and far between. In this Bhâjâ cave the frieze of dâgobas of a very early type round the verandah (Plate XCVII., figs. 1, 2, and 3) quite sets the question at rest, and though we have no wheels, which is very remarkable, we have tree worship, though of an unusual type, and the triśula only doubtfully once on a standard. There is certainly nothing in the sculpture that can be interpreted as a jâtaka, and altogether, though certainly Buddhist, the sculptures look as if they belonged to an earlier type than anything yet found in any other cave.

There is still one other subject connected with the Vihâra which I approach with diffidence, as it raises a question, to which I am not prepared with an answer, and which is still so important that some may think it neutralises all the other arguments that can be adduced to establish the antiquity of this cave. On looking attentively at the bas-relief that is found at one end of the verandah (Plate XCVI., fig. 4) it will be observed that the man on horseback, a little to the left of the centre, has his feet in stirrups, and there can be no doubt that this bas-relief forms part of the original decoration of the cave, and is coeval with the other sculptures. The winged horse (Pegasus) on the left, and the two primeval bulls fighting over the prostrate body of a man, and the whole character of the framework that surrounds the sculpture, all indicate an antiquity as great as that of any part of the cave. The two horsemen who accompany the chariot (Plate XCVIII.) certainly do not use stirrups, and there is not any such harness found either at Bhârhut nor even at Amrâvati, where the sculptures are so minute and realistic that it must have been detected if it existed, and there is only one doubtful example at Sanchi. On the western gateway there, a man mounted apparently on a mule does seem to have his foot in a stirrup,[1] but, so far as I know, it is a solitary example in these sculptures. This evidence of their use is certainly slight, but there is an engraved vase in the India Museum at South Kensington which seems to set the matter at rest. It was described by Mr. Charles Horne, late of the Bengal Civil Service, in the *Journal of the Royal Asiatic Society*, with two

---

[1] *Tree and Serpent Worship*, Plate XXXVIII., Fig. 2.

plates.[1] It was found on Lahoul in Kûlû in the Himalaya, having apparently been washed out of the ruins of some Buddhist buildings which had been undermined by the river. There was nothing, however, either in the vase or in the remains around it to indicate its age. Mr. Horne comes to the conclusion that, though "the drawing "indicates a period somewhat earlier than the carving in the Sanchi "topes," and everything points to a very early date, from the historical subject portrayed, he is inclined to place it about 200 to 300 A.D. (p. 375).

The sculptures in this cave may probably justify us in placing the age of the vase, as many years before our era, for the curious and interesting fact is, that the scenes portrayed on the vase are as exact a copy of those in this cave, as it is well possible to execute with a graver on metal, of bassi rilievi on a large scale in stone. We have the same prince driving his own elephant with an attendant of doubtful sex behind him. We have evidently another prince in his four-horsed chariot, accompanied by a female chauri-bearer, and another female who in the bas-relief sits behind, but on the vase who acts as charioteer. Both on the vase have state umbrellas over their heads. The chariots are almost identical in form, and the head-dresses of the females, and indeed of all, are of the same exaggerated type in both. There are no monsters on the vase, but instead a female, or it may be a male figure leading the procession, followed by a graceful female playing on a harp and another playing on a very long flute, which seems to have been the favourite national instrument in all the old sculptures.

These, however, are minor peculiarities, and do not interfere with the inference that the cave sculptures and the vase represent the same scenes whatever they may be, though it is probable they may not be of exactly the same age. The sculptures on the vase do indeed look more modern, though it is difficult to institute a comparison between them, the mode of expression and the material are so different. But be that as it may, the point that interests us most here is that the two men on horseback who accompany the chariot have, on the vase, their feet undoubtedly in stirrups, not of metal it is true, but a doubled strap serving the same purpose.

---

[1] *J. R. A. S.*, vol. v., New Series for 1871, pp. 367 to 375.

The question thus arises, is it conceivable that if the Indians used stirrups in the third century before Christ, neither the Greeks nor the Romans took the hint and adopted them also? It is one of those inventions which, like printing with moveable types, seem only to require to be suggested to be universally adopted, but the evidence of all antiquity seems against the idea. The Nineveh sculptures seem to prove that their use was unknown in Assyria, and if they were used either in Greece or Rome it is most improbable that the keen eyes of antiquaries would not have detected evidence of their employment. How on the other hand cavalry could exist and be efficient without the employment of stirrups is almost as mysterious, but that is a question that cannot be argued here. All that it is necessary to state here, is that in so far as the evidence now available can be relied upon, it goes to establish the fact that the use of stirrups was known in India in the third century before Christ.

Figure sculpture is so extremely rare in these western caves that it is very difficult to institute any comparison that will enable us to judge either of the relative antiquity or comparative merit of the sculptures in this cave. There are, it is true, groups in the caves at Kudâ and Kârlê (pp. 207 and 238), but they are only of two figures each, a man and his wife, apparently the founders or benefactors of the Chaitya, with very scant clothing and no emblems. There are also single figures, as at this very place of Bhâjâ and elsewhere, but nothing like an attempt to tell a story has anywhere been found, nor any mythological representations in any cave before the Christian era.

The sculptures in this cave are unlike anything found in the Katak caves, though how far that may be owing to distance of the locality, or to the nature of the material in which they are carved, it is difficult to say. They do not resemble those of the Bhârhut Stûpa. All these again are small and crowded, and applied to such different purposes that it would be dangerous to rely on any comparison that could be instituted between them. The same may be said of the Sanchi sculptures, though these are so much more methodical, and bring us so much more nearly within the circle of our knowledge of Buddhist literature, as we now know it, that it can hardly be doubted that they are much more modern.

If we had photographs of the sculptures of Buddha Gayâ, we might perhaps ascertain something of their age by a comparison with them. But the drawings that have hitherto been published of them are such that no reasoning can be based on them. The one that has been photographed[1] represents the Sun, Sûrya[2] driving a four-horsed chariot, from which his two wives, Prabhâ and Chhâyâ, shoot at the Râkshasas of darkness.[3] The subject is therefore different, and the chariot being seen in full front does not admit of comparison, but the two pillars on either side are as nearly identical with the two in the verandah here (Plate XCVI., figs. 2 and 3) as it is almost possible they should be. The one is bell-shaped, the other cushioned, and they are surmounted by sphinxes. They are unfortunately considerably worn, but their main features are quite unmistakeable. In so far, therefore, as architectural evidence can be relied upon there seems no doubt that this cave is of about the same age as the Buddha Gayâ rail. Which is the earliest may be allowed to remain an open question, but meanwhile it may be safe to assume 250 B.C. as the most probable date for this cave, and consequently there seems no reason for doubting that the sculptures in this Bhâjâ Vihâra are the oldest things of their class yet discovered in India. If there was any reason for supposing that Buddhism penetrated into Mahârâshṭra before the missionaries were sent there by Aśoka, after the great convocation held by him in 246 B.C., it might be considered an open question whether this might not possibly be even earlier than his reign; but that is a question that need not now be broached. A more important one, which I thought had been set at rest by the discovery of the Bhârhut Tope, must now be re-opened. The sculptures of that monument seemed to prove that a school of native sculptural art had arisen and developed itself in India, wholly without any foreign influence. If, however, the age of these Bhâjâ sculptures is admitted, it seems difficult to refuse to believe that it is not to some Baktrian or Yavana influence that they may owe their most striking peculiarities. The figure of the spear-

---

[1] Dr. Rajendralâla Mitra's, *Buddha Gayâ*, Plate L.

[2] There seems no doubt that General Cunningham is quite correct in identifying the Charioteer with the sun god, but the plate (*Reports*, vol. III., Plate XXVII.) in which he is represented is so incorrect as to be open to Dr. Rajendralâla's criticism.

[3] The same subject is represented in the Kumbharwârâ Cave at Elurâ (Plate LXXXIII., fig. 2), but in a much more modern, and less artistic form.

bearer, for instance (Plate XCVI., fig. 5), is so unlike anything else found in India, and so like some things found among the quasi Greek sculptures in Gandhara, with a strong reminiscence of Assyrian art, that the presence of a foreign element can scarcely be mistaken. It recalls at once the Assyrian, or as we were in the habit of calling it, the Ionic honeysuckle ornament of Aśoka's lâts at Allahabad and Sankissa,[1] and the strong traces of western influence that are found in his edicts as well as in his works. The bell-shaped quasi Persepolitan capitals which generally crown his lâts, and are the most usual features in this and in all the western caves anterior to the Christian era, tell the same tale. They are the only features that cannot be traced back to a wooden original, and must apparently have been imported from some western source.

The truth of the matter appears to be, that there was, in very early times a school of sculpture in India, represented by those at Bhârhut and Sanchi, which was wholly of native origin, and in which it is almost impossible to trace the influence of any foreign element. On the other hand the sculptures of the Gandhara monasteries are unmistakeably classical, and the influence of that school was felt as far as Mathurâ, certainly as early as the Christian era. Combined with an Assyrian or Persian element, it existed in Behar in Asoka's time and in this cave at Bhâjâ, and subsequently made itself most undoubtedly felt in the sculptures at Amrâvati. We have not yet the materials to fix exactly the boundaries of these two schools of sculpture, but their limits are every day becoming better defined, and may before long be fixed, with at least a fair amount of precision.

Whatever conclusions may eventually be evolved from all this, it probably will be admitted in the meanwhile, that the discovery of this Bhâjâ Vihâra, in combination with the Pitalkhorâ inscriptions, is one of the most curious and most interesting contributions that has of late years been made, and may yet do a great deal towards enabling us to elucidate the history and understand the arts of the Cave-Temples of India.

J. F.

[1] *Hist. of Indian and Eastern Architecture*, woodcuts 4, 5, and 6.

No. 73. S'ri, Consort of Vishnu, seated on a Lotus, with two elephants pouring water over her. From a modern image brought from Indore.

INDEX.

ERRATA.

Page 9, line 17, *for* Aryan, *read* Arrian.
„ 20, note 3, *for* Stœbus', *read* Stobæus's.
„ 21, note 1, *for* Ahyantra, *read* Abhyantra.
„ 22, note, line 9, *after* 68, *read* years.
„ 24, note 1, line 4, *for* Nerighssar, *read* Neriglissar.
„ 29, note, line 1, *for* accodring, *read* according.
„ 29, note, line 2, *for* σύλινον, *read* ξύλινον
„ 29, note, line 11, *for Protanto, read pro tanto.*
„ 32, note, line 11, *for* śtûpas, *read* stûpas.
„ 41, note 2 belongs to the third line of page 42.
„ 51, line 19, *for* Bikshus, *read* Bhikshus.
„ 53, line 26, *for Royal, read Bengal.*
„ 96, note, line 13, *for* road. The, *read* road—the.
„ 97 to 103, head lines, *for* Undavilla, *read* Undavilli.
„ 112, note 2, *for* Mantapan, *read* Mantapam.
„ 122, line 28, *for* S'hâlâs, *read* śâlâs.
„ 125, line 7, *for* Dharmaraga's, *read* Dharmarâja's.
„ 126, line 7, *for* boar, *read* lion.
„ 179, note 5, *for* Âryaheva, *read* Âryadeva.
„ 193, line 4 from bottom, *for* is nearly, *read* is as nearly.
„ 206, line 6, 7 from bottom, *for* Asalpamita, *read* Asâlbamita.
„ 219, line 7 from bottom, *for* Ambivlê, *read* Âmbivalê.
„ 229. Under the woodcut *for* a photograph)[1], *read* a photograph)[2]; and in the footnote *read* [2] Fergusson, *Ind. Arch.*, &c.
„ 232, line 3 from the bottom, *dele* from "mention, &c." to page 233, line 5, "identification," and *substitute* "state that the 'Sêṭh (or merchant) Bhûtapâla from Vejayanti established 'this rock-mansion, the most excellent in Jambudwîpa' and that 'Agnimitra son of Goti, 'a great warrior, presented the lion pillar;' but they contain no name of a king."

And add as a footnote to this:—Over the central door are two inscriptions of later date, the one of Usabhadata son of Dinika and son-in-law of Nahapâna, and the other in the 7th year of Vasiṭhîputa. Both record gifts to the *sangha* of Valuraka (Kârlê); so that the excavation must date before either of these kings.—J.B.

„ 243, line 3, *for* Devagaṛh, *read* Devagiri.
„ 261, note, line 2, *after* p., *read* 189.
„ 292, line 21, *for* façade has entirely fallen away, *read* lower façade, which was structural, has fallen away.
„ 313, line 4 from bottom, *for* Sihabaha, *read* Sihabâhu.
„ 334, line 5, *for* Mahâprajâpate, *read* Mahâprâjapatî.
„ 342, line 14, *for* Thsangs, *read* Thsang's.
„ 349, last line, *for* Samylla, *read* Semylla.
„ 350, line 2, *for* Staânaka, *read* Sthânaka.
„ 354, line 2, *for* t is, *read* it is.
„ 358, line 19, *for* litany, *read* compartment.
„ 360, note 2. *Add*:—The date is in "the 245th year of the Trikuṭakas," and Dr. Bühler regards it as dating from the Gupta era.—J.B.
„ 362, line 6, *for* Jñyâna, *read* Jñâna.
„ 386, line 10, *for* group, they, *read* group, that they.

Page 392, note 2, line 3, *for* he, *read* the.
" 397, note, *for* Kolvi, *read* Kholvi.
" 402, note 2, *for* 660 to 850 A.D., *read* cir. 600 to 750 A.D.
" 422, line 3 from bottom, *dele* the title LAKOLA'S CAVE, and insert it after line 4 on p. 423.
" 423, line 19, *for* hand, *read* hands.
" 424, line 4 from bottom, *for* sculpture, *read* sculptures.
" 429, last line, *after* platform *insert* a semicolon.
" 456, line 7. *Add* as a note: The first of these small shrines, that on the south, was dedicated to the Saptamâtrâs, the next to Chanda, the third, on the east, to Durgâ, the fourth to Bhairava, and the fifth, on the north side, to Gaṇêśa.—J.B.
" 461, footnote. For another list of the sculptures here referred to, see my *Rock Temples of Elurâ or Verul* (1877), pp. 47, 48.—J.B.
" 461, line, 28, and 463, line 25, *for* Vaishmave, *read* Vaishṇava.
" 470, line 13, *for* Airâvati, *read* Airâvata.
" 471, line 3 from bottom, *for* portice, *read* portico.
" 501, line 1, *for* Parwśanâtha, *read* Pârśwanâtha.
" 511, line 23, *for* Grinar, *read* Girnâr.

NOTE.

Since this work was printed off I have had occasion to refer to the fragments of sculpture now in the Louvre, brought by M. Texier from a Doric temple, erected at Assos in the Troad in the fifth or sixth century B.C., and have been so much struck with the similarities that exist between them and those in the ancient Vihara at Bhâjâ described in the Appendix, that I avail myself of this opportunity of directing attention to the fact, whatever the result of further investigations may be.

The principal ornaments of the façade, according to M. Texier's restoration,[1] are two groups of two bulls fighting, very similar to those represented on Plate XCVI., fig. 4, but without the prostrate man. In the centre are two sphinxes, winged, and their bodies leonine instead of bovine, as in the Cave, and between these two groups are lions devouring animals, as in the lower part of Plate XCVIII. Only two metopes were found. In one of these the sphinxes were repeated, in the other was a male centaur, and there can, from the general character of the sculptures, be little doubt that females of the same class existed in others. No fragment was found of the sculptures in the tympana, so that no complete comparison of the whole can be instituted.

The Architecture of the temple, of course, differs absolutely, as in every other known instance, both in principle and detail from that exhibited in this or any other Cave in India, but both the style and symbolism of the Sculpture seems undoubtedly to point to a common origin. The two monuments are too distant both in locality and date to admit of any direct copying being possible, but the similarity of their sculptures seems a satisfactory confirmation of the remark hazarded on page 523 regarding the influence of a strongly marked Yavana element in those of the Bhâjâ Vihara.—J. F.

---

[1] *Asie Mineure*, vol. ii. pp. 112 to 114 *ter.*; Texier and Pullan's *Principal Buildings in Asia Minor*, Plate 1. London. 1865.

SRI IN THE ANANTA CAVE

TREE WORSHIP IN THE ANANTA

TREE WORSHIP IN THE JAYA VIJAYA.

SCULPTURE IN RANI KA NUR.

SCULPTURE IN GANESA GUMPHA.

JUNÂGAṚH.

PLAN OF THE CAVES AT BÂWÂ PYÂRÂ'S MAṬH.

Plate II.

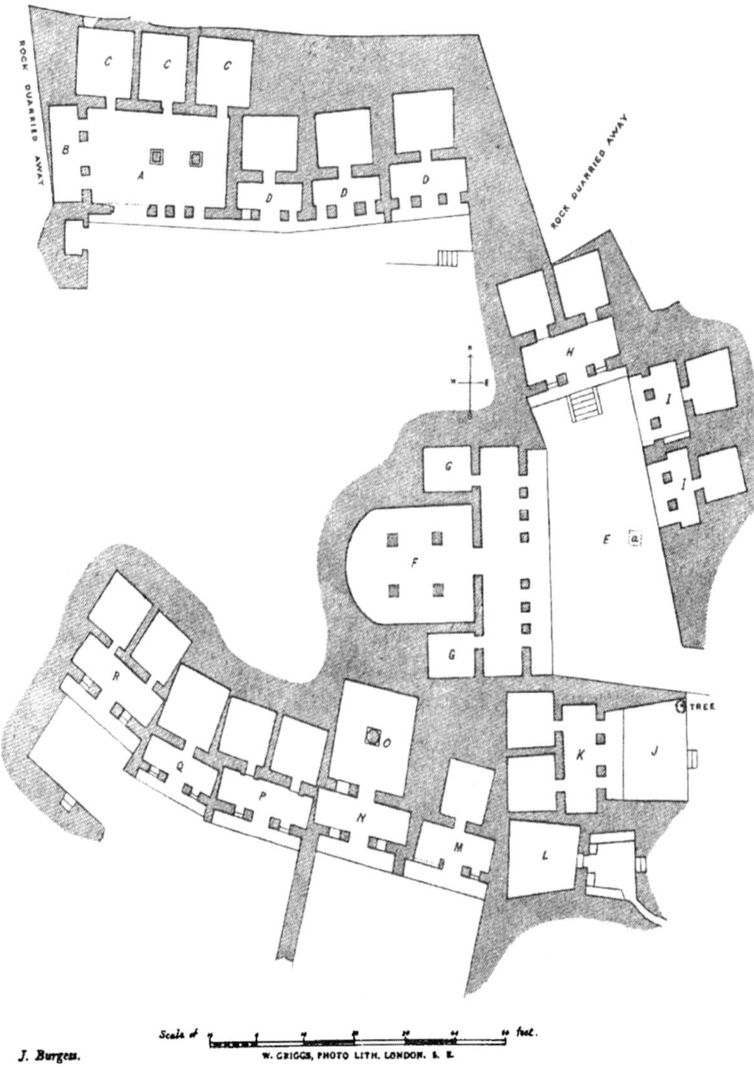

J. Burgess.

W. GRIGGS, PHOTO LITH. LONDON, S. E.

Plate III.

JUNAGARH.

3. COLUMN IN THE UPARKOT.
LOWER HALL.

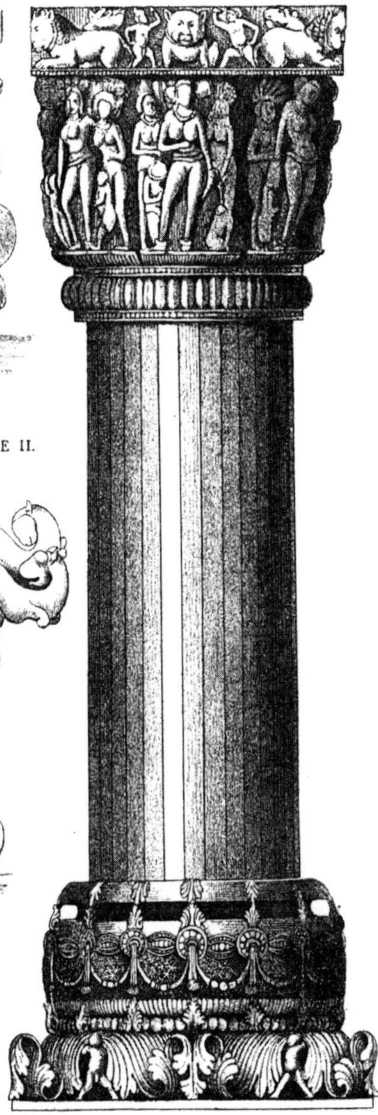

1. 2. DOORS OF CELL K ON PLATE II.

4

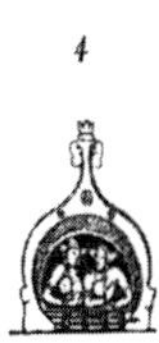

Scale of feet.

W. GRIGGS, PHOTO LITH. LONDON, S. E.

JUNÂGAṚH.

ROCK-CUT HALL IN THE UPARKOṬ.

Plate IV.

SECTION.

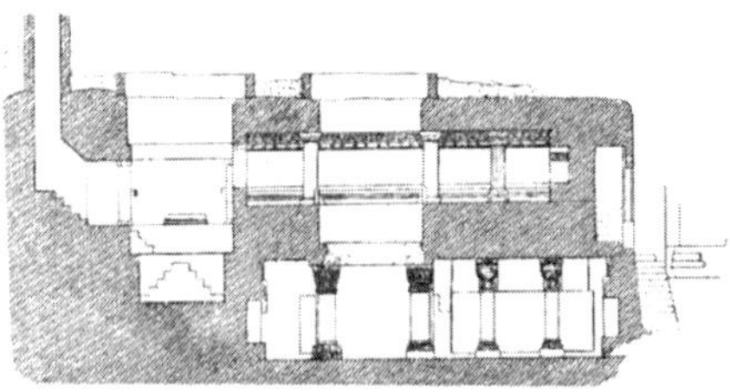

UPPER FLOOR.

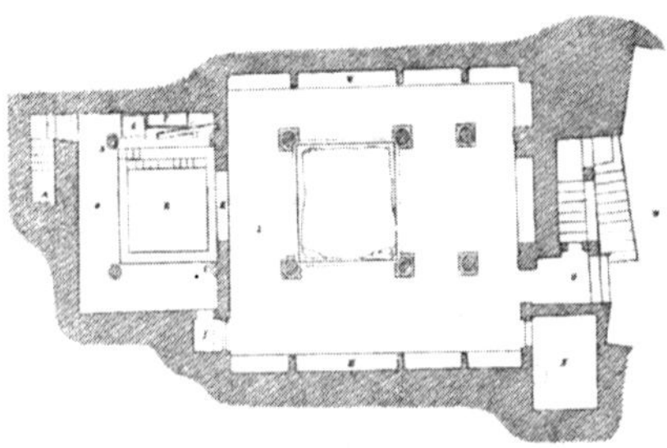

LOWER FLOOR.

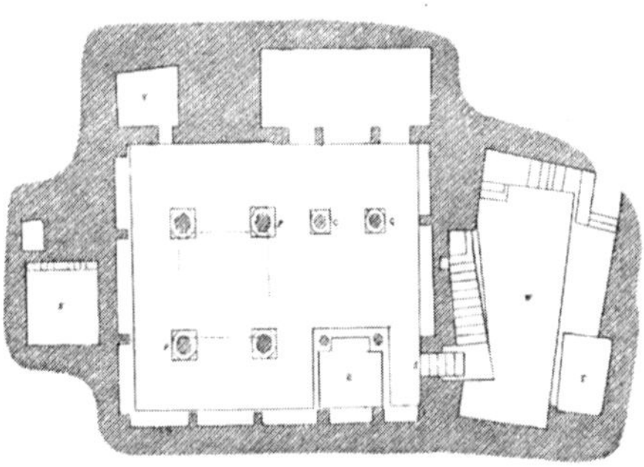

Scale of 0 5 10 20 30 40 50 *feet.*

J. Burgess.

W. GRIGGS, PHOTO LITH. LONDON, S. E.

1. KUḌÂ CAVE VI.

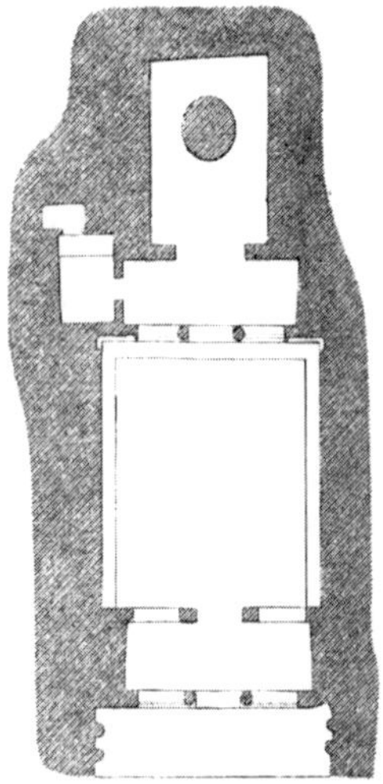

2. KARADH CAVE V.

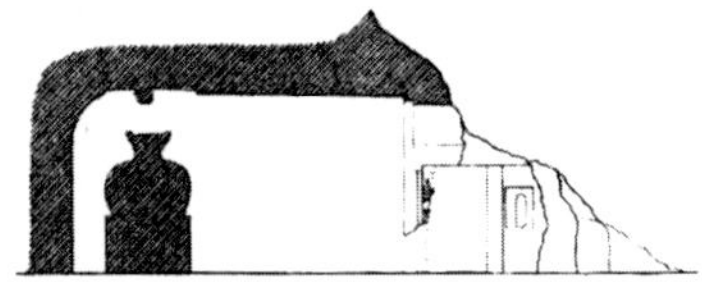

PLAN

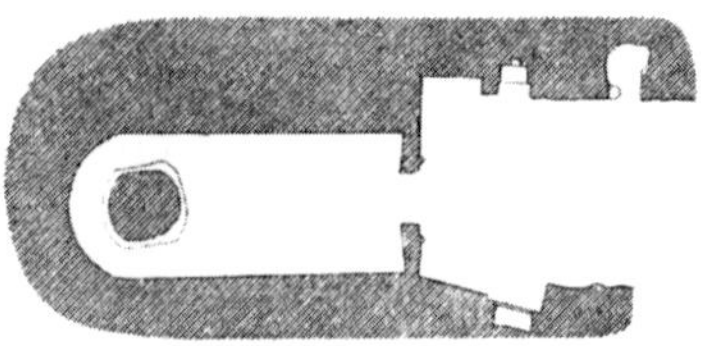

ŚAILARWADI CAVES.

3.

4.

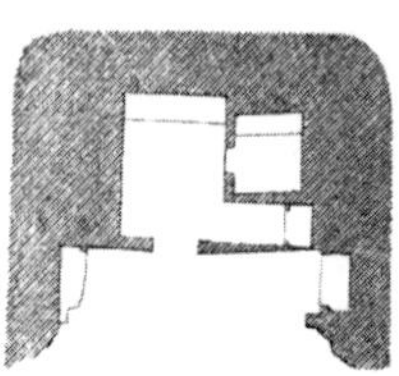

5.

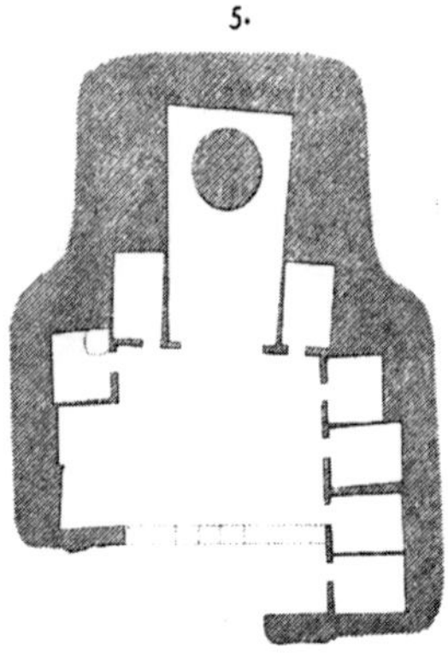

Scale of 10 0 10 20 30 40 50 feet

W. GRIGGS, PHOTO LITH. LONDON. S. E.

J. Burgess. *H. Cousens del.*

Plate. VI.

KARADH BUDDHIST CAVES.

SECTION AND PLAN OF CAVE XLVIII.

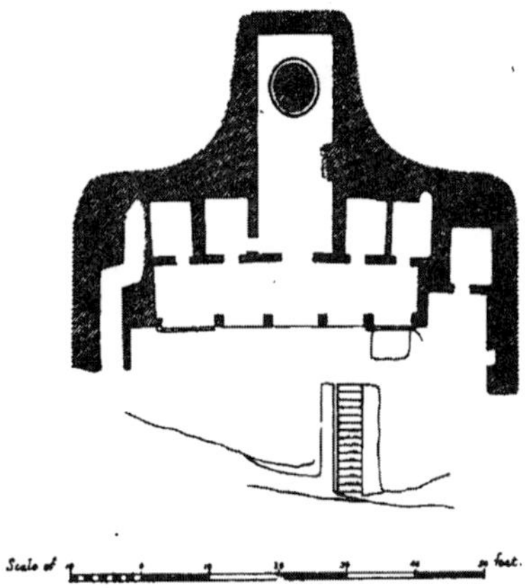

3. FRONT OF CAVE V.

J. Burgess. *S. J. Pacheco del.*

W. GRIGGS, PHOTO LITH. LONDON. S. E.

1. CARVED RAIL IN KÛDA CAVES.

KONDANE

BAUDDHA SYMBOLS.

2.

3.

4.

5.

6.

7.

9.

10.

11.

12.

8.

13.

14.

J. Burgess. W. GRIGGS, PHOTO-LITH. LONDON. S. E. *Jayrao Raghoba. del.*

Plate VIII.

KONDANE.

1. SECTION OF VIHÂRA.

2. PLAN.

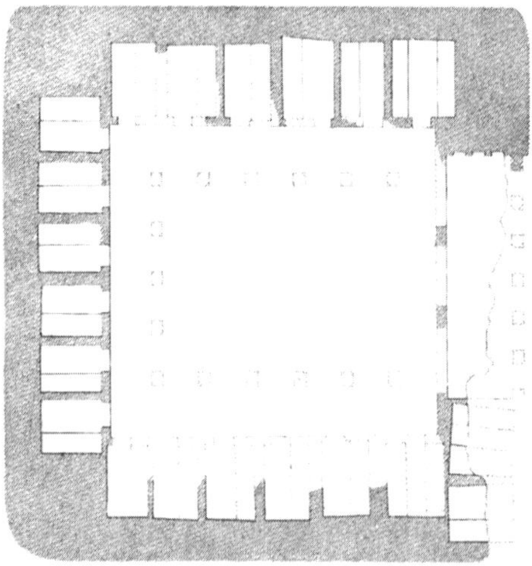

Scale of 10 0 10 20 30 40 feet.

3. PLAN OF CHAITYA.

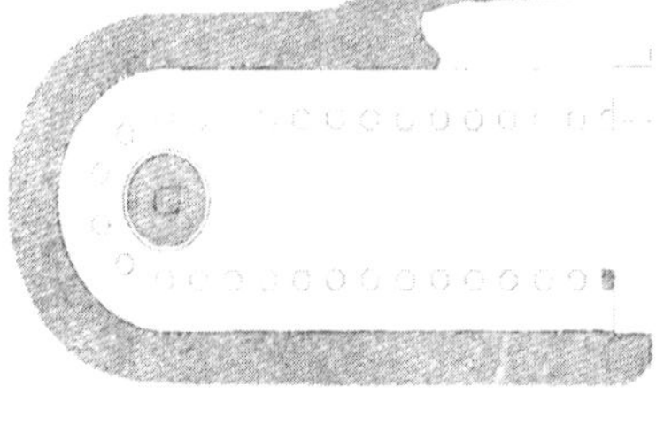

Scale of 10 0 10 20 30 40 50 feet.

J. Burgess. W. GRIGGS, PHOTO LITH. LONDON. S. E. Ganpat Purshotam del.

Plate. IX.

BHÂJÂ.

PLAN OF CAVES.

CHAITYA CAVE. SECTION.

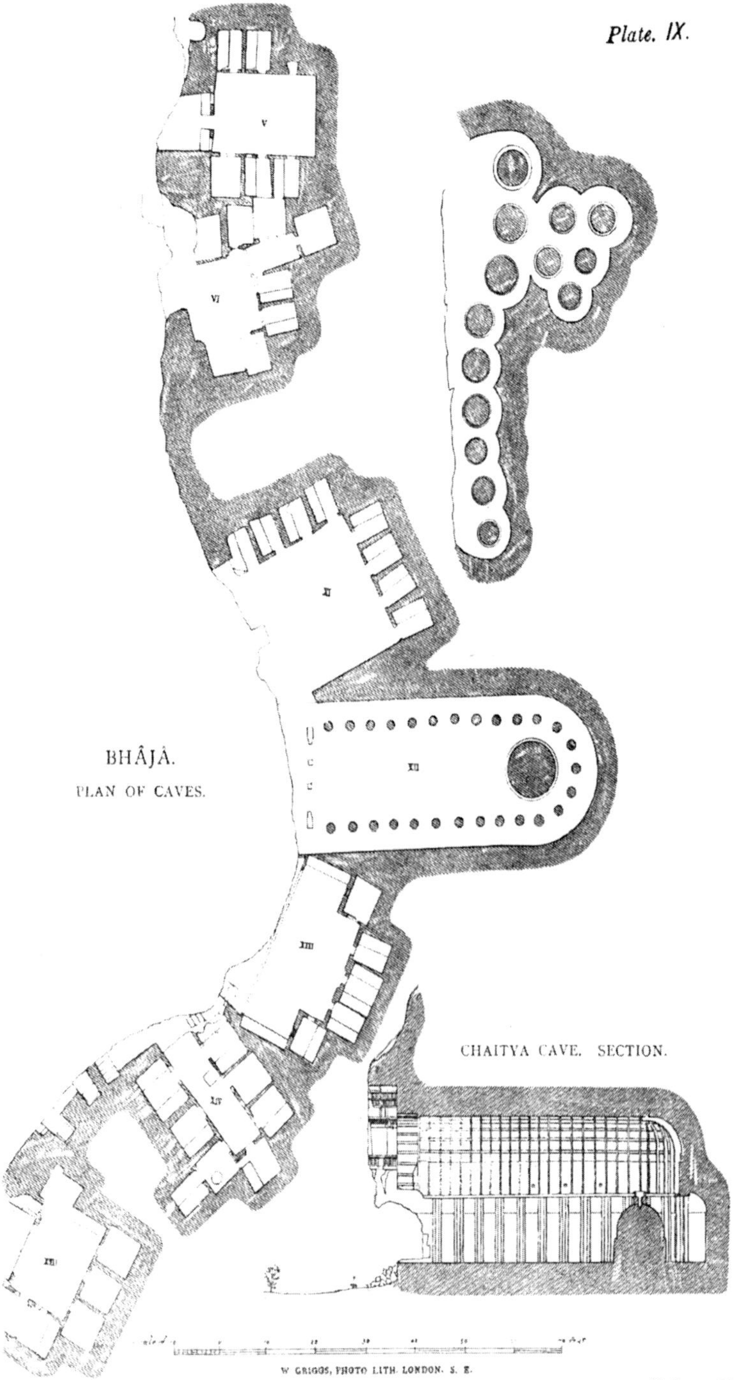

W GRIGGS, PHOTO LITH. LONDON. S. E.

H. Cousens del.

Plate X.

BEDSA.

VIHÂRA CAVE.

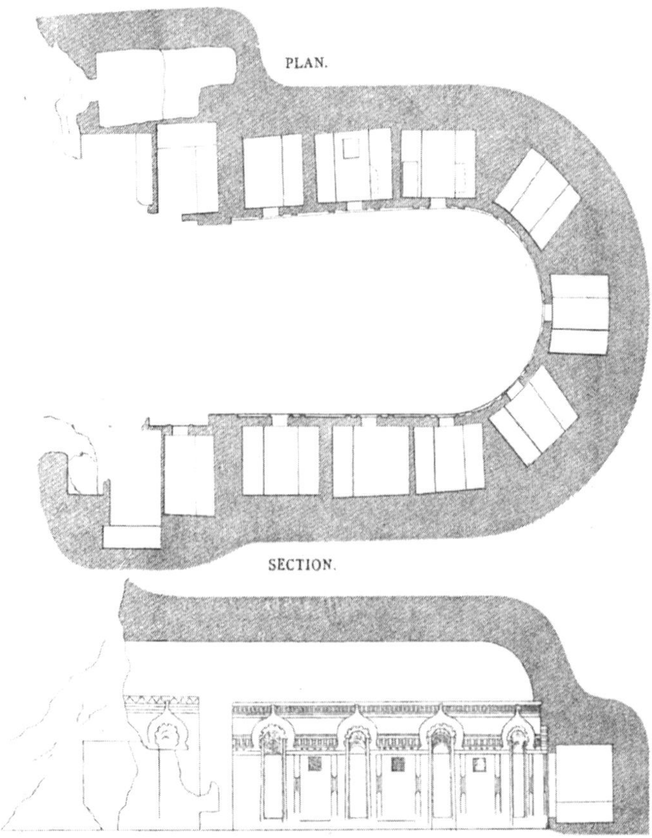

Scale of 10 — 20 feet.

W. GRIGGS, PHOTO LITH. LONDON, S. E.

H. Cousens del.

KARLE.

THE CHAITYA - LONGITUDINAL SECTION.

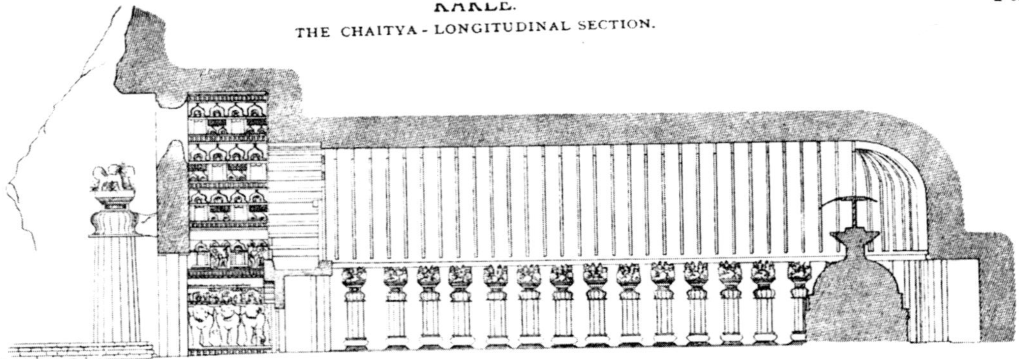

PLAN.

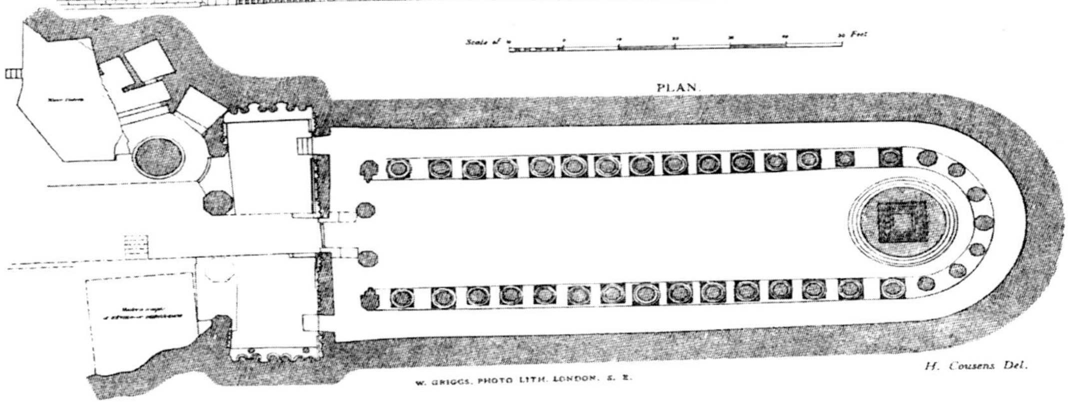

H. Cousens Del.

W. GRIGGS. PHOTO LITH. LONDON. S. E.

KARLÉ.

Plate XII.

CHAITYA CAVE. - PILLARS.

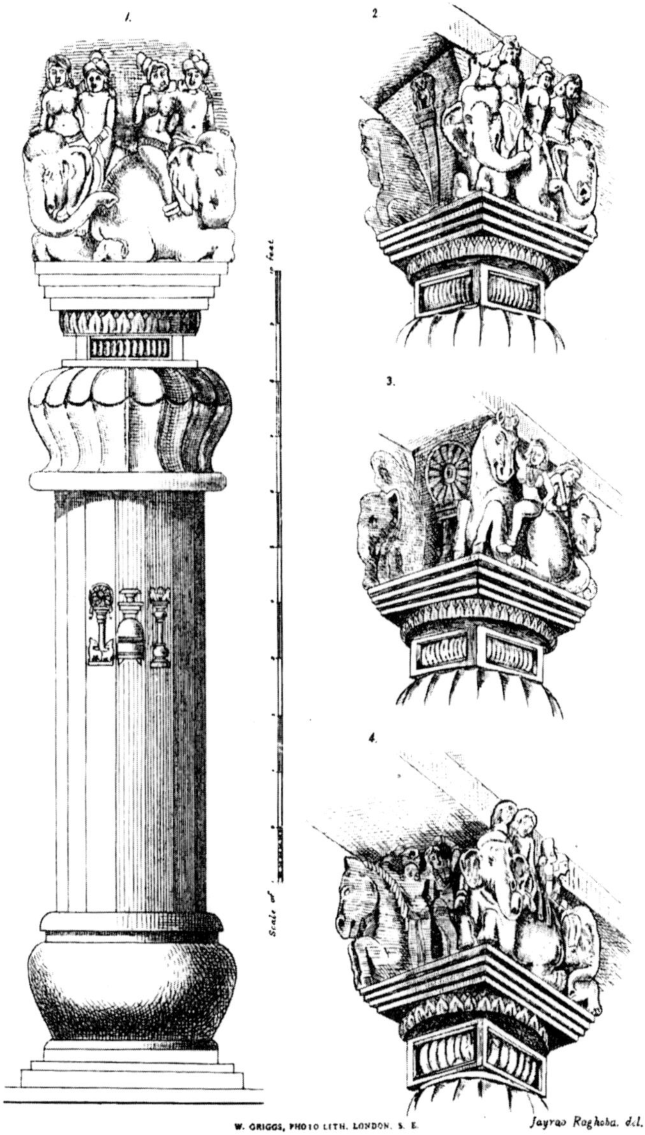

W. GRIGGS, PHOTO LITH. LONDON, S. E.

Jayrao Raghoba. del.

KÂRLÊ. **Plate. XIII.**

THE CHHATRA OR UMBRELLA.

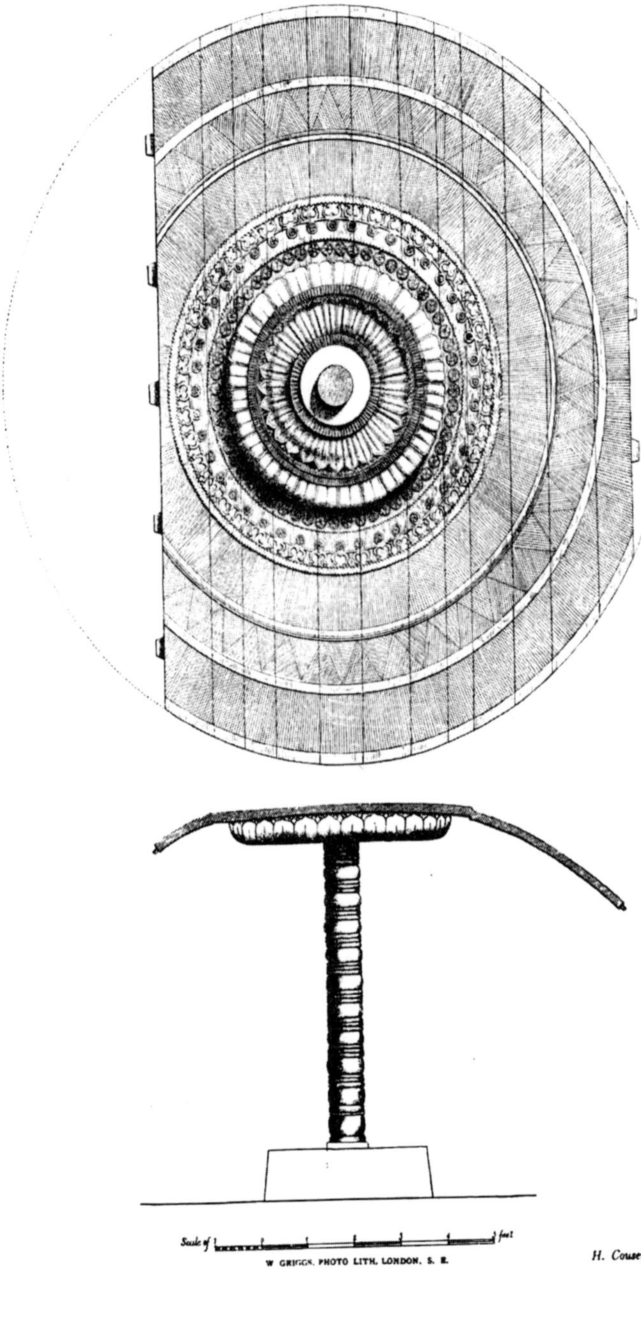

Scale of [1] feet

W. GRIGGS, PHOTO LITH, LONDON, S. E.

H. Cousens Del.

KÂRLE.

I. CHAITYA CAVE. - PART OF FRONT SCREEN. *Plate XIV.*

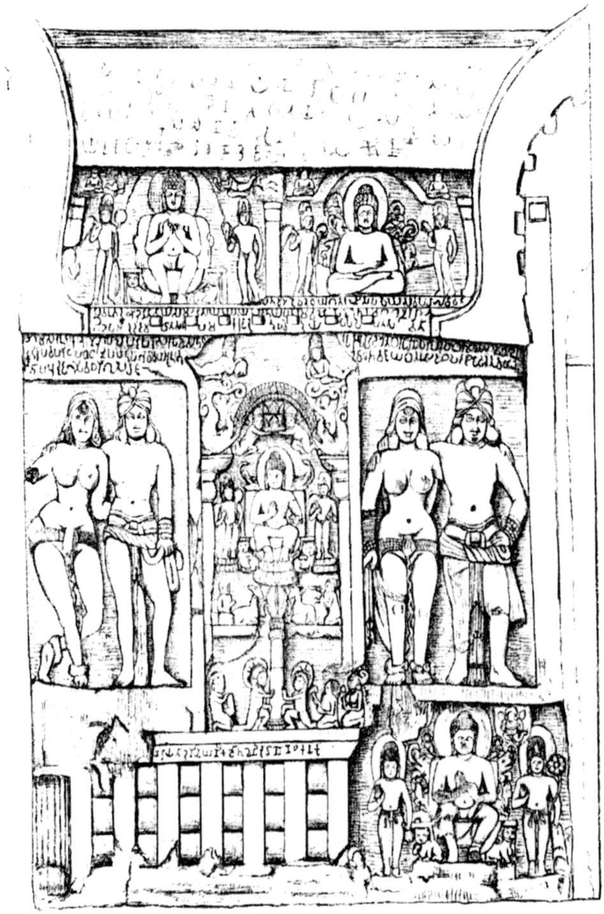

CAPITALS OF TWO PILLARS.

2. 3.

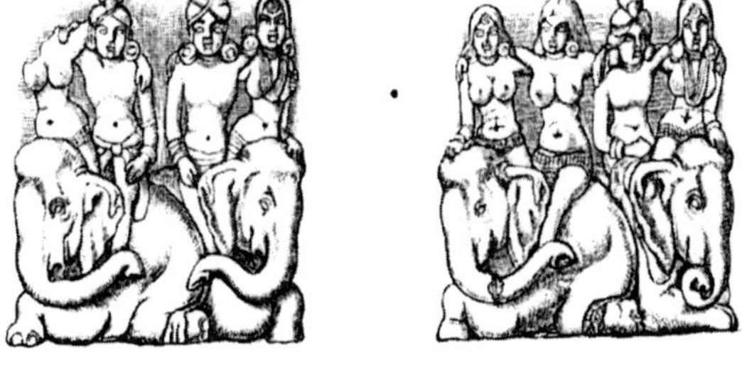

W. GRIGGS. PHOTO LITH. LONDON. S. E. *Jayrao Raghoba. del.*

1. SECTION OF THE CHAITYA CAVE.

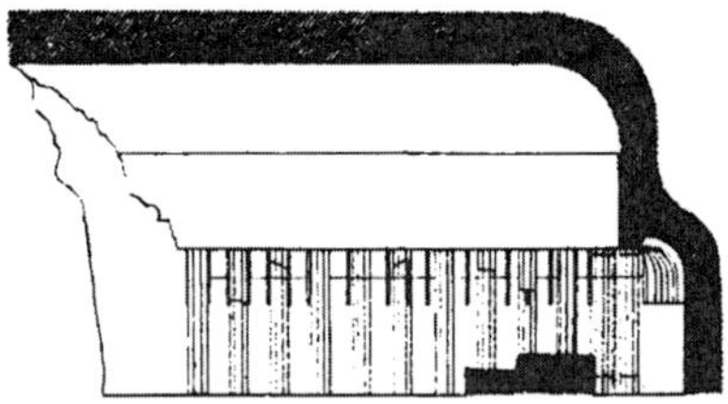

2. PLAN OF CHAITYA CAVE.

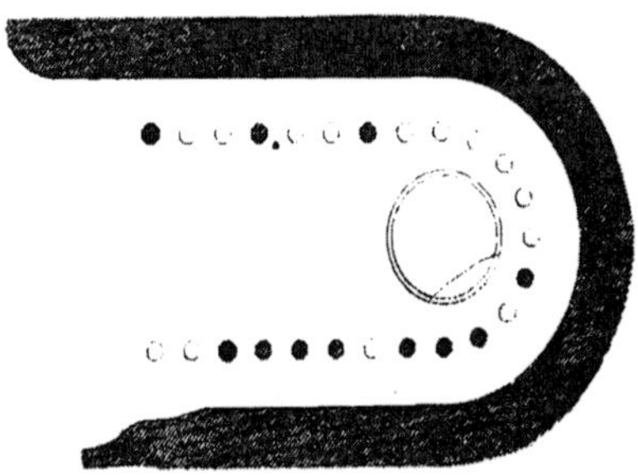

3. SECTION OF VIHÂRA.

4. PLAN OF VIHÂRA.

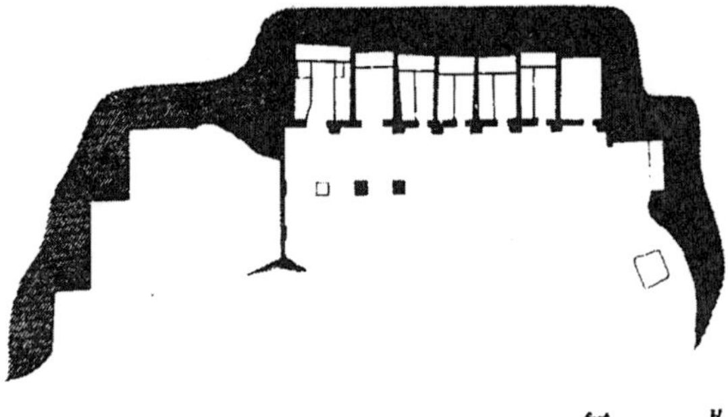

10 0 10 20 30 40 50 feet

H. Cousens del.

W. GRIGGS, PHOTO LITH. LONDON. S. E.

Plate XVI.

PITALKHORA.

CAPITALS FROM THE BUDDHIST VIHARA.

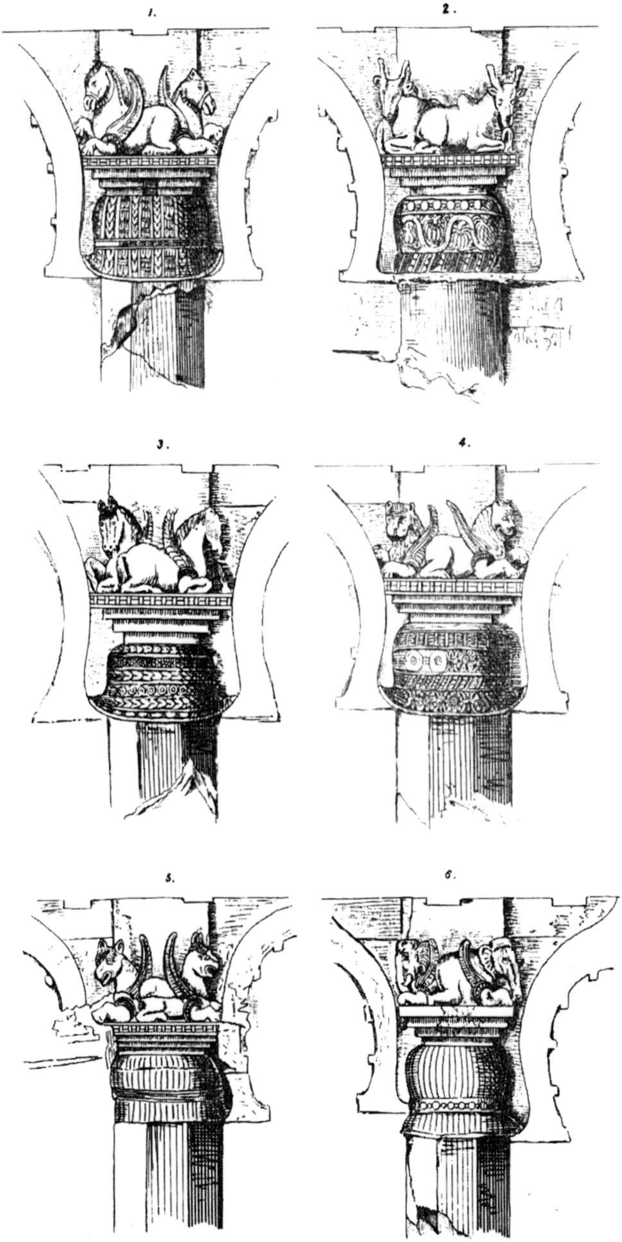

W. GRIGGS, PHOTO-LITH. LONDON, S. E. *Jayrao Raghoba del.*

Plate XVII.

1. SECTION OF CELL AT PITALKHORA.

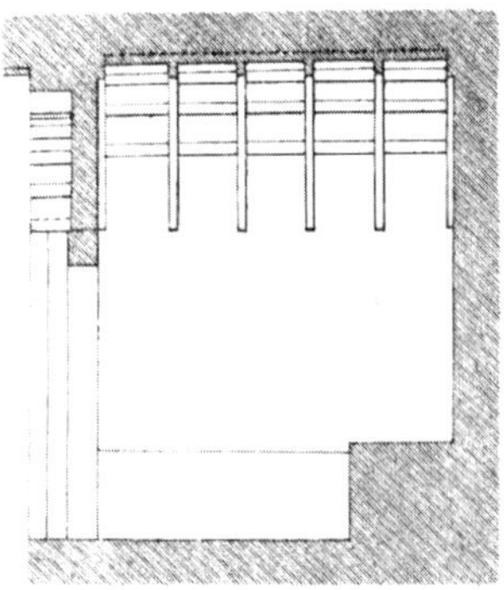

2. CROSS SECTION.

3. PLAN OF CELL.

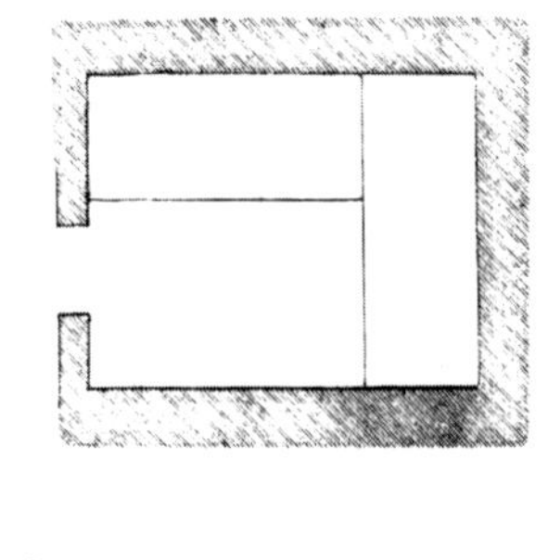

4. FRIEZE OF TULJA LENA, JUNNAR.

5. FAÇADE OF CELL AT MANMODI, JUNNAR.

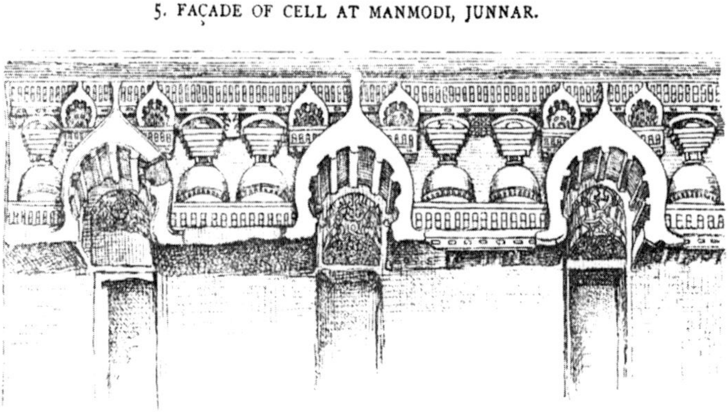

J. Burgess.

W. GRIGGS, PHOTO LITH. LONDON. S. E.

JUNNAR BUDDHIST CAVES. **Plate. XVIII.**

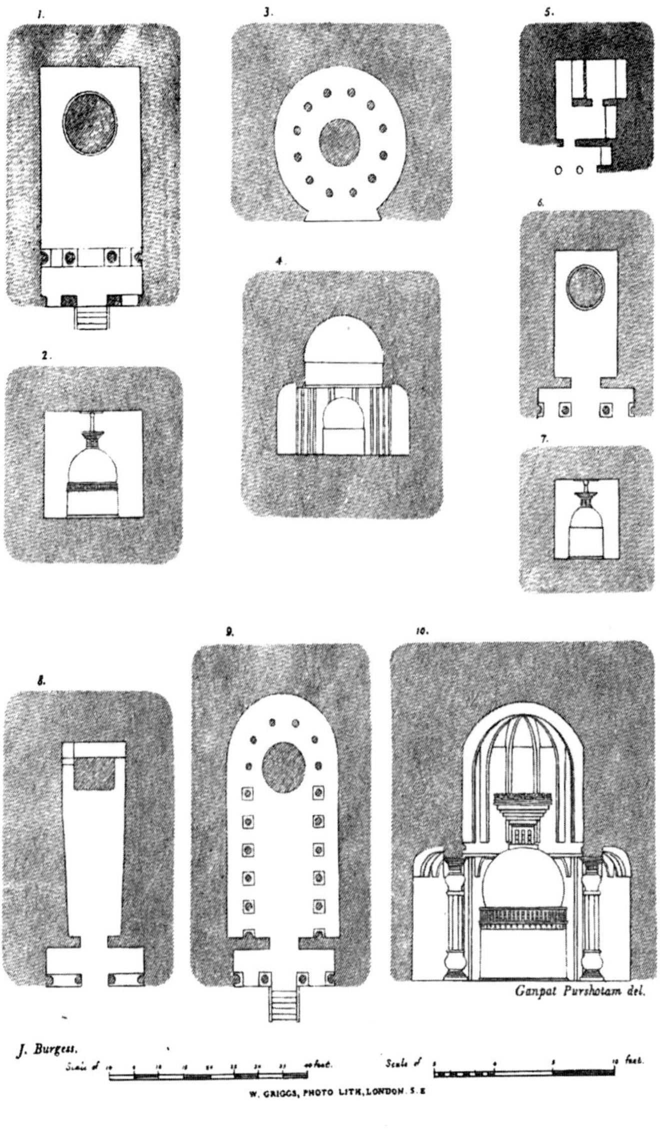

Ganpat Purshotam del.

J. Burgess.

W. GRIGGS, PHOTO LITH, LONDON. S.E

NASIK.

1. PLAN OF VIHÂRA, NO. III.

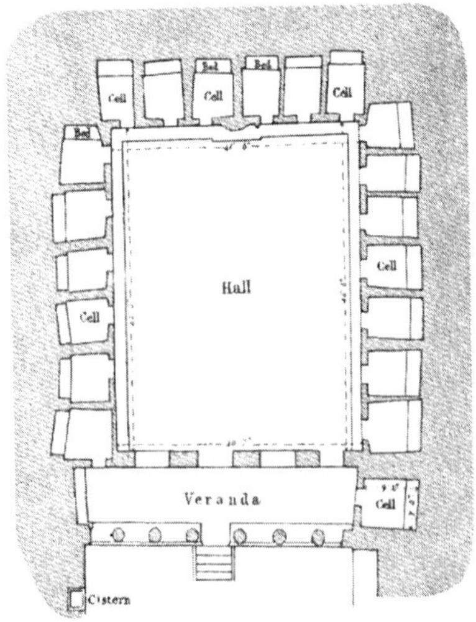

2. PLAN OF VIHÂRA, NO. VIII.

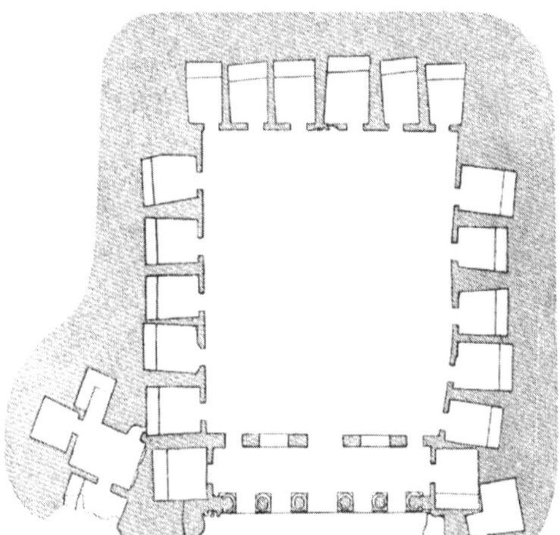

Scale of feet

J. Burgess.

W. GRIGGS, PHOTO LITH. LONDON. S. E.

Plate XX.

DOOR OF GAUTAMIPUTRA CAVE.

J. Burgess. C. M. Sykes Del.

Scale of 1 2 3 4 5 feet

W. GRIGGS. PHOTO-LITH. LONDON. S. E.

Plate. XXI.

NASIK.

1. PILASTER IN CAVE III.

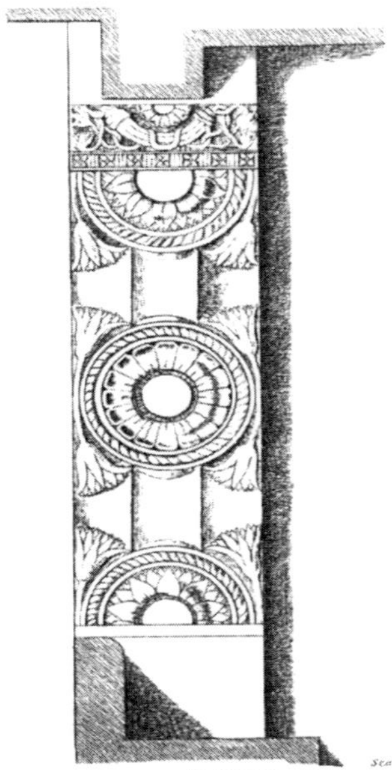

H. Cousens, del.

J. Burgess.

2. DÁGABA IN CAVE III.

scale of feet.

W. GRIGGS. PHOTO-LITH. LONDON. S. E.

3. PILLAR IN CAVE XV.

C. M. Sykes. del.

NASIK.

RIGHT HALF OF THE FRIEZE AND CAPITALS OF CAVE III.

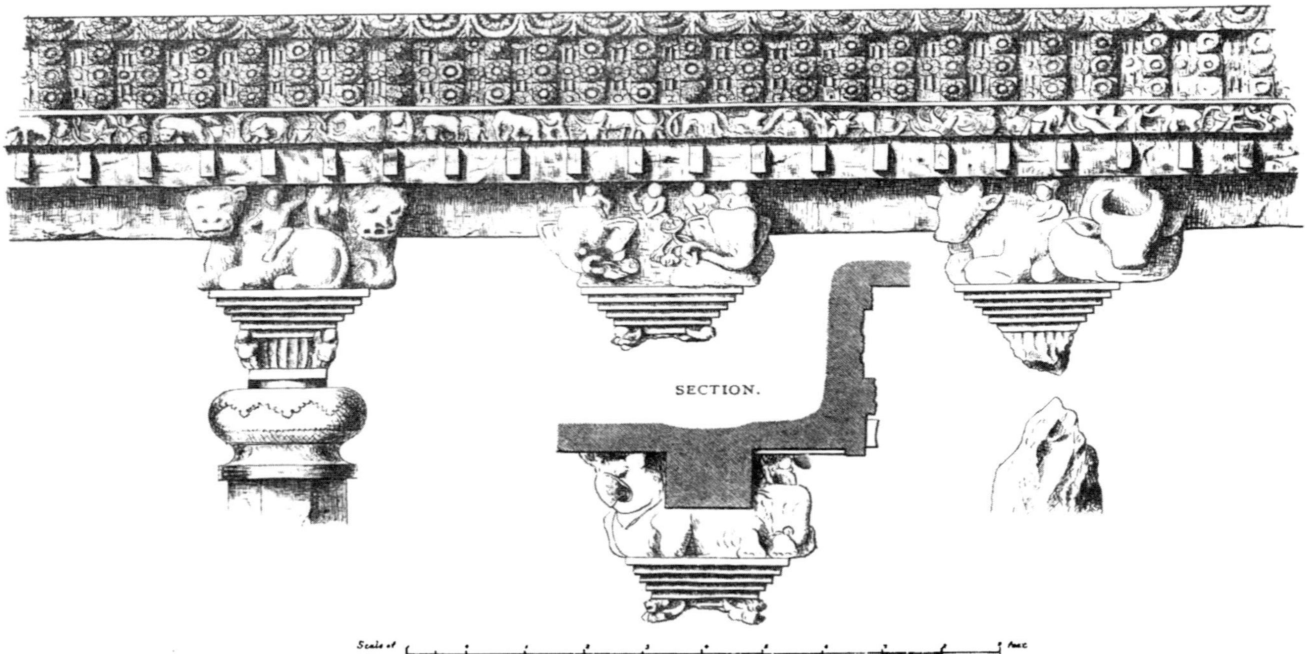

J. Burgess.

W. GRIGGS. PHOTO LITH. LONDON. S. E.

H. Cousens Del.

Plate XXIII.

1. FROM ŚAILARWADI CAVES.

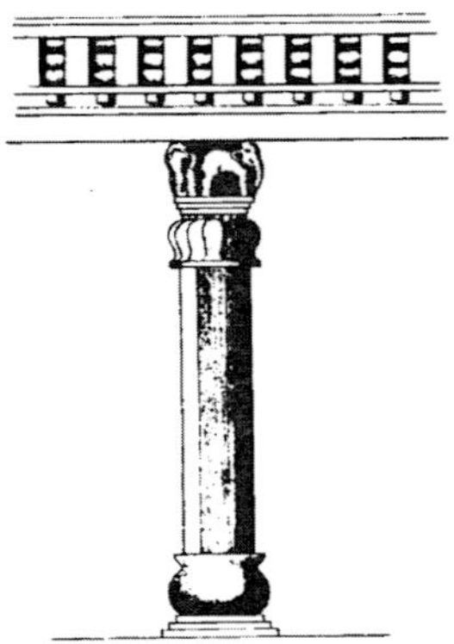

2. FROM BRAMCHANDRA CAVES

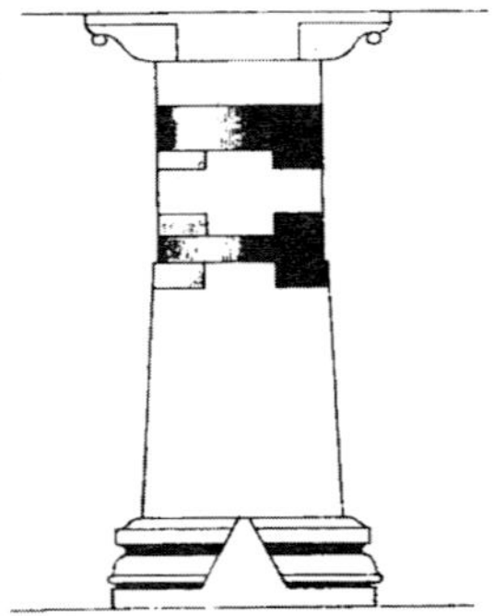

CAPITALS FROM CAVE VIII AT NASIK.

3.

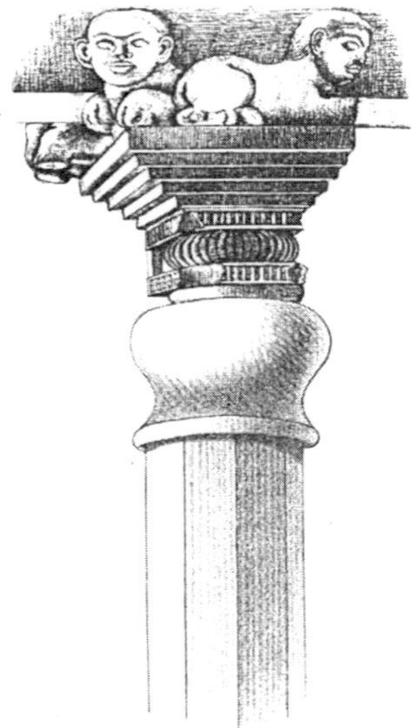

4.

J. Burgess.

W. GRIGGS, PHOTO LITH. LONDON. S. E.

Jayrao Raghoba. del.

Plate XXIV.

NÂSIK.

PANDU LENA CHAITYA CAVE-TEMPLE.

LONGITUDINAL SECTION.

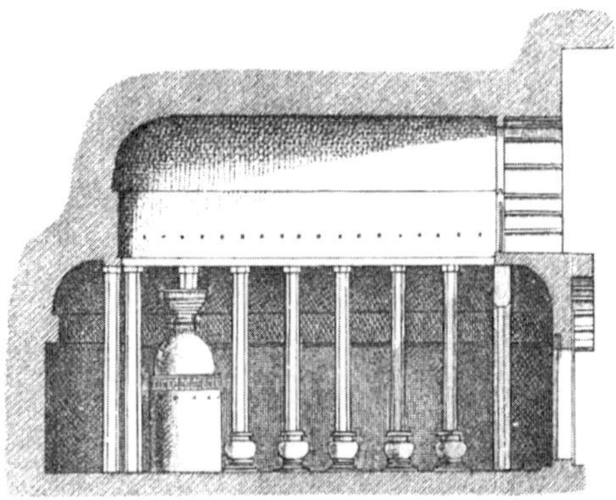

PLAN.

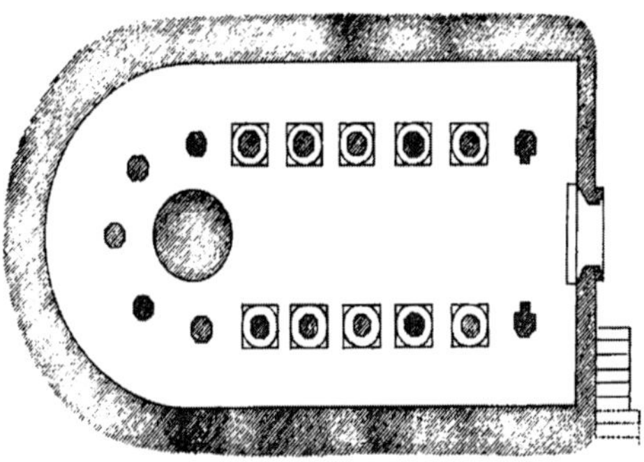

Scale of ... feet.

J. Burgess del.

W. GRIGGS, PHOTO LITH. LONDON. S. E.

NASIK.

DOOR IN CHAITYA CAVE.

J. Burgess. *C. M. Sykes del.*

W. GRIGGS, PHOTO LITH. LONDON, S. E.

Plate XXVI.

NASIK.

1. PLAN OF CAVE XV.

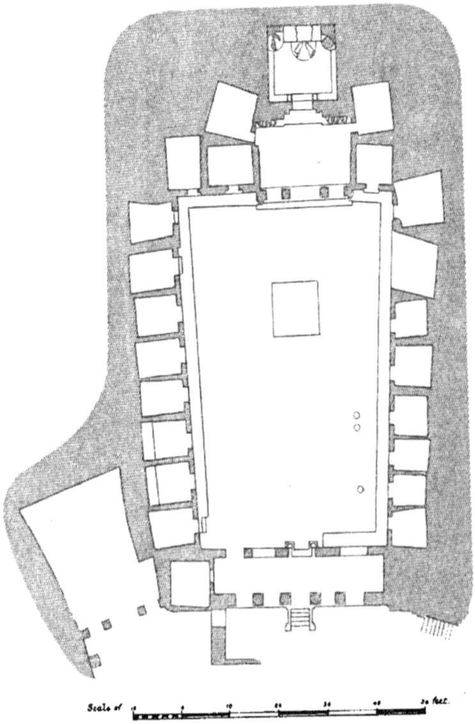

2. PLAN OF CAVE XIV.

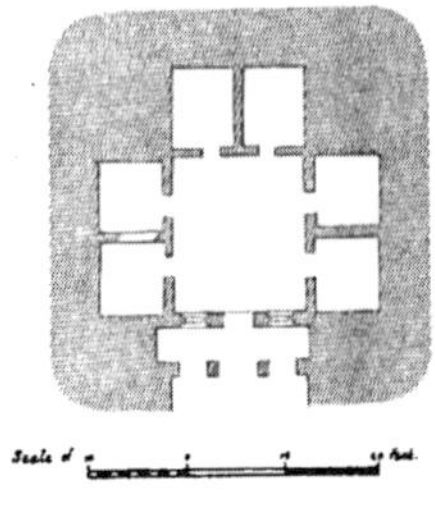

3. WALL ELEVATION IN CAVE XIV.

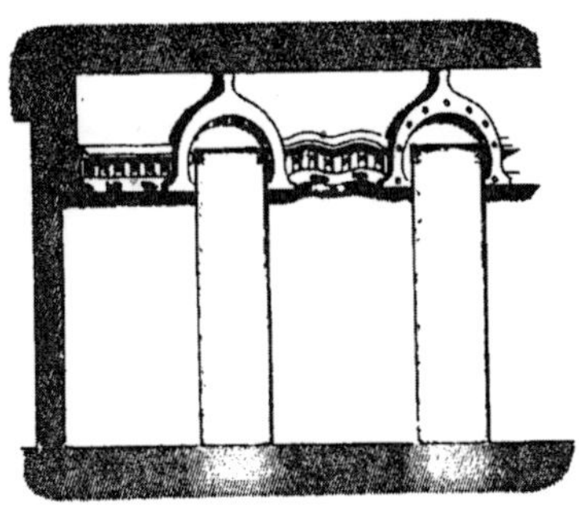

J. Burgess.

W. GRIGGS, PHOTO LITH. LONDON. S. E.

Plate. XXVII.

AJANTA.

VIHÂRA NO. XII.

SECTION.

PLAN.

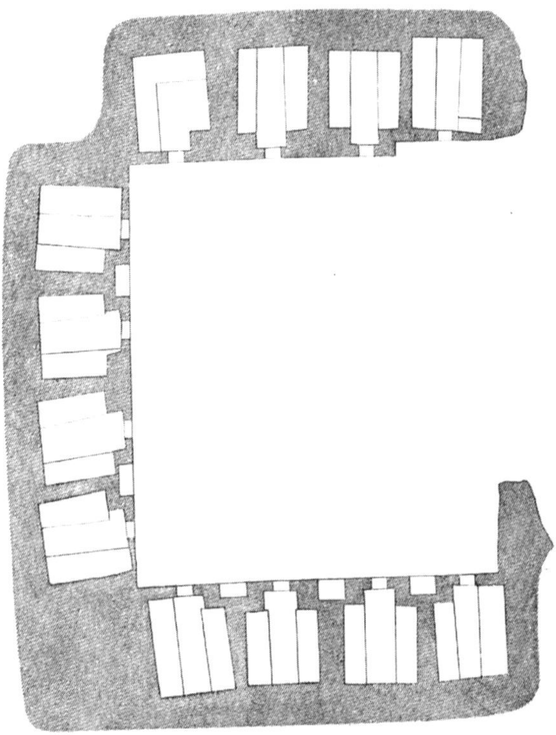

5 0 5 10 15 20 25 feet.

J. Burgess. W. GRIGGS, PHOTO LITH. LONDON, S. E. H. Cousens del.

Plate XXVIII.

AJANTA.

1. CHAITYA-CAVE. NO. X.—SECTION.

2. PLAN.

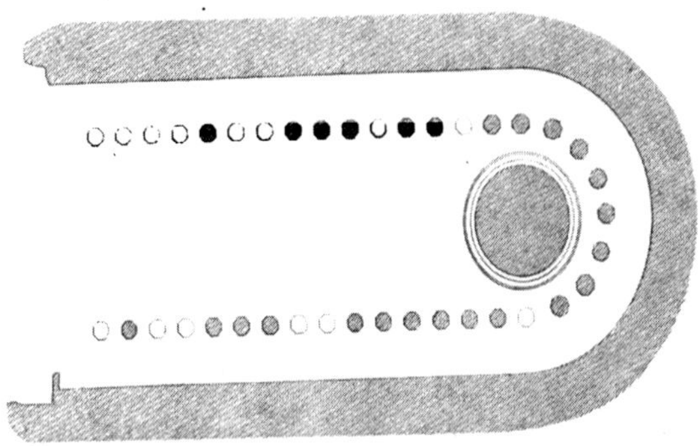

3. CHAITYA. NO. IX.—SECTION.

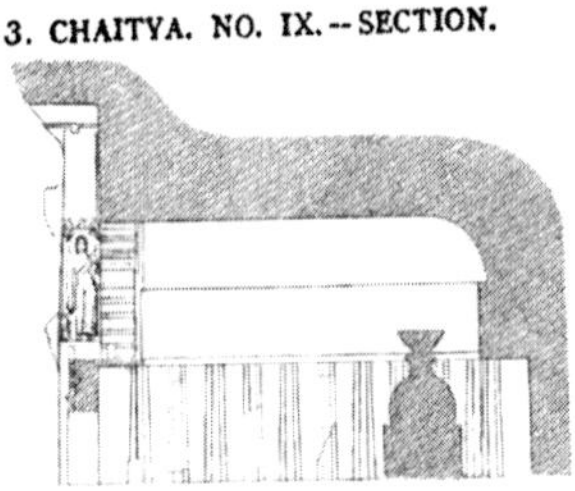

4. PLAN.

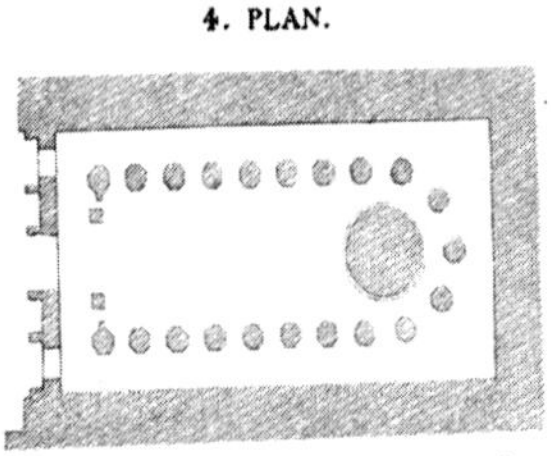

Scale of feet

J. Burgess. W. GRIGGS, PHOTO LITH. LONDON. S. E. Ganpat Purshotam del.

AJANTA. **Plate XXIX.**

FIGURES FROM THE EARLIEST PAINTINGS IN CAVE X.

J. Burgess. *Jayrao Raghoba, del*

W. GRIGGS, PHOTO-LITH. LONDON, S. E.

AJANTA.

Plate XXX.

1. PILLAR IN CAVE XI.

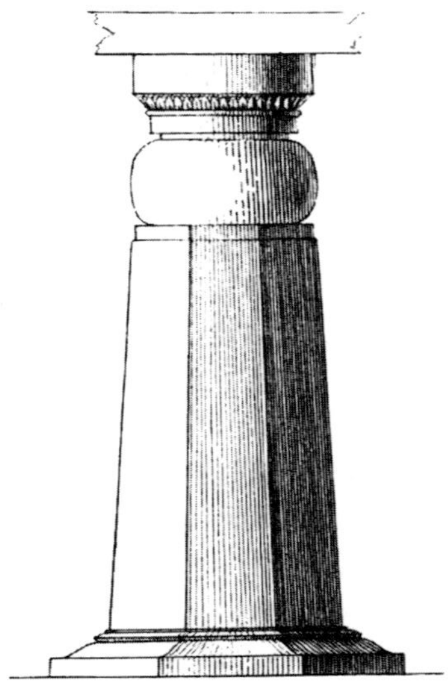

2. CAVE VI. SHRINE DOOR IN LOWER STOREY.

Scale of feet

J. Burgess.

H. Cousens del.

W. GRIGGS, PHOTO LITH. LONDON. S. E.

AJANTA. Plate XXXI.

SCULPTURE ON THE LEFT SIDE OF THE ANTECHAMBER, CAVE VII.

J. Burgess. S. J. Pacheco del.

W. GRIGGS, PHOTO-LITH. LONDON. S. E.

AJANTA: CAVE VI.

Plate XXXII.

UPPER STOREY.

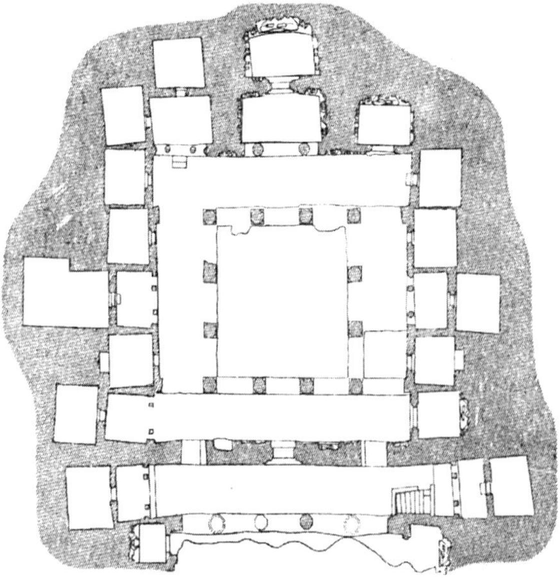

LOWER STOREY.

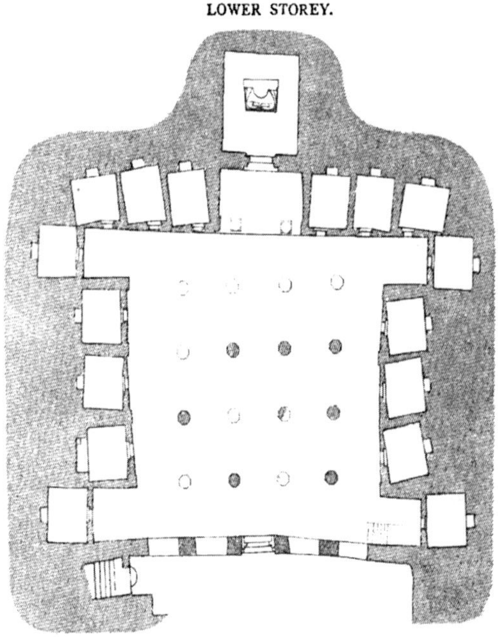

J. Burgess. W. GRIGGS, PHOTO LITH. LONDON. S. E. *Ganpat Purshotam del.*

Plate XXXIII.

AJANTA.

1. PLAN OF CAVE XVI.

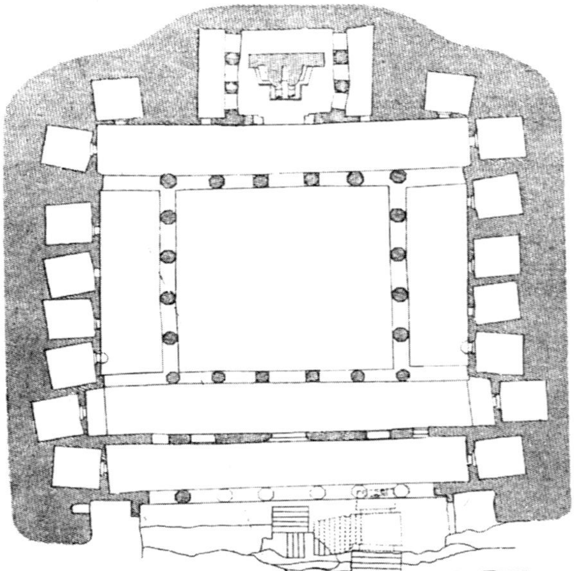

2. PLAN OF CAVE XVII.

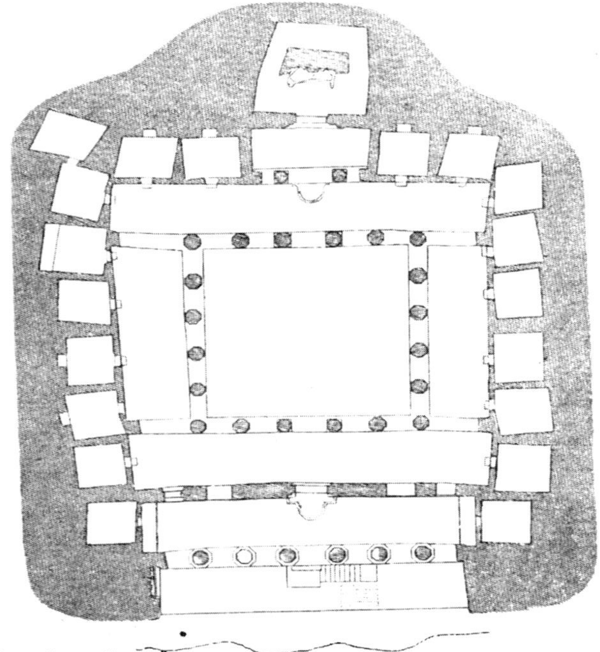

J. Burgess.

W. GRIGGS, PHOTO LITH. LONDON, S. E.

Ganpat Purshotam del.

AJANTA: CAVE XVII.

1. LEFT CENTRE PILLAR IN FRONT AISLE

2. LEFT PILASTER IN THE VERANDAH.

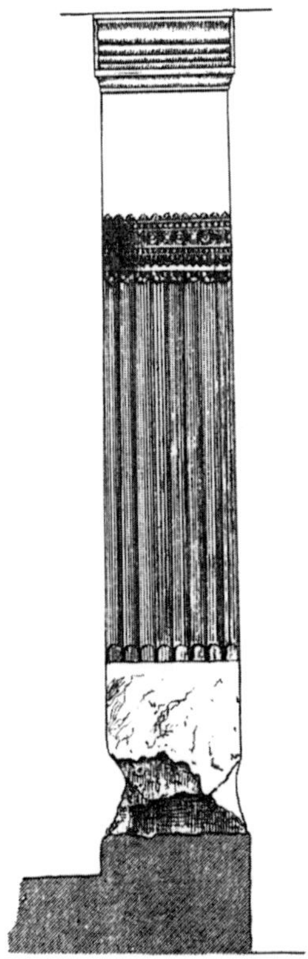

Scale of [illegible] *feet*

J. Burgess. W. GRIGGS, PHOTO LITH. LONDON. S. E. *S. J. Pacheco del.*

Plate. XXXV.

AJANTA: CAVE XVII.

1. IMAGE IN THE SHRINE.

2. PILLAR OF THE HALL.

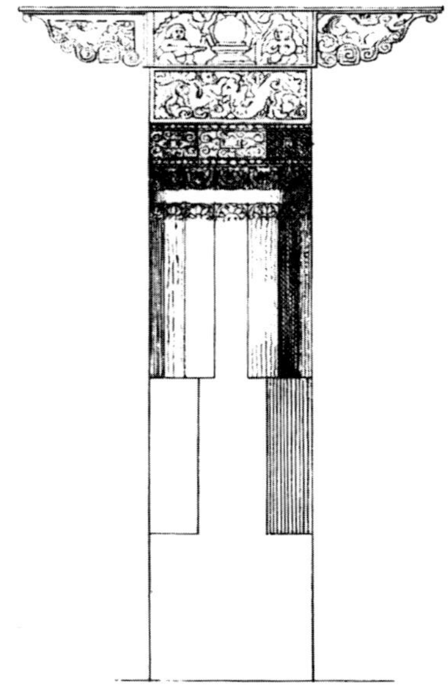

J. Burgess.

W. GRIGGS, PHOTO LITH. LONDON. S. E.

S. J. Pacheco del.

Plate XXXVI.

AJANTA.

LONGITUDINAL SECTION CAVE XIX.

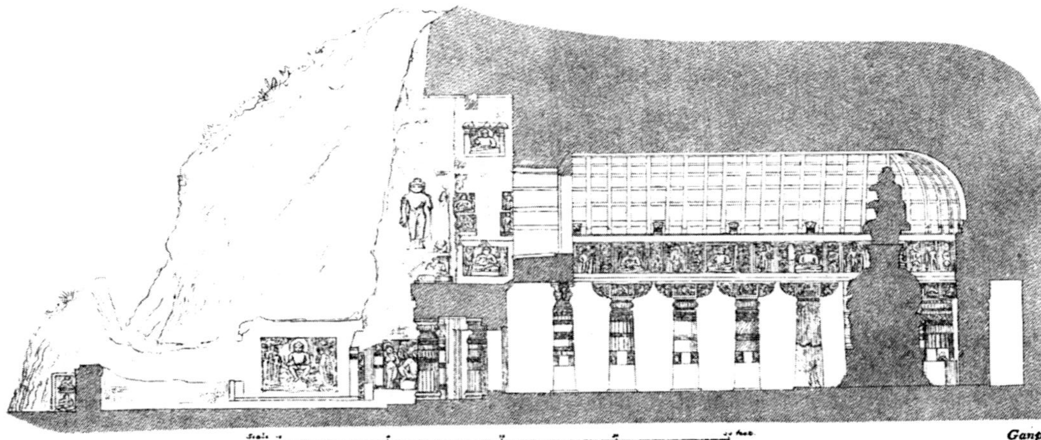

J. Burgess. Ganpat Purshotam del.

W. GRIGGS, PHOTO LITH. LONDON. S. E.

AJANTA.

CHAITYA CAVE NO. XIX.

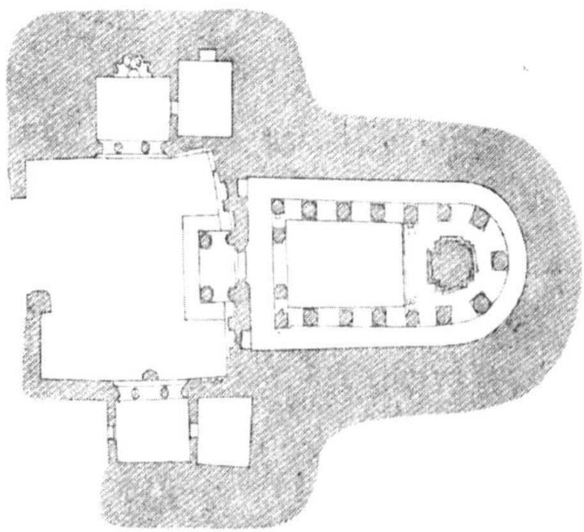

CHAITYA CAVE NO. XXVI.

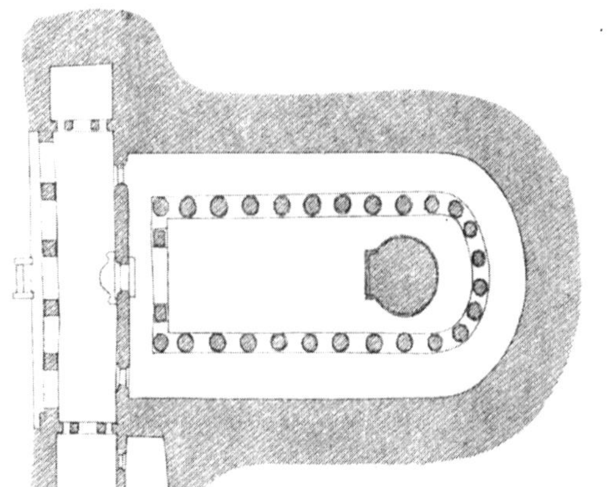

J. Burgess.

W. GRIGGS, PHOTO LITH. LONDON. S. E.

Ganpat Purshotam del.

Plate XXXVIII.

AJANTA.

1. DAGOBA IN CAVE XXVI.

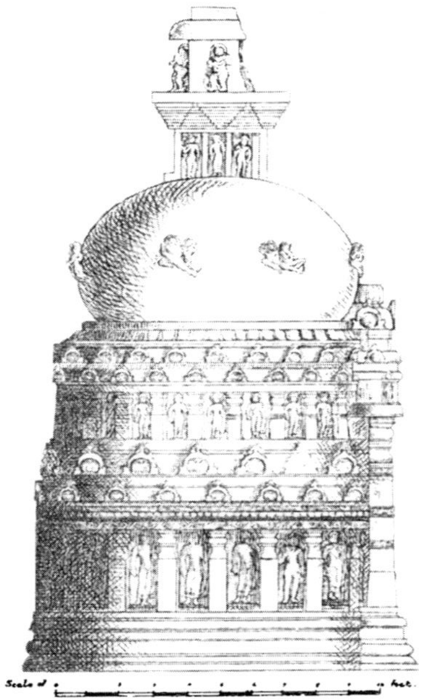

2. PILLAR IN NO. XIX.

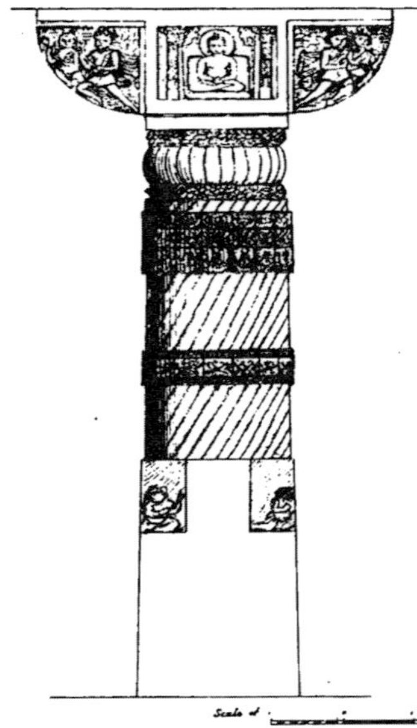

3. PILLAR IN CAVE I.

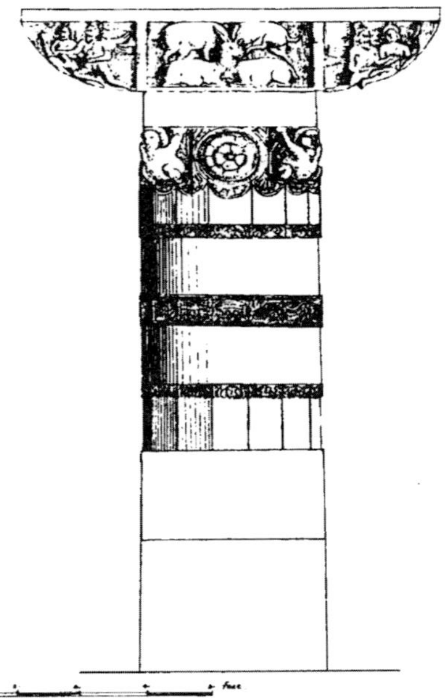

J. Burgess.

W. GRIGGS, PHOTO LITH. LONDON. S. E.

Plate XXXIX.

AJANTA. CAVE XIX.

NÂGA RÂJA.

J. Burgess.

W. GRIGGS, PHOTO LITH. LONDON. S. E.

Plate XL.

AJANTA.

CAVE I.

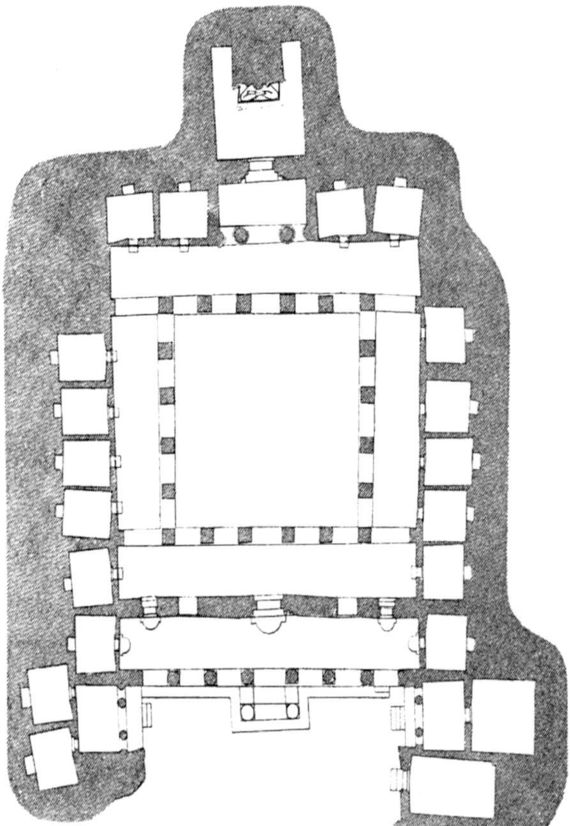

Scale of feet

J. Burgess. W. GRIGGS, PHOTO LITH. LONDON. S. E. Ganpat Purshotam del.

Plate XLI.

AJANTA.

FRIEZE OVER THE FRONT OF CAVE I.

J. Burgess.

H. Cousens Del.

W. GRIGGS, PHOTO-LITH. LONDON. S. E.

Plate XLII.

AJANTA.

1. SHRINE DOOR IN CAVE I.

Scale of [illegible] feet

W. GRIGGS, PHOTO LITH. LONDON, S. E.

2. PILLAR IN THE HALL OF CAVE I.

Jayrao Raghoba. del.

AJANTA.

WALL PAINTING IN CAVE I.

J. Burgess. W. GRIGGS, PHOTO LITH. LONDON, S. E. Jayrao Raghoba. H. Cousens } Del.

AJANTA.

I. PAINTED PANEL FROM CEILING OF CAVE I.

2. PLAN OF CAVE II.

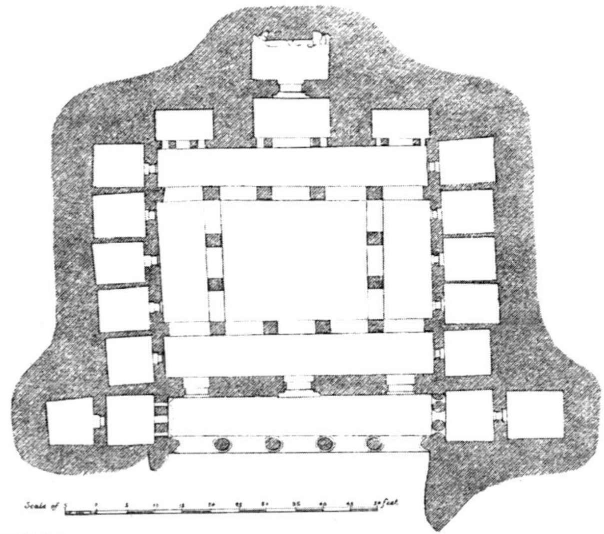

J. Burgess.

W. GRIGGS, PHOTO LITH. LONDON. S. E.

AJANTA.

CAVE II.

Plate XLV.

1. SHRINE DOOR.

2. PILLAR IN ANTECHAMBER.

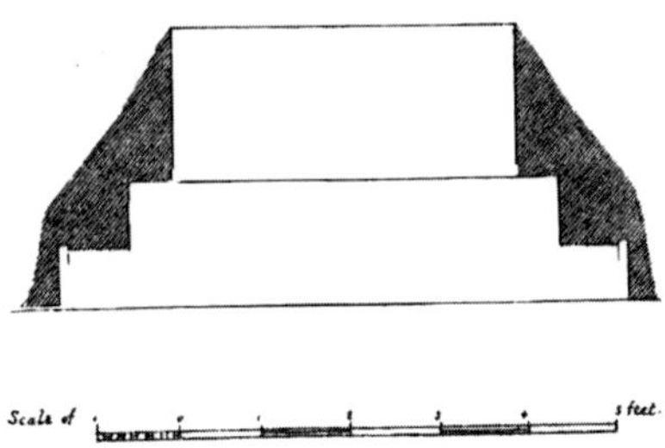

3. BRACKET IN CAVE XVI.

J. Burgess. W. GRIGGS, PHOTO LITH. LONDON. S. E. *S. J. Pacheco del.*

AJANTA.

PLAN OF CAVE IV.

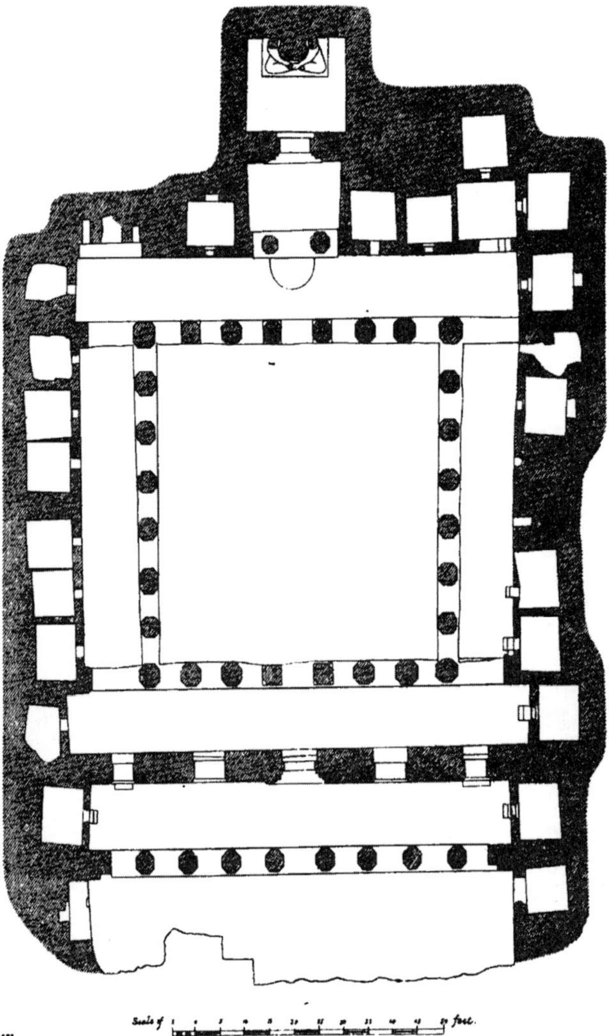

J. Burgess.

Scale of feet.

W. GRIGGS, PHOTO LITH. LONDON, S. E.

Plate XLVII.

AJANTA: CAVE IV.

HALL DOOR.

J. Burgess.

S. J. Pacheco del.

Scale of ... feet

W GRIGGS, PHOTO LITH. LONDON, S. E.

Plate. XLVIII.

AJANTA: CAVE IV.

1. LEFT CENTRE PILLAR IN BACK AISLE. 2. SIDE VIEW

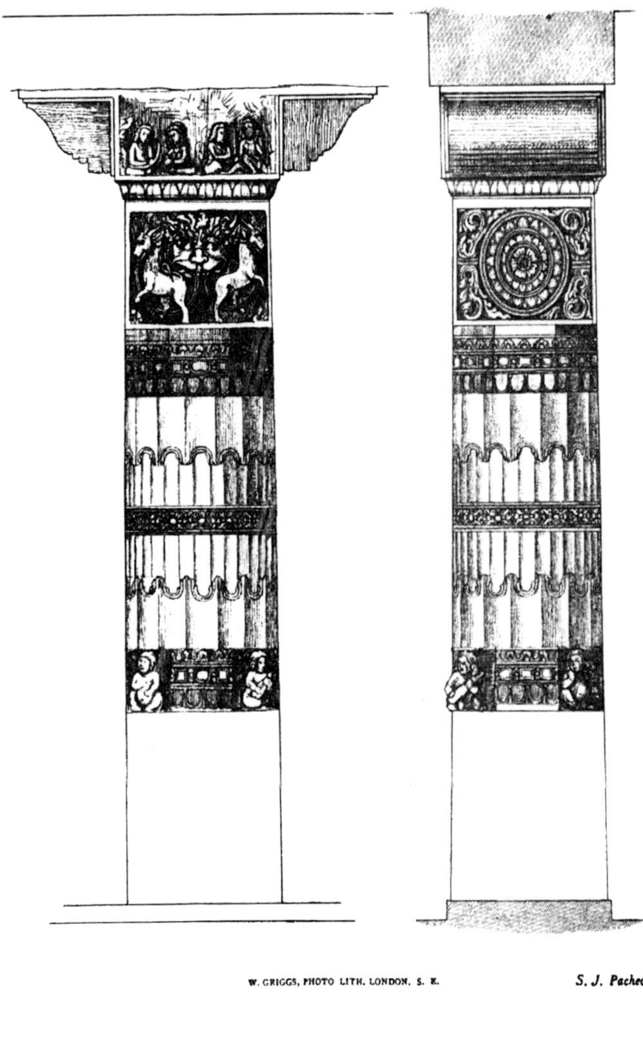

W. GRIGGS, PHOTO LITH. LONDON, S. E. S. J. Pacheco del.

Plate XLIX.

1. CHAPEL IN LEFT AISLE OF CAVE XXI.

2. PILASTER IN LEFT AISLE.

3. PILASTER IN VERANDAH OF CAVE VI.

Scale of feet.

J. Burgess. W. GRIGGS, PHOTO LITH. LONDON. S. E. Jayrao Raghoba. del.

AJANTA.

NIRVÂṆA OF BUDDHA. ON THE LEFT WALL OF CAVE XXVI.

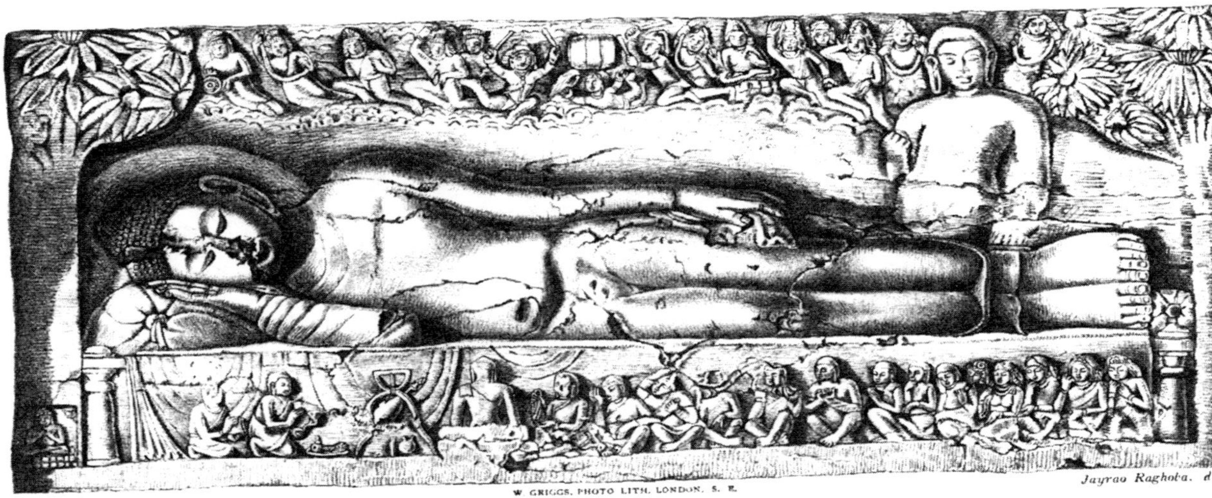

Jayrao Raghoba. del.

W. GRIGGS, PHOTO LITH. LONDON. S. E.

Scale of 12 feet

AJANTA.

TEMPTATION OF BUDDHA. CAVE XXVI.

J. Burgess. W. GRIGGS, PHOTO LITH. LONDON, S. E. *Jayrao Raghoba, del.*

Plate LII.

VIHÂRA AT GHATOTKACH.

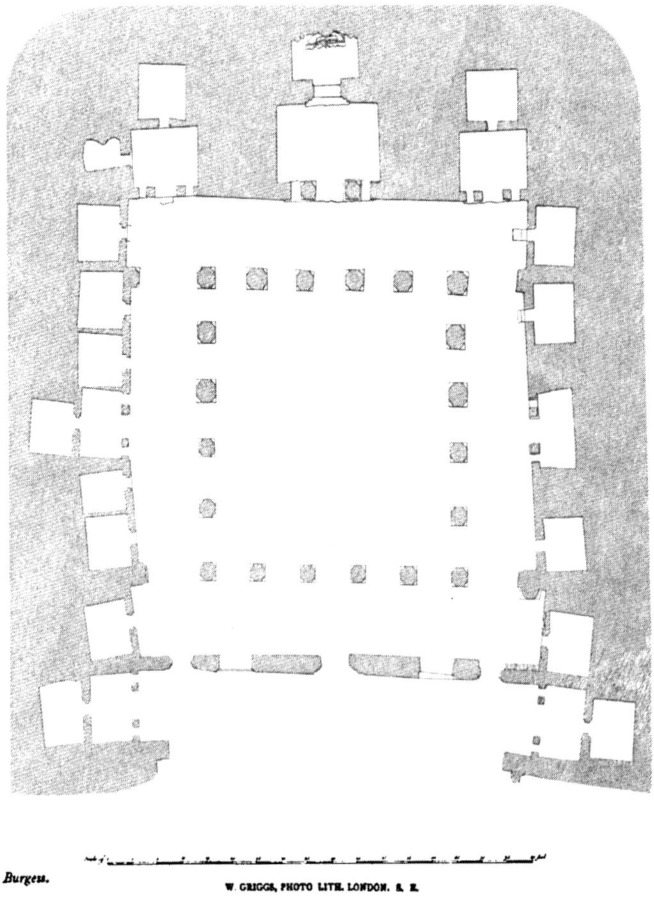

J. Burgess.

W. GRIGGS, PHOTO LITH. LONDON. S. E.

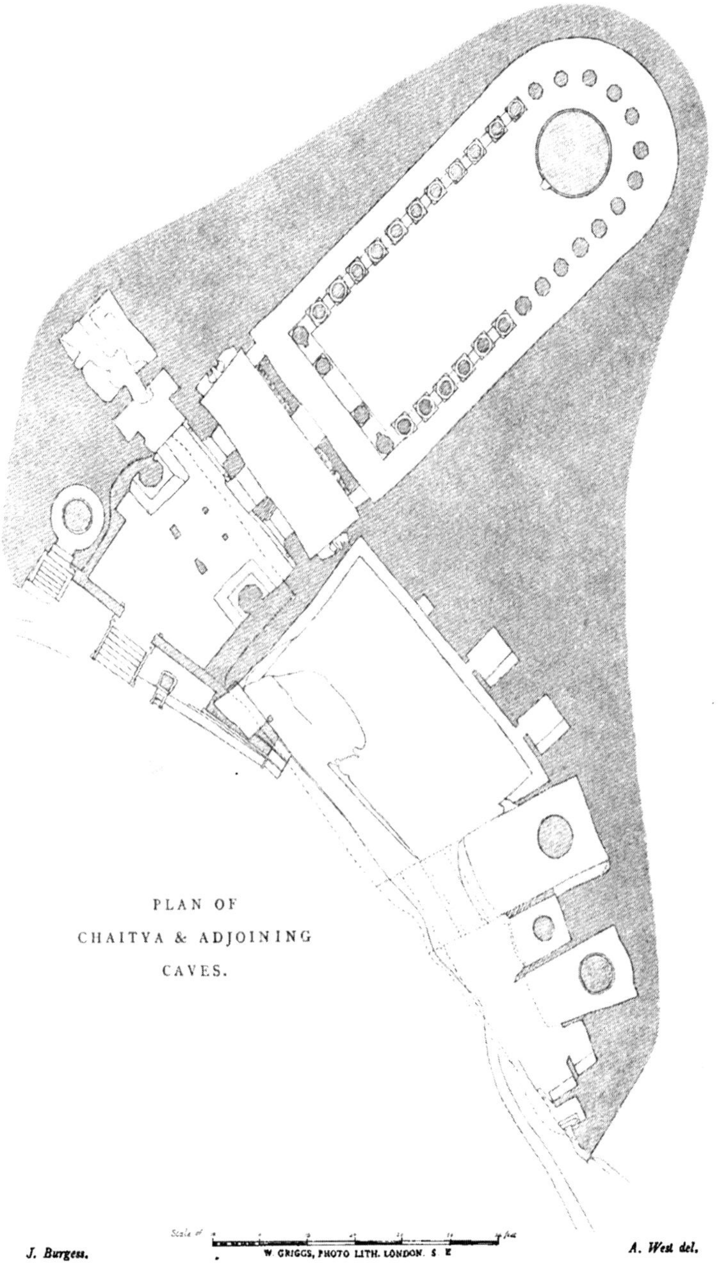

PLAN OF
CHAITYA & ADJOINING
CAVES.

J. Burgess. *A. West del.*

W. GRIGGS, PHOTO LITH. LONDON. S. E.

Plate LIV.

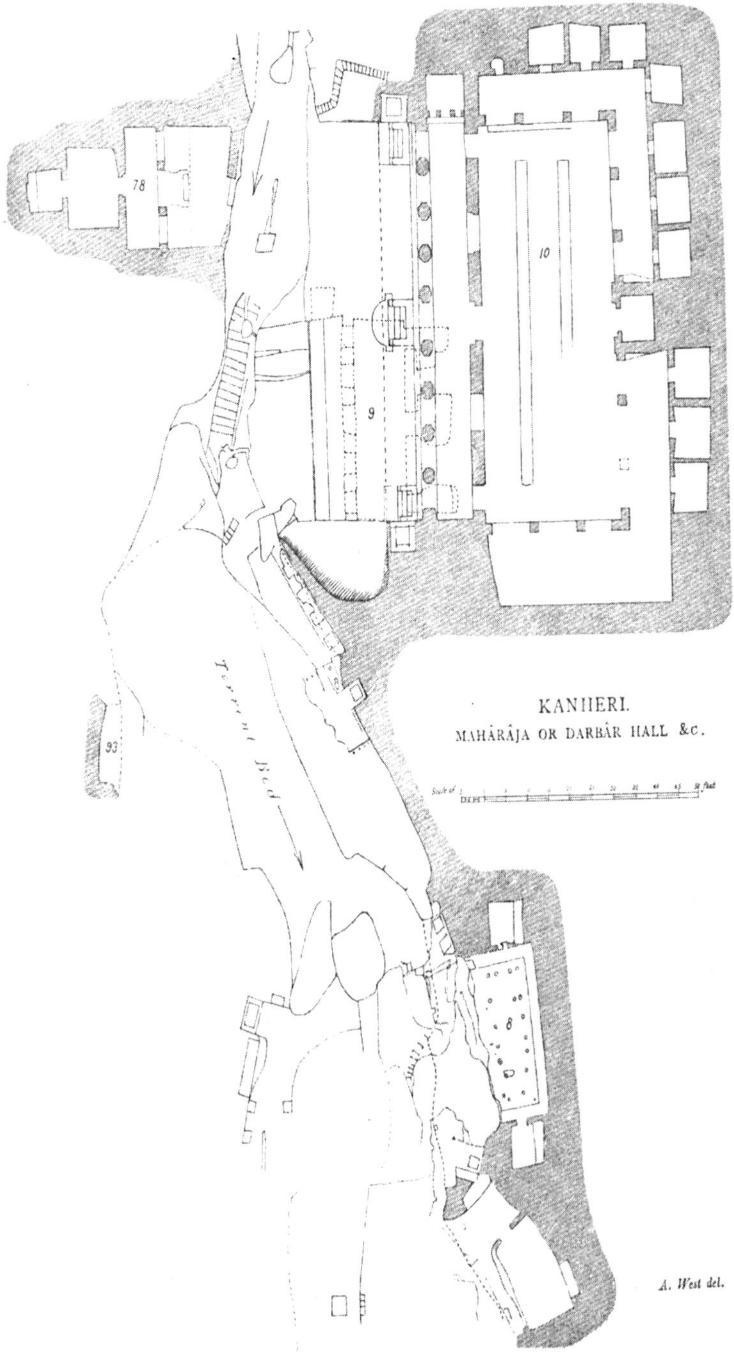

KANHERI.

MAHÂRÂJA OR DARBÂR HALL &c.

A. West del.

KANHERI.

1. BUDDHIST LITANY.

2. AVALOKITEŚWARA.

J. Burgess.

W. GRIGGS, PHOTO-LITH. LONDON. S. E.

Jayrao Raghoba del.

Plate LVI.

KANHERI.

BUDDHA ON PADMASANA WITH ATTENDANTS.

J. Burgess. W. GRIGGS, PHOTO LITH. LONDON, S. E. S. J. Pacheco del.

ELURÂ.

NORTHERN GROUP OF BUDDHIST CAVES.

Plate LVII.

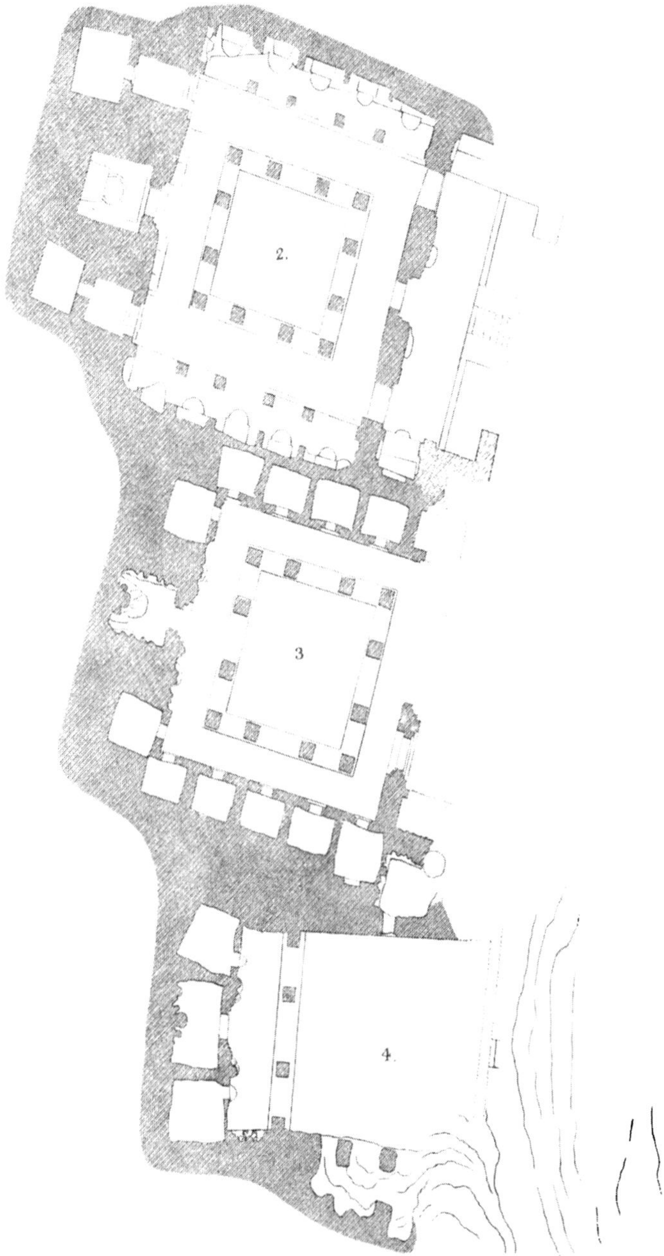

J. Burgess.

W. GRIGGS, PHOTO LITH. LONDON, S. E.

Ganpat Purshotam del.

ELURÂ.

1. PILLAR IN DHÊRWÂRÂ CAVE.

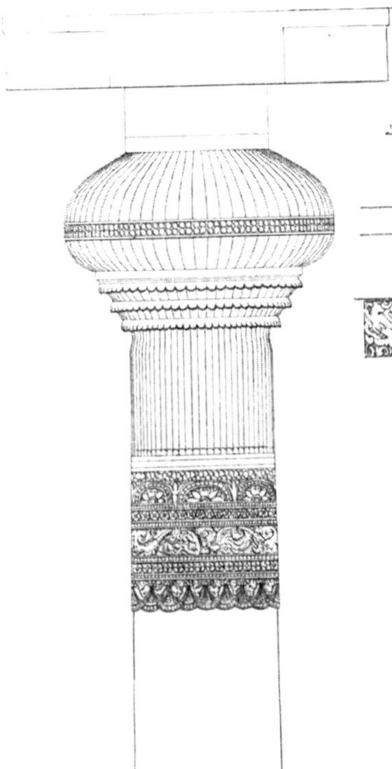

2. PILLAR AT THE ENTRANCE OF THE TÎN THÂL.

Scale of 1 0 1 2 3 4 feet

J. Burgess. C. M. Sykes del.

W. GRIGGS. PHOTO LITH. LONDON. S. E.

ELURÂ.

MAHARWAṚA BUDDHIST CAVE.

Plate LIX.

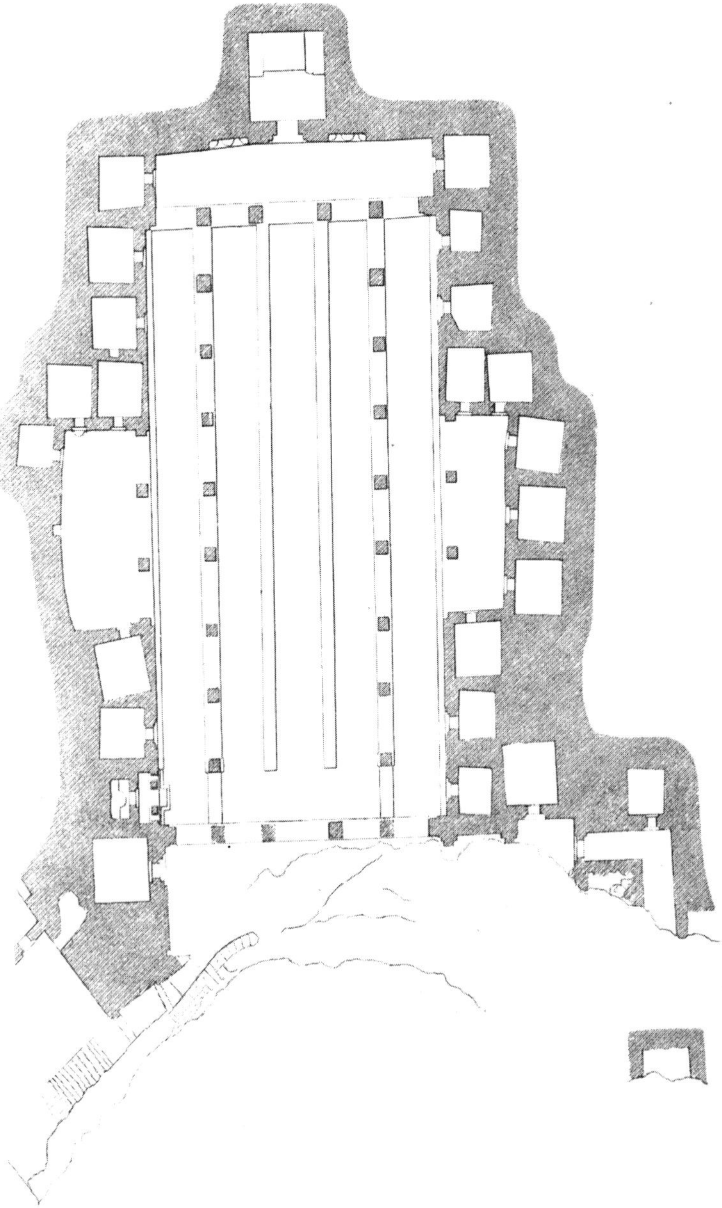

J Burgess.

Ganpat Purshotam del.

Scale of 10 0 10 20 30 40 50 feet.

W. GRIGGS, PHOTO LITH. LONDON, S.E.

ELURÂ.

BUDDHIST CAVES.

Plate LX.

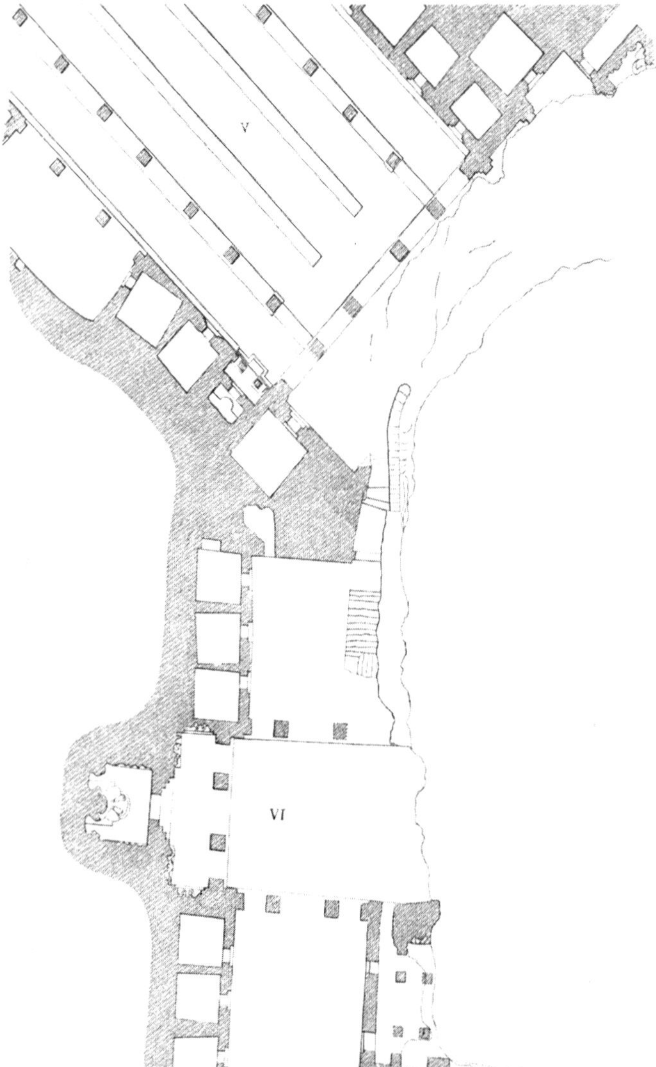

J. Burgess. H. Cousens del.

W. GRIGGS, PHOTO LITH LONDON. S. E.

ELURÂ.

FRONT OF THE SHRINE IN BUDDHIST CAVE NO. VI.

Plate LXI.

J. Burgess.

Scale of ... feet

W. GRIGGS, PHOTO LITH, LONDON. S. E.

Jayrao Raghoba. del.

ELURÂ. *Plate. LXII.*

VISWAKARMA CHAITYA CAVE.

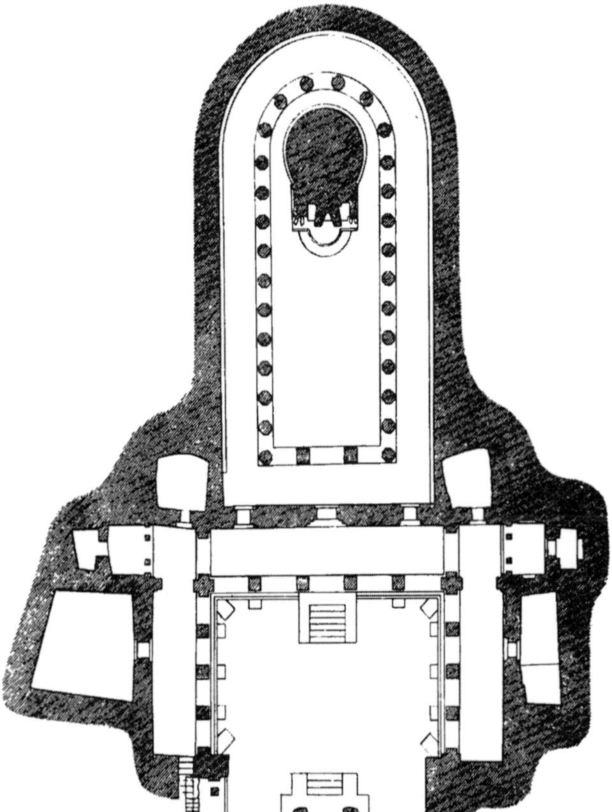

PLAN OF THE BALCONIES.

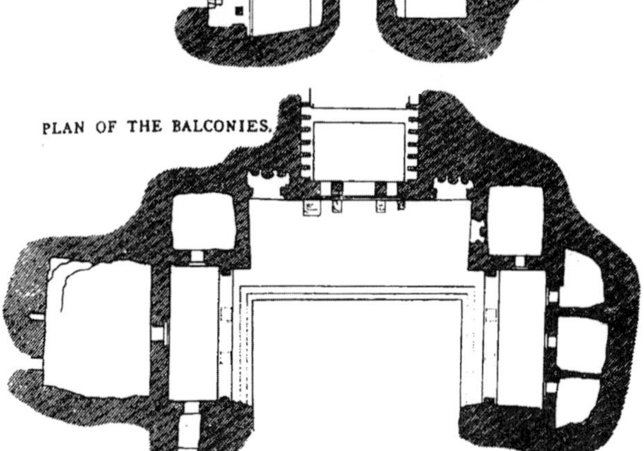

J. Burgess. W. GRIGGS, PHOTO LITH. LONDON, S. E. *Ganpat Purshotam Del.*

Plate LXIII.

ELURÂ:-VIŚWAKARMA CAVE.

COLUMN IN FRONT CORRIDOR.

PILASTER IN N. CORRIDOR.

PILASTER IN S. CORRIDOR.

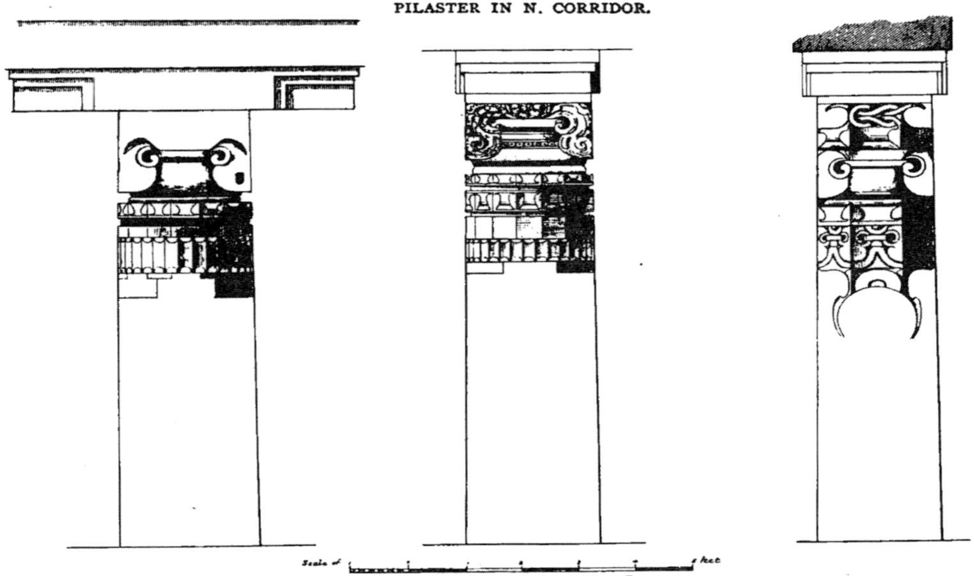

J. Burgess.

W. GRIGGS, PHOTO LITH. LONDON. S. E.

Dinkar Moreshwar.

ELURÂ. *Plate LXIV.*

GROUND PLAN OF THE TÎN THÂL BUDDHIST CAVE TEMPLE.

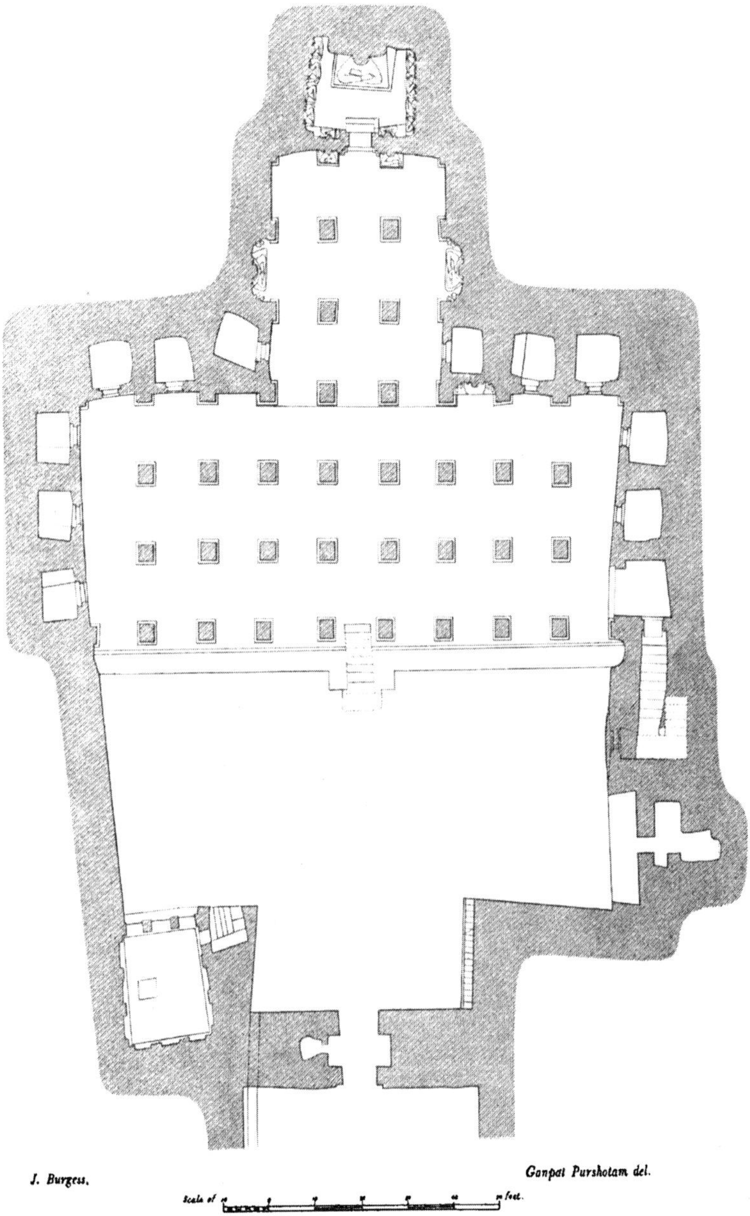

J. Burgess. *Ganpat Purshotam del.*

Scale of 10 0 10 20 30 40 50 feet.

W. GRIGGS. PHOTO LITH. LONDON. S. E.

Plate. LXV.

I. ELURÂ TIN THAL BUDDHIST CAVE
UPPER FLOOR.

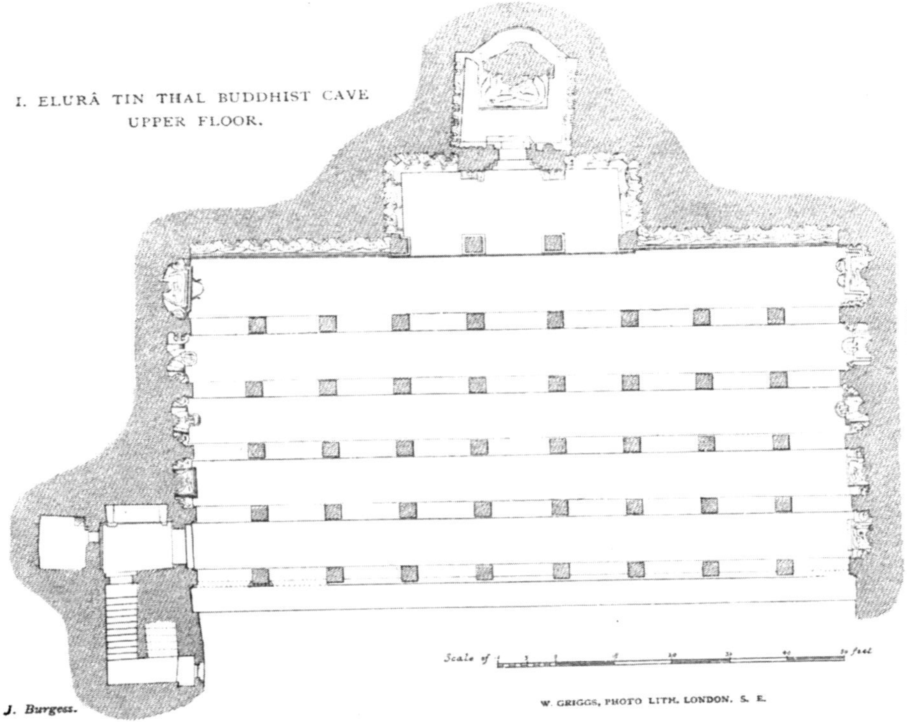

2. AURANGABAD CAVE VII.

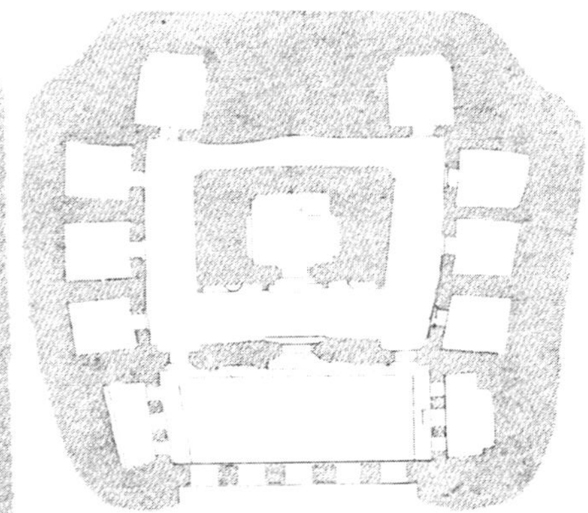

J. Burgess.

W. GRIGGS, PHOTO LITH. LONDON. S. E.

Ganpat Purshotam del.

Plate LXVI.

AURANGABAD. CAVE III.

2. PILLAR.

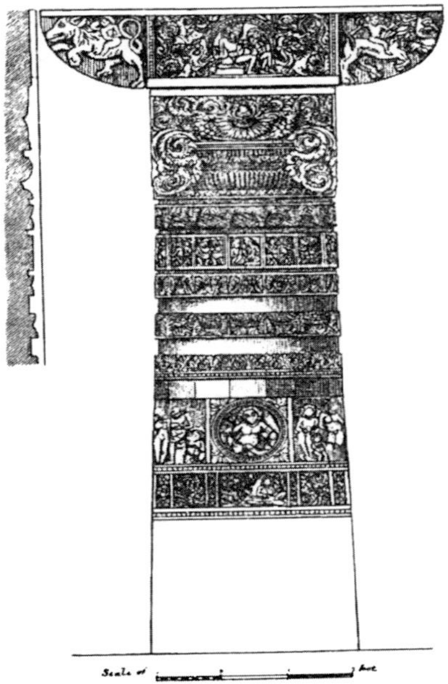

I. PLAN.

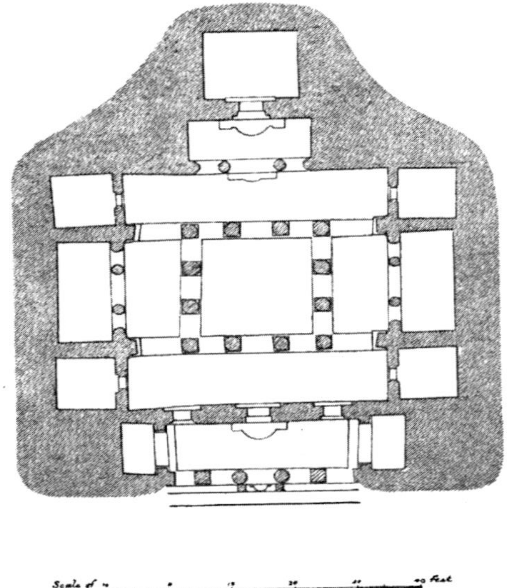

3. PILASTER.

J. Burgess.

W. GRIGGS, PHOTO LITH. LONDON. S. E.

Jayrao Raghoba. del.

Plate LXVII.

1. AIHOLE CAVE.

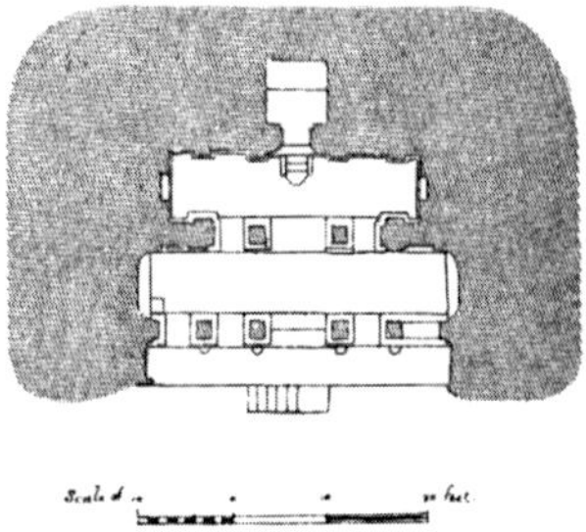

2. BADAMI CAVE I.

SECTION

PLAN.

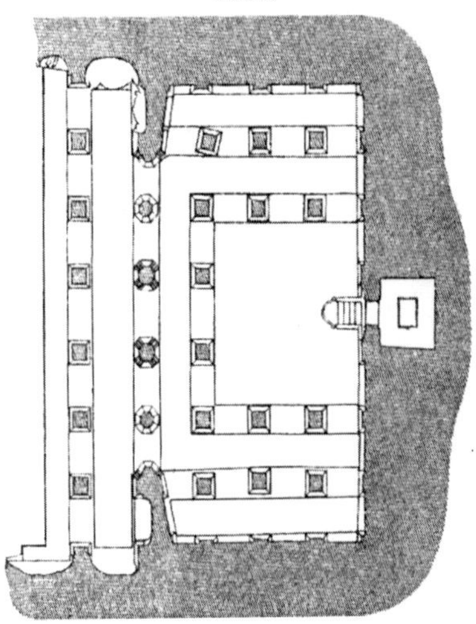

3. BADAMI CAVE III.

SECTION.

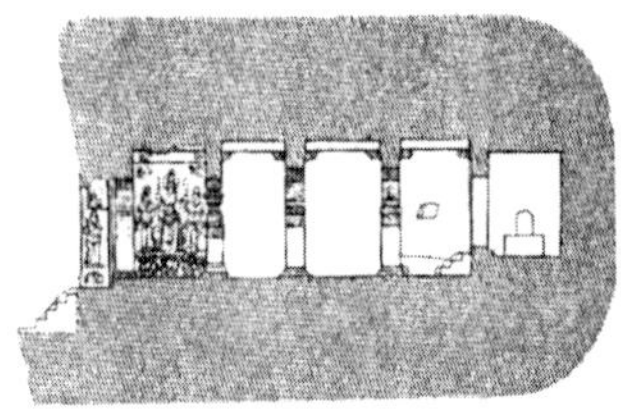

PLAN.

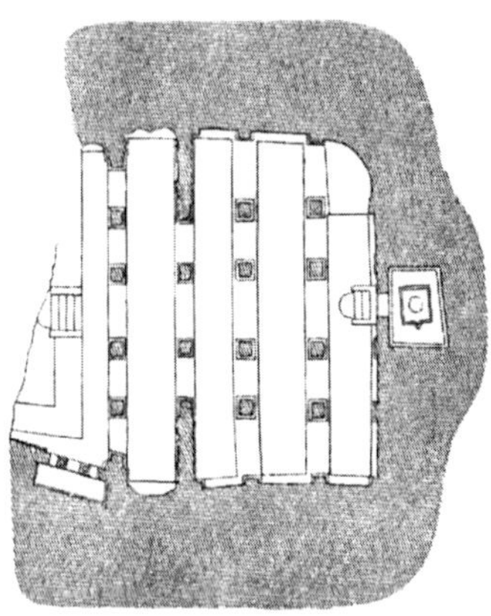

J. Burgess.

W. GRIGGS, PHOTO LITH. LONDON, S. E.

AMBÂ.

Plate LXVIII.

JOGAIS MANDAP.

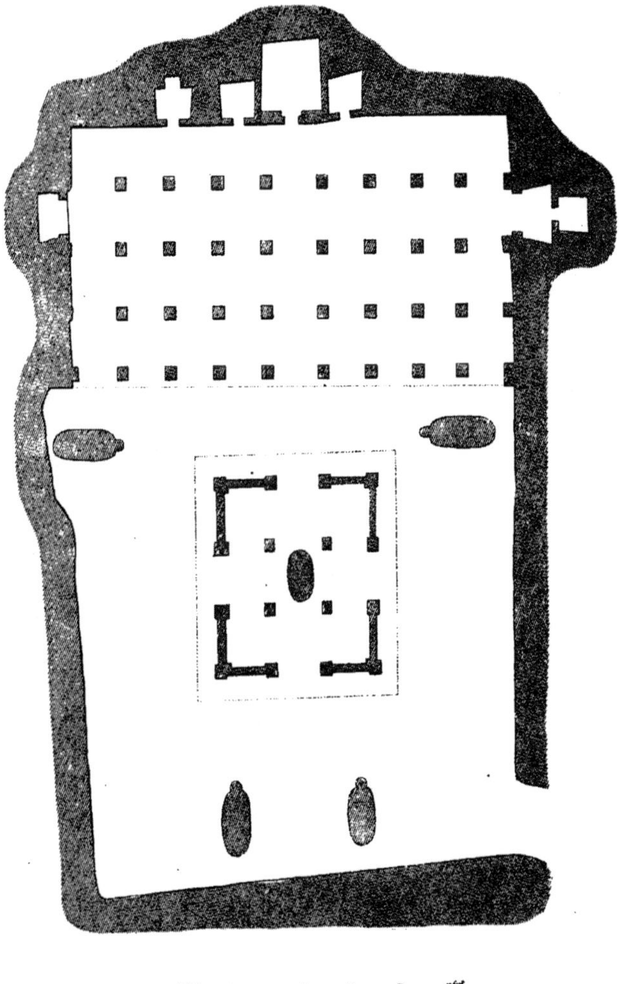

J. Burgess. W. GRIGGS, PHOTO LITH. LONDON, S. E. Ganpat Purshotam del.

BHÂMBURDÊ.

CAVE TEMPLE OF PANCHÂLEŚVAR MÂHÂDEVA.

Plate LXIX.

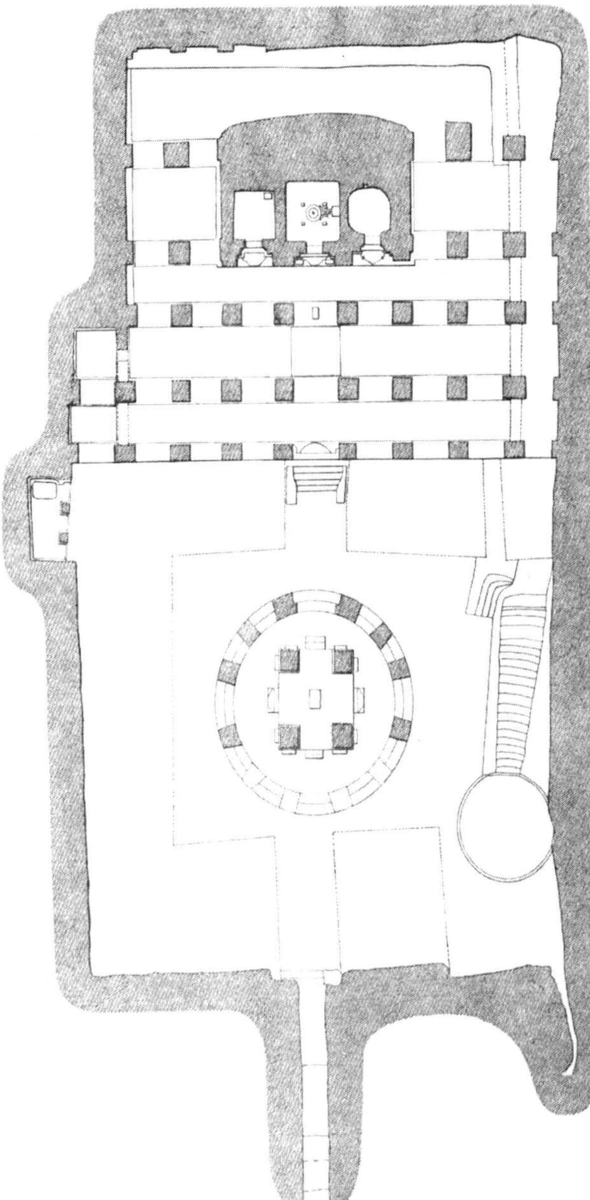

Scale of 10 feet.

J. Burgess.

W. GRIGGS, PHOTO LITH. LONDON, S. E.

Baluji Goomd.
Sakaram Gopal. } del.

I. DHOKE CAVE OF MAHADEVA.

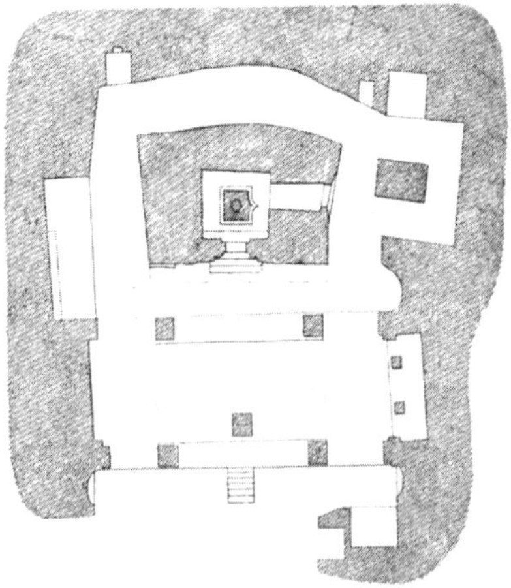

2. ELURA: RAVANA KA KHAI.

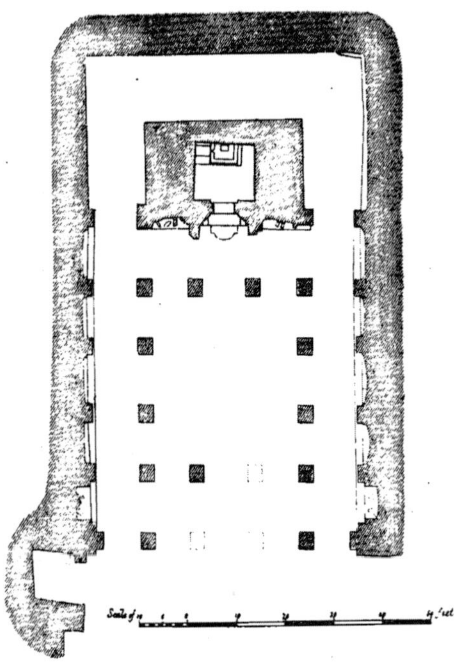

J. Burgess. W. GRIGGS, PHOTO LITH. LONDON. S. E. Ganpat Purshotam del.

RÂVANA KA KHAI. Plate LXXI.

1. PILASTER.

2. PILLAR.

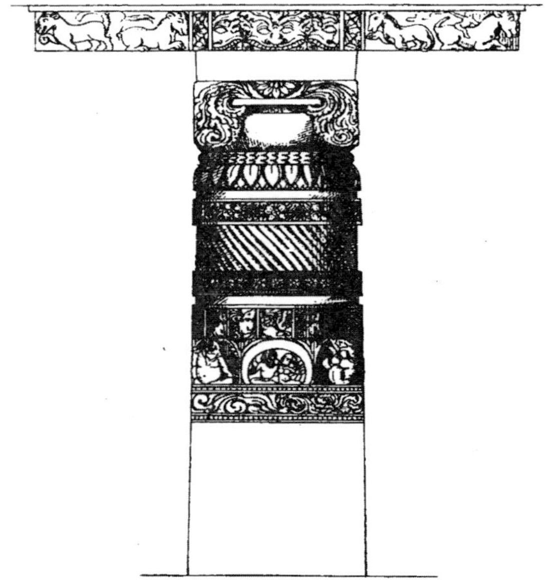

J. Burgess. W. GRIGGS, PHOTO LITH. LONDON. S. E. Jayrao Raghoba, del.

ELURÂ.

THE SAPTA-MATRA FROM RAVANA-KA KHAI.

J. Burgess. Jayrao Raghoba. del.

Scale of 5 4 3 2 1 0 5 10 15 20 feet.

W. GRIGGS, PHOTO-LITH. LONDON. S. E.

Plate LXXIII.

ELURÂ.

PLAN OF THE DÂS AVATARA - GROUND FLOOR.

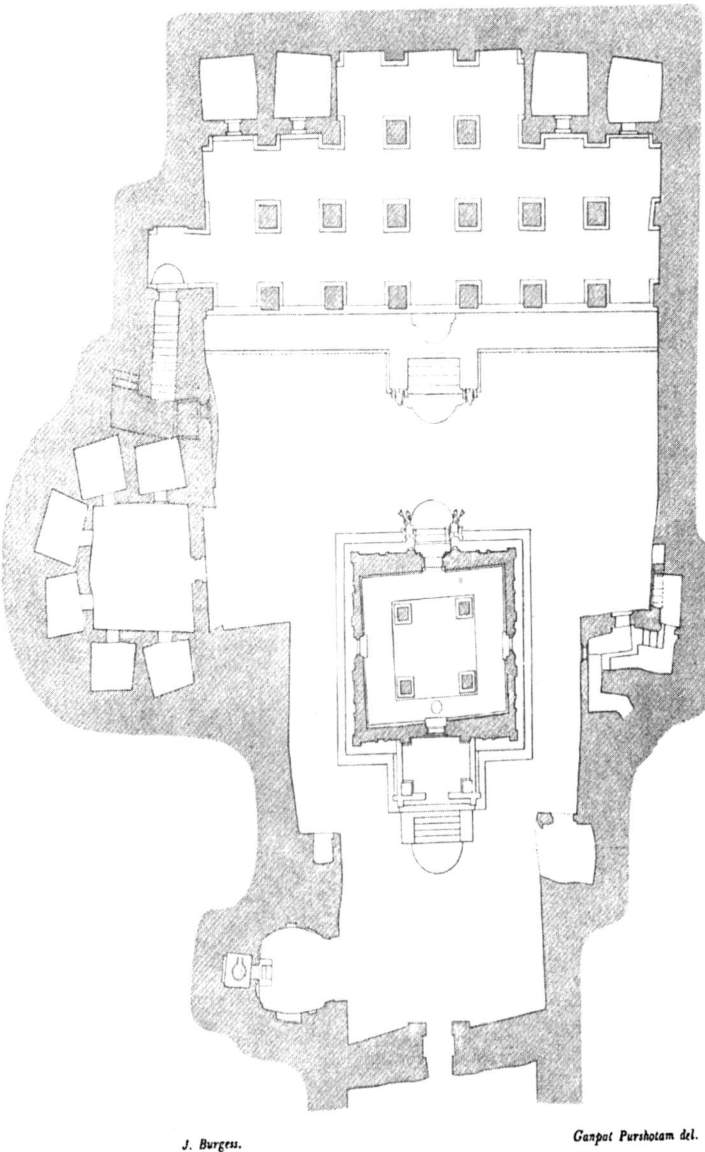

J. Burgess. Ganpat Purshotam del.

Scale of 10 0 10 20 30 40 50 feet

W. GRIGGS, PHOTO LITH. LONDON, S. E.

ELURÂ.

PLAN OF THE UPPER FLOOR OF THE DÂS AVATARA.

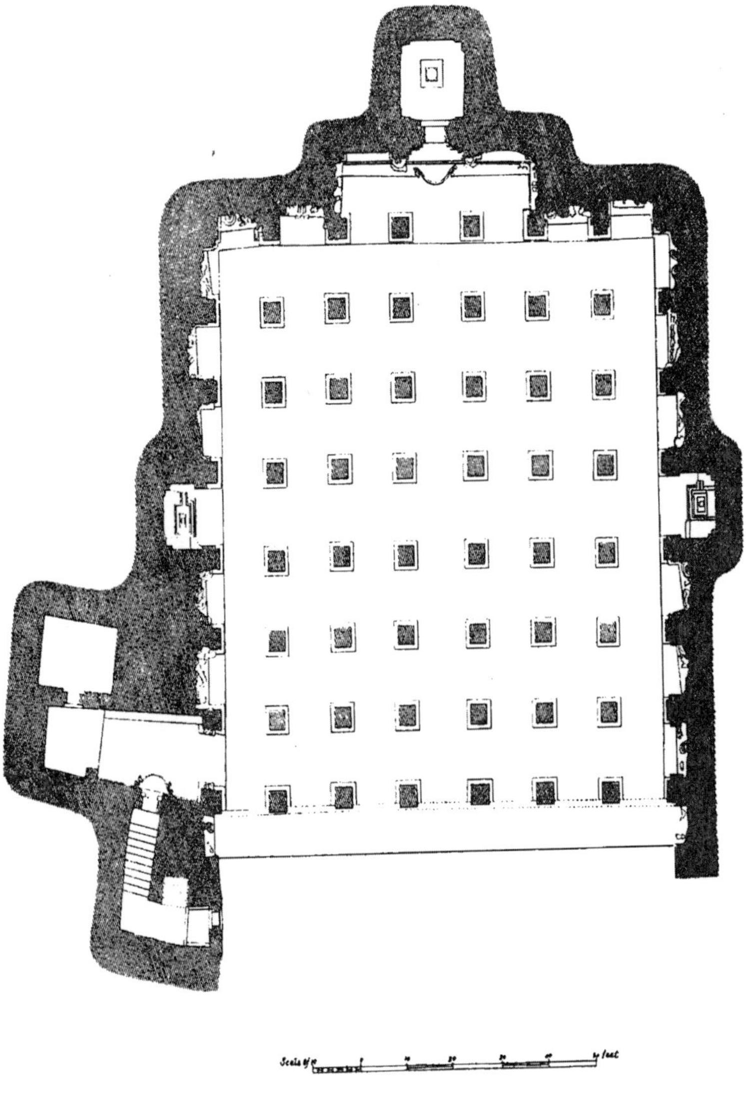

J. Burgess.

W. GRIGGS, PHOTO LITH. LONDON. S. E.

Ganpat Purshotam Del

ELURÂ.

1. NARASINHA AND HIRANYAKAŚIPU FROM DAŚ AVATARA.

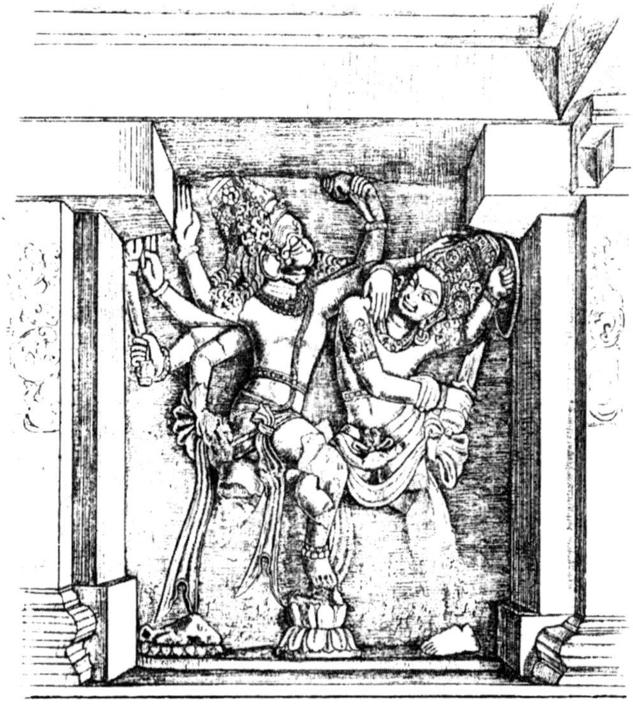

2. TRIMURTI IN CAVE ABOVE THE TELI-KA GANA CAVE.

J. Burgess. W. GRIGGS, PHOTO LITH. LONDON. S. E. Jayrao Raghoba. del.

ELURÂ. Plate LXXVI.

1. PLAN OF RAMÉSWARA.

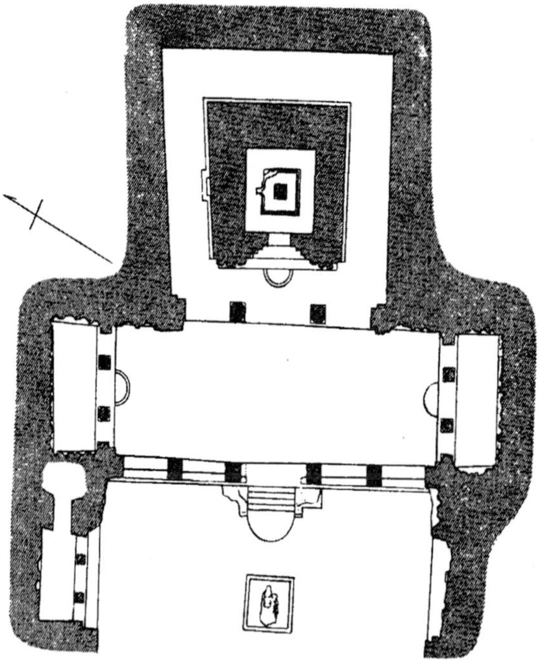

2. PLAN OF SMALL CAVES UP THE STREAM.

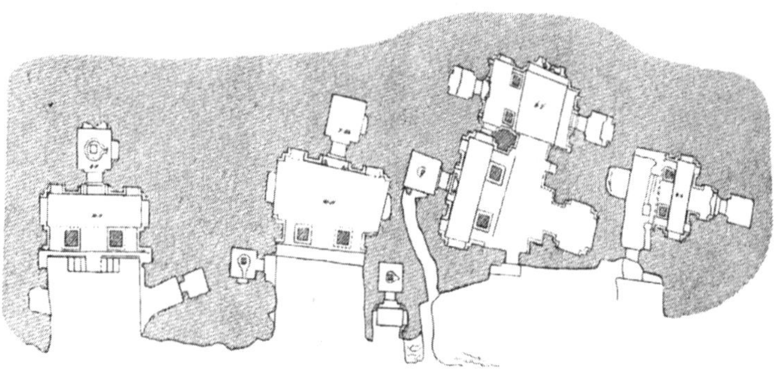

J. Burgess. W. GRIGGS, PHOTO LITH. LONDON. S. E. C. M. Sykes del.

Plate LXXVII.

ELURÂ.

DOOR IN RAMEŚWARA.

J. Burgess, C. M. Sykes Del.

Scale of 1 0 1 2 3 4 5 feet

W. GRIGGS, PHOTO-LITH, LONDON. S. E.

Plate LXXVIII.

ELURÂ.

FRONT OF SHRINE IN SMALL CAVE NEAR KAILASA.

J. Burgess. C. M. Sykes. Del.

W. GRIGGS, PHOTO LITH. LONDON. S. E.

ELURÂ.

PLAN OF DUMÂR LENÂ OR SITÂ'S NÂNI.

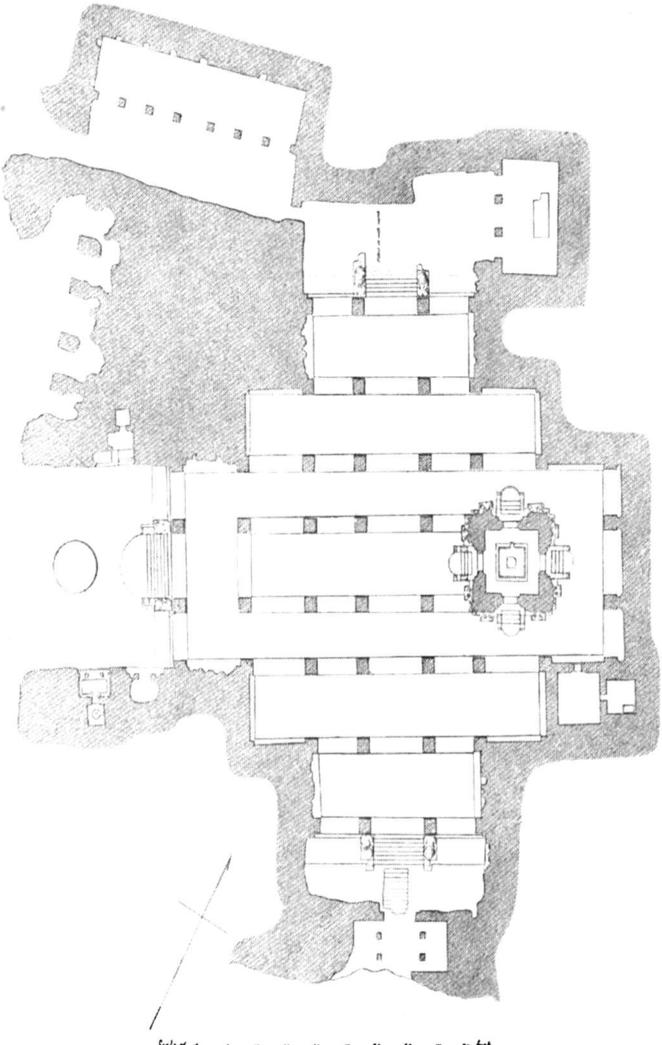

J. Burgess.

Scale of 10 0 10 20 30 40 50 60 70 80 *feet*

W. GRIGGS, PHOTO LITH. LONDON, S. E.

Plate. LXXX.

ELURÂ.

1. DWAJASTAMBHA IN KAILÂSA. 2. INDRA SABHA. MONOLITHIC COLUMN.

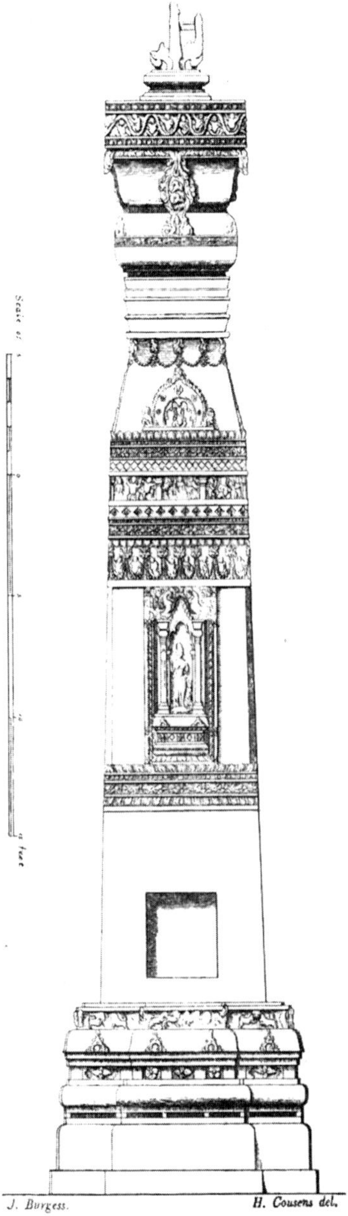

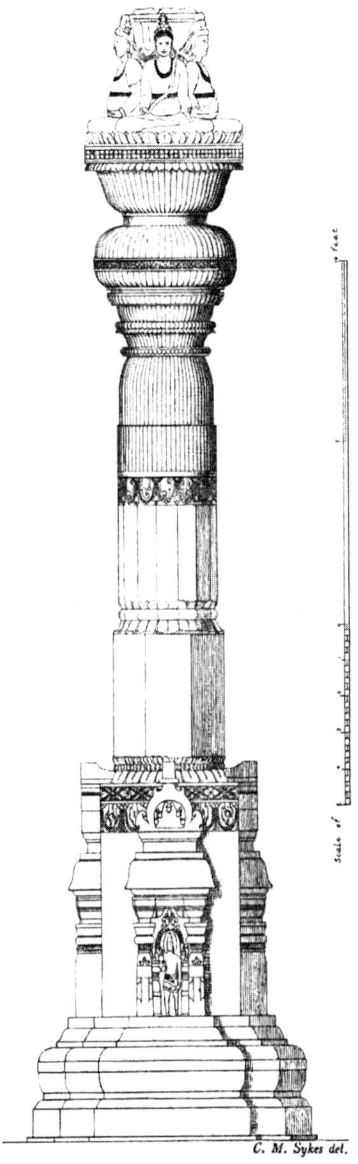

J. Burgess. H. Cousens del. C. M. Sykes del.

W. GRIGGS, PHOTO-LITH. LONDON. S. E.

Plate LXXXI.

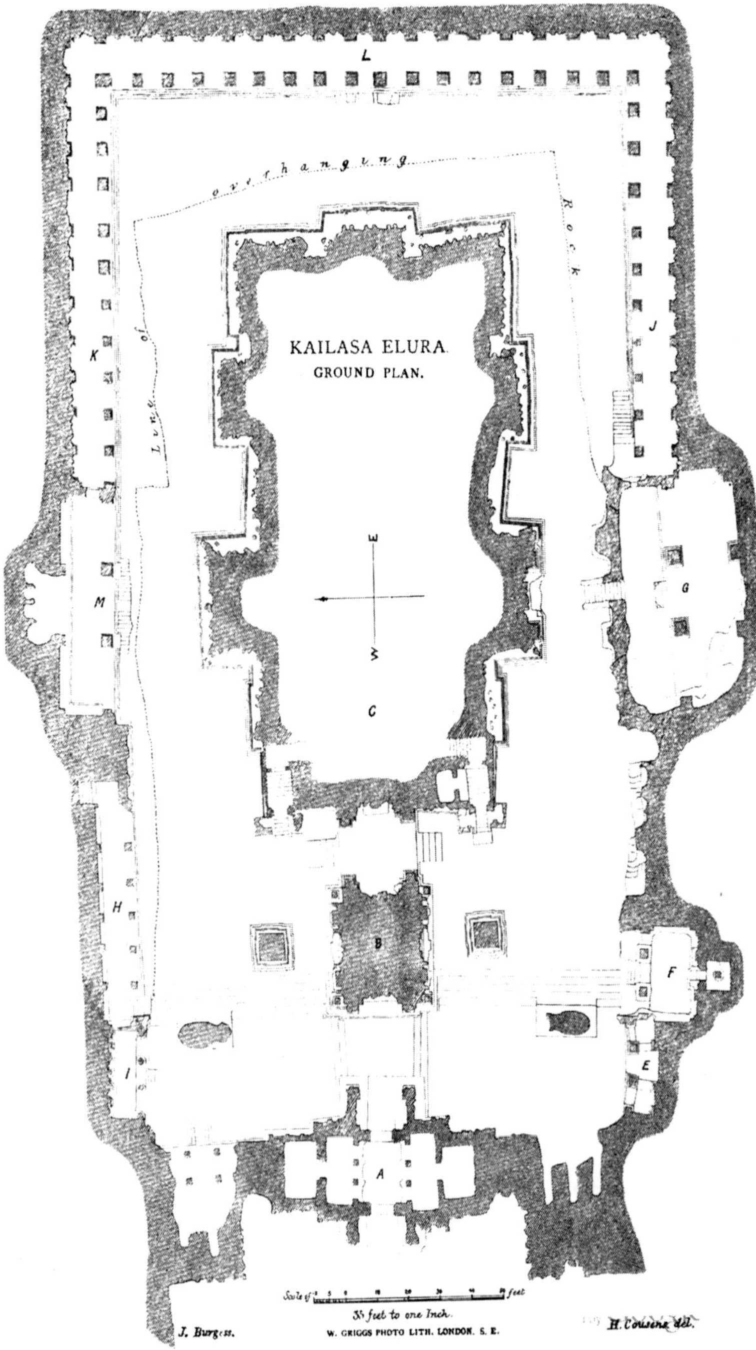

J. Burgess. W. GRIGGS PHOTO LITH. LONDON. S. E. H. Cousens del.

ELURÂ.

SOUTH ELEVATION OF KAILASA TEMPLE.

W. GRIGGS, PHOTO LITH. LONDON, S. E.

ELURÂ.

Plate LXXXIII.

1. ŚRÎ OR LAKSHMÎ IN KAILÂSA.

2. SÛRYA IN KUMBHARWAṚA CAVE.

J. Burgess.

W. GRIGGS. PHOTO LITH. LONDON. S. E.

Jayrao Raghoba. del.

ELURÂ.

Plate LXXXIV.

1. PILASTER IN KAILÂSA.

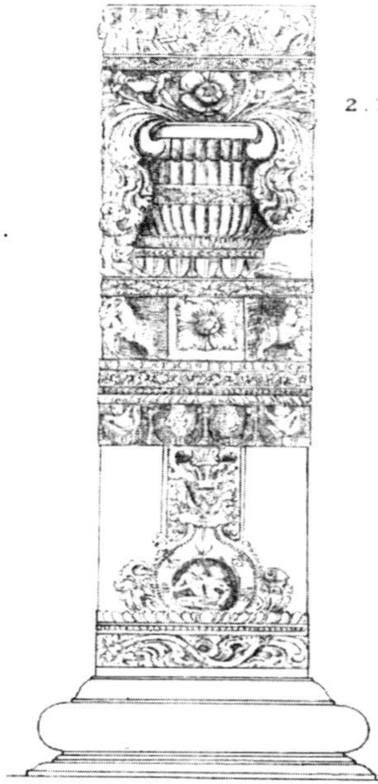

2. PILASTER IN N. PORCH OF KAILÂSA

3. PILLAR IN HALL OF KAILÂSA.

4. PILLARS IN LANKEŚWARA.

Scale of feet

J. Burgess.

W. GRIGGS, PHOTO LITH. LONDON. S. E.

C. M. Sykes del.

ELEPHANTA ROCK TEMPLE.

Plate LXXXV.

PLAN.

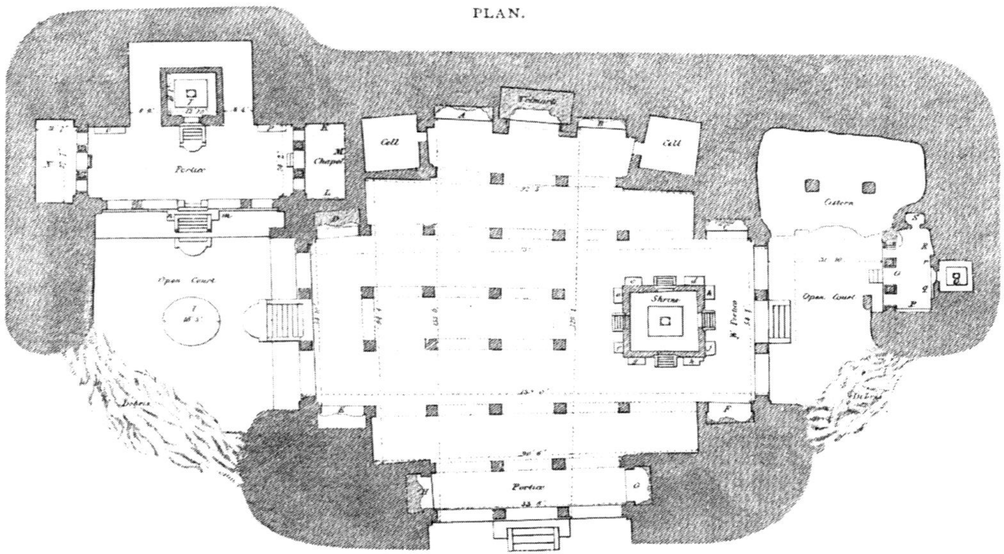

J. Burgess delt.

Scale of 100 feet.

W. GRIGGS, PHOTO LITH. LONDON, S. E.

ELURÂ.

PARŚWANÂTH FROM INDRA SABHÂ.

J. Burgess. *Jagannath Anauta del.*

W. GRIGGS PHOTO LITH. LONDON. S. E.

ELURÂ. Plate LXXXVII.

INDRA SABHÂ-LOWER HALL

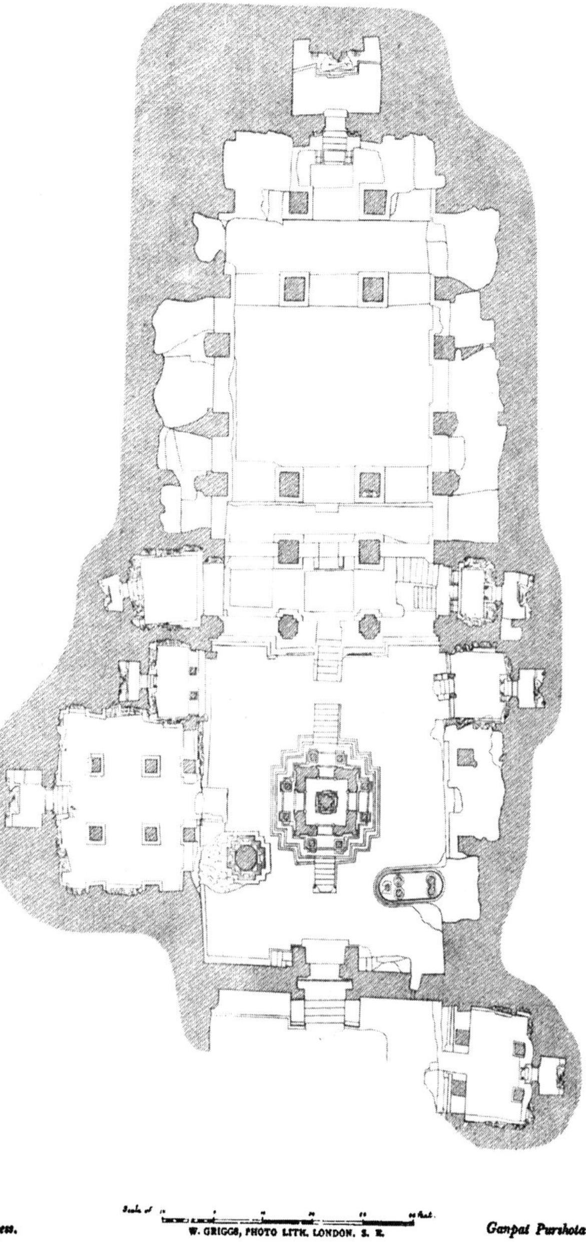

J. Burgess. W. GRIGGS, PHOTO LITH. LONDON. S. E. *Ganpat Purshotam del.*

ELURÂ.

INDRA SABHÂ—PLAN OF UPPER HALL, W & E. WINGS.

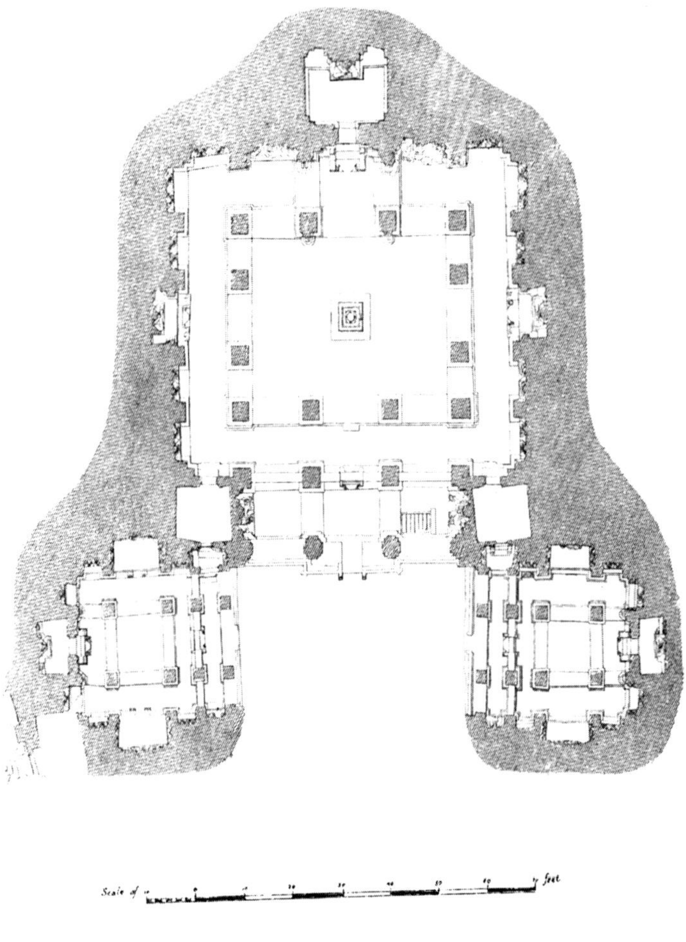

J. Burgess.

W. GRIGGS, PHOTO LITH, LONDON. S. E.

C. M. Sykes del.

ELURÂ.

INDRA SABHÂ SHRINE DOOR.

Plate LXXXIX.

J. Burgess.

C. M. Sykes del.

Scale of 12 ... 6 feet.

W. GRIGGS, PHOTO LITH. LONDON, S. E.

ELURÂ.

JAGANNÂTH SABHA, LAST JAINA CAVE.

Plate XC.

I. GROUND FLOOR.

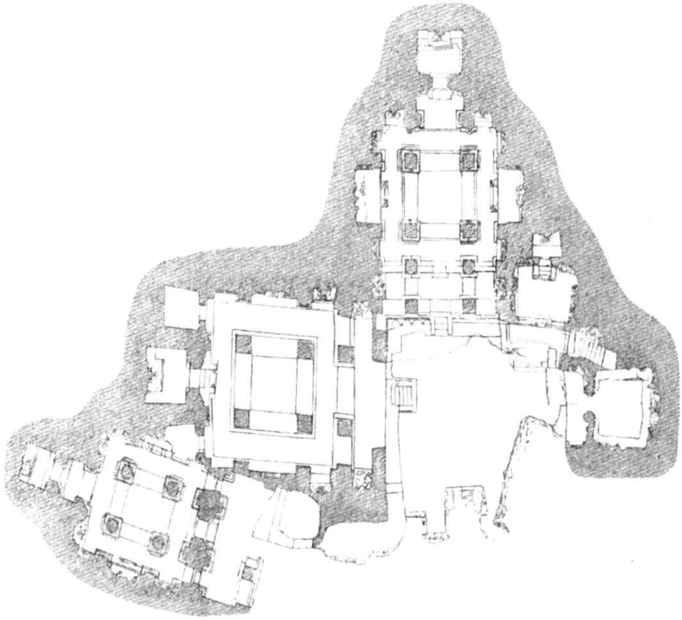

2. UPPER FLOOR.

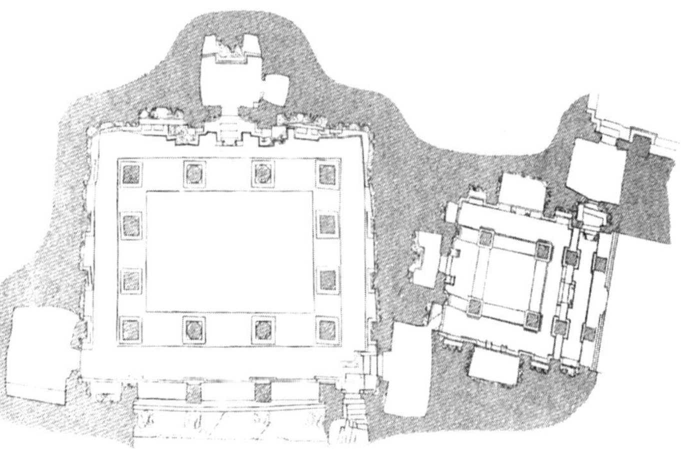

J. Burgess. W. GRIGGS, PHOTO LITH. LONDON. S. E. *Ganpat Purshotam del.*

ELURÂ.

Plate. XCI.

1. INDRA FROM THE JAINA CAVES.

2. TIRTHANKARAS IN THE JAINA CAVES.

J. Burgess. W. GRIGGS, PHOTO LITH. LONDON. S. E. Jayrao Raghoba, del.

ELURÂ JAINA CAVES.

Plate. XCII.

1. PILLAR IN HALL OF JAGANNÂTH SABHA.

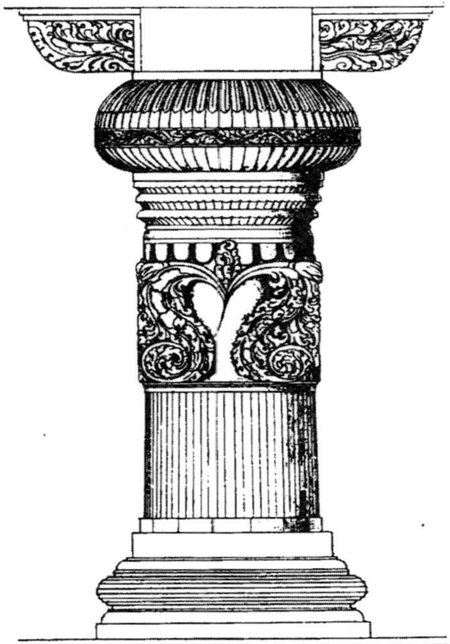

2. IN WING OF INDRA SABHA.

3. IN LOWER CAVE OF JAGANNÂTH SABHA.

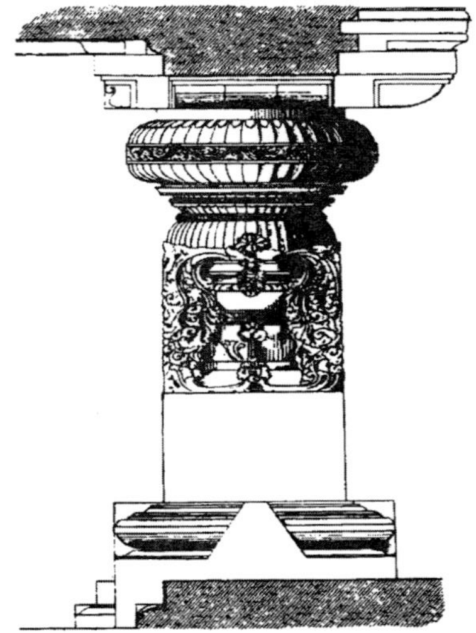

Scale of feet.

J. Burgess.

W. GRIGGS, PHOTO LITH. LONDON. S. E.

C. M. Sykes del.

Plate XCIII.

DHÂRÂSIṄVA-CAVE I.

PLAN.

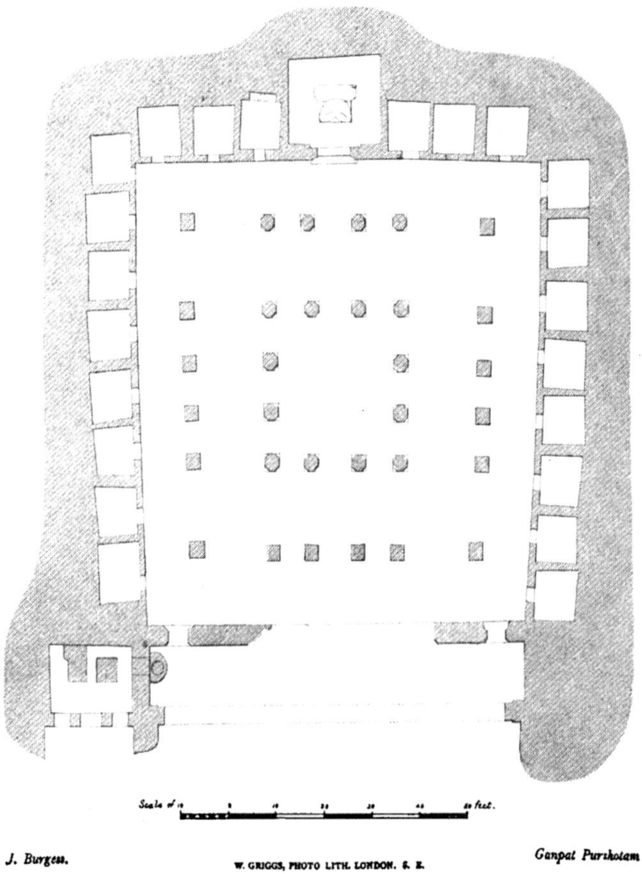

J. Burgess.

W. GRIGGS, PHOTO LITH. LONDON. S. E.

Ganpat Purshotam del.

ANKAI JAINA CAVE. NO. I.

Plate. XCIV.

1. SECTION.

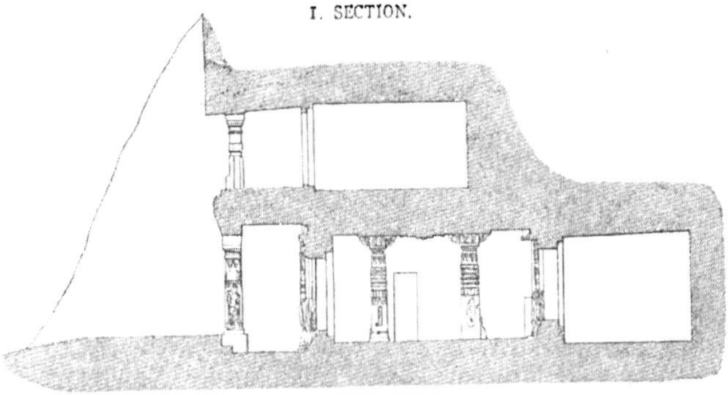

2. UPPER FLOOR.

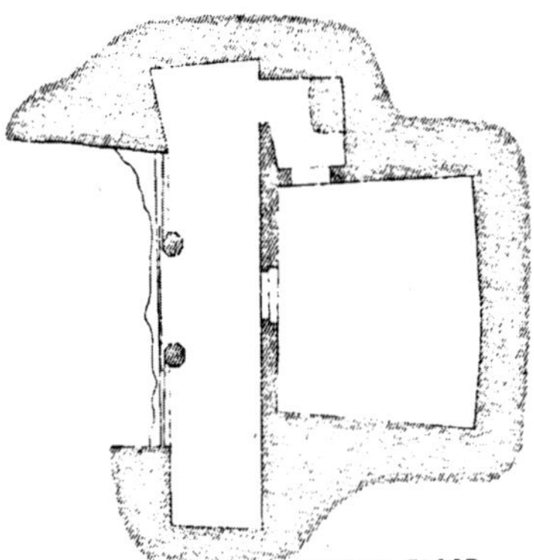

3. GROUND FLOOR.

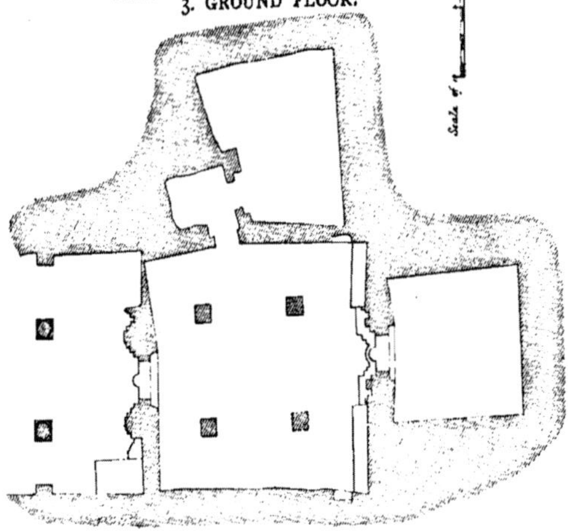

J. Burgess. W. GRIGGS, PHOTO LITH. LONDON. S. E. Ganpat Purshotam del.

ANKAI JAINA CAVES.

ENTRANCE DOOR TO LOWER STOREY OF CAVE I.

IMAGE OF TIRTHANKARA.

J. Burgess.

W. GRIGGS. PHOTO LITH. LONDON. S. E.

H. Cousens del.

Plate XCVI.

ANCIENT VIHARA AT BHÂJÂ.

4

5

J. Burgess.

1

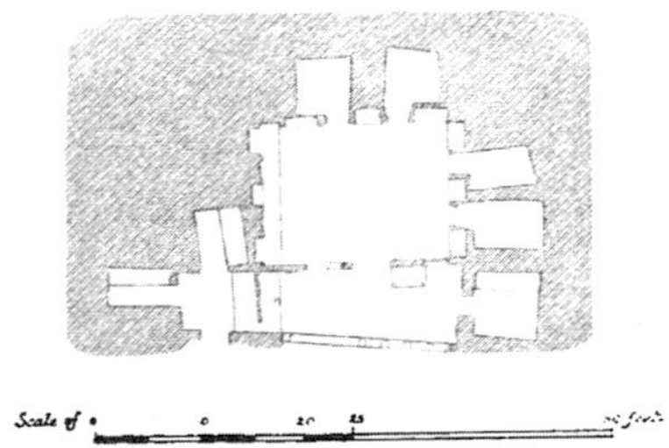

2

3

H. Cousens del.

W. GRIGGS, PHOTO LITH. LONDON. S. E.

J. Burgess. W. GRIGGS, PHOTO LITH, LONDON, S. E. H. Cousens del.

Plate XCVIII.

ANCIENT VIHARA AT BHÂJÂ.

BAS RELIEF AT END OF VERANDAH.

J. Burgess.

H. Cousens del.

W. GRIGGS, PHOTO LITH. LONDON. S. E.